TOM NAIRN, after serving time on the hulk of h
'Nationalism Studies' at Edinburgh Universit
sation and Nationalism' at the Royal Melbou___ _____ __ _____gy in
Victoria, Australia. His book *The Break-up of Britain* appeared in 1977 (Verso
Books, most recent edition Common Ground Publishing, Melbourne, 2003).
Faces of Nationalism (Verso) appeared in 1997 and *Global Matrix* (Pluto
Press, with Paul James) in 2005.

JAMIE MAXWELL is a political journalist. He writes for the *New Statesman*,
Bella Caledonia and the *Scottish Review of Books*, among other publications.
He is the editor of *The Case for Left Wing Nationalism*, a collection of his
late father Stephen Maxwell's essays and the co-author, with David Torrance,
of *Scotland's Referendum: A Voter's Guide*.

PETE RAMAND is the co-author, with James Foley, of *Yes: the Radical Case
for Scottish Independence* and a co-founder of the *Radical Independence
Campaign*. In 2013 he received an MSc (with distinction) in Nationalism
Studies from the University of Edinburgh.

ANTHONY BARNETT is the founder of *openDemocracy* and served as its Editor-in-Chief until 2007. He was the director of Charter 88 from 1988 to
1995. He is the author of numerous books, including *Iron Britannia: Why
Parliament Waged Its Falklands War*, and is a regular contributor to the *New
Statesman* and the *Guardian*.

Old Nations, Auld Enemies, New Times

Selected Essays

TOM NAIRN

Edited by

JAMIE MAXWELL and PETE RAMAND

Luath Press Limited

EDINBURGH

www.luath.co.uk

First published 2014

ISBN: 978-1-910021-64-4

The publishers acknowledge the support of

ALBA | CHRUTHACHAIL

towards the publication of this volume.

The paper used in this book is recyclable. It is made from
low chlorine pulps produced in a low energy, low emissions manner
from renewable forests.

Printed and bound by
Bell & Bain Ltd., Glasgow

Typeset in 11 point Sabon
by 3btype.com

Contents

Editor's Note		7
Foreword	Introducing Tom Nairn by Anthony Barnett	9
CHAPTER ONE	The British Political Elite *New Left Review* 1/23, January–February 1964	13
CHAPTER TWO	The English Working Class *New Left Review* 1/24, March–April 1964	21
CHAPTER THREE	The Three Dreams of Scottish Nationalism *New Left Review* 1/49, May–June 1968	37
CHAPTER FOUR	English Nationalism: The Case of Enoch Powell *New Left Review* 1/61, May–June 1970	53
CHAPTER FIVE	British Nationalism and the EEC *New Left Review* 1/69, September–October 1971	79
CHAPTER SIX	Scotland and Europe *New Left Review* 1/83, January–February 1974	107
CHAPTER SEVEN	The Modern Janus *New Left Review* 1/94, November–December 1975	135
CHAPTER EIGHT	The Radical Approach *Question Magazine*, July 1976	162
CHAPTER NINE	Scotland the Misfit *Question Magazine*, October 1976	169
CHAPTER TEN	1931 – A Repeat Performance? *Question Magazine*, October 1976	176
CHAPTER ELEVEN	The New Exiles *Question Magazine*, 1976	181
CHAPTER TWELVE	The English Dilemma *Question Magazine*, February 1977	186
CHAPTER THIRTEEN	The Twilight of the British State *New Left Review* 1/101–102, January–April 1977	191
CHAPTER FOURTEEN	The House of Windsor *Socialist Challenge*, June 1977	255
CHAPTER FIFTEEN	The Timeless Girn *The Claim of Right for Scotland*, 1989	261
CHAPTER SIXTEEN	Identities in Scotland Lecture to the International Congress of Scottish Studies, Grenoble, March 1991	275

CHAPTER SEVENTEEN   The Snabs
                           Scotsman, October 1991   286

CHAPTER EIGHTEEN   The Auld Enemy
                           Scotsman, March 1992   289

CHAPTER NINETEEN   Second-Rate Unionism
                           Scotsman, March 1992   292

CHAPTER TWENTY   Dark Forces
                           Scotsman, October 1992   295

CHAPTER TWENTY-ONE   Demonising Nationalism
                           London Review of Books, vol. 15 no. 4,
                           February 1993   298

CHAPTER TWENTY-TWO   Empire and Union
                           London Review of Books, vol. 17 no. 16,
                           August 1995   308

CHAPTER TWENTY-THREE   On Not Hating England
                           Independent on Sunday, September 1998   323

CHAPTER TWENTY-FOUR   Hooligans of the Absolute
                           openDemocracy, October 2001   344

CHAPTER TWENTY-FIVE   Gordon Brown: Bard of Britishness
                           First published in the book of the
                           same title, 2007   351

CHAPTER TWENTY-SIX   Union on the Rocks?
                           New Left Review 11/43
                           January-February 2007   382

CHAPTER TWENTY-SEVEN   Globalisation and Nationalism:
                           The New Deal
                           The 'Edinburgh Lectures', Edgelands
                           Project, March 2008   396

CHAPTER TWENTY-EIGHT   A Republican Monarchy?
                           England and Revolution
                           Foreword to *The Enchanted Glass:*
                           Britain and Its Monarchy, 2011 edition   406

CHAPTER TWENTY-NINE   A Nation's Blueprint
                           Foreword to *The Case for Left-Wing*
                           Nationalism, October 2013   413

CHAPTER THIRTY   Old Nations, New Age
                           openDemocracy, April 2014   416

Editors' Note

Tom Nairn's influence on Scottish politics has been huge. Much of the language used in the independence debate – particularly by nationalists – can be traced back to his work. Yet the Scottish media and academic establishments have never fully embraced him. For only a few short years since he rose to prominence in the 1960s has he held a formal position at a Scottish university, and just one mainstream Scottish title, *The Scotsman*, has published him on a regular basis (and even then it was only for a short time).

Nairn himself has never actively sought the spotlight, but his ideas are so thoroughly engrained in the way we think and talk about 'the national question' that we often reference them without realising it. So part of the reason we wanted to produce this collection was to ensure Nairn got the credit he is due. We hope *Old Nations* will bring Nairn's distinctive voice back to the forefront of our national debate.

Remarkably, up until now, there has never been a comprehensive collection of Nairn's work. We wanted to correct this and, in the process, illustrate how his thought has changed over the years. *Old Nations* starts with Nairn's early essays from the *New Left Review*, in which he developed a ground-breaking Gramscian analysis (alongside Perry Anderson) of the British state, progresses through his seminal 'Break-Up of Britain' essays from the 1970s and concludes with some of his more recent contributions to *The Scotsman, London Review of Books* and *openDemocracy*.

Although much of this book focuses on Nairn's serious theoretical work, it also includes a number of shorter, journalistic pieces which affirm Nairn's status as one of the great Scottish non-fiction writers of modern times. We have unearthed various articles from *Question Magazine*, a short-lived journal from the mid-1970s, which showcase the autobiographical side of his writing.

Old Nations is (we think) the definitive Nairn collection, but it is far from exhaustive. There are a number of important pieces we wanted to include but couldn't because we didn't have the space. We were editing in the run-up to September 18, so the dominant themes are, inevitably, Scotland, Britain and nationalism, even though Nairn's output extends well beyond these subjects. Finally, on a personal note, we both grew up reading Tom's work, have been hugely influenced by him and very much admire him. It's been an enormous privilege to work on this project.

Jamie Maxwell and Pete Ramand
September 2014, Edinburgh

Foreword

Introducing Tom Nairn

BY ANTHONY BARNETT

History is largely a tale of groping in the dark, a condition no person or class can miraculously escape from.

I'D LIKE TO ADDRESS this introduction to younger readers unfamiliar with Tom Nairn. You have the opportunity to greet a commanding European thinker who in person is gentle, modest and unassuming. I envy you the chance to read for the first time his wonderful, withering exasperation with the status quo. And the style of his argument: persistent, careful, demonstrative (in the sense of saying, 'Look! This is how it is.') and hard, urging us to stand up like humans from our bent, servile posture before the powers that are screwing up our lives.

Introductions to a collection usually go on about the range of the author's work and the intellectual path down which he has proceeded, or in Tom's case, led the way. But despite his unmatched scholarship and range of reading, anything that risks turning Tom into an academic would give a false impression. Tom is a writer. He is a writer first and foremost. You should bathe in his prose, let it take its time, and indulge yourself in it. Don't read him for a quick steer.

For Tom has a rare quality as a writer that is quite disturbing and difficult to accept, until you do; then laughter sets in and the world is never quite the same again. For in addition to being a writer Tom is a thinker. The supreme quality of his prose, whether in the form of anger, humour, seriousness or sarcasm, is that he shares his thinking with us. He searches for meaning and the real forces behind and within what is going on, and so teaches us too how to think. Or, as he might put it, to grope better in the darkness.

You might regard thinking as trivial or technical. But this depends on what you are trying to think about. Many philosophers, like the professional ones who fill university departments today, form a kind of conspiracy *against* thinking, as do most newspapers – all forms of sensationalism and celebrity culture. Tom, however, seeks to uncover the meaning of what is going on. Nothing could be more ambitious or necessary. Which is why there are no university departments openly dedicated to 'The study of what is going on'. That would be far too dangerous! Only a few exist where such work is pursued covertly.

What do I mean by 'What is going on?' I mean that Tom asks: Why are we ruled in the *specific* way we are ruled? How do they get away with it? Why do we let them? These are questions about us as well as them, about our weakness and passivity as well as their capacity and self-interest.

A fascinating example is provided in this collection with Tom's 1971 essay on Enoch Powell. Perhaps you are young enough never to have heard of Powell and his 'Rivers of Blood' speech opposing immigration. When he was in the Conservative opposition's Shadow Cabinet he issued a dire warning in Birmingham, 'As I look ahead, I am filled with foreboding; like the Roman, I seem to see "the River Tiber foaming with much blood".' Expelled from the Conservative front bench he nonetheless became a defining politician of the right and an instant bogeyman to the left. Tom engages with Powell and asks what it means that this bizarre figure could become such an influence.

In these days of stand-up comics, to say it is a polemic suggests taking up a position, making a shocking counter-attack for the sake of effect, in short posturing. What Tom does is quite different: he engages. He sucks in Enoch Powell, he reads his early poetry, he rolls him around his mouth, he tastes his toxic allure, he probes its attraction for British rule, he compares him to other types of far right leaders and then he spits him out.

This rare quality of engagement, of never reducing opponents to their shadow and considering all their living features and capacity to endure – *unless we do something about it!* – makes Tom as unpredictable as reality itself. You can see in this collection how he began as a Marxist, that is to say writing from the point of view of a body of thought taken to be correct. The more he engaged the more he abandoned the core Marxist belief that the meaning of history is known and that capitalism is having its grave dug by the working class it created; that this singular, proletarian class has no nation, and that like religion and aristocratic flim-flam, nationalism is a false-consciousness. Much later, he penned a fine critique of Hart and Negri's attempt to recreate the proletariat as the global multitude.

But this shift in Tom's thinking was not an abandonment of the method that Marx pioneered, the method of historical materialism. While Tom supports small nation civic nationalism, he investigates its economic advantages in relation to the direction of the modern world; he seeks out its deeper function and unravels its historical nature. He never takes such nationalism at its own word. He strongly backs civic nationalism, but not as a nationalist, for his perspective is international. He does not wear the Saltire as a badge of rank or any kind of uniform from which all else is judged. An intellectual of the left he is, but there is *nothing* of the policeman about Tom Nairn.

A small example, not to be found here, may illustrate his sensitivity to the historical influences that shape nationalism. In 1976 he went to a conference in Nicosia, Cyprus, on the fate of small nations. It took place soon after Turkey had invaded and captured the north of the island. Tom sets out how the Greeks had developed one of the earliest nationalisms in Europe at the beginning of the 19th century. Because it was so early it could take the form of a romantic pan-Hellenism. The Greek community in Cyprus, however, had suffered the longest colonial experience of any country in Europe, through to 1960 – with

British rule generating political lethargy within a relatively developed society. With independence, the Greek-Cypriots could not resist adopting pan-Hellenism as their nationalism, for they had none of their own. This then threatened the defensive nationalism of the Turkish minority – a nationalism that was historically as late as Greece's was early. I won't continue to try and précis Tom's analysis. This is enough to illustrate his approach. Nationalism always presents itself as an unchanging essence, especially for its ethnic proponents. But it is in fact never such, being always a historically contingent and economically shaped reality. This does not make it 'false'. On the contrary, because it is man-made it is all the more real for us – and can be more or less humane. At the same time, as a product of us humans in response to global development as we experience it in our very different ways, it also draws upon our shared nature.

Another reflection on this theme of humanity, progress and reaction to it, but this time central because about a turning point in world affairs, is Tom's article on 9/11. It was published in the *openDemocracy* debate four weeks after the World Trade Towers were brought down. 'Hooligans of the Absolute' is a robust dismissal of panic and alarmism and a devastating observation of the cost to the Middle East of its failure to develop secular nationalism. A far-sighted response, it draws on a deep theme in his writing: confidence in the long-term positive emancipation of global development.

It's an outlook that distinguishes Tom from many on the traditional and ecological lefts. Historically, the left felt confident about progress. We the progressives would shape the future. Today, the pessimism of defeat has captured the heart of many on the left, after the disasters of Communism, the collapse of social democracy and the impotence of Green politics. The result is a sometimes bitter contempt for the modern world. Tom does not share this attitude at all. Always seeking the forces that will shake and eventually break the existing order for the better, today in his work on globalisation he embraces the energy and real achievements of digital capitalism and the vital spirits of its popular cultures.

Any country that can produce a Tom Nairn deserves a fully independent place in world affairs, however modest. Likewise, a country that does not produce a political writer with such cultural depth, international range, profound reading, openness to argument, impatience with the status quo, biting wit and humane sympathy, may not deserve its independence. Such a country is England, alas. And this, as Tom has pointed out consistently and eloquently, is the heart of the problem with Britain that Scotland now suffers. (Not only Scotland of course.)

His wake up call to Scotland was a *basso profondo* within a wider chorus. His wake up call to my country, England, strikes a few lonely echoes against a stony reception – even when his diagnosis of the deep hysteria of the British elite is so well observed. Yet everyone in London who reads about politics is uneasily aware that he is the author of *The Break-Up of Britain*. The first to see it coming. And it is coming, in one way or another…

You can excuse his impatience for that book was published getting on for

40 years ago – way before you were born! But his seeing further and better has not stopped him from continuing to engage with the way that breathing fossil, the British constitution, 'a Coelacanth' Tom calls it, is actually lived – and how its history, interests and ideologies continue to entrap us.

His engagement with this, as across all his writings, is never morbid but never denies how close it gets to dancing with the dead. For Tom engages to make us free, self-governing and more human. He writes to rid us from stultified ways of thinking and the fetters of prejudice, cliché and received ideas of all kinds, from where so ever they come. In an era where every down-at-heel politico waves his or her 'values' at us like used five pound notes, Tom's writing is a genuine ethics: here is how to think, argue and stand up for ourselves. You may be young, you may be inexperienced, but don't let this prevent you from adopting a fully upright posture as you move forward, as you must, into the dark.

CHAPTER ONE

The British Political Elite

New Left Review, I/23

JANUARY–FEBRUARY 1964

CLASS-DIVIDED SOCIETIES have almost always been governed politically by a small minority. In general, this chosen few is a small group even in relation to the 'ruling class' itself, in the Marxist sense, the class which possesses or controls the economic wealth of society through the institutions of property, and in whose collective interests society is governed. The characteristics of such governing groups, especially in capitalist societies, and the nature of the relationship between them and the class or classes they represent – the social forces giving their power its fundamental meaning – is one of the most fascinating of historical problems. All too often, talk of 'the ruling class' – however polemically justified it may be in particular cases, in the face of antediluvian notions – tends by itself to obscure or at least leave aside such questions. Hence, argument remains on the level of the affirmation that there *is* a class which rules over the rest of society, and does not go on to describe *how* it does so. Or at best the idea of power is seen as indicating the obvious, universal instruments of power: the coercive State, the police and the army, deliberate propaganda for a way of life and certain sacred values.

But the modalities of power are infinite. In reality, the hegemony of one social class over subordinate classes in society may be extremely complex, a cultural tissue of great variety and subtlety, extending all the way from the education of infants to the naming of streets, present in peoples' inhibitions and mental blocs as well as in what they profess to believe – all that tradition of the dead generations 'weighing like a nightmare on the brain of the living', as Marx said. Mr Guttsman uses this remark to head his first chapter of his recent book.[1] Appropriately because the ancient bourgeois society of England is surely the most thoroughly conditioned by sediments of this kind, the most intimately burdened down by successive, often heterogeneous layers of historic culture deposited during the long good fortune of English capitalism. 'The revolution which did *not* happen in England', Edward Thompson has recently reminded us, 'is as important for understanding England as the French Revolution is for understanding France.'

---

1 W. L. Guttsman, *The British Political Elite*, Macgibbon & Kee.

The British governing class, for this reason, functioned as the centre or nexus of a much wider and deeper hegemonic system. Its political and administrative authority, its control of the State – the central bastion of power – was surrounded by a most formidable array of protective and concealing earthworks, gradually erected across centuries, and appearing almost as a feature of the natural landscape. In this fortress, it appeared as the incarnation of inevitable, timeless traditions, of an authority legitimate because always in existence and adapted like an ancient tree to the place of its growth. The rule of a class is most effective when it is least obvious, when the rôle of the State and coercion is minimal, when power exists not as constraint but as a kind of drugged, deeply conditioned consent on the part of the masses, as tacit inhibitions of the social consciousness which no effort of will can untie. It is by means such as these that British society has been ruled in the interests of the true dominating class – the industrial and financial bourgeoisie – for nearly two centuries. The bonds of such a system have proved themselves stronger than steel, stronger by far than Prussian bourgeois bureaucracy or French bourgeois logic.

The governing class, or élite, of the bourgeoisie was, of course, originally the aristocracy. This was the essence of the revolution – the bourgeois-democratic, rationalising, egalitarian revolution – which did *not* happen. The English bourgeoisie of the Industrial Revolution did not revolutionise society as a whole. Afraid from the beginning of the power of the new labouring masses brought into being by and for the Industrial Revolution itself, intimidated by the spectacle of the French Revolution and all it signified, the English middle class quickly arrived at a 'compromise' with the English *ancien régime*. Because of its basically capitalist structure (tenant-farming carried on by wage-labour for profit) and its absence of legal definition as a privileged estate, the aristocracy was such that a 'compromise' of this sort was possible. Nevertheless, the landowners were also the main protagonists of a distinctive civilisation, half-way between the feudal and the modern, with its own ways of life, its own values and culture – a civilisation still vital, at the period of the Industrial Revolution, and in spite of its bourgeois traits qualitatively distinct from the new social order of that Revolution. And no 'compromise' or 'alliance' – the usual terms employed – was, in fact, possible as between contrasting civilisations. No conscious tactical arrangement, no deal lasting for a season, was conceivable between social forces of this complexity and magnitude. Amalgamation was the only real possibility, a fusion of different classes and their diverse cultures into one social order capable of guaranteeing social stability and keeping the proletariat in its place. The history of England from the late 18th century onwards is in large measure the story of this fusion, its strains, achievements, and bizarre results.

Because the social and cultural factors in this process of mutual class absorption were disparate, the resultant civilisation was itself deeply *heterogeneous* in character. Inside this permanent, organic compromise the landlords kept control of the State and its main organs, as a governing élite trusted (on the whole) by the bourgeoisie. The contrast between this situation and most other bourgeois democracies is very striking; in general, bourgeois republics (like the different French republics, the United States, Italy after unification, the democratic periods of German history, etc.) give rise to a political élite recruited more or less directly from the ranks of the bourgeoisie itself, to a class of professional men of politics who represent the interests, the outlook, the culture of the bourgeoisie directly. They are part of a homogeneous social order. Pre-bourgeois elements have usually persisted in these societies, certainly – but generally in the shape of a peasantry, a subordinate rural order elbowed aside in the evolution of capitalism and of ever-diminishing importance. In England, paradoxically, the more advanced rural order preceding the rise of capitalism survived as the *master* of the latter. Not the peasantry but the aristocracy itself survived, in the face of the inevitable political and ideological feebleness of the emergent bourgeoisie, as the governors of the most dynamic capitalist system in the world. And landowning civilisation survived with them, as a mode of living, a culture and language, a type of personality and psychology, a whole dominant ethos.

For the successful functioning of the new composite social order, this ethos *had* to impose itself upon the mentality of society as large as the apex of civilisation, as the very image of genuine culture – the embodiment of the superior life – values outwit the economic process, the process of bourgeois accumulation and its 'materialism'. The political élite, therefore, does not in these circumstances appear in the least as a simple expression of the economically dominant class – as a 'committee' charged with looking after the collective affairs and interests of the bourgeoisie, in Marx's phrase. Instead, it appears as the emanation of a distinct social class, independent of and separate from the main conflicts and concerns of urban, capitalist society. It is not formed by the State and State institutions (the public educational system, State universities, technocratic colleges like the French *grandes écoles*) but has its own, natural, basis. It links the present to the past in an (apparently) unbroken tradition of authority, summing up this past in an effortless, natural assumption of the habits and posture of power here and now. This assumption is fortified by its association with the general social values of refinement – with life as something to be lived, not existed for the sake of accumulation. The State, political power, become in this way the centre of a vast social mystique – functioning within a set of ideas and attitudes and feelings and inhibitions that are, themselves, a form of hegemony.

It is often observed that all capitalist classes, as soon as their freedom of action economically is assured, become rapidly conservative in outlook. The English capitalist class, because of the peculiar circumstances attending its birth, was conservative from the outset. But it did not evolve its own conservatism, as the product of a unified bourgeois culture. The perfect model of social conservatism was before its eyes, in the social order of the English agrarian world. Modern English conservatism was the product, therefore, of a grafting process whereby the emergent society of industrial capitalism took this older world into itself, as its head, its directing organ capable of looking after its vital interests and able to provide a kind of authority, a many-sided hegemony superior to anything that it – in its notorious crudity – could develop.

This is not to say, obviously, that there were no conflicts between industrial capitalism and the landlords, at times difficult of solution (as in 1832 and 1846). But how secondary these episodes appear, in the longer perspectives of English social history! How profoundly this unique process of class assimilation has sunk into the very texture of English life, into the nature of our social conscious-ness and social relations, into our institutions, our customs, our feelings, our language! The very urban world, the bricks and mortar in which most of the population lives, is the image of this archaic, bastard conservatism – an urban world which has nothing to do with urban *civilisation*, as this is conceived in other countries with an old and unified bourgeois culture. That most bourgeois of Conservative premiers, Stanley Baldwin, could solemnly and characteristi-cally declare, as late as 1924, that he thought the countryside was 'the essential England', and that England would always be 'essentially in the countryside'. Few would have contradicted this sentiment then. In 1964, the aberrant obses-sion with the countryside is still a powerful feature of our culture – the country house, as the image of true civilisation and social cultivation, has sunk so deeply into the national soul. The modern British town is merely the obverse of this, in its meaninglessness. Culturally, as an artefact of real civilisation, it has never existed, because civilisation went on elsewhere, in the residences of the territo-rial aristocracy and gentry (or, just possibly, in the West End of the metropolis, where they customarily spent part of the year, and in the institutional embodi-ments of gentlemanly culture at Oxford and Cambridge). The squalid, crassly utilitarian town with neither shape nor centre; the suburb, which grotesquely mimics the rural ideal; the dignified country home in its landscaped park, an inevitable focus of taste, ideal social relations, and natural authority, all that the merely bourgeois town is not and has renounced: in this contrast of environ-ments (as in a thousand other contrasts and contradictions) the heterogeneous, paradoxical character of English society and culture is revealed – the true meaning of the 'slow evolution', the conservative empiricism of which (until yesterday) apologists were so proud.

Political life generally has to be studied in relation to its social background and meaning. This is perhaps especially so in the case of the traditional British political class – it is such a peculiar institution that observation of it which does not take the structure of British society very fully into account tends to be no more than another form of mystification. It has to be seen as one aspect of the complex, unique social drama of British bourgeois society. The principal fault of Guttsman's study is that it does not penetrate far enough into this drama. He is concerned, primarily, with the changing social composition of the political élite, with the social class and background of its individual members at different times: the élite was almost wholly landowning in 1832, became more 'middle-class' in membership from 1868 onwards, and eventually acquired a work-ing-class admixture through the Labour Party (although the latter, as he puts it characteristically, 'have, in the course of their rise in the governing hierarchy, tended to become absorbed in the wider political ruling class'). The core of the problem is, certainly, that:

> The persistence of aristocratic rule in a country which, thanks largely to its entrepreneurial middle class, had reached a position of economic and indus-trial eminence in Europe is an extraordinary historical phenomenon.

But Guttsman's somewhat narrow approach does not lead to any comprehen-sion of *why* this happened, of the underlying logic or *raison d'être* of the system. He describes, painstakingly, often admirably, what happened sociologically in the evolution of the political governing class; not what the process *meant*, in a more ample socio-historical perspective. For example, he describes at some length the ideological means by which the landlords justified their hegemony, such as the theory of the 'natural' political constitution expressing the real division of forces in society, the notion of the virtues of hierarchy and tradition as such, the concep-tion of the necessity of some ruling élite and its corollary – the idea of the 'rabble' below, always waiting to push its way into power and destroy civilisation. (Ch. III, 'The Self-legitimation of a Ruling Class'). But *why* was this archaic ideological concoction so palatable to the majority of the 'entrepreneurial middle class', whose level of intelligence – one must presume – was not particularly low?

Is it unduly carping to criticise a study in this way – because, in effect, it does not say or try to say everything? Especially a study so excellent in many respects as this one, so full of useful information about a vitally important topic that has been usually treated uncritically in the past? Hard as it may seem, I think it is better to refuse this obvious objection. We cannot afford to do otherwise. Studies of any aspect of society, even the most central, have their real meaning only in relation to all the rest – to a social structure as a whole, seen historically. And it is not the case that we have any sufficient idea of British society at this level – not the case that there is even a rudimentary historical debate regarding the total development of British society, in terms adequate to the difficult complexity of the subject. The immense mystificatory power of the old social order and its ideological arms; a self-satisfied lack of curiosity about British society; the false, atomistic 'empiricism' of the academic mentality; the conse-quent tardy growth and bias of British sociological thought – all these things stand between us and even beginning to understand what we need to under-stand about Britain, and ourselves. Until this has ceased to be so, it will be more important to ask questions and frame hypotheses (however 'vague' and 'specu-lative') about the whole than to be precise about the parts – in order that, ulti-mately, partial studies can be carried out still more precisely and significantly than is now possible, as features contributing to and clarifying some general, meaningful, intellectual landscape.

Nevertheless, it must be admitted that as a compendium of sociological information about the British political élite, Mr Guttsman's book is remarkable. His researches are summed up in a vast series of tables and diagrams that will be consulted by generations of students. Among these are, for instance: 'Occupations of Fathers of Aristocratic and Middle-Class Cabinet Ministers, 1868–1955', 'Background of Under Secretaries, 1868–1945', 'Religious Affiliations in the Group of Middle-Class Cabinet Ministers, 1868–1955', 'Composition of the Revolt inside Labour's Ranks in Post-War Years', 'Affiliations of Members of the Conservative Government, 1951–55, with other Elite Groups'; and so forth. There does not seem to be much that one could want to know about the political directorate, and that is expressible in this way, that Guttsman has not charted for us.

He concludes that: 'There exists today in Britain a "ruling class", in spite of all the changes he has described. The political élite does not 'stand out in almost singular eminence', as it used to do, nowadays 'it appears to share its position at the apex of power with a number of other élite groups' (all of which together are the 'ruling class'). But it is still supreme among these other élites, and is still an élite. The fact worries Guttsman. 'The strength and power of the British upper class has largely remained,' he sadly observes, and points out that only a determined optimist will think that those who happen to find their way into its persistent élite formation 'are inevitably or by definition the men best suited to govern us'. What is the answer? More democracy, more equality, he suggests, an effort to render our rulers more really representative of the nation and its talents. 'For our complex modern society to function efficiently talent and élite position ought to be closely linked.' Hence, the inefficient and privilege-ridden educational system should be reformed so as to eliminate this 'wasting of talent'. We have to smarten up our notions, and 'keep in step with the more widespread egalitarian feeling of the 20th century'. In a final, bold challenge to the reader's democratic instincts, he admonishes everyone to 'face squarely such issues as the selection of potential rulers, the control of the leadership, the widening scope for talent, the turnover of élites, the development of ability and the fostering of critical understanding throughout the population'.

Who disagrees with him? The conviction that something is wrong has penetrated into the darkest and most hopeless recesses of the national mind, and the suggested solutions which come forth are always the same: greater equality of opportunity leading to more efficient leadership, a reform of institutions and ideas for the sake of a more efficient and dynamic conduct of affairs, the liquidation of out-of-date customs in the name of progress and a more honourable showing on the international scene. But to see the familiar formulae emerging from such a large-scale historical study as this makes their oddness more evident. What do they *mean*, in the peculiar perspectives of British socio-historical evolution? In what strange, parochial world can such bourgeois banalities as these arise and be felt as boldly progressive answers to a crisis? Guttsman does not sense the paradox of the situation, because it lies outside the framework of reference he employs.

In part, surely, the unease one feels before programmes of this sort comes from their anachronism. They are, so to speak, by right part of the 'revolution which did not happen', 150 years ago, aspects of that general rationalisation and levelling of society that the emergent bourgeoisie ought to have accomplished but did not. They were on the programme of Jeremy Bentham and the Utilitarians, long before they reappeared on the programmes of Messrs Macmillan, Sampson, Shanks, Chapman, etc, etc. But the English middle classes chose an organic 'alliance' with the pre-existing forms of society, from fear of a radicalism that might over-reach itself, and because their easily attained economic domination of the world permitted them to bear the cost of the operation. In their peculiar historical situation, the advantages outweighed the disadvantages: the hegemony of a ruling caste was 'efficient' enough, it brought with it social stability in spite of the general, pseudo-feudal conservatism which it also clamped permanently on to bourgeois society. The classic era of imperialism succeeded the period of British industrial domination, and its effect was to harden further the arteries of this conservatism, to apparently justify in retrospect the path of the British bourgeoisie. Only in the most advanced stages of imperial decline have real doubts arisen on this score, in the last few years – but no sooner have they arisen than they become universal, trite diagnoses embraced by every newspaper and every commentator.

But false consciousness is not evaded as easily as that, even when circumstances demand some discarding of illusions. The new ideology brings us, at least, out of the medieval shadows and into a plainly bourgeois world of values. But what does such a step forward mean, in the second part of the 20th century? In a world where economic concentration has reached its present pitch, a world of State-supported monopoly capitalism and continental struggles for power? Under the new, harsher conditions confronting British capitalism, the British bourgeoisie has decided that the archaic historical baggage it has so far carried with it has become a mere dead-weight, a hindrance to necessary development, to be exchanged overnight for something more rational. But the reason it chooses, and must choose, is that of the bourgeois revolutions of the past – like a faint, rather comic, echo of great historical voices and movements long by-passed in the general evolution of capitalism. In order to catch up with events, it must try to make amends for past deficiencies, to advance to democracy, equality, and bourgeois dynamism, in a world ripe, or 'over-ripe', for socialism. In a world where, under ideal bourgeois-democratic conditions, the traditional pseudo-aristocratic élite can only be replaced by some British equivalent of Mills' 'power élite', where equality is falsified from the outset by vast new hierarchies of economic organisation and power.

This is not to say that such measures of rationalization should not be effected, even by socialists. But they must be seen for what they are, historically, and not in terms of the *inevitably* false consciousness in which they are now presented. The only aspect of the programmes of renovation which is clearly different is, of course, the demand for some kind of planning of the economy: a traditional *socialist* demand, taken over by the bourgeoisie and adapted to its own needs. This ought to remind us of where we are, in history.

We must hope, and do our best to ensure that the Labour Party remembers such elementary facts, if it comes back to power. It used to be taken in by the old mystifications. Can it avoid subjection to the new ones?

CHAPTER TWO

The English Working Class

New Left Review, I/24

MARCH–APRIL 1964

I

THE ENGLISH WORKING class is one of the enigmas of modern history. Its development as a class is divided into two great phases, and there appears at first sight to be hardly any connection between them.

It was born in conditions of the utmost violence, harshly estranged from all traditional and tolerable conditions of existence and thrown into the alien, inchoate world of the first industrial revolution. Formed in this alienation by the blind energies of the new capitalist order, its sufferings were made more hopeless by the severest political and ideological persecution. From the outset it inspired fear by its very existence. In the time of general fear produced by the French Revolution, such dread and hostility became chronic, affecting the old ruling class and the new industrial bourgeoisie alike, and creating a climate of total repression. What was possible but revolt, in the face of this? Humanity, pulverised and recast in this grim mould, had to rebel in order to live, to assert itself as more than a mere object of history, as more than an economic instrument. The early history of the English working class is therefore a history of revolt, covering more than half a century, from the period of the French Revolution to the climax of Chartism in the 1840s.

And yet, what became of this revolt? The great English working class, this titanic social force which seemed to be unchained by the rapid development of English capitalism in the first half of the century, did not finally emerge to dominate and remake English society. It could not break the mould and fashion another. Instead, after the 1840s it quickly turned into an apparently docile class. It embraced one species of moderate reformism after another, became a consciously subordinate part of bourgeois society, and has remained wedded to the narrowest and greyest of bourgeois ideologies in its principal movements.

Why did this happen? It is important for us to try and understand why, for many reasons. But above all, because the difficulties confronting any socialist revolution in Britain today are as much the long-term product of this astonishing transformation as of any development in the ruling class or any evolution in the structure and techniques of capitalism.

II

The problem of the English working class cannot be separated from that of the growth of English bourgeois society as a whole – that is, it is one part of a wider enigma, and is normally obscured like everything else by those liberal mystifications the English have erected in honour of their past. We have a long way to go in penetrating this general obscurity. Nevertheless, one vital fact surely emerges and imposes itself upon any serious consideration of the origins of the English working class.

Given the time and circumstances of its birth, this class was fated to *repeat*, in certain respects, the historical experience of the English bourgeoisie itself.

The revolutionary period of the English bourgeoisie occurred early in the general evolution of capitalism, earlier than that of any equivalent class in a major country. Those urban and rural middle classes who made the Revolution of 1640 were pioneers of bourgeois development, advancing blindly into a new world. Such blindness was the price of being in the van. Although the English Revolution attempted like other revolutions to escape from the general blindness and chance of historical evolution in a conscious remaking of society, the attempt was inevitably crippled by the lack of the very materials for an adequate consciousness of this sort. The final destruction of English feudalism in the period 1640–60 took place long before the full flowering of bourgeois ideology. Initiating the cycle of bourgeois expansion in this way, the English middle classes could not hope to benefit from a new conception of the world that was itself produced in the course of the cycle and reached maturity at a later date. Hence, although they contributed powerfully to the Enlightenment their practical struggles were necessarily conducted in terms of a pre-Enlightenment philosophy, a religious world-view unequal to what was at stake, English Puritanism. This fact explains a large part of those aspects of the Revolution which appear to us as a failure: its profound *empiricism*, the patchwork of compromise and makeshift it ended in, and the resultant organic coalescence with the English *ancien régime*.

But economically, of course, the Revolution was not a failure. Out of the mercantile society which triumphed in it, capitalist forms of production arose with giant force, threatening in their turn the equilibrium of that society. Dependent for their inception upon a new race of free, disinherited labourers, these forms in their violent rise soon swelled this labour force into a major social class, an even greater potential threat to society, to the old patrician order of mercantilism and the new industrialism alike.

Thus, the first bourgeois class to occupy the centre of the world historical scene engendered the first great proletariat. And the latter was inevitably forced into existence as far from the worldview it needed as the former had been. Any coherent and adequate proletarian ideology, the theory and practice of socialism, lay hidden in the future, the fruit of many struggles and debates in many countries. The English working class too was bound to grope its way in history.

To this central fact, the unavoidable darkness of its time, were added other constricting conditions derived from the peculiarities of English bourgeois development. The very precocity of the English bourgeoisie had, paradoxically, brought in its train a subsequent retardation of growth. 'The Revolutions of 1648 and 1789 were not *English* and *French* revolutions', according to Marx, 'they were revolutions of a *European* pattern... The Revolution of 1648 was the victory of the 17th century over the 16th century, the Revolution of 1789 the victory of the 18th century over the 17th century.'[1] The English bourgeoisie was to remain partly set within this pattern of the 17th century; it retains something of it even today. The conquests and prosperity of mercantile England, its emergence as one of the two world-powers, the great economic advance culminating in the Industrial Revolution – these were the real nerve and meaning of bourgeois development, its historical agency as creator of a new mode of production. Blind empiricism had opened the door to this triumph. Blind empiricism and its consequences were justified by it. The English bourgeoisie stood apart from the victory of the 18th century, isolated in a unique path of evolution, half innovator, half anachronism, bringing forth a new world from the very bowels of society while in heart and head it looked back to an older one. It was the most confident ruling class in modern history. What need did it have of the Enlightenment? It could take what it wanted from it, and produce its own limited, parochial Enlightenment in the shape of political economy and Utilitarianism. When the pattern of the 18th century finally erupted in 1789, it first greeted it, mistakenly, as a repetition of its own experience of the previous century, and then after realizing the mistake fought it to the death. This battle between the two great bourgeois revolutions crystallised all the peculiarities of English bourgeois development in a quite decisive way. Its estrangement from the central current of later bourgeois evolution was confirmed by this event, the insular destiny of its civilisation.

The English working class was to be the principal victim of such estrangement. For the bourgeoisie, it was simply the accompaniment to a world economic hegemony, a natural form of consciousness and conduct, justified by practice, a national pride. For a century, nothing was to contradict this confidence. But from the beginning, the fortune of the bourgeoisie was the undoing of the working class; the former's characteristic mode of appropriation of the world was a characteristic mode of expropriation of the latter, a unique way of preventing it from appropriating the world in its turn.

The French Revolution was in general the practical realisation of the Enlightenment, its translation into politics. Its most radical phase, the Jacobin dictatorship, was the realisation of the most advanced and democratic conceptions of the Enlightenment, and was enacted by the only stratum of the bourgeoisie capable of pushing the Revolution to its limit, the petite bourgeoisie, in alliance

---

1 *The Bourgeoisie and the Counter-Revolution*, pp. 67–68, Selected Works, Vol. 1.

with the workers, the peasants, and various dispossessed groups. The Jacobin ascendancy and Terror were what essentially distinguished the French Revolution from its great predecessor of the 17th century. The Jacobins of the English Revolution, the Levellers, had been defeated by Cromwell and his 'Girondins', the 'grandees', the forces of large landed and commercial property. But the French bourgeoisie, in its revolutionary struggle against the far more powerful and regressive French *ancien régime, needed* Jacobinism as the English had not. English feudalism and would-be absolution were swept away without the fire of Jacobinism.

Jacobinism, in one sense the apex of bourgeois progress, the most radical affirmation of its worldview, is nevertheless the most mixed of blessings in the future development of bourgeois society. Through it, capital comes into its inheritance by the active hegemony of classes destined to be expropriated by capital; it rises to dominance out of the herculean efforts and organised violence of its own future servants. But this origin is the worst of precedents for its own future stability. As the French bourgeoisie was to discover repeatedly in the 19th century, the great stamp imposed upon society by this critical experience – the noblest of all bourgeois achievements, a patrimony which it could not and cannot to this day fail to acknowledge – was also the never-ending source of its own weakness. It was a mark of Cain, perpetually visible as such to all the disinherited. While the bourgeoisie made a living museum of the revolutionary tradition, it remained a living inspiration, a promise surviving every defeat, to the masses.

Marx described this paradox of bourgeois development in the *Communist Manifesto*, claiming that the bourgeoisie 'in all its battles sees itself compelled to appeal to the proletariat, to ask for its help, and thus to drag it into the political arena. The bourgeoisie itself, therefore, supplies the proletariat with its own elements of political and general education, in other words it furnishes the proletariat with weapons for fighting the bourgeoisie.'[2] But in England the peculiar evolution of the bourgeoisie did *not* provide the English popular masses and the English proletariat with such a 'political and general education'. Not only had the English Revolution by-passed Jacobinism. The Revolution itself was buried in a morass of euphemism and misrepresentation, like some infantile trauma driven deep into the national subconscious. As a result, in this English bourgeois universe all appeared as 'locked fast as in a sort of family settlement; grasped as in a kind of mortmain for ever'.[3] The bourgeoisie, through its piecemeal entry on to the scene, was able to appropriate all the tradition of the dead generations and render it a living, oppressive, mystifying presence. What was written in the English sky, to correspond to the towering words of 1789, '*Liberté, Egalité, Fraternité*'? The shamanism of the British Constitution, an

---

2 *Communist Manifesto*, p. 43, ibid.

3 Edmund Burke, *Reflections on the Revolution in France*, p. 83 Oxford Worlds' Classics Edition.

assorted repertoire of (largely fake) antiquities, the poisonous remains of the once revolutionary ideology of Puritanism, and the anti-revolutionary invective of Edmund Burke.

The manufacturers, the new industrial bourgeoisie of the period 1789–1832, were certainly discontented with the old order, with the 'family settlement' inherited from 1688. They wanted a larger place in it, but not as the Third Estate had wanted its rights in France – that is, as an absolute necessity, a *sine qua non* of all further progress. They had already progressed so far that a revolutionary demand of this sort was ridiculous. A reform of the terms of the settlement was required, nothing more. Listen to the voice of their most rational and radical spokesman, expounding the characteristic English version of '*égalité*': 'A single mistake in extending equality too far may overthrow the social order and dissolve the bonds of society,' mumbled Jeremy Bentham. 'Equality might require such a distribution of property as would be incompatible with security... Equality ought not to be favoured, except when it does not injuriously affect security, nor disappoint expectations aroused by the law itself, nor disturb a distribution already actually settled and determined.'[4] It was too late for an English Jacobinism.

The English working class, therefore, was not only born far from socialism. This fact in itself, though inevitable, was not necessarily a fatal handicap. To proceed empirically is of no importance, if one can learn in time to do better – history is largely a tale of groping in the dark, a condition no person or class can miraculously escape from. Not merely time, but a concrete combination of historical factors positively *separated* the English working class from socialism. It was, so to speak, deprived of a whole dimension of growth from the beginning. This privation was also, in the widest and most authentic sense, a *popular* one. That is, it concerned not simply the emergent proletariat, but the numerous closely-related strata of the 'people' out of which it emerged historically, and from which it was for long scarcely distinguishable: artisans and out-workers, the urban crowds of casual workers and workless, the petty bourgeoisie of small producers in town and country. These heterogeneous subordinate masses, pre-capitalist or half-capitalist in nature and outlook, were the potential social force behind Jacobinism. It is only through the early revolutionary radicalism of the bourgeoisie that they can dominate the historical scene, that the 'petty' bourgeoisie ceases to be in any sense 'petty' and assumes a transitory heroic rôle. Capital, by the relative ease with which it conquered and transformed English society, always kept these classes in subordination. The English petty bourgeoisie was deprived of the chance to play its heroic part in history. English radicalism was permanently reduced to a phenomenon of *protest*, burdened with an 'oppositional' mentality the very reverse of 'Jacobin' mentality, spasmodic in its appearances and, of course, infected with religious mania. This was the terrible negative 'education' inflicted on the English working class.

---

4 *The Theory of Morals and Legislation*, pp. 119–129.

Alienated in this fashion from everything finest in bourgeois tradition, by the inner conditions of English social evolution, the masses suffered the *coup de grâce* from the new external conditions of the war against France from 1793 until 1815. Jacobinism became, not only something extraneous, but the face of an enemy, the object of patriotic hatred. National fervour became another weapon in the hands of the bourgeoisie, a reinforcement of its internal good fortune. English separateness and provincialism; English backwardness and traditionalism; English religiosity and moralistic vapouring; paltry English 'empiricism', or instinctive distrust of reason – all these features which, seen in an abstractly comparative perspective, may appear as 'defects' or 'distortions' of bourgeois development in England, were in reality hammered together into a specific form of bourgeois hegemony during the infancy of the working class. The British Constitution, claimed Burke, 'works after the pattern of nature'. That is, it and all the rest were made to appear as merely parts of nature, and so inevitable – aspects of an English firmament, like the south-west wind and the rain, not so many forms of domination of capital.

The French bourgeoisie could only triumph by forging a double-edged sword, a weapon the working class could in its turn develop and use against its rulers. The German bourgeoisie, frustrated in its early development, consoled itself with an intellectual world of heroic proportions and intensity, a world out of which, in spite of its abstractness and spiritualism, the seminal ideas of socialism could come. But the English bourgeoisie, more fortunate, could afford to dispense with the dangerous tool of reason and stock the national mind with historical garbage. Capital did not have to resort to self-wounding excesses to establish its reign in England; it could hide behind the Bible, and make of practically everything 'national' an instrument, direct or indirect, of dominion.

Such was the cage of circumstances into which the English working class was bound to grow up. Such were the full, daunting dimensions of the alienation awaiting it, above and beyond the economic and human alienation which was the stuff of its daily life. From the beginning, a giant's task confronted it.

III

British socialists are fortunate indeed to possess the great account of the origins of the English working class which has recently appeared: Edward Thompson's *The Making of the English Working Class*.[5] Above all, because it concentrates attention upon what must be our primary concern, the role of the working class as maker of history. Engaged in constant polemic against vulgar determinism, Thompson insists that: 'The working class made itself as much as it was made',[6]

---

5 Victor Gollancz, 1963.

6 op. cit., p. 194.

and indicates how by the time of the Great Reform Bill in 1832 the working class had become an active influence whose 'presence can be felt in every county in England, and in most fields of life'.[7] The working class was not merely the product of economic forces, but also realised itself in 'a social and cultural formation' partly directed against the operation of these very forces. Thompson's book is essentially the history of this revolt.

The popular masses out of which the working class arose remained for generations attached to pre-industrial traditions, their resistance to capitalism was also a reaching back towards this way of life, an attempt to recreate an ideal society of small, independent men controlling their own fate. The deepest sympathy with this aspect of popular sentiment is characteristic of Thompson's approach. Such aspirations were inevitably blotted out by the onward rush of capitalism, but were not for this reason unimportant or contemptible, and the author wants to 'rescue the poor stockinger, the Luddite cropper, the 'obsolete' hand loom weaver, the 'utopian' artisan, and even the deluded followers of Joanna Southcott, from the enormous condescension of posterity...'.[8] The slow, secular gestation of the first industrial revolution, the long phases of capital accumulation which opened the way to industrial capitalism, had created a rich, varied artisan culture with tenacious roots. During the period of formation of the working class, the most influential representative of this tradition was the journalist William Cobbett. Cobbett was typical in thinking of the misery and convulsion of the time as being an assault upon the immemorial rights of the 'freeborn Englishman'. These rights, located in a mythical past, had to be defended and reasserted as a peculiarly English heritage. Thus, the traditions and never-ending retrospection of the ruling class were to be fought with an even deeper and more backward-looking traditionalism: radicalism was in essence the restoration of a kind of English golden age. This was 'the ideology of the small producers', as Thompson admits.[9] But he also insists upon the extent to which this sort of thinking was developed by the contact with the new proletarian public, and shows how its particular defensive strength was employed in the new situation. Even the Protestant dissident sects, in spite of their abject otherworldliness, had preserved a 'slumbering Radicalism'[10] with elements of resistance in it. In the conditions of the time, the new working class was desperately short of means of resistance. It has to utilise everything to hand, and posterity has no right to be condescending about the terrible limitations of what ensued, the crop of hybrid, even pathological, unions which the workers were saddled with.

Here, as so often, the author's sympathy and passion carry us to a real understanding of happenings; in his company, we penetrate beyond the level of

7   op. cit., p. 807.
8   op. cit., p. 12.
9   op. cit., p. 759.
10 op. cit., p. 30.

mere chronology, into real history, into an imaginative recreation of the experience of the past. He is engaged in constant polemic with the academic 'objectivity' which sees history as a relation of the 'facts', and the 'facts' as whatever can be expressed statistically. He tries consistently to grasp for us 'the quality of life' under the Industrial Revolution. This requires 'an assessment of the total life experience, the manifold satisfactions or deprivations, cultural as well as material, of the people concerned'.[11] Only an imaginative effort of this sort brings us to the reality, the human dimensions of what happened. And it is in this sense that Thompson defends a 'classical' view of the period, as one of mass immiseration and suffering, against the empiricists who have maintained that, after all, it saw some rise in the standard of living. 'During the years between 1780 and 1840 the people of Britain suffered an experience of immiseration, even if it is possible to show a small statistical improvement in material conditions', he points out, 'the process of industrialisation was carried through with exceptional violence in Britain... This violence was done to *human* nature.'[12] The fundamental curse of the era was the very thing which raised the standard of living – the new economic conditions of life, the new alienation of the work-process itself which 'casts the blackest shadow over the years of the Industrial Revolution'.[13]

Besides the romantic, backward-looking resistance to industrialisation represented by Cobbett, the English people were presented with another ideology during the same years: that of Tom Paine. The English bourgeoisie had shut out the more revolutionary aspects of the Enlightenment. Paine did his best to make up for this. *The Rights of Man* and *The Age of Reason* are injections of pure Enlightenment rationalism, the militant and democratic optimism of a newer bourgeois world. Here was the authentic voice of an English Jacobinism, and Thompson reminds us how important it was: '... the main tradition of 19th century working-class Radicalism took its cast from Paine... Until the 1880s it remained transfixed within this framework.'[14] But if this was so, could not Paine fill the lacuna left by the cramped intellectual development of the bourgeoisie, could not this tradition educate the working class into the aggressive egalitarianism the masters had no use for? The ruling class had abandoned Reason for a footling reasonableness – why could its subjects not appropriate the lost heritage for themselves?

A book, however significant and popular, cannot itself permanently change and educate great masses of people. The presence and diffusion of the right ideas may be a necessary condition of advances in mass consciousness, but other conditions lie in the day-to-day awareness of people, their practical experience

11   op. cit., p. 444.
12   op. cit., pp. 445–6.
13   op. cit., p. 446.
14   op. cit., p. 96.

of reality. It is these which were decisive in this case. In considering what Thompson says on this theme, we approach the central nerve of his argument. 'Had events taken their 'natural' course,' he observes, 'we might expect there to have been some show-down long before 1832, between the oligarchy of land and commerce and the manufacturers and petty gentry, with working people in the tail of the middle-class agitation... But after the success of the *Rights of Man*, the radicalisation and terror of the French Revolution, and the onset of Pitt's repression... the aristocracy and the manufacturers made common cause. The English *ancien régime* received a new lease of life...'[15] There was to be no second revolution in England. 'The only alliance strong enough to effect it fell apart; after 1792 there were no Girondins to open the doors through which the Jacobins might come.'[16] Another instalment of bourgeois revolution was only possible if a significant enough section of the substantial middle class wanted it, and was prepared to risk the 'alliance' in question. Only this could have disrupted the forces of property and weakened the régime enough to launch a revolution, providing the circumstances under which the petty bourgeoisie and workers might have obtained power. By themselves, the latter were incapable of generating a revolutionary situation, whatever ideas were in their minds. But it is situations, and action, the bite of experience, which crystallise ideas from the 'mind' into the nervous system itself, making of them a dominating reflex and redrawing the limits of consciousness. Perhaps this is truest of all in the case of revolutionary ideas, struggling as they are against the dense weight of most historical culture – and how few those critical situations are that can be turned into hinges of history in this way, 1789, 1917 or 1949! Hence, neither Paine nor any other revolutionary ideology could really penetrate and dominate the 'subpolitical attitudes' of English subordinate classes. In several crucial passages, Thompson indicates what occurred instead.

The fundamental experience of the masses, in the period of the making of the working class, was the very opposite of coherent, aggressive self-assertion. It was an experience of being driven into revolt, and finding every means of expression cut away, every channel hopelessly blocked, every friendly element neutralised. In this historical nightmare 'the revolutionary impulse was strangled in its infancy; and the first consequence was that of bitterness and despair'.[17] Psychologically, a sort of withdrawal was the only possibility, the turning-in of a whole class upon itself. Escape was possible solely on the level of fantasy: in what Thompson describes, eloquently, as the 'ritualised form of psychic masturbation' provided by the Methodist Revival, or in the even more demented vagaries of Joanna Southcott and other prophets. The chapters on the ghastly religious terrorism into which Puritanism had degenerated at this period are, indeed,

---

15 op. cit., p. 197.
16 op. cit., p. 178.
17 op. cit., p. 177.

among the most instructive and impressive things in the book.[18] 'In the decades after 1795 there was a profound alienation between classes in Britain, and working people were thrust into a state of *apartheid* whose effects... can be felt to this day... Segregated in this way, their institutions acquired a peculiar toughness and resilience. Class also acquired a peculiar resonance in English life: everything... was turned into a battleground of class. The marks of this remain...'[19] Here was the result of the long, sporadic, ill-organised revolt of the proletariat, in the first generation of its existence: apartheid, apartness – within the new capitalist social order, whose laws supposedly abolished feudal ranks and levelled all relations to that of the business contract, the working class was beaten by repression almost into the condition of a feudal 'estate'. It was, so to speak, forced into a *corporative* mode of existence and consciousness, a class in and for itself within but not of society, generating its own values, organisations, and manner of life in conscious distinction from the whole civilisation round about it. Everywhere, the conditions of capitalism made of the worker something of an exile inside the society he supported. Only English conditions could bring about such total exile.

IV

But it is, paradoxically, precisely in relation to insights such as this that one feels the limitation of *The Making of the English Working Class*. We live in a society which, sociologically speaking, has been mainly working class for over a century. It is what it is, therefore, largely because of what the working class became, so that we must look with the most intense interest at any study of the formation of the class for clues as to this later evolution. There are many such hints in Thompson's book. But, exasperatingly, they remain hints. From his chosen period, 1789 to 1832, he looks backward in rich detail, describing popular traditions amply and appreciatively; while only occasional, almost incidental, remarks carry the reader forward in time to the maturity of the working class. This impression is aggravated by the inconclusive, even arbitrary, termination of the argument – the power of the work, the passion and enthusiasm animating it are such that one instinctively expects a more definite and sweeping conclusion. During the years of its terrible genesis, the English working class 'nourished, and with incomparable fortitude, the Liberty Tree. We may thank them for these years of heroic culture'. So the author ends. He is right, in their complacent embalming of the past the English have disfigured it, it is the duty, and the privilege, of socialists to rediscover and honour what deserves to be honoured, to make the past relive in the creative consciousness of the present. However, his study evokes other sentiments besides this gratitude, and Thompson has no words for them.

---

18   op. cit., v. Ch. xi, *The Transforming Power of the Cross.*
19   op. cit. pp. 177 & 832.

The formation of the English working class was a major tragedy. It was also one – and perhaps the greatest single – phase of *the* tragedy of modern times, the failure of the European working class to overthrow capital and fashion the new society that material conditions long ago made possible. The horrors of our time, Fascism and Stalinism, the agonising problems of 'under-development' and the Cold War, are all products of this disastrous failure. If the working class of only one major industrial nation had succeeded, the course of history would have been radically changed. And did not the English working class seem destined to lead the way? With what confidence Marx wrote, in 1854, surveying its prodigious growth, its irresistible numbers, the overwhelming contrast between this leviathan and the bogus façades of Old England!

> In no other country... has the war between the two classes that constitute modern society assumed such colossal dimensions, such distinct and palpable features. But it is precisely from these facts that the working classes of Great Britain, before all others, are called to act as leaders in the great movement that must finally result in the absolute emancipation of Labour.[20]

If, given the conditions of its origin, the English working class was bound to repeat to some extent the experience of the English bourgeoisie – should it not produce the first great and decisive working class revolution, the equivalent of 1640 in proletarian terms?

But the basic existential situations of the working class and the bourgeoisie are entirely different, and beyond a certain point this difference invalidates the comparison. Whereas the bourgeoisie arises as the agent of a new mode of production within medieval society, as a 'middle' propertied class established securely upon this basis, the working class possesses no corresponding foundation within capitalist society. It has nothing outside itself, its own organisation and consciousness. Hence, while the bourgeoisie was able to develop gradually, to transform the older order in stages as one kind of economic life fell apart before the piecemeal invasion of another, the working class cannot hope for the same sort of victory. In certain cases, the genesis of capitalism did bring about tremendous social tensions only resolvable by revolutions, in certain cases the bourgeoisie was compelled to evolve a pure, militant bourgeois consciousness as the weapon of its triumph – above all, in France. It was also possible for the bourgeoisie to transform society far more blindly and empirically, however, as the case of England shows – where 'empiricism' led to the most complete success of all, to the total subjection of society and economic domination of the world. And it is this kind of progress which is ruled out for the working class, and for socialism. Consciousness, theory, an intellectual grasp of social reality – these cannot occupy a subordinate or fluctuating place in the socialist transformation of society, no empirical anti-ideology or trust in the 'natural' evolution of affairs can substitute for them.

---

20 'Letter to the Labour Parliament', 1854, p. 402 *Marx & Engels on Britain*.

Consequently, in order really to 'repeat' the pattern of English history, the working class had to become what the bourgeoisie had never been – what it had renounced, what it had found effective replacements for, what it desired *not* to be with all its force of instinct. That is, a class dominated by reason. To become a new hegemonic force, capable of dominating society in its turn, the English working class absolutely required a consciousness containing the elements ignored by, or excised from, the consciousness of the English bourgeoisie.

This was the task that was completely, tragically, beyond the powers of the English working class. Nothing else was beyond its powers. In numbers, in essential solidarity and homogeneity, in capacity for organisation, in tenacity, in moral and civil courage, the English working class was, and is, one of the very greatest of social forces. And it has always existed in one of the least militarised of bourgeois states. No external fetters could ever have withstood this colossus. It was held by intangible threads of consciousness, by the mentality produced by its distinctive conditions and experience.

One of the chief virtues of *The Making of the English Working Class* is the writer's insistence on the role of consciousness in finally determining the character of a class, and of class relations. The new 'collective self-consciousness' was, he claims, the 'great spiritual gain of the Industrial Revolution'.[21] The positive aspects of this consciousness, its brotherliness and mutuality, its sense of dignity and community, are clearly brought home to us. But its limitations are not clearly presented, although they are no less important, and have lasted just as long. 'If we have in our social life little of the traditions of *égalité*,' he says, 'yet the class-consciousness of the working man has little in it of deference.'[22] The 'apartness' of working class consciousness, however, *implies* a kind of deference – for it resigns everything else, the power and secret of society at large, to others, to the 'estates' possessing authority or wealth. A corporative mode of consciousness turns aside from everything not the 'natural' or 'proper' affair of the corporation or class, all that does not belong to 'its' own world. A real sense of social equality – foreign to the English bourgeoisie – renders such a consciousness utterly impossible, for its nerve is the conviction that everything social is the proper affair of everybody, once and for all. Hence, the imposition of this profoundly corporative outlook on the workers was a fundamental victory for the ruling orders. It is true indeed that the working class 'made itself, as much as it was made' – but not *freely*, rather along the lines laid down by the bitter experiences Thompson recounts so well, lines which partly turned this self-activity of the working class into the instrument of its own subjection. In the alienation from certain universal values of the bourgeoisie – values vital to the farther evolution of society – lay a particularism, an ideological parochialism fatal to all revolutionary ideas. Revolution is the rejection of all corporative attitudes in the name of a vision of man.

---

21 Thompson, op. cit., p. 830.
22 ibid.

Yet this general reflection only conveys half of the tragedy, or half of the unique ascendancy the English bourgeoisie attained through it. The final bite of the process of formation of working class consciousness lay in the *integration* of the latter into an entire system of false consciousness, each element in which supported every other. The workers could not be transformed into this peculiar, densely corporate type of class, while the bourgeois became 'citizens'. There could be no 'citizens' in English society. The bourgeoisie had to remain a 'middle class' – as if feudalism was still in full vigour! – the 'backbone of the nation' functioning under yet another 'estate', the 'upper class' or ruling class. To the particularism of the working class, there had logically to correspond a whole web of particularisms, the weird heterogeneity and pluralism of society as a whole in England. The English social world *had* to become a world of the inexplicably concrete, the bizarre, the eccentric individual thing and person defying analysis. Is this not the true historical sense of the quiet madness of England? Even such endearing, exasperating, Dickensian lunacy had its historical function – the function, so to speak, of not seeming to have any function or meaning.

The final success of the system in subordinating the working class can be gauged, perhaps, in terms of the sheer *impossibility* of a *real* 'apartheid' of one class. The working class could not in reality create such a separate world. The separate, inward-turned class-consciousness could not be uniquely a means of protection of the positive values and 'way of life' of the workers – it was bound to be also a specific vehicle of assimilation, whereby bourgeois ideas and customs were refracted downwards into the working class. The result was not a *naked* imitation of the middle class, but a kind of translation – the kind of working class *caricature* of bourgeois ultra-respectability which puzzled and enraged Marx. The English working class transforms everything into its own corporative terms. Where in England can one find the perfect satirist's image of the bourgeois, if not among the older trade union leaders? But such mediate assimilation is more deadly than aping, precisely because it presupposes the self-activity of the class, because it reposes on a *genuine*, distinctly working-class consciousness.

Because of the intensive, apart character of working-class consciousness, no social or political doctrine ignoring the real economic position of the working class could grip it lastingly. It is possible to see the meaning of this, perhaps, if we recall Marx's observation on the French proletariat in its early days: 'The more developed and universal is the *political* thought of a people, the more the *proletariat* – at least at the beginning of the movement – wastes its forces on foolish and futile uprisings which are drowned in blood... Their political understanding obscures from them the roots of their social misery, it... eclipses their social instinct.'[23] The story of the English working class is almost the contrary

---

23 Article II, 'Vorwärts', 1844, pp. 236–37 of *Karl Marx: Selected Writings in Sociology and Social Philosophy*, ed. Bottomore & Rubel.

of this. This is the kind of *bloody* tragedy it escaped, thanks to the lack of development, the non-universality, of its political thought. The social instinct of the English proletariat could not be eclipsed; it was firmly embodied in a distinct class consciousness. But neither could it be expressed, realised positively in a non-corporative vision of the world, under the conditions of the time. Hence, the workers tried first of all to solve their problems with the Utopian-corporative ideology of Owenite trade-unionism, an attempt to build a kind of socialism in and for the working class itself, ignoring the rest of society. When this was proved impossible, their attention and force were directed to the question of hegemony over society as a whole – but in the totally inadequate forms provided by Chartism, a simple radical-democratic programme dissociated from the 'social instinct' of the class. No force on earth would have defeated a social movement and ideology really expressing and rooted in the social instinct of the English working class, not even if the English ruling class had imported all the gendarmes in Prussia. But the defeat of Chartism was absolute, because it was not so rooted. After the collapse of the movement, the working class was thrown back necessarily into itself, and into a more moderate and timid form of corporate action, into the trade-unionism which remains its basis to this day.

Unable to really 'repeat' the world-building experience of the English bourgeoisie, from 1850 onwards the working class indulges in a *false* repetition of that experience, in a kind of mimesis of bourgeois evolution as the latter was seen and misrepresented by the bourgeoisie itself. It behaves *as if* the workers, in their turn, could transform society in their own image by a gradual extension of their influence, by an accumulation of reforms corresponding to the bourgeois accumulation of capital. Customarily, this development is ascribed to external factors: the long prosperity of British capitalism after mid-century, at the zenith of its power, or the imperialism which followed and permitted the ruling class to 'bribe' the workers still farther and make them conscious of their superiority to foreign exploited masses. But *The Making of the English Working Class* brings us to a vivid realisation of the *internal* history that gave to such factors their true meaning and effect. It adds, or begins to add, a missing dimension to the history of the working class and of 'British Socialism'.

V

What could have made a difference, what could have prevented the fatal, closed evolution springing from the conditions Thompson describes? The temptation some will feel is to answer in one short, eloquent word: Marxism. Was not this the coherent, universal, hegemonic ideology of socialism alone corresponding to the social instinct of the English working class? But the word has only to be raised for the false simplicity of the answer to be obvious. The ideas of Marx penetrated the consciousness of the English workers less than anywhere else, when they eventually arrived on the scene.

The dialectical contradiction made evident by the failure of Marxism among English workers consists in this: the very type of intense class consciousness which preserves a fundamental authenticity of reflex and attitude – the prerequisite, the best guarantee of socialism – also conceals and renders inaccessible this vital area of awareness, beneath a carapace of dead matter. This carapace, the product of generations of the static, vegetative culture of working-class 'apartheid', with all its parochialism and elements of mimesis, cannot be split merely by the annunciation of Marxist ideas. Marxism is the product of the confluence and rethinking of all the major currents of bourgeois thought – it is the child of the Enlightenment and of German philosophy, as well as of English political economy. And in it, the ideas of classical economics assume a quite new significance and resonance. England, the home of political economy, is also historically estranged from the Enlightenment and German philosophy – consequently, in England Marxism encounters an environment in a sense estranged from, unaffected by, impervious to the very sources of Marxism itself, in spite of the national reverence for political economy.

This fact, together with the immense accumulation of historical peculiarities in England, on the level of the social superstructures and on the level of class consciousness and class relations, meant that Marxism as such – in the form of the commonly diffused basic schemes of 'vulgar Marxism' – was bound to be more or less *meaningless*. Presented in this fashion – as a kind of revealed truth on a plate – it could not possibly make fruitful contact with the actual experience and consciousness of the working class. If it could not enter into consciousness in this way, how could it change consciousness?

To put the matter in another way, very schematically: the characteristic of the English working class was its alienation from bourgeois reason, and an objective necessity for its self-realisation was the overcoming of this alienation. Hence, Marxism – which, of course, in content offered the possibility of just this – could only be absorbed in England through a truly gigantic process of thought, an intense and critical activity capable of compensating and remedying the deprivation. Marxism, to be effective, had to be the means whereby the working class threw off the immense, mystifying burden of false and stultifying consciousness imposed on it by English bourgeois civilisation. To be this, it had to be thought out organically in English terms as an unmystified consciousness of English history and society. But this was a prodigious cultural task. And in Victorian England there was no radical, disaffected intelligentsia to even undertake it.

All working class movements, all socialist movements, need 'theory'. The problem of consciousness and the changing of consciousness is always a crucial one. But in England, as Edward Thompson's book shows us, from the beginning the question assumed quite special acuteness, due to the special form of bourgeois hegemony in England and the special, distorted forms of consciousness this hegemony largely depended on. The problem was to create theory in an environment rendered impervious to rationality as such; to create the intense rational consciousness and activity which were the necessary pre-requisites of revolution in this society of totemised and emasculated consciousness, to generate the intellectual and emotional force capable of exploding the omnipresent weight of the tradition of the dead generations. The English working class, immunised against theory like no other class, by its entire historical experience, *needed* theory like no other.

It still does.

CHAPTER THREE

The Three Dreams
of Scottish Nationalism

New Left Review, I/49

MAY–JUNE 1968

MODERN SCOTTISH NATIONALISM has led a fluctuating, intermittent existence since 1853. Now, quite suddenly, it has become a more serious political reality. In the past it has gone through many renaissances, followed by even more impressive and longer-lasting collapses into inertia; but the present upsurge looks likely to last longer than others, at least, and to produce more of a mark on history.

Seen from without – from London, or in the perspective of British politics – the change appears welcome for many reasons. Like the companion Nationalism of the Welsh, it brings an element of novelty into the hopelessness and corruption of the post-imperial political scene. Obviously, fringe nationalisms will be good for the English, by forcing upon them a more painful reassessment of themselves than any they have yet undergone. The smug 'deep sleep' Orwell spoke of – the fruit of the oldest and most successful of modern imperialisms – would be more disturbed by the loss of Wales or Scotland then ever it was by the loss of India or Africa. And at the moment, a particular attraction to many must seem the near-destruction of the Labour Party's power which would result from the permanent loss of their Scottish or Welsh strongholds. In the slow, festering decay of British State and society, they are the most important forces of disintegration to have appeared yet: they prefigure the dismemberment of the united British society which built up the imperial system itself. They are at once a product of the collapse of the system, and the sharpest possible comment on the advanced state of this collapse. What justice it would be, if the Wilson Government which came to power to 'save the Pound' ended by losing Wales and Scotland as well!

The importance of the phenomenon demands that we should look at it less superficially, however. What is Scottish Nationalism in itself, as distinct from its external repercussions? Such a consideration of its meaning – as with other, comparable phenomena of modern nationalism – must lead to recognition of the deep contradictions embodied by it. Only some insight into these contradictions can allow us to try and form any real estimate of the movement's significance.

Dream-Country

Externally a positive reaction to the humiliating agony of a long era, Scottish Nationalism has another inwardness. For the Scots themselves, it is the late reflorescence of a dream, the hope of an identity, to which they have clung, obscurely and stubbornly, across centuries of provincial stagnation. Such a dream – and still more so, the time of its reflorescence – have a meaning which is bound to be far from clear outside Scotland.

Not that it seems too clearly appreciated within the country, either. Nothing demonstrates more surely the mythical nature of Scottish matter-of-factness and 'realism' than the small amount of effort the Scots have given to the prosaic understanding of what really matters to the country. Their dourness is at once a disguise, and a shield. A stony confrontation of the small change of living – counting the pence – protects them from a broader understanding that might threaten their identity: and also from what a Calvinist heritage apprehends as the sinful inner chaos. Behind the wary eyes and granite countenance of Scotland there lies not one dream only, but a whole inheritance of dreams, whose accumulation has made the psychology of modern Nationalism.

The now dominant dream of Scotland re-born should perhaps be seen as the third phase in the dream-psychology (which has very often been a dream-pathology) of Scottish history. It is deeply marked by both the great dreams that preceded it. Like them, its most important trait is a vast, impossible dissociation from the realities of history. The best short definition of Scottish history may be this: Scotland is the land where ideal has never, even for an instant, coincided with fact. Most nations have had moments of truth, at least. Scotland, never. The resultant chronic laceration of the Scots mind – most brilliantly conveyed to the world in Stevenson's fable of *Jekyll and Hyde* – is the thing which gives poignancy to the hope of a Scotland re-made, when seen from within. Scottish autonomy must appear there as the healing of the secular wound which has informed – and most often poisoned – Scottish consciousness ever since the Union of 1707. The real drama of the situation lies in its potential tragedy. It is not at all evident that the forms of autonomy one can reasonably foresee – whether partial or total – could cure the disease. They might perpetuate it, crystallising the long, central hopelessness of Scottish history within a framework of archaic bourgeois nationality.

But this is to anticipate. The logical place to begin is with the first tormented vision Scotland was subjected to: the Reformation. The great debate about Protestantism and Capitalism established a certain affinity between the two; it has not given us any formula for the easy interpretation of the actual relationship in any given society. However, this is not too hard in, say, 17th-century Holland, or in the London or Bristol of the same period. There the immediate value and efficacy of Protestantism as the ideology of a dynamic, mercantile middle class is evident. But the case of Scotland is radically different.

The fact is that the Reformation struck Scotland long before there was any significant mercantile or capitalist development there. Two centuries later, her native bourgeoisie was not strong enough even to retain its independence. Scottish capitalism did not flourish until after the Union, in the context of the British colonial empire. Yet, there is no doubt that Scotland was one of the most radically and successfully Reformed countries of Europe. The movement, which went on vigorously and progressively for over a hundred and fifty years, from the time of Knox to that of the covenanters, corresponds to the Revolutions which have left their stamp on the histories and national psychologies of other countries. Four centuries have passed since the Lords of the Congregation called John Knox home from Geneva to lead this Scottish Revolution. Yet their work is still felt, in every interstice of Scottish life. Often unacknowledged now, the ghosts still preside at every feast-day there, hidden regulators of the tongue.

This religious revolution derived its power and character precisely from its historical isolation. In the dreadful, chronic anarchy and mediaeval poverty of Scotland, it represented the one great effort of the Scottish people towards a meaningful order of their own. The effort was separated by centuries from the material conditions which – in Weber's or Tawney's thesis – should have corresponded to it, the processes of capital accumulation. This meant that originally the Reformation movement was an absolute attempt at moral and religious order, isolated from the very conditions that would have made it an integral part of history – at once 'corrupting' it, and bestowing upon it a real historical sense. Just because it could not be the veiled ideology of a class, the Scottish Reformation was bound to be an abstract, millennial dream – in effect, a desperate effort at escape from history, rather than a logical chapter in its unfolding. The Scots wanted, and needed, Salvation in the most total sense imaginable. Scotland's Revolution gave it them neat.

The harsh absoluteness of the Scots Theocracy reflected its historical displacement. It was a translation of theology into social relationships without mediation. Much more than an opiate, it provided a positive, partly democratic, intelligible social order that struck deep roots in a population whose historical experience until then had been a concentrated dose of everything worst about mediaeval Europe: dearth, weak central power, rapacious struggles for position, Church corruption, brigandage and wars. The divine, black dream divorced from time was also a form of civilisation. As one historian of the Kirk notes:

> The Kirk's Elders and Ministers who supervised the behaviour of every man and woman in the parish… were the nearest thing to a police force that most of Scotland knew till the 19th century. It was a force not because of any physical power but because of its prestige, because the people belonged to the Kirk and believed in it, even though they might grumble or tremble when it condemned their faults…'[1]

---

1   J. M. Reid, *Kirk and Nation: The Story of the Reformed Church of Scotland*, pp. 52–53.

The price the Scots paid, and still pay, for their possession by this dream was a high one. Long since, it turned into a detestable and crippling burden against which every form of creative culture has had to fight for life, from the 18th-century 'golden age' to the present day. Yet the very identity of Kirk and people – its 'national-popular' character, in Gramsci's phrase – meant that it, more than anything else, has been preserved in Scotland's long and stagnant twilight, far less than a nation yet not a province like any other. The denying demons are still alive. Addicts of the Christian-Marxist dialogue should try and shake hands with them some time, if they want a cure.[2]

Thus, the original character of the Reformation in Scotland was very far removed from the Weber-Tawney model. But of course this does not affect the fact that, when the conditions of capitalist development did arise in Scotland, much later, they found a country singularly well prepared. Undoubtedly the rapidity and success of the Industrial Revolution in Scotland had something to do with this. E. J. Hobsbawm suggests in *Industry and Empire* that the Kirk's educational system was particularly important here, as well as the more general factors of ethos and psychology.[3]

The strange, truncated condition of Scotland after 1707 made it natural to search for effective substitutes for the lost national identity. The Kirk was indeed such a substitute. But because of its unworldliness and its limitations of bigotry, inevitably an unsatisfactory one in the long run. In the later 18th century, Scotland produced two contrasting movements of culture that tried to compensate for the loss in their different ways. Basically similar to developments elsewhere in Europe, they acquired a particular meaning from the Scottish dilemma.

One was the Edinburgh Enlightenment associated with the names of David Hume and Adam Smith. This was, in effect, an escape from the peculiar destiny of Scotland, onto the plane of abstract reason (though possibly the taste for abstractions it revealed had something to do with the theological inheritance). There was a cutting edge to Hume's celebrated joke about wishing to be pardoned his Scotticisms, rather than his sins, when on his death-bed. The other movement was the same reaction to the Enlightenment as other cultures produced, towards feeling and the particular: Romanticism. It is difficult to exaggerate the importance of Romanticism for Scotland. While the Enlightenment was only an episode, Romanticism entered her soul.

Here was the second of the dreams still implanted in the subsoil of Scottish consciousness. European history shows a general relationship between Romanticism and the Nationalism of the 19th-century, not entirely unlike that between

---

2   Before doing so, however, they would be well-advised to read some classic descriptions of the demons: James Hogg's *The Private Memoirs and Confessions of a Justified Sinner* (1824), now available in a Cresset Press edition; or John Buchan's *Witch Wood* (1927).

3   E. J. Hobsbawm, *Industry and Empire: An economic history of Britain since 1750* (1968), chapter *The Other Britain*, pp. 252–268.

the Reformation and Capitalism, which we have already looked at. But again, Scotland was a drastic exception to whatever generalities hold in this field. There, the new freedom of expression and the discovery of folk culture could scarcely be the precursors or the supports of a new nation in the making (as in Italy, Hungary, Germany), nor the accompaniment of triumphant nationality (as in England and America). The Scottish nationality was dead. Scotland was once more severed from those real conditions which should have lent meaning to her culture. No revolution against the humiliations of the Union, no Scottish 1848 were to furnish a historical counterpoint to Robert Burns and Sir Walter Scott. The romantic consciousness too, therefore, could only be an absolute dream to the Scots. Unable to function as ideology, as a moving spirit of history, it too was bound to become a possessing demon. Elsewhere, the revelation of the romantic past and the soul of the people informed some real future – in the Scottish limbo, they *were* the nation's reality. Romanticism provided – as the Enlightenment could not, for all its brilliance – a surrogate identity.

Perhaps this function as substitute consciousness has something to do with the peculiar intensity of Romanticism in Scotland, and with the great signifi-cance of the country as a locale of the European romantic fancy. It had the right sort of unreality. Such unreality – in effect, the substitution of nostalgia for real experience – has remained at the centre of the characteristically Scottish struc-ture of feeling. David Craig has outlined the problem with admirable precision:

'Such nostalgia, in this 'national' form, was strong in many 19th-century literatures – in English poetry, for example, Arthurian romances and 'Merrie England' work, and in the German equivalents. It is indeed one form of Romantic escapism. What matters for integrity of feeling is the place or value this emotion is allowed to have in the whole experience, how far it is understood, and perhaps resisted...'

The point is, he continues, that in Scotland it never *is* resisted, from Scott himself up to Grassic Gibbon and MacDiarmid.

> It is a mark of the uncertain foothold for a national literature in Scotland that this weak ground of nostalgia should crop up in so many places. Emigration of our most notable talents thus both creates gaps in the imag-inative records of the country and tempts our writers into indulgence of their weaker sides... What again and again weakens them...is the feeling that the ground in their country is shifting under their feet, and this perhaps gets worse the greater the determination to *have* a national vantage-point, to take up one's stance inside exclusively Scottish territory.[4]

A most exact historical sense can therefore be given to the assertion that Scotland is peculiarly haunted by the past. She is doubly dominated by her dead generations. At bottom there is the bedrock of Calvinism, the iron, abstract

---

4   David Craig, *Scottish Literature and the Scottish People 1680–1830* (1961), pp. 290–293.

moralism of a people that distrusts this world and itself; then overlaying this, the sentimental, shadow-appropriation of this world and itself through romantic fantasy. Naturally, these strata are also in conflict with one another much of the time. But this is not the place to try and trace out the patterns of the conflict, present in some form in everything distinctively Scottish.

A Machinery of Myth

From this fertile soil has grown the myth-consciousness of modern Scotland, expressed in her Nationalism. Nationalism is her third dream. It is basically a dream of redemption. For the Scots, national existence must represent that magic, whole reality of which they have been cheated by history – in it, their maimed past will be redeemed, in more vivid colours than a history can ever provide.

It may seem surprising that such a consciousness should have emerged from the modern history to which most historians have paid attention: essentially, the grim story of the Scottish Industrial Revolution, with the destruction of Highland society as background.[5] Yet surely it is not. History has amply demonstrated the capacity of capitalist societies to harbour and transmit apparently archaic social forms and ideas – and, on occasion, to lend them new and monstrous life (as in Germany and Japan). For reasons not adequately studied, this sort of bourgeois society actually fosters these elements alien to itself, as counter weights to its own alienations. Surely there is no society, no landscape, more crassly impersonal and materialist than that of the Scottish Industrial Belt; yet this is the society which has secreted the past we have been looking at, as a dislocated and poignant inner reality.

The criterion of the success with which modern Scotland has done this is simple: the universality of its false consciousness, and the multiplicity of its forms. Scotland's myths of identity are articulated sufficiently to suit everyone. Though Ministers of the Kirk, lawyers, lairds, tycoons and educationalists all have their own contrasting angles on the *Geist*, the principle articulation is between two poles. Nationalist ideology draws all its real force from one or the other. On the one hand, there is the popular – or populist – complex of ideas, which coincides enough with the foreign image of the Scots to need little elaboration here. Sporranry, alcoholism, and the ludicrous appropriation of the remains of Scotland's Celtic fringe as a national symbol have been celebrated in a million emetic ballads. It is an image further blackened by a sickening militarism, the relic of Scotland's special role in the building up of British imperialism.[6] Yet any judgement on this

---

5   Described in, for instance, R. H. Campbell's *Scotland since 1707: the Rise of an Industrial Society* (1965), and John Prebble's *The Highland Clearances* (1963).

6   The significance of this is perhaps most easily comparable to that of the ANZAC day rituals for Australia and New Zealand: societies afraid of their own marginality and provincialdom seize on whatever they can as their indubitable contribution to world history, the proof of real identity.

aspect of Scottish national consciousness ought to be softened by the recognition that these are the pathetic symbols of an inarticulate people unable to forge valid correlates of their different experience: the peculiar crudity of Tartanry only corresponds to the peculiarly intense alienation of the Scots on this level. On the other hand, apparently (and very self-consciously!) remote from this, but part of the same machinery, there is the national consciousness of the intelligentsia. This is best seen as a sort of ethereal tartanry. Based upon rejecting the trash-image of Scotland, it aims to substitute something purer, but whose function will be the same: in effect, to seize the *real* soul of the land, beyond its blood-stained philistinism, beyond the Industrial Revolution ('This towering pulpit of the Golden Calf'), even beyond the Kirk and its progeny.[7] The precarious sense of identity renders it intolerable to a more reflective mind that 'Scotland' should be confused with any of these things.

> My native land should be to me
> As a root is to a tree. If a man's labour fills no want there,
> His deeds are doomed and his music mute.
> This Scotland is not Scotland...[8]

But then, what *is* Scotland? The fringe 'folk' culture that survived the Kirk's persecution and industrialism, and is unknown to most people now living in the country? The vivid dialect of the Lowlands, reworked into a limited poetic language by the Scots Literary Renaissance? Or some Jungian essence lying inside the living, like the dead generations, waiting on resurrection?[33]

There is no answer to the question. Whatever is chosen cannot possibly bear the weight put on it – be the 'root' of the tree – if one regards it prosaically, in the light of history. Perhaps this is why the Literary Renaissance had to be almost entirely poetical. Poetry in this sense is a kind of magic: it conjures up the dead and the non-existent into a semblance of the desired object. There is a profound and dangerous ambiguity in this whole movement of thought – of the greatest relevance to understanding Scotland's Nationalism – which has not been sufficiently studied in the past.

First of all, it is evidently tied to the peculiarly intense romanticism we looked at above. In McLuhanite terms, one might say that the content of the new dream is the old ones, however it seems to reject the past in form. David Daiches has also pointed out how Sentimentality '... lodged itself more deeply in Scotland than elsewhere, because of the division between the Scottish head

---

7   Edwin Muir, *Scotland 1941*, in *Selected Poems*, ed. T. S. Eliot, (Faber 1965), p. 34.

8   Hugh MacDiarmid, *Lament for the Great Music* (1934), in Collected Poems (1962), p. 258.

9   For that is the mask of the Scot of all classes: that he stands in an attitude towards the past unthinkable to Englishmen, and remembers and cherishes the memory of his forebears, good or bad; and there burns alive in him a sense of identity with the dead even to the twentieth generation.' Robert Louis Stevenson, *Weir of Hermiston* 1896), p. 198.

and the Scottish heart that history had already produced.'[10] Modern intellectuals are still struggling with this division. The more they get away from the stale, phoney solutions, the more obvious the sameness of their dilemma becomes. Its insolubility has the following consequences. 'This Scotland' – the real Scotland – is rejected as travesty, and can only be rejected *totally*. Here is a recent accurate gloss on MacDiarmid's well-known poem *Lament for the Great Music*:

> The Scotland of today is no longer Scotland, but a philistine travesty of itself. It is Scotshire, a county in the north of England, an ex-country, an Esau land that has sold its birthright for a mess of English pottage... He, as poet, presents the Scottish people with their own image, the thing they have become, and he calls them back, like a true bard, to their own heritage. But so lost are they that they do not recognise it, or him. This is the measure of how deep the rot has gone since 1707.[11]

What follows from such radical rejection of an impossibly corrupted reality? Either despair:

> Hauf his soul a Scot maun use
> Indulgin'in illusions,
> And hauf in gettin' rid o' them
> And comin – to conclusions
> Wi' the demoralisin' dearth
> O' onything worth while on Earth...[12]

Or, more sinisterly, the feeling that the 'real' Scotland which is worthwhile and has survived it all is – *one's self*. The poetical fantasy, and the poet himself, embody the sought-after *Geist*. There are then as many *Geists* as there are poets, or schools of Sentimentality currently operating. Hence, a widely diffused complacent narcissism – the true mark of cultural provincialism – from which Scottish intellectuals find it hard to escape. It is a structural state of Scottish culture, with roots in the history outlined above.

This, incidentally, is what explains something that has often puzzled the external observer of things Scottish. All references – however oblique – to the more vulgar and obtrusive forms of the *weltanschauung* are met with the confident, but slightly embarrassed assertion that Tartanry is now a thing of the past. It is always languishing since yesterday. This is invariably true, in one sense, and totally false in another. The flexibility of Scottish narcissism simply allows transitions from the heather-clad ballad to *Lament for the Great Music*, with any number of stops in between. This is, precisely, the unity and underlying sense of

---

10 David Daiches, *The Paradox of Scottish Culture* (1964), p. 82.

11 Tom Scott, on *Lament for the Great Music*, in Agenda, Autumn-Winter 1967–68, special issue on MacDiarmid and Scottish Poetry, p. 23.

12 From *A Drunk Man Looks at the Thistle*, (1926), in *Collected Poems* (1962), p. 141.

a deeply defensive culture on precarious foundations that are – as Craig put it – felt as shifting under one's feet.

The Politics of Narcissism

Inevitably, Nationalist politics are built upon this web of accreted myth-consciousness. No more striking illustration of this can be found than the common myth of Scottish Left-ness. Claud Cockburn recently fell foul of it in a *New Statesman* article called *The Bagpipes of Socialism*.[13] There he argued that Mrs Ewing's electoral triumph at Hamilton was not what it seemed, but '... the renewal of a great tradition: the potentially formidable alliance of Scottish socialism and nationalism.' A really cohesive system of false consciousness like the one we are examining must provide space for socialists as well as everyone else.

Useful as a North Atlantic Cuba would be, the conviction that this is Scotland's destiny rests on particularly shifting ground. Scotland is certainly a more egalitarian country than England, and in some ways a more violent one. It does not follow that she is a more revolutionary one. Scotland's gritty sense of equality derives from the old Theocracy, not from Jacobinism or Bolshevism. It is double-edged, like every other aspect of that heritage. It stands for the democracy of souls before the All Mighty, rather than an explosive, popular effort to *do* anything. It is extremely touchy, but passive. This passivity is intimately linked to something even more dangerous. According to the rabid forms of Protestantism that got the upper hand in Scotland, the democracy of souls is an uneasy one. Souls may be either saved, or damned, and which way one goes is by far the most important question of life on earth. Regrettably, there is no rational way of resolving the problem, so that argument about it is necessarily sectarian, and endless. The only solution is by fiat, from above, by an Authority that selects the Elect from the ranks of the Damned.[14] Hence, a kind of masochism, a craving for discipline, in fact, accompanies this Scottish sense of equality. Gramsci has pointed out the analogy between Calvinist and vulgar-Marxist determinism. In fact, there was no Stalinist like a Scottish Stalinist, a truth which must have impressed itself on many students of modern British politics.

Scottish Nationalism is not in the very least inherently 'Left'. It belongs squarely within a category quite familiar in the history of the world outside Scotland: bourgeois nationalism. This is, in fact, implied by the majority of Nationalist propagandists, in their favourite argument: why not Scotland? They

---

13 *New Statesman*, 23 February 1968.

14 The prevalence and intensity of the Elect-Damned psychology has a lot to do with the cultural narcissism previously described. The Elect – to which each individual is of course obliged to feel *he* belongs, however he categories the Damned – is by definition self-admiring, smug, and identified with the only reality that counts.

compare the case of Scotland to those of the many new nations and nationalities which have emerged since 1945, every one of them blessed with a seat at the United Nations. Surely Scotland's 'claim' is as good as any of theirs?

Claim to *what*? This is the question that the Nationalist myth-mentality appears largely consecrated to evading, with the assistance of all hands. The right to be free, territorial self-control, even the idea of nationality itself – these are not timeless truths, but the products of a certain logic in the historical process. They occupy a broadly recognisable place in history, and have a certain justification attaching to this place. Once, the world was without nationalities – and indeed, nationality appeared, not as the expression of 'freedom' and the right to be different and unique, but as the enemy of precisely these things, the leveller of tribal and feudal variety – and it will certainly be so again. Nations and Nationalisms are aspects of the bourgeois epoch of world history. Within this epoch it has (or in most cases, has had) two sorts of justification as a historical force. Firstly, as a necessary means of escape from feudal or other primitive systems that were an impossible barrier to economic and social progress. In this sense, Nationalism was a precondition of the formation of modern society, and such a vital one that bourgeois civilisation has on the whole remained cast in its mould; it is only now beginning to break away from it. Secondly – mainly in the 20th century – Nationalism has served as an analogous instrument for non-European societies to escape from another system which for them constituted an equally insuperable barrier to development: western Imperialism. It is unnecessary here to try and discuss the complexities of these issues. But surely it is clear that in both cases Nationalism had a double positive function: externally, as a means of sweeping away archaic or predatory social forms, and internally, as a means of mobilising populations for socio-economic development.

Where is Scottish Nationalism located in this perspective? In its present form, nowhere. That is, as a tragic dream comparable to the other dreams of Scotland's history precisely in its remoteness from those real conditions which could give it the historical significance it implicitly claims. Any reasonable political judgment on Scottish Nationalism must take into account both this remoteness, and its meaning in terms of Scottish history. True to their nature, the Scots usually voice their Nationalism in a very moral manner. Nowhere more so than in placing themselves within the great 20th-century anti-imperialist movement of national liberation. There can therefore be no harm in pointing out some of the moral truths which *do*, in fact, attach to the position of their country in the history of the world.

First of all, Scotland is not a colony, a semi-colony, a pseudo-colony, a near-colony, a neo-colony, or any kind of colony of the English. She is a junior but (as these things go) highly successful partner in the general business enterprise of Anglo-Scots Imperialism. Now that this business is evidently on its last legs, it may be quite reasonable for the Scots to want out. But there is really no point in disguising this desire with heroic irony. After all, when the going was good for

Imperialism, the world heard very little indeed for the Scots' longing for independence. It may not come amiss either to indicate the ludicrous phoniness of that comparison of themselves with the Irish the Scots are fond of in this context. The Irish rose up and wrenched their independence from Imperialism when the latter was at the apex of its power. With sleekit Presbyterian moderation the Scots have restrained themselves until it is abundantly plain that the English would be incapable of stopping an insurrection on the Isle of Wight. The Irish had to fight the Black-and-Tans. The London *Times* has already half-surrendered to the Scots.

The comparison between them is not a matter of 50 years in time. It is a matter of two worlds. When, after its own grab at colonial empire had failed with the disastrous Darien Expedition of 1698, the Scottish bourgeoisie joined forces with the English in 1707, the distinction became inevitable. The Scottish people ceased to belong to Frantz Fanon's 'Wretched of the Earth'. For two centuries they have belonged to the conquerors. Their industries were, as E. J. Hobsbawm puts it, 'the cutting edge of a world industrial economy'.[15] Their armies were the cutting edge of British Imperialism. Now, the bourgeois rhetoric of Nationalism blandly exorcises this history of blood and exploitation with a few readings from *The Rights of Man*. Indeed, one elder statesman of the Nationalist movement recently went on record with these remarkable words: 'The great mistake made by James VI in 1603 was to go to London. He should have governed the whole British Empire from Scotland...'[16] Unfortunately, this vein of delirium echoes the central uncertainty of Nationalism only too accurately. When in doubt, take refuge in bombast. The Scots have become vaguely conscious of having sold their national soul to the Devil. It is more painful to recognise that the bargain of 1707 cannot now be undone, except in name – unless of course the Nationalist movement had aspirations which went beyond the terms of that bourgeois world to which 1707 and its consequences belonged. But this is another question, and one of little relevance to existing Nationalism.

Admittedly, Scotland – along with the English North-East and South-West – has also long been the victim of the unequal development characteristic of advanced capitalism. Such areas are characterised by higher, chronic rates of unemployment, poorer housing, high emigration, and generally lag behind the favoured zones of growth (like the English South-East, or the Paris conurbation). It has been recognised that one way – perhaps a necessary way – of countering this tendency is to give more power over their own affairs to these regions. The Italian Republican Constitution of 1946 remains a model for such progressive bourgeois development, although only partially enacted to this day.

But this is to confer upon Scotland's problems a status quite different from the one enshrined in the Nationalist mythology. It makes the purpose of 'independence' into a minor administrative problem. Autonomy becomes an antidote

---

15 E. J. Hobsbawm, op. cit., p. 265.
16 Mr Douglas Young, quoted in *The Daily Telegraph* (Supplement) 9 February 1968.

for some of the worst damage done by the reckless past evolution of the capitalist system. Looked at in this perspective, regional Nationalisms could have a
usefulness to the system second only to its principal support through times of
crisis: the Labour Party. There is some formal analogy between such regional
distortions of development within capitalism, and the world problem of 'under-
development'; but there is such a difference of scale and quality that it is really
absurd to try and read the same political meanings into the two situations.[17]

In a capitalist world more unified every day by the great monopolies, Scotland occupies a position of particular dependence. The regional decay resulting
from her dependence upon English capitalism has only been remedied (very
partially) by the invasion of American capital and its chain of light-engineering
plants in the Lowlands. A bourgeois-national movement will create no new,
national heaven-and-earth in this situation. It is coming into an old world whose
crust hardened long ago. Its task is the anti-climactic one of administering more
efficiently and humanely what was created in the past. Nationalism belongs in
a young world in eruption, where the collapse of the ancient system releases
visionary possibilities of a new social order forged closer to the heart. Scotland's
Romantic Nationalism, which slumbered through this era of history, now emerges
from its grave like a *revenant* to confront the obsidian landscape of late capitalism.
Free, for the Spirit of National Redemption: the post of Local Under-Manager.

It might be objected that there are still anomalous forms of Nationalism with
much greater significance than this. The current Nationalist stirrings of Eastern
Europe, for instance, or – even more striking – France. We noticed at the beginning
that Scottish and Welsh Nationalism do indeed share something of this meaning,
at least in their external impact upon their context, as elements of disaggregation
in the aftermath of British Imperialism. But they appear – so far at least – to be
much less important than these other cases. In part, this is simply a matter of context.
It is the sclerotic oppression of Stalinism which gives positive and liberating
significance to Czech, Polish or Rumanian national movements. It is American
capitalism's growing domination of Europe that lends positive historical sense
to Gaullist Nationalism.

In part, however, it is also a matter of the character and aspirations of the
national bourgeoisie or ruling élite behind these national manifestations. After
all, the French bourgeoisie, with its revolutionary traditions (however faded),
its intense chauvinism and confident way of life, and its still great resources of
power, is one thing. The Scottish bourgeoisie is decidedly another.

The English have curiously little grasp of this aspect of the question – as if
confident that their long dominion over such provinces had necessarily produced
complete mimic copies of their own ruling classes there. In Scotland at least, this

---

17   An interesting study dealing mainly with this question, and with an emphasis very different
     from the present writer's is *The Revolt against Satellization in Scotland and Wales*, by
     Keith Buchanan, *Monthly Review*, March 1968.

naïve trust is quite unfounded. Here is one level indeed where a genuine analogy between the British provinces and the most hopeless areas of the ex-colonial Empire holds good. No West African or Asiatic *comprador* bourgeoisie has aped the external forms of English civility more sedulously – or remained more stubbornly itself, underneath them. This is the whole sense of the Calvinist mentality: cringing observance of external forms, for worldly purposes, and contemptuous disregard of them on another level. Inwardly, the Scots have absorbed little or nothing of the peculiar secrets of the English bourgeois régime: hegemony through tolerant compromise, 'permeation', the delicious mystification of traditionalism, the translation of impersonal power-relationships into subtle personal terms – all these are really closed books for them. That peculiarly heavy, gritty stylelessness, deaf to allusions and the subtler sorts of humour, that exasperating pedantry and solemn formalism, those alien and disconcerting silences and the clumsy intensity somewhere behind them tensed in relationship to a world felt as tragic and out of key with the ordinary spontaneity of living – these traits so familiar to the foreigner would be, written large, the characteristics of a Scottish bourgeois régime. They reflect that particular subordination to the past, described above. They also give a precise sense to the reactionary nature of Scottish Nationalism, and any government it produced.

The preoccupations of this parody of a ruling class are well laid out for us in A. J. C. Kerr's 1967 *Scottish Opinion Survey*.[18] Robert Burns would be vexed (but hardly surprised) to see that Republicanism is still well beyond its horizons. It is in fact deeply exercised by the difficult choice between Queen Elizabeth the I and II, and her offspring Prince Andrew, as suitable monarchs of the new realm. The real worry is the young folk, however. That odious, grudging tyranny of the older generations over youth which distinguishes Calvinism from civilisation will naturally be reinforced after independence. The truly worrying problem, is: how long should National Service be in the new realm? How much of it should be military, how much enforced 'public service'? This evil mélange of decrepit Presbyterianism and imperialist thuggery, whose spirit may be savoured by a few mornings with the Edinburgh *Scotsman* and a few evenings watching *Scottish Television*, appears to be solidly represented in the Scottish National Party. Those impressed by its 'radicalism' should turn to a towering portrait of the Scotch bourgeois, written in acid two generations ago:

> Hah! I don't understand that; it's damned nonsense! – that was his attitude to life. If 'that' had been an utterance of Shakespeare or Napoleon it would have made no difference to John Gourley. It would have been damned nonsense just the same. And he would have told them so, if he had met

---

18 *Scottish Opinion Survey* ('A study of educated and responsible Scottish opinion on the case for and against self-government'), conducted and edited by A. J. C. Kerr (William Maclellan, November 1967).

them... His thickness of wit was never a bar to the success of his irony. For the irony of the ignorant Scot is rarely the outcome of intellectual qualities. It depends on a falsetto voice and the use of a recognised number of catch-words... Not that he was voluble of speech; he wasn't clever enough for lengthy abuse. He said little and his voice was low, but every world... was a stab. And often his silence was more withering than any utterance. It struck life like a black frost.[19]

'John Gourley' is not dead. He surfaces in all his spleen every time anything in the least 'daring' appears at the Edinburgh Festival, and keeps a watchful eye on life during the rest of the year. Nationalism may or may not have this or that radical or progressive side-effect. This rough-hewn sadism – as foreign to the English as anything in New Guinea – will surely be present in whatever junta of corporal-punishers and Kirk-going cheese-parers Mrs Ewing might preside over one day in Edinburgh.

Hammer and Thistle?

For Socialists in England and elsewhere, the contradictions of Scottish Nation-alism are tricky going; but of course the problem isn't insoluble. For Scottish Socialists, these contradictions will be murderous unless they build up their own Nationalism to oppose the SNP and – beyond immediate politics – to come to terms with Scotland's complex cultural inheritance.

From outside its antagonisms, the contradiction appears as between the externally positive effects of Nationalism and its internally reactionary nature. That is, on the one hand it is necessary to support the claims of Nationalism, and to sustain its demand for more power, rather than less (the forms of mild devolution a British Government is likely to offer as a palliative). Not only for the reasons already mentioned – as a blow against the integrity of British Impe-rialism, and as a destructive factor of change in the reactionary equilibrium of UK politics. But also because it represents some transfer of power to a smaller arena, closer to the grasp of those subject to it – a process with which (in the long run, at least) Socialism must identify itself. On the other hand, it is neces-sary to distinguish such support from sympathy with the actual forces likely to benefit from it, and illusions about their success. The English Left has enough burdens to bear, without adding confusion over this issue to them.

From within the vice itself, where the problem is what to feel and do, this kind of distinction is largely meaningless. There, the temptation is to resign from the conflict, under the sway of Nationalist rhetoric: forget 'our differences' for the sake of unity, then 'sort them out' after independence. This would not be lunacy,

---

19 George Douglas Brown, *The House with the Green Shutters* (1908), pp. 23–24.

if there was an independent and combative Scottish Left capable of striking such bargains, instead of those spiritless provincial simulacra of the Labour and Communist Parties that actually exist. As things are, complicity in the pretence that the Nationalist movement and the obtaining of autonomy are 'neutral', a political events is merely suicide.

This study has not dealt with the tired legalistic arguments for independence, re-heated and served up in every Home Rule debate for the past 100 years. Anyone concerned with these fantasms – which keep Nationalist tongues wagging most of the time – will find their history in Sir Reginald Coupland's *Welsh and Scottish Nationalism*, and a good summary of them in H. J. Paton's recent *The Claim of Scotland*.

Nor has it dealt with that other major obsession of the petty-bourgeois mind: the totally Pickwickian 'economic problem' of whether Scotland would be 'viable' and could survive 'on her own' – as if she was some kind of small shop-keeper, in fact, not part of an international economic order. It has concentrated, instead, on certain aspects of Scottish history which may explain the larger depths of feeling, the structural (often half-conscious) attitudes of Nationalist psychology. Indeed, it is in relationship to this inwardness that a Left-wing Nationalism finds its true justification.

Modern Scotland is the product of a history without truth, a sterility where dream is unrelated to character, and both bear little relationship to what happens. Resisting the forces of assimilation with extraordinary strength, the country has retained through its half-life a dream of true existence: that is, of a wholeness expressing its life instead of hiding it, a three-dimensional being freeing the national will and tongue from their secular inhibitions, a realness to startle itself and the watching world.

What is vital to realise is that Nationalism, in its current forms, is not the possible attainment of this redemptive dream, but its ultimate betrayal. It is as out of touch with the real sense of contemporary history as the other delusions from which it has grown uncritically. It represents in some ways the logical outcome of Scotland's history: but precisely, the dénouement of a tragic half-history must itself be tragic.

The only possible sane reaction to the dilemma is a Socialist Nationalism, whose dream has dimensions which really correspond to those of the stubborn, visionary drive towards identity we have been considering – and which is a part of living contemporary history and of an arising future – not a stale memory of bourgeois nationality, to enshrine all the other stale memories the country has lived off for so long. It goes without saying that such a Nationalism must exist by sharply combatting the overpowering past which conventional Nationalism drools over, that it must see cultural liberation from Scotland's pervasive myths as a precondition of political action, and that it must utterly condemn the kind of garrulous, narcissistic windbaggery to which the intelligentsia has so often resorted – in the absence of anything better – as its special contribution to the problem.[20] It is simply not possible to escape from the provincialism the Scots fear so much in any other way. The SNP Nationalists are merely lumpen-provincials whose parochialism finds its adequate expression in the asinine idea that a bourgeois parliament and an army will rescue the country from provincialism; as if half of Europe did not testify to the contrary. Is it really impossible that Scotland, which has dwelt so long and so hopelessly on the idea of a nation, should produce a liberated and revolutionary Nationalism worthy of the name and the times?

---

20 How acute this problem is may be inferred from the fact that the great author o *A Drunk Man* and *Lament for the Great Music* was recently quoted (from the heights of his well-known command of Gaelic and Lallans) as declaring: 'I wont't have any English traditions imposed on Scotland. I don't even like the English language – it's a flabby affair too full of synonyms, a language for lazy and inexact people.' *The Daily Telegraph* (Supplement), 9 February 1968.

CHAPTER FOUR

English Nationalism:
The Case of Enoch Powell

New Left Review, I/61

MAY–JUNE 1970

> Every nation, to live healthily and to live happily, needs a patriotism. Britain today, after all the changes of the last decades, needs a new kind of patriotism and is feeling its way towards it...
>
> ENOCH POWELL, Speech at Louth, 1963

IN CERTAIN RESPECTS, the Right Honourable John Enoch Powell has long seemed the most original of Britain's bourgeois politicians – a figure whose every speech is awaited with eager interest and anxiety, who may be adored or hated but is universally felt to be important. Powell represents something new in British politics. If this something new is also something very old – nevertheless, in the present situation its impact, meaning, and possible results are all novel. Powell rose to this doubtful eminence mainly on the impact of his celebrated Birmingham address of 20 April 1968. This was the speech in which he met 'a quite ordinary working man' who suddenly told him 'If I had the money to go, I wouldn't stay in this country... In this country in 15 or 20 years' time the black man will have the whip hand over the white man.' After a scarifying catalogue of further such revelations, Powell concluded: 'As I look ahead, I am filled with foreboding. Like the Roman, I seem to see 'the River Tiber foaming with much blood". The message was that Britain's coloured immigrant population does indeed present a mortal threat to the British (or rather, to the *English* – for he pointed out that 'in practice only England is concerned') and must be got to return home whence they came. As Powell has modestly stated himself, the speech 'provoked a political furore without precedent since the end of the war'.

Naturally, he came to be regarded as the champion and chief spokesman of the various racist and anti-immigrant movements. He has also been widely accused of inconsistency (vis-a-vis his earlier statements on the issue) and of rabid demagoguery.[1] However, both the inconsistencies (which Powell of course presents

---

1   These charges are described and re-affirmed in Paul Foot's study *The Rise of Enoch Powell: An Examination of Enoch Powell's Attitude to Immigration and Race* (Penguin 1969), which also contains the relevant facts on the immigration issue up to 1969.

as the natural evolution of his views) and the blatant demagoguery serve a deeper, and perfectly consistent, purpose. This underlying purpose has been obscured by too narrow a concentration on the question of race and immigration. The narrow focus itself serves Powell's purpose very well, by turning what is really only a right-wing tactic into an obsession for left-wing and liberal opponents – while, in fact, there are wider and far more dangerous trends at work. Referring back to England's last bout of immigrationmania, against the Jewish immigrants of the period 1890–1905, Paul Foot remarks that in 1970 'all that has changed is that new scapegoats must be found for the homelessness, the bad hospital conditions, and the overcrowded schools...'² But in reality, though England's coloured population has of course become a scapegoat for capitalism's ills, very much more has changed than the scapegoat itself. Powell knows this. Indeed, it is his sense of these profounder historical changes which supplies the real bite to his attack on the immigration question. The 'New Right' he represents is rooted in such changes, as both symptom and aggravation of the historical decline of English conservatism, and so must be regarded in longer historical perspective.

The English Question

From Guilsboro' to Northampton, all the way
Under a full red August moon,
I wandered down... Yet the air
Seemed thronged and teeming, as if hosts
Of living presences were everywhere;
And I imagined they were ghosts
Of the old English, who by tower and spire,
Wherever priest and sexton's spade
In church or graveyard round about the shire
Their unremembered bones had laid,
Now in the warm still night arising, filled
The broad air with their company,
And hovering in the fields that once they tilled,
Brooded on England's destiny.

ENOCH POWELL, Poem XXVI, *Dancer's End*, 1951; written 1940–45

---

2   In this period, noted Elie Halévy, 'An unmistakable wave of anti-semitism came over public opinion... The Act of 1900 against usury was perhaps the first symptom... The (Conservative) Cabinet had succeeded in finding a question on which the working classes were naturally protectionist.' The culmination (then as now!) was the Aliens Act of 1905 which – Halévy continues – 'was a complete reversal of the previous legislation, or rather absence of legislation... and the foundation stone of an entire edifice of anti-alien measures, which amounted in the end not merely to protection, but absolute prohibition'. (*History of the English People in the 19th Century*, vol. 5, III, II, 5)

Powell's basic concern is with England and the – as he sees it – half-submerged nationalism of the English. His real aspiration is to redefine this national identity in terms appropriate to the times – and in particular, appropriate to the end of empire. England's destiny was once an imperial one; now it has to be something else. Powell is not really sure what it is. But he feels that he, Enoch Powell, carries some intimation of it within his own breast, and he has consistently striven to construe this sense of fate.

In 1964, speaking to the Royal Society of St George,[3] he returned to the theme of the 'old English':

> There was this deep, this providential difference between our empire and others, that the nationhood of the mother country remained unaltered through it all, almost unconscious of the strange fantastic structure built around her... England underwent no organic change as the mistress of a world empire. So the continuity of her existence was unbroken... Thus, our generation is like one which comes home again from years of distant wandering. We discover affinities with earlier generations of English, who feel no country but this to be their own... We find ourselves once more akin to the old English... From brass and stone, from line and effigy their eyes look out at us, and we gaze into them, as if we would win some answer from their inscrutable silence. 'Tell us what it is that binds us together; show us the clue that leads through a thousand years; whisper to us the secret of

---

3   This Society, unknown to most Englishmen, was founded in 1894 in the flood-tide of imperialist delirium. Its aim was aptly conveyed by the first number of its journal *The English Race*: 'There is some fear that the English stock is getting deficient in that healthy and legitimate egotism which is necessary to self-preservation... The Englishman must assert his indefeasible birth-right.' *The English Race* was uncomfortably aware that the Scots, Irish and Welsh (to say nothing of real foreigners) seemed to have more national consciousness than Englishmen: 'Above all other racial elements in the British system, the English needs to be distinguished and preserved.' Each issue contained a 235-strong list of 'names to remember on 23 April', ranging from Alfred the Great to William of Wykeham, patriotic poems and profiles, articles on such subjects as bell-ringing and Morris-dancing, and a thundering editorial, e.g.: 'Within the last century we English have absorbed an appreciable number of Scottish Celts and Saxons, Irish and Welsh Celts, and Jews... So far as the United Kingdom and the Empire are concerned, the knell of the pure-blooded Celtic race as a distinct element has sounded. The Celt will continue to undergo a process of gentle absorption, or share the fate of the aboriginals of America and New Zealand, the 'Redskin' and Maori... The racial instinct of the English is ever-present, far down and deeply-rooted; too dormant, too unassertive, unaggressive yet uneradicable.' (Vol. II, No. 16, April 1913). In 1939, *The English Race* changed its title to England. By 1950 even St George had gone from the cover, and (a parable of English imperial decline) it had dwindled into a genteel new sheet replete with pictures of thatched cottages and royalty, and appeals for funds. Powell's 1964 address is included in *Freedom and Reality* (Selected Speeches, ed. J. Wood, 1969). The reader's attention is drawn specially to the last section of the book, 'Myth and Reality', which Powell himself describes as the most important.

this charmed life of England, that we may in our time know how to hold it fast.' What would they say…?

In 1964, when the post-war Conservative régime ended, Powell still did not know what they would say. Twenty years of brooding on England's destiny had availed him little. By April 1968 the ancestors had, finally, said something: approximately, 'Go home, wogs, and leave us in peace!' This prodigious clue to a thousand years of history has, however, a meaning beyond its absurd manifest content. For the *dilemma* to which it appeals is a real one. It is quite true that the English need to rediscover who and what they are, to re-invent an identity of some sort better than the battered cliché-ridden hulk which the retreating tide of imperialism has left them – and true also (for reasons described below) that the politics of the last 20 years have been entirely futile in this respect. Powell's recipe for the growing vacuum is the – at first sight – incredible patchwork of nostrums expounded in his recent speeches: economic *laissez-faire*, Little England, social discipline, trade before aid, loyalty to Ulster, and racism. But no critique of such incoherence can afford to ignore the need upon which it works: in relationship to reality, it may possess a driving-force which it lacks when considered simply as a set of ideas. After all, very few past Conservative heroes have been noticeably 'coherent' in this sense: compared to those of Churchill, Joseph Chamberlain, or Disraeli, Powell's career so far is an epitome of logical sobriety. Only in the context of the twilit conservatism of the 1960s does his cynical opportunism appear startling, or even unusual. British conservatism has always been profoundly 'illogical' since the time of Edmund Burke, by an instinct rooted in the great historical conditions of its existence. It has been only too happy to rule, and leave logic to the 'opposition'.

The odd ingredients of Powellism are held and fused together by a romantic nationalism with quite distinctive cultural origins. Powell worked his way up from the lower middle-class (both parents were elementary school teachers) via a Birmingham grammar school to Cambridge. Thus early in life this solitary and rigid bourgeois industriously acquired the traditional culture of the English ruling élite: Greek and Latin. He became Professor of Greek at the University of Sydney at the age of 26, a remarkable tribute to ungentlemanly energy and self-discipline.[4] At the same time, he wrote verse in an appropriately archaic romantic mode derived mainly from A. E. Housman and the Georgians. The theme is usually death, or else the passing of youth, innocence, and love:

---

4   'A distinguished scholar and churchman (remembers)… visiting the prodigy on his arrival at Trinity College, Cambridge. He found Powell, on a bitter November morning, in an attic room in New Court. There was no fire in the grate and Powell, covered in an overcoat and rugs, was reading Thucydides. His visitor asked him if he would care to come to tea; Powell simply replied 'No'. In a renewed effort to break the ice, his school friend saun-tered across the room and lit a cigarette. 'Please don't smoke,' said Powell'. (T. E. Utley, *Enoch Powell: the Man and his Thinking*, 1968, p.48)

Oh, sweet it is, where grass is deep
And swifts are overhead,

To lie and watch the clouds, and weep
For friends already dead.[5]

These wholly sentimental reveries and sighing dramas tend to go on in the rustic English limbo first popularised by Housman:

I dreamt I was in England
And heard the cuckoo call,
And watched an English summer
From spring to latest fall,
And understood it all...
And I lay there in England
Beneath a broad yew-tree,
Contented there to be.[6]

This tradition of abstract upper-class kitsch arose in the same epoch which witnessed England's attempt at the Higher Imperialism, the Boer War, the Syndicalist Revolt, the Constitutional Crisis of 1911, and the Aliens Act.[7] It gives sublime expression to the hopelessly *rentier* mentality into which a large part of the English intelligentsia had now lapsed, to the despair of militarists like Lord Roberts, imperial administrators like Curzon and Milner, national-efficiency zealots like Sidney Webb, and such 'committed' intellectuals of the day as Rudyard Kipling and Henry Rider Haggard. As if knowing instinctively how impossible it would prove to save British imperialism from its own ramshackle self, the poets turned towards a safer past. This movement of involution led them – in a pattern which has also characterised other intellectual trends of the English 20th-century – to a conservative dream-world founded on an insular vein of English romanticism. Powell revelled in it. It never occurred to him that this week-end landscape was far more synthetic than the most plastic products of Hollywood. 'Ours is an age when the engines of bad taste possess great force,' he declared in his Inaugural Lecture at Sydney in 1938, 'With rare exceptions, the cinema, the newspaper and the wireless tend powerfully to promote vulgarity, by day and by night in our cities the eye and the ear are continually assaulted by objects of bad taste... I once heard Housman, when referring in a lecture to a certain corrupt epithet in Lucretius, remark that 'a modern poet, I suppose, might write such a phrase as that and fancy that it was good, but

---

5   Poem XXIX, *First Poems* (1937)

6   Poem XV, *Dancer's End* (1951)

7   The first of the five volumes of *Georgian Poetry* (a collection of verse signalling the new 'Georgian' as distinct from the old 'Edwardian' era) appeared in 1912, with poems by Rupert Brooke, Graves, Masefield, W. H. Davies, Drinkwater, and Walter de la Mare.

Lucretius could never have done so'. The words echo in my mind today; and whenever I have achieved a daring adjective in a poem 'and fancy that it is good', my conscience asks me whether Lucretius and Housman would have thought the same or not. That illustrates exactly what I mean by the cultivation of taste...'[8]

It goes without saying that he mastered the techniques of Georgianism, and produced suitably 'tasteful' rhymes. The same Prussian assiduity which took him to the Sydney Chair saw to that. Later in life, he even learned to fox-hunt, and penned a Housmanesque jingle on this important political experience. With this background, it was quite natural that the 'old English' should materialise to Powell primarily 'by tower or spire' or in old country churches – rather than, say, in a sooty Wolverhampton cemetery or the ruins of a factory. He still partially inhabits this Disney-like English world where the Saxon ploughs his fields and the sun sets to strains by Vaughan Williams.

This is, in fact, a romantic nationalism which retains nothing of the original energy of either romanticism or nationalism. In England, a country of ancient and settled nationality, romanticism did not serve as the instrument of national liberation, it could not help forge a new national-popular consciousness. It could not even function as substitute for a real national being and consciousness – as, for instance, it did in Scotland. All too easily, it turned into an escapist or conservative dream-world, negating the Victorian bourgeois régime at one level only to confirm it at another. By the time of Housman and the Georgians it has become a sickly parody of itself, expressive only of the historic stalemate into which the English bourgeoisie was falling. Powell's poetic nationalism, in turn, is nothing but a pallid echo of the parody, incongruously surviving into the later 20th century.

However, the very absurdity and archaism of this re-heated romanticism poses a problem. If English nationalism *can* still be identified with such inadequate symbols, it is because of an odd weakness at its heart. The saccharine countryside of the Old English is a reflection of something persistently missing, something absent from English national identity itself. In part, this void is clearly associated with the positive and distracting presence of something else, for so long: English imperialism.

The Imperial Crown

Still the black narrow band of shimmering road,
A thousand miles the same...
... Then on the Eastern hand
The skyline suddenly fell sheer away
And showed the smoky Delta; to the right
Rose sharp and blue against the desert's brown

---

8   *Greek in the University*, Inaugural Lecture to the University of Sydney, 7 May 1938.

The pyramids; and to our astonished sight
Descried, above it all, the Imperial Crown.

ENOCH POWELL, Poem XXXIII, *Dancer's End*

Powell was once the most passionate of imperialists. When he left Sydney for the Indian Army at the outbreak of war, India burst upon him like a revelation.[9] He admitted recently: 'I fell head over heels in love with India. If I'd gone there 100 years ago, I'd have left my bones there' (*The Times*, Feb. 12th, 1968). Here, surely, was the true sense and purpose of England's being. That the grandeur had been fatally undermined half a century previously, that England's imperialism was more and more of a theatrical charade, that the Imperial Crown was now held up by the dollar-sign – all this meant nothing. His enclosed imagination saw 'Edward the First, Plantagenet' as having held the imperial destiny in one hand already (in the 13th century):

The rod thou holdest in thy right
Is raised thy enemies to smite
And shatter their impuissant hate,
But in thy left already lies
The image of the earth and skies,
Foreboding universal power...

Poem L, *Dancer's End*

But in this imperial fervour there lay a basic uncertainty, an ambiguity which marks every facet of English imperialist culture in the era from the 1870s – when England began to become self-consciously imperial – up to the evident decline of the 1920s and '30s. On the one hand, English imperialism could scarcely avoid the most soaring ambition: it possessed so much, and had dominated so much of the world for so long, that its power could not help looking 'universal'. Yet on the other, the English were always uneasily conscious of the great discrepancy between this appearance and the substance behind it.

The old days of informal, economic empire were over, in the teeth of German and French competition; yet England's 'empire' remained a heterogeneous assemblage of units belonging to this bygone era, approximately held together by her navy. On one hand there was the boundless delirium of Rhodes and the music-hall: 'His Majesty rules over one continent, a hundred peninsulas, five

---

9 English political conservatism has always owed much to empire, and in particular to India. The most interesting statement of English conservative thought in the later 19th century, by that distinguished Victorian judge and bully James Fitzjames Stephen (*Liberty, Equality and Fraternity*, 1873), was also inspired by the author's Indian experiences. India, he wrote, was 'the best corrective in existence to the fundamental fallacies of Liberalism'. Out there 'you see real government'. (See Introduction to the 1967 edition, the first since 1874, by R. J. White).

hundred promontories, a thousand lakes, two thousand rivers and ten thousand islands... The Queen found the revenues of the Empire at £75million; she left them at £225 million... The Empire to which Victoria acceded in 1837 covered one-sixth of the land of the world; that of King Edward covers nearly one fourth. The Union Jack has unfolded itself, so to speak, over two acres of new territory every time the clock has ticked since 1800...'.[10] But on the other hand, the English universal power was incapable even of governing the British Isles, as the Irish proved every few years. The immensity was also empty. If the English had ever taken their imperial delusion seriously, it would have required the largest army in the world as well as their navy, a new and quite different English State, and a total reform of English society away from the lazy conservatism into which it subsided.

Whatever imperialist zealots like Kipling, Webb or Joseph Chamberlain said, there was never any real chance of such reform taking place. The great weight of English conservatism was against it. And if that were not enough, so was the pressure of the City of London, lender-in-chief to the world and – on the whole – happy with the slack old ways: there were as good profits to be had investing outside the English territorial 'empire' as inside it (in the USA or South America, for instance). The first issue of The English Race contained an appropriately vigorous article by the Duke of Gloucester on 'The Value of Pageantry'. There was, indeed, little behind the pompous pageantry of Edwardian imperialism which had not been there some decades before, when the governing philosophy had been that colonies were a political nuisance to be got rid of as soon as the march of Progress would allow. The hollowness sounds through the English imperialist mind in a thousand forms: in Rider Haggard's necrophilia, in Kipling's moments of gloomy doubt, in the self-pitying pessimism of Housman, in the sadness of Elgar, or in the gloomy cosmic truth of Forster's Marabar caves.

For Powell, however, it was all good as new a generation later. In this narrow, rigidly-focused sensibility, imperialism had joined forces with the English pastoral mode. He devoted his disciplined energy to crazy schemes for the retention of India by military force and, later, even to plans for its re-conquest when the Conservative Party came back to power in 1951.[11] This was, in fact, the main motive which had driven him into political life in the first place. The world was unthinkable without the British Empire. That is, Powell's imaginary world was unthinkable without it – the world where, now, Old English and grateful brown-skinned multitudes jostled bizarrely together.

The unthinkable happened. Independence was conceded to India and Pakistan by the Labour government of 1945, and after 1951 it became clear that even under Churchill it would not be undone. Powell's fantasia was rudely jarred by

---

10   St James Gazette, on the accession of Edward vii, January 1901, quoted in W. S. Adams, Edwardian Heritage (1949).

11   See Paul Foot, op.cit, p.19.

the fact: it took him some years to recover from the blow. England's destiny had received a mortal wound.

When he did recover, it was by a familiar machinery of over-compensation. The most truly remarkable speech of Powell's career has not been on immigration, or the virtues of capitalism, or the social services which he administered for three years as a Minister in the Macmillan government, from 1960 to 1963. It was on the British Empire. It was delivered, not to an audience of ravening Conservative militants, but in the academic detachment of Trinity College, Dublin, and is easily the most interesting comment on imperialism by a Conservative spokesman in this century – at least, since Joseph Chamberlain's famous 'Tariff Reform' address of 1903.[12]

'The life of nations' – he begins – 'no less than that of men is lived largely in the imagination.' Consequently, what really matters in national life is the nation's 'corporate imagination'. Within 'that mysterious composite being, the nation', nothing can be more important than 'the picture of its own nature, its past and future, its place among other nations in the world, which it carries in its imagination. The matter of this imagining is nearly all historical...' The *form* of such imagining, however, is myth. The politician's task – as Plato stated in *The Republic*, that bible of the English élite – is to 'offer his people good myths and to save them from harmful myths'. And (the point is) the current myths of the English corporate imagination are bad ones. The most important of such myths is the delusion that 'Britain was once a great imperial power, which built up a mighty empire over generations and then... lost or gave it up'. It is only because of the presence of this pernicious myth that the English believe they are in *decline*: they imagine they once stood upon a great height, hence they cannot help feeling in the shade today. But the conclusion (and by implication the whole of British politics since around 1918) is as mistaken as the premise.

'The myth of the British Empire is one of the most extraordinary paradoxes in political history,' continues Powell. Everyone believes it existed, but it never did: 'Until very nearly the Diamond Jubilee of Queen Victoria (1897) if you mentioned 'the Empire' to a man in the street in London, he would think you meant the United Kingdom, with its three capitals, London, Edinburgh and Dublin...'.[13] But what of India, Powell's old love, a British political dependency since the 18th century? Easy: 'India is the exception which proves the rule'. Otherwise, 'impe-

---

12 Speech at Dublin, 1964, in Freedom and Reality, op. cit., p. 245.

13 This is of course wildly inaccurate. As Richard Koebner's study of the introduction of terms like 'empire' and 'imperialism' into English usage shows, 'empire' was used in the early 1800s and 'imperialism' was perfectly familiar by the 1880s, both in more or less the modern sense. 'Imperialism' had made considerable inroads in the 1870s, in fact: Disraeli's first important imperialist speeches were in 1872, while Dilke's Greater Britain (which did much to popularise the imperial idea among the upper classes) came out first in 1868. See Imperialism: the Story and Significance of a Political Word, 1840–1960 (1964).

rialism' was largely invented by the Conservative government of 1895–1905, for narrowly political reasons ('because one could make stirring speeches about Empire without needing actually to alter anything') and the particular culprit was his own predecessor from the West Midlands, Joseph Chamberlain (then Colonial Secretary). 'And so it was' – he concludes – 'that just in the very last years when Britain's relationship with her overseas possessions could by any stretch of fiction be represented as imperial, the Conservative Party first, and then the British people, came to believe instinctively, implicitly, that they had an empire – a belief that was to colour their thoughts, emotions and actions for the next 70 years and to set a gulf between them and the rest of the world, the same gulf which exists between a man in the grip of a hallucination and those around him who do not share it.'

How familiar are these particular tones of disenchantment! In the 1950s the whole western world rang to them – the lugubrious exvotaries of Stalin who, unable to bear what their idol had become, turned to denounce the god that had failed them. Powell reacted in the same way towards the political collapse of imperialism. Given that the failure, the disenchantment, had occurred, what was once the all-embracing, seductive truth *could* only be a tissue of lies. There is in Powell's anti-imperialism exactly that weird mixture of sharpened perception and utter lunacy which one finds in ex-communist tirades on communism.

It is true indeed that England's high imperial moment was largely compounded of myth and pretence, that Chamberlainism was a practical impossibility, and that the Conservative Party had a strong vested interest in the charade. It is also quite true that the experience has left a deep subjective mark upon English national consciousness and culture (as Powell's own previous career had made abundantly clear). But it is grotesque to suggest that there was, literally, 'nothing' behind the theatricality of Edwardian imperialism. The reality behind it was, of course, the varied nexus of economic relationships built up by English trade and industry since the 17th century, which had made the English Industrial Revolution possible in the first place, and then been enormously extended by England's manufacturing primacy. There was all too little relationship between this mainly economic reality and the new pretentions aroused by military challenge and the desire to emulate Germany. It was impossible to systematise the conglomeration into an 'empire' in the Roman, French or German sense, except in fantasy. Yet this does not signify that such economic power (a different, more 'informal' empire than any other in history till then) did not *exist*.

This is, however, precisely what Powell is driven to maintain. He can allow no degree of truth or reality whatever to the cause which disappointed him. After the imperial myth, the second most notorious legend still gripping England's imagination is that England was once 'the workshop of the world'. In truth, it never was: this is no more than the 'identical twin' to the empire myth, and 'the characteristics of British industry which are supposed today to account for loss of ground to other nations were just as evident in the Victorian hey-day, when

Britain enjoyed the preponderant share of the world trade in manufactured goods.'
The very words belie the intended meaning. If Britain enjoyed 'the preponderant
share of world trade in manufactured goods' at that time, it could not possibly
have been for any other reason than that she enjoyed a preponderancy in world
manufacture, which is all that was meant by calling her the 'workshop of the
world'.

England's decline into 'her own private hell' has been – consequently – a
dream process, just as the myth of empire was 'our own private heaven'. To cure
herself, all England need do is wake up: 'If Britain could free herself from the
long servitude of her 70-year-old dreams, how much that now seems impossible
might be within her power. But that is another story, which has not yet begun...'
That was in 1964. One can scarcely resist the thought that, for Powell, the
awakening must have begun at last, with his racist speech of April 1968.

By May 1967, he already had some intimations. Referring with admiration
to General de Gaulle (one of his heroes), he commented: 'The face which we see in
de Gaulle's mirror is our own, and we had better look at it firmly and steadily...
What sort of people do we think we are? We have been hovering over the answer
for years... a nation of ditherers who refuse to make up our minds.'[14] After a
brisk review of the 'schizophrenia' which has long characterised British policy
(the Pound, 'peace-keeping', the growth fetish, and so on) he returned to the
question: 'What sort of people do we think we are? The question waits for its
answer. In psychiatry a sign of convalescence is what is called 'insight' – when
the patient begins to regain a self-knowledge hitherto rejected... How is Britain
to fulfil the Delphic command 'Know thyself'? How can you and I and the Tory
Party help in resolving the national dilemma, reuniting the split personality and
banishing delusion?' The reply was still cloudy, though. Powell concluded somewhat feebly, not in the tones of the Delphi Oracle: 'The politician is a voice...
We do not stand outside the nation's predicament: we are ourselves part of it...
All we can do is to speak out what we feel, to try and identify and describe the
contradictions, and the phobias which we see around us, in the hope that... we
may wake a chord that will reverberate.' Less than a year later, the Oracle had
spoken, and the chords had finally begun reverberating to his satisfaction. The
intimations of destiny in the Powell ego had at last found national 'contradictions and phobias' to identify with. The English had begun to know themselves
once more. In the obscene form of racism, English nationalism had been re-born.

---

14 Speech at Hanwell, 25 May 1967 (*Freedom and Reality*, op. cit.). De Gaulle had just admi-
    nistered another contemptuous rebuff to Britain's half-hearted desire to enter the Common
    Market, provoking near-universal resentment and wounded pride in Britain.

The Settled View

Conservatism is a settled view of the nature of human society in general and our own society in particular, which each succeeding generation does but re-express.

ENOCH POWELL, 'Conservatism and the Social Services', *The Political-Quarterly*, 1953

English nationalism has been travestied by romanticism and confused by imperialism. But no account of its calvary would be complete which failed to perceive how it has also been weighed down by *conservatism*. The 'matter of its imagining' (in Powell's phrase) is almost wholly conservative. This is not a question of the political Conservative Party but of that profounder, ambient conservatism which has marked the structure of English society for several centuries. The English national identity sags with the accumulated weight of its symbols and traditions, and is in consequence perhaps the least *popular* nationalism of any major country except that other island, Japan. This is in fact why the nationalism of the English appears so 'dormant' and 'unaggressive' (as *The English Race* put it): simply because the 'people' had so little positive part in creating it, or have forgotten the part they did play. On the whole, they have been forced into the stereotype of the plucky servant who 'knows his place' and, when the trumpet sounds, fights with the best of them. The fact poses a grave problem to would-be leaders of English national revival.[15]

An unintentionally comic clue to the problem is provided by Powell's own history of England, *Biography of a Nation*.[16] The 'Introduction' is a familiar, puzzled rumination on the subject: 'There is no objective definition of what constitutes a nation. It is that which thinks it is a nation... self-consciousness is the essence of nationhood... National consciousness is a sense of difference from the rest of the world, of having something in common which is not shared beyond the limits of the nation... This phenomenon of national consciousness remains almost as mysterious as that of life in the individual organism... This living thing, mysterious in its origins and nature, is perhaps the most difficult subject of purely human enquiry...'; and so forth. But, turning from this Ideal-

---

15   In this respect, the English right-wing dilemma is almost diametrically opposed to the American one. In America there is a popular, vividly-felt nationalism *without* a corresponding deeper structure of conservatism. Hence, for example, the recent American obsession with Edmund Burke, the founding father of modem English conservatism, and the interesting debate which surrounded and followed the publication of Russell Kirk's compendium *The Conservative Mind* in 1953 (see, eg. G. K. Lewis, 'The Metaphysics of Conservatism', *Western Political Quarterly*, vol. VI, and 'The Toryness of English Conservatism', *Journal of British Studies*, vol. I, No. I)

16   *Biography of a Nation: a Short History of Britain*, Enoch Powell and Angus Maude, 1955.

ist prologue to the text, the inscrutable secret reveals itself at once as all too simple: the shallowest imaginable montage of school-book clichés, wholly concentrated around the conventional symbols of conservative nationality (the Crown, Parliament, the Constitution, etc.). These are the unsurprising content of the national self-consciousness.

It is difficult to exaggerate the degree of Powell's symbol-fetishism. He literally worships every sacred icon of the great conservative past. Hence, for instance, his enraged opposition to the Royal Titles Bill of 1953, which did away with Elizabeth II's queenship of the Commonwealth. Faced with such desecration Powell was forced – to the dismay of his fellow-Conservatives in parliament – to identify himself with England's soul. Destiny had struck again: 'We in this House... have a meaning only in so far as in our time and in our generation we represent great principles, great elements in our national being... Sometimes elements which are essential to the life, growth and existence of Britain seem for a time to be cast into shadow, and even destroyed. Yet in the past they have remained alive; they have survived; they have come to the surface again and... been the means of a great flowering which no-one had suspected. It is because I believe that, in a sense, for a brief moment, I represent and speak for an indispensable element in the British Constitution that I have spoken.'[17]

He was both right and (in a sense important for understanding his whole political line) quite wrong. In one respect he does indeed represent very well an indispensable feature of English Constitutionalism – its obsession with the safe, fossilised forms of past authority and legitimacy. Yet of course the obsession must never be given free rein: its whole point, in England's traditional consensus-politics, was its function as an instrument of adaptation, a way of absorbing and neutralising *change*. When it becomes absolute, it becomes useless. But

---

17 Speech in the House of Commons, 3 March 1953. Powell has also contributed two farther volumes to the glory of the Constitution, *Great Parliamentary Occasions* (1960) or 'authentic glimpses into the past of Parliament', and *The House of Lords in the Middle Ages* (with K. Wallis, 1968), a history which devotes as much space as humanly possible to ritual and trivia – 'Every institution has a local habitation...the peculiarities of the place affect the behaviour and life-story of the institution itself. No scrap of information therefore about the place and arrangements of sitting of the institution... is to be despised... This is one advantage, at any rate, which a working member of such an institution has...'. The criterion of selection of Powell's 'great Parliamentary occasions' is the 'pedantic devotion' which the Englishman accords tradition: 'With almost incredulous delight we find that... Humanity, as represented and revealed in Parliament, does not seem to change at all as the centuries pass.' Real history is of no significance. It will come as a surprise to most readers, for instance, that the only 'great occasion' of the 20th century was the debate over the revised Church of England Prayer-Book in 1927. But what mattered was the purely parliamentary drama it gave rise to. John Jones, a Labour member, objected to this trivial squabble 'on behalf of the great mass of the workers of this country (who) are more interested in the rent-book than the prayer-book'. Powell comments: 'The House of Commons, like a mediaeval court, has its licensed buffoons and tolerated jesters.' (pp. 117–18).

Powell has a taste for absolutes. His destiny-filled solitude often blinds him to the wider logic of the Party, and the historic cause, which he wishes to serve. Utterly devoted to English conservatism, he is nevertheless also driven by a blinkered fervour which is alien to its way of working. Hence – as on the occasion in question – he easily finds himself far to the right of political conservatism. By a revealing paradox, this ultra-English bigot is compelled to feel and act in the most surprisingly 'un-English' fashion – that is, in a fashion which contradicts the real essence of the conservative political hegemony.

The mainstream of English conservative consensus has always effectively captured or suppressed left-wing disruption. The left, painfully conscious of its own dilemma, has not noticed how conservatism also had to control the right. Now, a retrospective penumbra of false consciousness eliminates them both. Not only does it politely pretend that the conservative hegemony has survived without difficulty (a fact of English nature), and quietly bury the history of the left, like syndicalism, the workers' control movement, and the other forces beaten in the great defeat of 1926. With almost equal effect, it expunges the grisly history of the English right. Mosley (like the British Communist Party) serves merely to underline the message: 'extremism' and foreign ideas never find a toehold here. When, finally, nemesis returns in the shape of Powellism, England is convulsed with astonishment: is it possible to be 'English', and extreme?

Yet the miracle of this long-lived conservatism lies, after all, in one word: war. Modern English conservatism was forged out of its 22-year war against the French Revolution and Napoleon. This was no war of popular nationalism, having as its stake the casting of English society in a new form: it was the opposite, a patriotic war of counter-revolution which reinforced the conservative social structure, and channelled and moulded popular forces in a fashion which made society able to bear the immense stresses of industrialization. It aimed to eliminate the people from history as other than a subordinate force, and fathered precisely that non-popular nationalism which, now, Powellism is endeavouring to inject life into from the right.

In old age, the imperialist system erected on this original basis has received two massive infusions of vitality from the two farther patriotic wars of the 20th century. Official legends regale the reader with tearful accounts of the tragic economic 'sacrifices' and 'losses' of 1914–18 and 1939–45. In fact, the First World War providentially saved Old England from collapse and civil war, and prepared the terrain for crushing the proletariat in 1926; while the Second World War furnished the perfect restorative, in the form of a victorious patriot drama where English conservatism could hardly avoid looking, and feeling, like a St George with one shining foot on the Nazi dragon's tail. Fortunately, the feet of the USA and USSR were on its neck. In both wars, England was on the right side, pursuing her long-established strategy of alliance with US imperialism. It is true that the war effort of 1939–45 produced much more social egalitarianism in England than any other event in her recent history, enough to result in the electoral defeat of Churchill in 1945. Yet – paradoxically – it also contained the social upheaval more firmly than ever in a renewed 'national' ideology of unity, a sense of patriotic purpose and regeneration. Hence (given the Labour Party's subordination to these myths) it led inevitably to the stifling new conservatism of the 1950s and 1960s.

So Powell's inheritance as an English nationalist is a very strange one. This stale, romantic, middle-class nationalism has survived on the surrogates of imperialism and foreign war for nearly a century. It is at the same time curiously underdeveloped (or 'submerged') because of its conservative, non-popular nature, and a living anachronism in a Europe from which nationalism has begun to pass away. How can it be made to live again?

The Logic of Prejudice

The music sounded, and in my breast
The ghosts of my fathers arose from rest...
Like the priests in Aïda they danced on my head
And sang savage hymns to the gods that are dead.

ENOCH POWELL, Poem XIX, *Casting Off*, 1939

England needs another war. This alone would recreate the peculiar spirit of her nationalism, rally her renegade intelligentsia (as in the 1930's), and reconcile the workers to their lot. Unfortunately, war of that sort – like her empire – is a lost cause. Her patriotic symbols are unlikely to receive any farther transfusions of blood. Nelson, Wellington, Haig and Churchill will – with any luck – never arise from rest to dance on our heads again.

The true-blue nationalist's dilemma is a serious one, therefore. His sacred traditions are visibly withering. There is a new generation which finds them meaningless, or comic. Even the school-teachers – once high-priests of national conservatism – are out on strike. When it is not an international bore, England has become an international joke: her only claim to distinction of any sort is a mainly anti-national pop culture and a (largely unmerited) reputation for *dolce vita*. How can England's silent majority be got to return to the fold, before it is too late?

War was the great social experience of England in this century – yet war served only to confirm and re-validate the value of the past, to affirm the essential continuity of the national tradition. The only *new* experience, going sharply counter to tradition, has been that of the coloured immigration of the 1950s and '60s. Hence, as Powell realised, it has become possible to define Englishness vis-a-vis this internal 'enemy', this 'foreign body' in our own streets. This is exactly what he tried to do in the speech of April 1968. It was more than a case of locating a new scapegoat: this scapegoat was to have the honour of restoring a popular content to English national self-consciousness, of stirring the English 'corporate imagination' into life once more, by providing a concrete way of focussing its vague but powerful sense of superiority.

How strong the force is which Powell began to tap in this way has been demonstrated by the rapid series of rightward steps which the Establishment took to deal with it. At each successive phase of the racial storm in the 1960s, more strict immigration controls were imposed. Writing in *Crossbow*, the organ of 'liberal' young Conservatism, N. Scott remarks that these were no more than fearful 'reactions to public opinion' which 'rendered respectable racially-prejudiced reactions to fears of unemployment and over-population'. But the same writer can only end his plea for tolerance and 'constructive race relations' by conjuring up precisely the phoney, old-style nationalism which Powellism goes beyond: 'Intolerance and racialism present Britain with a challenge to the values upon which life in these islands have been built... It is not, I hope, unfashionably nationalistic to recall Milton's words: 'Let not England forget her precedence of teaching nations how to live'.'[18] The fact is that intolerance and racialism did *not* present any challenge to national values, as long as (like military violence) they were comfortably located abroad; located at home, they represent a new situation to which rhetoric of this kind is irrelevant. As for the Miltonian precedent, it embodies very well a bourgeois moral high-mindedness which the English masses have never been particularly fond of. *Their* sense of superiority does not need them to pose as ethical models to an admiring universe.[19]

Six months after his April 1968, speech, Powell told the London Rotary Club (enjoying a week-end in all-white Eastbourne) that his words had 'revealed

---

18 N. Scott, 'Constructive Race Relations', Crossbow, Jan.- March 1970. In fact, modern English nationality also preserves a kernel of older identity derived mainly from the 16th and 17th centuries, which there is not room to discuss properly here. It was associated with the experience of Puritanism and the 'Puritan Revolution' of 1660, and as a result – 'English nationalism... has always been closer than any other nationalism to the religious matrix from which it rose... (to) a religious life and sentiment... full of social activism, of a feeling of responsibility for the betterment of the world'. (H. Kohn, 'The Genesis of English Nationalism', *Journal of the History of Ideas*, vol. 1, No. 1, 1940) Taine's lengthy account of this national high-mindedness in his *History of English Literature* is still unsurpassed. This strictly bourgeois element of English national feeling is of course also represented in Powellism. Indeed, his reputation for personal high-mindedness is such that, at the time of the Profumo scandal – 'The entire country waited for some time in suspense for Powell's judgement on his leader (Macmillan). He was already known to be a man of exacting conscience – some said a puritanical conscience – who would have no truck with lechery and lying. His positive affirmation that Macmillan had not erred was a powerful reinforcement to the Prime Minister in his distress' (T. E. Utley, op. cit., p. 88). Some of Powell's populist appeal comes from the fact that *such* a morally impeccable source should tell the people their instincts are sound, and need not be restrained by a middle-class morality.

19 Speech at Eastbourne, 16 November 1968 (*Freedom and Reality*, op. cit., p. 227).

a deep and dangerous gulf in the nation... a gulf between the overwhelming majority of people throughout the country on the one side, and on the other side a tiny majority with a monopoly hold upon the channels of communication, who seem determined... not to face realities'.[20] The populist intention is unmistakable: the new national spirit is of and for the overwhelmingly and decently prejudiced majority of English men and women, opposed by the 'aberrant reason' of a tiny minority who think they know best (and which actually included, as Powell knew very well, most members of both parliamentary parties and virtually the whole politico-cultural élite of conservative England).

In another sense, however, England's coloured minority is not such a fruitful choice for the New Right. It is quite a good scapegoat, and served to achieve a preliminary mobilisation of popular sentiment in the right direction. Yet there are inescapable limits to its farther development. In this way, the English coloured population contrasts oddly with the traditional victim of European right-wing nationalism, the Jews. It is, in fact, almost entirely proletarian in character, and unlikely to be anything else for some time to come – hence, it is impossible to pretend plausibly (as one could with the Jews) that it *is* the oppressive 'tiny minority', or at least is in league with it. England's Indians and West Indians can scarcely be identified with 'the system' by which the majority feels obscurely oppressed. They do not measure up to the task of re-defining England's destiny, as it were. In addition, they present the defect of being geographically concentrated in a few areas (whereas it hardly mattered where the Jews were, since they could so easily be imagined as everywhere). Above all, it should not be overlooked how vital immigrant labour has become to the British economy, as to the other West European economies, as Andre Gorz shows elsewhere in these pages. The Confederation of British Industries itself has always opposed restrictions on immigration and talk of repatriation.

Powell tried to extend the area and effect of the racial storm-area, first by his 'repatriation' proposals (offering himself, with characteristic moral integrity, as future Minister of Repatriation), and then by his new fantasy of a burgeoning, prolifically fertile coloured horde forcing the – evidently dried-up – native stock off the island altogether. But these did not repeat his initial shock-success. The new destiny was not emerging with the hoped-for speed. He turned to Ireland.

He showed evidence of stirring interest in England's most ancient problem only a week after the Londonderry riots of 1969. A letter of elevated moral tone appeared in *The Times* in August, rebuking the British Army commander in Ulster, General Freeland, for his 'political' comments during the crisis. Then in

---

20 *The Times*, 9 February 1970. On the day after this address, Powell said on television that his declaration was only 'logical', and something that needed saying. It was not at all calculated 'to increase animosity between those of different religions'. The Conservative shadow Home Secretary Quintin Hogg commented afterwards that 'Logic was not, perhaps, the friend of good politics.'

February 1970, Powell addressed an Ulster Unionist rally at Enniskillen. He declared that 'The ultimate fact in human society, and in the world of states and nations, is belonging or not belonging... The belonging of Northern Ireland and the not-belonging of the Republic are at present obscured by the condition of the law... The fiction of the Ireland Act, 1949, must go... (and)... the entry, the residence, the settlement and the franchise of the citizen of the Republic of Ireland will have to be determined exactly as those of a Frenchman, a Russian or an Australian are determined... Nothing, in my judgement, would conduce so much to banish strife and disorder as the plain and open assertion, in legal and constitutional terms, that the people of these countries belong, uniquely and solely, to the United Kingdom and are part and parcel of this nation, which is in process of defining and recognizing itself anew...'.[21]

This statement was made (it must be remembered) in a situation again approaching civil war, where a British army was supposedly 'keeping order' and in fact maintaining the Protestant police-state of Northern Ireland, because the Catholic 'people of these counties' objected with their lives to 'belonging' to this vestigial limb of Anglo-Scots imperialism. Not surprisingly, Powell 'received a standing ovation from the audience'. The Rev. Paisley and his Calvinist desperadoes had just been welcomed into England's destiny.

But to build destiny on such a basis is even more desperate than anticoloured racism. If England was ready to risk civil war for Protestant Ireland in 1914, it was because of the Empire and imperial prestige. Since these have disappeared, it will be somewhat difficult to turn Ulster into a popular cause again. Paisley and Major Chichester-Clark are not ideal heroes for the new national self-recognition. It might be possible to whip up some anti-Irish (or even some anti-Scots or anti-Welsh) feeling, given the right worsening conditions in any of these places, but this would not carry the national soul far either. It needs more serious fodder.

In English conditions, therefore, the logic of prejudice has its limits. Beyond race and Ireland, what would the main *social* content of the revived national mind be?

The Oak Tree's Roots

Often, when I am kneeling down in church,
I think to myself how much we should thank
God, the Holy Ghost, for the gift of capitalism.

ENOCH POWELL, quoted in T. E. Utley.[22]

---

21 op. cit., p. 114
22 op. cit., p. 114

Powell has indicated clearly what England's social future should be, in any number of perorations: 'Whatever else the Conservative Party stands for, unless – I am not afraid of the word – it is the party of capitalism, then it has no function in the contemporary world, then it has nothing to say to modern Britain…'.[23]

The capitalist market-place is another of the traditional fetishes Powell worships with total devotion, alongside the Crown and the Constitution. His view is a curious inversion of Fabian Socialism: the Webbs identified socialism with State ownership, control, and planning, while he identifies any form of State economic intervention (except currency issue and control) with 'socialism'. He cannot forgive his own party its corruption by 'socialism' in this sense. The modern Conservative Party has become a party of the State, it tolerates or even favours State power and bureaucracy almost as much as Labour. Powell even occasionally compares this State power to fascism: it represents, he claims, the true threat to our freedom – the inhumane, corporative dominance from above, from which only capitalism can preserve us. Hence, England must return as far as possible to the conditions of *laissez-faire*.

Two aspects of this odd rhetoric go some way to making it comprehensible, and help distinguish it from the ancient, over-familiar Conservative ideology of 'free enterprise' (a pedal which the Tories have had to lean on heavily ever since the Liberal Party died off, and they found themselves the main industrialists' party). Firstly, Powell's diatribes are not so much defences of the 'free market' as envenomed attacks on the mainstream of political consensus: the 'State power' against which he inveighs is no less than the tacit basis of agreement informing English political life, which (as always in the past) enables the two-party system to function smoothly and guarantees the peaceful evolution which is supposed to be the essence of English Constitutionalism. The slogan of 'laissez-faire' is the only economic one which distances his position sufficiently from the prevailing 'bad myths'. And, naturally, it appeals to at least one sector of the 'people' he is trying to galvanise into political life – the small business-man (still important in the West Midlands he represents) or the small *rentier* who feels oppressed and helpless in the face of today's great concentrations of economic power. This petty bourgeoisie is, after all, part of that historically absent or repressed English populism remarked on above – part of the historical 'people' kept in social servitude by the conservative hegemony.

Secondly, Powell's conception of the *laissez-faire* economy emphatically does not signify a *weak* or merely marginal State power – the State of classical English liberalism which was meant to do no more than 'hold the ring' for competing economic forces. Given what has happened in the past, a modern free-enterprise State must be *strong* (if only to cope with the much greater strength of business and financial organisation today). Hence, Powell's economics are more compatible than they seem with his evident authoritarianism. The 'freedom'

23 *Freedom and Reality*, op. cit., p. 10.

which his capitalist State would foster includes, quite logically, the 'repeal of the Trade Disputes Act of 1906'.[24] No less naturally, it includes repression of student agitation and of such infamous national scandals as the school-teachers' strike of 1969–70. To let capitalism off the leash again in the way Powell envisages would need, in fact, the strongest State action against workers, students, and intellectuals (the 'tiny minority who control communications', etc.). And obviously this face of Powellism appeals to an even wider stratum of discontented middle-class and lower-middle-class natives, like the Conservative Party militants he travels the country addressing.

Both these facets of Powell's ideology are very much the daily bread of nationalist, right-wing reaction in the past. They represent no more than the classical formula established succinctly by Charles Maurras long ago: 'Authority at the top, liberty below'.[25] If the nation is ill and led astray, then it follows that the prevailing political force must be corrupt and incompetent. It cannot be cleansed or put to rights except by a strong, decisive leadership able to express the true national will. By definition, the nation is always being betrayed. It must, therefore, be *redeemed*.

Powell has always been riveted by the notion of the national destiny re-emerging from betrayal and ruin. One of his early poems is about the Portuguese national poet Camões (Camoëns), who was shipwrecked in the Mekong Delta in the 16th century:

> Black the mountains of Timor
> Sweeping from the sea
> Watched Camoëns drift ashore,
> Rags and misery...

But the poet was to be saved from death, to compose the great national epic *Os Lusíadas*, and even in the depths of his degradation held in one battered hand 'a jointed fennel-stalk' –

> Hidden in that hollow rod
> Slept, like heavenly flame
> Titan-stolen from a god,
> Lusitania's flame.[26]

---

24 See *Freedom and Reality* ch. 10, 'Changing Trade Union Law', pp. 146–47. 'The evil of trade unionism', Powell states roundly, 'lies in the coercive power of combination which the trade unions possess, and which they use, either by threatening to withdraw their labour collectively or by actually doing so, in order to try to obtain more for their services than these would command in the open market without this coercion...'.

25 *Director and King* (1899), quoted in *The French Right* (selections ed. J. S. McClelland, 1970).

26 Poem VI, 'Os Lusíadas', *Dancer's End*.

In 1953, amid the humiliation of the Royal Titles Bill, he imagined 'a great flowering' that might still come forth from destruction. In 1964, at the Royal Society of St George, he compared England to Greece: 'Herodotus relates how the Athenians, returning to their city after it had been sacked and burned by Xerxes... were astonished to find, alive and flourishing in the midst of the blackened ruins, the sacred olive tree, the native symbol of their country. So we today at the heart of a vanished empire, amid the fragments of demolished glory, seem to find, like one of her own oak trees, standing and growing, the sap still rising from her ancient roots to meet the spring, England herself...'. Even now England must not despair: in spite of Heath, Wilson, and the Rolling Stones – 'we know not what branches yet that wonderful tree will have the power to put forth.'

In spite of all these classical features of right-wing destiny-mongering, however, Powellism still contains a glaring weakness at its heart: a far too overt identification with capitalism. This may appeal to capitalists, and particularly small entrepreneurs, but there is evidently a far larger area of the national soul to which it will never appeal at all. Most successful past brands of reaction have at least had the sense to conceal their links with capital from the public gaze. Powellism, by contrast, has its trousers down from the start: capitalism is nudely exposed as another cherished institution of Old England. When reminded by J. K. Galbraith at a Cambridge University Union debate that 'the competitive system was now an illusion, that the market was dominated by large monopolistic or semi-monopolistic concerns which have many of the attributes of the State and which... create rather than obey public taste,' Powell merely admitted that there was, indeed, much truth in this statement.[71] He knows perfectly well that his *apologia* for capitalist freedom are in practice justifications of existing, large-scale finance-capital.

It is all very well to say that 'capitalism is now the revolutionary cause', as Powell does. The English masses are not likely to see their destiny there – on the contrary. What odd naiveté is it that prevents Powell from perceiving the vital necessity to any counter-revolution of disguising its true nature, of pretending to be some kind of revolt *against* capitalism? As regards the prejudices Powellism works on, its power is (as we noticed) limited. Now, in its central social doctrine, it seems to present an inexplicable weakness, and to be manifestly incapable of furnishing the void of English nationalism. Why is this?

English Authoritarianism

Oh that this dull necessity
And mastering force of sanity,
This too strong texture of the mind

---

27 See T. E. Utley, op. cit, pp. 117–29.

That keeps me by its toils confined
In the world's badness,
Would break at last and set me free
Into the sunlit, halcyon sea
Of madness.

ENOCH POWELL, Poem XXI, *Dancer's End*

The central problem of Powellism arises mainly from asking the wrong questions about the phenomenon – from considering Powell, his Conservative Party back-woodsmen, and his potential mass following as a tendency, or even a movement. Then one must ask what this movement may tend towards, and the question of 'fascism' inevitably arises.

Nothing could obscure the real issues more. In England, even the home-grown fascism of Mosley or the National Front is largely a distraction. The genuine right – and the genuine threat it represents – are of quite a different character. One of the few things in politics that may be confidently predicted is that J. Enoch Powell will never lead a column of blue-shirts into Parliament Square.

The ideological weaknesses and absurdities of Powellism matter little, simple because *in itself* it probably tends towards nothing at all. It is not, and probably never will be, a 'movement' in that sense. However, unlike English fascism, it is certainly not a distraction. It is, on the contrary, directly linked to and expressive of profounder changes of the utmost gravity. Intellectually – or in terms of the history of right-wing ideas – Powell may be negligible. This does not remove his political significance in the least.

Powellism is a symptom: the true threat lies in the developing disease of which it is a symptom. Powell has emerged apparently as an active challenge to the existing political consensus from the right. In fact, he and his repercussions are symptomatic of the growing paralysis and deterioration of the consensus itself. There *is* a national insanity in the air, but it did not originate in Powell's second-rate ruminations. It is located squarely in the mainstream of English politics and – beyond that – in the harsh contradictions of English capitalism which the political consensus has been struggling with in vain for a quarter of a century.

Powell – as we saw – attributes the chronic crisis and historical loss of nerve of the English governing class to *consciousness*. It has fallen foul of unfortunate myths, and acquired a false self-consciousness – whence its dithering, its narcissistic isolation from reality, its feeble losing battle against economic crisis. The truth is the opposite. The continuity of England's incredible myth-consciousness, and her political decay, are the products of a material history – the shrinking material basis of an imperialist order still trapped in its own historical contradictions. And Powellism, the would-be trumpet-blast to cleanse the national mind, is only a belated echo of this decline. Its importance is, precisely, that it enables us to perceive just how advanced the rot has become.

Powell's pathetic nationalist demagoguery can reverberate only within this peculiar environment of decay and isolation. Somewhat earlier in the history of his nation he would have passed unnoticed, an obscure classicist and political conformist glumly turning over his own garden. Yet now this fossil epitome of Old England looms across the national scene, a mushrooming caricature of patriotic destiny. European nationalism generally is in poor shape in 1970. But England has become culturally and politically isolated, imprisoned within her dying imperialism, and here this archaic development can still have an impact. It can work upon the submerged nationalism of the English, trying at least to give a reactionary content to its uncertainty, and appeal to the (perfectly justified) national feeling of frustration and anger. Because this feeling is so inarticulate, and so divorced from the genteel clichés of the Establishment, the New Right can, at least, suggest convincingly that something is profoundly wrong and that something must be done about it, in a partly familiar idiom.

Yet what purchase it has is due to the fissure which has, slowly, opened up in the traditional mode of hegemony. The political Establishment has begun to lose its old grip on the nation, and on the masses. It has – so to speak – started to shrink out of contact with the social realities over which, traditionally, it exerted an all-embracing and conservative control. It is only from this new fissure in the socio-political structure that the stale fungus of Powellism has been able to sprout, so rapidly and with such effect. Where else could such mothballed platitudes resound so strongly, where else could fusty junk like Powell's produce quite such a sensation? Where, but in the stagnant, involuted atmosphere of a world near the end of its tether?

Because the political consensus lies within the area of rot, Powell under-stood intuitively from his solitude that it was necessary to go beyond and outside it, although it took him many years of groping to discover the way. Then, the new phenomenon of domestic racism – outside the grip of traditional hegemony *because* novel – suddenly disclosed the fracture which he needed. His destiny-fantasy at once acquired some leverage upon reality. This particular social problem has (as we noticed above) limits of exploitability, as does the Irish question to which Powell has now turned. But both are, nevertheless, deep running sores which the present English body politic can probably no longer cure. By thrusting a knife into them, Powell can quickly aggravate the patient's general condition; he already has.

It goes without saying that Powell, wrapped as ever in his conservative fetishism, does this in the hope of re-injecting life into the old political machine. He piously imagines that his words will send fresh red blood racing through the arteries of Westminster. It has probably never occurred to him that these aged organs may not be able to take the strain. He has often remarked, in his usual awed fashion, upon the amazing continuity which has characterised English political life in the past. He believes he is part of this continuity, engaged on giving it the new national basis it needs. It has never crossed his mind that he might be killing it. Yet there can be little doubt that this is the meaning of the astonishing spectacle that has begun to unfold itself: in Powellism, the English conservative Establishment has begun to destroy itself. Its secular hegemony has come to this: a solitary figure, solemnly and self-consciously identified with every fibre of the glorious past, who is nevertheless compelled to devour the patrimony he worships. His importance – and his seriousness as a phenomenon and as a political figure – is not intrinsic, but rather in his relationship to this wider process. It lies in his function as a ferment of disaggregation within a deeper contradictory movement. It is the logic of this movement that has carried him to where he is, and forced him to destroy his own idols.

To the left, absorbed in its own problems and the effect it is (or is not) having upon the social order, it comes as a surprise that this order should have begun to collapse in a different direction altogether. Now that Powellism has happened, however, the lines of force leading towards this result at least become clearer.

They radiate out from the underlying situation of stalemate, or irresolvable contradiction, in which British capitalism has been lodged since early in the century. This is not the place to try and analyse at length the main causes and features of the condition, or to distinguish specifically British traits from those which have also affected other capitalist States. In essence, the 'disease' is no more than the peculiar nature of British imperialism, or the complex of foreign and financial interests which the bourgeoisie acquired in its earlier development, which it preferred to the development of its domestic economy, and which – latterly – it has only been able to retain and develop *at the expense of* that economy. This contradiction has manifested itself in an 'economic crisis' lasting more than 20 years. It has become the near exclusive concern of government in this period. Everything else has been made to depend on it. According to the time of year and the stage each politico-economic cycle has reached, the perennial British crisis is 'growing', 'grave', 'very grave', 'on the mend', 'looking up', 'turning the corner' or 'finally on the verge of solution'.

Throughout this period, both great political parties have accepted the same definition of the 'economic crisis', and struggled hopelessly to resolve it in the same ways (the Labour Party perhaps somewhat more consistently than the Conservatives). Since the definition was superficial and mythical (a genuinely 'bad myth' in Powell's sense) and the remedies were and are only palliatives, the result has been a staple political diet of boredom and irrelevance, incomprehensible to most of the population. For practical purposes, the national soul has been the Bank of England for two decades, and political life has been tied entirely to a number of economists' fetishes ('the Pound', the 'balance of payments', 'Britain's reserves', etc.) in the name of political realism and common sense. It is not surprising that the natives have become deeply, angrily, inarticulately restless.

What is surprising is that they have taken so long to react. During this era of decline and attrition, the political consensus has lost much of its earlier vitality. It was not designed for conditions like these – the two-party system and the English constitutional machine assumed their contemporary form, in fact, within the successful economic empire whose remains they have been wrestling to defend. Then it ensured mass adhesion and averted class conflict in much easier circumstances. In the last ditch where the political Establishment has now been labouring for so long, it has shrunk into a parody of its former self. Originally it functioned by securing a consensus around great national ideas and policies; since there have been no such ideas since 1945, it has had simply to avoid social conflict at any cost. 'Consensus' has become something like paralysis.

It is in this feeble, palsied world that Powellism can arise and produce its effect – it refuses to play the (debased) 'game' of consensus politics, and actively stirs up conflict instead of conspiring to stifle or ignore it. Talk of Powellite 'fascism' or of 'Tory counter-revolution' wilfully ignores the real conditions under which Powell and racism obtained their remarkable leverage over the system. The fact is that there has been no 'revolution' to provoke the wave of reaction. It is true that at the same time as Powell has emerged there has been the beginnings of a challenge from the left: the nascent student movement, People's Democracy in Northern Ireland, and a rising tide of strikes. Yet these are no more than premonitory rumblings. They have not amounted so far to anything like the degree of social and political conflict which many other societies take completely for granted. Foreign visitors currently confront the bewildering sight of a 'law and order' campaign by the press, the media, and both political parties, in a society where (except for Northern Ireland) there is scarcely any lawlessness or disorder.

The point is, precisely, that Powellism has arisen and acquired its influence, and the political Establishment has moved effortlessly rightwards in response to that influence, *without* real provocation. The Labour Party is not only mainly responsible for the political paralysis and degeneration of the last years; it has also lost most of the stimulus which once came from its own left wing. As the New Right has grown up, the Old Left has dwindled away and ceased to function within the consensus. All that the system has been able to do is debate endlessly over mechanical remedies to the problem: 'bringing Parliament closer to the people' by revising the machinery of government, by appointing an 'Ombudsman', by televising parliamentary debates, and so on.

If this is so, and the English system drifts into a feeble authoritarianism without much pretext, then what will happen when it *is* provoked? So far, most of the provocation has come from it, as it has moved nervously towards more definite control over wages and the suppression of unofficial strikes. What will happen when the first large-scale factory occupation takes place? What will happen when the first effective worker-student alliance is formed? When one or other of the parties does finally pass anti-strike legislation, and embark on a more direct confrontation with the working class? What if any of these things should coincide with a further deterioration of the Northern Ireland situation, or with race-riots in England? What if they should cause, or accompany, a drastic down-turn of the perennial economic crisis, with the inevitable flight from sterling, loss of confidence, threat of devaluation, etc? None of these things is impossible. Any combination of them would, of course, presage a major upheaval in England.

In other words, when there is finally a real social conflict to test the political structure, how will that structure react? There is no point in making alarmist prophecies. But, with reference to Powellism, it is not in the least alarmist to indicate that this new right wing reflects (and derives its strength from) a general rightward degeneration of the political structure. It would be absurd to talk about an English fascism. But there is nothing absurd in remembering that in England, where there is no tradition of Caesarism, no domestic militarism, and no French or German-style army to incarnate national destiny, no reactionary régime could possibly neglect or overlook those priceless symbols of nationhood, Westminster, the Crown, and the Constitution.

Whatever the party in office, Powell has already demonstrated that he can pull the whole of the official structure of British politics in his direction. In a real crisis the impact of the new right would necessarily be qualitatively greater, whatever the formal political complexion of the Government. If the party system itself were strained by such a crisis, as is at least probable, then there is a ready-made formula to hand. National ideologies of reaction are very diverse. They seize upon and jumble up the materials to hand, with a logic which itself arises from the nation's history. The indigenous variety of authoritarianism, which has already occupied two decades of British political life in this century, is thoroughly established: in the longer-run, we might witness a National Government once again, which saves traditional values in the teeth of crisis. In this respect, Powellism may only be a preliminary ground-clearing exercise. Whatever political edifice would house English reaction, the furniture would doubtless still be that of British 'sanity'.

CHAPTER FIVE

British Nationalism and the EEC

New Left Review, 1/69

SEPTEMBER–OCTOBER 1971

Whatever is decided, the City of London should remain just as prosperous.
Moreover there is nothing in the Werner plan… to deter Britain.

The Banker, spring 1971

IN BRITISH POLITICS, agreement is traditionally more important than differences.
This is part of what 'consensus' implies. The points of agreement have to be
normally at a deeper level than those of discord, in order to minimise the latters'
effects. In fact consensus-points are best taken for granted: then, 'what we have
in common' stays in the background, the bass-note of national unity, an apparently neutral and uncontested framework for argument. There is no superior
technique of social conservatism.

But the current 'great debate' on whether or not Britain should join the
European Common Market is unusual in that for once this underlying framework is, at least, illuminated. However garbled some of its expressions may be,
it can hardly avoid being about fundamentals: it is about the nation and the
state. So it casts a rare searchlight over the rotting timbers, the massive but
badly rusted ironwork. 'What we have in common' – the political inheritance
of the Anglo-Scots bourgeois and imperialist nation-state and its extensions in
Britain and overseas – is more nearly the object of debate than its bland assumption. Like it or not, both 'points of view' in the debate can hardly help showing
the structure both stand upon.

The Rulers: Class Before Nation

What they stand on is, in the first place, nationalism. At first sight both the pro
and the anti-Europe factions may appear equally devoted to national sovereignty: that is, equally nationalistic. In his broadcast comments on the government's White Paper about the Common Market, Heath presented the operation
as a venture into new national glory: 'We have the chance of new greatness', he
said, 'we must go in if we want to remain Great Britain, and take the chance of
becoming Greater Britain'. The arguments for joining Europe have often been
very economic in content. But the point of growing economically stronger is

usually this: the restoration, even the improvement, of 'Britain's place in the world'. Only in this way can the British nation's prestige, influence and power among the other nations be ensured. For Britain as for the other big ex-imperial power in Common Market Europe, France, the Community is a surrogate for Empire: since Asia and Africa will no longer oblige, maybe we can use other Europeans to magnify the faltering *rayonnement*? Hence, as for De Gaulle, Europe might represent the continuation of the national saga: we can be imagined as joining our 'destiny' (the favoured concept of romantic nationalism) to the wider one of Western Europe, without giving up much that really matters.

On the other hand, among the anti-Common Market groups, it involves renouncing all that counts: the national saga itself. As from 1 January 1973, Britain will no longer control 'her' own destiny, and therefore no longer be 'her' self. Far from meaning more greatness and national self-affirmation, the European Community would lead to the erosion, eventually to the loss, of national identity. Foreigners, some of them bureaucrats, will tell us what to do. The leading weekly organ of intellectual reaction, *The Spectator*, believes for example that Britain must at all costs keep to the open seas and the fresh breezes of 'outward-looking' tradition. Claustrophobic, 'inward-looking' Europe would be ruin to this sailorly inheritance. The attitude is shared by the Monday Club's imperialists, the fascists of the National Front and – in somewhat different vein – by Enoch Powell. During the three years of his remarkable influence, the latter has reiterated the gospel of pure nationalism: the nation is re-discovering itself, 'defining itself anew' (with the help of the coloured immigrant community) after an era of degradation. After the long detour of Empire the English are home again, ploughing the Saxon field. The last thing they want now, evidently, is to have a lot of foreigners trampling over it. In this way imperialists, crypto-imperialists and post-imperialists of the right can all unite over the Common Market question. This is hardly surprising, since from the earliest days of English mercantilism up to Churchill a prodigious arsenal of patriot philosophy furnishes ammunition for exactly this sort of nationalism.

What is surprising is something else. Why, given these huge ideological resources, is this right-wing opposition to Europe so feeble? It clearly represents no more than a tattered fringe of the ruling class: a few MPs, a certain number of intellectuals, small and relatively impotent groups. True, it includes the right's most formidable single figure, Powell. But how isolated, how powerless he now appears! This is the man who exerted such a large influence on affairs only a year ago, and who only months ago seemed likely to lead a powerful movement against the Common Market. He toured Europe to prepare a campaign which has failed to materialise. There *is* no conservative revolt against Heath's government, either in parliament or outside it (where most of the big press supports him, with only predictable exceptions like the *Express*). How is it that the class and the party of Disraeli and Churchill, the prime repository of historic nationalism, can be so astonishingly united around the *less* nationalistic perspective? For, although the same national rhetoric often surfaces on both sides, there is of course no doubt that its intensity is far greater among the 'antis': as always, fervour is strongest among those defending the nation against outside enemies.

The problem is all the more startling if one considers for a moment the real situation in which Heath's bid for entry to Europe is being made. Most of those behind him are hound to have at least a marginal consciousness of what that reality is. The last decade has witnessed a vertiginous decline in British international power. It is false to think that the 1971 negotiations are – as is often reassuringly claimed – merely a re-presentation of the same old issues as Macmillan's government confronted in 1961. To read the speeches of 1961 now is to be instantly aware of a dizzying gulf. Those symbols of stardom round which opposition to Europe crystallised ten years ago, the Commonwealth and the American 'special relationship', have evaporated almost without trace. The Sterling Area is on its deathbed, still expiring quietly after the *coup de grâce* of the 1967 devaluation. A decade of economic crisis has cruelly and continuously underlined British isolation, impotence, and growing backwardness in the capitalist world. Chronic civil war has broken out in one British province. The immediate prelude to the new negotiations was a prolonged outburst of ethnic bemusement and half-hearted racism, culminating in the elections of 1970. Seen from abroad, Britain is obviously making the best of a bad job: its 20 years of dithering and crab-like advances issue in a pathetic last leap into the only hole left open, and the scuttling operation is solemnised as epochal 'decision' and ornamented by a great debate on destiny.

The Economic Field

Yet Conservatism has let itself be massively rallied behind this humiliating programme, and chosen to pretend that joining the European Community is patriotically possible, even desirable, even indispensable. The Conservative Union's special conference on Europe in July 1971 brought the spectacle of backwoods squires, old soldiers, Women's Institute militants and solid business persons from the North united in frenzied applause for Heath's 'success' in Brussels.[1] Almost every one of them must have entertained some sneaking doubts about the project, probably not long ago. But now all doubts were stilled. This unanimity is striking even though the general interests of British big capital make entry into the European Community imperative. The prospect for British big capital is clear enough. No important organ of bourgeois opinion has had any doubts about the matter for a very long time – indeed The Times and The Economist have waged a whole-

---

1 Something of the moment's madness can he gathered from the Chair-woman's closing remarks: it was most suitable, she said, that the conference had taken place on 14 July, anniversary of another great historic dawn of freedom and progress in European history. There was much cheering.

hearted and consistent campaign of support for entry for a decade. Three British Governments drawn from both parties have applied for admission to the Community. Familiarity with the reasons why British capitalism must enter the EEC should not be allowed to dull their force. This is now more urgent than ever. The economic difficulties of US capitalism have meant that any idea of some favoured relationship with the United States as an alternative to membership of the Community has had to be abandoned. The decisive question remains the small size of the UK internal market: British big capital needs a home base capable of sustaining its international operations. Not only do many sections of British industrial capital need a larger home market, but for many large companies the question of entry has already been settled. They are already in the Community in an economic sense and now vitally require political representation in its deliberations. Entry will also place these companies in a better position to participate in the mergers and alliances that will be necessary if they are to match the US giants and to withstand the onslaught of Japanese competition.

This by no means implies that entry will not be very painful to many sections of British capitalism – many smaller and middle size firms will go bankrupt or be taken over, and the same will happen to the less efficient of the larger concerns. Given the weak shape of British capitalism the sector which will be hit by entry is not small or marginal. But then there is no conceivable economic policy which could protect this sector very long – and if one could be found, it would simply extend indefinitely the sickness of British capitalism. The major financial institutions which play such a central role in the British economy are, on the other hand, likely to be able to profit significantly from entry. The position of these institutions seems to have been much strengthened over the last decade. Between 1964 and 1969 the total income of financial companies nearly doubled, while the income of industrial and commercial companies was almost stationary.[2] British financial capital has withstood the decline of sterling after 1967 in the most remarkable fashion, and has compensated for it by its large and growing share of the Eurodollar market. This sophisticated financial nexus is well poised to greatly extend its European operations. The only price that has to be paid is the ruin of the dense undergrowth of backward British industry in such fields as clothing, shoes, cotton, ship-building and machine tools. The averagely adroit financial institutions will entirely escape footing this bill – indeed they will be ready to re-conjugate the factors of production which it will release. Although no precise computation can be made of where entry will hit hardest, the great extent of the backward and uncompetitive sector is visible enough in its fruits, the retardation of British capitalism for which it is largely responsible. Under the circumstances, it might be thought that this sector would furnish the basis for a violent clash within the ruling class itself. The general tone of bourgeois comment on entry is restrained

---

2   See Andrew Glyn and Bob Sutcliffe, 'The Critical Condition of British Capital', NLR 66, p.25.

and cautious, impressed more by the absence of alternatives than by any relish for the struggle to come. All the same, the virtual absence of dissent from any sector of the ruling class does pose the question: what has persuaded a potent and numerous grouping of British capitalists to accept the probability of euthanasia with such good grace? After all it is one of the great achievements of the Conservative Party that it integrates not only the virtual entirety of the bourgeoisie proper but also the great mass of the petty bourgeoisie.

The Political Field

If one turns from the economic to the political field, two reasons for the display of unity at once suggest themselves. First of all, even the most backwoods British businessman must be sensible of the impasse of British capitalism. Entry to the Common Market represents *something*: an 'achievement', a step carried out in one direction rather than another. This should not be underrated, after a decade of nullity, especially when the last six years of it were presided over by the Labour Party. The beginning of the period saw the collapse of Britain's 'independent' nuclear force, along with the Blue Streak missile, and the failure of its last 'great power' initiative at the Paris summit conference of 1960. Since then little has happened but rot. It should not be forgotten either that if Wilson had managed to gain entry in 1967–8, we would have seen Labour conferences acclaim the historic achievement in similar excited fashion, with the relief of a party demonstrating that paralysis is not, after all, inevitable and that *it* can carry through what the other lot failed to.

Secondly, this particular ruling class has a deep instinct of unity often shown in the past. And in a situation of general decay and uncertainty, it becomes more not less important to support the side. Whatever the decision, for or against, it is vital to rally behind it and maintain a common front, repressing the doubts and suspicions many Conservatives must evidently have. Only a year ago, the elections made clear again that the British bourgeoisie is still far more actively class-conscious and politically aware than the working class. In this sense, the nagging anxieties and fears of the more vulnerable may only reinforce the determination to hold together and show the national way forward. Is it really 'forward'... or just sideways, anywhere, a blind last chance? Better than standing still, at any rate, and a proper class enthusiasm – the active will of 'those who know best' – is more likely to make it all work out.

Class political unity of this sort is itself a mode of domination. Its intensity at this moment must also reflect the fact that, on the European issue, the people are restive. The more fractious the lower orders become, the more vital it is to close ranks and keep cohesion at the top. Where the government is – apart from the Common Market – in a state of semi-siege, fighting an unpopular and dangerous battle against inflation and against the workers, in a grim and still deteriorating economic situation, the immediate political motives for unity are obvious. In other words, British Conservatism has inherited a certain amount of political, ruling-class sense from its long history as well as the chauvinist old clothes which (under more normal or relaxed conditions) it would enjoy wearing. This instinct perhaps enables it to distinguish the more from the less important: in Europe or outside it, the City of London will be prosperous and the rulers will keep most of what matters to them – but only if a decent class front is sustained.

At bottom, therefore, 'class' is more important to them than 'nation'. The fact does not appear in Tory orations, or in its manifestos about the Common Market. But it is registered in the political behaviour of the Conservatives since they won the elections of June 1970. At that time, after Powell's long assault on the party leaders, his mounting popularity, and the open feuds of the electoral campaign, Conservatism seemed quite badly divided. Now it does not. Class sense won it the election, against all the odds; the same combative class sense has now pulled it together on the unlikely (and in many ways unpromising) platform of entry to the European Community. Once, while it served their class interest, the Conservatives identified 'nation' with themselves. Now that the old clothes are less useful – and because the clothes actually *belong* to them, because the 'nation' *is* theirs, because they *are* the party of Disraeli and Churchill – they can be quietly dropped or turned into something a little more suitable. I'm as patriotic as the next man, old boy; but we must face facts.

The Labour Party: Nation Before Class

Our type of beer might disappear if Britain joins the EEC... we could not have our usual kippers because of their brown colouring, likewise our jelly marmalade falls foul of the draft directive on conserves. British sausages also do not conform and would have to change.

Bulletin No. 4, Common Market Safeguards Campaign (March 1971)

On the right, with few exceptions, class matters more than nation. On the 'left', nation is more important than class. For the fact is that the real opposition to European entry now extends from the majority of the Labour Party through most of the trade unions to the Communist Party. At this critical juncture, as the ruling class has drawn up tight round Heath's Europeanism, the traditional organisations of the labour movement have moved in the other direction to define themselves ever more clearly as the defenders of the nation-state, the island economy and patriotic tradition. While the ruling class – architect and chief beneficiary of nationalism – unites on a policy of abandoning old-style national sovereignty, the working class – principal victim of nation-state oppression throughout history

– is being mobilised in a rigid defence of nationality, virgin self-determination, the English Constitution and the New Zealand dairy farmers.

It was suggested to begin with that the 'great debate' throws unusual light upon the underlying framework of 'consensus' and the nation. The present distribution of roles is merely the unfamiliar truth, light falling upon what is always there. To employ another geological metaphor: there is implicit in the debate about Europe a fatal change of levels, which simply shows up strata faults normally concealed underfoot and taken for granted. Something of the true structure of hegemony is for once exposed to the air – and in particular, the part played by Labourism in sustaining it. The most useful place to begin reconstructing the political dynamic of the moment is nine years ago, at the Annual Conference of the Labour party in Brighton. During the previous three years, from 1959 to 1962, Labour had endured its worst antagonisms since the 1930s. The left and right wings had fought bitterly over the issues of unilateral nuclear disarmament and Gaitskell's proposed revision of the party's constitution. Intellectually, the right-wing revisionists led by Crosland had clashed with both Old and New Lefts as the movement searched for some way out of the stalemate that had overtaken it since the later days of the Attlee government. For the first time since the war a mass movement, the Campaign for Nuclear Disarmament, had offered some threat to Labour hegemony from outside. Although the right-wing leadership had won over the nuclear question, and the left had won a much more hollow victory over 'Clause 4', it scarcely looked in 1962 as if the trouble was over. Gaitskell was still detested as a traitor by the left, while the whole left was still despised as a group of behind-the-times trouble-makers by the right.

Yet at the 1962 Conference Gaitskell was able to rally the party behind him in the most remarkable way. He succeeded in forging a genuine sentiment of unity and purpose, for the first time in many years. And he did this by going beyond the dilemmas besetting the movement (which were quite insoluble as they stood, in the terms being employed) and appealing to something deeper, to what the antagonists had in common – he effected a 'change of levels' which gave him a hold on the real bedrock of Labourism. The party had fallen hopelessly apart about socialism; it could still be preserved and reinvigorated by an appeal to nationalism. The latter was structurally more important.

Gaitskell's Last Triumph

In 1961 the Macmillan government had made the first application for entry to the Common Market, and throughout 1962 Heath was conducting the negotiations at Brussels. At first the question had only added to the number of disagreements within the Labour Party: then as more recently, both the leadership and the movement at large were split into pro and anti-European factions. But as time went by the 'anti' group became stronger, especially to the left. The

National Executive issued a statement before the Conference which claimed that Great Britain could still 'go it alone': 'The prosperity of Britain rests far more on our ability to make intelligent use of our economic resources than it does on securing tariff-free access to the Six.'[3] At Brighton Gaitskell rose to defend this statement and, in what was to be universally regarded as an epoch-making speech, welded right and left wings together in emotional opposition to the Common Market. It is well worth recalling what he said.

The Leader did not accept that – as Macmillan was claiming – 'the only way Britain could put her house in order' was by entering the EEC and 'exposing industry to the blast of competition'. Under the Conservatives, perhaps; but under a Labour government it would not be so. Labour would enable the nation to stand on her own feet again. It was 'nonsense and rubbish' to say anything else. As for the political side of Europe – well, Europe meant Hitler and Mussolini as well as Goethe and Picasso. Could one be sure that in the long run the former would not be more important? We should allow the Europeans a few more years to prove they are really capable of behaving better, before thinking of joining them. Political federation would mean 'the end of Britain as an independent nation state'. The Liberals had been hot for this at their conference the previous week: 'They are a little young, I think', Gaitskell ironised, 'I am all for youth, but I like it to be sensible as well' (much hilarity). When the laughter had subsided he went on: 'We must be clear about this: it does mean... the end of Britain as an independent European state. I make no apology for repeating it. It means the end of a thousand years of history. You may say 'Let it end', but, my goodness, it is a decision that needs a little care and thought. And it does mean the end of the Commonwealth.' The Leader expressed his wish – evidently shared by the Conference – to cherish the Commonwealth. The latter 'owed its creation' to the Labour Party. It was at the source of our 'different history' from the continentals, our 'ties and links which run across the whole world'. 'When people say 'What did we get out of New Zealand; what did we get out of Australia?' ... I remember that they came to our aid at once in two world wars. We, at least, do not intend to forget Vimy Ridge and Gallipoli.' Then Gaitskell closed with a call for elections to decide the issue, implying that the people, stirred to patriotic opposition against the Common Market, would sweep Labour back to power again. If only an honourable old-style Conservative like Stanley Baldwin were still there, and there was some respect left for the old ways of the Constitution![4] Europe might yet be tolerable, but only 'upon our conditions...

---

3   NEC Statement, September 29 1962, quoted in *The, Second Try: Labour and the EEC*, ed. U. Kitzinger (1968).

4   The reference was to Baldwin's Conservative government of 1923, which allowed a general election on the proposal to break with Free Trade and erect tariff barriers around British industry. This was the election which carried the Labour Party to power for the first time, in January 1924. According to the theory of British Constitutionalism, yesterday's

only if it gives up, and shows that it gives up, the narrow nationalism that could otherwise develop.'[5]

The Leader was given what the normally sober *Report* calls 'an unparalleled ovation'. That year's Conference Chairman, the Rt. Hon Harold Wilson, at once leapt to his feet and proposed that 'this historic speech... be immediately sent to be printed and made available to every Party member in this country and to the wider areas beyond.' There followed an animated debate. Clive Jenkins said the moment reminded him of 1940, when Britain stood alone.[6] A. Wedgwood Benn declared: 'I believe that the historic speech that launched the historic debate at this historic Conference will carry us into historic battle.' As the day wore on, delirium increased. D. Healey MP rose to say he had divined what must inevitably be the task of the forthcoming historic Labour government: to alter the entire course and character of world history. 'A Labour Government will revitalise and invigorate the Commonwealth', he said. 'But we shall do more. A Labour Government under Hugh Gaitskell will revitalise and reintegrate the United Nations Organisations... the only instrument capable of solving the massive problems which confront us.' J. Stonehouse MP echoed these sentiments, after tearing up his previously prepared notes in order to speak from the heart: 'This man, this great man with ice-cold intellect but human, sincere emotions, can carry his country into a new era of world relationships' he cried, 'I believe that this Party will... (he faltered, as if overcome by the sheer grandeur of the vision)... bring about some new relationship in the world.'

Not long afterwards Gaitskell died, and was succeeded by Chairman Wilson. But he had prepared the way for the latter's triumph at next year's Conference – the famous Scarborough speech on Labour and the 'scientific revolution', now better remembered than Gaitskell's. Thus, there was the most direct connection between the 1962 melodrama and the historic Government which duly emerged. The party was emotionally reunited by nationalistic fervour (after the unsatisfactory compromises on nuclear arms and Clause 4) and in 1963 Wilson could furnish some spurious content for this renewed cohesion and impetus: the British nation-state could stand on its own two feet again with the help of advanced technology. Wilson is often considered as the man of reconciliation and party unity above all else, and his obsessive concern with these topics contrasted with

---

Conservatives are usually honourable men in contrast to today's scoundrels. A recent Commons oration by Douglas Jay (Chairman of the Common Market Safeguards Campaign) is studded with appeals to figures as diverse as Edmund Burke, Lord Grey, G. M. Trevelyan, Asquith, and Sir Winston Churchill (6 July 1970).

5   Labour Party *Annual Conference Report* 1962, pp. 155–65.

6   His actual words were: 'I am reminded of that day, 7th. May 1940, when the great debate was taking place on the Norwegian disaster, when Arthur Greenwood rose to speak for a Labour Opposition and a Conservative ex-Minister, Leo Amery, said: 'Arthur, speak today for Britain.' I believe that today this is what this Conference has done.' L. S. Amery was one of the most rabid spokesman of ultra-right military imperialism.

Gaitskell's narrow integrity of principle. Yet one cannot help noticing that it was Gaitskell and not he who began re-forging party unity, and that the technique was shamelessly simple: tear-jerking patriotism plus the invocation of the Empire's sublimated relics (Commonwealth and 'world-role').

Labour's New Cause

While the Wilsonian scientific-technological revolution has come and gone (without ever descending to earth), the basis of Gaitskell's anti-Common Market position remains as solid as ever. In 1971, we can see how it had outlasted everything else, even the Labour Party's decision in office to enter the Market. The Commonwealth, the 'special relationship' to the US empire, the world role, and the dream of British Socialism-in-one-country have all faded into scrap-book images. The six years of historic Labour government did not alter the course of world history; they prepared the conditions for Powellism and Heath's reactionary regime. They did not stand the nation back on its feet again, but left it flat on its back. The eager Chairman of the 1962 Conference was forced, only four years later, to do exactly what Macmillan had done before him: apply for admission to the European Community. When that failed, his government pursued a Conservative policy of economic deflation with far greater ruthlessness and consistency than ever before: the compensation for abject paralysis and national prostration was to be a balance of payments surplus (the conventional, but normally unobtainable objective of the City and British finance-capital since the 1920s). Under pressure, national interest and destiny turned out to be the Pound. Yet those six years of such impotence and confusion did not at all shake the Labour Party's self-identification with the *nation*. In 1971, it may have no new policies, no ideas, no vision, and no self-respect; but it still has the nation. It will give up – it already has given up – everything but this ideology. What really matters is not the revolutionary, radical, or reformist consciousness of the working class, but the right of the working class to control 'its' own nation-state through 'its' own political party. Since its political extinction in 1966–70, the movement has manifested scarcely one flicker of new political or social consciousness; for all the reaction it produced, the electoral defeat of 1970 might have happened to a corpse. Yet the mortal remains can still lay resounding claim, on behalf of the British people, to an immutable national sovereignty.

   Tribune, organ of the old Labour left, produced a 'Special Common Market Issue' on 4 June. It was prefaced by a bold-type excerpt from Gaitskell's 1962 speech – 'What Gaitskell Said'. Yesterday's reviled enemy is today's patriotic friend. Inside, the editor Richard Clements outlined the long history of the left's opposition to the Common Market. As a cold-war, capitalist conspiracy, the actions of the European Community contrast strikingly with those of the neutral and socialist Britain we have enjoyed since 1945. Are we to give all this up? The people will not have it. The Constitution of the British nation gives it a right to be heard. As Michael Foot has constantly repeated, it would be a fatal blow to 'our' democracy and 'our' parliament – the essence of 'our' nation – if we are precipitated into the European continent without so much as a general election.[7] '*Tribune* has explained all through the years why we believe that the consequences of entry into the EEC will be disastrous for Britain and damaging to the concept of a wider co-operation among all the nations of the world, both developed and under-developed.'

The concepts of the foreign 'plot', and of a 'narrow nationalist Europe', have always been of key importance in the left's anti-Market campaign. In a *New Statesman* article sulphurous with anti-French feeling, the former Labour Minister Peter Shore has claimed that the present entry proposals represent a plot going back *ten years*: yes, for ten years cunning Jules the Frenchman has been scheming to extract his pound of flesh from the British tax-payer, to give to his miserable poor peasants. 'It speaks volumes about the French meaning of a 'Community' and gives some indication of the 'Community spirit' we could expect to meet... that they should prepare this trap for Britain even before the negotiations began.'[8] No sir, in England we require no instruction in the true meaning of the term 'community'! Our Commonwealth tells us what it means, as does our copious national experience of harmony among the classes! 'Living communities are not built on statistical analysis alone', protests F. Judd MP in another issue of *Tribune*, 'It is the convictions and the will of those who lead them which provide the substance of their life. Just as I fear for the future of creative, participant democracy in the prevailing atmosphere of paternalistic Western European politics, so I fear that, despite the protests of sincere and well-meaning

7   For many years it has been obvious even to mildly liberal opinion that British democracy is by *bourgeois* standards very defective and steadily becoming more so; that popular pressures play less and less of a part in it, and public apathy is growing towards it; and that the whole system of government linked to it is ineffective, archaic and class-ridden. In the 1960s innumerable books and articles demanding radical reform of it appeared. Yet in the left-wing anti-EEC campaign one observes with stupefaction all these ancient and mouldering organs of class dictatorship reappear white as snow, pristine expressions of the national-popular will. When juxtaposed with the pestilential practices across the Channel (presumably) all the laboriously catalogued failings simply fade into insignificance.

8   At the Labour Party's special conference on Europe in July, Shore treated the audience to another outburst of paranoia on the same lines. The conspiracy had become fouler: we would have to pay out to Jules 'more than we paid out in two world wars!' There was a resonant tone to this oration which a later speaker was not ashamed to describe as 'Churchillian'. In fact, the only recent orator whose style Shore sometimes approached is Powell; nor was the resemblance merely form. He ended with a standard Powellite appeal against the 'act of *madness*' which entering the European Community would represent, after expatiating upon the 'great national *disaster*' facing us. He was rewarded with an unparalleled ovation.

colleagues in our party, the main driving-force for EEC enlargement is an old-fashioned and frustrated nationalism as irrelevant to the age in which we live as it is possible to be.' He goes on to contrast the 'narrow regional integration' of the Common Market with 'more meaningful international forums such as OECD, GATT and UNCTAD, or the multiracial, intercontinental and realistically hetero-geneous groupings of both the new Commonwealth and the United Nations itself.'[9]

Little need be said about the foreign plot fantasy. More interesting is the contrast between 'narrow, nationalist' Europe and generous internationalist Britain. The acrid savour of the plot comes from its desire to drag down 'outward-looking' Britain into 'inward-looking' Europe. One can never be internationalist enough for a true British nationalist, in short. It is necessary to examine briefly this curious mechanism by which patriots attribute their own half-repressed and half-ashamed chauvinism to an imaginary enemy, since it is central to the ideology of left-wing nationalism.

Now, as for Gaitskell in 1962, it provides just the right formula. It offers the ideal alibi for the *legitimation* of nationalism, enabling its champions both to vent jingoistic emotions and pretend they are something grander at the same time. Thus they can indulge in the sensations of a patriot while nominally standing up for some non-patriotic entity – Commonwealth, OECD, NATO, world free trade, the Third World, GATT, *anything* – against the hard-faced national egos of Europe. Extra spice is added to this effluvium of sanctity by concern for the poor. The Great-British nationalist feels that his proper place remains the whole world, nothing less will do: only the globe can measure up to the demands of this particular national ego. The sheer breadth of his largesse will naturally enfold the world's poor, shielding them from the flint-faced Bounderbys of Brussels.

The Legacy of Liberal Imperialism

If the historical roots of this – to borrow Judd's term – 'phoney internationalism' were not so clear, it would be merely a joke, a late and freaky offshoot of the protestant conscience. As things are, it represents bull-frog conceit and the very worst species of western hypocrisy. Like most of what passes for 'radical' in Britain, it is derived not from any kind of socialist experience or thought, but from 19th-century liberalism. In this case, from the abstract liberal internation-alism associated with Free Trade. Liberal internationalism found its economic rationale in free trade and the City's hegemony, and its crusading (or 'outward-looking') drive in the moral force of protestant conscience. Later, British impe-rialism merely gave a new content to liberal internationalism, while preserving

---

9   *Tribune*, 2 July 1971, 'Phoney Internationalism: That's the Common Market Policy towards Underdeveloped Nations'.

(as far as possible) its external forms. Thus, the British imperialists were not simply the first, the biggest, and the most successful plunderers on the international scene; they were also the best at pretending that *their* empire was really something else. It was this 'liberal imperialism' which the British workers' movements grew up within. From the outset therefore, nationalism was to assume for them this distinctive and tenacious colouring. Their 'living community', their 'participant democracy' was not that of a mere battling nation-state: it merged into a greater, spiritual, multi-racial, inter-continental and realistically heterogeneous something-or-other. Britain's greatness – unlike French or Prussian greatness – was somehow worldwide, Sunday-suited, unselfish and open-armed.

It was this imperialist false consciousness that provided one of the central vehicles for British nationalism. It remained important for the ruling class until the later years of the Macmillan government. In a perceptive bourgeois analysis of post-war British foreign policy, P. Nettl and D. Shapiro commented upon how phoney internationalism had systematically stultified that policy and turned it into a form of helpless immobilism.[10] Diplomacy became the pretence that a non-existent power was still there. Churchill had originally defined the *rayonnement* of British power as extending outwards in three circles: the Commonwealth née Empire, the Anglo-American relationship, and Europe. As regards the Empire, point out Nettl and Shapiro, the very rapidity with which it was dismantled militarily and politically led to exaggerated ideas about what was left: 'With the *fact* of Commonwealth relations comes a *myth*; from the real existence of some Commonwealth relationships we have made a mythology of our Commonwealth influence. This has served as a very real buffer to cushion the shock of our declining international power'. In this perspective, of course, it was the very 'heterogeneity, multi-raciality, etc.' of the Commonwealth which counted positively. Its hopeless conflicts of interest and outlook meant that nothing could be *done* with it. But it was big, a random, representative chunk of the whole globe – and hence valuable as a symbol, as a suggestive presence for speeches about brotherhood, global responsibility, and so on. Similarly, the Anglo-American rapport – that famous special relationship between old and new imperialisms – could be laboriously built up again by Macmillan after the Suez débâcle, upon one unspoken condition: that it should never be put to the test again. 'Once removed from the practical sphere of policy, however, it could grow in sentimental importance until it became, like the Commonwealth, an essential part of our mythology.' Europe's role in the pretence had been defined by Churchill himself and Foreign Secretary Bevin in the later 1940s. At that time, when they imagined that a debilitated Western Europe could be pressed into service, they had volubly *led* the movement for European unity with crocodile discourses about 'the spiritual unity of the West', Christian civilisation, and the rest. Even

---

10 'Institutions versus Realities – A British Approach', Journal of Common Market Studies, vol. II no. I (1963).

a European 'parliament' was applauded when it fitted in with their world-wide conceit. When the spiritual unity of Europe became the modest bourgeois reality of the Schumann plan, however, things brusquely altered: the Europeans had become 'inward-looking'. That is, they were no longer suitable raw material for global posturings and international moralising, for the non-stop hail of grandiloquent manoeuvrings, earnest consultations with innumerable 'partners' in this or that scattered everywhere round the globe, the treatyings, negotiations and edifying handshakes which testified to the continuing world-role of the British. Later another Labour Party foreign-affairs spokesman, Bevan, declared he had to have a hydrogen bomb in his pocket so that this charade could go on: it was worth almost any expense. At all costs the outward-looking goodness had to keep pouring outwards, and the globe would pay more heed if it knew that John Wesley *might* turn into Machiavelli overnight.

The ruling class has now spent a decade reluctantly and discreetly shuffling off this embarrassment. The entire basis of the phoney world-role crumbled away. Yet, one cannot avoid noticing, its hollow myth-consciousness remains strong on the left. In 1962 it was powerful enough to rally Labourism behind Gaitskell on an anti-Common Market programme. Even in 1971 it can inspire a majority of the movement to feel that Conservatism is *betraying* this essential liberal grandeur of the nation – and that therefore socialism should take up the standard and show itself the true repository of outward-looking tradition. And the inspiration is effective enough to have provoked something of a stampede in the same direction among the Labour leadership and the party's formidable strata of opportunists. This is a nationalism peculiarly confused with high-minded internationalist rhetoric, and it is easy to see historically how a certain style of liberal utterance was taken over by the Labour Party. Given the strength of Liberalism and the extreme dependence of early Labourism upon ex-Liberal Party intellectuals, it was probably inevitable. But what merits emphasis at this point is that, only a little way below the surface, it is really just nationalism. At crucial moments, Mr Hyde's hairy paw always bursts out of Dr Jekyll's frock-coat. The impulse behind this remarkable piece of historical transvestism is sheerly chauvinist. So was the *real* function and purpose of the internationalist psychodrama. For the oldest, biggest, and most scattered imperial power, it simply happened that national interest entailed global interest, or the pretence of it. Only now, when the pretence has shrunk to a thing of rags and tatters, is the hairy Id within left on his own. Yet he remains so vital to the Labour Party that its last surviving coherent aspiration is to keep the brute clothed and fed. Why is this?

The Last Refuge of a Social-Democrat

The world has so long been divided into geographical units, each developing at a different rate and in a different direction, that there is little basis or interest or sentiment to unite classes occupying roughly similar positions in the social pattern of their various states... The fact is that the nation state is by far the most important entity in world affairs. Nationalism is the one force strong enough to defeat all comers.'

D. HEALEY, 'Power Politics and the Labour Party', *New Fabian Essays* (1952)

Samuel Johnson said that patriotism was in essence the last refuge of a scoundrel; naturally, it is also the first, and last, refuge of a social-democrat. British nationalism belongs to Lewis Namier's select category of 'territorial nationalities' which – as distinct from the 'linguistic nationalities' fostered by 19th-century romanticism – are inherently conservative and result from a lengthy historical evolution in which 'It is the State which has created the nationality and not vice-versa.' In Britain, Namier commented, 'So close is the nexus between territory and nationality... that the English language lacks a word to describe a 'nationality' distinct from, or contrasted with, the citizenship derived from territory and State; and the meaningless term of 'race' is often used for what in Continental languages is covered by 'nationality".[11] At once total and – until the advent of Powellism – little disrupted by self-scrutiny, this sense of nationality stood historically upon a particularly homogeneous and geographically well-defined basis.

This basis survived the era of the European empires almost uniquely well. European imperialism came into its own from the moment when, among the older and larger states of western Europe, nationalism had apparently fulfilled its function. 'By 1870', wrote E. H. Carr, 'the constructive work of nation-building seemed complete,' as Germany and Italy joined the other great nation-states.[12] When this framework was established – although it was by no means complete in Eastern Europe – capital at once began to develop farther as imperialism. And in the resultant race for the world, the British national empire had easily the most successful career overall. It occupied the centre of the imperialist stage up to 1914. Yet it had already, from around 1900, reached a tacit accommodation – later an alliance – with the economic force of the United States, with the up-and-coming imperialism that challenged all the European empires from outside. It was on the winning side with the USA in both world wars. Hence, the nationalist foundation of its 'world-role' stayed remarkably intact. The nationalisms of the three great member-states of the European Community, by contrast, all suffered irreparable damage between 1939 and 1945.

Thus, in Britain, national labourism evolved towards a relatively pacific fulfilment in the years 1945–49, under the Attlee government. Thanks to the underlying solid cohesion of nationality in England, and to the good fortune of its empire – as well as to the final impetus of the wartime 'social revolution' – the

---

11   *Nationality and Liberty* (1948, also included in *Vanished Supremacies*, 1958). See also A. D. Smith, *Theories of Nationalism* (1971) pp. 177–8.

12   E. H. Carr, *Nationalism and After* (1945), p.17.

socialization of the nation was completed. Labourism's time of triumph (upon which it still lives spiritually) was not the dawn of a new era. It was exactly the opposite. It marked the long-delayed conclusion of the old social programme of liberal imperialism, launched by Joseph Chamberlain in the 1880s and carried forward massively by the Liberal government of 1906–14, but then obstructed by the confusion and reaction of the inter-war period. The Attlee government stood at the end of an era. It closed and sealed the epoch of British 'national social-ism', by the formation of a new totality in which reforms of the State effectively regained the allegiance of the proletariat, and so subordinated the class struggle to the 'national interest'. This real historic achievement was of course somewhat different from the one depicted in party propaganda and in the self-conscious-ness of the labour movement. But this is only to say that these represent a 'false consciousness' whose real function escapes it, not the most surprising of conclu-sions about the Labour Party.

It has become commonplace to observe that in material and measurable terms the British 'Welfare State' is no longer an outstanding achievement. Workers are, in this sense, better off in most parts of the European Community. Yet this observation often omits something fundamental. What counted about the Labour Party's reforms was the historical moment at which they were carried out, and the way in which they were carried out. They came in the wake of a great patri-otic war where – in contrast to the disintegration of the 1930s – national unity had been reintegrated at white heat. Moreover, they were carried out in a way which underlined the essential *continuity* of this national experience – which conveyed the vivid idea to the masses that reforms represented a natural devel-opment of 'society as a whole' rather than a disruption of the social fabric. It was here, at the level of ideology, that their astonishing success lay. As a material structure it may now look mediocre. But it represented as no other social-dem-ocratic system has done the reattachment of the workers to the State and the nation – the persisting conviction that this was 'their' work and achievement, that in certain respects the nation does belong to them.

British and US Imperialism

One of the most remarkable characteristics of Labour's 'phoney international-ism' in the last quarter-century has been its *practical* identification with the national and imperial interests of one other great power: the United States. So outward-looking wide-worldism is not only a camouflage for and a distorted expression of nationalism: it is also disconcertingly close to Atlanticism. It has always tended to locate its enemy not in the most appropriate and logical place for the second half of this century – across the Atlantic – but among the tradi-tional rivals of British imperialism on the Continent. In this perspective Europe emerges as 'narrowly nationalist' while the USA, in spite of its hugely greater world-power and its far greater impact on the old structure of British empire, is somehow in the same league as ourselves (and is rarely attacked with the same chauvinist venom).

This confusion is deep-rooted. It goes back to the tacit alliance concluded between the British and American empires before 1914. At that time the differing interests of the two systems – one increasingly devoted to the export of capital, the other to rapid industrial growth and the export of commodities – allowed an implicit accommodation between them. This material conjuncture provided the basis for a conflation of ideologies. Like the British 'liberal imperialism' which triumphed in 1906, American empire easily assumed the guide of an 'anti-imperialist' and 'internationalist' movement. Many elements in the common culture of the two nations fostered this development, and rendered it palatable to the left.

In this respect as in so many others, the immediate post-Second World War era was to prove decisive. For the triumph of Labour's national socialism also coincided with the maximal point of US hegemony, and with the period in which (under the Hull strategy) America set about constructing its own 'wide world' system under liberal and free-trade (or 'open-door') slogans similar to those familiar from the recent history of the British empire.

After 1945 the Empire could manifestly not be held together by the old means. However, the national patrimony could be astutely rescued by allowing the colonial territories to evolve to 'independence' while retaining control of the vital economic sinews of Empire: the gold mines in South Africa, the rubber planta-tions in Malaya, the oil fields in the Middle East. The forced sale of Britain's enormous holdings in Latin America during the war – in 1940 they had exceeded those of the United States – removed a dangerous obstacle to Anglo-American 'partnership'. Indeed, properly sensible of Britain's greatly reduced ability to play an international role, the Labour Government was positively eager to accept US sponsorship. Virulent anti-Communism furnished the perfect cement for this arrangement. Since its main political *raison d 'être* was to furnish a quite harmless surrogate for social revolution, naturally British social democracy was bound to be intensely hostile to Communism, even in its ultra-cautious and conserva-tive Stalinist guise. This epoch thus produced a double identification which has been stamped on the mind of British Labour for a generation. Both social reform and Britain's continued 'world role' were associated with the generosity of the senior partner, US imperialism. That is why Labour nationalism has a strongly Atlantic flavour added to the robustness of a more purely indigenous ideology. This is a nationalism which hopes to conserve and transmute the national essence by embracing the power which supplanted it. Labour's apparently 'anti-impe-rialist' opposition to the Suez expedition was in fact wholly consonant with its Atlantic nationalism. In tones of genuine outrage, it was pointed out by many a Labour spokesman at the time that the Tory Government had not even informed our American ally of what they were up to! When Labour's Foreign Secretary Bevin had sent gunboats to protect British oil interests from the designs of the upstart Mossadeq, naturally there had been punctilious prior consultation. The Wilson government's staunch defence of the US in Vietnam, its close cooperation with the CIA in Guyana and the Gulf, were consistent expressions of this orientation. Meanwhile at home the Dunkirk spirit was invoked in calls for national economic discipline and the notorious Labour MP and businessman Maxwell launched the ill-fated 'Back Britain Campaign'.

Only this time there were good reasons why the formula could not work so well. Where Marshall Aid had helped to finance domestic reform and restock overseas coaling stations, this time it was retrenchment and social service cuts that were dictated from Washington (quite literally, according to the Wilson Memoirs). Indeed the whole strategy of British deference to US imperialism had failed to foresee the approaching end of the latter's absolute global hegemony over the capitalist world. It seems entirely possible that there was US prompting behind Wilson's application to join the Community. Thus even once the decision to re-apply had been made, the Labour Government could not bring itself to make a clear deal with the French over the question, no doubt because it would seem incipiently disloyal to the benefactor over the Atlantic. Hence today the Labour Party finds itself in a situation where its attempts to exploit a nationalist opposition to the Community are doubly inhibited: most of the leadership knows that entry is the best, indeed only, option for British capitalism and not all of them are prepared to deny this for tactical reasons; secondly Labour's social patriotism is deeply alloyed by the Atlantic spirit. These two circumstances in no way prevent resort being made to the most hoary nationalist mythology – they simply mean that the resulting rhetoric is more than usually half-baked. Declamations in defence of the British sausage are not really the stuff out of which a crusading chauvinism is made. Then again there has been a definite seeping away of the nationalist sentiments to which even the most forthright jingoist demagogue could appeal. In short, we are not going to see Harold Wilson recreate the spirit of Mafeking Night or coast to electoral victory as Lloyd George did with a pledge to hang the Kaiser. But the fact that Labourist nationalism is a decadent one does not mean that it is any less poisonous so far as the working class is concerned.

The nationalism of the left in Britain, though in numerous respects illusory and counterfeit, is stubbornly rooted in history,[13] especially the history of the immediate post-war period which was so formative for contemporary Labourism.

---

13 It is not irrelevant to point out here how strongly national Labourism has been fostered and protected in the last 20 years by a left-wing culture overwhelmingly devoted to ideas of rootedness and continuity. Disappointment with the present has almost invariably issued in a search for new roots, a new and more real community and continuity – found especially in the 'real' nation of the working class. Thus, other more authentic roots are invented to support the weight of what is really a displaced nationalism. The notion is strengthened that the nation *does* in essence belong to the people, though incompletely. Hence a continuing, evolving process must complete what has been begun – as for instance, in Raymond Williams' *Long Revolution*.

From this history proceeds the logic of the last refuge – which was also the logic of Gaitskell's 1962 posture, and is now that of the labour movement's 1971 renewed attempt to beat the nationalist drum. Because the post-war Labour regime was the opening of a new era for British imperialism in which it would subordinate itself to the US Empire, there was never any question of simply inflecting the government to the left by a vote at a Party Conference or by forcing it to adopt one policy rather than another, taken in isolation. What was needed was a new political movement capable of challenging the whole social imperialist orientation of the Labour bureaucracy. Labourism was both in its organisational structure and in its ideological attitudes welded to the nation, a 'national' and not a class party. On the other hand – as Gaitskell grasped – this nationalist orientation could be easily exploited in order to *preserve* the movement, to arrest its disintegration and even give it a little new life. Criticised and hated for his 'betrayal' of Labourist socialism, he could compensate by stressing his (and the party's) utter fidelity to the nation-state, *our* heritage. And now, in a different context and with a different (and much more ominous) meaning, the same ritual is being gone through in 1971.

The Soul of the Nation

In both cases the Common Market has provided the ideal scapegoat, the perfect pretext for the exercise. It offers the image of a foreign, continental enemy against whom people can unite in a certain defensive, 'last-ditch' manner. But in this way Labour leaders simply gain direct access to what is a basic reflex of British nationalism. All sorts of nationalisms thrive on wounds, threats, insults, offended pride and assaults from without. British nationalism's peculiar imperialist confusion, its 'outward-looking' vagaries and lack of inward articulation or scrutiny, render it particularly liable to this effect. It scarcely knows what or where it is, except in a back-to-the-wall battle against odds (or something that can be presented as such). It becomes itself, spasmodically, under real or imaginary attacks from across the Channel. Suddenly at spiritual Dunkirks, a thousand years of history assume new and startling meaning; 'emergencies' define national identity. If there is no emergency, one can be invented. Class consciousness would threaten Labourism itself in the first place. So national socialism prefers the more reliable appeal to the national tradition and its sacred icons – in the British case, to an elephantine memory of those rare moments of felt unity against a European foe.

There is one other, more general, reason why social democracy can fall back so safely on the last refuge. Even at its most abject, a liberal or social-reformist movement is necessarily distinguished from conservatism by a certain amount of ideal projection into the future. It is bound to live to some extent in the reformed world of its ideals. Sometimes, however, the ideal universe may seem a little empty (the chronic state of Labourism since around 1950). But there is one thing which can always be included in it: the nation. Among nationalists of different ilks, the dispute is invariably for the soul of the nation. The left-wing nationalist has farthest to go in this struggle: he lives in the aspiration of possessing it, one day. His greater objective distance from the goal renders the subjectivity of desiring it all the more important. Thus, the better nation of the future is the excuse for continuing obsession *with* the nation: because it is not yet wholly ours, it is all the more vital that it remain there. If anyone objects that after all 'we' (workers, the people) have virtually no say in 'our' nation, living in the national house as servants, this is dismissed as defeatism. The point is the future, brother, the ideal nation to be constructed: we *intend* to own the house one day. That the Labour Party has not managed to scrape together a serious down-payment in its 71 years of life is neither here nor there. What matters in the Common Market controversy is the apparently fatal wounding of the intention, the dream: the owners are selling out before *we* have had a chance! The first necessity of national labourism is therefore to stop the fatal exchange of contracts.

In this way, the most valuable side of any working-class movement, its desire for change, for new times, is poisoned by nationalism. Idealism is tainted by ancient history, at the root. The best is changed into the worst, and wasted. The dignity of class is betrayed by the indignity of nation. A movement whose only hope would be to demolish the wretched old pile brick by brick, and renew itself in the process, is reduced to thinking of homeownership, of central heating and fitted carpets in the English Constitution.

The Labour Crisis

Under slogans like 'national self-determination' there lurks all the time a twisted and limited meaning. In a society based on classes, the nation as a uniform social-political whole simply does not exist... There is literally no social arena – from the strongest material relationship to the most subtle moral one – in which the possessing classes and a self-conscious proletariat could take one and the same position and figure as one undifferentiated national whole.

ROSA LUXEMBURG, *The Question of Nationality and Autonomy* (1908).

We have looked at the basic contrast between ruling-class and left-wing nationalism, and at certain features of the latter: its mystified expression as 'internationalism', and the real causes of its historical strength and persistence in Britain. Although this explains some structural aspects of the 1971 anti-European campaign, it does not amount to a specific enough diagnosis of the disease. For example, while 1971 certainly resembles 1962 in enough ways, it could hardly fail to differ in others: the Labour Party must have changed, like the nation, during these years of decline and futility. The current tide of social-chauvinism reacts to an appreciably altered situation, both in the labour movement and outside it, and may have correspondingly different consequences.

In the present situation, there is a crisis both in the development of the class struggle, and in the Labour Party. It is possible to interpret the latter's conflicts over Europe as a response to both of these together. More specifically, the function of left-wing nationalism's resurgence may be to try and contain or divert the social crisis, *and* at the same time reassert the party's control over its disintegrating traditional basis. In both ways Labourism struggles to remain itself. The most significant aspect of the whole picture, of course, is that it now quite evidently has to struggle much harder – even desperately. Labour's problems, in short, have much to do with the domestic class conflict in Britain, and even more to do with the movement's own inward drama; they have practically nothing to do with Europe.

At the Labour Party's July conference on the Common Market, there was a good deal of discussion about class, about the European threat to pay-packets, and about the good old causes of socialism and nationalisation. A foreign observer would have been in no doubt about the unpopularity of the Tory government and the need to get rid of it. On the other hand, he could not possibly have guessed that while this was going on, the class struggle in Britain was still traversing a most critical period – that the working class had recently suffered serious defeats and looked likely to endure others. At that very moment the new Industrial Relations Bill was on the point of becoming law. Only two weeks later workers were occupying Clyde shipyards in protest against the State's attempt to 'rationalise' their industry by sacking most of them. While the Labour Party plunged into rhetoric about precious national sovereignty, the most militant sectors of the proletariat were on the way to being hamstrung. Hence, as the State armed itself with measures to crush the main form of autonomous workers' action in Britain, the unofficial strike, the Labour Party was telling them their primary duty was the defence of the national State. As they fall to their knees under the rain of blows they are told to stand up again at once: to protect the *gendarme*! The argument seems to be that if John Bull happens to be battering them about the head at this particular moment, that is certainly unfortunate; but it's nothing to what they would get from the Brussels bureaucrats.

In the same way, the outside observer could scarcely have divined that a vicious and steadily escalating semi-colonial war was going on within the territory of the British nation-state. Here, silence reigned. At Belfast and Londonderry armoured cars and tear-gas testified to the virtues of outward-looking Anglo-Scots parliamentarism; what 'narrow nationalists' the Irish have always been! He would not have guessed, either, that just two years had elapsed since the Labour Party's own 'Industrial Relations Bill' was being discussed a few hundred yards away, and that the most perfect British continuity had in fact reigned between the essential policies of the old government and the new. Wise, progressive Labour rule had been replaced by the notoriously reactionary Heath regime. But somehow or other the vital 'national interest' of the British State flowed on unimpaired, both on the factory shop floor and in Ireland. And this is exactly the national essence – our control of our own affairs – which was being indignantly defended in Central Hall, Westminster.

The Wilson government failed to enact its own anti-strike legislation two years ago, simply because it looked likely to threaten the movement's very structure too closely. The Labour Party's distinctive and unenviable role in the national scheme of things is to reconcile the conflict of class and nation *within itself*: it has to *be* the 'nation' in miniature. The industrial legislation would have exposed too nakedly the contradiction upon which it rests. But the failure serves also to underline even more forcibly Labour's devotion to the 'national interest'. This is its essential myth. In July of this year, Tom Jackson, the leader of the Post Office workers' union which fought the most bitter and protracted strike of last winter, and suffered utter defeat at the government's hands, actually ended his speech with these words: 'The British people is sick and tired of a government which seeks to divide the nation.' Wilson echoed the sentiment in his closing words. It has become almost obligatory to reproach Heath with 'dividing the nation', naked subservience to class interests, and so on. And since of course Conservatives have always rebuked Labourites for being a narrow class party incapable of taking the national view, the overall logic is clear. Politics is a national-unity competition: who can divide the nation least, national-conservatives or national-socialists?

This concept of the 'national interest' is the pure practical expression of chauvinist ideology. And when focused upon an issue like the Common Market – where an all-British interest can plausibly be set over against that of foreigners – it serves to totally obscure both the interests of class and the political sense of the class struggle. That is its function. The *purpose* of nationalism in this context and at this time is quite obviously to betray the class struggle. It could not conceivably be anything else. It diverts a great deal of attention and energy away from the genuine battlefront of the social crisis, in a particularly difficult year. There are a million unemployed, economic growth is zero, Rolls-Royce is bankrupt, the inflationary tide rises, and the unions are on the defensive: yes, but we must save our national sovereignty. First things first. Also a pantomime battle against the European Community may cause people to forget how those faces on the Labour rostrum, now scarlet with sweat and patriotism, were themselves recently responsible for the policies leading to this black scene of crisis and reaction.

Chauvinism and the Class Struggle

This is of course the objective function of the demagogic lunacy which sparkles so brightly in the anti-Market crusade. Consider the speech delivered by Clive Jenkins at the July special conference. In it this prominent leader of a supposedly militant and left-wing union contrived to twitch every single chord of prejudice in the national-socialist *ensemble*. He started with an obligatory bow to the old

'internationalism': the 'Europe' we should be joining our destiny to is ridicu-
lously small and narrow – a mere fraction of the wide world we are used to. And
what a fraction! The European Community is a hot-bed of political reaction and
instability. France was on the verge of civil war scarcely three years ago. Italy is
now menaced by a right-wing militarist *coup d'état*. As for the Germans... Why
should we British endanger our national institutions with this contamination?[14]
Furthermore, the Common Market plainly serves the interests of the big corporations. He underlined their conspiracy by demanding that the Labour Committee
for Europe publish its accounts: have the poisoned tentacles of Fiat and Krupp
reached into our own party? 'We can look after ourselves', he concluded, and
intend to do so rather than pass under the sway of the Brussels bureaucracy.

Phoney wide-worldism, the lumpen-nationalism only a little way behind it,
bluff Britannic sanity versus European folly, the foreign plot fantasy, unctuous
invocation of our own folk-state, un-British bureaucracy: this Mickey-Mouse
mosaic vividly conveys the essence of Labourist national-populism. It is in this
perspective that it remains possible – to take another example – for the former
Labour Home Secretary and Chancellor James Callaghan to issue statements
like the one of early July. He announced he had uncovered an alternative policy
to entering the Common Market. It is simple. All that we (i.e. the next Labour
government) need to do is 'run the economy flat out for five years'. The proper
national programme is to sacrifice everything else to industrial growth, pulling
in belts, gritting teeth, and so on – if only we can pull our collective selves
together in this fashion, and man our national rigging properly, the open seas
may still be ours. But... wait a minute, is this not one of the leaders of the 1964-
70 government addressing us? One of the men who, after trying a timid policy
of autarky with the 15 per cent import surcharge of 1964, then led a five-year
stampede in the opposite direction? One of those *most* responsible for sacrificing industrial growth to years of savage deflation and the balance-of-payments
fetish? It is as if one of the Generals from the Dunkirk rout of 1940 had crawled
out of the water on to Dover beach and announced his new strategy for winning
the war: another British Expeditionary Force would solve all our problems! Yet,
with this all but unbelievable *pronunciamento*, Callaghan was staking his claim
to be leader of the anti-European movement. Nobody laughed. That is the point:
when nationalism takes over, almost anybody can say almost anything, and
remain immune from criticism or even ridicule.

The objective function of fantasies like this may be quite different from their
subjectivity. That this must be so in the present case is powerfully suggested by
another remarkable fact. The chauvinist mania has followed upon a period of

---

14 To the objector who might point out that France was near civil war in 1968 because of
    the greatest workers' strike in European history, and that Italy's social 'troubles' stem
    from the great wave of working-class militancy in 1968–70, it must of course be answered
    that these facts are of no importance whatever: they have to do with *foreign* workers.

strange silence in Labourist politics. It is universally conceded that there has been next to no real debate in the movement after the defeat of last year. If one looks back to the 1950s or the early 1960s, this at once appears odd. What sea-change had produced this weird, numbed acquiescence in fate where the only observable activity is the ritual airing of ancient totems? Yet a year of lifeless silence has, suddenly, given way to this outburst of patriotic excitement. The old fellow had subsided into his armchair so long one wondered if it was time to call the undertaker; now suddenly he is running about again, screaming of foreign plots and the threat to his kippers. It is hard to resist the thought that the frenzy must be in fact a *substitute* for the absent political and social debate. In 1962 Gaitskell found an escape from the party's antagonisms in nationalism; in 1971, the latter has replaced them. A decade ago the movement retreated into the last refuge; now it has nowhere else to go at all, since it can no longer summon up enough energy or confidence to think of an objective, or contradict itself signif-icantly. The nationalist psychology of defensive, last-resort struggle fits it only too well: this is the last ditch, and there are no other resources left. In 1962 this was not yet so: Gaitskell's national-populism had its effect before the decisive experience of another Labour government, before national-socialism was put to the test again and shown in its truth.

Look at the present social crisis from another angle. Although the main body of Heath's conservatism is continuous with the national policies of 1964 to 1970, there is one very important difference. The continuing deterioration of the economic situation and the war in Ireland have forced Heath to actions and tactics whose effect upon *consciousness* is considerably greater than the somnambulism of the former Labour government. This is the real sense of the lamentations about 'dividing the nation'. The free enterprise rhetoric of the Conservatives, certain of their deeds over the public industries and the social services, and – above all – the Industrial Relations Bill, have significantly accentuated class antagonisms in Britain. This at once creates an opportunity for the Labour Party and poses a grave threat to it. It is of course tempted to exploit the situation electorally – to foment the 'division' of the nation in order to regain parliamentary office. Yet, because the true line of class division passes through it (and not in between it and the Conservatives) this is an extremely dangerous manoeuvre. Its whole historic dilemma is that of a movement which expresses class consciousness and drive in order to contain and neutralise it in the 'national' framework. But, given its present utter poverty of ideas, it is scarcely in a position to dangle enticing new social-democratic visions before the masses. It cannot canalise discontent in this way (as Wilson did in 1963–64, for instance). However, it still has every-body's friend, the nation. The European question has dropped from heaven at the correct moment.

The Conversion of the Labour Leadership

The importance of the conjuncture has been demonstrated well enough by the 'conversion' of Wilson himself and a considerable section of the leadership to anti-Europeanism. He knows quite well that Heath will get Britain into Europe, that there will be no general election on the issue (barring inconceivable upheavals on the right), and that if he becomes Prime Minister again it will be in a member state of the European Community. Yet saving the cohesion of the movement is more important than the grotesque strip-tease of opportunist hypocrisy that was the only means to it. The point is that, objectively, this is perhaps the only way in which Labourism can go on trying to benefit from a sharpening class conflict, without being outflanked (or even torn apart) by it. The only channel left is nationalism. Hence any amount of sacrifice and ridicule are justified to use it. The resultant schism between the main body of party opinion and the right-wing pro-Europeans is, by any reckoning, far less dangerous than one between the leadership and a mutinous rank-and-file.

This is not to deny or ignore for an instant the reality of working-class anxieties about entering the Common Market. How could millions of people who have endured the inflation of the past year and appreciate the coming rise in food prices not be genuinely worried about the prospect? They have a shrewd suspicion – nourished among other things by six years of Labour government – that anything done to them 'in the national interest' will be bad. Such anxieties were vented at the July conference, and will be again in October. And the Labour Party's strategy is precisely to let them be vented, so that it can contain them and harness them for its own (and the nation's!) purposes. It 'explains' the grim economic facts as the result of Heath's policies, and seeks to mobilise opinion by focusing on the one policy which permits the maximum amount of safe emotion and generalised indignation: Europe. The suggestion is that it all hangs together: rising prices, 'dividing the nation', and going into the Common Market. By implication, there is an alternative which also hangs together and makes sense: a reasonable incomes and prices policy, uniting the country, and defending our national sovereignty.

The 'alternative' is, in the mouth of the Labour leadership, political trash. Its exhibition of slimy xenophobia and bare-fanged opportunism *is* the current 'radicalization' of the Labour Party, the most sternly left-wing posture it can now afford. Anything else must come from outside. One simple criterion should serve to clarify these judgements. No policy or strategy which is not directed *against* 'the nation' and the 'national interest' will do anything but betray the real interests of the workers and of socialism. The one thing with which no socialist could conceive of reproaching Heath is 'dividing the nation'. For unless the proletariat sets out to divide the nation more, to the utmost, it is lost. It has to put class before nation always, and class against nation where necessary. The peculiar semantics of 'unity' in the Labour Party, on the other hand, are both deliberate and central to its own form of mystification. Essentially, the great stress upon unity evokes the traditions of proletarian and trade union solidarity – the unity of *class* – and translates them into something else, Labour's own version of what is really the unity of the *nation*. This systematic translation is the heart of Labourism's character as a 'simulacrum' of the national whole. 'Unity' is turned by this dominant ideology from an *ex*pression of class into a mode of control or *re*pression of class.

Of course, the Labour Party needs to add some semblance of rationality and deliberation to its patriot's rallying-cry. It needs it because economistic reasoning plays a large part in the general ideological armoury of modern government. In this case it requires it particularly badly, because in the past it subscribed so heavily to the economic case *for* entering the EEC, alongside the *Times* and the CBI.[15] Hence the colossal, record-breaking outburst of mouth-pursing, brow-furrowing, on balance weighing-ups of the pros-and-cons in the Labour Party this year, those agonizing ruminations and stock-taking recogitations from which so many have emerged with the sad, strained conviction that, after all, in the end, when the really fine work with the scales had been done, the 'case' against entry was stronger on these particular terms.[16]

The De-Proletarianisation of Labourism

An important recent study, Barry Hindess's *The Decline of Working-Class Politics* (1971), attests to the basic wasting away of the Labour Party in the later 1960s. Examining the grass-roots decline in typical Labour Party urban constituencies, Hindess points out how the estrangement of workers from the existing political system is due to profound economic and social causes, and is irreversible. The 'decline and fall of social democracy', and consequently, of the 'great stabilising factor in British politics throughout this century', has occurred because of 'a breakdown of the social control which the Labour Party has been able to exercise

---

15 The main reference point of this side of the anti-Market campaign has been Nicholas Kaldor's article in the *New Statesman* in March 1971, reprinted and distributed by the Common Market Safeguards Campaign (alongside a gothic-script 'Petition to the Queen Her Most Excellent Majesty' urging the monarch to put a stop to the whole rotten business).

16 Rosa Luxemburg's chastisement of Bernstein in *Reform or Revolution* gives the correct perspective on this part of the performance: 'By saying good-bye to the dialectic, and resorting instead to the intellectual see-saw of the well-known 'on the one hand – on the other hand', 'yes – but', 'although – however', 'more – less', etc., Bernstein quite logically lapses into a mode of thought that belongs historically to the bourgeoisie in decline... The endless qualifications and alternatives of today's bourgeoisie are exactly like his quality of thinking and the latter is nothing but the most refined and accurate symptom of a bourgeois consciousness.' See *Rosa Luxemburg Speaks*, ed. M- A. Waters (1970), p. 86.

over such a large section of the population' – although this vital change is as yet masked by the persistence of old forms and labels at national level. The author believes that this inertia will carry Labourism along for some time yet, but that – 'in common with other mass spectator sports... it can be expected to resort increasingly to gimmicks in order to draw the crowds'.

It is tempting to see the anti-Common Market campaign as, precisely, a gimmick of this sort. With this and its attendant sideshows, the Labour Party is trying to hold on to its shrinking social basis. As if sensing the dwindling real power it can count upon, it attempts to squeeze the last miserable drops out of such ideological resources as are left to it, in order to regain a little terrain. Its real battle is a conservative one, in fact, and what it is struggling to conserve is itself, not the 'nation' – although, because nationalism is all that is left to fight with, it can only do so by hammering on this old chord. Hindess's analysis also suggests a plausible interpretation of the disposition of forces inside the party on the question. Though in some ways like the traditional left-right polarity, it is of course in others oddly different: the pro-Europeans are nearly all 'right', but far too many of their former colleagues have switched to join the 'left' (or remained non-committal) for such a simple schema to work. If, however, one perceives the new fissure as coming mainly between 'new men' and the 'conservatives' of both left and right who are more attached to and aware of the party machine, things make more sense. A large part of the old right-wing leadership has moved over to this stance, and so preserved the substantial cohesion of the *movement*, simply because for them the movement comes first. Thus, 'machine' men and frank opportunists looking to their career have for once allied themselves to the 'left' which is traditionally the mainstay of the movement and the local electoral apparatus. Labour pro-Europeanism, by contrast, must clearly appeal to what Hindess has diagnosed as the relatively ascendant force in the 'new' local Labour Parties – those middle-class activists who both exert growing control over the movement and apparatus and remain far less *dependent* upon them than previous generations of militants. To them, the old horse is simply less important. They are tuned in to a different career-wavelength, as it were, one farther away from the movement's conventional aims and preoccupations. In a few years' time, they probably feel, the 'movement' will need them more than they need it – in that dazzling future where alliance with Brandt and Serv-an-Schreiber will count for more than the increasingly reluctant Coronation Street vote.[17]

For the moment, though, the conservative 'movement' and its national-

---

17 The pro-marketeers are on the whole less 'party men', and the icons of the movement occupy a less distinguished place in their orations. The most enthusiastic admirer of Roy Jenkins could hardly claim he has a good party 'image' in the style of Herbert Morrison or James Callaghan. It may also be significant that the chief 'European' is one of the few authentic Liberals in the leadership (and a historian of Liberalism to boot).

socialist ideology are still much stronger, and can draw up the main body of Labourism behind them. They still struggle instinctively to maintain the 'great stabilising factor' which Labourism's control of the working class has repres-ented – the traditional and conservative form of socio-political mystification, as it were, whose nerve was the spurious identity of 'class' with 'nation'. In 1966–67, in the calmer conditions then prevailing, the Labour Party hoped to bring about a quieter transition from old to new, to carry the movement into the EEC in harmony with the ruling class and the 'national interest'. Now, under 'emer-gency' conditions of defeat and class aggressivity, it has had to choose the safer road of its national-socialist traditions, in the hope that this regressive tactic will dampen down the class-war *and* keep the movement intact – will give the workers something safer to worry about, and keep the trade unions and the constituency militants happy.

It goes without saying that the Labour leadership also hopes that, when things are calmer again and Britain is in the European Community, it will be forgiven its sins and allowed to return to the fold.

CHAPTER SIX

Scotland and Europe

New Left Review, 1/83

JANUARY–FEBRUARY 1974

FOR A NUMBER of reasons this seems an appropriate moment to reconsider the problem of Scottish nationalism. With its November 1973 electoral victory in the Govan Constituency the Scottish National Party has recovered from its setbacks in the 1970 general election. At the same time the Kilbrandon Commission has supplied a stimulus to regional self-government in the United Kingdom, by recommending the establishment of Scottish and Welsh parliaments. Both the tenor and the reception of these recommendations indicate, significantly, that nothing will come of them unless they are strongly and vociferously supported in Scotland and Wales. The English majority will not enact such reforms unless pushed. But then, why should it do so? In Ireland we are at the same time witnessing a wholesale alteration of the constitutional status of Ulster. But it is not only the United Kingdom's multi-national state which is in motion. In continental Europe too important movements have arisen in a similar direction. In a recent study of the present condition of the nation-state, Nicos Poulantzas wrote that we are seeing 'ruptures in the national unity underlying existing national states, rather than the emergence of a new State over and above them: that is, the very important contemporary phenomenon of regionalism, as expressed particularly in the resurgence of nationalities, showing how the internationalisation of capital leads rather to a fragmentation of the state as historically constituted than to a supra-national State...'.[1] More recently, *Les Temps Modernes* has devoted a special issue to an extensive survey of national minorities in France, perhaps the most strongly unified of the 'historically constituted' European nations at the state level.[2] In Italy, where regional self-government has become a question of practical politics, intellectual concern with the topic is also increasing. Perhaps the most valuable overview of repressed and resurgent nationalities in western Europe is provided by Sergio Salvi's *Le nazioni proibite: Guida a dieci colonie interne dell'Europa occidentale*.[3] Hence, it is indispensable to try and view Scottish or Welsh developments in a European perspective. This is the aim of

1   'L'Internationalisation des rapports capitalistes et l'état-nation', *Les Temps Modernes*, no. 319, February 1973, pp. 1492–3.
2   *Les Temps Modernes*, nos. 324–6, August–September 1973.
3   Vallecchi, Florence 1973.

the present paper.[4] I would like to look at certain aspects of Scotland's nationalism and modern history in a wider, more comparative, and more objective way than has usually been done in the past.

The Theory of Nationalism

What do the terms 'objective' and 'comparative' mean here? 'Real understanding of one's own national history begins only where we can place it within the general historical process, where we dare to confront it with European development as a whole,' writes Miroslav Hroch in his own invaluable comparative study of the genesis of nationalism in seven smaller European lands.[5] More generally still, it should be remarked that the history of theorising about nationalism displays two dramatic faults. One is a tendency to treat the subject in a one-nation or one-state frame of reference: so that each nationalism has to be understood, in effect, mainly with reference to 'its own' ethnic, economic, or other basis – rather than by comparison with the 'general historical process'. The second (and obviously related) tendency is to take nationalist ideology far too literally and seriously. What nationalists say about themselves and their movements must, of course, be given due weight. But it is fatal to treat such self-consciousness other than extremely cautiously. The subjectivity of nationalism must itself be approached with the utmost effort of objectivity. It should be treated as a psycho-analyst does the outpourings of a patient. Where – as is not infrequently the case with nationalism – the patient is a roaring drunk into the bargain, even greater patience is called for.

In short, the theory of nationalism has been inordinately influenced by nationalism itself. This is scarcely surprising. Nationalism is amongst other things a name for the general condition of the modern body politic, more like the climate of political and social thought than just another doctrine. It is correspondingly difficult to avoid being unconsciously influenced by it.[6]

---

4   This paper was originally presented at a post-graduate seminar of the Glasgow University's Department of Politics, held in Helensburgh in October 1973. I would like to take this opportunity of thanking the students of the Department who asked me to speak there. As printed here it still largely consists of notes for a talk, with only minor changes and the addition of some quotations and references. Only the concluding section is mainly new, and has been influenced by working on the preparation of the International Conference on Minorities, due to be held in Trieste from 27 to 31 May 1974. This will be the largest forum so far for the expression and consideration of minority problems in Europe, including those of repressed or resurgent nationality.

5   Miroslav Hroch, *Die Vorkämpfer der nationalen Bewegung bei den kleinen Völkern Europas*, Prague 1968, a study of the formation and early stages of nationalism in Bohemia, Slovakia, Norway, Finland, Estonia, Lithuania and Flanders.

6   There is no room to discuss this further. The reader will find useful surveys of nationalist theory in Aira Kemiläinen, *Nationalism: Problems Concerning the Word, the Concept and*

So we must try and avoid the empiricism of the nation-by-nation approach, and the subjectivism involved in taking nationalist rhetoric at its face-value. What exactly should we compare to what, in circumventing such influences? Broadly speaking, what merits consideration here is, on the one hand, the characteristic general evolution of European nationalism, between say 1800 and the major nationalist settlement of 1918–22; and on the other, whatever ideas and movements in modern Scottish history can be held to correspond to that general development. I am aware of course that the general category begs a number of questions. Nationalism did not come to a stop in Europe in 1922 after the Versailles agreements. Everyone knows that nationalism is still extremely alive, if not exactly in good health, everywhere in present-day Europe. But that is not the point. It remains true nonetheless that by the time of the post-World War One settlement European nationalism had gone through the main arc of its historical development, over a century and more. And the main lines of that settlement have proved, in fact, remarkably tenacious and permanent. Hence it is the outline provided by that century's development which – without in any way minimising Europe's remaining problems of *terre irredente* – should provide our principal model and reference point.

Scottish Belatedness

What corresponds to this now classical model of development in Scotland's case? Here, we encounter something very surprising right away. For what can reasonably be held to correspond to the mainstream of European nationalism is astonishingly recent in Scotland. As a matter of fact, it started in the 1920s – more or less at the moment when, after its prolonged gestation and maturation during the 19th century, European nationalism at last congealed into semi-permanent state forms. Thus it belongs to the last 50 years, and is the chronological companion of anti-imperialist revolt and Third World nationalism, rather than of those European movements which it superficially resembles. While the latter were growing, fighting their battles and winning them (sometimes), Scottish nationalism was simply absent.

I am aware that this assertion of Scottish belatedness also begs many questions. There is much to say about the precursors of nationalism in the 19th century, like the romantic movement of the 1850s and the successive Home Rule movements between 1880 and 1914. These are well described in H. J. Hanham's *Scottish Nationalism*. But all that need be said here is that they were quite distinctly precursors, not the thing itself, remarkable in any wider perspective for their

Classification, London 1964, and in Anthony D. Smith, Theories of Nationalism, London, 1971. One attempt to relate older theories of nationalism to contemporary developments is P. Fougeyrollas, *Pour une France Fédérale: vers l'unité européenne par la révolution régionale*, Paris 1968, especially Part I, chapters 1 and 2.

feebleness and political ambiguity rather than their prophetic power. While in the 1920s we see by contrast the emergence of a permanent political movement with the formation of the National Party of Scotland (direct ancestor of the SNP) in 1928. And, just as important, the appearance of the epic poem of modern Scottish nationalism (a distinguishing badge of this, as of most other European nationalisms), MacDiarmid's *A Drunk Man Looks at the Thistle*, in 1926.

So, we have to start with a problem – a problem written into the very terms of any comparison one can make between Scotland and Europe, as it were. Why was Scottish nationalism so belated in its arrival on the European scene? Why was it absent for virtually the whole of the 'founding period' of European nationalist struggle?

But we cannot immediately try to answer this. We must turn away from it and return to it later – for the simple reason that, as I hope to show, the belatedness in question is in no sense merely a chronological fact (as nationalists are likely to believe). It is intimately related to the essential historical character of Scottish nationalism. To understand the one is to understand the other. Hence to approach the problem correctly we must first make some progress at a more fundamental level.

The Tidal Wave of Modernisation

Let us turn back to the general European model. How may we describe the general outlines of nationalist development, seen as 'general historical process'? Here, by far the most important point is that nationalism is *as a whole* quite incomprehensible outside the context of that process's *uneven* development. The subjective point of nationalist ideology is, of course, always the suggestion that one nationality is as good as another. But the *real* point has always lain in the objective fact that, manifestly, one nationality has never been even remotely as good as, or equal to, the others which figure in its world-view. Indeed, the purpose of the subjectivity (nationalist myths) can never be anything but protest against the brutal fact: it is mobilization *against* the unpalatable, humanly unacceptable, truth of grossly uneven development.

Nationalism in general is (in Ernest Gellner's words) 'a phenomenon connected not so much with industrialisation or modernisation as such, but with its uneven diffusion'.[7] It first arose as a *general* fact (a determining general condition of the European body politic) after this 'uneven diffusion' had made its first huge and irreversible impact upon the historical process. That is, after the combined shocks engendered by the French Revolution, the Napoleonic conquests, the English industrial revolution, and the war between the two super-states of the day, England

---

7   'Nationalism' in the volume *Thought and Change*, London 1964, the most important and influential recent study in English.

and France. This English- French 'dual revolution' impinged upon the rest of Europe like a tidal wave. What Gellner calls the 'tidal wave of modernisation'. Through it the advancing capitalism of the more bourgeois societies bore down upon the societies surrounding them – societies which predominantly appear until the 1790s as buried in feudal and absolutist slumber.

Nationalism was one result of this rude awakening. For what did these societies – which now discovered themselves to be intolerably 'backward' – awaken into? A situation where polite universalist visions of progress had turned into means of domination. The Universal Republic of Anacharsis Cloots had turned into a French empire; the spread of free commerce from which so much had been hoped was turning (as Friedrich List pointed out) into the domination of English manufactures – the tyranny of the English 'City' over the European 'Country'. In short, there was a sort of imperialism built into 'development'. And it had become a prime necessity to resist *this* aspect of development.

Enlightenment thinkers had mostly failed to foresee this fatal antagonism. They had quite naturally assumed 'a link between knowledge and the increase in happiness', so that (as Sidney Pollard writes) 'Society and its rulers are increasingly able, because of greater knowledge, to combine the individual with the general interest, and the laws of nations will increasingly be changed to increase both. Thus the undoubted future progress of the human spirit will be accompanied by continuous social and individual amelioration'.[8] They imagined continuous diffusion from centre to periphery, from the 'leaders' to the regions still plunged in relative darkness. The metropolis would gradually elevate the rustic hinterland up to its level, as it were. It is, incidentally, worth noting that imperialists to this day always cling to some form or other of this pre-1800 ideology, at least partially.

In fact, progress invariably puts powerful, even deadly weapons in the hands of this or that particular 'advanced' area. Since this is a particular place and people, not a disinterested centre of pure and numinous culture, the result is a gulf (far larger than hitherto, and likely to increase) between the leaders and the hinterland. In the latter, progress comes to seem a hammer-blow as well as (sometimes instead of) a prospectus for general uplift and improvement. It appears as double-edged, at least. So areas of the hinterland, even in order to 'catch up' (to advance from 'barbarism' to the condition of 'civil society', as the Enlightenment put it), are *also* compelled to mobilise against progress. That is, they have to demand progress not as it is thrust upon them initially by the metropolitan centre, but 'on their own terms'. These 'terms' are, of course, ones which reject the imperialist trappings: exploitation or control from abroad, discrimination, military or political domination, and so on.

'Nationalism' is in one sense only the label for the general unfolding of this vast struggle, since the end of the 18th century. Obviously no one would deny

---

8   *The Idea of Progress*, London 1968, p. 46.

that nationalities, ethnic disputes and hatreds, or some nation-states, existed long before this. But this is not the point. The point is how such relatively timeless features of the human scene were transformed into the general condition of national*ism* after the bourgeois revolutions exploded fully into the world. Naturally, the new state of affairs made use of the 'raw materials' provided by Europe's particularly rich variety of ethnic, cultural and linguistic contrasts. But – precisely – it also altered their meaning, and gave them a qualitatively distinct function, an altogether new dynamism for both good and evil.

In terms of broad political geography, the contours of the process are familiar. The 'tidal wave' invaded one zone after another, in concentric circles. First Germany and Italy, the areas of relatively advanced and unified culture adjacent to the Anglo-French centre. It was in them that the main body of typically nationalist politics and culture was formulated. Almost at the same time, or shortly after, Central and Eastern Europe, and the more peripheral regions of Iberia, Ireland, and Scandinavia. Then Japan and, with the full development of imperialism, much of the rest of the globe. To locate at least some of the dimensions of the struggle today is simple. All one had to do was look around one in 1972 or 1973. Where were the storm-centres? Vietnam, Ireland, Bangladesh, the Middle East, Chile. Certain of these troubles may, or may not, have involved socialist revolutions and projected a non-national and Marxist image; there is no doubt that every one of them involved a *national* revolution quite comprehensible in the general historical terms of national*ism* (even without reference to other factors).

Europe's Bourgeoisies

The picture must be amplified and deepened in certain ways, however, to make it into a model applicable to a particular area like Scotland. We have glanced at the political geography of uneven development. What about its class basis and social content? Sociologically, the basis of the vital change we are concerned with obviously lay in the ascendency of the bourgeoisie in both England and France: more exactly, in their joint rise and their fratricidal conflicts up to 1815. Their Janus-headed 'modernity' was that of bourgeois society, and an emergent industrial capitalism.

And it was upon the same class that this advancing 'civil society' everywhere had the principal impact. In the hinterland too there were 'rising middle classes' impatient with absolutism and the motley assortment of *anciens régimes* which reigned over most of Europe. Naturally, these were far weaker and poorer than the world-bourgeoisies of the West. The gross advantages of the latter had been denied them by history's unequal development. Now they found themselves in a new dilemma. Previously they had hoped that the spread of civilised progress would get rid of feudalism and raise them to the grace of liberal, constitutional society. Now (e.g.) the German and Italian middle classes realised that only a determined effort of their own would prevent utopia from being marred by *Manchestertum* and French bayonets.

Beyond them, in the still larger Europe east of Bohemia and Slovenia, the even weaker Slav middle classes realised that 'progress' would in itself only fasten German and Italian fetters upon their land and people more firmly. And so on.

This 'dilemma' is indeed the characteristic product of capitalism's uneven development. One might call it the 'nationalism-producing' dilemma. Given the premise of uneven growth, and the resultant impact of the more upon the less advanced, the dilemma is automatically transmitted outwards and onwards in this way. The result, nationalism, is basically no less necessary. Nationalism, unlike nationality or ethnic variety, cannot be considered a 'natural' phenomenon. But of course it remains true that, as Gellner says, under these specific historical circumstances (those of a whole era in which we are still living) 'nationalism does become a natural phenomenon, one flowing fairly inescapably from the general situation'.

The Role of Intellectuals

Equally naturally, nationalism was from the outset a 'bourgeois' phenomenon in the sense indicated. But two farther qualifications are needed here, to understand the mechanism at work. The first concerns the intelligentsia, and the second concerns the masses whose emergence into history was – behind and beneath the more visible 'rise of the bourgeoisie' – the truly decisive factor in the transformation we are dealing with. 'The intelligentsia do, indeed, play a definitive part in the rise of nationalist movements – everywhere', remarks Anthony Smith.[9] In his history of the 'dual revolution' and its impact Eric Hobsbawm is more specific: the motor rôle is provided by 'The lesser landowners or gentry and the emergence of a national middle and even lower-middle class in numerous countries, the spokesmen for both being largely professional intellectuals... (above all)... the *educated* classes... the educational progress of large numbers of 'new men' into areas hitherto occupied by a small élite. The progress of schools and universities measures that of nationalism, just as schools and especially universities become its most conspicuous champions.'[10] The dilemma of under-development becomes 'nationalism' only when it is (so to speak) refracted into a given society, perceived in a certain way, and then acted upon. And the medium through which this occurs is invariably, in the first place, an intelligentsia – functioning, of course, as the most conscious and awakened part of the middle classes.

9 A. D. Smith, *Theories of Nationalism*, p. 83.
10 E. J. Hobsbawm, *The Age of Revolution: Europe 1789–1848*, London 1962, pp. 133–5.

Nationalism and the Masses

But if the intellectuals are all-important in one sense (spreading nationalism from the top downwards as it were), it is the masses – the ultimate recipients of the new message – that are all-important in another. As a matter of fact, they determine a lot of what the 'message' is. Why this is can easily be seen, on the basis of the foregoing remarks.

These new middle classes, awakening to the grim dilemmas of backwardness, are confronted by a double challenge. They have (usually) to get rid of an anachronistic *ancien régime* as well as to beat 'progress' into a shape that suits their own needs and class ambitions. They can only attempt this by radical political and social mobilisation, by arousing and harnessing the latent energies of their own societies. But this means, by mobilising people. People is all they have got: this is the essence of the under-development dilemma itself.

Consequently, the national or would-be national middle class is always compelled to 'turn to the people'. It is this compulsion that really determines the new political complex ('nationalism') which comes forth. For what are the implications of turning to the people, in this sense? First of all, speaking their language (or, over most of Europe, what had hitherto been viewed as their 'brutish dialects'). Secondly, taking a kindlier view of their general 'culture', that *ensemble* of customs and notions, pagan and religious, which the Enlightenment had relegated to the museum (if not to the dust-bin). Thirdly – and most decisively, when one looks at the process generally – coming to terms with the enormous and still irreconcilable *diversity* of popular and peasant life.

It is, of course, this primordial political compulsion which points the way to an understanding of the dominant contradiction of the era. Why did the spread of capitalism, as a rational and universal ordering of society, lead so remorselessly to extreme fragmentation, to the exaggeration of ethnic-cultural differences, and so to the *dementia* of 'chauvinism' and war? Because that diffusion contained within itself (as it still does) the hopeless antagonism of its own unevenness, and a consequent imperialism; the latter forces mobilisation against it, even on the part of those most anxious to catch up and imitate; such mobilisation can only proceed, in practice, via a popular mass still located culturally upon a far anterior level of development, upon the level of feudal or pre-feudal peasant or 'folk' life. That is, upon a level of (almost literally) 'pre-historic' diversity in language, ethnic characteristics, social habits, and so on. This ancient and (in a more acceptable sense of the term) 'natural' force imposes its own constraints upon the whole process, lending to it from the outset precisely that archaic and yet necessary colour, that primeval-seeming or instinctive aspect which marks it so unmistakably.

If one now relates these two central features of the bourgeois dilemma to one another, what is the consequence? One perceives at once the true nerve of political nationalism. It is constituted by a distinctive relationship between the intelligentsia (acting for its class) and the people. There is no time here to explore this interesting general theme in detail. For our purposes it is sufficient to note the name, and some of the implications, of the relationship in question. Political nationalism of the classic sort was not necessarily democratic by nature, or revolutionary in a social sense (notoriously it could be inspired by fear of Jacobinism, as well as by Jacobinism). But it *was* necessarily 'populist' by nature. The political and social variables to be observed in its development are anchored in this constant, which steadily expressed the class machinery of the process.

Thus, we can add to the 'external' (or geo-political) co-ordinates of nationalism mentioned above, a set of 'internal' or social-class coordinates. The former showed us the 'tidal wave' of modernisation (or bourgeois society) transforming one area after another, and soliciting the rise of nationalist awareness and movements. The latter shows us something of the mechanism behind the 'rise': the bourgeois and intellectual populism which, in existing conditions of backwardness where the masses are beginning to enter history and political existence for the first time, is ineluctably driven towards ethnic particularism. Nationalism's forced 'mobilisation' is fundamentally conditioned, at least in the first instance, by its own mass basis.

But then, we are in a manner of speaking still living in this 'first instance'. Nationalism arose after the French and Industrial Revolutions, at the very beginning of the 19th century. But the *anciens régimes* which the new nationalist middle classes had to get rid of in Central and Eastern Europe lasted for more than a century after that. Absolutism was far more tenacious than most bourgeois intellectuals admitted. It learned to borrow from the new world elements of technology and populism, to help it survive. Even when killed at last by the First World War and the 1917 revolutions, its ruinous mass of unresolved 'national questions' and fractured states was enough to poison history for another generation. And, of course, while this inheritance has become steadily less important in post-Second World War Europe, the expanding waves of extra-European nationalism are sufficient to hold us all still in this universe of discourse.

Let me now point out some important implications of this model of nationalism, before going on to consider the Scottish case. Its main virtue is a simple one. It enables us to decide upon a materialist, rather than an 'idealist' explanation of the phenomenon. In the question of nationalism, this philosophical point is critical. This is so, because of the very character of the phenomenon. Quite obviously, nationalism is invariably characterised by a high degree of political and ideological voluntarism. Simply because it *is* forced mass-mobilisation in a position of relative helplessness (or 'under-development'), certain subjective factors play a prominent part in it. It is, in its immediate nature, idealistic. It always imagines an ideal 'people' (propped up by folklore studies, antiquarianism, or some surrogate for these) and it always searches urgently for vital inner, untapped springs of energy both in the individual and the mass. Such idealism is inseparable both from its creative historical function and its typical delusions. Consequently a generally idealist mode of explanation has always been tempting for it. It lends itself rather to a Hegelian and romantic style of theorizing, than to a rationalist or Marxist one. This is one reason why Marxism has so often made heavy weather of it in the past.[11]

The Nation and Romanticism

I pointed out earlier, indeed, that theories about nationalism have been overwhelmingly influenced by nationalism, as the prevailing universe of discourse. This is really the same point. For they have been overwhelmingly influenced in the sense of idealism – whether their bias is itself pro-nationalist, or anti-nationalist.[12] The question is, then, which can explain which? It is a fact that while idealist explanations of the phenomenon in terms of consciousness or *Zeitgeist* (however acute their observation may be, notably in German writers like Meinecke) never account for the material dynamic incorporated in the situation, a materialist explanation can perfectly well account for all the most 'ideal' and cultural or ideological symptoms of nationalism (even at their most berserk).

---

11 I cannot refrain here from citing a criticism of the author made by the Scottish nationalist writer John Herdman, in his contribution to Duncan Glen's Whither Scotland?. He castigates my unduly material conception of the purpose of development (in an earlier essay called 'Three Dreams of Scottish Nationalism', *New Left Review* no. 49, May–June 1968, reprinted in Karl Miller's *Memoirs of a Modern Scotland*, 1970) and observes that: 'To my mind both these (material) purposes are secondary and subservient to the mobilising of populations for *spiritual* development. I dislike the word but cannot think of a better one...' (p. 109). And what does such spiritual development counter? The unacceptable face of 'progress', as shown in 'a nation which has become the very embodiment of anti-civilisation, of an amorphous mass culture which is ignoble, ugly and debased'. This is England of course. But it might equally well be France, as once seen by German nationalists; Germany, as once seen by Panslavism; America, as now seen by half the world; the USSR, as seen by the Chinese... and so on. By contrast Scotland's spiritual solution is (again very characteristically) 'the difficult assumption of a cultural independence which will give a new dynamic to the country' (Duncan Glen, op. cit., p. 22)

12 Naturally, the anti-nationalist bias tends to be somewhat more revealing; yet this is to say little. The most interesting strain of bourgeois anti-nationalism is the conservative one deriving from Lord Acton's essay on 'Nationality' (1862, reprinted in *Essays*, ed. G. Himmelfarb, 1949). But really very little has been added to it since, as one may see by consulting, e.g. Professor E. Kedourie's Actonian volume *Nationalism*, London 1960. It is significant in this connection that the first sensible progress in nationalism-theory was made after the First World War by scholars in America who had established a sufficient distance from Europe (the Hayes and Kohn schools). While with few exceptions further serious contributions have been made via the study of Third World 'development' since the Second World War, especially by sociologists. All three stances (social conservatism, the vantage point of an – at that time – less nationalist USA, and Third Worldism) have permitted varying degrees of psychic detachment from the core of the nationalist thought-world.

Start from the premise of capitalism's uneven development and its real class arti-culation, and one can come to grasp the point even of chauvinist lunacy, the 'irrational' elements which have played a significant role in nationalism's unfolding from the outset to the end. Start from the lunacy itself and one will end there, after a number of gyrations – still believing, for instance, that (in Hegelian fashion) material development exists to serve the Idea of 'spiritual development'.

Perhaps this can be put in another way. The politico-cultural necessities of nationalism, as I outlined them briefly above, entail an intimate link between nationalist politics and *romanticism*. Romanticism was the cultural mode of the nationalist dynamic, the cultural 'language' which alone made possible the for-mation of the new inter-class communities required by it. In that context, all romanticism's well-known features – the search for inwardness, the trust in feeling or instinct, the attitude to 'nature', the cult of the particular and mistrust of the 'abstract', etc. – make sense. But if one continues to adopt that language, then it becomes impossible to get back to the structural necessities which deter-mined it historically. And of course, we *do* largely speak the language, for the same reason that we are still living in a world of nationalism.

Lastly let me point out an important limitation of the analysis. So far I have been concerned with the earlier or formative stages of nationalism. That is, with the nationalism which was originally (however much it has duplicated itself in later developments) that of Europe between 1800 and 1870. This is – for reasons which I hope will be clear – what primarily concerns us in approaching the Scottish case-history. But it is certainly true that after 1870, with the Franco-Prussian war and the birth of Imperialism (with a large 'I'), there occurred farther sea-changes in nationalist development. These were related, in their exter-nal co-ordinates, to a new kind of great-power struggle for backward lands; and as regards their internal co-ordinates, to the quite different class struggle provoked by the existence of large proletariats within the metropolitan centres themselves. I have no room here to consider this later phase so closely, but it is important to refer to it at least. Not only has it deeply influenced the develop-ment of Scotland (like everywhere else in the world). Also, where I have stated that we still live in a climate of nationalism, it would, of course, be more accu-rate to say we still inhabit the universe of late nationalism: that is, nationalism as modified by the successive, and decisive, mass experiences of imperialism and total war.

Scotland's Absent Nationalism

Let us now turn to Scotland. How exactly are we to set it over against this general model? I pointed out to begin with the very surprising fact which confronts anyone trying to do this: that is, that for virtually the whole century of nationalism's classical development there is no object of comparison at all.

Between 1800 and 1870 for example, the dates just referred to, there simply *was* no Scottish nationalist movement of the usual sort.

It still may not be quite understood how disconcerting this absence is. To get it into perspective, one should compare certain aspects of Scotland's situation just prior to the age of nationalism with those of other European minor nationalities. With (e.g.) the Slav nationalities, Greece, Ireland, or Poland. In any such comparison, Scotland appears not as notably defective but, on the contrary, as almost uniquely *well* equipped for the nationalist battles ahead.

Nobody could, for example, claim that Scotland was a *geschichtsloses Volk*.[13] It had only recently ceased being a wholly independent state. The century or so that had elapsed since 1707 is a fairly insignificant time-interval by the criteria which soon became common under nationalism. Many new 'nations' had to think away millennia of oblivion, and invent almost entirely fictitious pasts.[14] Whereas the Scots not only remembered a reality of independence, they had actually preserved most of their own religious, cultural, and legal institutions intact. Their political state had gone, but their civil society was still there – still there and, in the later 18th century, thriving as never before. Most of backward, would-be nationalist Europe had neither the one nor the other.

Within this civil society Scotland also had at least two of the indispensable prerequisites for successful nationalism. It had a dynamic middle class, a 'rising' bourgeoisie if ever there was one. And (above all) it had an intelligentsia. In fact, it had one of the most distinguished intellectual classes in the Europe of that time, a class whose achievements and fame far outshone that of any other minor nationality. Given the key importance of the intelligentsia in early formulations of the romantic populism associated with 'nation-building', this was clearly a formidable advantage – at least in appearance.

As far as folklore and popular traditions went, Scotland was (needless to say) as well furnished for the struggle as anywhere else. Better than most, perhaps, since – as everybody knew then and knows now – one element in those traditions was an ancient, rankling hostility to the English, founded upon centuries of past conflict. These old conflicts gave Scotland a cast of national heroes and

---

13 The outstanding study of the problem of 'historyless peoples' from a Marxist point of view is R. Rosdolsky, *Friedrich Engels und das Problem der 'Geschichtslosen Völker'*, Hannover 1964, offprint from *Archiv für Socialgeschichte*, vol. 4, 1964.

14 Beginning with modern Greece, that first model and inspiration of nationalist revolts throughout Europe. There the gap between present realities and past history was so enormous that the new intellectuals had to create the new myths *de toutes pièces*. As one (notably pro-Greek) author says: 'Those who spoke the Greek language... had no notion of classical Greece or of the Hellenistic civilisation of Roman times... The classical ruins were quite unintelligible to early modern Greeks... From Roman times the Greeks had called themselves 'Romans' and continued to do so up to and during the War of Independence'. D. Dakin, *The Greek Struggle for Independence* 1821–1833 London 1973, pp. 11–22.

martyrs, popular tales and legends of oppression and resistance, as good as anything in *Mittel-europa*. True, the Scots did not have a really separate major- ity language. But any comparative survey will show that, however important language becomes as a distinguishing mark in the subsequent advance of nation- alism, it is rarely of primary importance in precipitating the movement. It is heavy artillery, but not the cause of the battle.

And in any case, the Scots had far heavier artillery to hand. They had – to consider only one thing – the enormously important factor of a clear religious difference. The Scottish Reformation had been a wholly different affair from the English one, and had given rise to a distinct social and popular ethos rooted in distinct institutions. There is no need to stress the potential of this factor in nationality-struggles today, looking across to Ireland (even in situations where both sides speak the same language). More important, and more generally, there was no doubt at the beginning of the 19th century – just as there is no doubt today – that 'Scotland' was a distinct entity of some kind, felt to be such both by the people living in it and by all travellers who ventured into it from outside. It had (as it still has) a different 'social ethic', in George Elder Davie's phrase. Analysis of the complex elements going into such a product, the recognisable and felt identity of a nationality-unit (whether state or province), may be diffi- cult. But usually the fact is plain enough. And this is what counts most, as the potential fuel of nationalist struggle.

So why, in circumstances like these, was nationalism to be conspicuous only by its absence in Scotland? This question is interesting enough. But it is time to note that behind it there lies another, much more important in any general perspective, and even more fascinating. If, in a European land so strikingly marked out for nationalism, nationalism failed to materialise, then it can only be because the *real* precipitating factors of the nationalist response were not there. And one may therefore hope to discern, through this extraordinary 'negative example', precisely what these factors were. To understand why Scotland did *not* 'go nationalist' at the usual time and in the usual way is, in my opinion, to under- stand a great deal about European nationalism in general. I hope the claim does not sound too large (or even nationalist). But, as well as understanding Scotland better in relation to the general European model discussed above, one may also understand Europe better by focusing upon Scotland.

Three Kinds of Nation

To assist us in focusing on what is relevant, let me recall a basic point in the crudely materialist schema adopted previously. I suggested there that nationalism is in essence one kind of response to an enforced dilemma of 'under-development'. What we must do now is define the latter term more concretely, in relation to Europe at the critical period in question – that is, during the original formation of nationalism. European countries at the beginning of the 19th century can for this purpose conveniently be assigned to one or other of three categories. Firstly, there are the original, 'historic' nation-states, the lands formed relatively early into relatively homogeneous entities, usually by absolute monarchy: England, France, Spain and Portugal, Sweden, Holland. Naturally, this category includes the 'leaders', the two revolutionary nations whose impact was to be so great, as well as a number of formerly important ones which had now (for many different reasons) dropped out of the race. Then (secondly) there are the lands which have to try and catch up, under the impact of revolution: the German-speaking states, Italy, the Hapsburg domains, the Balkans, the countries of Tsardom, Ireland, Scandinavia apart from Sweden. These account for by far the greater part of Europe geographically, and in terms of population. They were all to attempt to redeem themselves through some form of nationalism, sooner or later: they were all (one might say) forced through the nationalist hoop.

Finally – thirdly – one needs another category. The two main groups of bourgeois-revolutionary lands and 'under-developed' hinterland are easily clas- sified at this point in time. But what about the countries which either had caught up, or were about to catch up? The countries on the move out of barbarism into culture, those on or near the point of (in today's terminology) 'take-off'? Surely, in an age which thought so generally and confidently about progress of this sort, there were some examples of it?

This third group is a very odd one. It had, in fact, only one member. There was to be only one example of a land which – so to speak – 'made it' before the onset of the new age of nationalism. The European Enlightenment had an immense general effect upon culture and society; but it had only one particular success- story, outside the great revolutionary centres. Only one society was in fact able to advance, more or less according to its precepts, from feudal and theological squalor to the stage of bourgeois civil society, polite culture, and so on. Only one land crossed the great divide *before* the whole condition of European poli- tics and culture was decisively and permanently altered by the great awakening of nationalist consciousness.

North Britain

It was of course our own country, Scotland, which enjoyed (or suffered) this solitary fate. The intelligentsia at least had few doubts about what had happened. 'The memory of our ancient state is not so much obliterated, but that, by com- paring the past with the present, we may clearly see the superior advantages we now enjoy, and readily discern from what source they flow', ran the Preface to No 1 of the original *Edinburgh Review* (1755). 'The communication of trade has awakened industry; the equal administration of laws produced good manners... and a disposition to every species of improvement in the minds of a people naturally active and intelligent. If countries have their ages with respect to improvement,

North Britain may be considered as in a state of early youth, guided and supported by the more mature strength of her kindred country'.

A prodigy among the nations, indeed. It had progressed from fortified castles and witch-burning to Edinburgh New Town and Adam Smith, in only a generation or so. We cannot turn aside here to consider the reasons for this extraordinary success. Ordinarily it is no more than a sort of punch-bag in the old contest between nationalists and anti-nationalists: the former hold that Edinburgh's greatness sprang forth (like all true patriot flora) from indigenous sources, while the Unionists attribute it to the beneficent effects of 1707. It may be worth noting, however, that North Britain's intellectuals themselves normally thought of another factor as relevant. As the *Edinburgh Review* article mentioned above put it: 'What the Revolution had begun, the Union rendered more compleat'. It was by no means the fact of union which had counted, but the fact that this unification had enabled the Scots to benefit from the great *revolution* in the neighbour kingdom. As the great Enlightenment historian William Robertson said, the 1707 agreement had 'admitted the Scottish commons to a participation of all the privileges which the English had purchased at the expense of so much blood'.[15] That is, the Scottish bourgeoisie had been able to exploit (by alliance) some of the consequences of the English bourgeois revolution. After the black, the unspeakable 17th century, Robertson notes, it was 1688 which marked the real dawn in Scotland.

But many other factors were involved too, clearly. The character of Scottish absolutism, for example, the feudalism which 'collapsed as a vehicle for unity, and became instead the vehicle of faction', in T. C. Smout's words.[16] The character of the Scottish Reformation and its inheritance. I doubt if even the stoniest of Unionist stalwarts would deny that part of Scotland's 18th-century 'improvement' was due to her own powers, and the retention of a large degree of institutional autonomy. But what matters most in the context of this discussion is that Scotland's situation was almost certainly unique. It was the only land which stood in *this* relationship to the *first* great national-scale bourgeois revolution: that is, to a revolutionary process which, because it was the first, proceeded both slowly and empirically and therefore permitted in the course of its development things which were quite unthinkable later on. There was, there could not be, any situation like Scotland's within the enormously accelerated drive of 19th-century development. By then, the new international competitiveness and political culture's new mass basis alike prohibited gentlemanly accords like 1707.[17]

15   William Robertson, *History of Scotland*, 1803, in *Works* 1817. vol. 3, pp. 188–200.

16   T. C. Smout, *A History of the Scottish People* 1560–1830, 1969, p. 33.

17   Even more to the point perhaps, one need only think of the period just before 1707 – that is, the period of the Scottish bourgeoisie's last attempt at separate and competitive development through the colonization of Darien. This was destroyed largely through English pressures. Can anyone imagine that under 19th-century conditions this *débâcle* would have been forgiven and realistically forgotten? On the contrary, it would have

We know at any rate that the success story was never repeated quite like this anywhere else. There were a number of other zones of Europe where it clearly could have been, and would have been if 'development' had gone on in the Enlightenment, rather than the nationalist, sense. Belgium and the Rhineland, for example, or Piedmont. In the earlier phases of the French Revolution these areas were indeed inducted for 'improvement' into the ambit of the French Revolution, the Universal Republic. But as events quickly showed, this pattern could no longer be repeated.

Enlightenment and the Highlands

The most remarkable comment upon Scotland's precocious improvement was provided by Scottish culture itself, during the Golden Age. The country not only 'made it', in the generation before the great change (i.e. the generation between the failure of the Jacobite rebellion of 1745 and 1789) – it also produced the general formula for 'making it'. That is, it contributed proportionately far more than anywhere else in Europe to the development of social science. And it did so in the distinctive form of what was in essence a study *of* 'development': a study of the 'mechanics of transition', or how society in general can be expected to progress out of barbarism into refinement. Scottish Enlightenment thinkers were capable of this astonishing feat because, obviously, they had actually experienced much of the startling process they were trying to describe. Not only that: the old 'barbaric' world was still there, close about them. The author of Scotland's sociological masterpiece, the *Essay on the History of Civil Society* (1767), had been brought up in the Highlands.[18]

Scotland's progress was all the more striking because there was this one large part of it which did not 'improve' at all. Scotland beyond the Highland line remained 'under-developed'. This fissure through Scottish society had been left by the failure of later feudalism; now it was, if anything, aggravated by the swift rise of Lowland culture in the 18th century. A 'gulf' was formed which resembles in many ways the gulf that opened across Europe as a whole – that

---

been turned into a compelling popular reason for still more aggressive separate (i.e. nationalist) development. As things were, in the pre-nationalist age this tailor-made nationalist tragedy led straight to the 1707 Union.

18 As the editor of the recent Edinburgh edition of the Essay states: 'Adam Ferguson was a Highlander... and undoubtedly behind the *Essay* lies a deeply felt experience of the contrast between these two societies, and the question: what happens to man in the progress of society? Ferguson knew intimately, and from the inside, the two civilisations... which divided 18th-century Scotland: the *Gemeinschaft* of the clan, the *Gesellschaft* of the 'progressive', commercial Lowlands'. Duncan Forbes, Introduction pp. xxxviii-xxxix, 1966 edition.

is, the very gap I tried to describe previously, the development-gap with all its accompanying dilemmas and ambiguities. Highland Scotland, like most of Ireland, was in effect a part of Central or Eastern Europe in the West. Therefore it was bound to have a distinct development from the 'successful' civil society south of it. It had, as everyone knows, a distinct history of just this sort – one which painfully resembles the history of Ireland or many of the weaker peoples of *Mitteleuropa*, far more closely than it does that of the Scottish industrial belt. The Highlands were to suffer the fate characteristic of many countries and regions which generated nationalist movements in order to resist. But (here unlike Ireland) Highland society did not possess the prerequisites for *nationalist* resistance. Its position was too marginal, its social structure was too archaic, and too much of its life had been actually destroyed in the terrible reaction to 1745.

If this general analysis is right, then Scotland's precocious and pre-nationalist development must clearly be reckoned the true 'uniqueness' of its modern history. In European perspective, this emerges as much more striking than anything else. Nationalists always perorate at length upon the unique charms and mission of their object, I know: this is part of the structure of the nationalist thought-world. So is the fact that, seen from a distance, these ineffable missions resemble one another like a box of eggs. One has to be careful, consequently, before presenting a new candidate for the stakes. But I am comforted in doing so by one thought. This is that my emphasis upon the Enlightenment has never in fact (to the best of my knowledge) figured in such nationalist incantations in the past. On the contrary – for reasons that may be clearer below – if Scottish nationalists have ever been really united on one thing, it is their constant execration and denunciation of Enlightenment culture. In short, the real uniqueness of modern Scotland is the one thing which does *not* (and indeed *cannot*) be admitted into nationalist rhetoric.

There is logic behind this, of course. The same logic which drives one to the following thought: it simply cannot be the case that there is *no* connection between Scottish society's fulminating advance before 1800, and that society's subsequent failure to produce a nationalism of its own. There must, surely, be some relation between these two remarkable, peculiarly Scottish achievements. Let me now go on to suggest what it may consist in.

There are two questions which cannot help dominating much of the cultural debate upon nationalism in Scotland. One we have looked at already: it is the problem of how and why the Scots emerged, so suddenly, from backwardness to rise to the peaks of the Edinburgh Golden Age. The other is how and why – and almost as suddenly – this florescence ended in the earlier decades of the 19th century. So that, as far as the national culture is concerned – runs one typical complaint – 'The historian is left calling Victorian culture in Scotland 'strangely rootless'... We have to recognise that there did not emerge along with modern Scotland a mature, 'all-round' literature... In the mid-19th century the Scottish literary tradition paused; from 1825 to 1880 there is next to nothing worth attention'.[19] And, one might add, not much worth attention from 1880 to 1920 either.

It is inconceivable that the profoundest causes of this dramatic fall did not lie in Scottish society's general evolution. Yet where are these causes to be located? For, as Craig says, 'modern Scotland' – industrial Scotland, the economic Scotland of the Glasgow- Edinburgh- Dundee axis – continued *its* startling progress unabated. In his history T. C. Smout situates the beginning of the movement towards take-off in mid-century, after the 'Forty-five: 'The ice began to break. Slow and unspectacular at first, the process of change then began to accelerate in the 1760s, until by the outbreak of the American War in 1775 practically all classes in Scottish society were conscious of a momentum which was carrying them towards a richer society...'[20] The momentum continued until by 1830 the country had 'come over a watershed'. 'In 1828 J. B. Neilson's application of the hot-blast process to smelting the blackband ironstone of the Central Belt gave the Scottish economy the cue for its next major advance... it led to the birth of Scottish heavy industry with the swelling boom in iron towns and engineering in the 1830s and 1840s and the gigantic construction of shipyards on Clydeside in the last quarter of the century.'[21]

Thus, the economic 'structure' continued its forward march, across the developmental watershed and beyond, breeding new generations of Scottish entrepreneurs and a new and vast Scottish working class. But certain vital parts of the 'superstructure', far from sharing in this momentum, simply collapsed. On *that* level Scotland abruptly reverted to being a province again: a different sort of province, naturally, prosperous and imperial rather than theoretic and backward, but still (unmistakably) a very provincial *sort* of province. How is one to explain this remarkable disparity of development?

Let me relate it, first, to two other notable absences on the Scottish scene. One has already been several times referred to, since it is the main subject I am concerned with: that is, the absence of political nationalism. The other very striking absence is that of what one might call a developed or mature cultural romanticism. It is indeed the lack of this that constitutes the rootlessness, the 'void' which cultural and literary historians so deplore.

I know that this may be thought a paradoxical assertion. We are all aware of the great significance of both Scotland and Sir Walter Scott in the general mythology of European romanticism. And we are also conscious of the importance in Scotland itself of a kind of pervasive, second-rate, sentimental slop associated with tartan, nostalgia, Bonnie Prince Charlie, Dr Finlay, and so on. Yet I would hold that both these phenomena are misleading, in different ways;

---

19 David Craig, *Scottish Literature and the Scottish People*, 1680–1830, Edinburgh, 1961, pp. 13–14, 273.

20 T. C. Smout, op. cit., p. 226.

21 Ibid., pp. 484–5.

and that the existence of neither of them is inconsistent with the absence I am referring to.

Sir Walter Scott: Valedictory Realist

First of all Scott. In his essay on Scott in *The Historical Novel* (1962), Lukács points out that 'it is completely wrong to see Scott as a Romantic writer, unless one wishes to extend the concept of Romanticism to embrace all great literature in the first third of the 19th century'. Indeed, what Scott expresses himself – in spite of the great importance of his historical themes for later romantic literature – is rather 'a renunciation of Romanticism, a conquest of Romanticism, a higher development of the realist literary traditions of the Enlightenment'. Thus, to describe Scott as a 'romantic' is akin to describing Marx as a 'Marxist': he undeniably gave rise to a great deal of this European 'ism', but was not himself part of it. He was not, for example, a 'Romantic' in the sense that his compatriot Thomas Carlyle was, in the next generation (even Carlyle's misunderstanding and denigration of Scott are typically romantic).[22]

Scott's imaginative world arose from the same 'deeply felt experience of the contrast between two societies' mentioned above. That is, it belonged to the literary tradition of Scotland, as well as that of the Enlightenment in general. He brought to this an enormously heightened sense of the reality and values of the 'backward' or pre-bourgeois past – a sense which is, of course, characteristic of the whole period of awakening nationalism. But the typical course of his own imagination is never consonant with what was to be the general tendency of that period. It ran precisely counter to that tendency. As Lukács observes, it continued to run upon the lines of what he calls Enlightenment 'realism'.

For Scott, the purpose of his unmatched evocation of a national past is never to revive it: that is, never to resuscitate it as part of political or social mobilisation in the present, by a mythical emphasis upon continuity between (heroic) past and present. On the contrary: his essential point is always that the past really is gone, beyond recall. The heart may regret this, but never the head. As Scott's biographer J. G. Lockhart puts it, quite forcibly, his idea of nationalism was like his idea of witchcraft: 'He delighted in letting his fancy run wild about ghosts and witches and horoscopes... (but)... no man would have been more certain to give juries sound direction in estimating the pretended evidence of supernatural occurrences of any sort; and I believe, in like manner, that had any anti-English faction, civil or religious, sprung up in his own time in Scotland, he would have

---

22 Lukács' essay is also reprinted in *Scott's Mind and Art*, ed. Jeffares, Edinburgh 1969. Thomas Carlyle's influential essay on Scott appeared in the *London and Westminster Review* (1838), and is partly reprinted in *Scott: the Critical Heritage*, ed. J. Hayden, London 1970.

done more than other living man could have hoped to do, for putting it down'.[23]
For all its splendour, his panorama of the Scottish past is valedictory in nature.
When he returns to the present – in the *persona* of his typical prosaic hero-figure
– the head is in charge. It speaks the language of Tory Unionism and 'progress':
the real interests of contemporary Scotland diverge from those of the auld sang.

But in nationalist Europe the entire purpose of romantic historicism was
different. The whole point of cultural nationalism there *was* the mythical resus-
citation of the past, to serve present and future ends. There, people learned the
auld sangs in order to add new verses. Naturally, Scott was read and translated
in those countries according to this spirit – and as we know, his contribution to
the new rising tide of national romanticism was a great one. It was great everywhere but in his own nation. In his own national context, he pronounced, in
effect, a great elegy. But the point of an elegy is that it *can* only be uttered once.
Afterwards it may be echoed, but not really added to.

Consequently, Sir Walter's towering presence during the vital decades of the
early 19th century is not only consistent with the absence of a subsequent romantic-
national culture: to a large extent, it explains that absence. The very nature of
his achievement – whether seen in terms of his own politics, or in terms of his
typical plots and characters – cut off such a future from its own natural source
of inspiration. It cut off the future from the past, the head from the 'heart' (as
romanticism now conceived this entity). As for the second phenomenon I
referred to, popular or *Kitsch* Scotland, this is certainly a sort of 'romanticism'.
And it is certainly important, and not to be dismissed with a shudder as most
nationalist intellectuals tend to do. I shall have more to say about the great
tartan monster below. For the moment, however, I think it is enough to point
out that he is a sub-cultural creature rather than a performer in the elevated
spheres we are concerned with. Whisky labels, the *Sunday Post*, Andy Stewart,
the Scott Monument, the inebriate football patriots of international night:
no-one will fail to compose his own lengthy list or discern its weighty role in the
land. But this is a popular sub-romanticism, and not the vital national culture
whose absence is so often lamented after Scott.

What we have therefore is the relatively sudden disintegration of a great
national culture; an absence of political and cultural national*ism*; and an absence
of any genuine, developing romanticism, of the kind which was to typify 19th-cen-
tury cultural life. The three negative phenomena are, surely, closely connected.
In fact, they are different facets of the same mutation. And if we now set this
change over against the general explanatory model sketched out previously, we
can begin to see what it consisted in.

If one views it as a disparity of development, as between the ongoing economic
structure and a suddenly and inexplicably collapsed 'superstructure', then the

---

23   J. G. Lockhart, *The Life of Sir Walter Scott* (1837–8), Everyman's abridged edition, 1906,
     p. 653.

answer is contained in the very terms in which the problem is posed. That is, it is overwhelmingly likely that the cultural decline occurred *because* of the material development itself. Because Scotland had already advanced so far, so fast – to the watershed of development and beyond – it simply did not need the kind of cultural development we are concerned with. It had overleapt what was to be (over the greater part of Europe) the next 'natural' phase of development. Its previous astonishing precocity led it, quite logically, to what appears as an equally singular 'retardation' or incompleteness in the period which followed. This can only have happened because, at bottom, certain material levers were inoperative in the Scottish case; and they were inoperative during the usual formative era of romantic nationalism because they had already performed their function and produced their effect earlier, in the quite different culture-world of the 18th century.

The Absent Intelligentsia

We have some clues as to how this actually worked. Normally nationalism arose out of a novel dilemma of under-development; but it did so through a quite specific mechanism, involving first the intelligentsia, then wider strata of the middle classes, then the masses. The process has been admirably described by Hroch in his comparative inquiry. Initially the property of a relatively tiny intellectual élite (usually reacting to the impact of the French Revolution), nationalism passed through 'phase A' into 'phase B' (approximately 1815–48) where it was generally diffused among the growing bourgeoisie. It was in the course of this prolonged process that the new cultural language of romanticism and the new credo of liberal nationalism were worked out. But even so 1848 was still mainly a 'revolution of the intellectuals' (in Namier's phrase), and failed as such. It was only later that it turned into a mass movement proper ('phase C') with some roots in new working-class and peasant parties, and wide popular appeal. Thus, while the new *Weltanschauung* was (as we noticed) inherently populist in outlook, it took a long time to get to the people: that is, to the mystic source whence, in nationalist myth, it is supposed to spring.

Transfer this picture to the Scottish case: there was no real, material dilemma of under-development; hence the intelligentsia did not perceive it, and develop its perception in the normal way – it did *not* have to 'turn to the people' and try to mobilise first the middle strata then the masses for the struggle; hence there was no call to create a new inter-class 'community' of the sort invoked by nationalism, and no objective need for the cultural instrument which permitted this – 'romanticism'; hence the intelligentsia in Scotland (its previous eminence notwithstanding) was deprived of the *normal* function of an intellectual class in the new, nationalist, European world.

But – it may be objected here – even given that this was so, and that the underlying situation decreed a different politico-cultural fate for the Scots, why did it have to take the sad form of this *collapse* into provinciality, this bewildering descent from great heights into the cultural 'desert' of modern Scotland? Why could the Enlightenment not have continued there in some form, in a separate but still 'national' development? This is another of those questions whose very formulation guides one towards an answer. It was, of course, *impossible* for any such development to take place. Impossible because no one intellectual class can ever follow such a separate path in Europe. Once the general intellectual and cultural climate had altered in the decisive way mentioned, in consort with the unfolding of nationalism, it has altered for everybody.

This was by no means just a question of fashion, or the fact that intellectuals heed what goes on abroad. Nationalism was a general, and a structural state of the whole body politic. Although it was born in the 'fringe' lands under the impact of modernity, its subsequent impact transformed everyone – including the 'source' countries of the bourgeois revolution themselves, France and England. The new, enormous, growing weight of masses in motion broke down the old hierarchies everywhere and forced more or less similar cultural adaptations everywhere. In this violent process of action and reaction, no one part of the wider area concerned could 'escape' nationalism and its culture. It had either to evolve its own nationalist-type culture, or succumb to someone else's (becoming thereby 'provincialised').

Against the Fall

Under these new conditions, what in fact happened to the great Scots intelligentsia? As an intellectual class it belonged, with all its virtues, *entirely* to the pre-1789 universe. Both its patrician social character and its rationalist world-view were parts of that older, more stable, hierarchical world where the masses had scarcely begun to exist politically. Claims have been made for its 'democratic' intellect. 'Democratic' in the deeper sense which now became central it emphatically was not. It was pre-Jacobin, pre-populist, pre-romantic; and as a consequence, wholly pre-nationalist. In the drastically different geological epoch which now supervened, it could survive only for a short time, in somewhat fossil-like fashion. The sad tale is all there, in Lord Cockburn's *Memorials*. 'We had wonderfully few proper Jacobins,' he comments wryly upon the Scottish élite's wholesale slide into reaction, 'but if Scotch Jacobinism did not exist, Scotch Toryism did, and with a vengeance. This party engrossed almost the whole wealth, and rank, and public office, of the country, and at least three-fourths of the population.'[24] Sir Walter himself was, of course, in the front rank, battling (literally) to the death against the 1832 Reform Bill.

Elsewhere in Europe this suicide of former élites did not matter. They were displaced by what Eric Hobsbawm called the 'large numbers of 'new men", who

---

24   Memorials of *His Time*, by Lord Cockburn (1856), abridged edition, 1946, pp. 64–5.

were educated into nationalism and the other new rules of populist politics. These new men were awakened into radical dissatisfaction with their fate, and had the sense that without great collective efforts things would not improve much for them in a foreseeable future. They tended to come (as Hroch observes) from 'regions of intermediate social change' – from small towns and rural zones whose old life had been undermined, but for whom industry and urbanization were still remote (and dubious) realities.[25] Out of such regions there arose a new and broader intelligentsia to take the place of the old: modern, romantic, populist, more mobile, mainly petit-bourgeois in background.

But – precisely – in Scotland it did not. No new intellectual class at once national in scope and basically disgruntled at its life-prospects arose, because the Scottish petty bourgeoisie had little reason to be discontented. In the overwhelming rush of the Scottish industrial revolution, even the regions of intermediate social change were quickly sucked in. Hence no new 'intelligentsia' in the relevant sense developed, turning to the people to try and fight a way out of its intolerable dilemma. Hence Hroch's phases 'A' and 'B' were alike absent in Scottish development: there was, there could be, no nationalism or its associated romantic culture fully present in that development. There could only be the 'void'.

This kind of analysis will stick in a number of throats for two reasons: it is materialist in content, and rather complicated in form. How simple the old nationalist theory of the Fall appears, in contrast! It can be compressed into one word: treachery! The old Edinburgh élite was guilty of the (Romantic) original sin: cutting themselves off from the people. Second only to 'community' in this value-vocabulary is the unpleasant term 'roots'. The Enlightenment intelligentsia sold out its birth right – its roots in the Scottish national-popular community – for the sake of its pottage of tedious abstractions.[26] Sir James Steuart may be forgiven, as he happened to be a Jacobite. The rest were cosmopolitan *vendus* to a man: they may have invented social science, but their attitude towards Scotticisms was unpardonable. It was this wilful rootlessness that started the rot. 'The cultural sell-out of Scottish standards… the failure of Scotland's political and cultural leaders to be their Scottish selves has created the intellectual and cultural void which is at the centre of Scottish affairs,' states Duncan Glen in *Whither Scotland?* (1971). As for David Hume and that band: 'We should give the opposite answers to those of the great philosopher who failed to rise above the attitudes

25 Hroch, op. cit., pp. 160–1; see also E. J. Hobsbawm, 'Nationalism', in *Imagination and Precision in the Social Sciences*, London 1972, p. 399.

26 An interesting recent example of this was provided by the nationalist Stephen Maxwell, in censuring some favourable remarks I had made about the Scottish Enlightenment in *Scottish International* (April 1973). Replying in the following issue of the review he condemned their 'intellectualism' as 'a symptom of the schizophrenia in Scottish culture that eventually issued in the 'kailyard' and was partly responsible for obstructing an adequate radical response in Scotland to the problems of 19th-century industrialism…'. Exactly: the 18th century is to blame for everything, even my own lamentable views!

of his time. Since then, however, we have had 200 years of the Scottish waste of the potential of the Scottish people and we should surely have learned the correct answers by now...'.

The simple idealism and voluntarism of this diagnosis should need no further stressing. It amounts to saying, *if only* the intellectuals had behaved differently, then our national history might have left its banks, and changed its course. It is not explanation, but retrospective necromancy. But it has as a consequence that the Scottish Enlightenment (as I pointed out above) recedes into a curious limbo of non-recognition, in the nationalist perspective. That is, the country's one moment of genuine historical importance, its sole claim to imperishable fame, literally does not count in the saga of the Scottish national Self. The triumph of Reason produced a wasteland void, as still thriving Romantic clichés would have us believe: not for the first or last time, the nationalist and the romantic 'theories' are really one.

The Reformation as Scapegoat

Lest it be thought that I am treating romanticism too cursorily, and dismissing its view of Scotland too lightly, I shall turn briefly to the most influential study of this kind. Edwin Muir's *Scott and Scotland* appeared in 1936, and has never been reissued. This is a pity, and rather surprising, for it is a book which has reappeared in other people's books and articles ever since. The copies in the Scottish National Library and the Edinburgh City Library must be particularly well-thumbed. No-one who has spent any time in the archives of literary nationalism can have failed to notice how often Muir is quoted, nearly always with approval.

How did he diagnose what happened to Scotland in the time of Scott? Muir is impressed particularly by what he calls 'a curious emptiness' behind Scott's imaginative richness. The void is already there, as it were, within the work of the Wizard of the North. What caused it? It reflects the fact that Sir Walter lived in 'a country which was neither a nation nor a province and had, instead of a centre, a blank, an Edinburgh, in the middle of it... Scott, in other words, lived in a community which was not a community, and set himself to carry on a tradition which was not a tradition... (and)... his work was an exact reflection of his predicament'. Scott's predicament was, of course, also one 'for the Scottish people as a whole... for only a people can create a literature'. England, by contrast, is 'an organic society' with a genuine centre and true *Volksgemeinschaft*. The English author has something to sink his roots into, while his Scottish colleague cannot 'root himself deliberately in Scotland' since there *is* no soil – no 'organic community to round off his conceptions', and not even any real wish for such a society (i.e. no real nationalism).

The mainspring of this, as of all similar arguments, is that it bestows eternal validity, or 'natural' status, upon certain categories of 19th century culture and politics. It is true that all 19th-century nation-states, and societies which aspired to this status through nationalism, had to foster what one may (although somewhat metaphorically) call 'organic community'. That is, for the specific motives mentioned previously their middle classes invented a type of inter-class culture, employing romantic culture and ideology. It is true also that Scotland was structurally unable to adapt to an age in which these categories and motives became the norm. What is not true – though it is the crux of Muir's position – is that this represented some sort of metaphysical disaster which one must despair over.

Muir then goes on to trace (again in very characteristic terms) the dimensions of both disaster and despair. One learns, with some surprise, that the trouble started in the middle ages. The Enlightenment and capitalism are only late symptoms; it was in fact the Reformation which 'truly signalised the beginning of Scotland's decline as a civilised nation'. The last of 'coherent civilisation' in Scotland was at the court of James IV (early 16th century). The metaphysical ailment of the Scots, a split between heart and head, began shortly thereafter, that '... simple irresponsible feeling side by side with arid intellect... for which Gregory Smith found the name of 'the Caledonian Antisyzygy".[27] So, after the Catholic 'organic community' had ended there was no hope, and Scotland was simply preparing itself for 'the peculiarly brutal form which the Industrial Revolution took in Scotland, where its chief agents are only conceivable as thoughtless or perverted children'.

A markedly oneiric element has crept into the argument somehow, and one wants to rub one's eyes. Can anybody really think this? Not only somebody, but most literary nationalists: it should not be imagined that this position represents a personal vagary of the author. It does have a bizarre dream-logic to it. Muir himself took his pessimism so seriously that not even nationalism seemed a solution to him. But broadly speaking the dream in question is that of romantic nationalism, and the logic is as follows: modern Scottish society does not fit it, and one has to explain why; since the idea-world (roots, organs, and all) is all right, and has unchallengeable status, it has to be Scotland which is wrong; therefore Scottish society and history are monstrously misshapen in some way, blighted by an Original Sin; therefore one should look further back for whatever led to the frightful Enlightenment ('arid intellect', etc.) and the Industrial Revolution; the Reformation is the obvious candidate, so before that things were pretty sound (a safe hypothesis, given the extent of knowledge about the 15th century in modern Scotland).[28]

---

27 This curious bacillus can be traced back to G. Gregory Smith, *Scottish Literature: Character and Influence* (1919). It explodes unpronounceably in the archives of literary nationalism quite often after that – e.g. MacDiarmid: 'The Caledonian Antisyzygy... may be awaiting the exhaustion of the whole civilisation of which English literature is a typical product in order to achieve its effective synthesis in a succeeding and very different civilisation' (*Albyn*, 1927, p. 34).

28 Edwin Muir, op. cit., pp. 22–4, 73–5.

Start with Idealism and you end up embracing the Scarlet Woman of Rome. I do not wish to dwell longer on this paradox now (though I shall need to refer to it again below). The aura of madness surrounding it is surely plain enough. Farther exploration of the oddities of nationalist ideology in Scotland had better wait until we come to the formation of the nationalist movement itself, in this century. Before I get to this, some more remarks have to be made about the consequences of the Scottish inability to generate a nationalism in the last century.

The Emigre Intelligentsia

I suggested above that Scotland can be seen as a 'negative image' of general European nationalist development, and one which tells us much about that development. There is a sense in which it tells us more than any 'positive' example could: for, of course, in all actual case-histories of nationalism general and highly specific factors are fused together almost inextricably. Whereas in Scotland, where so many particular factors favoured nationalism so powerfully, it is easier to detect (simply by its absence) what the basic causative mechanism must have been. It is in this sense that one may argue that Scotland furnishes a remarkable confirmation of the materialist conception of development and nationalism outlined previously.

But so far the argument has been couched in over-negative terms. We have seen why the development of bourgeois society in Scotland did *not* decree a form of nationalism, and the various 'absences' which followed from this peculiar evolutionary twist. The Scottish bourgeoisie was *not* compelled to frame its own pseudo-organic 'community' of culture, in order to channel popular energies behind its separate interest. Hence there was no serious romanticism as a continuing 'tradition', and the indigenous intellectual class became in a curious sense 'unemployed' or functionless upon its home terrain. The new Scottish working class, in its turn, was deprived of the normal type of 19th-century cultural 'nationalisation': that is, such popular-national culture as there was (vulgar Scottishism, or tartanry) was necessarily unrelated to a higher romantic-national and intellectual culture.

One of the most striking single consequences of this overall pattern was massive intellectual emigration. The 19th century also witnessed great working-class and peasant emigration, of course, but these were common to England and Ireland as well. The Scottish cultural outflow was distinctive, although it had much in common with similar trends in Ireland and the Italian south. The reasons for it are clear enough. The country was well provided with educational institutions and its higher culture did not vanish overnight. However, it certainly changed direction, and assumed a markedly different pattern. Its achievements in the century that followed were to be largely in the areas of natural science, technology and medicine – not in the old 18th century ones of social science, philosophy, and general culture. And of course it was what happened to the latter that is most related to the problem of nationalism, and concerns us here. It is in *this* crucial zone that one may speak of 'unemployment', and hence of the forced emigration of the sort of intellectual who elsewhere in Europe was forging a national or nationalist culture.

After the time of Sir Walter Scott, wrote the Victorian critic J. H. Robertson, '… we lost the culture-force of a local literary atmosphere; and defect superinduces defect, till it becomes almost a matter of course that our best men, unless tethered by professorships, go south'.[29] In his *Scottish Literature and the Scottish People* the contemporary critic David Craig makes a similar point: 'During the 19th century the country was emptied of the *majority* of its notable literary talents – men who, if they had stayed, might have thought to mediate their wisdom through the rendering of specifically Scottish experience. Of the leading British 'sages' of the time an astonishingly high proportion were of Scottish extraction – the Mills, Macaulay, Carlyle, Ruskin, Gladstone'.[30] This last is an especially characteristic judgement, with its suggestion of retrospective voluntarism: *if only* the émigrés had chosen to stay at home, then it might all have been different. The point was that in reality they had no such 'choice': 'specifically Scottish experience' in the sense relevant here would have been a product of culture, not its natural, pre-existent basis – and since Scottish society did not demand the formation of that culture, there *was* no 'experience' and nothing to be said. This phase of the country's history demonstrates, with exceptional vividness, both the social nature and the material basis of 'culture' in the usual intellectuals' sense. It may look as if it could have simply come 'out of people's heads', by free choice; in reality it could not.

There is no time here to say more about the fascinating history of the émigrés and their impact upon the neighbour kingdom. But in a broad sense there is no doubt what happened: unable, for the structural reasons described, to fulfil the 'standard' 19th-century function of elaborating a romantic-national culture for their own people, they applied themselves with vigour to the unfortunate southerners. Our former intelligentsia lost its cohesion and unitary function (its nature *as* an élite) and the individual members poured their formidable energies into the authentically 'organic community' centred on London. There, they played a very large part in formulating the new national and imperial culture-community. We must all be at times painfully aware of how England to this day languishes under the 'tradition' created by the Carlyle-Ruskin school of mystification, as well as the brilliant political inheritance nurtured by Keir Hardie and J. Ramsay MacDonald.

In one way this can be considered a typical form of 'provincialisation' which went on in all the greater nation-states. Everywhere hungry and ambitious intellectuals were drawn out of their hinterlands and into the cultural service of their respective capitals. If there was a significant difference here, it lay surely in the

---

29 J. H. Robertson, *Critiscisms* Vol. II (1885) p. 67.
30 Craig, op. cit. p. 276.

higher level and stronger base from which the Scots started. These enabled them, perhaps, to make a contribution at once more important and more distinctive in character. They did not come from a province of an *ancien régime*, but from an advanced quasi-nation with a high (if now anachronistic) culture of its own, and so had a head-start on other backwoodsmen.

To be concluded.

CHAPTER SEVEN

The Modern Janus

New Left Review, I/94

NOVEMBER–DECEMBER 1975

THE THEORY OF nationalism represents Marxism's great historical failure. It may have had others as well, and some of these have been more debated: Marxism's shortcomings over imperialism, the State, the falling rate of profit and the immiseration of the masses are certainly old battlefields. Yet none of these is as important, as fundamental, as the problem of nationalism, either in theory or in political practice. It is true that other traditions of western thought have not done better. Idealism, German historicism, liberalism, social Darwinism and modern sociology have foundered as badly as Marxism here. This is cool comfort for Marxists. The scientific pretensions and the political significance of their ideas are greater than those of such rivals, and no one can help feeling that they ought to have coped better with such a central, inescapable phenomenon of modern history. My thesis is that this failure was inevitable. It was inevitable, but it can now be understood. Furthermore it can be understood in essentially materialist terms. So as a system of thought historical materialism can perfectly well escape from the prolonged and destructive impasse in which it has been locked on the issue. However, the cost of doing so is probably 'Marxism'. Materialism cannot escape unmarked and unchanged from the ordeal, for an obvious reason. The reason is that to perceive the cause of *this* failure is to see something of Marxism's real place in history, some of its limitations, some of the unconscious roots which tied it blindly to the course of modern historical development. It means seeing Marxism itself as a part of history in a quite uncomplimentary sense, one which has nothing to do with the holy matrimony of theory and practice. It means losing for all time that God-like posture which, in the guise of science, Marxism took over from Idealist philosophy (and ultimately from religion).

Marxist 'failures' over nationalism appear to us in the first instance as philosophical, conceptual ones. The great names from Marx himself to Gramsci did not pay sufficient attention to the subject, dealing with it incidentally or tangentially rather than head-on. Those who did tackle it more directly, the Social-Democrats of Tsardom and the Hapsburg Empire, disagreed wildly among themselves. After the trauma of 1914 Marxists never had the stomach to return to this debate on anything like the same level. Had they desired to after 1925, the complete fetishisation of Lenin's supposed positions on the question made it both politically and psychologically very difficult.

The *coup de grâce* to their dithering was administered by Stalin's essay on *The National Question* (1912). By the most sinister of coincidences, the one text most suitable for canonisation in the new creed was by the great dictator himself. That this essay was one of the more modest relics of the great unfinished pre-1914 debate mattered little. Under the new conditions it riveted Stalin's name to the halo of Lenin. This is why it is still almost universally parroted by every brand of party Marxism. For half a century, organised Marxism has relied almost entirely upon this inadequate instrument in grappling with this most baffling and dangerous historical opponent – whose force seemed set fair to annihilate it altogether until the turning-point of Stalingrad.

This is a sad chapter in the history of ideas. But in itself it explains nothing. If one thinks it does, then the temptation will remain to say that surely, somewhere or other in the prodigious variety of revolutionary talents Marxism assembled, there *must* be a theory of nationalism. We are not cleverer than Rosa Luxemburg or Otto Bauer. We are not more painfully conscious than them of the critical and devastating nature of this phenomenon for socialism. So if we excavate assiduously enough the theory will surely emerge, like a crock of gold, from between the lines of the classics, maybe even from the scattered remarks and letters of Marx and Engels themselves.

In other words, if one believes that the 'failure' was essentially a conceptual, subjective one, the temptation remains to lend a retrospective helping hand. This exercise appeals strongly to the devotional side of Marxists. 'What so-and-so *really* meant was of course such-and-such, bearing in mind the following (commonly overlooked) texts...'; 'the insights of Lenin-Stalin or Engels-Marx must be complemented by Luxemburg's observations on...'; and so forth.

Real respect for our forebears demands we recognise the futility of these rituals. Their 'failure' was not a simply conceptual or subjective one. No amount of brass-rubbing will compensate for it. The fact is, that if they could not put together a tolerable theory about nationalism, nobody could, or did. Historical development had not at that time produced certain things necessary for such a 'theory'. The time was not ripe for it, or for them. Nor would it be ripe until two further generations of trauma had followed 1914. There is nothing in the least discreditable to historical materialism in the fact, although it is naturally lethal to 'Marxism', in the God's-eye sense.

The philosophical failings lead us back in turn to real history. They lead us back to the material conditions under which the enigma of modern nationalism presented itself to these past generations. Lacking angelic perspicuity, they had to confront it under very severe limitations. Nationalism is a crucial, fairly central feature of the modern capitalist development of world history. Time-bound like other systems of speculation, Marxism did not possess the power to foresee this development, or the eventual, overall shape which capitalist history would assume. As regards nationalism, the trouble is that not much less than this is required for approaching the problem.

Idées Reçues of Nationalism

So much by way of introduction. To go farther let us remember how most Marxist (and other) thinking about the subject oscillates between the horns of an over-familiar dilemma.

On one hand nationalism can hardly help seeming a good thing, a morally and politically positive force in modern history. It has been the ideology of weaker, less developed countries struggling to free themselves from alien oppression. From the time of the Greek and Latin-American independence wars up to the recent struggle in Indo-China, it appears as in this sense an aspect of progress. But on the other hand we know quite well that the term applies, and applies no less characteristically, to the history of Italian fascism and the Japanese military state of the 1930s, to the careers and personalities of General de Gaulle, General Amin and the Shah of Iran.

The task of a theory of nationalism – as distinct from a stratagem for living with the contradiction – must be to embrace both horns of the dilemma. It must be to see the phenomenon as a whole, in a way that rises above these 'positive' and 'negative' sides. Only in this fashion can we hope to escape from a predominantly moralising perspective upon it, and rise... I will not say to a 'scientific' one, as this term has been subjected to so much ideological abuse, but at least to a better, more detached historical view of it. In order to do this, it is necessary to locate the phenomenon in a larger explanatory framework, one that will make sense of the contradictions.

The question arises of what this framework is. My belief is that the only framework of reference which is of any real utility here is world history as a whole. It is only the general process of historical development since (at least) the end of the 18th century which can serve to give us the focus we need on such a huge and complicated problem. Most approaches to the question are vitiated from the start by a country-by-country attitude. Of course, it is the ideology of world nationalism itself which induces us along this road, by suggesting that human society consists essentially of several hundred different and discrete 'nations', each of which has (or ought to have) its own postage-stamps and national soul. The secret of the forest is the trees, so to speak. Fortunately, this is just the usual mangled half-truth of common sense.

No – it is the forest which 'explains' the trees, in the sense which interests us today. It is certain general conditions of geography, topography, soil and climate which determined what trees should grow, how thickly, how far, and so on. In other words, 'nationalism' in its most general sense is determined by certain features of the world political economy, in the era between the French and Industrial Revolutions and the present day. We are still living in this era. However, we enjoy the modest advantage of having lived in it longer than the earlier theorists who wrestled with the problem. From our present vantage-point we may be a little more able than they were to discern some overall characteristics of the process and its by-products. Indeed it would not say much for us if we were not able to do this.

Next, we must inquire what are those features of general historical development which give us some clue about nationalism. At this point it may help to
dip briefly into the mythology of the subject. If someone were producing an up-dated
version of Gustave Flaubert's *Dictionnaire des idées reçues* for the use of politics
and social-science students, I think the entry 'Nationalism' might read as follows:
'*Nationalism*: infrequently used before the later 19th century, the term can nonetheless be traced back in approximately its contemporary meaning to the 1790s
(Abbé Baruel, 1798). It denotes the new and heightened significance accorded
to factors of nationality, ethnic inheritance, customs and speech from the early
19th century onwards. The concept of nationalism as a generally necessary stage
of development for all societies is common to both materialist and idealist
philosophies. These later theoretical formulations agree that society must pass
through this phase (see, for example, texts of F. Engels, L. von Ranke, V. I.
Lenin, F. Meinecke). These theories also agree in attributing the causes of this
phase to specific forces or impulses resident within the social formations concerned.
Nationalism is therefore an internally-determined necessity, associated by Marxists with, for example, the creation of a national market economy and a viable
national bourgeois class; by Idealists with the indwelling spirit of the community,
a common personality which must find expression in historical development. Both
views concur that this stage of societal evolution is the necessary precondition
of a subsequent, more satisfactory state of affairs, known as 'internationalism'
('proletarian' or 'socialist' internationalism in one case, the higher harmony of
the World Spirit in the other). This condition is only attainable for societies and
individuals who have developed a healthy nationalism previously. While moderate, reasonable nationalism is in this sense praised, an immoderate or excessive
nationalism exceeding these historical limits is viewed as unhealthy and dangerous (see entry 'Chauvinism', above).'

The gist of this piece of global folklore (which unfortunately embraces much
of what passes for 'theory' on nationalism) is that nationalism is an inwardly-
determined social necessity, a 'growth-stage', located somewhere in between traditional or 'feudal' societies and a future where the factors of nationality will become
less prominent (or anyway less troublesome in human history). Regrettably, it is
a growth-stage which can sometimes go wrong and run amok. This is mysterious.
How can adolescence become a deadly disease?

Whatever the doctors say about this, they agree on the double inwardness
attaching to nationalism. It corresponds to certain internal needs of the society
in question, *and* to certain individual, psychological needs as well. It supplies peoples
and persons with an important commodity, 'identity'. There is a distinctive, easily
recognisable subjectivity linked to all this. Whenever we talk about nationalism,
we normally find ourselves talking before too long about 'feelings', 'instincts',
supposed desires and hankerings to 'belong', and so on. This psychology is obviously an important fact about nationalism.

The Maladies of Development

The universal folklore of nationalism is not entirely wrong. If it were, it would be unable to function as myth. On the other hand, it would be equally unable to function in this way if it were true – that is, true in the sense that concerns us in this place. It is ideology. This means it is the generally acceptable 'false consc-iousness' of a social world still in the grip of 'nationalism'. It is a mechanism of adjustment and compensation, a way of living with the reality of those forms of historical development we label 'nationalism'. As such, it is perhaps best regarded as a set of important clues towards whatever these forms are really about.

The principal such clue is the powerful connection that common sense suggests between nationalism and the concept of development or social and economic 'growth'. It is true that the distinctively modern fact of national*ism* (as opposed to nationality, national states and other precursors) is somehow related to this. For it is only within the context of the general acceleration of change since about 1800, only in the context of 'development' in this new sense, that nationhood acquired this systemic and abstract meaning.

However, it is not true that the systemic connotation derives *from the fact of development as such*. This is the sensitive juncture at which truth evaporates into useful ideology. It is simply not the case (although humanity has always had plenty of reasons for wishing it were the case) that national-ism, the compulsive necessity for a certain socio-political form, arises naturally from these new developmental conditions. It is not nature. The point of the folklore is of course to suggest this: to award it a natural status, and hence a 'health' label, as if it were indeed a sort of adolescence of all societies, the road we have to trudge along between rural idiocy and 'modernity', industrialization (or whatever).

A second significant clue is that pointing towards social and personal subjec-tivity. It is true that nationalism is connected with typical internal movements, personnel and persons. These behave in similar ways and entertain quite similar feelings. So it is tempting to say (e.g.) that the Italian nationalism of the 1850s or the Kurdish or Eritrean nationalism of the 1970s rest upon and are generated by these specific internal mechanisms. They express the native peculiarities of their peoples, in a broadly similar way – presumably because the people's soul (or at least its bourgeoisie) needs to.

However, it is not true that nationalism of any kind is really the product *of these internal motions as such*. This is the core of the empirical country-by-country fallacy which the ideology of nationalism itself wishes upon us. Welsh *nation-alism*, of course, has much to do with the specifics of the Welsh people, their history, their particular forms of oppression and all the rest of it. But Welsh national*ism* – that generic, universal necessity recorded in the very term we are interested in – has nothing to do with Wales. It is not a Welsh fact, but a fact of general developmental history, that at a specific time the Welsh land and people are forced into the historical process in this fashion. The 'ism' they are then compelled to follow is in reality imposed upon them from without; although of course to make this adaptation, it is necessary that the usual kinds of national cadres, myths, sentiments, etc., well up from within. All nationalisms work through a characteristic repertoire of social and personal mechanisms, many of them highly subjective. But the causation of the drama is not within the bosom of the *Volk*: this way lie the myths of blood and *Geist*. The subjectivity of nationalism is an important objective fact about it; but it is a fact which, in itself, merely reposes the question of origins.

The real origins are elsewhere. They are located not in the folk, nor in the individual's repressed passion for some sort of wholeness or identity, but in the machinery of world political economy. Not, however, in the process of that economy's development as such – not simply as an inevitable concomitant of industrialisation and urbanisation. They are associated with more specific features of that process. The best way of categorising these traits is to say they represent the *uneven development* of history since the 18th century. This unevenness is a material fact; one could argue that it is the most grossly material fact about modern history. This statement allows us to reach a satisfying and near-paradoxical conclusion: the most notoriously subjective and ideal of historical phenomena is in fact a by-product of the most brutally and hopelessly material side of the history of the last two centuries.

The Metropolitan Fantasy

Uneven development is the verbal opposite of even development. The opposition is verbal, not real, since all the actual 'development' human society has been forced through since the Industrial Revolution is uneven. Nevertheless, the notion and aspiration of even development is so powerful that we ought to start from it. It is, after all, close to being the nerve of a Western or 'Eurocentric' world-view the *Weltanschauung* which still tends to govern the way we think about history, and so (amongst other things) about nationalism. It is noticeable, for instance, that the mythology referred to previously is a way of pretending that nationalism is somehow part of an even, natural evolution of social events.

The idea of an even and progressive development of material civilisation and mass culture was characteristic of the European Enlightenment. It reflected a forward view natural to the élites of that time and place. Like their predecessors in eras of high culture they still thought in terms of civilisation versus 'barbarians' in the outer mists. But the new convictions of Progress made the outlook for the barbarians more favourable: given time, and help, they might catch up. This redemption was conceived of as a process of steady acculturation, both outwards and downwards. Outwards from the centre to these peripheric regions, and sociologically downwards, from the cultivated classes to the servants and labouring people.

Capitalism was to be a powerful instrument in this diffusion. As regards the nationality factor, Kant put it very clearly. The national divisions of mankind were an excellent thing in themselves: in Europe, for example, they had helped prevent the formation of a universal despotism, an Empire of the Eastern sort. In the future, it was middle-class trade which would ensure they did not get out of hand. 'The spirit of commerce, which is incompatible with war, sooner or later gains the upper hand in every State', he wrote, and 'the power of money' (which he thought the 'most dependable of all powers') will compel ruling classes to see sense. That is to get rid of their atavistic urges and make peace at all costs (*Perpetual Peace, a Philosophical Sketch*, 1795).

As we now know, the real developments implicit in the ideas and forces Kant was counting on were quite different. Nor could they possibly have been foreseen by the grand universalising tradition Kant represented, a tradition still Christian even in its new secular forms. In reality, the spirit of commerce and the power of money, as they invaded successive areas of the globe, would lead to the renewal of atavistic urges. They would produce an intensification of warfare. Instead of growing less significant *as* barriers, national divisions would be erected into a new and dominant principle of social organisation. History was to defeat the Western Philosophers.

The defeat has been permanent. This is perhaps the true, longer meaning of Marxism's 'failure' over the National Question. Unable to foresee the real contradictions of Progress, its catastrophic side, this tradition of thought has also thereafter found it consistently impossible to apprehend and digest the fact properly. In turn, this blind spot has consistently become the fertile source of all modern irrationalism. It is the complex of refractory, unassimilable phenomena linked to nationalism and its many derivatives (racism, anti-Semitism, etc.) which time and time again appeared to undermine and thoroughly discredit Western rationality. This opened the door to anti-rational and pessimistic philosophies – that *série noire* which has so closely counterpointed the march of Western Progress over the globe, and occasionally threatened to break it up for good.

The unforeseeable, antagonistic reality of capitalism's growth into the world is what the general title 'uneven development' refers to. It indicates the shambling, fighting, lop-sided, illogical, head-over-heels fact, so to speak, as distinct from the noble uplift and phased amelioration of the ideal. Modern capitalist development was launched by a number of West-European states which had accumulated the potential for doing so over a long period of history. The even-development notion was that this advance could be straightforwardly followed, and the institutions responsible for it copied – hence the periphery, the world's countryside, would catch up with the leaders in due time. This evening-up would proceed through the formation of a basically homogeneous enlightened class throughout the periphery: the international or 'cosmopolitan' élite in charge of the diffusion process. But no such steady diffusion or copying was in fact possible, and neither was the formation of this universal class (though there have been and are caricatural versions of it, in the shape of comprador bourgeoisies allying themselves to metropolitan capital instead of to their own people).

Instead, the impact of those leading countries was normally experienced as domination and invasion. The spirit of commerce was supposed to take over from the traditional forms of rapine and swindle. But in reality it could not. The gap was too great, and the new developmental forces were not in the hands of a beneficent, disinterested élite concerned with Humanity's advance. Rather, it was the 'sordid material interests' (as Marx and Engels relished saying) of the English and French bourgeois classes which were employing the concepts of the Enlightenment and classical political economy as a smokescreen. Even with the best will in the world (which they did not have), progress could not help identifying herself to some degree with these particular places, classes and interests. And in this way she could not help fomenting a new sort of 'imperialism'.

On the periphery itself, outside the core-areas of the new industrial-capitalist world economy, people soon needed little persuasion of this. They learned quickly enough that Progress in the abstract meant domination in the concrete, by powers which they could not help apprehending as foreign or alien. In practice as distinct from the theory, the acculturation process turned out to be more like a 'tidal wave' (in Ernest Gellner's phrase) of outside interference and control. Humanity's forward march signified in the first instance Anglicisation or Frenchification, for as long ahead as the people most conscious of the change could see. As was said later on, more globally: 'Westernisation' or 'Americanisation'.

There was never either time or the sociological space for even development. The new forces of production, and the new state and military powers associated with them, were too dynamic and uncontrolled, and the resultant social upheavals were far too rapid and devastating for any such gradual civilisation-process to take place. There was to be no 'due time' in modern history. All time was undue once the great shock-wave had begun its course. For those outside the metropolis (where in unique and unrepeatable circumstances things had matured slowly) the problem was not to assimilate culture at a reasonable rate: it was to avoid being drowned.

The Enlightenment was borne into wider reality by bourgeois revolutions which shook the older social world around them to pieces. In these less-developed lands the élites soon discovered that tranquil incorporation into the cosmopolitan technocracy was possible for only a few of them at a time. The others, the majority, saw themselves excluded from the action, rather than invited politely to join in; trampled over rather than taught the rules of the game; exploited rather than made partners. It was no consolation to be told that patience was in order, that things would even up in the next generation, or the one after that. Was this true at all? Would not the actual configuration of the new forces of change merely put the English even more firmly in charge of an even more un-Indian India; the Germans even more in control of second-class, Slav lands? True or not, the point came to seem academic. Given the violence and rapidity of the changes in act, patience and time were no longer human possibilities anyway.

The Necessary Resort to Populism

Huge expectations raced ahead of material progress itself. The peripheric élites had no option but to try and satisfy such demands by taking things into their own hands. 'Taking things into one's own hands' denotes a good deal of the substance of nationalism, of course. It meant that these classes – and later on some-times the masses beneath them, whom they felt responsible for – had to mobilise *against* 'progress' at the same time as they sought to improve their position in accordance with the new canons. They had to contest the concrete form in which (so to speak) progress had taken them by the throat, even as they set out to progress themselves. Since they wanted factories, parliaments, schools and so on, they had to copy the leaders somehow; but in a way which rejected the mere implantation of these things by direct foreign intervention or control. This gave rise to a profound ambiguity, an ambivalence which marks most forms of nationalism.

Unable to literally 'copy' the advanced lands (which would have entailed repeating the stages of slow growth that had led to the break-through), the backward regions were forced to take what they wanted and cobble it on to their own native inheritance of social forms. In the annals of this kind of theo-rizing the procedure is called 'uneven and combined development'. To defend themselves, the periphery countries were compelled to try and advance 'in their own way', to 'do it for themselves'. Their rulers – or at least the newly-awak-ened élites who now came to power – had to mobilise their societies for this historical short-cut. This meant the conscious formation of a militant, inter-class community rendered strongly (if mythically) aware of its own separate identity vis-a-vis the outside forces of domination. There was no other way of doing it. Mobilization had to be in terms of what was there; and the whole point of the dilemma was that there was nothing there – none of the economic and political institutions of modernity now so needed.

All that there *was* was the people and peculiarities of the region: its inherited *ethnos*, speech, folklore, skin-colour, and so on. Nationalism works through *differentiae* like those because it has to. It is not necessarily democratic in outlook, but it *is* invariably populist. People are what it has to go on: in the archetypal situation of the really poor or 'under-developed' territory, it may be more or less all that nationalists have going for them. For kindred reasons, it had to function through highly rhetorical forms, through a sentimental culture sufficiently acces-sible to the lower strata now being called to battle. This is why a romantic culture quite remote from Enlightenment rationalism always went hand-in-hand with the spread of nationalism. The new middle-class intelligentsia of nationalism had to invite the masses into history; and the invitation-card had to be written in a language they understood.

It is unnecessary here to explore the process in detail. Everyone is familiar with its outline, and with much of its content. We all know how it spread out from its West-European source, in concentric circles of upheaval and reaction:

through Central and Eastern Europe, Latin America, and then across the other continents. Uniformed imperialism of the 1880–1945 variety was one episode in this larger history, as were its derivatives, anti-colonial wars and 'de-colonisation'. We have all studied the phenomena so consistently accompanying it: the 're-discovery' or invention of national history, urban intellectuals invoking peasant virtues which they have experienced only through train windows on their summer holidays, schoolmasters painfully acquiring 'national' tongues spoken only in remote valleys, the infinity of forms assumed by the battle between scathing cosmopolitan modernists and emotional defenders of the Folk... and so on.

But before we go on, let me try to sum up this part of the argument. Real, uneven development has invariably generated an imperialism of the centre over the periphery; one after another, these peripheric areas have been forced into a profoundly ambivalent reaction against this dominance, seeking at once to resist it and to somehow take over its vital forces for their own use. This could only be done by a kind of highly 'idealist' political and ideological mobilisation, by a painful forced march based on their own resources: that is, employing their 'nationality' as a basis. The metropolitan fantasy of even development had predicted a swelling, single forward march that would induct backward lands into its course; in reality, these lands found themselves compelled to attempt radical, competitive short-cuts in order to avoid being trampled over or left behind. The logistics of these short-cuts brought in factors quite absent from the universalising philosophy of Progress. And since the greater part of the globe was to be forced into detours of this kind, these factors became dominant in the history of the world for a long period, one still not concluded.

In the traditional philosophical terminology, this amounts of course to a 'contradiction'. The contradiction here is that capitalism, even as it spread remorselessly over the world to unify human society into one more or less connected story for the first time, *also* engendered a perilous and convulsive new fragmentation of that society. The socio-historical cost of this rapid implantation of capitalism into world society was 'nationalism'. There was no other conceivable fashion in which the process could have occurred – not, that is, unless one resorts to the metropolitan fantasy of a gradual, secular, contradiction-free 'development' imagined in purely economic or statistical terms. It is a matter of everyday observation that apologists of developed-country Progress still do resort to arguments like this; and that the protagonists of under-developed country nationalisms still do passionately rebut them with talk about human nature, sturdy popular wisdom, and all the rest. The world market, world industries and world literature predicted with such exultation in *The Communist Manifesto* all conducted, in fact, to the world of nationalism. They were supposed to lead to a contradiction much more palatable to the Western-philosophical taste: that between social classes, a proletariat and a bourgeoisie essentially the same everywhere – two cosmopolitan classes, as it were, locked in the same battle from Birmingham to Shanghai.

The Anti-Imperialist Theory

It is only too easy to deduce from this picture a certain theory of nationalism. I will call this the anti-imperialist theory. It lays primary emphasis upon the successive waves of peripheric struggle, from the early nineteenth century up to the generalised Third World rebellion of the present day. And, of course, it views the phenomenon in a highly positive moral light. There may have been aberrations and excesses, but nationalism is mainly with the angels of progress. This point of view is given its most cogent expression at the end of Gellner's celebrated essay on nationalism. 'By and large this does seem a beneficent arrangement', he argues, because if the nationalist response to development had not occurred then imperialism would have simply intensified, and 'this politically united world might well come to resemble the present condition of South Africa…'.[1] The anti-imperialist theory is better than stories about demonic urges and irrepressible atavism. It does relate nationalism to the wider arc of historical development (in the way we saw was necessary), and it does encompass some of the mechanisms of that process. It combines a degree of theoretical consciousness with its strong practical and political impulse, the impulse of solidarity with the under-development struggles which are still proceeding over most of the globe. Yet it is really incorrect. In effect, it is a sort of compromise between historical materialism and common sense: between the much more ambiguous truth of nationalism and those mythologies I mentioned previously. As such, it renounces the difficult task of gripping both horns of the dilemma and – for the most sympathetic of motives – clings aggressively to one of them. In many cases (though not in Gellner's), it comes down to little more than a more sophisticated justification of romantic nationalism, now transformed into 'Third Worldism'.

The truth is less palatable. Anti-imperialist theory lets go of the real logic (or illogic) of uneven development, because it lets go of the totality of the process. It forgets or disguises for its own purposes what the central drive, the main dynamic of this whole contradictory movement has been. That is, the irresistible and transforming impact of the developed upon the under-developed, of the core-areas upon the world's countryside. Nationalisms do 'resist' the impact, true, and with some success – but only to be transformed themselves, as they adopt the forces which attacked them. And this whole pattern of resistances could not avoid changing and informing the entire developmental process – it could not help making nationalism a kind of world norm, a standard for the advanced and industrialised countries as well as for the awakening ones.

From the very outset, part of the 'superiority' of the development leaders lay in their political and state systems. It lay in the fact that they had invented the national state, the real proto-type of the national*ist* ideal, by quite empirical processes extending over many centuries. They discovered and proved its power

---

1   Ernest Gellner, *Thought and Change*, London 1964, pp. 177–8.

long before nationalism had been formulated as the general, systemic response to that power's incursions throughout the world. When it came, that response could not help being highly over-determined ideologically.

In this general sense, nationalism was obviously generated as a compensatory reaction on the periphery. Its ideal intensification corresponded to the absence of a material reality: the economic and social institutions of modernity, those developmental arms now being wielded with such effect by England, France and later on by the other territories that achieved them. It was the absence of these arms, and despair about getting them, which made the compensating ideological weapon of nationalism a necessity: the idealist motor of the forced march out of backwardness or dependency.

Hence, as the most basic graph of nationalist history will demonstrate, the ideology has always been produced on the periphery (or at least, by people thinking about its dilemmas, whether they are themselves in it or not). The *locus classicus* was in Germany and Italy, during the era when these were march-lands endeavouring to re-order themselves to face the threat from the West. And the rhetoric and doctrine of nationalism have been constantly re-formulated and replenished by spokesmen of the periphery ever since, up to the time of Amilcar Cabral and Che Guevara. The power and omnipresence of this ideology require no emphasis here.

However, this very influence has also meant that the ideological dimension of nationalism has always loomed too large in reflection about the phenomenon. There is a distinct sense in which this dimension has been far *too* important for theorists. The point is that the ideological over-determination is itself a forced response, and what forces it is a material dilemma – the crudest dilemma of modern history. That is, 'underdevelopment', the fact of not having and the awareness of this intolerable absence.

But then, this being true, something else follows. The march-lands and the countryside may have formulated the ideology of nationalism. In the nature of things, it was unlikely to be they who translated this rhetoric into fully-functioning reality. They did not have the power to do so: this is the entire *material* point of the dilemma around which nationalisms revolve. On the contrary, once the advanced states and economies took over the doctrines of 'nationalism' they were certain to give these ideas real muscle. England and France and the United States did not invent 'nationalism'; they did not need to, originally. They were in front, and possessed the things nationalism is really about (as distinct from the things its ideology displays). The Enlightenment and classical political economy were great statements about being in front. But – precisely – statements of a type utterly different from what came into fashion with the age of nationalism.

'Uneven development' is not just the hard-luck tale of poor countries. It dragged the wealthy ones in as well. Once the national state had been ideologised into 'nationalism' and turned into the new climate of world politics – the new received truth of political humanity – the core-areas themselves were bound to become nationalist. As the march-lands caught up in the later 19th century, as Germany, Italy and Japan emerged into the extra-rapid industrialisation made possible by their 'revolutions from above', was it surprising that England and France developed their own forms of 'nationalism'? There resulted a struggle between founder-members and *parvenus*, where great-power nationalism was forged from the new notions and sentiments. Forged, naturally, with far greater efficacy than on the periphery, for the simple reason that these societies had the media and the abundant human and material resources to do so.

In other words, 'uneven development' is a dialectic. The two sides involved continuously modify each other. Nationalism may have originated as a kind of 'antithesis' to the 'thesis' of metropolitan domination. But it was rapidly, and inevitably, transmitted to the whole process. However, the term 'dialectic' should not be allowed to mislead us any more than the inebriants of romantic-nationalist ideology. It does *not* mean (as Gramsci once put it) that history is a boxing-match with rules, where we can be secretly sure what kind of 'synthesis' is going to emerge. In the quite un-Hegelian reality, for which 'uneven development' is merely an approximate label, there has never been any certainty as to who would win. As a matter of fact, the 'antithesis' came near to destroying the 'thesis' altogether; and the states denoted by the latter term only won in 1945–6 by the development of powers so enormous as to threaten the annihilation of historical humanity itself. It is not impossible that in some later stage of the same struggle they will be employed.

Nationalism and the Irrational

'Uneven development' is a politely academic way of saying 'war'. The process it refers to is warfare – that 'development war' (as one might call it) which has been fought out consistently since the irruption of the great bourgeois revolutions. The causes which disproved Kant's predictions about national divisions also disappointed his dream of a Perpetual Peace. For much of the time, naturally, the struggle has been conducted in socio-economic or diplomatic terms. But this essentially conflictual process has always tended towards real warfare. And we all know, it is the simplest matter of historical fact, that from the Franco-Prussian war to the present day, modern history has degenerated into military conflicts of a type and scale unimaginable previously. Instead of the social revolutions forecast by the men of the 1840s, there have been World Wars. Instead of civil strife, there has been imperialist and nationalist slaughter; and the social revolutions which have occurred have done so as by-products of these wars – so intertwined with nationalist motifs as to have a sense quite different from the one envisaged by Marxist universalism.

In this world at war, it is absurd to award 'nationalism' a sort of patented right on one side. This moralising perspective not only prevents one from grasping the importance of great-power nationalism in the unfolding of the whole process. It fatally impedes one's view of what must be considered a central sector of the phenomenon: fascism. Beyond this, it deforms any theoretical effort to approach the problem of nationalism's so-called 'irrationality'.

I pointed out already that core-area nationalism was, in the long run, as inevitable as peripheric nationalism; but likely to be more effective. The most potent versions of all were to be found in a distinct location within the larger history we are analysing. That is, in nationalities which to some degree combined both factors: a painful experience and fear of 'under-development', *and* modern socio-economic institutions enabling them to mobilise and indoctrinate their masses effectively.

There is no doubt where this explosive combination was found: in the notorious 'late developers' of this century's history. What were the factors that Germany, Italy and Japan combined together in the trajectories which made them the Axis Powers of 1939–45? All three were societies with a relatively recent experience of 'backwardness' – a deprivation and impotence suddenly made humiliatingly evident to them by the impact of outside powers. All three reacted to this dilemma with particularly strong, compensatory ideological mechanisms – mechanisms which, as far as the two Western members are concerned, comprise virtually the whole panoply of nationalist beliefs and sentiments. Then they rapidly evolved some of the real substance of nation-state power through break-neck industrialisation and State-imposed societal regimentation. Their capacity to do this arose, of course, from their general position in the world political economy: they were not in the real periphery, and occupied an intermediate place between it and the centre – the march-lands or semi-periphery of the process.

In this way these societies were able to realise the ideology of 'nationalism' with unprecedented force. How effective this embodiment was would be shown by the subordination of the German working class – once the vanguard, the great hope of European socialism – to Hitler. However, in spite of these successes, the late-comers' position remained precarious. In the first half of this century all three were confronted with the fact, or the immediate likelihood, of breakdown. For all of them this implied relegation: permanent confinement to the secondary, semi-peripheric status, exclusion from the core-area's 'place in the sun'. Physical or moral defeat, the menace of internal collapse, or (as they saw it) continued or renewed aggression by the central imperial powers – these were the motives that impelled them into a still more intensive form of nationalist mobilisation. It is not surprising that the country weakest in those real developmental factors I indicated, Italy, should at this point have generated the especially strong and influential 'ideological' response of the first fascist movement. Nor that this ideology should have been rapidly appropriated and turned into effective power by the late-developer with the real sinews of imperialist force, Germany.

What counts in the present argument is a simple recognition of fact. It was these countries, that location in the uneven-development process, which engendered the full historical potential of 'nationalism'. In a perfectly recognisable sense, it was here that nationalism was carried to its 'logical conclusion', as an autonomous mode of socio-political organisation. To theorise about nationalism without seeing this is worse than Hamlet without the Prince of Denmark. Nationalism is such a Protean phenomenon, it informs modern history to such a large extent, that one may of course maintain there is no such thing as an 'archetype' for it, no one single form which displays its meaning. Still, if forced to pick out one specimen in a compressed history lesson for some inter-galactic visitor, one would have little choice. Seen in sufficient historical depth, fascism tells us far more about nationalism than any other episode.

There is a larger theoretical issue behind this. As I said earlier, nationalist folklore has an easy answer about the more evidently disastrous aspects of modern history: they represent accidental aberrations or excesses. The anti-imperialist mythology adds something to this. For it, these catastrophes arise from the appropriation of nationalism by the imperialists and its abuse. Great-power chauvinism, or 'reactionary nationalism', is a metropolitan ruling-class conspiracy that borrows the ideas and feelings of the world's national-liberation struggles and employs them to dupe the proletariat. Regrettably, this often seems to work.

So, there are two kinds of nationalism. The main, essentially healthy sort we applaud in Indo-China and Mozambique; and the derivative, degenerate sort we oppose in, for example, the American working class, Gaullism, the Chilean *Junta* and so on. It is this difference which explains the 'irrationality' of some nationalist phenomena. While the mainspring of nationalism is progressive, these abusive versions of it are regressive, and tend towards the encouragement of social and psychological atavism, the exploitation of senseless fears and prejudices, and so towards violence.

Without for a moment denying that these political and moral distinctions are justified, and indeed obvious, one is none the less forced to point out that the *theoretical* dimension attaching to them is quite mistaken. The distinctions do not imply the existence of two brands of nationalism, one healthy and one morbid. The point is that, as the most elementary comparative analysis will show, all nationalism is both healthy and morbid. Both progress and regress are inscribed in its genetic code from the start. This is a structural fact about it. And it is a fact to which there are no exceptions: in this sense, it is an exact (not a rhetorical) statement about nationalism to say that it is by nature ambivalent.

The Collective Unconscious

This ambiguity merely expresses the general historical *raison d'être* of the phenomenon. Which is the fact that it is through nationalism that societies try to propel themselves forward to certain kinds of goal (industrialisation, prosperity, equality with other peoples, etc.) *by a certain sort of regression* – by looking inwards, drawing more deeply upon their indigenous resources, resurrecting past folk-heroes and myths about themselves and so on. These idealistic and romantic well-springs adhere to every form of nationalism. It is a perfectly banal fact about nationalist history that such soul-searching quite easily becomes sheer invention, where legends take the place of myths. Indeed, this fabrication of an imaginary past was a prominent feature of that original 'progressive' national-liberation struggle, the Greek War of Independence of the 1820s.

Again, this is emphatically not to say that all forms of nationalism are as good, or as bad, as one another. It *is* to say that the huge family of nationalisms cannot be divided into the black cats and the white cats, with a few half-breeds in between. The whole family is spotted, without exception. Forms of 'irrationality' (prejudice, sentimentality, collective egotism, aggression, etc.) stain the lot of them. Hence, while we must, of course, distinguish among different national movements and ideologies to make any kind of political sense of history, these judgements do not really mark out one sort of nationalism from another. They repose upon different criteria: for instance, the supposed class character of the society in question, or its supposed rôle in the unfolding of international relations.

In short, the substance of nationalism as such is always morally, politically, humanly ambiguous. This is why moralising perspectives on the phenomenon always fail, whether they praise or berate it. They simply seize upon one face or another of the creature, and will not admit that there is a common head conjoining them. But nationalism can in this sense be pictured as like the old Roman god, Janus, who stood above gateways with one face looking forward and one backwards. Thus does nationalism stand over the passage to modernity, for human society. As human kind is forced through its strait doorway, it must look desperately back into the past, to gather strength wherever it can be found for the ordeal of 'development'.

This is also the situation which helps us understand why, in a quite general sense, the 'irrational' could not help arising into the process. Because, so far from being a 'natural' growth-phase, this is a *rite de passage* so terrible, so enforced by outside power, so fiercely destructive of all custom and tradition that there could never in the nature of things be any guarantee it would succeed. Let me put this in terms of a personalised metaphor. In mobilising its past in order to leap forward across this threshold, a society is like a man who has to call on all his inherited and (up to this point) largely unconscious powers to confront some inescapable challenge. He summons up such latent energies assuming that, once the challenge is met, they will subside again into a tolerable and settled pattern of personal existence.

But the assumption may be wrong. In the social trauma as in the individual one, once these well-springs have been tapped there is no real guarantee that the great forces released will be 'controllable' (in the sense of doing only what they are supposed to do, and no more). The powers of the Id are far greater than was realised before Freud exposed them to theoretical view. In the same way, the energies contained in customary social structures were far greater than was understood, before the advent of nationalist mobilisation stirred them up and released them from the old mould. Unfortunately Marxism – which should have accomplished a 'Freudian' analysis of the historical case, and still must do so – remained on the level of myth and guesswork here.

Extreme difficulties and contradictions, the prospect of breakdown or being held forever in the gateway – it is conditions like those, surely, which may lead to insanity for an individual or nationalist dementia for a society. Given the colossal strains of industrialization, and the variety and intensity of forces which this challenge unchained into more conscious activity, there is *in a general sense* nothing amazing about the emergence of irrationality in modern history. It would have been really amazing had there been *no* temporary triumphs of the anti-Enlightenment like Nazi Germany. But the forces behind its imperialism and genocide were 'demonic' only in a manner of speaking. To be exact, in the manner of speaking of those unable, or perhaps sometimes rather unwilling, to locate them intelligibly within the general framework of modern developmental history. It was easier to pretend the Germans had been assailed by some a-historical propensity – a natural (or even supernatural) *Geist*.

I cannot refrain from at least mentioning the alternative superstition now more common, though only *en passant*. If one rejects the *Doktor Faustus* mythology then it becomes hard to deny that fascism and genocide are somehow part of the 'logic' of modern history. Then it becomes all too easy to assert that they *are* the logic of modern history. That is, modern capitalist institutions, even industry and democracy as such, are all intrinsically fascistoid and evil: the totalitarian nationalist states of the 1930s show where we are all heading. There is no call to say more about this here. As a sort of lay diabolism, I suppose it must be considered one of the odder by-products of the defeat of Western Philosophy by nationalism.

Nation Triumphs Over Class

I have said nothing about the sacrosanct subject of class so far. This has been deliberate, of course. In any materialistic approach to a problem like this, one does not only find the road blocked by the abundant mythology of common sense; Marxism has its own cottage industry working away. We have our own half-truths, our own garbled ideology, our own glib evasions to distinguish us from the common herd. And our speciality has always been 'class'.

As I said before, the bourgeois Enlightenment had its own comforters in this field. The *philosophes* thought that war and blind patriotism were by-products of the rule of the landowning classes. Dynasties were supposed to have a vested interest in conquest and bloodshed. It was they who maintained the archaisms and irrationalities of human life in being – so, get rid of aristocracy and this would wither away also. Feudalism would be replaced by the rule of a genuinely universal class, a class whose interests coincided with those of humanity in general: the bourgeoisie. As Kant said, *this* class's vested interest seemed to be promoting peace and lowering barriers among peoples, in the name of economic and cultural development.

The radicals who lived into the earlier stages of this promised land, and realised that it was going to be extremely different from the blueprints, quickly formulated a new edition of the idea. The middle classes were far less than 'universal' in their interest. They too had an inescapable stake in chaos and warfare; indeed this would get worse, if only because of the superior means of destruction science now made possible. So nationalism became 'bourgeois nationalism': and it followed that if only one got rid of this class and its forms of economic and social organisation, then nationalism too would disappear. Again, narrow folly and blind sub-rational instincts were kept alive and fed by those forms. Once the class whose aims really *were* consonant with those of humanity, the proletariat, acquired power then chauvinism would no longer have any *raison d'être*.

Naturally, the myth was modified later on. Narrow folly and revived archaism proved so popular that it had to be. It was diluted down into uncertain compromises of the sort that infuriated Rosa Luxemburg. Mass nationalism was good up to a point, in certain specific conditions, in the fight against alien oppression, and so on. Beyond that point it immediately degenerated again into a morbid delusion and an instrument of bourgeois reaction. In effect, the essence of the myth was saved by tactical retreats and manoeuvres. Lenin was the most brilliant exponent of these.

The basis of the belief here being defended was that class is far more important in history than the petty *differentiae* nationalism seems to deal in. Class struggle was the motor of historical advance, not nationality. Hence, it was literally inconceivable that the former should be eclipsed by the latter. Exceptions to the rule demanded exceptional explanations – conspiracy theories about the rulers, and 'rotten minority' speculations about the ruled. Finally, these exceptions blotted out the sun in August 1914.

I suppose this ought to have led to a radical investigation into what was wrong with Marxism's theory of history. But it did not, for reasons I hinted at earlier and cannot explore further here. Instead, after the revolution in Russia, the Third International engendered what was really an extreme intensification of the myths: internationalism had failed through lack of will-power and organisation – for subjective reasons. The conspiracies and rotten apples had not been exposed and fought with enough determination. Had they been (the implication was) then the factors of class might well have triumphed over those of national division, there might have been a great social revolution instead of the war. This was the patched-up mythology with which Marxism moved towards its encounter with the fascist revolutions of the '20s and '30s.

When an ideology is preserved and defended with such intensity, against such enormous odds and evidence, it can only be because what is protected is felt as of incalculable worth. What was at stake in this long defensive battle was, clearly, Marxism's conviction of being the true heir to the positive or universal aspects of the Enlightenment. Unable yet to come to terms with the new world of nationalist development, Marxism clung with all the greater determination, with a practically religious faith, to this basic part of its creed. 'National frontiers have long been anachronistic for capitalism itself...': in the last century, how many exercises in justification have started or ended with these words!

It must be obvious from the tenor of these remarks that I share the conviction which always lay behind all this mass of sophisms. Socialism, whose intellect and heart lies more in the Marxist tradition than anywhere else, *is* the heir of the Enlightenment. The defensive battle was right, in spite of all its obscurantism and piety. Socialism was a premature birth. So far from being 'ripe' (or even 'over-ripe') for it, as its protagonists told themselves, conditions in the earlier half of this century were to remain locked in the vice of primitive, uneven development and nationalism. Hence, the faith could probably only have been defended in this way.

It does not in any sense detract from the honour of that fight, or from the ultimate value of what is protected, to point out that it involved theoretical errors. The main such error concerned class. A defective grasp of the overall nature and depth of capitalist development implied certain mistakes. It meant that it was not yet possible to employ the concepts of historical materialism in relation to their proper object, the only object which gives them genuine meaning: that is, the world political economy. This is the only genuine 'structure' which can be held to explain the assorted 'superstructures' of capitalist reality (including nationalism). The lacuna was only very partially remedied by the Marxist theory of imperialism, and the initial use this made of the notion of uneven development.

The Dominant Contradiction

Unable to perceive the dominant contradiction of capitalism's growth into the world *as* dominant, Marxism insisted it represented a chain of accidents. The real, basic contradiction still at work everywhere was, therefore, the class struggle. The more hidden it appeared to be, the more it was necessary to insist. The cloud of accidents was always on the point of dispersal. The social struggle was always just about to shed its irrelevant national or patriotic form and let the universal meaning show through.

There is no need here to explain the elements of exorcism and bad faith in all this. No need either to show how such attitudes colluded (as they really could not help doing) with the nationalism of the era, by counter-posing quite abstract internationalism to a pragmatic support of nationalist struggles and wars over half the planet. This is not past history. It can be studied fairly exhaustively by anybody who can read a newspaper.

In the present context it is more important to say something about the underlying theoretical issue. The story of uneven development is one of how the primary contradiction I have tried to outline has enveloped and repressed the secondary antagonism upon which Marxism laid such stress: the class struggle. As capitalism spread, and smashed the ancient social formations surrounding it, these always tended to fall apart along the fault-lines contained inside them. It is a matter of elementary truth that these lines of fissure were nearly always ones of nationality (although in certain well-known cases deeply established religious divisions could perform the same function). They were never ones of class. Naturally, in innumerable cases the two things were inextricably confused, where an upper class of one nationality ruled over peasants and workers of another. But the point is that the confusion could only be regulated in terms of nationality, not in terms of class. As a means of mobilisation, nationalism was simply incomparably superior to what was contained in a still rudimentary (often, one should say, a merely nascent) class consciousness.

The superiority was not accidental – a sort of unfair advantage temporarily won here and there, but soon to recede before the truth. It derived from the very structure of those 'modern' societies cast out of uneven development. There was never any chance of the new universal class which figured in Marxist doctrine emerging *as* 'proletarians', rather than as 'Germans', 'Cubans', 'Irishmen' and so on. The most serious difficulty the new western philosophers faced here was something entailed by this fact.

There is, after all, a sense in which it is manifestly true to say that class is crucial to an understanding of nationalism. Nationalist regimentation was to a very large extent determined in its actual form and content by the class nature of the societies it affected. Their social stratification posed certain problems which it had no alternative but to solve; and the 'solution' lies in the crudity, the emotionalism, the vulgar populism, the highly-coloured romanticism of most nationalist ideology (all the things intellectuals have always held their noses at). So what is actually being exorcised by the draconian insistence that class is more significant than nationality is a larger maleficent spirit than appears at first sight. It is, if you like, the fact that the 'solution' worked.

Nationalism could only have worked, in this sense, because it actually did provide the masses with something real and important – something that class consciousness could never have furnished, a culture which however deplorable was larger, more accessible, and more relevant to mass realities than the rationalism of our Enlightenment inheritance. If this is so, then it cannot be true that nationalism is just false consciousness. It must have had a functionality in modern development, perhaps one more important than that of class consciousness and formation within the individual nation-states of this period.

Marxists (and other internationalists) have the old way out of this dilemma, I know. It can be deduced from the central myth-store we have dipped into several times already. But of course – it can be repeated, in the tone of down-to-earth heartiness appropriate for unbearable contradictions like this – any fool knows that the struggle of the proletariat is in the first instance against its own national bourgeoisie, and is, to that extent, itself national (*Communist Manifesto*). So *of course* workers are first of all Germans, Cubans, etc., nor will they cease to be so at the Last Trump. There is no real contradiction between the attributes of nationality and those of proletarian or socialist internationalism: the former is only a phase on the way to the latter (etc.).

This is where the bite is. What these rotund platitudes exorcise is the truth that there *is* such a contradiction. Under the actual conditions of capitalism's uneven development, with the actual frontier-delimited class consciousness which that process threw up, there is a deadly contradiction at work. Had 'even development' taken place in the world, then presumably national awareness would have evolved also, as peoples became literate and politically conscious; and presumably this would have been the placid, non-antagonistic awareness, the 'natural' fact which still haunts the mythology of the subject – that should-have-been history which to a surprising extent still governs reflection on what there has been and is. In the world of national*ism* things are different. Its war-like circumstances constantly engender real antagonisms between nationality and class. And in these conflicts – as long as the primary contradiction of the world economy dominates it – the position of nationality will remain stronger.

At this point let me return to the original suggestion I made. That is, to the idea that the 'failure' of Marxism over this problem was inevitable, not an unfortunate accident which could have been overcome by trying harder.

The inevitability lay in the fact that, during the era when Marxists struggled most desperately and brilliantly with the enigma – before the onset of Stalinism – the general process of capitalist development had not gone far enough. The overall characteristics of 'uneven development' had not yet been sufficiently delineated by history itself. Only partially aware of this emerging framework, socialists continued to believe they were living in the Latter Days of capitalism's progress. Their conviction remained that the process *would* straighten out and become more logical, sooner rather than later. A great social revolution where it ought to occur in the developed heartland, would ensure this – thus restoring the basis for even development, and vindicating western philosophy in its Marxist variant.

It took the great fracture of 1914 to begin to destroy the conviction. And this was only the start of the demolition process. After the war itself came the renewed failure of revolutionary class struggle in the west, the eruption of fascism in its stead, and still another imperialist Armageddon. Ever more clearly, socialism became the main ideological arm for the forced march of a whole new range of under-developed territories. It fused effectively with their new nationalism, rather than with the class-consciousness of workers in the developed countries. As uniformed imperialism was swept away by the generalised revolt in the Third World, the cumulative sense of uneven development began to become clearer.

Only then, perhaps – i.e. only in the past decade or so – has it become more possible to perceive the general outline and structure of the process. Until it had really extended everywhere on the globe and reached even the remotest areas of Africa and Asia (as it is now doing), the possibility remained an abstract one. But today the 'end' (in one sense) of development has begun to render it concrete. Capitalism has indeed unified humanity's history and made the world one. But it has done so at the cost of fantastic disequilibria, through near-catastrophic antagonisms and a process of socio-political fragmentation (numbering 154 states at the latest count) still far from complete. The momentum of the conflictual phenomena denoted by 'uneven development' has so far proved greater than the other, more unitary and rational tendencies of capitalism's growth. They and all their ambiguous progeny have become lodged in the resultant global order. Those national frontiers that have been 'anachronistic' since an early stage of capitalist expansion continue to multiply. In the 1970s there has even reappeared some likelihood of new barriers inside some of the oldest, most stably unified states of western Europe: France, the United Kingdom and Spain.

But there is a consolation in this picture for the theorist. For it is in admitting and looking at it more steadily that it does, at least, become possible to get some bearings on the question of nationalism. It is in relation to this framework that a better theoretical orientation towards the phenomenon may arise. One can start locating and defining it more clearly – because there is, at last, a more settled and inescapable landscape which it can be related to. We can at least glimpse something of the forest – it might be more accurate to say the jungle – and of those wider, outer conditions which have precipitated its fierce internal growths.

Nationalism and Philosophy

The task of making such a plausible theoretical definition is of course a huge one. I am not trying to do this here, only to indicate in the scantest outline how it might be done. Even among the few signposts I have sketched in there are great gaps I can only refer to *en passant*.

For example, I have said nothing about the economics of uneven development, a topic essential from the point of view of historical materialism. There is little I can do to remedy this omission here, except mention some notable contributions to it, like those of Arghiri Emmanuel and Samir Amin.[2] Nor is there time to even touch upon the problem of socialism's place in the dialectic of unbalanced development, although this also is a key topic in any effort to grasp the process as a whole. One might say, for example, that the displacement of socialism from metropolis to periphery has been in many ways the most significant sign of the triumph of uneven development. Of all the weird mixtures and alliances

2   Arghiri Emmanuel, Unequal Exchange, NLB, London 1971; Samir Amin, Le développement inégale, Paris 1973.

engendered by 'combined development' – the direct transference of advanced ideas or techniques into under-developed lands – this may be the most important. Nationalism defeated socialism in the zone of high development, forcing it outwards into successive areas of backwardness where it was bound to become part of their great compensatory drive to catch up – an ideology of development or industrialisation, rather than one of post-capitalist society. In this position within the world economy, it has of course become a subordinate ally of nationalism. Yet this defeat has also implied the worldwide diffusion of socialism, at a tempo far more rapid than that imagined by the founding fathers – it has meant that capitalism could not, finally, unify the world wholly in its own image. Even in its American age of unprecedented prosperity and power after the Second World War, it was forced to confront its own end from a direction quite different than the one envisaged by theorists of even development.

As I say, the task of framing a 'theory' of nationalism is that of understanding the destructive mechanisms and contradictions of uneven development – and this, in turn, is the task of re-interpreting modern history as a whole. In this sense the puzzle of Marxism's 'failure' over nationalism is simple: the problem is so central, so large, and so intimately related to other issues that it could not be focussed on properly before. History itself is now helping us towards a solution. It would be presumptuous and unnecessary to say much more about the problematic itself here.

But there are certain wider, more philosophical implications of it which may be briefly mentioned. The most striking of these concerns the ancient, archetypal opposition of idealism and materialism. It is not quite true that the real subject of modern philosophy is industrialization (as Gellner has said). But I think it is true that the real basis of philosophical speculation is the complex of issues surrounding economic development: more or less those indicated previously, uneven development and all its implications of nationalism, 'irrationalism', inescapable ambivalence, and so on. In this context it is important to note some things about the way reality now re-presents itself.

It is not true that the conception of nationalism outlined earlier is reductionist in character. It does not wish or think away the phenomena in question (political romanticism, the idealism of under-development, subjectivism, the need to 'belong', etc.) by asserting that these are merely manifestations of economic trends. It does exactly the opposite. It awards them a real force and weight in modern historical development – one quite distinct from the groanings of metaphysical irrationalism – by explaining the material reasons for this newly-acquired leverage. It locates them in relation to the material dilemmas of backwardness, and so makes of them an objective fact, not a demonic mystery; but the objective facts of nationalist passion, the awakened mass of modern instincts, and the organisation of these into total or racial warfare have their own decisive impetus. To show they are the other face of capitalism's invasion of our world does not entail their demotion to mere appearance or epiphenomenon.

'Materialism' in this sense does not indicate a mechanical or metaphysical pseudo-explanation of what we have been talking about. It does not indicate another battle in an ancient philosophical war which (precisely because of its 'philosophical' character) can never be won or lost. Rather, it points the way towards leaving this war behind. It is the 'real' or historical explanation which enables us to understand the modern war of words – that is, the inability of 'Marxism' to escape from the level of philosophy in the past, its own erection into the aberrant philosophy of 'dialectical materialism', and the consequent renaissances of philosophical idealism.

In discussing the question of irrationalism earlier, I suggested that Freud's mode of explanation was in some ways applicable. Let me extend this analogy a little. To say that the assorted phenomena and bric-a-brac of nationalism have a 'material' basis and explanation is akin to saying that individual neurosis has a sexual explanation. We all know the generations of indignant evasion which have now gone into denying and disguising the latter theory (degrading, reductionist, undervaluing consciousness, etc., etc.). These evasions were largely ideological misunderstandings of Freud. His theory does not really 'dismiss' the higher things of human consciousness at all: it enables us to appreciate their genuine weight, their true function in the individual's history, by relating them to the unconscious and buried segments of that history – to the underlying, forced dilemmas of personal development which have been willy-nilly 'solved' in neurosis. Following the metaphor in our own terms, one might say: 'nationalism' is the pathology of modern developmental history, as inescapable as 'neurosis' in the individual, with much the same essential ambiguity attaching to it, a similar built-in capacity for descent into dementia, rooted in the dilemmas of helplessness thrust upon most of the world (the equivalent of infantilism for societies), and largely incurable. Socialism over a sufficiently large part of the world *may* represent the necessary condition for a cure one day. But this is hazardous speculation.

The Angel of History

The failure I have been talking about has always engendered pessimism in the West, as well as regurgitations of Hegel and Spinoza. These philosophies of defeat and anguish increasingly informed western Marxism after the First World War. Their most impressive and sophisticated formulation was of course that given by the Frankfurt School. Theodor Adorno's *Minima Moralia* is the masterpiece of this dark intelligence: with its reflections on life in the United States, it also provides the most interesting connection with the great revival that Frankfurtism is now enjoying there. But the single most extraordinary image of their world-view (which I make no apology for quoting once more here) was Walter Benjamin's angel of history: 'His face is turned towards the past. Where we perceive a chain of events, he sees one single catastrophe which keeps piling wreckage upon wreckage and hurls it in front of his feet. The angel would like to stay, awaken the dead, and make whole what has been smashed. But a storm is blowing from Paradise; it has got caught in his wings with such violence that the angel can no longer close them. This storm irresistibly propels him into the future to which his back is turned, while the pile of debris before him grows skyward. This storm is what we call progress.'[3]

In the last quarter of Benjamin's century, the storm has blown into the most remote areas of the world. Beyond the wreckage it has aroused the great counter-force of anti-imperialist struggle. But – as I suggested before – the theoretical truth of the angel's strange trajectory does not lie only here. The terror of his vision comes from the whole process of which Third World nationalism is a part, from the original west-wind of progress as well as the multiform reactions it has produced in the east and the south. The defeat suffered by imperialism was a precondition of philosophical advance, but only a precondition.

In that advance itself, what was 'Marxism' must become for the first time an authentic world-theory. That is, a theoretical worldview (the successor of religion and philosophy) which is actually founded upon the social development of the whole world. This is the meaning to be attached to a statement I made earlier on, concerning Marxism and historical materialism. In itself the announcement of the umpteenth forthcoming transcendence of Marxism into something else would be meaningless. Has a month passed since 1890 without the solemn announcement of this quasi-divine rebirth? But philosophy alone would never have accomplished this act. It is history itself which has slowly created the real, new conditions for the change I am referring to. And it is these conditions which in turn allow us a better understanding of historical fate, and prepare the way for theoretical reformulations upon a basis far sounder than those of the past.

It is in dealing with the enigma of nationalism that 'Marxism' is inexorably thrust against the limits of its own western origins, its Eurocentric nature. Yet it could never overcome these limits in theory, until they had been thoroughly undermined and broken down in practice – that is, by the events of the past decades, where the reflorescence of western capitalism was accompanied by its persistent defeat and degeneration on the periphery. It is in this sense perhaps much less fanciful than may appear at first glance to suggest that the years that witnessed the end of the great struggle in Indo-China, the oil-producers' revolt and the revolution in Portugal will appear in retrospect to mark a turning-point in the history of ideas, as well as in American foreign policy or international relations.

What actual course will the thought of historical materialism follow, as it tries to build beyond these over-narrow Enlightenment foundations? In seeking a stronger and worldwide basis (as distinct from claiming it in the abstract, as Marxism always did) it would seem to follow from the argument advanced above that an essential step must be a return to sources. That is, to the real historical sources of Benjamin's single catastrophe, the home of the wind that has propelled

3   Walter Benjamin, *Illuminations*, London 1970, p. 259.

us so far and so erratically. This means the history of western-founded 'progress'. It is only now that a distinctively non-occidento-centric version of this story is becoming possible, a version which will be something like the world's picture of modern development – a picture in which the Enlightenment, and the bourgeois and industrial revolutions of the West figure as episodes, however important.

This reflection permits me to try and situate the theory I have been schematically outlining for you. It should be seen as belonging within the same broad current of thinking as – to take the most evident examples – Immanuel Wallerstein's *The Modern World System* and Perry Anderson's *Passages from Antiquity* and *Lineages of the Absolutist State*. These are works by scholars originally concerned with Third World questions, impelled subsequently to a general re-interpretation of the origins of capitalist development itself. They do not arise from Eurocentrism but from the reaction against Euro-centrism – a reaction which has, nonetheless, the achievement of a better understanding of the European sources of modern development as one of its main responsibilities. In dealing with nationalism, we have of course been examining later stages of the process, the colossal chain-reaction set up by the fuller impact of the West upon the body of older world society in the later 19th and 20th centuries. But this is recognisably part of the same broader task.

The 'sources' referred to in this conception are different from what has normally hitherto been meant by the term in the polemics of Marxism. They do not lie within Marxism itself, as a system of doctrine and belief. The movement of thought in question is outward-going, not inward-looking. It is a motion made possible by the new matter of history itself – a reflection of that matter, therefore, and not the expression of our own iconoclastic will, of a more intensive meditation upon ideas and data already in existence. It is for this reason that it cannot assume the form typical of so many past 'revisions' and counter-revisions in Marxist history – that is, prescient re-readings of texts, more rigorous and unassailable editions of old concepts.

I do not mean to imply that the internal re-exploration of our thoughtworld is futile, or uninstructive. This would be to dismiss too much of the French Marxism of the past decade as worthless. It is reasonably obvious that such re-exploration should accompany and complement the *external*, historical critique of Marxism. The two tasks ought to be one. The problems connected with what Marx and his disciples 'really meant' by their ideas and actions should issue into the consideration of what these actually did mean, as the actions of distinct generations of intellectuals in determinate historical circumstances. But the dilemma consists in where one puts the centre of gravity. If it is placed internally, the result is bound to be the perpetuation of sectarian theology in some form, however refined. This is the main, indispensable commodity in Marxism's corner of the world market in ideas, and there are bound to be buyers. If by contrast one's primary focus is external, and perceives one time-bound (though still unconcluded) chapter in the history of ideas, then the exegesis of ideas is serving a different purpose altogether.

I do not know what that purpose is. Like everyone else my back is turned to the future, and like most others I am chiefly conscious of the debris reaching skywards. However, there is no point in fabricating new totems for history to hurl in front of our feet after desacralising the old ones. This is not a pessimistic stance, though I suppose there is a degree of wilful disenchantment about it: I would like to believe that it is no more than being compelled at last to face with sober senses our real conditions of life, and our real relations with our kind. Marxists have often been secretly afraid that they were wrong, and the reactionaries were right, on this crucial subject: that the truth behind the sphinx's riddle of modern nationalism might really destroy them for good. Then the wreckage would end by burying us all and the angel will never close his wings.

This fear is as unfounded as the instant-formula utopias of proletarian internationalism. A better decipherment of the riddle can only serve to separate out the durable – the 'scientific', or as I chose to call it above 'historical materialism' – from the ideology in our *Weltanschauung*, the grain from the husks represented by the defeat of Western Philosophy.

CHAPTER EIGHT

The Radical Approach

Question Magazine

JULY 1976

THE OLDEST QUARREL between socialists and nationalists about Scottish independence turned on a familiar commonplace. The nationalists were supposed to want independence for its own sake, regardless of the quality of society after self-determination. Socialists told them that the whole business could only be justified if a startlingly new quality of society was made possible; otherwise it would be mere 'bourgeois nationalism' – and, in fact, probably a large step backwards instead of forwards. Kailyard or Communism: such were the stark emblems that dominated the old debate.

Although far from extinct, this quarrel is now becoming mercifully outdated. The recent congress and policy documents of the SNP make this clear, as does the new collection of SNP essays edited by Gavin Kennedy, *The Radical Approach*. Opponents can no longer claim that our nationalists are mere sovereignty-fetishists without positive policies. On the contrary, there is now a very recognisable ideology of independence, to some extent worked out in terms of policies in different fields, and fairly distinct from both kailyard conservatism and socialism. The label attached to this new product is 'radicalism'.

If the old quarrel is losing its relevance, what will the new one be like? This is the question I want to discuss. What does this new brand of 'radicalism' mean? And what new questions does it pose for socialists?

There certainly are such new problems for the socialist and Marxist left. And yet – this constitutes the crux of my argument – these are as nothing compared to the dilemmas which 'radicalism' creates for the nationalist movement itself.

The Common Pattern

In all newly constituted national states, the state itself plays a crucial, all-important role. This is virtually a law of history. There have been no exceptions to it during the era of ascendant nationalism, from the early 19th century up to the present day. Centralisation, increased state intervention in the economy, and a centrally directed mobilisation of social and cultural resources – these have been the invariable watch-words of new nation-states.

The general causes of this are obvious. These new countries have almost always won independence in conditions of great difficulty, frequently through wars and revolutions. They have always had to confront continuing difficulties after the attainment of self-government, difficulties arising from disruption, external and internal hostility to the new regime and general unpreparedness for independence. Coping with these problems needs a great social effort. The only way of summing up the necessary support and resources is centrally, through the new state apparatus.

So, whether or not a genuine social revolution accompanies the new birth, it always brings about a 'revolution from above' that implies the strengthening of state authority in every field. Nationalist movements are usually supported by freedom-minded people; but libertarians usually have a hard time of it afterwards, because they find themselves in an 'emergency' situation where considerable state regimentation seems unavoidable. They don't even have the consolation of seeing beyond the emergency. For as everyone knows such emergencies tend to perpetuate themselves: the first ten years last for ever. Much of modern history can in fact be interpreted as a chronic, enforced 'emergency' of this kind, the enduring legacy of revolutionary circumstances.

The Scottish Exception

But the ideological perspective now established by the Scottish national movement is in striking contrast to all this. It looks forward to a very different pattern of events. It is anticentralising, anti-statist, and antibureaucratic; its watch-words tend to be local power, employee or tenant participation and consumer sovereignty.

'Decentralisation of industrial control... should be pursued in an independent Scotland in the first instance with the aim of limiting the growth of state power', writes Stephen Maxwell in his essay 'Beyond Social Democracy', perhaps the most important general statement of the new view (*The Radical Approach*, p. 15). To succeed, this attack on the overgrown state must be pursued on many levels. As well as in industry 'we must radically disperse the points of power and initiative and communication in society', says Isobel Lindsay (p. 25). This implies a new emphasis on cultural factors in politics – 'the intricate, pervasive arid distinctive way in which societies have evolved, and individuals take identity and meaning from them', as she puts it. In marked contrast to the movement's past strain of philistinism, she argues that it is only for the nationalists that 'issues of culture and cultural change are of real importance' (p. 24).

This philosophy is currently being applied in a number of policy fields. In *The Radical Approach* readers should study, for example, the essays on housing, industrial relations, the Highlands and the Orkney and Shetland Islands. Environmentalism lends itself easily to the perspective, while David Hamilton – attacking 'the bureaucratic organisation of medicine' in his article on health –

points out this is made easier by the fact that 'This attack on bureaucracy is a theme running through the SNP manifesto' (p. 70).

It is interesting to observe that the theme will probably also figure to some extent in the outlook of the Scottish Labour Party. This party's policies are still in course of formation, so it would be premature to draw definite analogies. But the SLP will most likely evolve its own version of the revolt against centralism and old fashioned state nationalisation, workers' control, 'community-centred development', and so on. It would be surprising if it did not, since it exists partly in reaction against the great all-British centralist and state-bureaucratic political party, the Labour Party. What this distinctively socialist version will be like remains to be seen, but it wold be no less surprising if it didn't cover some of the same ground as the new nationalist world view.

A Political Contradiction

Much should be said – I will not try here and now on the origins of these ideas, on the manifold connections between neo-nationalism and the general wave of New Left thinking in the 1960s. Without too much effort one can find similar notions at work in new nationalist and regionalist thinking everywhere. The creed of smallness is beauty, anti-Leviathan and mini-community is already fairly defined and has received some philosophical anointment.

In the Scottish context; something else is more important, and more urgent. For the situation in Scotland, I believe, compels one to review the anticentre *Weltanschauung* critically. It compels one to treat it more sternly, not in the sense of questioning its values, but in the sense of questioning its possibility. The foreseeable perspectives of Scottish development do not cast doubt on the ideology's humanity, on its populist credentials or ultimate desirability. But I think they do make one question its feasibility, its adequacy, *as* an ideology of independence.

What are the particular features of Scottish politics today that provoke this reaction? The movement for Scottish self-government is one of a large number of more or less kindred national revivals. Looked at comparatively along this spectrum it presents one odd combination of features. It is the national movement which has advanced farthest towards winning effective power of some sort. No other can presently be described as on the threshold of power, or as having been promised a considerable part of what it wants within the next two years by the presiding government. But it is also the movement that has come to this point against the least external resistance. No other has been so unqualifiedly constitutional and pacific in its evolution and methods.

In that more typical pattern of nationalist development I referred to previously, external resistance and internal conflicts go hand-in-hand. The one leads to the other. It is the determined opposition of the presiding imperial power which hardens the position of the nationalists, and encourages the anti-nationalists to back-track. No special cunning is needed to pursue this policy of 'divide and rule', only a few *gendarmes* and a little brutality. The result is the normal internecine conflict between a militant, independenceminded minority and those who cling passionately to the status quo. The ruling power's object in this conflict is of course to steer the indifferent, wavering, conservative, more or less silent middle into the second of these camps.

In Scotland and Wales, the absence of the one has led to the absence of the other. The relative tolerance of the British constitutional state towards them has made possible a relative mildness in their own affairs. And it is in this mildness that the relaxed ideology of anti-centralism and power dispersal can flourish – flourish to the extent of becoming the identity of the most advanced of neo-nationalist movements. The paradox is obvious. But what one must now wonder is: will this paradox not turn, fairly rapidly, into a serious contradiction?

The Limits of Britishness

The paradox of a relatively conflictfree nationalism is currently summed up in one word, the magic invocation, the wish-bone of current British politics: 'Devolution'. What the term implies is a transfer of substantial political authority by peaceful agreement. With amicability on both sides, the recipients of the new power can proceed about their business without crisis. Because there will be no emergency, no civil war, no battle for survival, there need be no embattled state, no enforced centralisation. This more civilised political process should permit direct progress to a more libertarian and spontaneous social order.

Many people on the nationalist side desire independence but still instinctively believe in this scenario. Sometimes one hears about devolutionists who are really nationalists at heart. But how many Scottish nationalists are really devolutionists under the skin? How many are convinced, at bottom, of this British miracle – of a negotiated transubstantiation, a reasonableness deeper than back-lashes and oil revenues?

Those who do feel this retain an implicit faith in the political constitution of England (however scornful they may occasionally be about Michael Foot or Mrs Thatcher). It is because they feel or half-feel this security that they are free to imagine a decentred utopia, a Scottish state that will – so to speak – wither away rather than grow like all the others. *The Radical Approach* is itself a remarkable comment on this underlying attitude. With the exception of a contribution by Owen Dudley Edwards (focused on a comparison between Scotland and Ireland) and a very few pages about sharing North Sea oil revenues, there is very little about the outside world at all; and nothing at all about England or the UK state. The future of Scottish society is projected into a curious, rather unreal vacuum.

Yet at the very moment when this new radicalism is being projected, it is becoming plain that the old British-style security is on the way out. In her foreword to the collection, Margo MacDonald writes that the new radical image should hold out hope, and 'go some way to allaying the fears of those faint-hearts, and Devolutionists, amongst us who dread the loss of London's over-bearing influence'. But that influence has also been supportive of an overbearing, frequently insufferable *paterfamilias* who, none the less, could be counted on to do the right thing in the end. The supports are vanishing. We can no longer be so sure he will do the decent thing.

The devolutionary wish-bones are still being rattled, I know, but they give off an increasingly hollow sound. It is not going to be as easy as many people thought. This gathering unease was strongly present at the Motherwell conference, and influenced some of the debates. There is now much less likelihood of a calm, basically orderly progress into self-government (whether 'independent' or not), within the limits of the British state system. It looks as if 'Devolution' is going to test that system to the limit; and it might easily break it down. It also looks increasingly as if the process might go on for some years, even decades, generating a far higher level of political conflict.

The Problem of Transition

What does this more realistic perspective imply, for the new 'radicalism' and the relations between Scottish socialists and nationalists? Seen comparatively, it is of course only a slight 'normalisation' of the conditions for Scottish nationalism. We are not (or we will not long remain) as exceptional as we appeared to be hitherto. Any change in this direction has considerable meaning, especially for the new SNP radicals.

This is not to maintain, incidentally, that the alteration of climate entails a precipitous descent into violence. Rash predictions of this order have been made quite often in the past. The deeply British assumption behind such warnings seems to be that any serious break with Westminster constitutionalism will plunge us at once into an Ulster or Lebanon situation. But (as far as I know) this assumption is never properly argued; and in fact it would be very difficult to defend.

However, there will be greater uncertainty, disappointed expectations, higher tension, franker opposition and resentment – there may even be further pugilistic exchanges in the Mother of Parliaments. What all that will lead to we do not know. But even such a relative 'normalisation' of the Scottish situation is enough to pose new questions. Enough (that is) to pose questions new here, but fairly standard everywhere else.

Decentralisation?

How can a newly formed state both deal with external resentment and internal enemies *and* practise decentralisation? How can it take up arms (even in an unmilitary sense) and at the same time distribute power to people, enterprises, regions, classes who may be hostile to its existence? 'The institutions of the radical economy would be manageably small, democratic and responsible', says Gavin Kennedy in his *Radical Approach* essay (p. 56). What if they were also pining to restore the English connection? Developments could be community-centred, but travelling in quite the wrong direction. 'In an independent Scotland the diversity of the country acts as an insurance against the oppression of any one region over another', claims Owen Dudley Edwards (p. 108). Perhaps but what if this old, tenacious, prickly diversity were used as an obstacle to governing the nation at all? What if, in the manner of the American South, it was exploited as an excuse for the sabotage of democracy?

I am not posing these dilemmas to discredit the values of the new Scottish radicalism. But the fact is that they are values which will only be attainable – even partially – through a difficult dialectic between state and society, between the new centre and the diverse forces in the Scottish community. How that dialectic actually works is likely to be determined by two things especially, which I would like to conclude by emphasising.

The Political Culture

The first is the nature of the new Scottish centre itself. I believe we should spend more time worrying over the character of the new state, and the new Scottish constitution, and less time cultivating our diversities; more time on the future political culture, less time on the old economic chestnuts of self-sufficiency and North Sea oil.

The Scots may be right to want a radically devolved and self-regulating society. But it does not follow that a weak or disarticulated state 'must accompany and foster such a society. Only a strong state is likely to be able to promote and sustain such a big alteration in the social order. Since – as I have also argued – a strong, rather centralist state is likely to be forced on us anyway by the real circumstances of self-rule, something else follows. Radicals and socialists alike should be anxiously concerned to get a state capable of working towards the sort of society they are blueprinting. They ought to be far more concerned, in a distinctly un-British way, with the form of the state. The chances are that the kind of state we shall end up with will be different from the old English model, and will stand in a substantially different relationship to society. If so, then we also need a new political philosophy – again, a non-British philosophy – to try and chart our movement in this direction.

The second crucial but usually neglected factor concerns the outside world. What happens to new selfgoverning societies is determined as much – often far more – by external forces and relations as by their own dreams. It is those external pressures which cause the habitual patterns of militancy and mobilisation. We ought therefore to be far more preoccupied by the study of these forces and relations. Scottish socialists and nationalists alike should be far more outward-looking. Concern with international relations or the study of other nations and national movements is not a marginal luxury we can leave until some remote date, when we have finished deciding just how we want the kail to be planted in the new Scottish backyard.

Radical v Socialist

No radical or socialist approach that overlooks these elements in the political culture is likely to take us far. I put 'radical' and 'socialist' together here, because clearly, in so far as nationalists have become genuinely radical, and socialists have become Scottish, they have the most powerful common interests here. In the old quarrel the nationalists used to say: keep the ranks closed until independence. The socialists used to answer: what kind of independence? Independence for what? 'Independence' was an abstraction in that kind of argument. As it ceases to be so, the argument has to change, because all parties who accept the change seriously – however different their ideologies remain – acquire a mutual interest in the construction of a viable arena to conduct their affairs in. They will have to redefine their quarrels in the new Scottish context. And this presupposes a context capable of supporting them meaningfully: that is, a strong democratic state able to cope with a sea of troubles externally and regulate internal conflict.

So, that new or future quarrel between socialists and nationalists I referred to at the start does not yet exist – it cannot be pulled ready-made out of a hat, because it is no longer only a matter of ideology. It will have to be reconstructed in this new context in order to be really meaningful; it will have an element of common interest built into it; and it will be quite different from the old, British-style contests within the UK state. But we are at the beginning of this new process; it will take a long time to work out the terms of the new battle satisfactorily.

CHAPTER NINE

Scotland the Misfit

Question Magazine

OCTOBER 1976

AS STEPHEN MAXWELL said, debate about this country's future swings too easily 'between the banal and the melodramatic.' (*Q*, September 1976), and left-wingers have indeed over-cultivated the apocalyptic strain... So the choice is between 'We'll be alright, Jock!' – a popular refrain in the SNP – and lurid predictions of doom in which MacNasties rampage through the kailyard while Brian Wilson and the Buchans hold lonely exiles' meetings at St Pancras Town Hall.

While correctly criticising this over-easy pessimism, Mr Maxwell none the less ends up too far into the company of the banal. He argues that neither American nor English intervention is really likely to distort and side-track Scotland's progress to independence. Hence, 'Scotland's political options remain open', and she will be able to follow a reasonably independent line in external affairs, cultivating (especially) an 'opening to the North' in the sense of relations with Scandinavian countries. 'The Left-wing vision of an independent Scotland besieged and coerced by hostile forces has little substance', he concludes, and we will become another 'small European democracy' like Norway, Austria, or Denmark.

Without indulging in leftish hysteria, one may doubt whether it will be as easy as this. There is, I believe, a more rational calculation to be made about independence, and more genuine anxieties than those of the cultural pessimists. There is more substance than Stephen Maxwell allows in the socialist apprehension about hostile forces outside; and much more than he admits in our fears concerning the internal allies of these forces.

Where Scotland Stands

The core of the problem is what kind of country one believes Scotland is, and where one would locate a Scottish state in the world order. At the moment, there are amazingly different answers to these questions floating around. Few of them show any signs of being derived from actual study of the country or its international context. This is of course partly why argument coups so disconcertingly from one extreme to another – as if no real land existed between the preconceived visions of Nationalist and Anti-Nationalist.

Unfortunately, the problem is really difficult. It is not in fact at all easy to discern where an independent, or even a semi-independent, Scotland would stand. Yet, without such a comparative perspective, how can we advance far in serious consideration of external affairs and foreign policy?

There is one particularly important factor here, rarely included in any prediction. Like the SNP draft policy on External Affairs (*Scots Independent*, September 1976), Mr Maxwell's perspective takes in the immediate geographical and political context: the North Sea littoral and the British Isles, NATO and the Common Market, and the Soviet Union in the distance. But is there not also a wider framework to be taken into account?

This is what one may call the development factor. The decisive issue for a nation's political location is not necessarily its immediate geopolitical context. It may be where it stands in terms of the development process – that is, its comparative grade of socio-economic development, its specific developmental problems, and the political conflicts with the outside world which these entail.

Under- or Over- Developed?

What one is seeking in this perspective is Scotland's place in the larger world drama of development. Most people would concede that the world's prime problem is 'under-development', and that the dominant conflict of the coming century will be between this impoverished majority and the few nations who have successfully industrialised. Hence any country's fate (and its foreign policy) is likely to be determined by where it is located in this development war.

The SNP-Maxwell conception of this is too simple: Scotland is a developed society which is going to become more so ('oil-financed expansion will make Scotland into one of the fastest growing markets in the world', etc.), so that self-government implies instant graduation into the development elite. In reality, while no one would of course deny that the Scots were 'developed' in broad comparison with the Third World, it is not so clear that they belong in the well-to-do suburbs of the world either ('countries economically favoured and relatively rich in basic resources', like Sweden or Norway).

There are, after all, a lot of places which are neither the one nor the other. Modern historical development is not in fact neatly divided into the haves and the have-nots: it also displays a restless, contentious 'middle class' of societies that believe they belong in the upper stratum but, for many different reasons, are frustrated in their aspiration. These are mainly small nations, relatively developed and either dominated or heavily overborne by larger, more backward neighbours.

In short, not all who think themselves chosen are allowed in the ranks of the Elect. They end up Damned – damned for being too small in population yet too big for their boots, damned for getting in the way of greater powers and stubbornly insisting on their rights, damned for being in the wrong place and being too advanced and too conceited to lie down and be walked over like provincials.

Misfits

This awkward squad has played a significant part in the history of Europe, and one that shows no sign of diminishing. As far as the contemporary period goes, it probably began with the Belgian Revolution of 1831–32.

Here was an example of a relatively over-developed middle-class society – at that time the spearhead of the Industrial Revolution on the continent – which grew impatient with the somnolent imperial monarchy to the north of it, and realised that statehood was necessary for more dynamic growth. The Belgians had been consigned to King William I's Empire of the Netherlands by the Congress of Vienna, for strategic reasons. But at almost the same moment they launched on an era of vigorous development fuelled by the rich sub-soil resources of Wallonia. For its part, Holland merely declined farther into fossilised inertia founded on colonial exploitation; it had a strongly anti-entrepreneurial culture, replete with nostalgia and an exaggerated respect for a long-dead 'Golden Age'.

Belgian independence was a success. Like the Swiss before them, the Belgians found themselves in a pivotal position among surrounding great powers: the latter were interested in encouraging the balancing-act, and King William lacked strength and incentive to reclaim his divine rights.

But in the nature of things such conditions were rare. Most other small, thrusting nationalities became cuckoos in somebody's nest and suffered accordingly. The list of such misfits is interesting, and longer than one would think: Bohemia-Czechoslovakia, Catalonia, the Basque Country, Croatia, Ulster, Cyprus. This is to confine the argument to Europe alone, ignoring outside examples like the Ibo nation in Nigeria, Singapore, or Kurdistan.

All these Switzerlands *manqués* find themselves standing, in the words of the SNP draft policy, 'at a point of convergence'. 'The fact that Scotland stands at a point where such diverse influences (England, the EEC, North America, the USSR) converge immediately distinguishes her position', elaborates Maxwell in his article. This sounds good, and profitable. The trouble is that when a frontier 'point of convergence' *is not also a zone of tolerable equilibrium* or neutrality, it can be disastrous. This is perhaps the most important single factor in small-nation geo-politics.

Misplaced Resources

What goes wrong in misfit development is partly a question of location: these minor, intrusive people have the impudence to stand on someone else's toes, and this is because they think they have the right to develop where they happen to exist. Regrettably, this is the wrong place from the point of view from the prevailing political order.

Thus, during the declining years of the Hapsburg Empire, it was developing, bourgeois Bohemia which provided the main challenge to the fossil-state in Vienna. Like the Belgians, the Czechs saw that escape from this palsied and retrograde regime was a precondition of prosperity. Why should they not become an island of industrialisation – a progressive, democratic Switzerland of *Mitteleuropa*, exploiting their cross-roads situation? But as a matter of fact genuine Czech independence was to prove insupportable to all three of the empires which have controlled the wider area since that time: the Hapsburgs, the German Third Reich, and the Soviet Union.

In the same way, the Catalans and the Basques would have liked to develop into successful intermediary states. They should have turned into southern Belgiums, capitalist societies linking mainland Europe and Iberia together through commerce and industry. They too had to extricate themselves from a larger, backward mass: the irredeemably parasitic state power of Castile. But again, Spain was too strong, and the interest of other big powers in their independence was too weak. So, with the exception of short-lived republics in the 1930s, their convergence-position proved fatal to their national aspirations.

Sensitive geographical location is not the only important factor in the game. Very often crucial natural resources play a part too. The coal and iron were uncovered in the 'wrong' places, politically speaking: in southern Belgium rather than Holland, in the ethnic fringes rather than on the Castilian plateau, among the Czechs rather than in the Hapsburg heartlands. Later, petroleum was also bound to lie in the wrong places: in Kurdish Iraq rather than in the south, in the eastern Ibo country and not in northern Nigeria – and so on.

Geological good fortune, a crossroads situation, a restless and enterprising bourgeoisie: some combination of these factors may give new political life to small nationalities, but it is not so common for that potential to be realised smoothly. In at least as many case the conjunction has produced series conflicts.

Realpolitik

Those Scandinavian lands which figure so prominently in the SNP *Weltanschauung* did not only get thriving independence for the reasons Stephen Maxwell gives: being 'ecologically favoured and relatively rich in natural resources'. They were also lucky enough not to be in a convergence-point. Located on the northern fringe of Europe, they were away from the line of fire during the great imperialist contests, at least until 1940. Benefiting from the great-power markets, they were nevertheless largely free from their rivalries and so able to cultivate their under-populated gardens in peace.

The small northern nations had another advantage. No one claimed that their vital national resources (Norwegian water power, Swedish ore, the timber of the northern forests) belonged to somebody else. But as we have seen, most of the small peoples in the continental land-mass could not be so lucky, particularly those which developed late. They could usually be depicted as thieves: egotistical 'narrow nationalists' stealing what rightly belonged to the larger populations and states around them. What right have the Basques to keep the iron and oil of Vizcaya to themselves, instead of sharing it with Castile, Andalusia and Extremadura? Why should the Welsh think they can exploit 'their' water by selling it to the English Midlands? – and so forth.

And the Scots? The Maxwell-SNP position is that we too will be left in peace, for the following reason. Although conceding that 'England... might appear to have the means to abort the very emergence of an independent Scotland', Mr Maxwell goes on to suggest that 'the British state could not survive the denial of Scotland's right of self-determination' because 'in terms of *Realpolitik* the crisis which would result... would destroy what remains of the international confidence on which sterling and the UK economy now so precariously depend'.

The trouble is that one can easily re-write this judgement, using nearly the same words: 'The British state could not survive the full attainment of Scotland's right of self-determination, because in terms of *Realpolitik* the resulting crisis would have destroyed what remains of the international confidence on which sterling and the UK economy now so precariously depend'.

Which version is more likely to be true? This may well be clearer in a few weeks' time. But is there much doubt which way the wind is blowing? Until quite recently the idea of forcing a referendum on Scottish independence was a minority view. During August and September it seems to have hardened into – at least – a strong probability. The promise of a referendum will be the instrument for getting the Devolution Act through Parliament, against the growing resistance of the Great-English majority.

The aim of such an exercise (as nearly everyone in Scotland, and almost no one in England, appears to understand) is of course 'to abort the very emergence of an independent Scotland'. This is normally done with gendarmes and armoured cars. But under the peculiar conditions of Britain – a constitutional state with precarious economy, already heavily committed to 'internal security' operations in Ireland – these classic procedures can only be a last extremity. The referendum will (as they hope) be a palatable substitute: a solemn and binding oath by the Scottish people not to actually steal England's oil and bring down the old family mansion for good.

Turning Nasty

Once the Scottish silent majority has croaked out this promise – so the thought goes-provincial peace will reign again. The North Britons will already have as much self-government as they really want; certainly as much as is good for them. Demands for more will be the work of manifest, irrepressible trouble-makers. If these do not succumb to the moral truncheon of the referendum, then – in what will really be a quite different political climate – other means can be used.

It is perhaps in this perspective that one ought to reconsider those outside interests (especially US interests) which the Maxwell position dismisses so lightly. He suggests that the Americans are not likely to be very concerned about Scottish independence, and that if they intervene seriously it is more likely to be on our side. 'The United States... would seek to obstruct any English response which might induce Scottish opinion to look for alternative security policies based on Nordic examples outwith NATO', as he puts it, a trifle gnomically. In any case – 'Scotland should prove stony ground for US covert operations. No politically significant section of Scottish society will feel its interests so threatened... as to seek the serious patronage of external interests'.

There is something distinctly askew about this position. If there is anything obvious about Scotland, it must be that quite a large sector of the population feels uneasy and threatened by the prospect of independence. This is not just the 'Keep-Britain-United' faction or left-wing *Kulturpessimismus*; there is also that much larger 'English partly' founded upon centuries of civil closeness. In turn, this merges into what one may call the 'American party', a conservative move- ment that has nothing much to do with Dr Kissinger or the US multinationals on our soil. It is based on the fact that every other Scottish family has one or more relative 'doing well' in a comfortable suburb or small town of North America (or somewhere similar in South Africa, Australia, etc.). Nearly all members of this party have no doubt that *this* is the world to which they want Scotland to go on belonging, independent or not.

If these tendencies are not 'politically significant', it is simply because they have not yet been mobilised. The process is beginning now. The referendum is meant to be its key instrument: a massive appeal to the forces of *Gemütlichkeit*, against 'going too far'. John Smith, the Minister of State with Responsibility for Devolution, was kind enough to outline the programme for us recently. 'For every separatist there are four or five Scots less stridently, but just as passionately, committed to the unity of the United Kingdom', he said. The referendum will put lead in their pencils. We shall soon be oxter-deep in blabbering invocations of 'the magnificent history of the United Kingdom partnership' (as he puts it: *Scotsman*, 14 September).

Stephen Maxwell believes that 'a confident and assertive nationalism' will render the country impregnable to external subversion and the CIA. He is quite right to castigate the left for replying exclusively and easily on the myth of 'a militant people's Socialism' as the only viable content of independence.

However, there does not actually have to be a militant people's Socialism in office to cause trouble: the vague threat of it will do. And it is an objective fact about Scotland that this possibility is rooted in its social structure. Here again we would seem to have more in common with Catalonia than with the Scandi- navian nations. Fortunately or not, none of the latter contain city-states like Barcelona or Glasgow.

Eyes to See

In the same issue of *Q* as the article I have been discussing with Duncan Glen wrote about Glasgow in these terms:

> Surely there are enough people with eyes to see... the awfulness of the poverty
> of social emptiness... To see and to say: we have waited too long. Dramatic
> social chance is required – now – on a massive scale. I hesitate to say a revo-
> lution as I have no wish to scare off anyone...

But there are eyes to see in Madrid, London and Washington too; and their owners
are ready to be scared off by the complications of independent politics in countries
with problems like those. Maxwell hopes that the SNP myth of classlessness will
keep the hounds at bay. But that Myth works better in some places than in
others: better, I suspect, in Nordic countries or Holland than in a future independent Scotland.

Actually conditions are worse in the West of Scotland than in any other of the
listed nations except Ulster (the least soothing of exceptions). So in the comparative framework I outlined Scotland might appear something like this: a country
moving into developmental conflict with the backward state controlling it, impelled
by a typically thrusting, middle-class nationalism – yet also bearing with it a
uniquely large inheritance of working-class depression, urban squalor, and assorted
'social problems'.

Foreign Affairs

One needs only sketch in this striking combination of external and internal problems
to raise conflicting cries. From the SNP-Maxwell side come accusations of pessimism; from Tam Dalyell and the anti-Nats the shouts of 'I told you so!' and
demands to cease this madness now.

These are both stances with a lot of preconceived truth in them. So is the
left-wing catastrophism Mr Maxwell attacks. But I am reluctant to believe that
any of these conclusions really follow from a more realistic analysis of Scotland's
place in the world.

That place may be more difficult, ambiguous and conflictual than most people
have realised. But this is an argument against independence only in the heads of
those who still suffer from Great British delusions. They think there is somewhere
to go back to. For others who know that there is no place else to go, it has simply
become vital to understand what the reality will be like.

The tougher it is, the more important foreign policy will be. External relations
are of crucial significance for most small countries; and of course, they matter
even more in the ranks of the Damned than in those of the Elect. This is why there
should be a searching, wide-ranging debate about Scotland's future relations with
other countries – a discussion that shakes us out from those deep-laid provincial
idées reçues, and forms an integral part of the search for genuine self-government.

It may even be that, as we pursue it, we shall find out what we are really like
more effectively than by the traditional techniques of introspection and literary
spirit-raising.

CHAPTER TEN

1931 – A Repeat Performance?

Question Magazine

OCTOBER 1976

IN A MULTITUDE of ways, the new crisis seems like the old. A Labour government in office, struggling desperately against the effects of a world depression; a plunging exchange rate, so-called 'speculation' against sterling, the sacrifice of all positive social policies to the demands of survival; mounting rumours of coalition and increasing conflicts within Labour ranks; preposterous tranquillising utterances from the Chancellor of the Exchequer interspersed with talk of 'totalitarianism' as the sole alternative – the analogies with 1931 are indeed numerous and increasing. Yet in reality this resemblance is quite deceptive. Only a little way beyond the appearances lies a very different situation, and an even more different prospect. Were the analogy justifiable then the conservative forces of the United Kingdom would have little to fear in the long run. For the implication would be that, after the fall of Callaghan's government and left wing split in Labour, some new all-party regime would successfully impose draconian deflation; the British working class would loyally endure it, hoping for better luck 'next time'; and then slowly improving economic conditions would give the old British state another half century of life.

While nobody knows what will happen, we can be reasonably sure that this will not. There are, fortunately, limits to the farcical repetition of history even in England.

While things have gone on much as usual upon the small stage of British politics during the 1960s and '70s, these limits have inexorably encroached upon the actors. They are now left on a tiny proscenium, far away from both their national audience and the outside reality they once commanded, executing the ancestral drama of the British Constitution in faltering tones and threadbare costumes.

New Era

Although perceived at the time as possibly the 'end of capitalism', 1931 was also the beginning of a new era for capitalism. And it was in England that a vital part of the formula for this new epoch was discovered. Even as the great crisis proceeded, J. M. Keynes was laying down the outline for a recovery programme.

This plan for state action was to take several decades to implement. And probably the most significant single thing about it for UK politics was that it allowed Labourism to find a new reforming role after the catastrophe of 1931. As Robert Skidelsky put it in an interesting article last week:

> What finally enabled a government perspective to emerge in line with Labour expectations was the post-war Keynesian revolution. Keynesianism promised to restore British capitalism to health by means which also furthered trade union and (moderate) socialist goals. It provided for an increased state role in managing the economy, which pleased the Fabians... but by indirect controls, which preserved free collective bargaining...'

TIMES, 12 October

It did not actually 'restore British capitalism to health' of course. But it patched it up sufficiently to keep the play going (and even, in the abnormal conditions of the post-war recovery, going quite well). The real problem now is that this entire epoch seems to have revolved. And there is no sign of another Keynes.

Friedman

Instead, the ascendant star of economic theory is monetarism. After the Great Crash the West turned towards a real saviour. In the crisis of today it has turned to a tribe of cranks who think money supply is the new elixir of economic life. Indeed the High Prince of this faith, Milton Freidman, has just been crowned with the Alfred Nobel memorial prize and £90,000 by the Swedish Academy of Sciences.

'Many of the 'monetarist' policies now favoured by governments, including half-heartedly the British government, may be traced to Professor Friedman's Work', noted the Daily Telegraph (15 October). Unlike the notoriously obscure Marx and Keynes, this Mickey Mouse of the economics world 'is not the sort of clever man who blinds you with science, who tells you in elaborate and incomprehensible terms what you know to be a bit fishy. On the contrary, he represents common sense, systemised and rendered articulate'.

The chief British disciple of Friedmanism, Enoch Powell, is temporarily estranged from power. Still, others can pick up the banner. The new post-Health Conservative Party is well sown with monetarists, and many calls to be less half-hearted about it all rang out at their Brighton Conference.

The great liberal thinkers of the 1930s and '40s formed a new framework capable of reconciling capitalism with socialism (or at any rate with statist and welfare policies which could be called that). In the 1950s Gaitskell and Anthony Crosland set the Labour seal on this consensus. But no sooner had this happened than the conditions of the Keynes–Beveridge 'social contract' began to alter. In stronger capitalist countries this has not been so important. But in Great Britain, where continuing external good fortune had only concealed underlying structural weaknesses, the effects were to be graver.

Debate continues about the causes of these changes – the growing force of multi-national corporations, the loss of state economic power, etc. – but the results are undeniable. Wilson's new Keynesian regime collapsed into a pathetic rout in the 1960s. From 1974 to 1976 he returned to erect a funambulesque 'Social Contract' disguising the disappearance of the real one – wisely shuffling off the stage himself some months before the scenery started to fall on the players. At the same time, the outstanding remaining liberal-Keynesian in Labour ranks, Roy Jenkins, strode off in the different and more rewarding direction of Brussels.

Behind them, greyer successors struggle more feebly with the old dilemma of governmental half-heartedness: how to avoid the harsh logic of outright deflation and plain capitalist remedies. Like all governments since the later 1950s they are dependent upon external pressures over which they have very little control: upon the remaining big holders of sterling, upon the IMF and the Federal Reserve Bank in America, upon the EEC's 'green pound' policy, upon Helmut Schmidt.

Such outside powers may of course decide to prop up the show for some time yet, for their own good reasons: mainly in order to avoid the repercussions which British collapse would have upon a still uncertain economic recovery. If they do not, or cannot, what is likely to happen?

The National Government's programme of cuts and restrictions impinged upon working people already deeply demoralised. The organised part of the working class had been defeated twice, in the years leading up to the Great Depression. The immediate post-war unrest had been quashed in 1921–22; then there was the final, bitterly symbolic humiliation of 1926.

Nothing remotely like those setbacks has been experienced in the last 20 years. On the evidence of 1972–74, it is very difficult to believe that the workers would put up with savage austerity from a Conservative government. They tolerate the Healey-Callaghan measures because they retain a (half-hearted) belief in Labourism, and because the dominant trade union leadership (dating from the 1960s) is unusually 'left' politically and has over-committed itself to the government.

Myths

This has led to an odd change in the general estimation of what is happening. Only two years ago there was widespread subscription to the myth of irrepressible militancy: a decade of unofficial actions, the Industrial Relations agitation and the great miners' strikes had fostered belief in the crypto-revolutionary nature of British labour. Now, after a year of the 'Social Contract', an opposite myth has taken over. People who once thought workers capable of anything now think they will put up with anything in the name of National Salvation, like their fathers of the 1930s.

It is not necessary to plunge back into the old myth to see something wrong in the new. Nobody knows how the working class would now react to being struck forcibly on the cranium by a new National-cum-Conservative regime of the familiar sort which has ruled Britain for 21 years of this century. Presumably it will not join the CPGB or the marxist sects *en masse*. But it is still extremely likely to produce some form (perhaps quite novel) of aggravation.

Admittedly, the old constitutional regime has great social strength. Few states could have survived the shocks of winter, 1974, and proceeded with a seedy pretence of 'business as usual'. If the creditors allow it to, it might therefore muddle on for years yet. By deep-rooted instinct the Westminster system puts middle-of-the-road cohesion before everything else. In spite of what Edward Heath (that supreme middle-of-the-roader) declaimed at Brighton, we may be some way from 'the end of the road' as usually envisaged.

The trouble is that the end is envisaged wrongly. In spite of all the appalling difficulties – the falling pound, the destruction of government economic strategy, the lack of even a theoretical hope of any new way out, the prospect of renewed class struggle – a social crisis is by no means certain. English society is superbly resistant to class conflict. On this front it may still have resources to draw upon.

Political

But a political crisis in the sense of a crisis of the constitution and the state, does seem quite certain. This is something totally different from the 1931 situation. Here also 1976 stands at the end of an era to the beginning of which Ramsay Macdonald and Stanley Baldwin were near.

Forty-five years ago Great Britain was a concept as unchallenged as the mother of Parliaments and Constitutions. Scottish and Welsh nationalism were recently conceived, obscure groups of enthusiasts. 'Home Rule' had lapsed from being a secondary, anodyne issue into the neglect from which it would not re-emerge until after 1945.

But now the decline of the British state is not registered solely in terms of ambiguous 'apathy' or mass indifferentism. It has assumed the shape of positive disaffection by two nations. In the case of Scotland this movement is likely – without a quasi-miraculous recovery in the south – to unseat the very basis of the two party order, and so infirm the old state in the period when it is most in need of consensus. In a quite objective sense that has nothing to do with the internal character of Scottish or Welsh nationalism, these are clearly the 'revolutionary' forces successfully at work in the new crisis.

One suspects that it is really in the shadow of this realisation that new and startling conversions to the cause of constitutional reform are made. In 1931 neither the *Economist* (9 Oct. editorial) nor anybody remotely resembling Lord Hailsham (Richard Dimbleby Memorial Lecture, 14 Oct.) preached radical overhaul of the state as a precondition for solving the crisis. If such pillars of the Britannic ancient regime now feel the building coming down, it must be because the situation is genuinely extreme.

The social strength of the old regime lay in its willingness and capacity to strike bargains. Fortified by Keynesianism during the generation now past, it rested upon effective 'compromises' with working class. But compromises depend upon giving and taking in (more or less) calculable terms: so much conceded here, as against so much exacted here. The demands of Scottish and Welsh nationalism are not of this kind at all. Even without exaggerating their strength or support, they are – unlike the sort of demands that have regulated working-class politics in Britain – claims for real power.

In the current devolution legislation the state is of course trying to bargain with them as if 'compromises' of the hallowed sort were possible, as if a certain amount of reasonable give-and-take among reasonable British gents might allow the old regime to wallow on. This assumption is almost certainly wrong (even if some people in the SNP or Plaid Cymru hold it too). If real power and real nationalism are in the game, then the ancient regimes will fail: the game is actually a new one, not even imagined in 1931.

CHAPTER ELEVEN

The New Exiles

Question Magazine
1976

I HAD NOT SEEN Jonathan Barker or his wife Susan since we were at university together. We had pursued almost opposite courses. Mine was the usual one of emigration to the south, and ever rarer visits home from London or farther afield. Theirs had been the less common experience of English implantation in Scotland – that is, a chosen adoption of our country, as opposed to merely coming here for a job.

Our spasmodic contacts had given the impression of a deep adoptive patriotism. This was not only due to their shifts of address, from the university city to a small north-western town, and then to a remote Inverness-shire glen. Jonathan's writing, his research and his teaching had been mainly on Scottish problems. Through them he had sought to combat and remedy the stuffy parochialism which had so incensed us as students. He had exposed small town corruption and incurious provincialdom. The kailyard had withered in his blasts. He had launched local newspapers and fostered community projects. His name was familiar in many correspondence columns, as was his Home-County accent on radio and TV programmes.

Fortunate

It had struck me sometimes how fortunate Scotland was to attract and benefit from this kind of liberal gadfly. I even felt guilt about it: so many of us (as Jonathan often said) left the country for regions where we were needed less, and appeared to care little for Scotland. His lonely battle accused us from a distance, when we happened to hear of it. This nobler form of exile reproached our own: the Barkers were paladins of civilisation, we were careerists in the softer southern world, hard-shelled exploiters of an indifferent host body.

Turning westwards off the main road towards their village, I felt this old mixture of pleasure and guilt. But I could not help imagining how pleased they must be at the new conditions in Scotland, and the signs of new life appearing. After all, they had fallen in love with the place in the stygian '50s (incomprehensibly to most of us) when it looked as if the gloaming would last forever. How happy they must be in the awakening '70s.

In the morning the children took me for a walk around the house, then into the tiny scattered village. How well they had chosen! The three converted and modernised cottages nestled in a hollow some way from the road, overhung by birks. Inside there was the comfortable chaos remembered from students days: piles of books and papers, Habitat furniture, worn rugs, toys and empty wine-bottles. The end cottage was Jonathan's work shop and office and 200 yards away stood the abandoned school which he was currently trying (with the somewhat grudging assistance from the District Council) to turn into a community centre and art gallery. They seemed on the best of terms with the natives of the Strath, even if (as Susan insisted) these often betrayed a *Brigadoon*-esque cynicism about improvement and the fight against authority.

Idyll Crumbles

The idyll began to crumble after breakfast. I was curious to know how they viewed devolution, and my very questions must have manifested a positive interest in the topic. There was an awkward silence.

'Eh… maybe I should show you some things I've been writing recently', said Jonathan stiffly. He rose and went through to his workroom to get them. When he was out Susan moved closer, and nervously broke the silence.

'Jonny's very worried, you know, and he's quite right. So am I. It's all these attacks on the English.' Once launched, she could scarcely stop. 'Those people… that man Henderson, didn't you see his speech at the SNP conference? …All these letters in the *Scotsman*. People looking at us and noticing the way we speak. Just because we happened to be born on the wrong side of the border…'

Jonathan returned, and I read through his *Socialist Worker* and *Guardian* articles, and his many missives to the *Scotsman* and *Herald*. It was a deeply depressing moment. A fearful anxiety now corroded their rural bliss. Far from thinking of self-government as a justification of their efforts, they saw sheer disaster. It did not fulfil their love of Scotland, but destroyed it. Independence promised not emancipation and the release of the liberal and socialist tendency they were devoted to – quite the contrary, it could stand only for the triumph of the narrowest nationalism. The moving forces behind it were our old enemies, small-town bigotry, football tartanry, Calvinical intolerance.

As the day went on this heart of darkness intensified. The sun bathed the Aird in an incongruous honeyed light while my hosts returned obsessively to the one theme. What would become of them, and people like them, in a country gripped by fascist-style racism and foreigner-baiting? Half-forgotten anti-Eng-lish jokes and incidents of the kind always endured by their countrymen now flooded back to them with new, sinister significance.

'I don't mind telling you, I'm afraid of the knock on the door, really afraid…', Jonathan concluded one of his tirades, crouching over the Swedish wood-stove and glaring at me with a new mixture of appeal and accusation. Had we not fought the same enemies, with the same values? Wasn't it now time to rally as one against the madness of an independent Scotland? 'Devolution' did not mean the end of benighted provinciality – it represented a narrowing, black tunnel with a midnight knock on the door at the conclusion: *Sturmbannfuhrer* Henderson and his racial purification squad, with an expulsion order.

Obsessions are difficult to argue with – and I was still somewhat stunned by their vehemence. It had not occurred to me (and obviously it hadn't to the Barkers) that nationalism might entail changes on this level – personal, emotional shifts as well as institutional ones.

The key to their present alarm – I now realise belatedly – lay in the nature of their past love for Scotland. Though genuine – they had reorganised their whole lives round it – this love had retained within itself some elements of unconscious superiority. With the due qualifications, it had not been wholly unlike the profound affection felt by so many British imperialists for India, or by the French in North Africa. Jonathan and Susan had been crusaders, the missionaries of civilised values. But some missions acquire their point from an ambient darkness. More precisely, from a society at once picturesque, humanly interesting, and romantically in need. The aim is to help such a people up without damaging its Rousseau-esque charm. By embracing white-liberal standards the natives may overcome peasant prejudices, yet remain themselves. It is this guided self-affirmation which would have answered the progressive passion of my old friends.

The nationalist movement was worse than a different story altogether. It contradicted the basis of the crusade – and hence, the very personality of the crusaders. They felt rejected in the soul: this was the sense of the door-knocking fantasy and their bewildering fear of the future. By nature a nationalist movement jumbles together backward and progressive attitudes in its general advance unrepentantly assuming that it must learn from its own mistakes – that for example (an incident which had featured in our conversations) the agonised growing pains of the Scottish Labour Party were, for all their violence, preferable to the imperial anaesthesia and safe corruption of British Labourism.

At the time I saw them I had recently returned from Catalonia and witnessed an inflamed cultural nationalism at its strongest and most oppressed. The truth is that this is a dimension largely absent from Scotland's nationalism. English accents figure prominently in the National movement and in the SLP. For all its dourness and pock-marks, the Scots' particular feeling of superiority is not racist in nature but religious. Only if the entire English nation by some unimaginable act relegated itself to the ranks of the Damned would it be likely to turn 'anti-English'; and even then it would hardly pick on such utterly commendable Immigrants for eviction.

But it might – of course – wonder whose side they were on. This is precisely what they cannot stand. Wrong in so many obvious ways, they are aware that a new line is being drawn. Faint and uncertain as yet, it is bound 'to grow deeper through struggle. As it does so, an authentic dilemma is certain to be posed to more and more English people in Scotland. The Barkers had a true premonition of this, however luridly they expressed the feeling.

What is the real problem? In one sense, the most banal one in the world: that of being people living in another country, exiles or emigres. Having myself existed largely in that condition, I felt a degree of impatience with all the panic.

Estrangement is a challenge, a delight, an opportunity, as well as a threat: why couldn't they see this?

No Adaptation

The answer was that they had got used to 'belonging' in another country without this normal process of adaptation, alienation and self-definition. Such was their right – or so they felt. How, suddenly and belatedly, they apprehended this ordinary dilemma being forced upon them. It appeared quite abnormal to them: a matter for irrational fright, or flight, rather than adjustment. Naturally, they projected this fear as an image of our barbarism. The people they had loved and felt at home among were – when it came to the bit – mainly small-minded lunatics pining for Nazism. Naturally again, this prospect made illusion of much of their lives, and had to be resisted with desperate anguish.

On the subject of barbarism, Jonathan had not failed to remind me of the Scots who had joined him in wielding the scourge. This is true: once upon a time, it was we who embarrassed *him* with excessive denunciations of our pre-democratic tribe and its incestuous rituals. But we and our vehemence were of the tribe, he was not; while our opinions and standard's ran parallel courses, they did not have the same basis or inner meaning. And, this was the meaning now externalised by the new situation.

In the same way (as no Englishman fails to do) he reminded me of our reception in the south. How unfair it was, that their lack of discrimination against us and the Welsh should be rewarded by such narrowness! Like all parallelisms between metropolis and margin, this one is false: the number of English intellectuals or professors in Scotland is not balanceable against their Scottish equivalents in England, because there is no underlying symmetry. The asymmetry of English preponderance is the ground-arithmetic of the British Isles. No longer neutralised by empire, not yet countered by the vitality of a European state, this arithmetic has resurfaced in Westminster's latter days. Nostalgia for the old indifference is futile (which will not prevent it becoming an industry). And the rules of a new, more conscious and genuine tolerance have to be constructed.

Provinciality has an allure far greater than our customary political language allows. Those who despise and mock it may still be half-consciously in love with it on another plane. At heart they have defined themselves against this romantic, rear-guard seclusion and do not really want to see it go.

The quandary is worst for English intellectuals like Jonathan. In reality they have little or nothing to fear – probably less, for example, than the numbers of English people who stayed in Ireland after 1922. Yet their subjective dilemma of redefinition is genuine: it involves a status-change peculiarly hard for the English, who – because of their very pre-ponderance – have no acceptable, delimited political identity to fall back upon. They simply cannot help construing the nationalist challenge as an assault upon civilisation itself: the finer standards upheld by their own persons.

I would die to defend my friends from anything remotely like the persecution they are busy fantasising. This is perhaps the bitterest, most obscure confusion of all. For I would defend them as citizens of Scotland, or of a reconstructed British state; not as subjects of the United Kingdom. And because they have not really questioned or renounced the latter, they regard this distinction as a betrayal of them in themselves. Retreating into their rage, they are bound to be driven into the political camp of Unionism. Their unconscious imperialism of outlook will re-emerge as 'Keep-Britain-United' or 'Scotland-is-British'. Their old love of the country will become a hardened conviction that its good, simple people are being led astray by criminals.

A few days after leaving the Barkers I found myself in a pub in Kensington. 'I don't mind the Scots', said the loud man at the bar, 'never have done. Known lots of them. I welcome their accent, same as the Welsh or the Northerners… don't mind the way they carry on either. No: it's when they claim to be expressing Scottish *thoughts* that … well', he paused for a reflective sip at his gin and tonic, '… I have my doubts.' Better than before, I understood that this was not just bar-room wisdom.

CHAPTER TWELVE

The English Dilemma

Question Magazine

FEBRUARY 1977

THE SCOTSMAN'S correspondence page is under constant bombardment on the subject of racism. The target of these anguished correspondents is the supposedly racist outlook of the SNP – or, sometimes, the racism of all nationalist movements whatever. Every small sign of bigotry or unwary remark about 'the English' is pounced on and exhibited as proof to the thesis.

These correspondents imagine a truly 'Balkanised' British Isles, divided not only territorially but by ethnic hatreds and border or minority problems. They perceive the motor of the nightmare as lying in Scotland, Wales and Ulster. This is conveyed most notably by the notion of the 'English backlash' against the smaller countries: infuriated by the petty chauvinism of its old partners, even liberal England will be driven into its own defensive version of the same thing.

Nobody should take these fears lightly. They carry too great a burden of real history with them. Yet, while humanly understandable, they are in the British context curiously – and revealingly – misdirected. The small country nationalists have the upper hand in British politics just now, and it is possible that the intra-British relations become strained or even violent. But this will not amount to the anti-nationalist's apocalypse. If that ever happens it will be produced by a machinery quite different from the one they depict: not by 'backlash' but by the intrinsic character of England's own society and state. It is in England, not Britain, that race and nationality are deeply confused. It is England alone that could be the motor of the catastrophic tendency the letter-writers imagine.

While in London over Christmas I attended a meeting of the National Party, a recently formed breakaway from the better known National Front. It was held in – of all the places – Conway Hall, Red Lion Square, the traditional venue of the metropolitan fringe left. More surprising still, the event had been organised by the hall's owners, the South Place Ethical Society, after a sustained argument over the propriety of letting the premises be used by such right wing movements. The Chairman for the evening was Nicholas Walter, a prominent voice of English anarchism. It was at his invitation that I attended. The theme of this weird debate was 'Nationalism versus Internationalism'. David McCalden, 'National Activities Organiser' of the Party, duly gave a conventional defence of nationalism. Its healthy variety, opposed to the levelling of both capitalist and communist 'internationalism'; its popular and democratic nature, distinct from the elitism of the internationalists; putting one's own people first does not entail bigotry, or hatred of others – and so on. Mike Lobb, another NP official, followed him on the same anodyne path. Hitler came in for particular excoriation, as a notorious internationalist lunatic.

On the other side, Peter Cadogan and Peter Cronin advanced a Conway Hall version of internationalism, with emphasis upon individual liberty and face-to-face community. The *Internationale* of decent souls respects many of the national values the fascists had been evoking: 'the Anglo-Saxon shires are with us still', cried Cadogan in the course of a paean on romantic Englishness. But this kind of thing has nothing to do with national*ism*. Their libertarian sees the state as the canker which corrupts nationality: get rid of it, and there would be a natural international concord. 'We may be making history tonight' suggested one of the South Placers. Was not this staggering confrontation of extremes an example of what the society had always sought, the truths in the middle of the road?

At this point, a foreign observer might have been pardoned some puzzlement. What did such a mild parade of commonplaces have to do with the notorious problems of immigrants in England? How could fascists be mixing so easily with the milk of London progressivism? But the problem was soon cleared up. When the debate was opened to the floor it instantly acquired a wholly different cast.

The polite, Jekyllish mask of the platform orators was thrown away. There was no concern whatever for respectable 'nationalism' among the National Party rank and file. Every one of their interventions played the same obsessive tune: race. The white man's superiority (inventions, Shakespeare etc.); the alien threat to our British bloodstock; the farther brown-black millions poised to invade and complete the mongrelisation of Britain; betrayal of the race by all parts of the Establishment. The accents were all working class. Like a rusty barrel-organ they grated out the same old fantasy over and over again, to the positive embarrassment of the leaders who had clearly planned, in such odd circumstances, to project a more elevated image.

Appalled silence fell on the other side of the hall. Obviously there was no *via media* with this lot: one might as well discuss Plato with a grizzly bear. His Ulster accent thickening with embarrassment, McCalden conceded defeat and suggested weakly that 'Racialism versus Multi-racialism' might have been a more appropriate topic for the evening. It was, indeed, the only possible theme for any discussion whatever with members of his movement. Racialists and libertarians trooped out in the rain, towards the common dejection of public-house post-mortems and the last tube home.

Without reading so much into this strange cameo of English existence, it did demonstrate one singular truth quite powerfully: the *effective* dominance of racialism over the contemporary condition of English nationalism. This has of course nothing to do with the much-celebrated wealth of cultural raw materials the English have at hand if they want to feel national, a bottomless quarry reaching from the Saxon Shires to Melvyn Bragg. The point lies in the weak political deployment of those riches. Somehow they are being overshadowed and neutered by the preposterous hairy beasts of the far right.

Why have blood-myths, utterly discredited and vilified since 1945, obtained such leverage over a great liberal state? In the 1960s their popular force (or the fear of it) inflected the entire body politic in an illiberal direction. This movement was damaging to capitalism, as well as to the left and the better instincts of the liberal élite. Yet it is doubtful whether the harm has been undone by attempts at counter-legislation in the 1970s. And in the meantime, almost any conversation with a liberal or a socialist can be counted on to raise the spectre, if it turns towards nationality or the future.

It is time to point out in the current debate that this persistent, sickening undertone of English life is not accidental, or a passing aberration time and tolerance will cure. The paradox of a liberalism that lapses into racism is in appearance only. In reality, that sort of liberalism breeds this kind of racialism. The latter is no lapse, but rooted in the nature of the state, and giving that experience a new turning. It could only be remedied by changing the state, and giving that experience a new turning.

For several centuries a great, decisive part of England's energies was directed outside itself. English identity was already significantly blurred by the illogical muddle of the pre-modern 'United Kingdom' - that assortment of anachronistic links which 'devolution' is a feeble effort to rationalise. Then this original 'British Empire' was enormously extended by the sustained, successful adventure of overseas conquest. Colonisation and the industrial revolution placed England in the vanguard of modern development for far longer than any other state. Slow to accumulate, this privilege was also slow to disappear: even in the 1960s, the Commonwealth was still seriously perceived by some as a better future than Europe – more in tune with the 'outward-looking' customs of Britishness, etc.

Except from Hong Kong, most of the apparatus of the old imperialism is gone. But not its effects on us. The imprint of this long saga upon English society and consciousness is extremely deep, and the struggle to really get rid of it has hardly begun. The heartland of the British myth, England has been conditioned by it to regard itself not as a nation in the ordinary sense but as a central element in some larger, vaguer, much more glorious thing. National redefinition is imposed by the end of empire: it will take place, in some form. Yet this inheritance is a major obstacle for the English in doing so.

It prevents any realistic, limited focus upon the English nation as such. Instead, the characteristic form of self-consciousness there is a grotesque oscillation between complacency and self-flagellation. Governments see that everything is hopelessly wrong and lurch into Candide-like schemes of regeneration founded on the notion that, basically, everything is alright. When accosted on the subject, intellectuals say that England is by nature above the plane of nationalism (actually what they often *say*, in the key of self-denigration, is that the English are below it – too mixed up, all with Scotch grandmothers, and so forth)

Defective Nationalism

When encountered among intellectuals or the political class, this vaguery is easily turned to a joke. Deeper down in the social fabric the humour vanishes. For English society is in a special, debilitating sense class-bound, and the same facts or ideas assume wholly distinct meanings seen through different layers of its prism. Defective nationalism becomes the open wound of racism.

Internally, British imperialism made possible a unique form of social conservatism. The ruling class used its external success to foster an interior stability, sacrificing growth and mobility to consensus. This particular social harmony rested upon the famous, incorrigible gulfs of the English class-system – on those castle-like distinctions that still amaze outside observers. The English state functions through the ruling élite's benevolent, patrician hegemony; and that real hegemony relies on the inert conservatism of the mass beneath – what Disraeli called the 'angels in marble', the cultivated conservative instincts of an imperial proletariat.

Politically, these instincts breed the anti-egalitarian deference of 'Us and Them'. But these two mental worlds are now being prised apart in the crisis of the old state. In this era of chronic failure and fading allegiance, 'We' are losing faith in 'Them'. And in the collapsing fabric the question of England's immigrant communities has assumed a particularly divisive role.

It means something quite different to the different strata of England's societal hierarchy. For the liberals in charge, it represents a problem of humane civilisation: 'integration' and better-engineered 'community relations', appeals to a quite non-national ethos of reasonableness. In the huge urban deserts of London, the West Midlands and Yorkshire, it assumes the shape of a near-incomprehensible human plight: growing 'alien' presence in a universe of rotten housing, unemployment, job dissatisfaction, and closing escape-routes. Unable to put the economy on its feet properly, They have nonetheless chosen to inflict this new burden on Us. Then They expect us to be liberals about it!

At this level, the ideological formulation is starkly different from the polite one of the responsible classes – yet similar in being quite non-national. What the broad vaguery and evaporating grandeur of Britishness decays into here is racism. The fact is that this ex-imperial habit of mind translates much more easily into racial fantasy than into nationalism. Among the ill-educated, illiberal, non-responsible strata confronting the daily dilemmas of 'race relations' such shameful myths provide only the means of self-assertion. Hostility to their socio-political system flows obsessively into one narrow, debased channel, an underground river of petty rancours, raging resentments and fermenting emotions – a Hyde-like sewer that is the obverse, and the compliment, of the humane, patrician *régime* up above.

Hence it is not the case – as most English commentators assume – that the salience of racism is simply a form of nationalism. This simplistic idea has encouraged their denunciations of what is happening in Scotland and Wales.

The truth is almost the opposite: the peculiar force of racialist fantasies in England is the result of the absence of a more ordinarily defined nationalism there. Unable to find this more limited identity in its available culture, the popular imagination launches into an extreme substitute. The immigrant presence is the pretext of this movement; but the real impulse derives from the special maladies of English class-consciousness, and the lingering traditions of Britishness.

So the 'disease' is probably chronic rather than infectious. While the rulers labour with desperate, humane energy over devolution and race-relations, the very structure they stand on compels all the rising, inchoate resentments of society into this river of filth. Their nation is weary of failure, of disenchantment and retreat. But all this subdued anger and half-conscious longing for renewal is forced into the berserk counter-revolution of the racists. The younger intellectuals express their estrangement from the state in an abstract, sectarian marxism; the most deprived part of the working class is an equally abstract inverted universalism of race. In between, the Establishment – as it used to be called – muddles down the long decline of bankruptcy, appointing Royal Commissions on invalid carriages and crutches to ease its passage. 'England' is, as yet, hardly visible politically.

CHAPTER THIRTEEN

The Twilight of the British State

New Left Review, I/101–102

JANUARY–APRIL 1977

External conflicts between states form the shape of the state. I am assuming this 'shape' to mean – by contrast with internal social development – the external configuration, the size of a state, its contiguity (whether strict or loose), and even its ethnic composition... We must stress that in the life of peoples external events and conditions exercise a decisive influence upon the internal constitution.[1]

OTTO HINTZE, *The Formation of States and Constitutional Development*
(1902)

ONLY A FEW YEARS AGO, the break-up of Britain was almost inconceivable. Southern, Catholic Ireland had broken away from the United Kingdom in 1922; but there seemed little reason to believe that the Protestants of Northern Ireland or the other minor nationalities of Wales and Scotland would follow their example. Conditions were different in these other cases. Southern Ireland had been a conquered country, displaying most of those features which in this century have come to be called 'under-development'. Upon that basis, and mobilising the deep-laid cultural differences provided by Catholicism, a largely peasant society had produced the classical nationalist reaction against alien rule which ended in 1922. As the century's history of anti-imperialist struggle unfolded, this seemed more and more a typical episode of it. Although unusually close geographically to the metropolitan centre, southern Ireland had in fact been separated from it by a great socio-political gulf, by that great divide which was to dominate so much of the epoch: the 'development gap'.

For this very reason, it appeared improbable that other regions of the British Isles would follow Eire's example. There were episodes of conquest in the histories of northern Ireland, Wales and Scotland, true enough. But these had been followed or accompanied by episodes of assimilation and voluntary integration – and until the 1960s it looked as if the latter tendencies had triumphed. All three societies had, at least in part, crossed over the main divide of the development process. Unlike southern Ireland, they had become significantly industrialised

---

1   *The Historical Essays of Otto Hintze*, London 1975.

in the course of the 19th century. All three had turned into important sub-centres of the Victorian capitalist economy, and around their great urban centres – Belfast, Cardiff and Glasgow – had evolved middle and working classes who, consciously and indisputably, gave their primary political allegiance to the imperial state.

Through this allegiance they became subjects of one of the great unitary states of history. Absorption, not federation, had always been the principle of its development. From the period of Norman feudalism onwards, the English state had expanded its hold over these outlying areas and peoples. Until in 1800 – as one constitutional authority puts it – 'there existed the United Kingdom of Great Britain and Ireland, and in the process of its development there was not the smallest element of federation'. None of the constituent countries of this multi-national state 'retained even a modified sovereignty: that of each was melted in the general mass'.[2]

Such is the theory of the British state, and the notion of the British parliament's total sovereignty still praised and defended in current debate. To understand it as more than that would be misleading. The 'general mass' has not, on the whole, been taken to mean civil society. The 'unitary state' in this form was compatible with civil variety in the different countries composing it: it did not necessarily seek to impose a uniform culture, language, or way of life. There have been examples of forced levelling, for instance in Wales or the Scottish Highlands; yet in the main 'Anglicisation' was left to the slower, more natural-seeming pressures of one large central nationality upon the smaller peripheric areas.

In spite of the pressure, a lot of latitude was left by the system to the personality of the smaller nations. Nineteenth- and early 20th-century British imperialism even encouraged such circumscribed patriotisms. A conservative pride in local colour and traditions went well with the grand design. Hence, until the secession of southern Ireland in 1922, a general formula of 'Home Rule' for all three countries was widely discussed and approved of. While the centre remained strong, such an approach did not appear too threatening. On the other hand, for the same reason – the strong, magnetic pull the metropolis had over its fringe lands – pressure for genuine self-government was not very great. Apart from the exception, Catholic Ireland, it remained weak until the 1960s.

Since then, in only a decade, it has swelled into the major political issue of the 1970s. It is worth underlining how quite unexpected and puzzling this change has been. Vague expectations about a possible transformation, or even collapse, of the British system after the defeat of its empire had been commonplace not for years but for several generations. Worried prognostications of this order go back to the 1890s or even earlier. It never took much political imagination to grasp that: 1. Great Britain was quite unusually and structurally dependent upon external relations tied up with its empire; 2. Britain was due for demotion or outright

---

2   C. F. Strong, *Modern Political Constitutions*, 8th revised edition, London 1972, chapter 4, section IV.

defeat at the hands of the bigger, more dynamic capitalist states that expanded from the late 19th century onwards. Hence the loss of its critical overseas wealth and connections was bound to promote internal readjustments – or perhaps, as left-wing observers imagined with relish, a real social revolution. There was something suitable about this: the most inveterate and successful exploiters ought to suffer the most sensational punishment.

There is no doubt that the old British state is going down. But, so far at least, it has been a slow foundering rather than the *Titanic*-type disaster so often predicted. And in the 1970s it has begun to assume a form which practically no one foresaw. Prophets of doom always focused, quite understandably, upon social and economic factors. Blatant, deliberately preserved inequities of class were the striking feature of the English social order. Here was the original proletariat of the world's industrial revolution, still concentrated in huge depressed urban areas, still conscious of being a class – capable of being moved to revolutionary action, surely, when the economic crisis got bad enough. As for the economic slide itself, nothing seemed more certain. A constantly weakening industrial base, a dominant financial sector oriented towards foreign investment rather than the re-structuring of British industries, a non-technocratic state quite unable to bring about the 'revolution from above' needed to redress this balance: everything conspired to cause an inexorable spiral of decline. The slide would end in break-down, sooner rather than later.

Clearly the prophecies were out of focus, in spite of the strong elements of truth in them. The way things have actually gone poses two related questions. Firstly, why has the old British state-system lasted so long, in the face of such continuous decline and adversity? Secondly, why has the break-down begun to occur in the form of territorial disintegration, rather than as the long-awaited social revolution? Why has the threat of secession apparently eclipsed that of the class struggle, in the 1970s? In my view the answer to both of these questions depends mainly upon one central factor, unfortunately neglected in the majority of discussions on the crisis. This central issue is the historical character of the British state itself.

The Logic of Priority

The most important single aspect of the United Kingdom state is its developmental priority. It was the first state-form of an industrialised nation. From this position in the general process of modern development come most of the underlying characteristics of the system. A specific historical location furnished those 'external conditions', in Hintze's sense, that 'exercised a decisive influence upon the internal constitution'. Critical analysis of the state-form has been retarded by two inter-related factors. The conservative account which has always insisted on the system's uniqueness is in reality a mythology, and has been an important ideological arm of the state itself. But critical rejection of these mystifications, above all by Marxists, has normally reverted into complete abstraction. Thus, a pious bourgeois cult of British priority and excellence has been countered by insistence that there is 'in reality' nothing special about the British state: like all others, it represents the dominance of a capitalist class.[3]

In development terms, it represented the dominance of the first national capitalist class which emancipated itself from city or city-state mercantilism and created the foundations of industrialisation. From its example, much of the original meaning of 'development' was derived. For this reason the English – subsequently 'British' – political system was, and still remains, 'unique' in a non-mystifying sense. These are peculiarities that owe nothing to the inherent political virtues of the British, and everything to the conditions and temporality of capitalist development in the British Isles. The multi-national state-form that has ruled there from 1688 to the present time could not be 'typical' of general modern development, simply because it initiated so much of that development.

This initiation goes back to the revolutionary era of English history, between 1640 and 1688. It is not necessary here to discuss the various accounts which

---

3 'Marxist political analysis has long suffered from marked deficiencies... notably in relation to the nature and role of the state, and has shown little capacity to renew itself...', notes Ralph Miliband in *The State in Capitalist Society* (London 1969, pp. 6–8). Apart from Gramsci, 'Marxists have made little attempt to confront the question of the state in the light of the concrete reality of actual capitalist societies'. But his own analysis remains focused upon 'the many fundamental uniformities... the remarkable degree of similarity, not only in economic but in social and even in political terms, between the countries of advanced capitalism' (p. 9). However, theory-construction equally demands advance on the terrain of differentiation and specific analysis: the developmental uniqueness of states as well as their uniformities. A characteristic example of the traditional application of Marxist theory to Britain is *The British State*, by J. Harvey and K. Hood, London 1958 – see particularly chapter 2, 'The Marxist Theory and the British State'. On the other side, there is of course a huge literature devoted to panegyric of the Constitution, along the lines of Sir David Lindsay Keir's *The Constitutional History of Modern Britain since 1485*: 'Continuity has been the dominant characteristic in the development of English government. Its institutions, though unprotected by the fundamental or organic laws which safeguard the 'rigid' constitutions of most other states, have preserved the same general appearance throughout their history, and have been regulated in their working by principles which can be regarded as constant.' These institutions 'have all retained, amid varying environments, many of the inherent attributes as well as much of the outward circumstance and dignity which were theirs in the medieval world of their origin. In no other European country is the constitution so largely a legacy from that remote but not unfamiliar age...', and so on (8th edition, London 1966, chapter 1). By far the most useful and disrespectful classic of constitutional lore is Walter Bagehot's *The English Constitution*. Sir Ivor Jennings's *Parliament* (London 1939) contains two exemplary mainstream summations of myth in its opening sections, 'Authority Transcendent and Absolute' and 'The Importance of Being Ancient'.

have been given of the causes or unfolding of the upheaval.[4] But few critics would dispute that it signalled the end of absolutism in the British Isles. By the beginning of the next century, only the Celtic areas in the north and west retained a basis for restoring the absolute monarchy; and this attempt failed finally in 1746. Thus, the late-feudal state had effectively disappeared by the end of the 17th century, and the way had been opened – at least – for the development of a bourgeois society.[5] To the conditions of that society there corresponded a new type of political state, first theorised by Thomas Hobbes and John Locke. 'In the aftermath of the crisis... it became clear that despite differences in emphasis there was a strong converging tendency so that by the early 18th century the search for sovereignty was moving almost all the European countries towards the concept of the impersonal state', writes one historian of the idea of the state.[6] This common tendency, in time, produced the modern constitutional state of the 19th century. In 1843 Marx delineated the latter's emergence as follows. The political revolution which had destroyed feudalism 'raised state affairs to become affairs of the people, (and) constituted the political state as a matter of *general* concern, that is, as a real state, necessarily smashed all estates, corporations, guilds and privileges, since these were all manifestations of the separation of the people from the community...'. It posited a collection of abstract individuals – 'citizens' – whose collective will was supposedly represented by the abstract authority of the new state. The real life of these individuals, as property-owners, religious believers, workers, family men and women, etc., was consigned to the realm of 'civil society'.[7]

This relationship between society and state was – as Marx indicates in the same place – first completely formulated by Rousseau, and realised in practice by the French Revolution. This second revolutionary era, from the American revolt of 1776 up to 1815, marked the definitive establishment of modern constitutionalism. Absolutism has been far stronger over most of the European continent than in England. Hence, 'On the Continent, the full development of constitutionalism was delayed until the 19th century, and... it took a series of

---

4   These are summed up in Lawrence Stone's *The Causes of the English Revolution, 1529–1642*, London 1972.

5   In England, Absolutism was 'felled at the centre by a commercialised gentry, a capitalist city, a commoner artisanate and yeomanry: forces pushing beyond it. Before it could reach the age of maturity, English Absolutism was cut off by a bourgeois revolution', writes Perry Anderson in *Lineages of the Absolutist State*, London 1974, p. 220. An earlier bourgeois revolution had occurred in the Netherlands, but this model did not lead to a comparable sustained priority of development. There, the 'transitional' state form quickly decayed into a highly conservative patriciate.

6   J. H. Shennan, *Origins of the Modern European State*, 1450–1725, London 1974, p. 113.

7   Marx, 'On the Jewish Question', in Marx and Engels, *Collected Works*, vol. 3 (1843–4), p. 166.

revolutions to achieve it.'[8] It was these revolutions which formed the typical modern idea and practice of the state, imitated and reduplicated on an ever-increasing scale up to the present day. 'With the exception of those of Great Britain and the United States', points out the same author, 'no existing constitution is older than the 19th century, and most of those which existed in the first half of that century have since either entirely disappeared... or been so fundamentally amended and revised as to be in effect new.'[9] But, of course, the association of the English and American systems is misleading here: the American was the first-born of the moderns, and only the English represents a genuine survival.

Alone, it represented 'a slow, conventional growth, not, like the others, the product of deliberate invention, resulting from a theory'. Arriving later, those others 'attempted to sum up at a stroke the fruits of the experience of the state which had evolved its constitutionalism through several centuries'.[10] But in doing so (as panegyrists of Westminster have always said) they could not help betraying that experience, which remained (in a sense far less flattering than the panegyrists believe) inimitable. Because it was first, the English – later British – experience remained distinct. Because they came second, into a world where the English Revolution had already succeeded and expanded, later bourgeois societies could not repeat this early development. Their study and imitation engendered something substantially different: the truly modern doctrine of the abstract or 'impersonal' state which, because of its abstract nature, could be imitated in subsequent history. This may of course be seen as the ordinary logic of developmental processes. It was an early specimen of what was later dignified with such titles as 'the law of uneven and combined development'. Actual repetition and imitation are scarcely ever possible, whether politically, economically, socially or technologically, because the universe is already too much altered by the first cause one is copying. But this example of the rule had one interesting consequence it is important to underline in the present context.

Most theory about the modern state and representative democracy has been, inevitably, based upon the second era of bourgeois political revolution. This is because that era saw what Marx called 'the completion of the idealism of the state', and the definition of modern constitutionalism. It established and universalised what is still meant by the 'state', and the relationship of the political state to society. Hegelian-based idealism and Marxism were both founded upon study of 'The *classic* period of political intellect... the *French Revolution*' and its derivatives.[11] As such, they naturally – even legitimately – neglected the preceding evolution of the English state. Far less defined and universalisable, this process

---

8   C. F. Strong, op. cit., p. 25.

9   Ibid., p. 36.

10   Ibid., p. 28.

11   'Critical Marginal Notes on the Article 'The King of Prussia and Social Reform, by a Prussian' ', in Marx and Engels, op. cit., p. 199.

embodied, and retained, certain original characteristics that in the later perspectives seemed 'anomalous', or even inexplicable.[12] These traits have remained the preserve of worshippers within, and puzzled comment without. It is for this reason that the present political crisis in Britain raises such far-ranging and theoretical problems. While comparable to other problem-situations in Western Europe in a number of ways – e.g. Italy, as regards its economic dimensions, or Spain and France as regards its neo-nationalism – there is something important and *sui generis* about the British case. It is, in effect, the extremely long-delayed crisis of *the* original bourgeois state-form – of the grandfather of the contemporary political world. The passing of this ancestor calls for more than superficial commentary.

An Imperial State

The non-typical features of the British state order can be described by calling it 'transitional'. More than any other society it established the transition from the conditions of later feudalism to those of modernity. More than its predecessor,

---

12 The 'marked deficiencies' of analysis noted by Miliband (note 2 above) have unfortunately an influential origin in the history of Marxist writing: the deficiencies of Marx's and Engels' own views on the British state. The odd situation these views represent has been insufficiently emphasised by their biographers. From mid-century onwards the main theorists of the following century's revolutions lived in the most developed capitalist society, and the central part of their main achievement, Capital, was based to a great extent on study of its economy. Yet they wrote very little on its state and hegemonic structures. Compilations of their writings on Britain (e.g. Marx and Engels, *On Britain*, Moscow 1953) are among the thinnest of such volumes. Also, their outstanding writings touching on relevant political questions were all early, and were never improved upon: the striking examples here are Engels's *Vorwärts!* articles on 'The Condition of England' (now in Collected Works, vol. 3) and his *The Condition of the Working Class in England* (Collected Works, vol. 4). These date from 1844 and 1845. Marx's own general political ideas were formed before his exile in England. As Colletti observes in a recent introduction to the *Early Writings*, he 'already possessed a very mature theory of politics and the state... (and)... Politically speaking, mature Marxism would have relatively little to add to this' (*Early Writings*, Pelican Marx Library, London 1975, p. 45). This 'mature theory' was wholly drawn from Continental study and experiences. There were to be no further experiences compelling them to a more searching inquiry into the prior universe of the British state: their long exile coincided largely with an era of quiescence and growing stability in Britain, and this seems to have rendered them largely incurious about their immediate political milieu. The absence of curiosity led them to persist in a view (very marked in their occasional articles and letters on Britain) of the state as a façade or mask of capitalist realities. The evident archaism of the state did not, therefore, qualify their vision of these realities as the prefiguration of what other, later-developing societies would have to undergo. But their enormous authority in other directions has always tended to justify this blind spot, and so underwrite the 'marked deficiencies'.

the Dutch Republic, it gave impetus and direction to the whole of later social development. Yet for this very reason it could not itself be 'modern'. Neither feudal nor modern, it remained obstinately and successfully intermediate: the midwife of modern constitutionalism, perhaps, as much as a direct ancestor.

Internally, this system presents a number of 'peculiarities' related to its historical location. It replaced late-feudal monarchy by a rule which was – as it remains today – patrician as well as representative. Because in this original case a spontaneously emergent bourgeois 'civil society' created the state, pragmatically, civil society retained an unusual dominance over the state. The only comparable examples were to be in social formations directly hived from England, like the white colonies or North America. Elsewhere the armature of the state itself was of incomparably greater significance in development: all the progeny of the '*classic period of political intellect*' were to be relatively state-dominated formations, reflecting the harder circumstances of historical evolution in the 19th and 20th centuries. In turn, this original English civil hegemony had certain implications for the nature of civil society itself, to which I will return below.

But for the moment it is essential to stress something else. From the outset, all these internal conditions were interwoven with, and in reality dependent on, external conditions. As well as England's place in developmental sequence, one must bear in mind its place in the history of overseas exploitation. As Marx indicated in *Capital*, success on this front was bound up with the primitive accumulation of capital in England itself.[13] The new English state's ascendancy over its competitors in colonisation accompanied the crystallisation of its internal forms. Hence, a double priority was in fact involved: the temporality of England's new capitalist social system was in symbiosis with the country's maritime and conquering adventures. The latter remained a central feature of world history until the Second World War – that is, until long after English industrial capitalism had lost its pre-eminence, and indeed become a somewhat backward economy by many important indices. It was the extraordinary external successes of the transitional English state that permitted it to survive so long. Otherwise, it would certainly have gone down in the wave of new, state-ordered, nationalist capitalisms which developed in the course of the 19th century. It too would have been compelled to suffer a second, modernising revolution and the logical reorganisation of its constitution and state: precisely that second political upheaval whose absence has been the constant enigma and despair of modern Britain.

But in fact the advantages gained through developmental priority were for

---

13 See *Capital*, chapter XXXI, 'The Genesis of the Industrial Capitalist': 'The colonial system ripened trade and navigation as in a hot-house... The colonies provided a market for the budding manufactures, and a vast increase in accumulation which was guaranteed by the mother country's monopoly of the market. The treasures captured outside Europe by undisguised looting, enslavement and murder flowed back to the mother-country and were turned into capital there.' (Pelican Marx Library, London 1976, vol. I, p. 918.)

long decisive. As the 'industrial revolution' waned from the mid-19th century onwards, the more conscious and systematic exploitation of these advantages compensated for domestic backwardness. A 'New Imperialism' took over from the old, with the establishment of a financial control of the world market as its core. This mutation accorded supremely well with the character of the patrician state. It safeguarded the latter for another half-century, at the cost of ever-greater external dependency and ever more pronounced sacrifice of the domestic economy. As will be suggested in more detail below, this pattern has reproduced itself without fail not only into the last years, but into the last months and days of the present crisis: a slow, cumulative collapse determined not by the failure of 'British capitalism' alone, but by the specific underlying structures of an archaic state and the civil class-system it protects.

'Imperialism', in the sense pertinent to this prolonged trajectory, is somewhat different from the definitions now customarily given to the term.[14] As with constitutionalism, theory has naturally been pre-occupied in the main by later and more systematic developments: in this case the formation of modern European empires between 1880 and 1945, and the nature of the informal US system which followed them. However, England's pattern of foreign exploitation and dependency has lasted from the 16th century to the present, uninterruptedly. Like the state-form it made possible, it preceded and conditioned the rise of later rivals and – even while adapting to this new world, as in 'New Imperialism' – remained itself of a somewhat different nature.

This nature is best understood in terms of the social order which it fostered in England. A régime so largely concerned with overseas and naval-based exploitation required, above all, conservative stability at home. It demanded a reliable, respectful hierarchy of social estates, a societal pyramid to act as basis for the operations of the patrician élite. This was, of course, quite a different need from the later forms of imperialism. These emerged into an England-dominated world: 'late developers', often with far greater real resources than the British Isles, impelled by a restless internal dynamic of development. This was to be the case, above all, of Germany. The later empires were either industrial-based, like Germany; or else strongly militaristic in outlook, by compensation for the lack of economic potential, like the Italian, French and Portuguese systems. Indeed, more or less aggressive militarism was the general accompaniment of later 19th-century

14 The best review of theories of imperialism is Benjamin Cohen's *The Question of Imperialism: the Political Economy of Dominance and Dependence*, London 1973. The general view of imperialism advanced there perceives it as rooted in 'the external organisation of states' (p. 234), and to that extent accords with the theory of this book. Unfortunately, Cohen fails to relate this theme of external state-order sufficiently to that of uneven development, and so is forced to fall back on nationality and nationalism as 'given facts' rather than as developmental functions (see pp. 255–7). In reality uneven development generates these 'given facts' of imperialism and nationalism for the contemporary era (c. 1750–2000), not vice-versa.

colonisation and expansion. The British empire alone was not in essence either of these things. It had been constituted before the others, on a scale which gave it lasting advantages in the later conflicts. And it had been formed overwhelmingly by naval and commercial strategy in which land militarism was of small account.[15]

The following paradoxes must therefore be taken into account. The pioneer modern liberal-constitutional state never itself became modern: it retained the archaic stamp of its priority. Later the industrialisation which it produced, equally pioneering and equally world-wide in impact, never made England into a genuinely industrialised society. Even more evidently, the cramped foundations of the Industrial Revolution quickly became archaic and *dépassé* when set against the unfolding pattern of general world industrialization from the late 19th century onwards.

The two paradoxes are, of course, organically connected. No recovery from industrial 'backwardness' has been possible, precisely because no second revolution of the state has taken place in England: only the state could have engendered such a recovery, by revolution from above – but the old patrician structure of England's political system, incapable of such radical action, has also resisted every effort at serious reform up to the present day. This astonishing resistance, in turn, must be explained in terms of external relations.

During the very period when industrial backwardness began to present itself as an inescapable problem, between the 1870s and 1914, and foreign competition began to overwhelm England's economy, the archaic mould of society and state was greatly reinforced there. This was the work of the 'New Imperialism', consolidating and reorienting the vast inheritance of previous colonisation and overseas trade. Less and less able to compete with the new workshops of the world, the ruling élite compensated by extended control of the world's money market – by building up a financial centre in the City of London. During the long period when sterling was the world's main trading currency – it lasted until after the Second World War – these unique and formidable financial institutions remained at one level the nucleus of world capitalism. Long after the industrial centre of gravity had moved to North America and Continental Europe, they kept their pre-eminence in the area of capital investment and exchange.[16]

Thus, one part of the capital of England was in effect converted into an

15 In his article 'En Route: Thoughts on the Progress of the Proletarian Revolution' (*Izvestia*, 1919, reproduced in *The First Five Years of the Communist International*, vol. 1, New York 1945), Trotsky commented: 'England's insular position spared her the direct burden of maintaining militarism on land. Her mighty naval militarism, although requiring huge expenditures, rested nevertheless on numerically small cadres of hirelings and did not require a transition to universal military service.'

16 The modern imperialist turning of the UK economy is outlined, and its long-term significance suggested, in S. Pollard, *The Development of the British Economy 1914–1950*, London 1962; see especially 'Foreign Investment and the Problem of Empire', pp. 19–23.

'offshore island' of international capitalism, to a considerable degree independent of the nation's declining domestic capitalism. This type of finance-capital imperialism rested, in other words, on a marked division within British capitalism itself. The latter became the victim of a split between the consistently declining productive sector and the highly successful City sector. Naturally, City institutions monopolised the outstanding talents and energies of the business class; in addition, they exerted virtual hegemony over the state in virtue of the élite social solidarity so strongly rooted in English civil society. This hegemony provided the material basis of the state's 'backwardness'. It was a 'backwardness' perfectly congruent with the demands of the controlling elements in British capitalism – elements which enjoyed the conservative societal hierarchy of 'traditional England' and which, if they did not actually approve of the industrial degeneration, had no urgent reasons for redressing it.[17] External orientation and control implied external dependency. In this sense, it is true to say that such external dependency provided the essential condition for the original accumulation of capital in England; for both the industrial revolution *and* its 'failure', or at least its incomplete and limited character in England itself; and for the one-sided compensatory development of liberal, City imperialism that has carried the old order into the last quarter of the 20th century.

English Civil Society

In his critique of Hegel's theory of the state, Marx insisted that it was not the idea of the state which constituted civil society; rather, the real new nature of civil society – modern or bourgeois society – was responsible for the state. He posited a typical duality of modern conditions, therefore. The competitive, material anarchy of middle-class society evolved as its necessary complement an abstract political state-order: the new liberal or constitutional state. The key mystery of this relationship was representation. The representative mechanism converted real class

---

17 At a number of places in his celebrated Imperialism (1902), J. A. Hobson used southern England as an image of the successful, imperialist side of British capitalism: a countryside of plush 'parasitism' drawing tribute from overseas via the City, supporting 'great tame masses of retainers' in service and secondary industries, and riddled with ex-imperialist hirelings. 'The South and South-West of England is richly sprinkled with these men', he continued, 'most of them endowed with leisure, men openly contemptuous of democracy, devoted to material luxury, social display, and the shallower arts of intellectual life. The wealthier among them discover political ambitions... Not a few enter our local councils, or take posts in our constabulary or our prisons: everywhere they stand for coercion and for resistance to reform' (pp. 150–1, 314, 364–5). Not a few of them were active very recently, in forming para-military and strike-breaking organisations during 1973 and 1974. The only big difference brought by 75 years is that the 'niggers' they were aiming to put down were mostly white: the other, 'unsuccessful' side of British capitalism north of them.

inequality into the abstract egalitarianism of citizens, individual egoisms into an impersonal collective will, what would otherwise be chaos into a new state legitimacy.[18] However, as noted previously, Hegel and Marx alike were in part theorising the later, 'typical' circumstances in which middle classes developed a form of dominance more hastily and competitively, against much greater feudal obstacles, and often by revolutionary effort. Although Marx's view of the priority of civil society applies with particular emphasis to England, the accompanying abstract duality does not. The latter reflected the historical experience of the Continental states.

In the English evolution which had gone before, the middle classes developed more gradually and created a civil society which stood in a substantially different relationship to the state. The conquering social class of the mid-17th-century civil wars was an agrarian élite: landlordism in a new form, and with a new economic foundation, but emphatically not the urban bourgeoisie which later became the protagonist of modern European development. Although no longer feudal, and allied increasingly closely to the urban middle class, this class remained a patrician élite and concentrated political power entirely in its own hands. In a way quite distinct from later 'ruling classes' it constituted the actual personnel and machinery of the English state. The latter was not the impersonal, delegated apparatus to be formulated in 19th-century constitutionalism. On the contrary, in a way which was not repeatable by any typical bourgeois stratum, one social class *was* the state. Hence, one part of civil society wholly dominated 'the state' and lent it, permanently, a character different from its rivals.

In a standard work on the subject, Samuel Finer points out how: 'The importance of this tradition is that it has preserved not only the medieval forms but the medieval essence: this was that the king governed – but conditionally, not

---

18 'The most important characteristic which distinguishes the burghers (*bürgerliche Gesellschaft*) from the other sections of the national community is their individualism... (Civil society) remains basically a multitude of self-seeking individuals, impatient of customs, traditions, and privileges, and apt to conceive freedom as the absence or at least the minimum of political obligations. Such a society threatens not merely the rest of the nation but the supreme public authority itself...'. This is Z. A. Pelczynski's summary of Hegel's view of the political challenge of bourgeois society (*Hegel's Political Writings*, 'Introductory Essay', Oxford 1964, p. 61). This political challenge is taken up much more trenchantly in Marx's early critique of Hegel and (as Colletti emphasises in his presentation of the Early Writings, op. cit.) taken to a supremely logical conclusion, 'a critical analysis of parliamentarism and of the modern representative principle itself' (p. 42). The only way forward was the dual dissolution of egoistic 'civil society' and the state power corresponding to it. But this was an enormous short-circuit historically, which failed to question the basic assumptions of Hegel's view sufficiently: it was not in fact true that bourgeois society is necessarily 'impatient of customs, traditions', etc., etc., and wholly dependent upon an alienated state power for its cohesion. It employed customs and traditions (England was the striking example of this), invented others, and generated the cohesive power of nationalism to hold itself together.

absolutely. At the heart of the English political system – now embracing the entire United Kingdom – there was always a core of officials, who initiated, formulated and executed policy... (and)... political opposition has never sought to abolish this key-nucleus of the working constitution, but only to control it... The form taken by an Act of Parliament links the present to the past and attests the under-lying continuity of the medieval conception of government.'[19] This continuity has not been one of 'medievalism' in a literal sense. But what was preserved was the essence of rule from above, in that 'transitional' mode established by 1688: an élite social class took the place of the failed English absolute monarchy – a collective 'Prince' which now employed the symbolism of the crown for its own ends. This class framed representative rules for its own members, in the most limited version of property-owning parliamentarism: less the foundation of 'demo-cracy' (in the Enlightenment meaning) than a new variety of constitutional aristo-cracy, like a medieval republic upon a grand scale. Its landlords became akin to the self-perpetuating and co-optive élite of such a republic – but in a city-state become a nation-state.

In relation to the body of civil society, this ruling class established a tradition of informality (as opposed to the formality of the 'normal' state-form); personal or quasi-personal domination (as opposed to the impersonality inseparable from later states); non-bureaucratic and relatively de-centralised control with a weak military dimension (as distinct from 'rationalised', rigid and militarised control.) It established a low-profile state which, with the rapid economic development towards the end of the 18th century, easily became the minimal or *laisser-faire* state depicted by classical political economy. The patrician state had turned into the 'nightwatchman state' of the Industrial Revolution, and presided over the most dramatic initial phase of world industrialisation.[20]

---

19 S. E. Finer, *Comparative Government*, London 1970, chapter 5, 'The Government of Britain', p. 139.

20 Marxist and other commentators have often been unable to resist the inference that the minimalist Victorian state so devoted to laisser-faire must have registered an internal change of nature: the mythical middle-class takeover (after which Britain's ruling class merely looked archaic, and was actually an instrument of industrialism, etc.). Perhaps the most striking expression of this view recently is Harold Perkin's *The Origins of Modern English Society, 1780–1880*, London 1969, an analysis justly influential for its account of 18th-century hierarchy and the birth of modern class consciousness. He points out that 'It was... the peculiar relationship of the English landed aristocracy to society and hence to the state which created the political climate for the germination of industrialism' (p. 67), and that *laisser-faire* was not in essence an industrialists' ideology at all: 'The truth is that the English landowners had sold their souls to economic development long before the Industrial Revolution (and) when it came they were more than ready to accept its logic, the freedom of industrial employment from state regulation' (p. 187). Yet he is unable to refrain from depicting a mid-Victorian Triumph of the Entrepreneurial Ideal, and the conventional view that 'the entrepreneurial class ruled, as it were, by remote control, through the power of its ideal over the ostensible ruling class, the landed aristocracy which continued to occupy

This minimalist, crypto-bourgeois state form reposed upon two vital conditions. One we have already noticed: the successful commercial and colonial
strategy that embraced the interests of both élite and middle class together. The
second lay in the constitution of civil society itself. The relative absence of a strong,
centralised state armature in the nation dominating world development was possible only because that national society possessed a different kind of cohesion. It
is the nature of this cohesion which in many ways presents the main problem of
modern British development, above all in comparative perspective.

It is clearly not the case that English bourgeois society resembled the para-
digms imagined by Hegel and Marx: the dissolution of feudal integuments into
a 'state of nature', an unadulterated morass of conflicting egoistic drives, the war
of each against all first theorised by Hobbes. Certain sectors of the new industrial bourgeoisie may have looked like that; they were certainly pictured as like
it in some celebrated literary vignettes of the 19th century. Yet on any broader
view the picture is quite unsustainable. The new stratum of 'economic men'
were never more than a minority, and a relatively powerless minority (indeed,
one way of looking at the subsequent problems of capitalism in England is to
say that they have never become nearly strong enough politically and culturally). They existed inside a larger civil order whose striking characteristics were
(to a degree still are) practically the contrary of the great anti-bourgeois myths.

In a sense not true of any other contemporary state, Finer notes that the English
Constitution is 'a facet, a particular aspect of the wider life of the community.

---

the main positions of power down to the 1890s and beyond... Neither contemporaries nor
historians have doubted that the capitalist middle class were the 'real' rulers of mid-Victorian England, in the sense that the laws were increasingly those demanded by the busi-
ness-men and... their intellectual mentors' (p. 272). In fact, there was no such Triumph, or
change of nature, for the reasons he himself indicates: the ruling élite could adjust relatively
easily to the *laisser-faire* conditions of primitive industrialisation – 'seizing on Adam Smith'
(in his own words) 'as in an earlier age they had seized on Locke, to justify their instincts by
the borrowed light of reason' (p. 187). If one seriously, believes that the 'entrepreneurial
class' took over 19th-century Britain, them the entire subsequent history of entrepreneurial
backsliding and chronic industrial failure becomes incomprehensible. In fact, successful
enterprise moved away from industry altogether after the first cycle of industrialization
and, far from dislodging the élite or the state, formed a new alliance with them on the foundation of City-centred imperialism. A generation later this ruling complex discovered a
new 'borrowed light of reason' in J. M. Keynes. Important studies stressing the continuity
of the ruling class include W. L. Guttsman, *The British Political Elite*, London 1963, and
The English Ruling Class, London 1969. Ivor Crewe's Introduction, 'Studying Elites in
Britain', to *The British Political Sociology Yearbook*, vol. 1, London 1974, contains a devastating critique of the failures of social science in Britain to confront its main problem: 'So
far no sustained empirical analysis of the British power structure has appeared', he points
out, in a society where 'it is natural to conclude that a small, economically and education-
ally privileged group of high traditional status possesses a pervasive and decisive influence
in British affairs' (pp. 13–15).

It is an emanation, not an epiphenomenon: it springs out of British social structure and values, it is not something that some group has superimposed upon these.' One symptom of this is what he calls 'the powerful and pervasive role of interest groups... related in turn to the wide proliferation of autonomous private associations' in English life.[21] This aspect of social structure probably derives from the original, spontaneous development of the state in England. State power was appropriated by a self-regulating élite group which established powerful conventions of autonomy: that is, of forms of self-organisation and voluntary action independent of state direction. By their efficacy, these in effect came to function as a civil substitute for the state. They imparted to the body of civil society a consistency that rendered the state-skeleton less significant under English conditions. Such traditions of autonomous responsibility had a class basis: they represented originally the civil-cum-political authority of the agrarian élite. However, they could be imparted to the bourgeoisie also, given the relatively gradual emergence of the latter class within the old patrician mould. There was a sufficient common basis of interest to make this possible.

There were at least three dimensions to this common interest. One lay, of course, in the successful expansion and defence of overseas empire. A second can be found in the degree of economic homogeneity between the governing landed class and the bourgeoisie: while remaining a genuine social aristocracy, the former had long ago ceased to be a feudal estate economically. During the 18th century it consolidated its position by a successful revolution from above, the 'agrarian revolution' which provided one of the necessary conditions for the better-known industrial development that followed. Using its state hegemony to expropriate the peasantry, the landowning élite built up a capitalist agriculture that prospered in harmony with the industrialisation process until the later 19th century, by which time Great Britain had become overwhelmingly dependent on imports of food and the agrarian sector had become relatively unimportant. The third binding factor – and the one which has aroused most critical attention – consisted in the joint front formed by the landowners and the bourgeoisie against the proletariat which arose in the Industrial Revolution. There is little doubt that this is the key to understanding the class composition of modern English civil society, for the pattern lasted from the 1840s until after the Second World War. It is also the key – for the reasons already advanced – to an understanding of society-state relations, and so of the state itself.[22]

---

21   S. E. Finer, op. cit., p. 131.

22   In a critique of my and Perry Anderson's earlier views about this crucial point, Richard Johnson writes that 'their main explanatory notion, aristocratic hegemony, *turns out to be nothing more than the principal theme of English Liberal ideology*... (where)... the roots of evils has been seen *precisely* as 'feudal', 'aristocratic' or 'military' residues in an industrial-democratic world. *The New Left Review* analysis conforms to this very English tradition of radical liberalism: it does not surpass it, still less unmask it.' ('Barrington Moore,

The most common pattern in the formation of modern states was that the middle classes, whether in a social revolution or in a nationalist movement, turned for help to the people in their effort to throw off the burden of 'traditional society' (absolutism, feudalism, or the imported oppression of colonial régimes). During the '*classic* period' the French Revolution had given the sharpest and most influential definition to this conflict. However, developmental priority was to impose and retain quite a different pattern on England. The Civil War of the 1640s was the English conflict that most nearly corresponded to the later model (the 'first bourgeois revolution'). Yet, while ending absolutism and opening the way to capitalism, it had given in many respects the weakest and least influential definition to the general movement which followed in Europe. In spite of its importance, its *political* imprint on subsequent developments was almost nil.

The patrician class and state provided the necessary conditions for industrialisation. Thus, these material conditions encouraged the middle class to bury its revolutionary inheritance, at the same time as the spread of Enlightenment ideology made the concepts of the previous century (the 'Puritan Revolution') outmoded and useless for farther political progress. Towards the end of the century, external forces were again decisive in cementing the alliance. The prolonged overseas struggle with France ended in a successful war against the French Revolution – that is, against most of the political meaning of the 'classic period'. This crucial victory in the great-power struggle consolidated the paradox: already an archaism in certain obvious respects, the English (now 'British') patrician state none the less remained able to lead and dominate world development for another half-century. No rival comparable to the French *ancien régime* would appear until the unification of Germany. During these noon-day generations, Great Britain accumulated reserves of capital – and not only economic capital – which would sustain its antique forms for far longer than the radicals and early socialists of the 19th century dreamed.

In effect, these conditions prevented the 'second bourgeois revolution' in the British Isles – that 'modernising' socio-political upheaval that ought to have

---

Perry Anderson and English Social Development', in *Cultural Studies*, No. 9, Birmingham, Spring 1976, p. 21.) In reality, the author continues, both the élitist phenomena which we stressed and the more blatantly bourgeois aspects of British existence were '*pressed into the service of capital as a whole*' (p. 25). However, this critique answers itself. What is 'capital as a whole' in the specific circumstances of British social development? Not an undifferentiated and abstract category, but an imperialist formation with a meaningful and sustaining relationship to the retrograde forms our analysis underlined: it was the capture of Liberalism by Imperialism which nullified the former's radical aspect, and gave the working class the task of recovering and accentuating that radicalism as a necessary part of its own political advance. This 'second bourgeois revolution' remains in that limited sense on the historical agenda, but it is surely not the case that recognizing this entails a general ideological retreat to old-fashioned radicalism. It is true that we did not 'unmask' radicalism; but then, no Marxist analysis ever 'unmasks' any phenomena in this Phantom-of-the-Opera sense.

refashioned both society and state in logical conformity with the demands of the new age. This was not because radical intellectuals and movements did not call for such a change. On the contrary, both before and after 1789, a good deal of the blueprints for modernity were drawn up in Britain (and to a remarkable extent they were conceived in the most curious 'stateless society' of the 18th century, Scotland). In the 1830s and 1840s, what seemed at the time the strongest radical movement in Europe, Chartism, struggled to realise these ideas. In the *Manifesto* Marx and Engels supplied the most celebrated formula for bourgeois revolution: 'At a certain stage in the development of those means of production and exchange, the conditions under which feudal society produced and exchanged, the feudal organisation of agriculture and manufacturing industry, in one word, the feudal relations of property became no longer compatible with the already developed productive forces; they became so many fetters. They had to be burst asunder; they were burst asunder.'[23] The radical formula was not enactable in Britain partly because the 'conditions of feudal society' had already been burst asunder and replaced by pre-modern, transitional ones; partly because of the external triumphs of these transitional forms; and partly because of the threat which the dispossessed and the new proletarian masses presented to them.

This 'threat' would, of course, have been the opportunity for a bourgeois class desperate to get rid of real feudal 'fetters'. But classes embrace political revolution only when they see no other route forward. In spite of the enormous social tensions of the industrial revolution, this was never the case for the English middle class. It was possible, though not easy, for them to arrive at a workable compromise with the political ruling class. This possibility always determined their long-term course, fortifying them against the social threat from underneath and removing most of the substance from their radicalism. Bourgeois radicalism did not vanish from the British political scene: it reappeared in many guises later in the 19th century, between the 1870s and 1914, represented by leaders like Joseph Chamberlain and David Lloyd George, and it is still represented today by certain aspects of both the Liberal and Labour Parties. However, its relegation to a secondary (and often regional) status proved permanent. Patrician liberalism had defeated radical liberalism, and its victory has marked the whole evolution of the political system since then.

This was a 'compromise' quite distinct in nature from the ones arrived at in late-developing nations like Germany and Japan. There also the new bourgeois classes were driven into alliances with landowning élites against the threat of revolt or social turbulence – alliances which also sacrificed the enlightened inheritance of egalitarian progress and democratic politics, and encrusted capitalism with all sorts of pre-modern features. But in these other cases a new, forced industrialism was entering partnership with more genuinely archaic landlord classes – with social orders which had never gone through an equivalent of 1640, let

23 Marx and Engels, *Collected Works*, vol. 6, p. 489.

alone a 1789. This linkage with military late-feudalism was different in its whole developmental character from the English alliance with a post-feudal, civilian, parliamentary élite. It subordinated capitalism to militarised 'strong states' whose inevitable external aim was to contest Great Britain's already established territorial and economic domination.

Both the cost and the gains from the English class-compromise were less dramatic, more long-term (and, of course, not so much of a threat to world peace). The cost was the containment of capitalism within a patrician hegemony which never, either then or since, actively favoured the aggressive development of industrialism or the general conversion of society to the latter's values and interests. Permanent social limits were thus imposed upon the 'industrial revolution' and the British entrepreneurial stratum. As we shall see later, in a curious – and again unique – fashion, the emergence of working-class politics would merely confirm these limitations, and in its own way render the 'second political revolution' even more distant.

The gains were represented by the effective social subordination of the lower classes – a structural domination achieved by the re-formation of civil society and the enactment of a long-term social strategy, rather than by state or military means. What the re-formation created was a clearly demarcated order of classes, in the stable form most appropriate to overseas-oriented exploitation. High social mobility, individualism, egalitarian openness, *la carrière ouverte aux talents*, restless impatience with tradition – the traits of dynamic capitalism were systematically relegated or discounted, in favour of those which fitted Britain's particular kind of empire. From the latter half of the 19th century onward a similar neglect and relegation of technical and applied-science education was noticeable – the type of formation most important in all later stages of industrialisation, after England's pioneering lead. This imbalance was never to be corrected, in spite of (at the time of writing) almost a century of complaints on the subject.

The Intelligentsia

What did this social strategy of containment consist of? It was pointed out earlier that the civil conventions of self-organisation and regulation were imparted to the middle class, on the foundations of growing common interests. This, rather than state bureaucracy or armed repression, would furnish the cohesion of English progress. However, such a strategy needed an instrument – the civil equivalent of state-directed authority, as it were, a pervasive power capable of acting upon civil society at large. This instrument was the English intellectual class. In a broad sense of the term, stretching from literary and humanist thinkers on one side to the Church and 'civil servants' (the English word for functionaries) on the other, the 'intelligentsia' played an unusually central and political role in promoting social integration.

The more habitual use of the term indicates an intellectual stratum distanced from society and state: thinkers and writers distanced from and critical of the status quo. In the English social world, however, almost the reverse is the case. This is undoubtedly another of those anomalies that have made the comparative grasp of British development so difficult. From the inside the phenomenon has been elusive simply because virtually everyone concerned with analysis of the British state has been a member of the class in question: myths of British civilisation have rendered self-scrutiny unnecessary. From the outside, judgement has been impeded by the developmental singularity of the thing: an intellectual class of great power and functionality, yet not either created by or in critical opposition to the state – neither a state-fostered technocracy (on the French model) nor an 'alienated' intelligentsia (on the Russian model). In addition, of course, it should be remembered that both sociological and Marxist analysis of intellectuals has been very slow in advancing any adequate general theory of intellectual groups.[24]

The nucleus of the English intellectual class was formed by civil society itself, not the state. From the mid-19th century up to the present day, this civil armature has been created by a small number of private, élite educational institutions: the 'Public Schools' and the old universities. Although, in recent times, the latter

---

24 The *locus classicus* for critical analysis of this phenomenon has become Noel Annan's essay 'The Intellectual Aristocracy', in J. H. PLumb (ed.), *Studies in Social History: a Tribute to G. M. Trevelyan*, London 1955. This at least gives some overall sense of the authority of this informal tradition. Unfortunately little advance has been made upon it, not surprisingly in view of Crewe's strictures (see note 19, above). The most useful, though still quite inadequate, way to approach it is via study of the educational system. On the principle that the anatomy of the ape is contained in that of *homo sapiens*, the reader could do worse than begin with the report *Elites and their Education*, by David Boyd (National Foundation for Educational Research, London 1973). This demonstrates that since the Second World War there has been very little alteration in élite formation: a slight decrease in 'Public School men' in the ranks of the state bureaucracy has been compensated for by a slight but appropriate increase in the army, the navy, and the banks. Dr Boyd (an American) concludes that the outstanding trait of this immutable mafia is the near-complete absence of 'inter-generational mobility': the clerisy perpetuates itself to an astonishing extent simply by breeding, and the occasional co-option of a few lower-bourgeois upstarts who normally become the most impassioned defenders of the system. Commenting dolefully on the last of many efforts to 'modernise' the recruitment of higher state cadres, Leslie Moody of the Civil Service Union said: 'The point is, that you can lay down as many provisions as you like, but if the appointment to top jobs is by selection boards, then the preferences of those on the boards will be reflected. You can't legislate prejudice out of people's minds...' (*Guardian*, 30 October 1973). Mr Moody's hope was that by the 1980s things might be a little better. On the Marxist side, it is Gramsci's *Gli Intellettuali* which furnishes some elements for the analysis of intellectual strata in traditional societies; but here too little has been added by subsequent work. For a critical account of Gramsci's concept of 'hegemony', see Perry Anderson, NLR 100, 1976–7. Most treatments of the subject have tended to focus on the question of revolutionary intelligentsias (e.g. Alvin Gouldner's recent work) rather than on their role in stable societies like England.

have become financially dependent upon the state and enlarged the social basis of their recruitment, this has not altered their essential mode of operation. Originally, patrician liberalism depended upon a supposedly 'natural' governing élite: a land-based stratum with certain social characteristics of caste. The functional intelligentsia formed from the 1830s onwards was in essence a still more artificial perpetuation of this, where civil institutions gradually replaced landowning as the foundation of hegemony.

Discussion of this issue has often been clouded rather than clarified by theories of general élitism. It is often argued that all states depend on some form of élite stratification and specialisation, and that democracies engender oligarchies. But the British state is in this respect also distinct: it is a case, and really the only case, where oligarchy engendered democracy through an organic social strategy that preserved its own nature (and, naturally, deeply marked and infirmed the 'democracy' which emerged). In this case, élitism was neither fossil survival nor aberration: it has remained the enduring truth of the state. British Labourism is the story of how working-class politics made its own compact with that truth. The bourgeoisie made an alliance with the English form of landlordism, and this was expressed by the formation of the liberal intelligentsia; in turn, that stratum took charge of the emergent political force of the proletariat in the first quarter of the 20th century. In the archetypal person of J. M. Keynes it conceived the new, most general formula for this second alliance, which has lasted from the Great Depression to the present and seen the Labour Party become the main support of the declining state.

From this forward glance one gains already some idea of the astonishing social strength of the system. Embodied in the intelligentsia, the social strategy responsible for this endurance was neither that of revolution from below, nor that of revolution from above – the two main avenues whose interaction has defined so much of modern history. It averted the former, which remained a possibility until the defeat of Chartism; but without embarking on the latter either. It exorcised the spectre of a second, radical revolution – yet without creating the 'strong state' and the right-wing or nationalist social mobilisation which was the alternative way of catching up. Alone among the major powers of 1815–1945, Great Britain was able to evade the choice. Priority and external success let the country remain socio-economically 'backward' (at least from the 1880s) without driving either the lower class and intellectuals, or the economic ruling class, to despair. And throughout the epoch, such adjustment as proved necessary to maintain the system in being was conceived, publicised, and largely enacted by this exceptionally active, confident and integrated intellectual class. If the external secret of old England's longevity was empire, the internal secret lay here: in the co-optive and cohesive authority of an intelligentsia much more part of the state, much closer to political life and more present in all important civil institutions than in any other bourgeois society.

The world-view of this social group is a conservative liberalism, and in terms of socio-political strategy this entailed the preservation of rule from above by constant adaptation and concession below. The general social conservatism of modern England demanded the retention of fixed distinctions of rank: stability before mobility. Yet in modern conditions such stable cohesion was only possible where the lower classes acquired a minimum of confidence in the system – that is, in English terms, a trust in 'them', the rulers. This belief in the concrete nature of the constitution – our way of doing things, etc., as different from the abstraction of post-1789 constitutionalism – depended in turn on 'their' capacity to offer sufficient concessions. Adequate adaptation thus conserved the patrician essence, and strengthened its accompanying mythology, in a continuing dialectic against the new pressures from below.

A misplaced mysticism has been natural enough, considering the success of the machinery. But in reality such a political order worked through the unique conjunction of two factors: a social stratum able to enact it – the governing intelligentsia – and the material or external conditions enjoyed by the whole society. The long-term strategy in question has certainly never been employed anywhere else (giving rise to the idea of the peculiar 'cleverness' of the British ruling class). It could not be. More centralised and rigid state-systems do not work in that way at all: no administrative bureaucracy – even in the shape of the most dazzling products of the French *grandes écoles* – can function with the powerful, pervasive informality of England's civil élite. Neither the feudal absolute state, nor – in the Marxist phraseology – the democratic committee-state of the bourgeoisie could possibly imitate it. But this is merely to state that the *typical* forms of pre-modern and contemporary polity are different.

A strategy of compromise presupposes the restriction of the political dialogue to what can be demanded or conceded in this fashion. As we saw, the social formula was originally contrived between the post-1688 landlord class and the middle classes, and grew from common interests. The latter furnished sufficient homogeneity among the upper strata for mutual adjustments to be possible, and for the question of power never to be made too acute. This is the point of a flexible compromise-strategy. It keeps the issue of command, or the source of authority, at a distance; instead, the political process is restricted to the apparent exchange of influences – to trading within a social continuum, certain of whose features are seen as unalterable.

However, this plainly poses a problem regarding the integration of the working class. Since the First World War the final form of the English political world, and of its myth, has been the inclusion of the working class. In 1844 Engels wrote that Toryism had begun to alter course (under Peel), because 'it has realised that the English Constitution cannot be defended, and is making concessions simply to maintain that tottering structure as long as possible.[25] The new, alien element

---

25 'The Condition of England, II', in *Collected Works*, vol. 3, p. 491 and pp. 512–13.

of democracy would destroy it; and in British conditions, democracy would become '*social* democracy', the transition to socialism itself. This was in an essay explaining the Constitution to the readers of *Vorwärts*. It did not occur to Engels, Marx or other radicals that the tottering structure would absorb the proletariat politically without even becoming 'democratic' in the sense intended. Still less could they conceive how the resultant non-democratic proletarian movement might turn into an essential prop of the archaic state and the essentially in-egalitarian society they contemplated with such contempt. The strategy of 'concessions' was enormously stronger than then seemed likely; the 'tottering' aspect of the system was merely its constant motion of adaptation and containment. Provided with both an internal mechanism of development and highly favourable external conditions, it was able to broaden its social basis in successive stages between 1832 and 1918. At the latter date, the concession of universal male suffrage coincided with the maximum territorial extension of the British Empire after its victory in the First World War.

The Working Class

The working class did not have interests in the social order in the same sense as the middle classes; there was no basis for the same sort of compromise as the latter arrived at with the landlords. However, another proved possible – and indeed so satisfactory that after 1945 the labour movement was to play in many respects the major part in securing another generation of existence for the old state. Far from diminishing with the latter's slide towards collapse after the 1950s, this alliance has if anything grown stronger. It was to be the Labour Party that made the most determined effort to restore the fortunes of British capitalism in 1964–7; when this attempt failed, it became in turn the main political buttress of the state in a more straightforward conservative sense. It rebuilt consensus after the outbreak of class conflict under the Heath Conservative government. This consensus took the form of a negotiated suspension of the economic class struggle – the 'Social Contract' – as the precondition for another, more cautious effort at capitalist restoration.

Like its predecessors, this policy was associated with complete (if not rather exaggerated) fidelity to the Constitution and all its traditions. The House of Lords has become the target of some attacks as an 'anachronism'; this is the limit of Labour's iconoclasm. The very fact of the existence of the 'Social Contract' at this late hour, and with these implications, shows the depth of the real social-class alliance behind it.

The most common version of national class alliance – as I remarked above – lies between the popular masses and a middle class which undertakes the establishment of a modern state. That is, of a constitutional democracy with standard forms. It is also true that numerous 'deviant' versions exist: the popular support for the middle-class counter-revolutions of 1918–39, and mass acquiescence in many third-world military and one-party régimes. Yet it should be acknowledged that all have something in common, as would-be modernizing states (even if in some cases, as with the fascist dictatorships, this revolutionary side was mainly appearance). The British variety has been very different. It is a social alliance based not upon a modernising bourgeois revolution, but upon the conservative containment and taming of such a revolution. Whereas in the former process the masses are normally led by middle-class cadres into the overthrow of an *ancien régime*, in the latter they are deprived of such leadership. Under British conditions the intellectuals were not radicalised: they moved more and more into that peculiar service of the old order mentioned previously, as an extensive, civil-based, autonomous corps of *chiens de garde*. Without the leadership of a militant radicalism, the masses were unable to break the system.[26]

The waves of social revolt generated by early industrialisation, from the period of Luddism to the 1840s, fell away in mid-century and revived only in very different forms towards the end of the century. Had there existed a true confrontation between the bourgeoisie and a feudal caste closer to its origins, the political reforms of 1832 would have figured as simple palliatives – a doomed effort to arrest the tide. In fact, they signalled a turning-point in the other sense. After 1832, the bourgeoisie became steadily more positively reconciled to the state. And in the wake of this reconciliation, through the defeat of Chartism, the working class became negatively reconciled to the same old corruption, to élite hegemony, class distinctions, and deference to tradition.

Having failed to break through, the working class was forced to retreat upon itself. Political defeat and the accumulation of powerful social pressures from above compelled the formation of a deeply defensive, somewhat corporative attitude. This was to be defined most clearly – as the basis of the 20th-century workers' movements – by the trade-unionism that arose in the later decades of Queen Victoria's reign. Devoted to the piecemeal improvement of workers' conditions within the existing conservative social framework – a status quo now strengthened by two further generations of imperial success – this movement moved only very slowly and reluctantly back towards any political challenge to the state. Though increasingly strong in itself, trade-unionism remained mainly deferential

---

26 Connoisseurs of these debates on the UK Left will know that no statement like this can be made without provoking accusations of crazed idealism, subjectivism, historicism, mere radicalism, neglect of mass struggle, or worse. To anticipate: the specific (imperialist) character of UK capitalism and its place in general development led to a particular state-form marked by 'continuity' (traditionalism, etc.) and a high degree of integrative capacity – both of the 'new' entrepreneurial classes and of the working class; but this historical success had as its other face equally distinctive failures (in 'modernisation', adaptability, etc.) which, since the 1950s, have become steadily more dominant, presaging a general mutation of the state; the passage towards this crisis is so far led by renascent 'bourgeois radicalism' (in the shape of Scottish and Welsh nationalism), rather than by the class struggle in the metropolis, although this may soon change.

to the state and Constitution. Rather than perceiving political revolution as the road to socio-economic betterment (like so many Continental movements), the British workers preferred to see a pragmatic politics evolve bit by bit out of their economic struggle. This lower-class corporatism has remained easily satirisable as a kind of quasi-feudal life-style: insisting on one's limited rights, while continuing to know one's humble position in the wider scheme of society.[27] Conservative apologists have naturally made much of British working-class political Toryism, undeniably a principal source of straight political conservatism ever since the extension of the suffrage.[28] However, it is difficult to see what alternative pattern of development was available, in a country where all the upper orders had so successfully exploited their unique position of developmental priority, and evolved such a strong civil hegemony at the core of the most successful of imperial systems.

The upper-class compromise carried a certain cost with it, in spite of its irresistible seduction: social sclerosis, an over-traditionalism leading to incurable backwardness. So did the lower-class alliance – though here the cost has been harder to identify, and slower to make its burden apparent. This dilemma is best understood in terms of the peculiar traits of English nationalism. The more characteristic processes of state-formation involved the masses in a positive role. As I argued in 'The Modern Janus' (NLR 94), the arrival of nationalism in a distinctively modern sense was tied to the political baptism of the lower classes. Their entry into history furnished one essential precondition of the transformation of nationality into a central and formative factor. And this is why, although sometimes hostile to democracy, nationalist movements have been invariably populist in outlook and sought to induct lower classes into political life. In its most typical version, this assumed the shape of a restless middle-class and intellectual leadership trying to stir up and channel popular class energies into support for

---

27 Two recent articles giving a vivid impression of the current condition of working-class attitudes are Michael Mann, 'The New Working Class', *New Society*, November and December 1976.

28 For example, R. McKenzie and A. Silver, *Angels in Marble: Working-Class Conservatives in Urban England*, London 1968. Discussing the 'deference' ideology of lower-class conservatism, the authors point out: 'One of the pervasive conditions promoting the survival of deference is the modest role accorded 'the people' in British political culture. Although it is a commonplace of research on stable democracies that general electorates are typically uninvolved in politics... it is only in Britain that this is so largely consistent with the prevailing climate of political values. Though modern constitutions typically locate the source of sovereignty in 'the people', in Britain it is the Crown in Parliament that is sovereign. Nor is this a merely technical point. The political culture of democratic Britain assigns to ordinary people the role, not of citizens, but of subjects...' (p. 251). So far from being a 'technical' point, the concept referred to has dominated the debates on devolution (see below): the crucial constitutional issue (and impossibility) is the conservation of the absolute sovereignty of the Crown in Westminster. At a far deeper level, such distinctions are not bourgeois-constitutional trivia (as so many Marxists have held): they manifest the nature of the state, and the whole material history which produced that state.

the new states. When successful – and of course, though many other factors are involved and nationalist ideology has always exaggerated its part, it has succeeded more often than not – this positive rôle has been prominent in the later political histories of all societies. It has often established the key myth of subsequent political development. At its most characteristic this is perhaps the myth of popular revolution or national-liberation struggle – a model of popular action and involvement which haunts the state, and is returned to repeatedly by later generations (often very blindly and conservatively).

Obviously, this has the implication that where mass initiative was little used in national histories such 'myths' may be correspondingly negative, or easily travestied by states that owe nothing to them: modern Germany and Japan are possibly the most usual examples here. But Britain is also a case in point. The older 17th-century revolutionary tradition of the major nationality, England, had been effectively buried. There was no second political revolution, so that the more radical tendencies of the bourgeoisie were diverted and absorbed into the dense machinery of civil hegemony. As this happened the new working class was also diverted and repressed: the defeat of early 19th-century radicalism forced it into a curious kind of social and political *apartheid*. This condition was almost the opposite of the active intervention from below which figured in so many modern revolutions; so, therefore, was the mythology, or underlying political consciousness, which it generated.

Nationalism is always the joint product of external pressures and an internal balance of class forces. Most typically it has arisen in societies confronting a dilemma of uneven development – 'backwardness' or colonisation – where conscious, middle-class élites have sought massive popular mobilisation to right the balance. But obviously the position of Britain – and in the present argument this means mainland England on the whole – was unusual in this regard. Here was a society which suffered far less from those external pressures and threats than any other, during a very long period. Now we can see how unusual was the internal class dynamic which corresponded to such external good fortune. The working class was not 'mobilised' in the ordinary sense, except for purposes of warfare: it was neither drawn into a revolution from below nor subjected to a 'revolution from above'. Instead it was contained and stratified into a relatively immobile social order – the one world society which faced practically *no* developmental problem until well into the 20th century.

Thus, the popular 'great power' nationalism formed on this basis could not help being especially conservative. It was innocent of the key, populist notion informing most real nationalism: the idea of the virtuous power of popular protest and action. In its peculiar, dignified concept the people are the reliable backbone of the nation; not the effective source of its authority, not the real makers of the state. This makes for a subtle yet profound difference in the stuff of modern English politics. In its long struggle against economic decline, the political world has been in fact struggling – although largely unwittingly – against the particular absences and defects deriving from this class structure. Bourgeois radicalism and popular mobilisation were eschewed for the sake of conservative stability. This led to a politically inert nationalism, one too little associated with internal divisions and struggle, too socially complacent and deferential. Given the position of the British Empire until the 1950s, this nationalism was periodically and successfully mobilised for external war – each episode of which further strengthened its inward conservatism, its conviction of an inherited internal unity. But this very conviction and complacency made it extraordinarily difficult to achieve any kind of internal break – any nationalist renaissance *against* the now hopelessly stultifying inheritance of the state. There was simply no tradition of this kind. Stability had become paralytic over-stability; the adaptive conservatism of the successful 19th-century system had turned into the feeble, dwindling, incompetent conservatism of the last generation.

All efforts to break out from this declining and narrowing spiral have failed, whether to the right or to the left. The reason is in part that neither the political right nor the left has any tradition of effective internal popular mobilisation at its command: there is neither a revolution nor a counter-revolution embodied in the substratum of popular awareness. Hence, governments have invariably appealed to the nation as a whole, much too successfully. Spurious conservative unity is the bane of modern British politics – not, as so often maintained by superficial critics, insuperable class divisions or party oppositions. Seen from the side of the working class too, therefore, imperialist society in Britain presents a development paradox. This is the country where a deep-laid strategy of class alliance achieved the highest degree of popular integration into the affairs of the state. But this was never 'integration' in the more typical sense of individualistic breakdown of the proletariat, through upward mobility and an aggressive capitalist ideology. Instead, it assumed a more corporate and passive form, in accordance with the traits of post-Industrial Revolution development under imperial conditions. The result was a particularly powerful inter-class nationalism – a sense of underlying insular identity and common fate, which both recognised and yet easily transcended marked class and regional divisions. However, far from being a model of politically effective nationalist ideology, this complex was to become useless outside imperial conditions. The reason is that its pervasive strength is inseparable from an accompanying conservatism – which in turn serves as an inhibitor of radical change or reform.

The bulk of the intelligentsia continues to subscribe to this peculiar variety of nationalism (not surprisingly, since it played such a big role in building it up). But so does the working class, under the aegis of British Labourism. Hence the two main sources of change have remained tied into the old structure. They maintain their historic allegiance to a form of nationalism which is in fact reverence for the overall nature of the modern (post-1688) British tribe. This is a faith in the mystique of that system, not in the people who made it (*they*, the revolutionaries of the 1640s, have been suppressed and travestied throughout the era in which this modern tribalism arose). Such faith is in 'the Constitution', and beyond this fetishisation in the capacity of 'we all' to surmount difficulties, win battles, etc. But 'we all', as 'we' are actually organised, means those who effectively control the social order; hence the sentiment is very close to belief that 'they' will continue to see we are cared for (though of course they may need to be reminded of their duties sometimes).

There have been numerous analyses of the economic contradictions of post-empire Britain, depicting a society hoist by the petard of its own past success in industry and finance. But the economic vicious circle is mirrored – and rendered inexorable – by this corresponding contradiction on the plane of politics and ideology. Here also imperialism cast society into a shape inadaptable to later, harder conditions of existence. It forged a state which, although very 'flexible' in certain respects – those most noticed and revered by apologists – is incapable of change at a deeper level. On *that* plane, where the modern political principle of nationality really functions, it is bound by a suffocating, paralytic pride in its own power and past glories.

Nationalism, whether of the right or of the left, is of course never really independent of the class structure. Yet its particular efficacy as a mobilising ideology depends upon the *idea* of classlessness – upon the notion that, at least in certain circumstances and for a period of time, what a society enjoys in common is more important than its stratification. In England, the specially strong stratification created by the failure of the 'second bourgeois revolution' made the normal egalitarian or radical version of this notion impossible. The ordinary texture of English social life denies it. Hence the only effective version has been one which ignores these class divisions against an 'outside' enemy – at the same time implicitly re-consecrating them, as the tolerable features of a 'way of life' basically worth defending against the world. Time and time again this defence has in turn fortified in-built resistance to radicalism. That is, to all tendencies (democratic or reactionary) which might aim to really demolish the creaking English snail-shell of archaic pieties, deferential observance and numbing self-inhibition.

Origins of the Crisis

'Moderate', 'orderly', 'decent', 'peaceful and tolerant', 'constitutional'; 'backward-looking', 'complacent', 'insular', 'class-ridden', 'inefficient', 'imperialist' – a realistic analysis of the British state must admit these two familiar series of truisms are in fact differing visages of the same social reality. That Arcadian England which appeals so strongly to foreign intellectuals is also the England which has, since the early 1950s, fallen into ever more evident and irredeemable decline – the United Kingdom of permanent economic crisis, falling standards, bankrupt governments, slavish dependence on the United States, and myopic expedients. The appealing, romantic social peace is inseparable from the twilight. Though imaginatively distinguishable, resistance to modernity is in reality not separable from the senility of the old imperialist state. They are bound to perish together.

The preceding analysis suggests that the origins of this long crisis, still unresolved, go back a long way.[29] They may also suggest the basic reason why resolution is so difficult, and has been so long delayed. The fact is that emergence from the crisis demands a political break: a disruption at the level of the state, allowing the emergence of sharper antagonisms and a will to reform the old order root and branch. But in this system, possibly more than in any other, such a break has become extremely difficult. The state-level is so deeply entrenched in the social order itself, state and civil society are so intertwined in the peculiar exercise of the British Constitution, that a merely 'political' break entails a considerable social revolution.

The governing élite and the liberal intelligentsia, and the dominant sector of the economic ruling class, all have an obvious vested interest in the state. The industrial bourgeoisie and the working class do not.[30] Yet the latter have never succeeded in undoing and modernising the state, in spite of their potential power. As far as the entrepreneurial class is concerned the absence of will is more understandable. The combination of British-Constitutional ideology, their weak political position in relation to the City, and their fear of 'socialism' has turned them into a particularly supine and harmless sub-bourgeoisie. Since the defeat of Joseph Chamberlain's more industrially-oriented 'social imperialism' – a right-wing attempt at a new, more radical class alliance – they have exerted little substantial influence on the state.[31] As for the working class, the main lines of their own

---

29 The original analysis to which this one (and all others like it) owe a great debt is Perry Anderson, 'Origins of the Present Crisis', NLR 23, Jan – Feb. 1964.

30 In this and comparable analyses, the split between finance and industrial capital always receives a great deal of attention, as a basic feature of the underpinning of the state-structure. But in an acute comment in his article 'Imperialism in the Seventies – Unity or Rivalry?' (NLR 69, Sept.–Oct. 1971), Bob Rowthorn points out how a division of interests within the industrial sector itself has enormously accentuated the political results of that split. 'Paradoxically', he observes, 'the weakness of the British state is to be explained not by the simple decline of British capitalism as such, but by the very *strength* of the cosmopolitan activities of British capital, which has helped to undermine further its strictly domestic economy' (p. 46). Imperialism left a legacy of very large firms with overseas operations, as well as the City: it is their combined interests which have remained largely independent of the UK state and its 'strictly domestic' economy, and so have helped cripple all vigorous efforts to revive the latter (by import controls, action against overseas investment, etc.). Hence, he concludes: 'Leading sections of the British bourgeoisie have been effectively 'de-nationalised', not through their own weakness but through the weakness of the British state and their own home base. The overseas strength of British big *capital* has compounded the debility of British capitalism...' (p. 47).

31 Recent emphasis upon 'buried history' excluded from the Establishment versions has focused mainly upon working-class and popular material; but there is an outstanding quantity of bourgeois data that has suffered a similar fate, no less relevant for understanding the

integration into the 20th-century state were decided by the same defeat: the defeat of right-wing imperialism was the triumph of 'liberal imperialism', from 1906 onwards – the permanent victory of the City over the British economy, and of patrician liberalism over the class strategy and outlook of the British state. The era of New Imperialism had put the old class alliance under severe strain, from the 1880s onwards. The external threat from a more militarised and competitive world combined with new internal menaces, from a more restless and organised working class and a tiny yet significant trend to disaffection among the intellectuals.

However, that period of crisis was resolved by a reaffirmation of liberalism – in effect, a reaffirmation of the underlying strategy laid down in the earlier 19th century, and described above. This has become the traditional mode of hegemony, most identified with the Constitution, the British road of compromise, and so on. Now, the problem before it was the more effective incorporation of the working class – of a working class, which, in the two decades before 1914, had begun to emerge from trade unionism and demand a limited political voice of its own.

Previously the enfranchised part of the working class had given its allegiance to the Liberal Party. But at the very period of that Party's triumphant return to power, in 1906–14, a new Labour Party had been formed. Although extremely moderate in ideology, and more an expression of trade-union interests than a socialist party in the Continental sense, this movement none the less clearly represented a class point of view. Between 1914 and 1924, when the first Labour government took office, this point of view was effectively subordinated to the underlying consensus. It may be that this achievement was only possible so quickly and so decisively because of the First World War. Indeed, maybe the general strategic victory of liberalism should be attributed as much to this factor as to its electoral and reforming successes in 1906 and 1910–11. It is certainly true that neither the Tory right nor the more militant and syndicalist elements of the working class were really reconciled to the solution up to 1914. The clear threat of both revolution and counter-revolution persisted until then, and the old order was by no means as secure as its later apologists have pretended.

But external success settled the dilemma, in accordance with the main law of British history. The victory of the *Entente* drew both Tory and revolutionary dissidents back into the consensus. The war effort itself signified a huge development

---

overall pattern's significance. Chamberlain's right-wing, tariff-reform imperialism is an outstanding example of this – the buried relics of a forsaken ruling-class strategy which prefigured a very different state-form in the 20th century. As L. S. Amery put it, for tariff-reformers the State 'should be a creative force in economic life, vigorously directing the nation's energies... developing the empire', etc. (*The Fundamental Fallacies of Free Trade*, London 1906, pp. 5, 17, 92). Chamberlain himself predicted that if his social-imperialist strategy was defeated by the Free Traders, Britain would fall into a long decline comparable to that suffered by Holland and Venice – see *Imperial Union and Tariff Reform*, his 1903 speeches.

in state intervention, upon lines already present in the Liberal Party's reform programme of Edwardian times: public enterprise and control of the economy, and social welfare. As was to happen also in the second world conflict, the ideological reinforcement of all-British patriotism coincided with important structural developments favourable to working-class interests. These developments took the form of the constant extension of state activity and influence, and ultimately – after the Second World War – of the pioneer 'welfare state' which for a brief period served as a model for other capitalist countries. In the above analysis, the emphasis has been placed on the strong élite character of the British state, and its bond with a markedly hierarchical yet cohesive civil society. This may appear in some ways at odds with the great expansion of state functions initiated first by Liberalism and then by Labourism. But the contradiction is only apparent. In fact, the growth of the state – a theme which fuelled polemic and political debate from the 1880s onwards – has never seriously changed its underlying nature. This has been demonstrated by the character of the growth itself: random, *ad hoc* formation of new agencies and functions, which rarely question the basic principles of government. This amoebic proliferation has merely surrounded and preserved the essential identity of the British Constitution. The endless pragmatic expediency of Westminster governments has multiplied state activity in response to successive challenges and demands, above all the challenges of war; it has done so (normally quite consciously) in order to conserve the vital mystique of Britishness, not to change or dilute it.

Externally, this line of development was of course made feasible by imperialism. The ruling class retained a position strong enough, and secure enough psychologically, to pursue the strategy of concession in graduated doses to more organised pressures from below. There was – or seemed to be, until the 1960s – surplus enough for the exercise to be valid. While the particular evolution of the class struggle in Britain strongly favoured its continuation, in spite of the difficult passage of Edwardian times. Working-class politics evolved on the back of trade unionism in Britain, emerging quite empirically as a kind of collective, parliamentary voice for a corporate class interest. Hence internally too there was a notable tendency to accede to the concession strategy. It was only rarely that the political leaders of 'British Socialism' perceived a new state and constitution as the precondition of achieving class demands. Normally, the perception was that *the* state could be bent in the direction of these demands. Class political power of the type which became feasible after 1918 (year of the foundation of the contemporary Labour Party) was only the strongest way of doing this.

The class alliance of 20th-century Britain is essentially devoted to the exorcism of 'power' in any disruptive sense, and to the maintenance of social consensus at almost any cost. Obviously the decisive test of this strategy was the attainment of elective power by a working-class based movement. It was argued previously that the intelligentsia had played a key, often ill-understood role in the mechanism of hegemony, as the agents of the state-society bond – the 'state-substitute' officers of civil society, peopling the profusion of para-state or semi-official bodies the English state characteristically depends on. But now a definitely lower-class political force had emerged into the state arena under war conditions, in an irreversible way: the 'masses' whom the patricians were supposed to look after were threatening, though still quite mildly, to look after themselves. This could only be coped with in terms appropriate to the system by the formation of a new intellectual leadership – the creation of a new bond between this awakened sector of civil society and the old state. Fortunately, the very conditions which had presided over the birth of Labourism were highly conducive to this. The corporative aspect of working-class politics meant that it was weak in ideological leadership, and relatively unaware of the problematic of power: the most articulate ideology of nascent Labour politics, Fabianism, was at its feeblest on this issue. 'Gradualism' did much to pave the way for the shift in power relations that actually occurred.

This shift took the form of the transfer of a substantial part of the old Liberal intelligentsia into the ranks of the Labour Party itself. The 'ranks' is, of course, a formal way of speaking; what they actually migrated to were the higher echelons of the movement, rapidly finding themselves promoted and elected into posts of power. From 1918 onwards an ever growing stream of intellectuals who would previously have adhered to the Liberal Party (or at least been satellites of Liberalism in the wider sense) moved to the Labour Party. They took Liberalism (in the crucial deeper sense) with them. Their liberal variant of the British state creed was readily accepted as the guiding light of the new movement: British Socialism with that unmistakable, resonantly moderate and pragmatical emphasis on the 'British'. From the same moment onwards, the Liberal Party itself declined. No significant part of the intelligentsia shifted back towards it until the 1960s, when it began to look as if Labour might be drifting into a bankruptcy of its own.

One does not require even the most tenuous form of conspiracy-theory to explain the change. The Liberal Party, after laying the foundations of the 'welfare state', had been deeply discredited by the war experience, and still more by the experiment in coalition government with Conservatism after 1916 – a régime presided over by the one-time chief of Liberal radicalism, David Lloyd George. Reaction against the war and the post-war slump (when working-class militancy was severely defeated) was therefore also against Liberalism in the old form. The progressive arm of the intellectual class turned to the new movement, where it was overwhelmingly welcomed. In the guise of socialist novelty, tradition established a new lease of life and the integration of the proletariat into the British state assumed a new level of expression. By then, it was only in that guise that the system could perpetuate itself. Liberalism developed better without the vestment of the old Liberal Party. The change took time, naturally. It was not until the end of the Second World War in the 1940s that the process was complete. But by that time, liberal thinkers like Keynes and Beveridge had forged the intellectual and planning framework for the new era of reform, and the political leadership of Labourism had become wholly dominated by traditional, élite cadres. These created the more interventionist state, and the social welfare systems of post-Second World War Britain, in continuity with the Liberal Party pioneers of the early 1900s.[32]

Earlier, middle-class radicalism had been defeated, and a continuity established which 'contained' capitalist development within a conservative social nexus. Now, working-class radicalism had been diverted and blunted in an analogous fashion, and with similar results. This second solution of continuity carried the working class into its own version of 'containment'; proletarian opposition to free capitalist development united politically with that of the élite traditionalists. The weakening, ever more backward industrial basis was made to carry not only the old snail-shell but a modern 'welfare state' as well. Its triumph, which has only recently become its disaster, lay in evolving a system which both Dukes and dustmen could like, or at least find tolerable.

British Socialism, when perceived in its underlying relationship to the state (or equally, in its inner morality and reflexes) should be called 'Tory Socialism'. In the later 1930s and 1940s a new generation of liberal thinkers invented 'social-democratic' forms for the Labour Party, based upon largely spurious parallels with Continental socialist reformism: Evan Durbin, Hugh Gaitskell and (in the 1950s) Anthony Crosland. Failing as completely as most Marxists to focus upon the specific character of the English state and constitution, these pretended that the Labour Party was a movement of modernising egalitarianism – in effect, that it was engaged on (if indeed it had not already achieved) the second, radical social revolution which the middle class had failed to produce. The events of the period 1964–70 were an ironical refutation of these ideas. The cringing Labour

---

32 In his *Politicians and the Slump: the Labour Government of 1929–31*, London 1967, Robert Skidelsky warns commentators on attributing too much to the formulated Keynesian doctrines themselves: 'The absence of developed Keynesian theory was not a decisive barrier to the adoption of what might loosely be termed Keynesian policies, as is proved by the experience of the United States, Germany, France and Sweden which in the 1930s all attempted... to promote economic recovery through deficit budgeting.' (pp. 387–8). But in Britain such 'social engineering' depended upon 'a resolute government exploiting the differences between industry and the City' (as these had been outlined in the major document of the era, the Macmillan Report on *Finance and Industry*, London 1931, Cmnd. 3897). Although correct in the abstract, what such analyses ignore is that the nature of the state is incompatible with this sort of strategy: no such 'resolute' régime has ever come into being, even with the modest equipment in 'social engineering' Labour acquired during and after the Second World War. The reason is that a strategy of 'making capitalism work' *in* that sense remains semi-revolutionary in British conditions (i.e. it implies radical re-formation of the state in a more than simply administrative way). As Skidelsky has indicated elsewhere, the most 'resolute' proponent of that kind of reform, Oswald Mosley, was driven into the ranks of counter-revolution by the sheer impossibility of the task: see 'Great Britain', in *European Fascism*, edited S. J. Woolf, London 1968, and his subsequent biography of Mosley.

conservatism of 1974–6 has been their annihilation. The Labour Party's so-called 'social revolution' of the post-war years led not to national revival but to what Tony Benn now describes as 'de-industrialisation': that is, to rapidly accelerating backwardness, economic stagnation, social decay, and cultural despair.

The immediate origin and political condition of this long-delayed crisis was the political harnessing of the working class to the socially conservative British Constitution. In many polemics this process has been crudely mistaken for 'surrender to capitalism', or 'reformism' – for instance, the social reformism of German Social-Democracy since the Second World War. In fact the Labourist 'surrender' has been to a particularly antique form of bourgeois society and constitution, and the resultant balance of class forces has been to a significant extent directed *against* capitalism, in the sense of industrial modernity and the individualistic, mobile but more egalitarian social relations accompanying it. The form of capitalism which it actively assisted – foreign-oriented investment and finance capital – was itself a constant impediment to more dynamic industrial growth. Labourism allied the proletariat to the inner conservatism and the main outward thrust of imperialism; not to domestic industrialism. As a result, it became a principal agent of 'de-industrialisation'.

One may also argue that it turned into *the* main cause of 'the British malady' (etc.), at least from around 1965 onwards. Nobody would rationally have thought that a capitalist class so socially conservative and so tied to monetary imperialism could easily change its historical skin, and quickly give birth to a régime of dynamic modernisation. It was the Labour Party which channelled the 'radical' elements and social forces capable of that. It was Labour which returned to office in 1964 with the only plausible-sounding scheme of radical change – a programme of combined and concerted social and technological modernisation, envisaging the ending of social privilege, and 'putting science and industry first'. Within three years this programme was utterly defeated, and the Harold Wilson of 1970 was reduced to posturing as the Premier of a 'natural governing party' – the party now thoroughly at home with the traditions of British state hegemony, wielding an easy Tory authority over the propertied class once afraid of it.[33]

---

33 Among many lugubrious chronicles of conceit and decay, perhaps the most compact and useful is *The Decade of Disillusion: British Politics in the Sixties*, edited by D. McKie and C. Cook, London 1972, especially the chapter by Peter Sinclair, 'The Economy – a Study in Failure'. The latter's account of the National Plan fiasco conveys the oscillation between megalomania and incompetence that has characterised most key state operations in recent decades: 'The impression brilliantly conveyed to the electorate in 1964 was that some undefined negative attitude implicit in 'stop-go' and some unspecified kind of governmental amateurism were all that had deprived Britain of rapid growth in the '50s and early '60s. Purposive and dynamic government would suddenly restore her rightful rate of growth (i.e. by Planning).' In reality the National Plan was to consist 'of little more than the printed replies to a questionnaire sent to industries about their estimates of inputs and outputs on the assumption of 25 per cent real growth by

External Solutions

Since the final failure of Labourism to achieve (or even seriously attempt) Britain's second political revolution, the state has entered into a historical cul-de-sac from which no exit is visible – that is, no exit along the sacrosanct lines of its previous development. British political life has revolved helplessly in diminishing and sinking circles, from which both main political parties try to strike out in vain. They imagine that 'left' or 'right' wing solutions are feasible without a radical break in the crippling state form which corsets them both and forces all new policies back into a dead centre of 'consensus'. The party-political system itself (of which Labour has become the main defender) makes it next to impossible to obtain any new departure from within the system. The two-party equilibrium, with its antique non-proportional elective method and its great bedrock of tacit agreement on central issues, was formed to promote stability at the expense of adventure. It was never intended that stability should become catalepsy. But all that 'stability' meant was the comfort of external supports which rendered internal growing-pains unnecessary; now that these have vanished, inert conservatism has inevitably turned into increasing non-adaptation to the outside world.

Nothing is more significant during this last era of thickening twilight than the role of what one might label imaginary external solutions: the magic escape-routes indulged in by one government after another as their economic growth-policies collapse around them, broken in pieces by the contradiction of a non-growth state. Since the 1950s boom, the most important of these has been the European Economic Community. British governments refused to join the EEC earlier, during its expanding phase, because they retained too strong a faith in imperialism. Re-baptised as the 'Commonwealth', they still thought the system might go on furnishing Britain with the external support-area it was used to. This illusion dwindled away in the 1960s. Each administration after the Macmillan Conservative government then turned to the Common Market as the only possible realistic alternative. The Labour Party mouthed strident patriotic opposition to Europe when out of office, in 1961–3 and again in 1970–74; but when returned to power, it always moved back into a negotiating stance with the EEC, and finally staged the referendum that confirmed British membership in 1975.

British entry can therefore be described by the two words which apply to

---

1970...(!)... The hope was that this stated assumption would justify itself by encouraging business to create the additional capacity required to make its 'prediction' come true... The truth is that its targets could not conceivably have been achieved.' (pp. 103–4) Shortly afterwards the agency set up to perform this feat of levitation, the Department of Economic Affairs, 'withered away unnoticed and unannaled'. Perhaps the most sobering picture of the actual capitalist reality beyond the various new styles, starts and visionary scenarios punctuating governmental life from 1964 to the present is *British Capitalism, Workers and the Profit Squeeze*, London. 1972, by Andrew Glyn and Bob Sutcliffe.

almost everything in post-Second World War history: 'too late'. It took place when the long developmental phase of the EEC was nearly over, and world depression was looming – so that the British entered a Community itself falling into stalemate and self-doubt. In addition, entry had taken place for a predictable and illusory reason. Although not exactly a surrogate for Empire (like the Commonwealth or EFTA), the Common Market was beyond any doubt seen as the external answer to the British disease. The stimulus of entering a vigorous, competitive capitalist area was intended to do what domestic economic policy had so obviously failed to do: force the fabled 'regeneration' of British industry. Internal levitation had failed, with a dismal succession of thuds; exposure was supposed to accomplish the miracle instead.

Painful as the effects were expected to be, the assumption was that they would be less awful than drastic internal reform. Europe was perceived essentially as bracing bad medicine. But the point of the treatment was revival of the patient, not decent burial. Even fervent Europeanists still regularly transmitted surreal notions on how good it would be for the Continent to have lessons in democracy from the Mother of Parliaments. Neither side in the debate relaxed its grip on the udders of island constitutionalism for a moment.[34] In fact it is dubious whether entry could have had much beneficial effect on the British economy even ten years sooner, unless a much more radical internal programme had been adopted – unless (e.g.) the Labour 1964 policies had been taken seriously and fought for, instead of being thrown overboard at the first signs of trouble. Without a programme of (in Benn's sense) 're-industrialisation' in some sort of conjunction with the new EEC external field of forces, it was always possible (as opponents argued) that these forces would have been overwhelming economically. But 're-industrialisation' is not really a question of economic policy in Britain. This is the characteristic empirical-minded error made by successive governments since 1945 (and still made by Benn and his supporters on the Labour left wing). It is, in fact, a call for revolution. More exactly, it is a call for the 'revolution from above' which the British state-system has been built upon denying and repressing ever since the Industrial Revolution. It is a call – therefore – which has not the most remote chance of being effectively answered by the existing state, and the deeply rooted civil structures which sustain it.

This impossibility is the immediate context for both the so-called 'economic crisis' and the problem of peripheral nationalism; as such it deserves closer study. The keynote of all appeals for economic renaissance between the 1880s and the present day has been the industrial sector: the wish is to re-establish the primacy of the productive sector over the City and finance-capital – and hence,

---

34 I wrote a short account of this passage in our affairs which appeared as NLR 75 and as *The Left Against Europe?*, London 1973, arguing that from any progressive standpoint ranging from the mildly reforming to the revolutionary no fate could be worse than national isolation in the grip of an unreformed UK state.

of the technologist and the industrial entrepreneur over the banker and the broker, of the 'specialised' scientist or business man over the non-specialised (or 'amateur') gentleman-administrator who has governed both the political system and the state bureaucracy. The exercise is presented as the formation of a new, healthier equilibrium: righting the balance left by aristocracy and empire, 'stimulating' industry to a better performance in comparative terms. Once achieved, this more competitive industrial basis will provide export-led growth, leading to a harder currency and so to a renewed foundation for London finance capital also. Sterling will regain its place as a valid international trading currency (even though second to the US dollar), and this all-round revival would signify new life for the state.[35]

Sometimes the operation has been seen as state-contrived or directed (as under the Wilson government of the 1960s); sometimes as a matter of 'liberating capitalism', freeing the entrepreneurial spirit from state obstructions and burdens (e.g. the Heath government of 1970–72, whose rhetoric has now been taken up by Mrs Thatcher, with the usual empty radicalism of opposition). Yet these prescriptions are not as different as they appear. Since the whole problem lies in the fact that Britain does not possess a dynamic but frustrated capitalist class capable of responding to 'liberation' in the simple-minded Friedmanite sense, state intervention is in fact inevitable (as Heath swiftly found out). The historical 'balance' that has to be righted is in reality so ancient, so buttressed by manifold social customs and ideology, and the domestic capitalist class is so short-sighted and dependent, that nothing except vigorous intervention from above can conceivably make an impact.

However, there exists no state-class of 'technocrats' or administrators capable of doing this. The political and administrative class is irremediably compromised, socially and intellectually, with the old patrician order. Such 'strategies' exist only as recurring fantasies of liberation: perpetual 'new starts', bold dreams of dynamism solemnly enunciated in manifestos and dramatic 'reports' every year or so when the government changes hands (or even when it does not). These furnish a fleeting euphoria to commentators, wholly founded upon the fact that they and their readers have forgotten the previous instalments. The predictable failure of each new bold initiative is simply suppressed, even as it takes place; by oniric magic, a new dream-corner materialises which the nation has to get round, into the land of the righted balance and 'soundly-based' prosperity. The external observer perceives a constant decline, with occasional plateaus; the

---

35 The most interesting general analysis and verdict on economic policy and the state is that provided by *The United Kingdom in 1980: the Hudson Report*, London 1975. Its main argument was that failure in economic policy was inseparable from the structure; personnel, ideology and recruitment of the state. This abrasive commonplace produced an unprecedented chorus of abusive dismissal from virtually the whole corps of *chiens de garde*: the intelligentsia choked as one over this bitter foreign pill. I tried to describe the spectacle at the time in *Bananas*, No. 1, London 1975.

English spirit sees constantly-repeated hard luck, and Chancellors of the Exchequer who failed to 'get it quite right' *this* time, but, *next* time...

To interrupt this cycle of delusions would require a change of élites. It would entail the radical removal of the entire traditional apparatus of state and civil intelligentsia – that is, of that stratum which, in spite of its liberalism and constitutional gentility, is as much of a stranglehold upon English society as were the Prussian Junker class, the Italian Risorgimento Liberals, the Spanish landowners or the old Dutch burgher class on their respective countries. Élite changes of that kind never occur by modulation and negotiation: they need a break (which may, of course, assume many different forms). No state ever reforms itself away into something so strikingly different – least of all one with this degree of historical prestige, residual self-confidence and capacity for self-deception.[36]

From the early 1960s to 1975 the European Community provided a constantly recurring external support for illusions of re-juvenescence: the vital outside succour which would render internal revolution unnecessary. But as faith in this empire-surrogate evaporated (almost from the instant of entry) another and still more potent formula took its place. The procession of quasi-divine strokes of good fortune and helping hands that had helped the wheelchair through the 20th century received an incredible climax. From around 1970 it became steadily clearer that oil exploration in the North Sea was going to yield great results, with the obvious promise of an eventual reversal of the chronic British balance-of-payments crisis, a restoration of sterling, and a state-aided industrial investment programme of modernisation. After furnishing the British state with the greatest colonial domain, the Gold Standard, victorious allies in two world wars, the EEC and the protective American Empire for its old age, God out-did his own record of generous favouritism. The final version of imperial exploitation was discovered in the mud of the North Sea. Practically from the grave itself there seemed to arise the last great, miraculous escape route, the ultimate external cornucopia.

---

36 It should not be assumed that the UK state's immutability implies absence of wish to reform itself; on the contrary, as with other *ancient régimes*, the drowning sensation produces an almost ceaseless quest for insignificant change. 'In the ten years between 1964 and 1973', notes one authority, 'this Constitution's quality of flexibility has been predominant. Never before has there been so much talk or so much actual change, always within a framework which has been kept intact...' P. Bromhead, *Britain's Developing Constitution*, London 1974, p. 217. This wave of frenetic tinkering was devoted to making the old machine more 'efficient' while keeping it intact: a contradiction in terms pondered over by many Royal Commissions and Inquiries (described in, e.g., Frank Stacey, *British Government 1966–1975*, Oxford 1975, see especially chapter XII). Possibly the finest monument to this 'stage army of the good' (Stacey, op. cit., p. 215) was the Redcliffe-Maud reform of Local Government, a superbly unradical and unpopular administrative overhaul that conveyed the maximum impression of novelty with the minimum of real change. The only genuinely radical reform to emerge, from the Kilbrandon Commission's Report on Devolution, was brought about by a threat of death to the framework itself: the political eruption of Scottish and Welsh nationalism in 1974.

This last phase in the pattern of external dependency has, of course, been perceived by most political leaders in the usual way: salvation at the 11th hour. Providence will pay off Great Britain's debts, and allow her ancient state to slither into the 21st century. In an outbreak of euphoria without precedent, one Minister after another has conjured up the light at the end of the tunnel. If only the British can hang on, in a few years all will be well. The North Sea income will pay off the debts many times over, and leave a huge surplus for industrial invest-ment. What all Chancellors of the Exchequer failed to do, nature will accom-plish. At the same time, like any heir expecting a fortune, the government has hugely expanded its borrowings from abroad. Combined with the soaring infla-tion of 1974–6 (which afflicted Britain more than her main industrial competitors), this led to a chronic sterling devaluation crisis. Partly 'managed' by government – in order to favour export industries – this collapse none the less threatened to become total in 1976. While waiting on the oil revenues to flow in, shorter-term salvation was obtained by a loan from the International Monetary Fund in December.

Foreign governments, and foreign observers generally, naturally have a differ-ing perspective on this conjuncture. There is no reason why they should take this latest version of the British redemption myth seriously. But there are plenty of reasons why they should conclude that both the IMF loan and North Sea oil will merely be another chapter of false hopes.[37] They will be used to avoid painful changes, not to promote them; to put off drastic reforms once more, not to make them palatable. Consensus and inertia will see to that. To furnish one or two extra 'chances' for a state like this one is meaningless. It involves placing more credence in the re-birth ideology of politicians than in the character of the state which they serve. The former deals in round-the-corner optimism; the latter in a trisecular accumulation of imperial complacency and slow-moving certain-ties, all firmly cemented into the instinctive reflexes of the huge extended family that really governs England. As long as that family is there, conducting its busi-ness in the drawing-room conversational monotone of tradition, further stays of execution will be used for its real historic aim: to change just as much as is necessary for everything to go on as before.

Class and Nationalism

The conservative essence of the British political drama occupies a smaller and smaller stage, and goes on in an ever-dimmer light. In the declining spiral each new repetition of the play, although advertised by the players as the same, has

---

37 They need only read J. P. Mackintosh's astringent account of the behind-the-scenes
    manoeuvrings around the loan, in *The Times*, 13 December 1976, should a doubt have
    crossed their mind that contemporary British statesmanship is invariably myopic farce
    acted out like Greek tragedy.

a new note of hollowness or approaching night. Each time the forces capable of extinguishing the performance move a little closer to the actors and the ancient scenery, and loom more noticeably over events.

There are the outside forces, upon which this analysis has placed so much emphasis. The disappearance of empire and the dwindling place of its child, the City, in the fabric of international capitalism; the failing industrial sector and currency, and the gathering intolerance of the capitalist powers for this chronic malingerer who, in spite of every assistance and sympathy, still cannot shake himself into new life. Internally, the class struggle also advances with its own threat of disruption. Since 1974, when the miners' strike led to the overthrow of a Conservative Government, the Labour Party has accomplished apparent miracles in restoration of the consensus: this was (as *The Times* stated then) what it was elected to do. The latest round of crisis-and-redemption has only been possible at all on the frozen ice of the class struggle, obtained by means of the 'Social Contract' – perhaps the last desperate form of that deep class-alliance the state has always relied upon.

How thick the ice looks, in the declarations of Labour Ministers and trade-union leaders who have supported the agreement! How thin and short-lived it may soon become, as inflation and unemployment continue to increase during 1977! It would be broken altogether by the return of the Conservative Party to office, even before it melts under force of circumstance. And under the ice of this traditional nation-first solidarity, real tradition has been put in reverse. The point of the old, secular social strategy was concession to mounting pressures from below: there was always something to concede, and some reason for the lower classes to retain faith in the British firmament. Sacrifices were made for later gains that came from empire and warfare – but which really did come, until well after the last world war. Under the Social Contract, sacrifices and falling standards are being accepted in exchange for rewards that now hinge (when one discounts the escapism of North Sea oil) genuinely on the capacity of the British state to reform its own society – upon the enactment of the long-awaited, incessantly heralded 'British economic miracle' putting the country back on a level with its old rivals in Europe.

If (one should say 'when') this does not take place, a massive reaction is bound to occur and shake even the very strong structure of English hegemony. Even English patience is not endless. Were it to happen in conjunction with a further phase of the external crisis – accompanied by a currency collapse, for example – then not even the beleaguered optimists of the Establishment would imagine the political system going on as usual. The very least they foresee is the conventional British 20th-century formula for crisis, a 'National Government' of emergency.[38]

---

38 'National' or coalition governments, in the sense of 'emergency régimes' where the state faces a crisis, account for 21 years of this century's political history in Britain: 1915–22,

But in any case, to these two menacing forces has now been added a third – a third force which, though less powerful and significant than the others, is likely none the less to function as the precipitant of the conflict. The underlying dynamic of class alliance has altered; but so have the rules of the political system itself. The one has been forced by Britain's shrinking economic stature and relations; the other by peripheral nationalism – that is, by a different kind of opposition to the same declining world and philosophy. Different aspects and modes of this opposition are described in some of the essays in *The Break-up of Britain*. But in the context of British state-history what counts most is the common element they display: however varied in background and aims, these situations of breakdown and gathering nationalism fall outside the characteristic contours of English constitutionalism. They are not the kind of problem it was slowly formed to deal with, and they will resist or destroy the typical remedies which it inspires. In summary, almost emblematic form, one might say: London government invents habitual class remedies to nationalist ailments. Its instinct is to concede, when sufficiently prodded, then consolidate tradition on the new, slightly different balance of forces that results. Although notoriously effective on the front of class struggle and negotiation, the strategy has no real application to national questions. The philosophy and practice of conservative empiricism presupposes a stable, consensual framework; the new nationalisms challenge that framework itself. British constitutionalism makes an arcane mystique of power, removing it from the arena of normal confrontation and enshrining it as a Grail-like 'sovereignty'; but nationalism *is* about power, in a quite straightforward sense. It is a

---

1931–45. The corresponding figures for party rule are: Conservatives, 28 years; Labour Party, 18 years; Liberal Party, nine years (British Political Facts, 1900–1968, London 1969, by D. Butler and J. Freeman). It is the normal formula of retrenchment, and will undoubtedly be employed again when the situation becomes critical enough. More important than the time-span of emergency régimes is their pivotal role in state history: the genuinely massive adaptations and changes of balance have taken place in war-time – when the impact of external forces became literally irresistible – and under 'non-party' tutelage. The collapse of the Liberal Party, the crystallisation of Labourism, the emancipation of women, the Welfare State, liquor licensing hours, widespread sale of contraceptives, trade-union 'partnership' in the state, juvenile delinquency – very many of the big turning-points and most recognizable traits of modern British life were products of war-time. Warfare provided a forced rupture in the normally stifling continuum of the state Establishment – in effect, a partial, controlled social revolution which gave the system a new lease of life on each occasion (but above all after 1945). This thesis is conveyed in Arthur Marwick, *The Deluge: British Society and the First World War*, London 1965, and *Britain in the Century of Total War: War, Peace and Social Change 1900–1967*, London 1968. On the Second World War, Angus Calder's *The People's War*, London 1968, argues cogently for an interpretation of the War as an abortive, ultimately betrayed, social revolution. The congruence of the thesis with the general emphasis on external relations put forward here is obvious.

demand for the Grail, or at least a bit of it (this is, of course, a demand for the impossible, in English ideological tradition).

This pattern has been followed to the letter in the development of intra-British conflict so far. When Welsh and Scottish nationalism began to advance politically in the 1960s, London government from the outset assumed that these developments would have to be adapted to, and nullified, in the habitual way. It noticed that the demands were different in Wales and Scotland, as were the relative strengths of the nationalist parties. So of course different concessions would be in order in each region. A Royal Commission was appointed to work out how this should be done, in the customary hope that the problem would have solved itself by the time this body's deliberations were finished. When completed, its recommendations were greeted with universal derision and cynicism.[39]

The derision vanished with the new election results of 1974. The new Labour government hastily produced legislation embodying some of the Commission's ideas, which became the 'Scotland and Wales Bill' of December 1976.[40] Now that the problems were not going to disappear spontaneously, concessionary tactics would have to be employed. With limited degrees of self-government in domestic

---

39 The *Royal Commission on the Constitution, 1969–1973*, London 1973, Cmnd. 5460, two vols, chaired (latterly) by Lord Kilbrandon. The general reaction of parliament and metropolitan opinion to its appearance in October 1973 leaves one in no doubt that the whole thing would have been consigned to the dungeons as a lost cause, had the Nationalists not made their dramatic electoral break-through only a few months later. The lost cause then speedily turned into the dominant theme of parliamentary existence, as it was seen that the future of the political order itself was at stake. Among the neglected but entertaining sections of the Report are those on the Isle of Man and the Channel Islands, tiny territories that cast a minor yet revealing light on the vaster fabric they (somewhat vaguely) belong to: 'Unique miniature states with wide powers of self-government', as the Commissioners recorded, 'not capable of description by any of the usual categories of political science... full of anomalies, peculiarities and anachronisms, which even those who work the system find it hard to define precisely. We do not doubt that more logical and orderly races would have swept all these away long ago...' p. 410, p. 441. Not having made enough nuisance of themselves, these authentic feudal relics have been left in peace: 'We have not approached the Islands in any spirit of reforming zeal', confessed the Commission, 'Indeed, if only the constitutional relationships between the United Kingdom and the Islands could remain as they have been in recent years... everybody would be happy, and our task would disappear.'

40 The progress of 'devolution' from universal contempt to a critical issue of state is best epitomised in Hegel's reflections on the Great Reform Bill of 1832. Reluctantly, it was conceded that – 'The right way to pursue improvement is not by the moral route of using ideas, admonitions, associations of isolated individuals, in order to counteract the system of corruption and avoid being indebted to it, but by the alteration of institutions. The common prejudice of inertia, namely to cling always to the old faith in the excellence of an institution, even if the present state of affairs derived from it is altogether corrupt, has thus at last caved in...', *Hegel's Political Writings*, 'The English Reform Bill', op. cit., p. 298.

matters (extremely limited in the case of Wales), it was believed that the regions
would soon relapse into their traditional subordination. Are they not full of
basically loyal folk who may have a few grievances but know that Britain is best?
Once reasonable note is regally taken of their grudges, surely they will fall into
line again, acknowledging their limited yet honoured place in the greater scheme
of things? A great deal of fulsome rhetoric of 1960s vintage went into the deal:
the legislation was titled 'Our Changing Democracy' and sanctified by speeches
on bringing government 'closer to the people', combating impersonal centralism,
etc. When set in the historical perspectives of English élitism, this was indeco-
rous to say the least of it: few have seen it as anything but an ideological façade.
Like the Local Government reforms which had preceded devolution, the changes
were at heart ways of preserving the old state – minor alterations to conserve
the antique essence of English hegemony.

There was no real belief in a new partnership of peoples. And in fact, such
a partnership – in other words, genuine 'transfer of power' from the old state –
was never conceivable without the most radical reform of the centre itself. To give
effective power away meant examining, and changing, the basis of power itself:
the Constitution, the myth-source of sovereignty, and all that it depends upon.
The whole British political system had to be altered. There has been no serious
question of doing this, for the sake of the Scots, the Welsh and the Ulstermen. The
only political party which advocates it is the one permanently removed from
power, the Liberal Party.[41] Unable to contemplate radical reform of the centre
(since its whole modern history has been built on avoiding it), London government has blundered empirically into the usual tactic of graduated response. One
commentary after another has explored the self-contradictory nature of the
proposals, their liability to generate conflict and escalation of nationalist sentiment and demands.[42] These criticisms have had little effect on the policy. At the

41 The Kilbrandon Commission formulated the view of federalism which has become standard
    in the debates on devolution: 'As far as we are aware no advocate of federalism in the
    United Kingdom has succeeded in producing a federal scheme satisfactorily tailored to fit
    the circumstances of England. A federation consisting of four units – England, Scotland,
    Wales and Northern Ireland – would be so unbalanced as to be unworkable. It would
    be dominated by the overwhelming political importance and wealth of England. The
    English Parliament would rival the United Kingdom federal Parliament; and in the
    federal Parliament itself, the representation of England could hardly be scaled down in such
    a way as to enable it to be out-voted by Scotland, Wales and Northern Ireland, together
    representing less than one-fifth of the population. A United Kingdom federation of the
    four countries... is therefore not a realistic proposition.' *Royal Commission*, op. cit.,
    para. 531, p. 159. The most persuasive version of the Liberal Party's argument for a federal
    Britain is Jenny Chapman's *Scottish Self-Government* (Scottish Liberal Party, 1976).
42 But no commentary has done so more devastatingly than the main parliamentary debate
    on devolution itself, during the four days of the Scotland and Wales Bill's Second Reading,
    Monday– Thursday 13–16 December 1976 (Hansard *Parliamentary Debates*, Vol. 922,

time of writing it may still be obstructed or dropped altogether, because of the vicissitudes of economic crisis and UK politics; there is small chance of its being amended into a workable form of federalism.

The Slow Landslide

The foregoing analysis has tried, in all too summary a fashion, to isolate some of the elements of fatality in Great Britain's current crisis. It has discovered these, above all, in the historical structure of the British state. As far as 'devolution' is concerned, these are the only sort of reforms which such a state *can* enact, while remaining bound by its distinctive historical identity. That identity was the product of extraordinarily successful earlier adaptation. Although a development oddity belonging to the era of transition from absolutism to capitalist modernity, its anomalous character was first crystallised and then protected by priority. As the road-making state into modern times, it inevitably retained much from the medieval territory it left behind: a cluster of deep-laid archaisms still central to English society and the British state. Yet the same developmental position encouraged the secular retention of these traits, and a constant return to them as the special mystique of the British Constitution and way of life. Once the road system had been built up, for other peoples as well as the English, the latter were never

---

Nos. 14–17). The student is advised to begin at the end, with the speech of the Lord President of the Council and Leader of the House of Commons, Michael Foot. This poem of embattled Constitutionalism begins: 'The central issue was mentioned by my hon. Friend the Member for Walton (and numerous other hon. Friends and Members)…They expressed their genuine belief that there was a danger of the Bill's undermining and destroying the unity of the United Kingdom. That is the central feature of the debate… My reply is that there are many other hon. Members on both sides of the House who support the Bill precisely because they believe it is the best way to strengthen and sustain the unity of the United Kingdom…'. Pursuing his theme of mystic unity, the Lord President underlined the point with ever greater emphasis: the whole structure of the measure upholds, even enhances the Sovereign Supremacy of Parliament: 'The fundamental explanation for the way we have devised the Bill is that we want to ensure that this House retains its supremacy…' so that, in the event of conflict among the nations, 'We sustain the proposition that the House of Commons… and the decisions of Parliament must be respected. That is the way in which we say these matters must be settled. Because we set up other Assemblies with specified powers, rights and duties *does not mean that the House of Commons need not retain its full power to deal with these matters in the future…*' (my emphasis). Not only is federalism out of the question; the unitary state will remain as mythically One as all past apologists have depicted it. A Scottish National Party MP, Gordon Wilson, objected to this ghost of Absolutism being conjured up once more: was it not the case that in some countries, Scotland for example, the people were held to be sovereign, rather than Parliament (more precisely, the Crown in Parliament)? This was, again, the far from 'technical' point referred to by McKenzie and Silver (see note 27, above). But, of course, it was not even noticed in the context of Foot's Westminster fustian.

compelled to reform themselves along the lines which the English revolutions had made possible. They had acquired such great advantages from leading the way – above all in the shape of empire – that for over two centuries it was easier to consolidate or re-exploit this primary role than to break with it.

In terms of modern developmental time, this has been a very long era. During it, English society has become thoroughly habituated to the conservative re-exploitation of good fortune; and for most of the period the leaner, marginal countries around England were associated with the act. They too received something of the impress of the curious English class system, and were deeply affected by the traditions of patrician liberalism. They also were for long integrated into its peculiar success story, in a way quite different from most other minor nationalities, and only possible in these singular developmental conditions. At bottom, this freer, less painful, less regimented form of assimilation was simply a function of the unique imperialism England established in the wider world, and of the state-form which corresponded to it internally.[43]

The critique of that form is still at an elementary stage. This is partly a result of the mystifications referred to earlier; but also partly because of the general tardiness with which the study of comparative development has arisen. I suggested in 'The Modern Janus' that the whole question of nationalism has remained enigmatic for the same reason. Both the general principles of the nation-state and the particular examples of these principles at work, in fact, can only be properly discerned in this relatively new developmental perspective. Although formulated originally to explain backwardness, it has turned out to be the intellectual framework most appropriate for understanding the 'advanced' states as well: in this case, the original schoolmaster of the process, long left behind by his first disciples and overtaken by others every year now, yet congenitally unable to renounce the habits of primacy.

---

43 This is related to the criticism which must be made of what is in many respects the best, most comprehensive attempt at an overall analysis of British development and its impact on the smaller nations: Michael Hechter's *Internal Colonialism: the Celtic Fringe in British National Development 1536–1966*, London 1975. His account is conducted essentially in terms of over-abstract models of development: the orthodox evolutionary and diffusionist model (which foresaw the gradual elimination of peripheral nationalism) is replaced by the 'internal colonialist' one emphasizing the factors of uneven development, discrimination, etc., present even in the oldest West European states. Although enlightening, the application of the theory to Britain is insufficiently historical, and misses too many of the specifics. It omits the key question of the character of the unitary UK state, and has too narrow a view of the significance of imperialism for the whole British order. The differentia of this variety of 'internal colonialism' was that – like the state itself – it was a pre-modern (Absolutist or transitional) form of assimilation, which survived and acquired new vitality through successful external depredations – thus enabling real integrative tendencies to outweigh those of 'uneven development' for a prolonged period. Nonetheless, a discussion founded upon Hechter's analysis would probably be more useful than any other in the future (he himself conceded that 'the models employed here are painfully preliminary', p. 6).

Many elements have been quite left out of even this bare outline. The nature and ambiguous function of the English Common Law system, for example, as both guarantor of individual liberty and central buttress of social conservatism. In both senses, the mystique of law extends and supports those aspects of the constitution and legal system mentioned previously. Or the particular importance of modern religious developments in England: as in other contemporary democracies, these have certainly contributed powerfully to the actual substance of the political order, especially on its left-wing side. Both Liberalism and Labourism are structurally indebted to the long-drawn-out English Reformation which extended from late Tudor times until Victorian Nonconformity.[44] Or the undoubted significance of emigration, continuous yet hard to quantify in its effects, as the perennial safety valve of society's restless and unstable fraction. In this basic human sense, 'empire' was anything but an abstraction to many generations of British workers and their families.

However, in spite of these and other omissions, I hope a sufficient idea of this strange, declining social world has emerged. It has always been too easy, at least in modern times, to either praise or condemn the Anglo-British state. On the one hand, its historical role and past grandeur impose themselves on most observers. During the Cold War in particular Britain's faltering economy was compensated for by a renewed cult of ancient Constitutional Liberty and wise pragmatism: an especially holy wayside shrine of the Free World. On the other hand, since the end of the last century nobody who has looked at all critically

---

44 Stein Rokkan's study, 'Nation-building, Cleavage Formation and the Structuring of Mass Politics', in *Citizens, Elections, Parties: approaches to the comparative study of Processes of Development*, Oslo 1970, gives an interesting comparative view of the persisting significance of religion in the structure of modern party politics; see especially pp. 101–7. This significance is substantially different in all four British nations, and still constitutes one of the deepest agencies of diversity at work: Catholicism and militant Protestant anti-Catholicism in Ireland; Radical Nonconformity in Wales; and Calvinism in Scotland. In England itself, debate on this question has always rightly focused on the famous Halévy thesis: among recent discussions, see particularly Bernard Semmel's edition of Halévy's *The Birth of Methodism in England*, London 1971, and the same writer's *The Methodist Revolution*, London 1974. The latter attempts to relate the theme to the character of Anglo-British nationalism, pointing out how: 'having long abandoned their 17th-century revolutionary inheritance, the sects, implicitly following the logic and in part the rhetoric of Cromwellian policy, could see a liberal, Protestant Britain as an elect nation with a divine mission. This was a view which... Methodism came to share' (pp. 172–8). In terms of the 'second revolution' argument outlined above, Methodism is perhaps more plausibly interpreted as a surrogate, merely 'cultural' revolution, whose intensity and effects were intensified by the failure of revolution at the state level – rather than as a spiritual barrier to revolution as such. Implicitly following the rhetoric of a lost revolutionary inheritance, without its reality, such 'cultural revolutions' end as reinforcements of the existing state-form. In both England and China they have also served as partial mechanisms of adjustment to industrial or urban existence.

at the economy or the class structure has been able to avoid sarcasm, often tending towards despair. Incurious worship and flagellation (including self-flagellation): it has always been hard to steer any sort of critical course beyond these poles, and yet keep the whole object in view. If critique is becoming more possible, it is probably because the object itself has at last decayed to the point of disintegration. The different Britain now being born may be better able to consider its ancestor dispassionately. The new fragmentation may also bring more space and distance into the British world, mental as well as regional and political. If so, it will become easier to weigh up the old contradictions and form a more balanced, overall estimate of the state's decline. The factors of grandeur and of misery are bound together, in the peculiar dialectic and tempo of Great Britain's fall from empire.

That kind of imperial greatness led inexorably to this kind of inert, custom-ridden, self-deluding misery. In its fall as in its origins, this empire differs from the others. It revolved around a remarkably non-regimented society, civilian in its direction and peaceful in its politics, and informed by a high degree of responsible self-activity. But the absence of bureaucracy was always the presence of an extensive, able, co-optive patriciate: rule from above was stronger, for being informal and personally mediated, not weaker. Peace was paid for by democracy – that is, in terms of the loss of any aggressive egalitarian spirit, in terms of 'knowing one's place' and quietism towards the state. The civility was tied to this permanent malady of class, in a unity essentially archaic in nature, whatever its gestures towards modernity. 'Responsibility', that liberal glory of the English state, was never separable from the huge, passive irresponsibility underneath. It depended on and fostered this working-class apathy, the particular social inertia of England. For its part – with the same long-term inevitability – Labourism merely occupied the terrain of this passivity, camping on it like a new set of well-meaning landlords.

A specific form of containment of capitalism, and an accompanying anti-capitalist spirit, were notable merits of the old order. They too made for a kind of peace, and for a muddled, backward-looking social consensus. Perhaps there are some elements of Arcady in all social formations, premonitions of a future ideal mixed up with the usual nostalgia for lost worlds. In modern England this has always been obvious and operative in the state. Too many people have been unable for too long to free themselves from the ghost of social harmony these conditions created – unable therefore to withdraw belief from the evolutionary myth which sees the authentic harmony of socialism one day emerging from that ghost. Yet in reality the anti-capitalist consensus has been the slow death of the old system: it gave it longevity, with some help from the Labour Party, but only to render senility and ultimate collapse more certain. In studying this strange slow-motion landslide, one begins to see the answer to the two questions posed earlier: why has the decline lasted so long, without catastrophe? And, why does its final disintegration seem to be taking the form of nationalist revolt, rather than social revolution?

The very archaism of the Anglo-British state – its failure to modernise and its slow competitive death – was connected to a remarkable social strength. Its 'backwardness', epitomised in industrial retreat and stagnation, and the chronic failure of government economic policy, was inseparable from its particular kind of peaceful stability, from its civil relaxation of customs, its sloth, even its non-malicious music-hall humour. The Siamese twins of anachronism and social cohesion belonged to each other. It was never in reality feasible to infuse the American or West German virtues into them without the effective destruction of this unique body politic. In English mythology, the uniqueness is ascribed to a mixture of racial magic and 'long experience'. In fact, it should be ascribed to empire. In a sense quite distinct from the habitual icons of imperialism – militarism, uniformed sadism, cults of violence, etc. – this was (as should surely be expected) the most profoundly and unalterably imperialist of societies. Of all the great states, the British was the most inwardly modelled and conditioned by prolonged external depredations, and the most dependent on fortunate external relations. From the time of its Indian conquests to that of its cringing dependence on the United States, its power was the internal translation of these fortunes. An incorrigibly overseas-oriented capitalism removed much of the need for internal reformation and dynamism; but the absence of this pressure was the ideal ground for maintaining and extending the patriciate, and for imposing a conservative straitjacket on the working class. Time and success were the conditions for this slow, anomalous growth; but these were what the British state had, because of its prolonged priority of development. Hierarchy and deference became the inner face of its outward adventure. Alone among the modern imperialisms, it evolved some of the semblance of an ancient empire, with its mandarinate and its placid urban peasantry.

The contrast between Britain and the more brittle imperial systems that were convulsed by losing their colonies does not lie – as often thought – in the former's less great dependence on empire, or in its ruling class's more civilised deportment. Externally, it rested upon the far greater success of British empire, a system so extensive and so deeply deracinated that it could survive the end of formal colonisation. Internally, it lay in the superior strength and cohesion of British class society, proof against shocks fatal elsewhere. No other nation was so dependent on imperialism, or had got more out of it; but also, no other nation had made so much of that accumulated riches, socially speaking, in the shape of a contemporary tribal state of such formidable complacency and endurance. This archaically based security, in turn, made possible the elements of liberalism in the élite's policy – both at home and abroad.

Slow decline has been the joint product of inner social strength and altering external relations. The former has failed bit by bit, in the successive spirals of the inevitable 'economic crisis' and futile governmental tactics to reverse the trend; the latter have changed less abruptly, and on the whole less unfavourably, than is now remembered in a climate of generalised economic gloom. After the

1939–46 war, Britain was still within its long victorious cycle, although nearing the end. It would still enjoy another brief phase of relative advance and prosperity, in the 1950s, before the European and Japanese economies had reasserted themselves. Even then, American hegemony continued to furnish an important surrogate external force-field, both economically and politically. I have already mentioned the EEC and North Sea Oil as further extrapolations of this quest for imperial substitutes.

The actual degeneration has been slower than most ideological pictures of it; it is also, of course, different in nature from them. In Great Britain itself Doom has been cried every Monday morning for many generations, following an ancient patrician principle that such announcements instil courage in the masses, and help to exorcise the real peril (whatever that may be). Like internal secrecy, this form of magic appears natural to English-style hegemony. Outside commentators naturally find it difficult to avoid an apocalyptic path influenced by these largely ritual warnings and exhortations. But actually, no one can predict the conjunction of external and internal circumstances that may one day cause the collapse of this resistant state. It might survive the present world recession with at least its main social structures intact.

It is, of course, the character of these dominant structures which leads to the answer to the second question, why peripheral bourgeois nationalism has today become the grave-digger rather than the intelligentsia or proletariat. The smaller nationalities have lost faith in the old state long before its social opposition. More rapidly and decisively than either the mainstream English intellectuals or the English working class, they have acknowledged the only genuinely predictable verity of British state-history: under *this* socio-political system, no conceivable government can reverse the trend, or fight successfully out of the *impasse* left by an empire at the end of its tether. The reinforced archaic solidarity of metropolitan society has numbed awareness of this truth in England. So it has sunk in to the periphery more readily – that is, into societies which, in spite of their modern political subservience, still retain an alternative historical reality and a potentially different vision of things. This is the wider context that ought to form the foundation for any political judgement on Britain's new nationalisms. It is insufficient to judge them in terms of their own self-consciousness and ideology, or – the commoner case – quite abstractly in terms of an idealised internationalism versus a supposed 'Balkanization' of Britain.

Against Internationalism?

Politically speaking, the key to these neo-nationalist renaissances lies in the slow foundering of the British state, not in the Celtic bloodstream. This is not to deny the significance of ethnic and linguistic factors – the things usually evoked in accusations of 'narrow nationalism', above all in the Welsh example. However, in the Scottish case these are relatively unimportant: this is overwhelmingly a politically-oriented separatism, rather exaggeratedly concerned with problems of state and power, and frequently indifferent to the themes of race and cultural ancestry. Yet it incontestably leads the way, and currently dominates the devolutionary attack on the British system. Before long (and depending partly on the fate of the declining Spanish state) it may figure as the most prominent and successful new-nationalist movement in Western Europe.

A more general theoretical argument lies behind this apparent paradox. In the general analysis of nationalism presented in *The Break-up of Britain*, it is suggested that in any case those ethnic-linguistic features so prominent in the ideologies of nationalism have always been secondary to the material factors of uneven development. The undoubted weight of nationalist ideology in modern history is owed, none the less, to a chronically recurrent dilemma of socio-economic development – a dilemma so far quite inseparable from the actual capitalist nature of the 19th and 20th centuries. This material contradiction of uneven development has itself assumed many forms; so have the compensatory ideologies which it has invariably generated. Yet it remains true that the notoriously subjective or 'irrational' elements in nationalism are always functionally subordinate to an economic reality, *provided one takes a wide enough developmental context*. This usually means looking beyond the particular state or variety of nationalism one is interested in (and often it means taking continental, or even world history into account). It means, therefore, looking far beyond the sort of ideas about nationalism normally entertained by nationalists themselves, and also by the most passionate opponents of nationalism.

In the case of the British Isles, the factors of internal uneven development are clear. They were of course clear in the older example of southern Irish nationalism; but essentially the same kind of dilemma, 'under-development' and ethnic-linguistic exclusion, has continued in north and west Wales, and furnished the basis for the more politicised and state-oriented nationalism of the present-day *Plaid Cymru*. In Scotland, a similar but much less important form of under-development has persisted in the Highland area: it still contributes something to the character of Scottish nationalism, and will not be without significance to a future Scottish state. But what has decisively changed the Scottish situation is a different variety of uneven development altogether. The factors operative there are closer to those observable in Catalonia or the Spanish Basque region: a tendential relative 'over-development'. Obviously linked to the discovery and exploitation of North Sea oil, this new awareness has proved particularly effective in the face of the English decline and political immiseration discussed above. It has awakened the Scottish bourgeoisie to new consciousness of its historic separateness, and fostered a frank, restless discontent with the expiring British world.

These differing patterns of uneven development do not suffice in themselves to explain the basis of neo-nationalism, however. The material basis is completed by recognition of the decisive effect exercised *by the uneven development of Great Britain as a whole* upon these, its constituent parts. This is, of course, the very theme I have been studying, from the angle of the British state. From the angle of the constituent nations – and this has come to be true even of Northern Ireland – it means that their own contemporary development, and the particular problems they confront in it, have become both entrapped and amplified by this larger drama of developmental failure. The latter's reverberations fuse with the more strictly nationalist initiative and energy now functioning in the British periphery. Both together widen the fissures making for a break-up of the British state.

This wider context furnishes a better basis for estimating the place of peripheral British separatism in history. A better foundation, hence, for pronouncement on their political significance. The larger story is that of the fall of one of history's great states, and of the tenacious, conservative resistance of its English heartland to this fate. Within the more general process, the disruptive trends of the periphery emerge as both effect and cause; products of an incipient shipwreck, they also function – often unwittingly – as contributors to the disaster itself, hastening a now foreseeable end. Consequently, judgement of their role hinges upon one's view of the dying state itself. If one does not recognise that it is moribund, like most of the English left, then naturally Scottish and Welsh nationalism will appear as destructive forces – as a basically irrational turning back towards forgotten centuries, as involution at the expense of progress. Whether conservative or socialist, belief in a continuing unitary state of the British Isles entails viewing these movements as a threat – whether the menace is to be countered by 'devolution', or eventually by other means. Of course, a good deal of the opposition to peripheral self-government is not even as articulate as this, and has no definite idea of the British state at all: it simply takes it for granted, with or without its more feudal ornaments. But the upshot is the same, politically.

On the other hand, if one perceives the United Kingdom as an *ancien régime* with no particular title to survival or endless allegiance, then the breakaway movements may appear in a different light. The phrase 'We must preserve the unity of the United Kingdom' is currently intoned like a litany by most leaders of British public life. Its magic properties are obviously derived from the cults of Constitution and Sovereignty. Merely to refuse this sacrament allows the observer to begin, at least, to acknowledge some positive side in the cause of the smaller nations. While, of course, the view put forward in *The Break-up of Britain* that the all-British régime is an increasingly contradictory and hopeless anachronism entails another shift in judgement. Countries struggling to free themselves from a sinking paddle-wheel state have, on the face of it, much justification for their stance. As the ancient device goes further down, this justification will increase, in their own eyes and those of the outside world. If at any point the collapsing metropolis attempts to quell their rise by force or constitutional chicanery, it will become absolute.

The logic of the anti-nationalists is most often obfuscated by another idea, which one might describe as the concept of the viable larger unit. New small-nationality movements tend in this somewhat abstract light to be condemned for opting out of an already achieved and workable progress on some larger scale: lapses into pettiness, self-condemned by a broader common sense. The notion surfaces to some degree in the commonplace of the devolution debate: 'You could never manage on your own'; 'Surely we're better all together, in one big unit?'; 'It's just putting the clock back'; 'It's irrelevant to people's real problems' – and so on. From a metropolitan angle of vision, these bluff platitudes carry a lot of conviction. Any opponent of them seems to define himself as some kind of dark fanatic.

The mistake in this attitude does not lie in its assertion that bigger units of social organisation are good, or necessary, or inevitable. A tendency towards larger-scale organisation and international integration has indeed accompanied the growth of nationalism and the proliferation of new national states, through-out modern times. This is certain to go on. Scarcely anyone believes that this dialectic will cease, or that the historical clock can be 'put back' in this sense. Certainly very few of Europe's new nationalists think anything of the kind. The crucial point is the quite characteristic elision in the metropolitan world-view. What it invariably does is to identify the existing larger state-form with his historical necessity. Yet what neo-nationalism challenges is not the general necessity as such, but the spurious identification hung on to it. In their own day, the Napoleonic Empire, the Hapsburg Empire, Tsardom, Hitler's New Europe and the old British Empire were 'justified' by precisely similar arguments; and in certain of these cases the 'internationalist' defence was put forward by mani-festly sincere, progressive thinkers – sometimes by socialists, and Marxists. It requires little counter-argument, surely, to point out that not all 'larger units' are equivalent, or equally 'viable', or represent progress. Thus – to make the roughest classification – one finds on the one hand workable federations or confederations of states, or communities, associations like the Nordic Union, the Andean Pact, the European Community, or the United Nations Organisation; on the other, an assortment of multi-national units imposed by heredity or conquest, most of which mercifully vanished in one or other of the world wars and the remainder during the anti-colonial movement after 1946.

To which category does the existing Great-British state belong? Clearly, defend-ers of the British union locate it unthinkingly in the former camp, as a modern, reasonable sort of wider integration. In fact, an in-depth historical analysis shows that, while not directly comparable to the most notorious relics of the 20th century, like the Hapsburg, Tsarist or Prussian-German states, *it retains some-thing in common with them*. This derives from the features we have examined. Although not, of course, an absolutist state, the Anglo-British system remains a product of the general transition from absolutism to modern constitutionalism: it led the way out of the former, but never genuinely arrived at the latter. Further-more, the peculiar hybrid nature impressed by this unique experience was confirmed by its later imperialist success. Possibly only the most successful and long-lived of modern empires *could* have preserved such an anomaly, and kept it in working order until the 1970s. Hence, both in its origination and in its surprising longevity, the British state belongs to the first category rather than the second. It is a basically indefensible and unadaptable relic, not a modern state-form. In its prolonged, empirical survival it has, of course, gathered many of the latter's aspects and appearances; but this must be distinguished from authentic transmutation, via a second political revolution. No less evidently and profoundly, the modern history of the British state is about the absence of such a change: although in one sense a question of comparative structural analysis, this recessive character is also written openly upon the institutions, rituals and self-advertisement of the system, in ideological terms.

If this is the case, then what is the situation of the British state in the (admittedly) necessary world of new, wider international units and co-operation? Far from belonging there as of right, the existing United Kingdom of Great Britain and Northern Ireland *is not even a possible candidate* in the field. It is not important here to speculate upon how long the International Monetary Fund and the other capitalist states will go on providing for the UK's old age. But it is certainly significant that, in this company, the only useful kind of speculation has assumed a geriatric odour: a motorised wheelchair and a decent funeral seem to have become the actual horizons of the 1980s, without design or conscious consent.

Other new-nationalist movements have other dilemmas to deal with, of a broadly analogous kind. It is interesting – but too much of a digression at this point – to ask what kinds of reproach they address to (e.g.) the Fifth French Republic, the states of Spain and Italy, or the Federal Government of Canada. Over-easy generalisation has dogged the theory of neo-nationalism, and erected an over-abstract defence against metropolitan sermons on Progress and Common-sense. There are undoubtedly different kinds of state failure or inadaptation at work, different grudges and demands, and (presumably) quite different solutions in order. It should be the task of independence movements in these various countries to work out an analogous critique of the dominant state. It may be that these critiques have a common element to them, though I believe that it is not yet clear what this is. Perhaps (to quote the most frequent suggestion) the post-Second World War development of the capitalist economy, with its US-centred multinationals and internationalisation of the forces of production, has to some extent infirmed and de-legitimised all the older sovereign states – diminishing 'independence' everywhere, therefore, but by the same token making it more plausible to demand this status, even for regions and peoples that would never previously have thought of undertaking the whole armament of nation-state existence.

But even if this is so, such very general economic causes will work to discover widely differing problems and dilemmas. And none of these is likely to resemble the British case very significantly: here, neo-capitalist uneven development has finally exposed the most genuinely anachronistic state of the economically-developed world to the light, an archaic palimpsest covering the entire period from Newton's theories to the thermonuclear bomb, and conserved (above all) by empire and successful warfare. Acceptance of *this* entity as the 'viable larger unit' of British-Isles development strains credulity to the uttermost. Like other social fossils before it, it struggles to survive by utilizing the counter-law of combined development, and importing remedies: the 'white hot' technological revolution, French planning and 'technocracy', non-élitist higher education (as in the Polytechnics), even West German workers' representation (as in the proposals of the Bullock Commission). In reality, that law works the other way, and merely generates grotesque failures (as in the British 1960s) or partial successes which underscore the system's futility, and make plainer the need for a radical change.

As we have seen, doom has been cried too often about the UK, too stridently and (above all) in too foreshortened a fashion. None the less, doom of a sort is genuinely inscribed in this historical pattern. Sufficiently – at any rate – to wholly discredit the easy metropolitan assumption that it, or something like it, should be defended against nationalist wreckers. Viable larger units of social organisa-tion ought to be defended against 'narrow nationalism', or an ethnic parochialism indulged in for its own sake. But defence is only possible when they actually *are* 'viable': which really means, when they are the most modern, democratic, and decentralisable form of organisation that current development permits – when, therefore, they are capable of progressive accommodation to the tensions of uneven development, and of contributing positively to new international rela-tions and the foundation of socialist society.

The point is of course underlined farther by consideration of the present character of the British independence movements. Preachers of UK unity at all costs imagine latent fascisms, and seize on every scrap of patriotic or anti-Brit-ish utterance as evidence of this. In reality, the Welsh national party is without doubt the least parochial or 'narrow nationalist' mass movement in British poli-tics. Strongly influenced in earlier times by a sentimental, medievalist universal-ism, it is if anything rather exaggeratedly attached to European examples and ideas, and has consistently perceived 'nationalism' as a largely cultural escape route from the peculiar isolation of Wales. The Scottish National Party has a very different historical basis. But its recent successful development has carried it too towards a far more catholic and outward-looking position. It advances the concept of an Association of British States as the successor to the United Kingdom, to preserve what is indeed functional or 'viable' in the union: nego-tiated agreements among the constituent parts would separate this out from the reactionary and fetishised London slogan of 'essential unity'. For its part the more recently-founded Scottish Labour Party has from the outset linked the cause of self-government to that of membership of the European Community – seeing in the latter, obviously, a preferable wider unit of organisation from a point of view at once nationalist and socialist.

More generally, the question of the Common Market emphasises still more cruelly the absurdities in any unreflecting defence of the UK *ancien régime*. It is only a year or so since the British state at last reconciled itself to membership of that particular larger unit. And the debate surrounding the event demonstrated that 'nationalism' in the familiar disparaging sense is by no means confined to the smaller nations. 'Narrowness' has nothing whatever to do with size. There is a narrow US, Soviet and Chinese nationalism, as well as a Welsh or Scottish one. The difference tends to be that the greater nations remain grandly unaware of their narrowness, because their size, their culture, or their imagined centrality makes them identify with Humanity or Progress *tout court*. Great British chauvinism belongs to this camp. But it does so – of course – with diminishing reason and increasing delusion. The whole bias of the British imperialist state has led the English people to feel themselves as something naturally bigger, more open and more important than just another nation-state. In reality, this museum-piece has dragged them from empire to something less than a modern nation-state, without letting them become one; the missionary expansiveness has turned into the narrowest, most dim-witted of nationalisms. This is what was deployed (especially by the Labour Party and other sectors of the Left) in the futile attempt to 'keep Britain independent' between 1971 and 1975. The vulgar hysteria and patriotic kitsch of *that* 'independence movement' easily eclipsed anything tried in Scotland or Wales.

Metropolitans have often accused those who (like myself) both supported entry to the European Community *and* self-government for smaller nations. There is no contradiction in this. None, that is, unless one thinks that the Community and the old British state are equivalently healthy and acceptable 'larger units' – so that it must be illogical to accept the one and reject the other. In fact, there is no common measure between them. In one of the essays in *The Break-up of Britain*, the reader will find a rather pessimistic analysis of the EEC's development. But whatever the shortcomings and contradictions of the new Europe, it is still a modern, voluntary, genuinely multi-national organisation, capable of farther progress and influence. By contrast, the United Kingdom long ago ceased to be a multi-national entity in any ennobling or forward-looking sense: the nerve of its larger unity passed away with empire, and should not be mourned or resuscitated for that reason. The problem of preserving positive elements left by that union – civil and personal closeness, individual liberties, forms of civilised association – is a genuine one, of which nationalists are conscious.

As things stand, the formula most likely to damage these relations permanently is exactly that which the paladins of UK unity at all costs have chosen. This is because another field of forces altogether lies behind their cause, concealed from them by the peculiar missionary nostalgia and phoney *grandeur* of Britishism. Most of *The Break-up of Britain* is about the British periphery, or about the theoretical context of nationalism; all too little of it is on England, the heartland. Yet this is certainly where the longer-term political direction of the British Isles will be settled. The paralytic decline of the old state has given a temporary ascendancy to Scotland and other peripheric problems. Beyond this moment, it is bound to be the post-imperial crisis of the English people itself which takes over – the crisis so long delayed by the combination of inner resilience and outward fortune we have discussed.

However, this social crisis is rendered enigmatic by the cryptic nature of English nationalism. A peculiar repression and truncation of Englishness was inseparable from the structure of British imperialism, and this is one explanation of the salience of racism in recent English politics. The growth of a far Right axed on questions of race and immigration is in fact a comment on the absence of a normal nationalist sentiment, rather than an expression of nationalism: this Mr Hyde represents a congruent riposte to the specific character of the Dr Jekyll state outlined above – to the tradition of gentlemanly authority and liberal compromise. It is less surprising than one would think at first sight that such an antithetical phenomenon should have acquired a degree of leverage over the state power (in the 1960s), and a remarkable prominence in terms of public debate and intellectual apprehension.

The longer the *ancien régime* endures, the more defined and worrying this trend is likely to become. On the analysis presented here, it corresponds to an underlying reality – not mere aberration, or a transient mood of intolerance. The fall of the old system must force a kind of national re-definition upon all the British peoples. This process is most important, but also most difficult, for the English metropolis where all the main roots of the British state are located. There, the very strength of those bases means that is far harder for system-directed resentment and loss of allegiance to find tolerable expression: the growing exacerbation is forced into an exaggerated antithesis to the state as such. Among the younger intelligentsia this has assumed the progressive shape of Marxism (albeit sectarian Marxism); but among the masses – separated from the intellectuals by the specific abyss of English class – it has too often taken the form of racist populism. As a matter of fact, the particular breadth and vaguery of residual all-British consciousness decays more readily into racialism than into a defined, territorially restricted nationalism. Once divorced from the powerful liberalism-from-above that previously regulated it, it displays obvious affinities with the old fantasies of the white man's blood and genetic aptitude for civilisation.

Hence, it is not mere alarmism to suggest that the persistence of the British régime fosters the most regressive possible side of an eventual English nationalism. Those who defend it *l'outrance* against the supposed petty patriotism of Scotland and Wales do so in honour of its liberalism and past achievements, hoping these can somehow be saved and perpetuated; they ignore the limitations and central defects tied structurally to these traits, defects which are becoming disastrous as the external situation of the state deteriorates. The latter process is irrevocable. So is the emergence of a new English national awareness, as drastic reform (or even political revolution) is forced by the decline. The more it is delayed, the more certain this awareness is to be inflected to the right, and captured by the forces feeding off the wounds and failures of decline.

There exists in modern history no example of a national state afflicted with this kind of decline and traumatic loss of power and prestige which did *not*, sooner or later, undergo a strong reaction against it.[45] In this sense, England has not yet undergone its own version of Gaullism: the prophet of this kind of conservative-nationalist resurgence, Powell, has been so far rendered impotent by the cohesion of the régime, which gave insufficient purchase for such 'outside' opposition to the system as such. Will this go on being true, as Britain lurches still farther downwards on the road of relative under-development? Nothing is pre-determined as regards the political nature of the break and one may, of course, argue that it could be radical or left-nationalist in outlook, rather than reactionary. But it is hard to overlook the fact that the very conditions of degeneration and all-British impotence are themselves 'determining' events in one way rather than the other. Another brief era of ephemeral 'recovery', another plateau of 'stabilisation' on the secular path of British decline, and these forces may well become even stronger.

There is a final interesting implication attached to this prospect. The sharpest 'internationalist' opponents of fringe nationalism in the current debate – like Eric Heffer in England, Leo Abse and Neil Kinnock in Wales, or Norman and Janey Buchan in Scotland – perceive a Britain 'Balkanised' into ethnic struggle and mutual hatreds by the agency of movements like the SNP or *Plaid Cymru*. There is an element of justified alarm in their vision, which should be taken seriously. But their idea of the machinery by which such conditions could come about is revealingly mistaken. As far as England is concerned, all they see is a rather justifiable 'backlash' against peripheral extremism: in reality, that 'backlash' is the frustrated political potency of the English people, and the dominant force in the British Isles – a force which did not wait on the rise of separatism to take on retrograde and alarming forms. One must distinguish between the movements precipitating the break-up at this moment (which are led by the nationalists) and the deeper causes at work, which have little to do with Scotland and Wales, and everything to do with the long-term, irreversible degeneration of the Anglo-British state. It is these, and these alone, which could in the long run provoke the kind of generalised feuding and resentment such critics fear.

It is, of course, perfectly true that the minor nationalities of Britain might be forced into a wave of regressive 'narrow nationalism'. This possibility is inseparable from any form of nationalism (the causes of the connection lie in the very nature of the uneven-development dilemma underlying nationalism). And this is the grain of truth in the internationalists' alarm. Yet their misconception of

---

45 The obvious exceptions in post-Second World War terms are Germany and Italy (although previously they were leading exemplifications of the rule). On the other hand, it can be maintained that in these cases the reverses were so absolute, and the externally-imposed constitutions so successful, that (above all in Germany) there was total interruption of the continuity which such national reactions depend upon. In a more than rhetorical sense, 'new nations' intervened in both cases.

the state and their unwillingness to focus upon the specifics of the English situation bring a false perspective to that alarm. Regression is never far away, in the ambiguous reality of any nationalist movement. But a definite triggering mechanism is required, none the less, to compel it into that pattern – to make the recessive trends finally outweigh or cancel its liberating, progressive potential. These critics ignore what that mechanism is virtually certain to be, in British conditions. By ignoring it, they encourage its development. In their panicky defence of the old state and Westminster's sovereignty, they help preserve those very things which are the root cause of their nightmare: the hopelessly decaying institutions of a lost imperialist state.

The Marxist Argument

The new debate about nationalism in the British Isles recalls some old ones. The most important of these is the mainly pre-1914 argument among Marxists, which resulted in the most influential single theory of political nationalism and indirectly determined nationality policies over a large part of today's world.[46] To a great extent that dispute still shapes the Marxist left's views of nationalism. Although it was complicated, the significant opposition most relevant to the new case lay between the positions of Rosa Luxemburg and those of Lenin. In this sector of the Left, the period of the Second International was dominated by expectations of imminent social revolution. The general conviction was that upheaval would come fairly soon, and in the most advanced capitalist countries. When it arrived, it would rapidly become international in character: although born in one nation, its example would be irresistible elsewhere, and in this diffusion the international solidarity of the proletariat would become a proven reality. Hence, the basic task of revolutionary movements lay in preparing the way for this process.

But this formula left one major uncertainty. The era that culminated in 1914 was not only marked by developing class struggle and the growth of organised socialism; it was equally one of maturing national struggles, both in Europe and outside it. Inside Europe, the remaining multinational states like Austria-Hungary and Tsarist Russia experienced growing strains from their dissident nationalities, and the Ottoman Empire came near its end. In the other continents, alert observers perceived the beginnings of a general, predominantly nationalist revolution against the newer European imperialisms. Nearly all these movements of national liberation took place in relatively backward areas (though with notable exceptions like Bohemia and Catalonia).

How were these two sorts of revolt related to one another? This was the key problem. On one hand, thinkers like Rosa Luxemburg took the view that

---

46 J. Stalin, 'Marxism and the National Question', in *Works*, vol. 2, 1907- 13, Moscow 1953. There is unfortunately no critical edition of this very important text.

nationalist struggles ought to be allotted a distinctly secondary place. This was
the case above all where the two threatened in any way to come into conflict with
one another. Where this did not happen (straightforward anti-colonialist wars
were the obvious example) there was no dilemma, and it could be conceded that
nationalism had still a positive function. But wherever (as in her native Poland)
it seemed that workers or intellectuals might have to make a choice between a
national struggle and a class struggle, the former should *never* be given priority.
Thus, given the situation of the Poles, 'integrated' into the Tsarist domain but
occupying a sensitive buffer position vis-a-vis Germany (perceived at that time
by most Marxists as a centre of the coming revolution), it was their duty to
renounce 'narrowly nationalist' aspirations. In similar European situations, the
national struggle was a distraction, if not a positively hostile barrier, to what
really mattered: the imminent break-through of the class struggle. It mattered
relatively little just where the latter happened. Its non-national values and impetus
would quickly render the whole realm of nationalist preoccupations anachronistic in any case.[47]

Luxemburgist anti-nationalism was criticised and qualified by Lenin, in a
series of writings on the issue.[48] Even in Europe, even much closer to the scene
of metropolitan revolution, he argued that the nationalist revolts had a more
positive meaning. The social forces and passions they harnessed were too great to
be genuinely 'renounced'; and in any case they worked to unseat the old dynasties,
and so foster conditions generally favourable to social revolution. The break-up of
these old states was a necessary (though admittedly far from a sufficient) condition of the kind of change Marxists were working towards. In this pragmatic spirit
the nationalism of liberation struggles ought to be encouraged, at least up to the
moment of their seizure of state power. After that it would, of course, become

47 The best introduction to Luxemburg's views is Appendix 2, 'The National Question',
    of Peter Nettl's *Rosa Luxemburg*, vol. 2, London 1966. Her main assumption was that
    '... national and Socialist aspirations were incompatible and that a commitment to
    national self-determination by Socialist parties must subordinate those parties to bour-
    geois nationalism instead of opposing one to the other. A programme of national self-
    determination thus became the first of Rosa Luxemburg's many indices of an opportun-
    ism which tied Socialism to the chariot of the class enemy...' (p. 845). The text Nettl
    refers to as her principal statement, *Przeglad Socjaldemokratyczny*, August 1908, No.
    6, 'The question of nationality and autonomy', has only recently been translated from
    Polish to English, in Horace B. Davis (ed.), *The National Question: selected writings by
    Rosa Luxemburg*, New York 1977.
48 Collected together in, e.g., *National Liberation, Socialism and Imperialism: selected
    writings*, New York 1968. Most of Lenin's articles and speeches on the question can be
    found in vols. 20, 21 and 22 of the *Collected Works* (December 1913–July 1916). I am
    grateful to Yuri Boshyk for letting me see his unpublished paper 'Lenin and the National
    Question in Russia: 1913 to February 1917', part of his work on the history of Ukrainian
    nationalism.

the task of the revolutionaries to disassociate themselves from the nationalists: national liberation would then turn into 'bourgeois nationalism', a force hostile to the broader revolutionary cause.

Both these stances were informed by what actually happened after 1914. The decisive non-event was the 'advanced' social revolution, which had been the common assumption of the whole argument. Revolutionary failure rendered Luxemburg's position an abstract one: defiant moral grandeur, in perpetual rebuke of a fallen world. There had been no room for the ambiguous and yet central phenomenon of nationalism in her heroic world-view. Nothing existed between socialism and barbarism; and the latter appeared to have won, as the European working classes drowned in their various 'anachronisms'.

Leninism was less starkly refuted by the evidence of events. However, their development implied that his more pragmatic attitude to the problem became permanent. It was no longer a provisional, tactical formulation holding good only until revolution came. There was nothing but pragmatism, for generations: the provisional became ever-lasting, as capitalism continued to endure and develop, and uneven development and nationalism prospered along with it. The Central and East European national movements attained their goals, but the result was a generation of mainly authoritarian régimes linked to a resurgence of conservatism, or fascism, in Western Europe. The anti-colonial struggles also won, but over a far longer period of time than was imagined. Their political consequences were equally ambiguous: unaccompanied by revolution in the metropolis, such newly independent nations were formed as the 'under-developed' sector of a still capitalist world – exposed, therefore, to forms of exploitation and to developmental dilemmas which long outlived uniformed imperialism. In 'The Modern Janus', national liberation and statehood was depicted as a doorway, like the gate over which the Roman god Janus gazed into both past and future. In reality, this threshold of modernity has been a prolonged, dark passage for most of the world, and has occupied most of the 20th century.

Already made problematic by the post-1914 course of history, Lenin's pragmatism was then fossilised by post-1917 history. He himself went on wrestling with the question until his death. With splendid, agonised clarity he had perceived that it was far from any satisfactory resolution even within the territory won by the revolution, and that the latter could easily fall victim to a renascent Great-Russian nationalism.[49] Locked in one under-developed area dominated by one nationality, the revolution could not help itself becoming joined to a 'narrow nationalism'. In the past, other revolutionary nations had harnessed universalising, missionary ideologies to their national interests: England had done so with Protestantism, and France with the Enlightenment. Now the Russians employed Marxism in the same way, as a legitimising creed of state. And as part of this

49 For the part played by national questions in Lenin's last days, see especially chapters 4 and 5 of Moshe Lewin's *Lenin's Last Struggle*, London 1969.

process the Leninist view of the national question was hypostatised, and treated as a largely ritual formula for consecrating judgements convenient to Moscow.

Unfortunately, it was a position that lent itself in some ways to this exploitation. Its virtue had lain in its 'realism', in its cautious recognition that nationalism was a double-faced phenomenon central to revolutionary strategy. In the actual dynamics of its era, before the 1914–18 deluge, this was doubly positive: as practical tactics, and as the basis for a theoretical development of Marxist ideas on nationalism. But the post-1918 deformations of communism emptied it of all real content, on both counts. All that remained was a double-faced position, the ambiguity of the formulae without their inquiring, restless tension: polemic mummified into priestly cant. None the less, it is not impossible to separate out the original impulse from the accretions of mechanical dogma. In my view an emended version of Lenin's old conception is the only satisfactory position that Marxists can adopt towards the problem of neo-nationalism, in the British Isles or elsewhere. Neither Austro-Marxism nor Luxemburgism offer this possibility.[50]

What are the emendations required by this exercise? They are of two kinds, both essential to any intelligible re-employment of these philosophies of sixty years ago. The first concerns the nature of those states and multi-national societies (including the Soviet Union) where revived nationalism is, or is likely to become, a key issue. The second concerns the general theoretical level – that is, Marxist concepts of nationalism's place in historical development, the theoretical reformulation towards which Lenin's ideas pointed, but which never took place. Advance on these fronts, of course, precludes the sort of ghostly archaeology and hushed citation of texts normally associated with Leninism.

The old argument took place in a context of indubitably archaic state forms: the surviving absolutisms of Central and Eastern Europe. Thus, it could be acknowledged without too great difficulty (as Lenin did) that merely nationalist revolt against these entities had a strongly positive side to it. As we saw, this acknowledgement rested upon a second assumption. There was another category of 'modern' capitalist states, against whom only socialist revolution was justifiable, or indeed conceivable. They were the crux of the future revolutionary process, and as such played a part in the justification of pre-socialist revolution elsewhere. These

---

50 The Austro-Marxist theory, crucial to the whole pre-1914 debate, conceived of a solution to the question by distinguishing between autonomy in 'cultural' areas (language, education, etc.) and inter-dependence in the field of economic relations and external affairs. A useful collection of the Austro-Marxist material (largely untranslated) can be found in G. Haupt, M. Löwy, C. Weill, *Les marxistes et la question nationale 1848–1914*, Paris 1974: see 'Anthologie', sections IV, V, VI, on the Brünn Programme, Renner and Bauer. The basic criticism made of their position was always that it was simply unrealistic to posit such a distinction: 'cultural' matters of the sort dear to nationalists are in fact intertwined with economic issues, and no effective 'autonomy' can be confined to the former area alone (except in the ideal, somewhat god-like state conditions which the traditions of the Hapsburg Empire encouraged social-democrats to believe in).

categories have ceased to apply in contemporary terms. The world of dynastic empires disappeared in war and revolution; while the second category of relatively 'modern' (or at least non-feudal) capitalist and non-capitalist states has expanded, altered and ramified in a way that makes simplified overall judgement about it impossible. The failure of the social revolution ensured this. It meant that capitalist state-forms would go on proliferating and evolving internally; and also that socialism, confined to relative backwardness and isolation, would develop its own highly ambiguous forms of state-life in a still nationalist universe. Nothing of this was foreseeable in 1913. It follows that any attempt to recuperate the sense of the political judgements made then can only be in a renewed and much more complex perspective – one that admits, above all, the receding horizon of the socialist revolution and the permanent difference which this has made. It is still possible to do this. There is still a distinction to be made on the left between nationalist and socialist revolutions, and an inter-relationship and order of priorities to be recognised – but how much more nuanced and analytically demanding the judgement has now become!

For example, is the French state of the Fifth Republic still identifiable with those Jacobin 'colours of France' which have impassioned one generation after another of radicals, ever since the Great Revolution? Did the events of May 1968 demonstrate this continuity – or the very contrary, a situation in which the best traditions of *la Grande Nation* had succumbed to an ineradicably conservative, centralised machine capable only of great-nation posturing and oppression? One's view of the significance of Breton or Occitan nationalism, of the place of the French Basques or the Alsatians, is partly dependent on this judgement. Is the United States of President Nixon and the Vietnamese war still in essence the democratic state of President Lincoln, which Marx defended against the secessionist nationalism of the Confederacy? Can Federal Canada be upheld, ultimately, against the nationalism of Quebec? In Yugoslavia a revolutionary socialist state has defended the most original multi-national régime in the world for a quarter of a century – yet there are still unsolved, and apparently growing, difficulties which cannot be merely dismissed as relics or temporary relapses. In the Soviet Union the same problem is posed much more acutely. Is the new national unrest and agitation against a 'socialist state' explicable and justifiable in the same terms as under the Romanovs or the Hapsburgs? The list is endless. As endless (one is almost tempted to say) as the reality of the world where the metropolitan revolution is so delayed. The point of presenting it here is not to make principled judgements impossible. It is only to suggest that they are more difficult, more relative, and finer than the prevailing Marxist or *Marxisant* slogans allow. It is the element of caution and relativity in Lenin's old position that ought to have been developed, as revolution receded or went wrong; instead, it was the element of dogmatism which triumphed, a sectarian icon extracted from its historical context.

Understanding of the state – both the particular state and the inter-state order – is one prerequisite. But this factor of autonomous political judgement implies the second amendation I mentioned above. The point here is (as the case of Great Britain demonstrates most graphically) that the analysis of the state's meaning and function itself depends upon an accompanying view of the inter-state order. States are formed by that order, not only (or even primarily) by an inner dynamic of classes, or a 'national economy' perceived as a separate entity. Consequently, one's general conception of modern historical development is called into play: the overall nature of capitalism's uneven development, which alone can provide an explanation of contemporary state-formations and so of the problematic of secession or resurgent nationality. This means that the very essence of the Marxist world-view is called into play. But, of course, the entire aim of dogmatism is to avoid that: it is to cultivate the pretence that the world where the revolution has not gone according to plan is the same as... the original, imagined, heroic world where it *will* go by the plan, because it must. In short, these 'amendations' are actually demands for the growth of Marxist thought. The first in an area where it has proved congenitally weak: the analysis of political structures and the state, above all the bourgeois-democratic state. This weakness underlies, and partly accounts for, Marxism's more notorious inability to come to terms with modern nationalism. The second demands revision in area where Marxism is basically strong, the general framework of historical development – but where, neverthe-less, orthodoxy largely paralysed creative revision until the great growth in development studies of recent years.

As to the British case, I suggest that analysis shows the definitively moribund character of this particular state, the reasons for its longevity and the (closely affiliated) causes of the difficulty of social or political revolution within its heart-land. This is simply one chapter in the history of the missing metropolitan revo-lution. It happens to be about an especially anomalous state-history, and may have small bearing on the other chapters due on other countries. But as far as it goes, it seems to demonstrate the case for the separation of the smaller countries. In relation to *this* specific 'metropolis' (or ex-metropolis), and as long as it endures on its old constitutional tracks, they have good reason to want out, and good cause for claiming that their exit is a progressive action – a step forward not only for their own peoples, but for England and the wider state-order as well.

Lenin argued that nationalist upheavals could contribute to socialist revo-lution where it counted, in the great centres. With appropriate modifications, one can surely make roughly the same case here. The fact is that neo-nationalism *has* become the grave-digger of the old state in Britain, and as such the principal factor making for a political revolution of some sort – in England as well as the small countries. Yet, because this process assumed an unexpected form, many on the metropolitan left solemnly write it down as betrayal of the revolution. Forces capable of unhinging the state finally appear, out of the endless-seeming mists of Brit-ish-Constitutionalism; not to be greeted as harbingers of a new time, however. Instead, they are told to mind their own business.

I referred previously to those on the socialist left who still believe in the

Constitution, and their consternation is natural enough. But the Marxist left which totally spurns Westminster and (on paper at least) wants nothing more than its overthrow, also criticises the separatists. Their reason is that proletarian socialism is supposed to be the grave-digger, and no one else will do. So they tell the nationalists to drop their shovels and put up with the pathetic limits of 'devolution': the revolution will solve their problems along with the others. Meanwhile they should wait until the time is ripe – i.e. the time for socialism – taking a firm grip on their petty-bourgeois, backward-looking impulses. The essential unity of the UK must be maintained till the working classes of all Britain are ready.

The fact is that the new nationalisms of the British Isles represent a detour on the way to revolution, and one which is now generally familiar in terms of 20th-century history. It is 'unexpected' only in terms of the rigid anticipation of an imminent social revolution about to break through and lead the way. The crux of Lenin's view was that nationalism could constitute a detour in some degree valid – contributing to the political conditions and general climate favourable to the breakthrough, undermining conservatism and the inertia of old régimes. Why should this not be true in the British case also? If the social revolution is on the agenda of the heartland at all, then it will be enormously advanced by the disintegration of the state. It cannot fail to be, as the old party system becomes unworkable through the detachment of Scotland and Wales, as the Constitution itself fails and has to be reformed more or less radically, in circumstances of political flux and innovation not known since the earlier nineteenth century.

If it is not on the metropolitan agenda, then the problem is different. Different, but scarcely unfamiliar: as we saw, the dominant truth in any reconsideration of the older Marxist conceptions is the non-arrival of the metropolitan revolution – whether this be due to 'delay' or a deeper impossibility, whether it implies more patience or a drastic critique of the world view itself. We have looked at some of the causes of slow change and blocked reform in the UK state. But at a certain point clearly this analysis leads into the larger scene: notwithstanding all its many 'peculiarities', it is hardly surprising that Britain has not yet done what nobody has done anywhere in the industrialised world, conduct a successful social revolution.

Should *this* still be the case, then neo-nationalism needs no farther justification at all. Escape from the final stages of a shipwreck is its own justification. If a progressive 'second revolution' still does not take place in England, then a conservative counter-revolution will; and in that case the movements towards Scottish, Welsh, and even Ulster independence will acquire added progressive impetus and lustre, as relatively left-wing causes saving themselves from central reaction. One can readily imagine the sudden sectarian rediscovery of Celtic political virtues under those conditions.

At the moment, the prevailing nostrum is inevitable general approval of 'the right of national self-determination' (not even the Scots or Welsh can be exempted from this, although it has been argued the Ulstermen are) combined with Lenin's supposedly sage qualification that 'we do not in all cases advocate the exercise of that right'.[51] Advocacy depends upon the influence which the nationalism in question is imagined to exert upon the general course of revolutionary politics. As far as the above analysis goes, it will be obvious how that influence is estimated. Obvious, too, the nature of the resulting dilemma. Should there be the possibility of a radical, left-directed breakthrough at the centre, in which the English people finally shakes off the old hierarchical burden of the British state-system, then the nationalist upheavals will assist them – even though the path should be a tormented one, with a higher degree of intra-British political antagonism and misunderstanding. And in that eventuality, the question would then arise of building up a new, fairer, more federal British order: not the dingy, fearful compromise of 'devolution' but a modern, European multi-national state. Should this possibility not exist, then what the small British (and other) nationalities are facing is another prolonged era of capitalist uneven development, stretching into the next century. It is certain that at some point in this period the British régime will finally founder, and very likely that this will be accompanied by a new, indigenous variety of conservative reaction. Who, in that case, can deny them effective self-determination, not as a moral piety but as an urgently necessary, practical step?

---

51 The most often-quoted passage in this connection occurs in 'The Right of Nations to Self-determination', Feb.–May 1914 (Collected Works, vol. 20): 'To accuse those who support freedom of self-determination, i.e. freedom to secede, of encouraging separatism, is as foolish and hypocritical as accusing those who advocate freedom of divorce of encouraging the destruction of family ties...' (p. 422). Whether one advocates divorce or not in any concrete case depends upon one's judgement of the 'family ties' already existing, and especially of the *paterfamilias*. Should the case be hopeless, and the foreseeable prospect of amelioration dim, then it is correct to move on from affirmation of the 'right to self-determination' to encouragement of actual separation. In that movement (in Nettl's words) the 'autonomous role of the proletariat' implies 'alliances with all elements who historically have to move forward (in a revolutionary sense) before they move back' (op. cit., vol. 2, p. 851).

CHAPTER FOURTEEN

The House of Windsor

Socialist Challenge

JUNE 1977

GENUINE SOCIALISTS have always detested the Windsor monarchs. They appear to confront a nation sucked into helpless crown-worship, without a single ounce of decent republicanism in its make-up. While they dream of communism, the country has not advanced out of this old feudal rhapsody. The 'serious' bourgeois Sunday papers lead their bloodshot cousins into new levels of hysteria. Given the opportunity Labour councillors slobber over the Regal fingers and the Dynastic feet. Huge crowds and street fêtes in Jubilee year testified to the continuing popularity of monarchy.

Yet the socialist challenge to this vast bewitchment is often noticeably feeble. 'Parasites and Scroungers!', to quote a recent anti-Jubilee leaflet handed round by one group. 'The cost of all this frippery!', as William Hamilton and others from the fading non-conformist traditions of the labour movement tend to say. Marxists sometimes go beyond these homilies, but it is usually to give a standard, somewhat mechanical dismissal in their own terms: monarchy is a deliberately maintained illusion, a class opiate meant to dull and divert class consciousness. Our ruling class has always been strong on ideology, far superior to coercion as a method of domination when it can be made to work; this is one of its strongest ideological arms, and certainly one which works.

This is good enough, as far as it goes. However, few really feel it *is* far enough. Confronted by the appalling popularity of monarchy, it is not enough to choke with despairing indignation, or console oneself with tales of the one or two honest Queen-haters there were in the pub last Saturday night. Such attitudes lead either to a sort of disgust with popular unreason – the masses who let themselves be duped by a meretricious show – or to romantic notions of a people not *really* fooled by it all, secretly commonsensical behind the Union-Jack façade.

Both notions are dangerous to socialism. It is much more important to ask what are the historical reasons for the Great-British monarch's specific character. These cannot be reduced to abstract considerations of ideology and class. Furthermore, it is these same characteristics which help us to grasp the causes of the institution's popularity. The British people are not daft because they still adore a Crowned Head; but they *are* the victims of a political culture which is in certain definable aspects retarded and limited. These peculiar limitations descend from the experience of empire, and are rooted in the nature of the existing state.

It is useless to criticise monarchy in isolation from these things. On the death of Queen Anne in 1714, the British ruling class invited the monarch of an obscure German princely state to step into her shoes. They did this to ensure the preservation of the social order established by the limited bourgeois revolutions of the previous century – 1640 and 1688. It was essential that the new dynasty should be controllable, and Protestant. No other formula would guarantee the 1689 Bill of Rights, and the union with a mainly Presbyterian Scotland achieved only seven years earlier.

The dynastic pretext for the change lay in the Hanoverians' distant blood connection to the old Stuart line. However, this was a secondary (though still quite important) technical question. Their distance, their Protestantism, and their foreignness were what counted. At home the Electors of Hanover were petty absolute rulers of the kind that still dominated the European political landscape. But the British élite calculated, correctly enough, that the culture-shock of transplantation from their small homeland to a great mercantile state would keep them quiet.

Much more was at stake here than the desire for a quiet life. The post-1688 ruling caste of landlords and merchants dreaded the return of absolute kingship – still the normal form of government almost everywhere else. To gain some idea of the universe of mummified reaction which kingship represented at that time, one need only consult Perry Anderson's analysis of the period in his *Lineages of the Absolutist State*. It was still a world of benighted despots, showing few signs of following the Dutch or English path of revolution. The closer Stuart pretenders – with a far better blood-claim to the throne than George I – yearned to return the British Isles to that world of sanctified traditionalism. We should remember that the threat was not finally dispelled until 32 years after George was brought in, with the defeat of Charles Edward Stuart's rebellion at Culloden in 1746.

This was the negative side of the installation of the House of Hanover (who only retitled themselves as the House of Windsor in 1917, driven by a wave of anti-German feeling). But the positive aspect of the operation was more important. As well as preventing the return of Catholic Absolutism, the new family was forced to adapt itself to the character of the post-1688 state. This was – and still remains – the crucial point. From the outset the modern UK monarchy has been one part of a distinctive state-system.

Betraying the Revolution

In the late-feudal world the British state was of course a revolutionary force. It was the first great achievement of bourgeois revolution, transcending the city-state limits of earlier forms of middle-class power. The enormous impetus it gained from the break-through would carry it, in a short space of time, to the defeat of France and a headlong career of colonial expansion.

And yet, this astonishing creation still unavoidably bore the marks of its epoch.

This first-born capitalist state – like the first-born socialist states of the 20th century – suffered profound deformations which reflected its struggle against the hostile world-environment. Until 1746 its very existence was in doubt. The Bourbons and Hapsburgs were at the door, waiting on one false move from the upstart. They had powerful internal allies still eager to undo the Revolution Settlement, not all of them in Ireland or the Scottish Highlands.

The monarchy was an important part of the pattern of betrayal of the revolution. The penalty of being first into the new political universe was that the ruling clique had to feel its way into permanent hegemony, through a long process of shifts and strategems. Judged in the light of the radical republicanism that had flowered during the revolutions themselves, these were shameful concessions. The gilded empiricism of the 18th century state could easily be depicted – and was – as an abject surrender to the epoch. Just as Soviet Russia can be caricatured as re-born Tsarism, so the Old Corruption of Walpole and Pitt could be seen as no better than the other *anciens régimes* of the continent.

In effect, the post-1688 political system could not help being a bastard form. It cleared a path towards bourgeois egalitarianism, the more rational constitutional order of the 19th century – yet never, itself, quite arrived in that novel world. The original great capitalist state never became a typical one. The ruling class fell foul of its own pragmatism, and became locked in the bizarre illogic of its transitional polity. To begin, with the Hanoverian kings were merely a part of that odd compromise position. Afraid of a return to Divine Right, the governing class did not feel able to dispense with kingship altogether. Quite rightly, they thought that a show-crown would help them to keep authority, both internally and in foreign affairs. Such a stage or 'constitutional' monarchy could help over-awe a still un-politicised people at home, and keep their end up in transactions with the continental despots. To this purpose, the oligarchy embarked upon a mighty programme of showmanship whose fruits are with us still. They were helped by the 1745 revolt, and the paroxysms of bourgeois relief which followed its defeat.

However, this primitive version of *la société du spectacle* registered quite limited success. It was not in fact simple to transfigure the 'wee German lairds' into an acceptable simulacrum of Great-Power Monarchy, and – as early 19th century radical history showed – popular scepticism about the institution remained fairly strong. The personal limitations of early specimens of the family had constricted the campaign; George III's dotage and the debauchery of the Prince Regent threatened to cripple it altogether. In the Royal Pavilion at Brighton, the true spirit of absolute kingship wreaked comic vengeance upon its phoney successors.

The usual myth is that Queen Victoria cured all that, through the personal charisma of a genuinely bourgeois monarch: prudish, sober, penny-pinching and deferential to the norms of a middle-class state. School text books have always dropped a veil of decency over the preceding decades, with suspect insouciance (incidentally, this is one reason why the Regency has qualified so notably as a period for romantic historical fiction). One recognises here a typical idealist inversion of the historical process: a personality is made responsible for the change, rather than a material change for the personality. In reality it was military and colonial success that transfigured the stodgy British monarchy into the Disneyish charade of modern times. The British state's victory over the more radical bourgeois revolution in France had been the key. It is as if – pursuing the analogy with socialist states mentioned before – the Brezhnev régime were to conduct a successful conquest of China and carve up the whole Asian continent afterwards. Even the most doltish and reptilian of Establishments could hardly fail to acquire a new lease of life.

In the context of the times, the Windsor regime's successes were if anything greater than that. For a period, it virtually 'occupied' the world. The advances of its industrial revolution delivered continents into its paws, in a way that no subsequent state would ever be able to emulate. The rich life-blood of a world's wealth rushed to its head, lending a new magnificence and meaning to its mediocre dynasty. It is true that only a distinctly more *petit-bourgeois* life-style in the Royal Household made it quite acceptable to the newly-rich middle classes; however, this was only the necessary condition of the apotheosis, not its cause. Moral retrenchment was a petty price for external glory; and the glory was reflected from the state's position of primacy and imperial dominance.

Imperial Counter-Revolution

It was imperial domination that provided the Crown with its brightest jewel in both the figurative and literal senses of the word. India provided the material basis for enveloping the working class in bourgeois mythology. It also provided the Koh-i-noor, the largest uncut jewel in the world, which to this day is mounted in the ceremonial Crown.

Such remarkable external success had deep internal repercussions. It served to fix the old, transitional polity of England into an unbreakable shell. What could possibly be wrong with a society which had won these triumphs? The newer bourgeoisie of an industrial century was won over, first to tolerance then to love of the bastard-state. All the marks of crypto-feudalism were rhapsodised into supreme virtues. That generally backward-looking, shambolic character inflicted upon it by historical isolation turned into a manifestation of racial wisdom: the British gift for peaceable non-radical change.

Basking in its 'golden age' of colonial depredation, the new Anglo-Scottish bourgeoisie felt no particular need to reform and modernise its state system. The ramshackle machinery was simply patched up and expanded where necessary. Dynasty and all. Political sloth was justified as *laissez-faire*; ideological somnolence was under-written by the new, romantic myth of origins – a sickly travesty from which the Revolution drained away altogether, and where Charles I became a tragic hero. At the core of this system, all the vital features of the 18th century compromise remained intact (as they do today): hierarchy, deference, a civil-based elitism, gentlemanly secrecy in government, 'amateur' administration, and so on. This is the context that explains the new role of the monarchy in modern Great Britain – or, it is more strictly accurate to say, in a Britain which has refused to become 'modern' for so long that it is now incapable of the jump without a revolution. From mid-Victorian times onward, as the Westminster polity slumped into ever more convinced inertia and self-satisfaction, dynastic matters grew proportionately more significant. Under the Empire, socio-political conservatism was registering a success without precedent. Kingship became *the* mighty expression of this tendency – a tendency which, of course, could not help being really popular in nature, and basically affecting the development of Britain's working class movements.

The British monarchs do not stand alone in the social sky (as fairy-tale accounts pretend). They are surrounded by a necrophiliac state-order groaning with beautified relics, rusty talismans and mystic precedents. Reconstruction of this tomb was a first priority of the post-1945 Labour Government. The Crown rests, as it has done since the Revolution, upon a narrow but determined civil élite devoted to the sapient management of that mass passivity linked to empire. It is the whole pre-modern hegemony which supplies the climate of British Royalty. Without the former, the latter would at once lose the peculiar ideal power and popularity it still enjoys.

This is why it is quite misleading to compare the Windsors to other surviving forms of monarchy. It is true that some modern states (like Denmark or Sweden) have retained a ceremonial dynasty in preference to an elected president. But this is the obverse of what happened in the United Kingdom. Here an archaic state-order has employed – one might say over-employed – the symbolism of monarchy to avoid modernisation. The Windsors are not really bicycling kings and queens, egalitarian monarchs. They are the essential tools of a social conservatism which has successfully disabled both egalitarianism and political democracy.

Compensation for Defeat

As British imperialism shrank and the regime wobbled on the long downward course, the Crown swelled in importance. Each new retreat was accompanied by louder Royal salvoes, more obsequious slaverings from the high bourgeois Establishment and more hystrical flag-waving down below. In general, a Crowned Head is supposed to function as a palpable image of continuity and reassurance; here, it acts as a powerful guarantee of stifling over-continuity and Empire-style complacency.

It would be a much happier situation if Queen Elizabeth were functioning as an opiate to forestall the coming socialist revolution. The truth is many degrees more dismal. She and her pyramid of lackeys constitute a dead-weight repressing – so to speak – the revolution before last in Britain. Their ideological force is built upon a now ancient loss of radical nerve by the bourgeoisie itself – upon the inner capitulation of last century, most strikingly expressed for us by the virtual disappearance of middle-class republicanism in Victoria's reign. The 'magic' of our monarchs is the sweet odour of decay arising from this mountainous dung-hill of unfinished bourgeois business.

The particular, exaggerated popularity Royalty enjoys is the voice of a still-active social conservatism. It is one manifestation of a nation which turned its back on the pains of progress generations ago, then grew unable to do anything else. Now, each new half-hearted and knock-kneed failure to 'put Britain on its feet again' is followed by a relapse into Tolkien-like reveries of compensation. The Dynasty is essential for this. Thus, the Labour Party launched its last white-hot painless revolution in 1964–67; a decade afterwards it presided over the Silver Jubilee and quite openly prayed for North Sea oil to make the Golden event of 2002 possible. Oil will keep the invalid carriage going as the empire once did. At the end Sir David Owen's Government will stage a 21st Century Spectacular making the Jubilee look like a village fête.

It is odious, but not surprising, that so much of the working class in four countries remains enthralled by this geriatric symbolism. The social conservatism in question is *not* a confidence-trick practised on them by the governors (although of course there are elements of this in the stage-management of the Royals). It is a deeply-embedded cast of mind, and one not yet shattered by mass experience. Imperialism has left behind a detritus far bigger than superficial judgements on the left admit, and several generations have squeezed this substance into compacted, resistant form. It is transmitted in a thousand ways through the capillary vessels of popular culture, as well as whipped up by Ministers and press barons.

For this reason counter-hysteria against the Queen has small effect. Denunciations of what she costs, or how many acres she owns, are a futile side-track. This is not in any way a counsel of despair. It goes without saying that an uncompromising republicanism will remain central to all the non-Labourist forms of socialism in Britain. However, there is little value in abusing the Monarch herself, in isolation from the decrepit Cathedral-State where she is enthroned. When this edifice is at last shaken down it will bury her dynasty in its ruins. Unable to raise much public protest against these orgies, socialists can take some comfort from the fact that the ruling class is losing its marbles. As one stone after another falls on its head off the crumbling old pagoda, the ancient Windsor *Weltanschauung* will give way too. The *Observer* and the BBC will go on stuffing royalist polyfilla into the cracks as long as they can. But the foundations themselves are collapsing under the added stresses of world recession, political divisions and nationalist agitation in Ireland, Scotland and Wales. Rather than squirming socialists ought to plan – I hope with at least a measure of optimism – for the day when the rulers admit that the old building is uninhabitable, and come out of it fighting.

CHAPTER FIFTEEN

The Timeless Girn

The Claim of Right for Scotland
1989

THE SNP'S DRAMATIC desertion of the Scottish Constitutional Convention at its crucial opening meeting has already won its place in tradition; a theatrical coup in all respects worthy of 1979, 1843, and before. It superbly evokes all the aberrant, self-destructive grandeur of our nation's history: everything (in short) which has over the centuries made the Scots a people of gallant losers and political imbeciles.

I well recall a personal rediscovery of this Scotch-pessimist philosophy of history, one freezing January morning back in 1975. It came back to me in the hardy shape of William Thompson, the Liddesdale postman. He made his way among the hundreds of molehills to the door of a cottage with some re-directed mail, noticing as he left again the piles of political and history books standing inside the front door.

'Ach, politics', he said as if the most natural of conversation opener, 'the trouble wie' us is we've never been able tae agree amang wirselves'. I had only returned to Scotland the night before, after some years abroad, and it was the first thing anyone bad said to me, apart from road directions. Still in the grip of returnee fever, I didn't know what to reply; but no doubt thought something along the lines of 'Have they been left a bit behind, in God-forsaken places like this?'.

The conversation turned to getting rid of moles. He gave me a long and useful account of the local methods of mowdie-trapping and disposal. That moment has often come back to mind over the years. Especially, since our great *Claim of Right* appeared and all those serious moves took place to turn it into the political reality of a Constitutional Convention. At last, I thought, Willie is being proved wrong. Yet in the same breath (having reacquired much of the equipment of 'Scottishness' in the intervening years) I couldn't help simultaneously feeling 'How will it go wrong?' And as all other sufferers know, in the God-forsaken sub-conscious 'It's bound to go wrong!' sits in sour-breathed proximity to another timeless, girning old drunk: '*Who* will ruin things this time?'

Well, we ken noo.

Problems of Identity

In the 'Prologue' the *Claim of Right* presents itself as an 'articulation' of Scotland's need for political institutions: the voice of a common identity as yet unrepresented by institutions of its own. The task of the Constitutional Convention proposed by the *Claim* will be to design and legitimate these bodies before – 'in due course' (p. 20) – presenting the plan to a British government and negotiating with it. This of course assumes the Convention's right-its effective if *de facto* embodiment of the Scottish national sovereignty. It will be asserting only those 'rights of the people' inscribed in all contemporary constitutional systems: all (that is) except the one which Convention spokespeople will be confronting in such a situation.

Now this is sure one day to raise many genuine problems of the 'What happens when Mrs Thatcher says "no"?' kind. The SNP's Convention delegation made flamboyant use of that question, and has been brandishing it remorselessly ever since. The great walk-out was done on the pretext that (unlike the SNP) the other bodies represented there had no answer to it now. Mrs Thatcher's 'No' and the party's new magic charm, 'Independence-in-Europe', have been the main part of the Nationalist argument against the Constitutional Convention process.

But it was Jim Ross, secretary of the committee which produced the *Claim of Right,* who outlined the problem of a British 'No' better than anyone else in his comments on the SNP victory at the Govan by-election. Independence may indeed, eventually, prove 'the least of the evils available to Scotland'; but, he pointed out quietly, this is unlikely to happen 'without fighting in the most literal sense of the word':

> The nature of power in Britain breeds a thicker skin than most. Even if the SNP won a majority of Scottish seats in a general election, a Tory Government wouldn't hesitate to profess that such a vote had nothing to do with independence the attitude of any United Kingdom Government will be conditioned by the interests of England and at present these demand the continued attachment of Scotland... The day when Scottish independence will be a friendly process is not in sight, nor is there any sign that Scots are yet ready to tough out a thoroughly unfriendly process.

Scotsman, 14 November 1988

For the unfriendly process, however, what counts is widespread support going far beyond voting: the participation of different classes and social bodies in their own way and to varying extents, the transformation of the social and cultural climate, a massive rather than an elite consciousness. The Convention process is part of this. Only a part, true: but – given Scotland's peculiar fragmentation on the relevant plane of consciousness – probably a vital one.

It can't do it on its own; but it may be a precondition of serious advance beyond the shallow mobilisation of the '70s. Beyond (that is) the kind of

mobilisation historically associated with the electoralism of the Scottish National
Party.

'They're Stealing Ma Scones!'

Although verbally similar, it must be stressed that Ross's sombre problematic is
not really that put forward by the SNP delegates to the Convention, and reiterated
ever since by its leadership. He is envisaging the transformation of Scotland's new,
emergent political identity into a movement of national resistance or liberation;
the disappearance of the 'Scottish cringe' in a political rather than a metaphorical or psychological sense. This process is still at an early stage, and its later
development (if it happens at all) is inevitably hard to imagine. What the SNP is
playing with, by contrast, is best understood as a kind of strip-cartoon version
of the independence scenario; 'national liberation' for British idiots to be attained
by the simple short-cut of voting SNP at Her Majesty's next General Election.

Ross and CSA's Convention wonder (and have earned the right to wonder)
what a rediscovered Scots political identity might do to us and to Britain. The
SNP's comic-book edition wonders nothing of the kind. Why should it, since it
owns the monopoly on national political identity? The latter's terms and conditions arc set out in a policy-booklet and purchasable along with the party card.
'Scots' prove themselves such by voting SNP. Other Salvation is there none. And
all true party-folk are naturally suspicious of any competition undermining the
Godly simplicity of this assumption.

For a time it may have suited SNPers to be nice to the assorted small-'n' nationalists arising in other movements. They were lost, poor things, and deserved a
little time to find the light. A little, but not too much; for there can be no real
need for the 'rediscovery' or development of something long ago awarded the
Royal Patent for exclusive sale to the Scottish electorate. Still less (therefore) for
a tedious Convention aiming to debate for a year or so and set out alternative
wares; so many devolutionary distractions from the only significant flag in the
wind, the tattered one with the 'VOTE SNP' on it. We already have as much political identity as is good for us, 'Conversion' is really the game not persuasion or
strategic compromise. Anyone thinking differently just can't have seen the old
flag (held up higher than ever after Govan). If they have, and yet still draw back
from the light, they may well be hireling knaves.

In the same article Ross underlines how disenchanted the Scots generally have
grown with 'the total sovereignty of Westminster' and the special kind of dry-rot
destroying the United Kingdom's political system. But such despair was premature, back in November. Only three months later we can see the dry rot is in good
hands; British 'Parliamentary cretinism' (to use Lenin's old phrase) has found its
last abiding refuge within the SNP, where sectarian infantilism seems likely to
keep the old thing warm until a true Doomsday comes. The strange SNP version
of *Sinn Fein* ('ourselves alone') we can now see means not the Scottish people

alone, but the Scottish National Party alone: sole and Providentially-nominated guardians of the national ballot-box. Their first duty has come to be protecting the imaginary Grail from the Constitutional Convention – a new parcel of rogues, assembled together to pinch it from them.

Once more the primal scream of offended British Scotia rings out: 'They're stealing ma scones!' This soul-cry came from Labour in the 1970s, when it first saw serious competition arising in the SNP. Now we hear it the other way round as in the 1980s a broader nationalism has arisen to challenge that party's mortgage upon the national heart. The insult could be tolerated, even wanly smiled on, while the SNP was still hard up for votes. But since Govan the prospect of redeeming the mortgage by traditional means has suddenly reappeared. So, protection of both SNP property-rights and (for the time being) of Her Majesty's Constitution have become a first priority; fundamentalism under the Crown, a rapid rush to Westminster, and then triumphant exit (without too much of all that 'unfriendly' business, thanks to Europe).

The Tough and the Toothless

In Ross's perspective, the point of the Convention is to forge a wider and more popular Scots political identity – that separate democratic identity and self-confidence which contemporary Scotland so evidently lacks. It was this lack (not flaws in 'devolution' as such or economic slump) which brought the ruin of the later 1970s. The main tide of events since 1707, whatever it has preserved, inevitably brought near-obliteration at the political level – an annihilation derived from submergence in one of the greatest State-polities of modern times. And re-emergence from this is naturally slow, and halting. In a country where (Praise be) religious, linguistic and ethnic factors don't automatically underwrite political identity, the latter has inevitably to be constructed 'in its own terms': just what the Scots (overshadowed by Anglo-British political grandeur, and moulded by their own collusion in it) find most difficult. Even with Thatcher to help them, decades may be needed to reverse these centuries of responsible paralysis.

Ross's point is, surely, that without the formulation of such an identity – the popular sense of 'Scotland' as a distinct *political community*, erected on a far broader basis than one electoral party – there can be no chance of our 'toughing out' any of the less friendly aspects of nationalism. A kind of bubble-nationalism – a longing for identity rather than the actual building of it may blow up now and then in favourable conjunctures: we saw it in the 'seventies and it may be happening again now. But such balloons are always likely to deflate again under real challenge. This is because they are filled by windy but fugitive enthusiasm, rather than the steadier mixture of accumulated collective resentment and offended interest which fuels enduring nationalism. When such mixtures discover a valid contemporary myth of mobilization, national-political identity is born. But contemporary Scotland is still in search of such a myth; while the SNP's surrogate wobbles back and forth between Bannockburn (1314) and the ballot-box ('next time').

'Toughness' here is not to be confused with the vulgar and toothless rhetoric of SNP fundamentalism. All this spluttering creed of 'Independence, nothing less!' actually means is 'Send us to Westminster!' (to pull independence from the constitutional hat). In reality 'toughness' can only refer to mobilisable identity, not rhetorical posturing; to a more resistant and many-sided communal consciousness which, if it's to amount to anything historically, must eventually be determined upon its rights *at all costs*. These costs may (and customarily do) include action outside the law, forms of civil war, the risk of economic upset, and eventually a willingness to rock (or sink) every boat in sight, starting with the Westminster Ark.

The Constitutional Convention is of course (and must remain) a peaceable body: but what it is actually doing is far more revolutionary than anything which can be undertaken by any British system party like the SNP. That most of those doing it are so un-revolutionary is merely a comment on the times. We are living through a successful counter-revolution, and the Campaign for a Scottish Assembly is trying to make the Scots opt out before it's too late. Mild-mannered, over-respectable folk have been drawn into this effort, as into all similar political upheavals of the past. Elements of our corporate, canny Establishment have entered the fray at last; and 'devolution' and Utopian federalist schemes do indeed often figure among their motives. But these motives and ideas are no true measure, either of the process itself or of its consequences.

Here, the hammer-effect of Thatcherism seems to have brought about a curious reversal in the Scottish arena. While the histrionic radicalism of 'Independence, nothing less!' has turned into a form of 'dowdy' conservatism, along the Convention's route a certain pragmatism which once underwrote the Union has become, for the time being, a profoundly unsettling and formative force, the Convention, after all, is trying to set out a principled political alternative – a Scottish constitutional way – incompatible with the very nature of the United Kingdom State. This is plainly spelt out in the *Claim of Right*'s argument, with its sober denunciation of Westminster's 'illusion of democracy' and the *de facto* tyranny concealed behind it. In his reflections on Govan, Ross put the same point in another way. 'Pay no attention to comparisons with Norway and Sweden: in 1905', he advised:

> The economic and social interactions of Norway and Sweden then were far different from those between Scotland and England now. Also, Norway's big brother was Sweden, ours is England, a very different and much more brutal polity.

'Nationalism' Versus Nationalism

However, the Convention's prelude to effective presentation of this alternative has now been threatened (and possibly aborted) by the sectarian posturings of the SNP leadership. The principal immediate barrier to the development of nationalism has, paradoxically, become Nationalism itself. In other words the current expansion of democratic consciousness in Scotland has now collided with the older narrower version of nationalism pioneered by the SNP. Beyond a certain point the new, more realistic and resistant form of national awareness hammered out under 'Thatcherism' has turned out to be profoundly unwelcome to old philosophy. SNPism remains what it always was: the conviction that one body is *the* irreplaceable, Historically-patented stand-in for political Scottishness party, Movement and embryonic State all in one, complete with foreign and economic policy, doormen's uniforms, 'Flooer o' Scotland' and an Independence Scroll up for the Queen to initial. What need is there to plan a new State, when we can already boast an Independent Scotland-in-Waiting, chafing for its solemn procession from No.6 North Charlotte Street up to Parliament Hall?

In a recent TV debate about 'Independence in Europe'. Mrs Ewing replied to a cheeky jibe about a possible Socialist Republic of Alba in these words:

> This is an easy question to answer. Ever since 1926 the SNP's policy has always been Commonwealth Status, Loyal to the Crown. This position is so invincible that we've never even debated it, it's never been called in question once.

Left Right & Centre Dec. 1988

Anybody recalling a relatively recent SNP conference debate about a referendum on Republican status might have questioned this Presidential verity (the motion got substantial support, but did not end up defeated). However, the secure tone and refulgence of *Madame Ecosse* were making a much more important point (before proceeding to her inevitable encomium on Norway and Sweden). She was underlining SNPism's impregnable home base in the identity of the 1920s, when George V was National Dad and Councillor Alfred Roberts had just been blessed with a daughter.

Some optimists thought that this addled identity-surrogate had died off years ago. Though occasionally taken down and lovingly dusted at moments like the one just mentioned, the presumption was that it might really have gone the way of the Labour Party's 'Clause 4', and would cause little more trouble. That happy notion was apparently confirmed after Jim Sillars' election triumph last November when the victor of Govan made a remarkable series of measured statements seeking out new common ground with Labour and the other likely Convention participants. These were important in preparing the atmosphere for the Convention's preliminary moves, and suggested that progressive nationalism had indeed consigned political Lauderism to the wings, if not to the back exit and the dustbin.

Now the truth is clearer. We have seen the old mummy leap malignantly out of its specimen-jar and take over the SNP's National Executive again. Its cheeks appear suffused with rosy new life, as if the rest had done it good. The rows of sober-suited young politicos have melted away from the centre-stage limelight, and confine themselves for the time being too embarrassed choruses of the old fundamentalist ditties. 'A rush of blood to the head' is how one or two of them have been overheard describing the shame, with the implication that such tides have – however reluctantly – to be swum with rather than resisted then and there. Poll-intoxicated atavism might be another description.

People are supposed to remember what they were doing when President Kennedy was assassinated, I will certainly always recall the moment of realisation that the Convention had been crippled (whether mortally or not remains to be seen). It was during the suspenseful day following the initial 28 January meeting; there was still some lingering hope in the air, as the SNP delegation debated its final stance. Then a radio announcer brought the grim news; SNP President Mrs Winifred Ewing had pronounced herself 'largely satisfied' with the decision reached (and due to be formally divulged next day).

Hope dropped dead on the spot, and a darkly inebriated *fin-de-siècle* swam suddenly into focus, where loyal 'Scots' might still be sending *Madame Ecosse* up to Strasbourg and the 1997 batch of Lauderite fundamentalists down to Westminster – all still crystalballing helplessly about what to do if England keeps on saying 'No!' to Commonwealth Status and Independence-in-Europe-under-the Crown into the next Millennium.

Tartan Sectarianism

'Atavism' entails harking back. But just what is SNPism reverting to in such moments of crisis and decision? It's hardly the first time that the syndrome has been observed. In fact it is the third time since the last general election in June 1987 that this unmistakable style has been seen in operation.

'SNP-ism' was forcefully displayed (for instance) in September 1987, when the STUC sponsored a march and 'Rally for Scottish Democracy' at Glasgow Green. Then too the Nationalists refused to take part. Hence what had been conceived as a new popular-front response to the tightening grip of Thatcherism declined (inevitably) into an old-fashioned Labourite event – a culturally adorned celebration of their one-legged 'victory' in Scotland. And the following year, after prolonged arguments, the SNP withdrew from the united anti-poll-tax campaign (again STUC-led) in order to set up its own ordained version, 'Say No to Poll-tax'.

As with the later Convention walk-out, these gestures were carried out amid a fuliginous reek of embittered accusations about Labourite treachery and conspiracy; no movement which that detested party is involved can, it seems, be other than imprisoned from the outset – a 'front' for continued English domination rather than Scottish common interests.

What does this common pattern express? The Scottish National Party's general outlook and credo -its reflexes, rather than its policies were formed in that other era so dear to Mrs Ewing I already mentioned. It is chronologically quite recent yet already spiritually and developmentally remote. They belong integrally to a pre-Thatcher Britain of Imperial decline, 'consensus', evolution and Labourism, where 'class' (in the quaint old Queen's-English sense) was all, and British Constitutional problems (finally solved in 1832) did not exist. The first half-century of the SNP's existence was passed under those conditions – that is, in a Scotland still pre dominantly (sometimes overwhelmingly) loyal to Empire, Throne and Labour's turn.

In such circumstances, political nationalism could only exist as an embattled, more or less hopeless, minority sect. To say that a movement is a 'sect' does not imply triviality or worthlessness; this case alone will prove that point. From the 1920s until well after the Second World War the SNP and its predecessors sought to revive the idea of Scottish independence and they should be honoured for that. However, they did so under such cripplingly adverse conditions that both the idea itself and the politics which grew up around it suffered badly. Suffered such deformation, in fact, that a 'Scottish National ism' arose not only very different from other nationalist movements but – in the end – at odds with the wider nationalist movement which would later develop in Scotland itself.

SNPism anticipated the more normal situation of the 1980s; the aggressive assimilationism of 'the Englishing of Scotland' and the Poll tax, and signs of real mass disillusionment with the political Raj and its more markedly colonial effects. But – precisely – it *anticipated* them from a pre-natal position, rather than expressing a democratic-popular nationalism already in existence. It was the voice of a land as yet without mass political identity, and looked forward (instead) to a curious, stage-managed resumption of Scotland's pre-democratic Statehood. The party was bearing the gift of modern political identity to the nation, rather than vice-versa. That gift being (of course) itself: an ideological stance even more favourable to egomania than the normal theatre of Westminster politics.

Now, it can be argued that in the circumstances this was better than nothing – a lot better (e.g.) than the national nullity of Scottish political consciousness once Labour had forgotten about Home Rule after 1918. Equally one could maintain that only such a blinkered and narrowly arrogant creed could have accomplished the break-through of the early 1970s: a broader, less philistine movement would have been too caught up in (or 'contaminated' by) all the compromises of British culture. However the price for such limited success had to be a confirmation of the traits in question – the formation of that contemporary SNP 'fundamentalism' predicated wholly upon the need *not* to 'change with the times', not to compromise and accommodate for fear that any inflexion may sabotage the Gift. Fifteen years after its historic 'high' of 1974 this legacy is not only alive but quite capable at crucial moments of reasserting its command over the movement. However, since reality has changed – for the good as well as for the bad – this capacity has now become destructive as well as preservative. It is holding back progressive nationalism as well as – in effect *rather than* -combating the Auld Enemy.

In the United Kingdom politics most sects have based themselves upon purist doctrine of 'class', a Marxist concept filtered (inevitably) through the weird prisms of a primarily English hierarchy and backwardness. On the extreme right there are also sects like the National Front using the concept of white or Anglo-Saxon 'race'. SNP sectarianism owes nothing to either of these. Its rigidly idealised picture is of a pure 'Scotland' embodying certain mythic social and psychological virtues regardless of class, race or creed – the nation of undefiled 'Scots' who, once awakened to their virtuous inheritance, will cast aside the false garb of Englishness and vote pure Nationalist. Although SNP discourse blames 'the English' for everything (exposing itself to accusations of ethnic narrowness) this rhetoric is in function most akin to Trotskyite denunciations of 'capitalism'; something which ideology renders inevitable but is very rarely meant literally or personally.

In these ideological terms, what anti-Englishness so conveniently obscures is *Britain*. But politically speaking, the SNP's 'Scotland' is also a function of Britishness: the obedient, constitutional path of Her Majesty's electoral system, restoring full partnership in Crown, Commonwealth and (nowadays) 'Europe' too. It has always been hard to explain to southern observers that all those anti-English tirades were only studio-Tibers, foaming with much ketchup. The 'England' in them is an ideal construction made necessary by the other one, 'Scotland'; and both belong within a wider structure of signs and silences which takes 'Britain' for granted. Inside that, over-emphasis upon 'England' consistently distracts attention from many profoundly British aspects of the actual Scots (including their Nationalists). After all, the Scots and Welsh invented 'Britain' and retain a (sometimes unwittingly) large stake in the notion, while the English rarely view it as more than a tiresome if necessary overcoat. The reason 'Britain' *has* to be all an English plot in Nationalist rhetoric is in order to legitimate a 'Scotland' whose claims were *not* – or not yet sufficiently – justified by persecution and minority status. Yet at the same time, the factor of pretence in such pretend-nationalism could be sustained in practice solely by tacit, grudging allegiance to a British Crown and Parliamentary system which couldn't (therefore) all be just an English plot. Were that so, Nationalists would hardly be pinning all their hopes upon the Constitutional path, and electoral success at Westminster: they would probably have been in jail.

Thus, nationalist sectarianism and Crown-and-Commonwealth Britishism have in fact propped one another up in an increasingly contradictory and odious symbiosis. The SNP's sect mentality derives from the need rigidly to adhere to this idealised pretence factor – the principal ideological bond of the movement: that's why it has always been so suspicious of intellectual culture, in the way so memorably described by H.J. Hanham:

The SNP was to be a party fighting for the small man to whom culture was something that he had already...'.

Hanham, *Scottish Nationalism* (1969), pp. 175–6

Culture one doesn't have already contains a display of theoretical doubts and alternatives, constantly menacing the explosion of the contradiction and the sabotage of party-spirit by egg-heads. Hence, consciousness-raising is best avoided. The special philistinism which sets the SNP apart from every other variety of modem national movement derives from this underlying dilemma. And now, in the 1980s, it is under threat from an evolving political culture too – the nascent, more concrete sense of national identity generated by the mounting oppression and political brutalism of the Thatcher years.

The Fossilisation of SNPism

The tenacious after-life of SNPism (in honour of the charismatic spirit one might also call it 'Ewingism') can probably be explained in a number of ways. The sheer conservatism of political movements -notably those with revolutionary goals – should never be underestimated. Also, until the shocks of the Thatcher era, the profoundly apolitical nature of Scottish society offered little intellectual stimulus or opposition to the Nationalist belief system. It let the philosophy of the *Scots Independent* be embalmed in a strange time-warp.

But the main explanation must surely be that already referred to: the success of the early 1970s. After the decisive failure of British social-democracy in the mid-1960s (when it became evident that British modernization could never assume a left-wing form), political restlessness began to mount in both Wales and Scotland. Along with the English North, these were the principal fiefdoms of a Labour corporatism now doomed to stagnation and decline. But unlike the North, both had a long-stifled, national dimension capable of mobilizing some of the result-ant resentment and uncertainty, In Scotland this happened quite quickly and (as everyone said at the time, and ever after) 'sensationally'; Winifred Ewing's by-election victory at Hamilton in 1967 led on to a fitful electoral advance culminating in the 30 per cent and 11 seats of the October 1974 parliament.

What this rapid fluctuation of voting patterns did was to carry forward an essentially sectarian movement into a position of partypolitical power. Carry forward, but not transform; the very speed of the changes, as well as the nature of the support behind them, meant that there was a big change in 'support' (defined mainly in voting and opinion-poll terms) but very little another ways. That was why sectarianism emerged confirmed by the experience, not discredited. After all, an astonishingly large proportion of Scots had apparently responded to the call – had nodded assent to SNP 'Scottishness' at least in the polling booths.

It was soon realised how shallow and unreliable this gesture towards political identity still was, as support dropped away again in 1977. 'Sensation' was succeeded by relapse into normal shoulder-shrugging apathy. Yet its effect upon the political plane were to be lasting. Here – where 'Scottish' consciousness is at its feeblest and most ambiguous – the consequence could only be the ratification of the party's world-view: the 'fundamentalist' certainty that 'we can do it again', on essentially the same grounds and by the same means – do it again but (obviously) with more votes next time round, correspondingly bigger leverage over the Crown, and an even quicker Constitutional exit to Commonwealth and European status. Among the faithful, the intensification of such certainty occluded the alternative perspective on the 1967–77 decade. This other explanation was that SNPism's heady surge forward of the early 1970s was due to one particular conjecture of events, unlikely ever to be repeated. It was a shallow-level mobilisation made possible by the impact of 'Scotland's Oil' in what were to be closing years of that 'decent' old British regime to which Mrs Ewing's 1920 philosophy integrally belonged.

During these years, after Edward Heath's brief experiment with pre-Thatcherism in 1972, it was Labourism which found itself struggling to sustain consensus and compromise on (inevitably) too many fronts at the same time. One of them was the partially reborn 'national question' in Wales and Scotland. Its operations in that direction were (like most of its policies) futile. But they did prolong the crucial fantasy SNPism depends on; that of a Crown-State reluctantly making way for the Scots to renew their rightful 1707 place. The brutal and thick-skinned polity behind 'Parliamentary Sovereignty' continued to be hidden or made light of.

Hence the abortion of 1979. Post-euphoria did produce a shift to the Left among Nationalists, associated with the 79 Group which (after expulsion and readmission) went on to produce so many new leaders and spokesmen in the 1980s. However, improvements within this Left-Right policy spectrum occur on an axis quite distinct from that of Realism versus Sectarianism – and it is the latter, unfortunately, which remains most fundamental to the SNP's self-image and ideology. It used to be a rather right-wing sect with as many members as voters. It has now turned into a rather left-wing sect which a large number of people vote for.

It has always been erroneous to identify SNPism primarily in terms of this Left-Right polarisation; popular distrust of the movement has rested as much upon perception of its inherent crankiness and unreliability, as upon its right-wing or 'Tory' character. Recent history has shown all too well how parts of the working class can be won over to the political Right. But it is far less likely to move over and stay with a palpably sectarian movement – with the politicos who still put up with *Scots Independent* in the age of satellite broad casting and desktop publishing. In the sense, the real connotation of the old 'Tartan Tory' jibe may lie as much with the adjective as on the noun. Tartan purism is not necessarily right-wing, but remains an inescapably friable and indeterminate quantity -somehow more likely to turn the key in the door to open it up. I need scarcely add that the often ultra-conservative antics of many SNP leaders and spokespersons – including, notably, the current President of the Party – have done nothing to allay the distrust.

Modernising Scottish Politics

I suppose it all means a lot more disagreement amang wirselves before we can fight back effectively. In both the Labour Party and the SNP, new generations will have to kill off the old before the promise of the *Claim of Right* can be fully realised. And the rest of us? We belong to that big movement 'Without a name or a leader, which loves none of the political parties and judges them by how they go about getting Scotland a democracy' wrote Neal Ascherson in *Observer Scotland* on 5 February 1989. In this perspective, what we need is the national movement prefigured by the *Claim* and the Convention, and not (as he concludes) 'an Independence League of Purity in the desert'.

His diagnosis of the last Independence League gesture is that it reveals 'just that miserable, contemptible weakness for which the SNP have with justice mocked Labour: the fear of power'. However, fear of power in this sense is the same as sectarian desire *for* power: a moral might imaginable solely as patented property-right and justification by the Almighty. Sects fear power, in fact, *and* think of nothing but the awesome power which reality so unrighteously denies them – a thought so compulsive that it may (usually in the name of realism) wipe out all that threatens to contradict it. Marxist sects end up in this way with a fantasy proletariat unfairly prevented from following *the* recipe for Socialism; the SNP equivalent is its fantastic Nation of 'Scots' betrayed by most really existing Scottishness – the weirdly apolitical projections of an apolitical and anti-cultural nationalism unique in the world.

What the Ascherson-democratic Party sees in the Convention row is the likelihood of relapse into the climate of inveterate feud and denunciation which, until 1988, was Scotland's substitute for national political debate. After the great betrayals of the 1979 referendum, the 40 per cent clause and the 'Labour Says 'No'!' campaign, all serious strategic arguments about Scottish political identity had for well over a decade been locked into this vicious, seemingly inescapable circle of hatred and recrimination: Scotland's Corsican-style war between an undemocratic mass movement and a democratic sect. Journals like *Radical Scotland* have provided a valuable forum for the battle, and tried to move it as a whole into a more constructive direction: is this to be their reward too defeat by the *Geist* of *Scots Independent*?

I won't try to deal here with the Labour side of it. However, having been in quite early in the business of denouncing Labourite backwardness and structural hopelessness (around 1965), I feel no great need to apologise for this. Most of the grim things said about Labourism in most situations of the kind we are dealing with here are likely to be true. In defence of SNP non-participation Jim Sillars has argued that taking part would have been liking 'putting the party's head in a noose' held by the Labour Party (*Scotsman*, February 1989). How could he, of all folk, ever have imagined it would be anything else? In a Scotland dominated by the electoral system which had just returned him to Westminster and the SNP to the top of the opinion polls?

The point, perhaps, was that all movement towards a Scottish democracy must start from a situation of preposterous unfairness: our historical part-interest in the collapsing legacy of Britishness. But what the Convention process offers is a broader way of challenging that legacy; a challenge which, had Labourism later betrayed it for its own ends, Nationalists could then have effectively defended in the name of (Scottish) democracy and popular sovereignty. The withdrawal tactic might than have been a national success, rather than a national disgrace.

By contrast, no amount of corruption and conniving mediocrity can itself justify a response of hysterical purism. The fact that it has, returns us to the real dilemma; Labour's dreadfulness, however unreformable and depressing, remains that of a political party; the SNP's stridency and abstraction, its passionate substitution of rhetoric for reality, remain the attributes of an incorrigible sect. And no embryo polity worthy of the *Claim of Right's* new initiative can be made from the collision of these elements alone.

About 'Europe' too I won't say much here. I supported European political integration as a form of modernisation when most of the UK Left and the Scottish National Party were still denouncing it as a fiendish conspiracy, and see no need to rehearse old arguments again. But of course, SNPism's version of them can only be a sectarian one: a new achievement upon plane of electoral rhetoric for Britain's most important electoral sect. Its use of 'Independence in-Europe' is as a deeply ambiguous slogan to take the sting out of 'separatism'. It invites voters to a wider horizon, beyond insular British parochialism; but simultaneously conjures up there a *Deus ex machina* who will somehow smooth the forward path, history's 'Yes' to set against the English 'No'. In practice, this now means one more reason to vote SNP – *rather than* organizing in the broader, pragmatic spirit of the *Claim*. Thus, the new urge for autonomy in Scotland is transposed on to the foggy plane of a post-1992 Europe whose overall political configuration is unclear.

The new Europe is absolutely preferable to the United Kingdom as a broader political arena; but the question of what new forms of self-government that arena will favour (or disfavour) can only be fought out well into the coming century. And Scotland's influence on that argument will (again) depend upon the nature of the national-constitutional movement she evolves now, in her struggle to get out from under Anglo-British hegemony. On her national *movement*, not upon this or that electoral party pretending to be the Nation.

'We've never been able tae agree amang wirselves' – and for a time it looks like being harder than ever. Unity isn't an unqualified marvel, or something to fight for at any price at all. However, there's a difference between disagreeing or even fighting within a framework of some agreement, and trying to wheedle or extort some scraps of agreement out of a sub-politics of endless paranoid feud and vendetta. The Constitutional Convention remains Scotland's best chance to move from the latter to the former – to translate conflict on to a higher level of achieved identity, as the necessary condition for getting out of the UK and getting anywhere in the new Europe.

CHAPTER SIXTEEN

Identities In Scotland

*Lecture to the International Congress of
Scottish Studies, Grenoble*

MARCH 1991

L'Ecosse a été redoutable tani: qu'elle n'a pas été incorporée avec l'Angle-
terre; mais, comme dit M. Voltaire, un état pauvre, voisin d'un riche, devient
vénal a la longue: et c'est aussi le malheur que l'Ecosse éprouve.

Encyclopédie (1765), art. 'Ecosse'

Auld Claes

'IDENTITY' IS A VERY contemporary term.1 Contemporary, that is, in the sense
of being at once newly puzzling and politically significant. Older meanings like
'being the same', 'personal identity', a classical philosophical problem or the
humble bureaucratic insignia of 'identity cards' seem to have given way to something else.

It might be described as a terrain of uneasy collectivity. Upon it whole nations
or peoples can now be described as looking for, and perhaps less often as finding,
'their own identity', the things that make them different and worthwhile, or, at
least, peculiar. In one sense this usage may look like new clothes for the distinctly
old-fashioned beasts of 'national character' and 'destiny'. Yet it is not really so.
On such ultra-sensitive ground, alterations are never 'merely verbal', matters of
stylistic whim.

The word use is new because there is something new. 'Identity' has emerged
from neutrality and become a positive term because new claims are instinctively
attached to it. Nationalities have always had identity. But now it seems they
must have it. No longer taken for granted, identity has to measure up to certain
standards. The comfortable old clothes won't do: identity must toe a line of
uniformed respectability. If defective, its shames call out for remedy, or at least
a cover-up; if 'rediscovered', it must then be 'preserved' from further violation;

---

1   Based on a talk given at the International Congress of Scottish Studies held in Grenoble in
     March 1991. This appeared in another version in the Congress Proceedings, *Etudes écos-
     saises*, no. 1 (Grenoble, 1992) as 'Scottish Identity: A Cause Unwon'.

and above all it has to be asserted ('proudly') and so get itself recognised by outsiders. Yes, it's time the world stopped smirking about *our* identity.

It is no coincidence that the most critical investigation of this theme is by a
Scotsman, W.J.M. Mackenzie. Though often jocular in approach ('Murder of a
Word', 'Life Story of the Victim', etc.), his *Political Identity*[2] is a serious work
consciously reflecting the Scottish confusion of the 1970s. 'A discussion of political identity', he concluded, 'is primarily a discussion of the conditions in which
it is possible to realise 'common purpose''. Conscious, collective 'identity' in other
senses – cultural, linguistic, religious – may figure among these pre-conditions; but
only when common purpose and action emerge can their significance be complete.

New Clothes from Nowhere

The new self-consciousness, as Mackenzie realised, would bring particular vexation
to the Scots. At a recent Glasgow dinner party I found all the wounds and grudges
on open display. Its presiding spirit was a prickly yet strangely helpless nationalism: a passionate will to look forward driven – by what weird machinery of
self-contradiction? – into fits of backward-looking self-laceration.

An animated political debate about the state of the British Union led, as
intended, to speculation on our own future in the crumbling *palazzo*. But the
very use of 'our' in the heavyweight sense reminded everyone present that when
Scottish politics and nationality meet, nothing can ever be taken for granted.
Modem patriotism has no natural persona in Scotland. Our old clothes are
romantic rags, yet – embarrassingly, inexplicably – none of the' new uniforms seems
to fit either. Hence the whole company – conservatives, Labourites, nationalists,
anti-politicals – found itself pitched onwards into the morass of 'Who are we?'
Or, more portentously, 'What is Scottishness?'

But the forward motion is often in a backward direction. An exit is hard to
find from this bog, and soon the point was proved once more. The familiar spec-
tres broke surface and sank again, one by one – that somehow pre-destined
succession of abandoned hopes and touchy debating points which reduce most
dialogues about Scottishness to furious silence, or alcoholic despair. 'How the
Scots love a good argument!' a French friend once observed. He was right, but
failed to notice how what they love most of all is a fiery debate edging on violence,
yet leading safely nowhere. 'Nowhere' is in this sense a distinctive Scottish place.
What it means is the reassuring void we ken, rather than unfamiliar gestures of
political agreement or compromise: the limbo in which our nation happens to
have settled down, as distinct from the common ground of modernity.

Most of our rhetorical ghosts were summoned to this particular feast. There
was the deliberate tunnel vision of Scottish Toryism, bluntly happy with the
auld-claes identity and obdurately convinced that adding politics would bring

---

2   New York, 1978.

Cambodian disaster: 'Independent Scotland? Fine – just as long as my seat's booked on the last train out!' Snowflake cultural nationalism featured prominently on the other side, an ancestral soul too precious for rough political beasts to trample on: 'What we really need is a new Enlightenment, Scotland's direct line to the Absolute – why ruin the great gift with shoddy politics?' In this way, bluff conservatism and a craintive intellectual purism have met and reinforced one another over the generations: united in dread of native narrowness.

Topography of Nowhere

The fatal terrain was further delineated by what one might call 'fragmentosis Caledoniensis'. From their earliest bookish encounters Scottish intellectuals imbibe a form of national nihilism, the sense of a *Heimat* lovable yet incurably divorced from the modem. The road is short to belief that the charm must depend upon the backwardness. So the divorce becomes permanent; and one consequence is a disarmed love, constantly beset by fear. But there is a way of countering this dread – by the wilful dissolution of 'Scotland' into just so many competing parishes and social classes. The crucial weakness of Scottish identity – political nervelessness, absence of common purpose – ends wrapped up in assertions that after all there's ('really') no such thing as Scottish identity.

These claims are invariably pursued with a suspect intensity, which derives from the nature of what is being asserted: a paradox so absurd that passion alone can enunciate it without shame. Scotland? Which Scotland? – Highland or Lowland, Hugh MacDiarmid or the *Sunday Post?*'; 'Scotland': *if* that word means anything – which I doubt – then surely it means utterly different things in Grampian and in Clydebank?' Scotland's internal contrasts (actually no greater than in most other nations) are thus weirdly elevated into mountain ranges of peculiarity – barriers exclusive of all possible consensus and common interest.

Exclusive, therefore, of both the ambitions and the risks of a national politics. Haven't other peoples acted to overcome or balance their variegated inheritance, and not invariably by suppression? Yes: but such calm comparisons slither around the main point at issue – the fact that the Scottish middle class wants to feel paralysed in advance by this problem. Self-inflicted stalemate gives them two things at once: a dramatic, if somewhat doleful, sense of uniqueness, and continued absolution from political sin.

Elective Idiocy

No doubt because we were in Glasgow, Edinburgh New Town was the parish pump provoking most spleen among the participants. What few national vitals may be left us, it was implied, are now being devoured in a feeding trough of Anglicised depravity. The task of resurrecting Scots identity, superhuman in any case, will before long be unthinkable amid Edinburgh's sell-outs and south-eastern incomers: the 'fragmentosis' will soon be terminal, thanks to this *quartier maudit* devoted to the trashing of all native virtues and institutions.

That stance too is laughable to outsiders. They know that only an hour away the roles are always comically reversed. In the capital 'Scotland' is perceived as menaced primarily by the other city's 'Miles Better' capitulation to everything most frenzied and flatulent about Mrs Thatcher's enterprise culture. Socialism has had its problems; but why this wilful infatuation with a capitalism run to seed? In a recent show Victor and Barry described themselves as 'quite the funniest duo in Scotland… or even Gle-e-esgow!' And the great city-state does believe its identity to be, in some inscrutably bloated sense, larger than that of the nation as a whole. European Culture Year is bound to do further damage here.

What has this delusion ever shown, but that our largest village has its normal share of idiots? *Invisible Country: A Journey Through Scotland*,[3] Glaswegian James Campbell's nicely titled voyage of discovery around the *Heimat*, contains some relevant remarks on the too famous contrast. He points out that his own city has been stamped mainly by all 'the metropolitan influences of industrialism' – non-native forces like Empire, immigration, an outward looking socialism and, we can now add, post-modern capitalism. In contrast – and however many sleekit demons patrol her streets – Edinburgh has resisted these influences to remain a place where 'the past is 'imperative… and strengthens the feeling of belonging to a distinct tribe with its own myths and traditions'. In other words a Scottish society may exist, and, arithmetically speaking, has to exist, around Glasgow; but the Scottish nation will always be unimaginable without Edinburgh. So, therefore, will any identity in that newly crucial sense I began by mentioning.

Politics: The Scottish Knot

It often happens at such discussions that foreigners strike a lonely note of sanity, and in this case an Irishman obliged, periodically intervening to chide the brawling factions. He seemed particularly moved by the sight of one journalist – a saintly man renowned for personal forbearance and Olympian judgement – who snapped suddenly under the strain, thumped the table, and declared that he had positively nothing whatever further to say on the subject. There were a few seconds of silence. During them the black hole behind 'Scottishness' was visible to everybody. Then we all fell back into it again.

Observers find these situations of divisive self-flagellation absurd, even demeaning. A *nation sans état* like Scotland has many faults; but not enough, surely, to justify intellectual suicide? What they sense is the lurking self-indulgence – a contradiction still more enjoyed than resented, the posture of an elite

---

3   London, 1984.

suffering from mounting exasperation and fear, yet unwilling, so far, to shake itself free from the customs of a once remunerative impotence.

That is exactly the knot of attitudes which paralyses the formation of 'identity' I mentioned earlier. New identities have to be made. Nationalists like to imagine them as pre-existing – Sleeping Beauty awaiting her Prince's speech – but they are not in fact a ready-made inheritance. Politics alone brings them into effective being: Mackenzie's 'common purpose', struggle or movements bestowing a sense of possibility and of a strategy pursuable against obstacles and over time. These alone create a practical standpoint in the present from which an 'inheritance' can be estimated, or rendered less ambiguous. Great risks and defeats are the usual accompaniment of such struggles.

What is most worth underlining here is that while this 'making' may be of a nation, it is also of a class – those social groups and alliances with enough passion for the novelty to run its risks, and face the initial defeats. Though in the name of an indeterminate 'people', national-liberation struggle can only be led by certain people with more determinate and vested interests in the process; nor could it conceivably be otherwise.

But in that case a less comfortable converse must also be true. The familiar argument has a shadow implication, falling heavily upon us in Scotland. Because national movements require such a motive force, they may be stymied by the lack of one. Nationalism may find itself paralysed and indefinitely held back where the class in question remains unable to seize the initiative. If the most likely identity-forming and identity-bearing groups remain stuck in the Gordian knot of their own past, then even favourable objective circumstances may permit astonishingly little forward motion – a movement always too little and too late to grasp its chance.

The point can be put another way. Social forces bent upon national self-assertion are unlikely to avoid excess and rashness: with nationalism, overdoing it tends to be the only way of doing it. But by the same token, can one not also imagine a class so afraid of rashness that challenge makes it retreat into compromise and prevarication – into a craintive moderation whose very 'reasonableness' is a kind of alibi for failure and retreat?

Institutional Identity

Well, of course there is such a class. I am a member of it. I happen to be a recalcitrant offshoot who stopped paying his dues years ago, and as a result gets labelled 'intellectual' (though the tedious thing about renegades is the way they always bear their class – and their nation – with them). This class runs Scotland. No collective presumption is involved here, for the important term is 'runs': the Scottish institutional middle class has never ruled this country, it merely manages it.

Its dilemma of the present day – under the Thatcherite onslaught – is one of both conscience and consciousness. Round dinner tables and elsewhere we find it fretting characteristically about whether or not the moment has come for it to rule, rather than merely administer. But that needs a new common purpose, a determination fed by a new consciousness – by, precisely, a renovated sense of 'identity'. And the awful, paralytic truth is that an upper-servant class may find it far harder to take such a decision than those who are genuinely below stairs – the outcast or dispossessed whose life chances have, suavely or brutally, been defined for them. The latter may quite easily tell itself there is nothing to lose. The Scots managing class is not brought up to think that way at all; and it has permeated the nation with its caution.

After all, its main articles of faith derive from the history of a not-so-petty bourgeoisie. Until very recently, post-1707 experience seemed to be showing it that a country – and for a time an empire – comfortably in the hand was worth any number of other possible ones, out there in history's dark bush. Even when the country then rots in the hand – some parts of it surviving on sufferance, others snatched away by assimilation – such a stratum finds it congenitally difficult to let go. To risk letting go, that is, and reach out more determinedly for a visionary one, the one which measures up, in the new clothes, etc. The old 1707 gene structure goes on regulating its primary reflexes: 'canniness', the crippling sense of how much there is to lose.

Other segments of the Scottish 'people above', like the landowners and the industrialists, may have had different attitudes; so may the working class at times. But neither have had the importance for 'identity' which these organised middle ranks have so consistently borne since the 18th century. In this sense the institutional cadre has been like a continuing armature of the wider Scottish bourgeoisie – had it been annulled by the Union, then both capitalism and class relations would have assumed quite different forms here, and Thatcherite Conservatism would not be facing the problems it does. All comparative studies of nationality have underlined the crucial place of such professional strata in generating the identity shifts behind nationalism: it is teachers, clerics, lawyers, journalists and loose screws who cause the trouble, far more than landlords, bankers, manufacturers or trade-unionists.

A Too Civil Society

But by the very same token, may not the same people be able to stop and contain 'the trouble' – to *prevent* identity from getting political and stirring up a common purpose? The Scots middle-class complex is of course rooted in the autonomous 'civil society' bequeathed us by 1707. In this descriptive, and quite uncomplimentary sense, we are too civil to be nationalistic. The old trinity of Kirk, Law and Education still accounts for most of it. But in recent times it has been heavily reinforced by a devolved bureaucracy; and then, after the reforms of the early

1970s, by a formidable new apparatus of local government as well. It is during this era that the Labour Party has become the stratum's dominant political expression: terminal-condition socialism in the service of major-domo politics.

The result is a uniquely castrate formation, devoted to low but uncomfortable with high politics. It 'represents' Scotland's working class in much the same mythic fashion as the *nomenklatura* once did in Eastern Europe, but with a lot less power over it. Since 1979 it has also found itself somewhat furtively half standing in for the nation, like a butler unexpectedly offered the keys of the mansion. In that situation, what would Gordon Jackson/'Hudson of *Upstairs, Downstairs* have done but muddle through meantime, hoping desperately that he could follow the Admirable Crichton 's example and hand them back again as soon as possible? With, maybe, just a bit more self-management downstairs?

It's quite true that nowadays Hudson/Crichton has a disreputable younger brother who has left service and taken to tearaway rhetoric and fulmination. Every now and then he breaks out and dispenses enough ideological firewater to assemble a crowd. For a time this glowers threateningly at the old mansion (seen as peopled by 'traitors', 'hirelings', etc.), and chants 'Independence now!' When nothing happens it gets depressed and goes home again. No windows are smashed, and the hirelings of the top civil society (now including poll-tax registrars and a swelling number of sheriff-officers) continue responsibly about their business. 'Something-must be-done' editorials make their seasonal appearances in *The Scotsman* and *Herald*. There is some tut-tutting down south (less and less with the passage of time and the regular postponement of 'doomsday'.

If such 'SNP revivals' have become Heritage-events it is for a good reason which Scotland's main *mittelstands* myth quite easily explains: firewater-Hyde is of course none other than feartie-Jekyll in altered guise – blowing off his repressions with another bout of noisy inaction.

Common in all pre-political societies, millenarist movements have often preceded the growth of statehood, fostering a dream-like identity which may or may not, eventually, flow into the aggressive 'common purpose' of nationalism. However, such versions of identity tend to be based upon utopian purism, religious in form (if not always in content) and can never themselves be that purpose. Rightly scorning the marsh politics of self-colonisation, they count on quasi-divine mass conversion to put things right. This is of course the pure nationalism so dear to SNP fundamentalists, and manifestly in the ascendant since January 1989. However, pure nationalism remains inseparable from pure fantasy: 'one bound, and we shall be free', on that day when the pure Scot in all of us sees the light.

Circles of Identity

So the SNP is 'bourgeois' all right; a fact which, unfortunately, has nothing to do with tartan, the Tories or CBI (Scotland). It is much more like the alter ego of the institutional bourgeoisie: a *Doppelgänger* which, though intuited in the past by Stevenson and others, has only grown up and become really important during the era of the larger state's decline. Paradoxically, an institutional elite deprived of an elite's most important characteristic – command power – is far more comfortable with a rhetorical than with a practical nationalism. The verbal apocalypse of anti-English raving suits it fine. Through this a sense of 'national character' is preserved without the vulgarity of actual rebellion or practical over-assertiveness. Since the magic bound will never be made, we see a 'nationalism' which, disconcertingly, has become another way of going round in circles, rather than of escaping from them. Doomsday would mean getting *them* off our backs now. But an apocalypse always postponable to next time keeps dependence in business: in actual, historical time all those 'next times' will inexorably become never, as actual people just give in, give up or emigrate.

These perennial circles of 'Scottishness' – our identity complexes – all derive from a compensated impotence: 'venality' as the *Encyclopédie* authors diagnosed it. But this is a chronic condition with a definite class backbone, not a question of individual hand-outs or petty corruption. It is structure, not an endless series of individual 'sell-outs'. And the basis for it is inscribed into the circumstances of an early-modern nation-state decapitated and then offered – instead of the usual oblivion – very substantial and long-lasting advantages. Though enjoyed by all classes, some have got a lot more out of it than others.

I believe that the one I'm focusing on here derived the most enduring benefits: that petty and middling bourgeoisie involved in what George Davie once euphemistically called 'the balanced harmony of our institutions ...the steady rhythm of independent institutional life'. This was the class most devoted to what he described as 'the formula of unification in politic, separation in ethics', a mode of existence 'still national, though no longer nationalist'. *The Democratic Intellect*, and its many imitators, have often praised the marvels inherent in such separation, and then gone on to mourn their attrition and eclipse: a national distinctness mercifully free from political evil, and maybe best uncorrupted by it.

In reality that 'formula' was a pre-modern one, increasingly useless in a reformed state – in the modernity where, as Gramsci put it, 'politics is everything'. After 1832 'harmony' became the entrenched routines of a provincial sub-Establishment, ever more stupefied by its steady rhythms of 'responsible', and unchallengeable, dependency. National-legal dignity collapsed into a prostrate legalism. The broad-based educational system mutated into a sickly hermaphrodite: the British worst of both worlds, Knox below and Oxbridge on top. Only the Kirk rebelled, in the 1843 Disruption: but, inevitably, to produce something worse, 'free' clerics determined to guarantee their purity by withdrawing from political modernity altogether.

Without political democracy, the important democratic strain in Presbyterianism was bound to be drowned by the authoritarian. I once tried resentfully to sum all that up in a phrase which caught on, about Scotland's rebirth depending on the strangling of the last Minister with the last copy of the *Sunday Post*. With hindsight, I can see that what the gibe really aimed at wasn't just dog-collars and publisher D.C. Thomson. It was the whole self-strangulating class presence of which these have become symptoms: the unique Scots phenomenon of a national sub-mandarin class cringeingly proud of its 'responsible' addiction to political *coitus interruptus*.

Modernity summons us to show our identity passes. But all the Scots have to pull from their pocket is a set of identity malfunctions rooted in this decrepit corporate persona. Unable to escape from nationality, the latter has devoted itself to containing the beast and evading its political consequences, including democracy. Hence its innumerable and complex alibis for the avoidance of common purpose and action, its prolix labyrinths of subterfuge and bombast, its deft and wordy combinations of the parochial and the evasively 'outward-looking' (often ennobled as philosophy, a talent for abstraction), and its penchant for self-dramatisation. In a structuralist perspective, 'Scottishness' appears as a deliberately exit-less maze. Its whole point is permanent circular wandering, punctuated by ritual offerings at one sacred lamp-post after another: nostalgia, the divided soul, 'equality', moderation, *esprit de clocher*, 'use of England where the UK's meant' and a prescribed daily prayer for Gaeldom.

What the Jekyll-&-Hyde mythology actually expresses is an unnaturally united stratum glumly yoked to higher British servitude. Inevitably, its principal political task has been to reproduce self-colonisation – a process which, against mounting odds, demands both a constitutional cringe and the retention of some national dignity and substance. And, as with the 'fragmentosis' malady mentioned before, one way of accomplishing that is via a collective fantasy of really being unspeakably different. The dourly apparent persona hides a 'real' one. In MacDiarmid's phrase, 'an upswelling of the incalculable' must always be just round the corner. Impotence flows not from what we are, but from a more distinguished sort of soul malady. We are being sent down the plug-hole not by abject mediocrity but by fated contradictoriness: being forever in two minds and out of our heads, the 'tragedy' of instinct versus intellect and so on. MacDiarmid's 'Antizyzygy' symbolises the condition of being politically nobody; but also colours and disguises it, in a way palatable to the sufferers themselves.

The Castration Metaphor

So, it is hardly surprising that the new identity garments won't fit the Scots. They have been manufactured for more recurrent and standard situations where factors like language, ethnic culture, religion and the memory of forced integration prevail. In this mainstream of modern nationalism, institutionally forged identity has almost by definition been unimportant: national movements normally have to demand 'their own' civil institutions on the basis of other identity signposts. Hence politics is an ethnic-cultural, sometimes a religious, mobilisation foregrounding such signs – a process in which intellectuals naturally take a high profile.

In our odd historical sidestream, however, things are the wrong way round. Certain bequeathed institutions are the real if unpicturesque signposts. Among such fossils of statehood, the more usual form of nationalist militancy – mobilisation via language or culture – is something of a dead end. Sometimes effective against colonialism, it is relatively useless against our kind of institutional self-colonisation. Our *auld claes,* Walter Scott's tartanic romanticism, have been an all too effective spiritual antidote against the least romantic, the most boring of bourgeois societies. This has been very upsetting for intellectuals like Hugh MacDiarmid. But it also explains why he and others have gained so little influence on nationalist politics, or – reversing the argument – why Scottish nationalism, alone among European nationalist movements, has proved so remorselessly philistine.

Since 1979 things have felt different. Until then grumblingly at home within a patriarchal *ancien régime,* the civil corporatism of the Scots instantly detected and bristled against the new metropolitan challenges. Such second-in-command class knew instinctively that it could never survive drastic overhaul of the UK command structure. What counts here is that 'Thatcherism' is an alteration of the state, as well as a range of economic reforms. It set out to destroy not just public-sector economics but the old tradition of patrician liberality within which these had grown up. Quickly discovering that this tradition already had one foot in the grave, Thatcher's' new court understood it could soon be toppled over for good.

But as it did so the south-eastern government was unwittingly demolishing the external buttress upon which the old balancing-act identity of the Scottish middle class had so Jong depended. The term 'castrate' I used earlier may have seemed merely a literary insult. But there is a serious point to the metaphor, the one Ernest Gellner describes in his *Nations and Nationalism.* He points out there how techniques of 'gelding ' were often employed by antique empires to sustain their power: actual eunuchs, but also 'priests... foreigners whose kin links could be assumed to be safely distant; or members of otherwise disfranchised or excluded groups who would be helpless if separated from the employing State'.

For such subordinate strata, everything depended upon the absolute stability of the 'unwritten' elite structures of central power: the dispensation of privileges and rewards by, in the old UK sense, 'decent chaps' who could be counted on to see a eunuch's point of view. If some crazed sultan or warlord got rid of these intermediary cadres, however, eunuchdom was obviously in deep trouble: although either physically or culturally conditioned against initiative and command, it could not tolerate the sacrifice of all separate status and dignity. Self-subordination is one thing; the dissolution of its whole social universe is quite another.

Planks of Identity

So it was from 1979 onwards that suddenly we began hearing so much about'
'community', and the humane anti-materialism of the Scots – 'our way of doing
things', so distinct from the vile egotism of the south-east. After 1987's doomsday
debate these seeds of identity started sprouting everywhere – far more widely than
in the SNP's ideological greenhouse. The most unlikely voices could be heard
saying that we, responsible folk, had not abandoned responsibility for 'the philosophy of greed', or the vulgar individualism later extolled in Mrs Thatcher's
Edinburgh speech to the Kirk. Suddenly, reminders of Scotland's many past tributes
to greed and the capitalist road fell on deaf ears.

This is because they had, in a new sense, become irrelevant. A new, more
broadly based identity is in formation: the middle classes are being compelled to
defend their old civil corporatism by new and more aggressive ideological means.
Ideology apart, they are doing so with the canniness and circumspection one would
expect: 'responsibly' and in thought-out, collaborative stages. The political form
this process has assumed is the Scottish Constitutional Convention: the high
point so far of a resumption of real, rather than rhetorical, common purpose.
In this way the Campaign for a Scottish Assembly has come to reflect the middle
class's still very sideways and hesitant motion towards political nationalism,
rather than the SNP. Not surprisingly, the latter greatly resents this fact.

A German journalist I met after the Convention's inaugural session in Edinburgh commented on the sight, remarkable in today's Europe, of representatives
from so many institutions and walks of life actively talking and trying to accommodate to one another – a living and civil corporatism. 'But, my God'; he
concluded, 'it was all so boring, too!'

A good sign, I replied, and deeply reassuring. True, nationalism can 't be made
from boredom alone; but the point is that our upper-serving or 'eunuch' classes
are at last trying to educate themselves out of their inheritance, and can 't help
being rather boring about it. They gave up independence in an odd, one-off
fashion and are only likely to resume it in some similar, sidelong, untypical way:
nerving themselves for the break through lengthy corporate rituals, elaborate
charters and stuffy proclamations redolent of both court- and class-room.

In this sense, perhaps, the SNP version of national identity has never been half
'bourgeois' enough – it was a two-penny populism aimed at a bit of everyone
and no one in particular. Hence the boredom-producing classes never took it
seriously. But now at last, under the lash of Thatcherism, they have started to
take identity seriously. The identity alibis have begun to acquire a political edge.
Our own 'common purpose' is a sort of formation – probably the only sort really
possible. It's still far from the fully upright posture, I know.

CHAPTER SEVENTEEN

The Snabs

Scotsman

7 OCTOBER 1991

'STANDS SCOTLAND WHERE SHE DID?' The stock quotation from *Macbeth* haunts many who return to this country, finding again that home is somehow the opposite of what it should be. For some travellers, crossing the hearth brings no reassurance, only an uncertainty deeper than when they left. Of course the morning air and the rolls are the same, and the reflexes of daily community – the 'small fields back of the house', as American poet Carl Dennis called them. But within the house itself things are also the same; and this is not so good.

The effect is hideously magnified should the traveller have the misfortune to come back during the party-political conference season. While abroad I have found that a more benign and flattering image of the homeland almost inevitably imposes itself. One tends to think of – and to casually mention – *The Wealth of Nations*, mealy puddings and Speyside in autumn, rather than the *Sunday Post*, Irn-Bru or Breich.

This image is easily habit-forming. A few weeks, and one already has the beginnings of émigré syndrome. If the latter has grown at all pronounced, my advice must be to avoid brusque re-entry in the late-September to early-October period.

It's like coming back to a household of grief-stricken drunks. The front door inches open to the sound of Ma and Pa Broon shrieking at one another. Not even new insults, the recycled abuse of 20 years ago. Later – one knows with sinking heart – they will be pelting one another with the kitchen rubbish, while the kids will be sprawled upstairs with a video of *Terminator 2*, wishing they had been conceived in a test-tube.

Thus does an ancient nation ponder its future. Since the 1970s the pathological parent-figures have been the Labour Party and the SNP. There have been other parties to vote for of course, but more and more eclipsed by the unceasing brawl in the centre of the stage.

Were this merely theatre of the absurd it would be bad enough: a suicidally repetitive form of brain-damage, insulting to its captive audience. Though (it should be noted) over time the Scottish public has at least evolved defences against it: apathy (better than being poisoned), and the grim humour of internal exile. Once widespread throughout Eastern Europe, this perceives all politics as an activity of 'them' – something so obviously depraved that, rationally, one can only be in it for whatever can be got out of it.

Regrettably, more than theatre is involved. Sufferance is not enough: loyalty is demanded too. The audience will have to support them at the next British general election and the recent conferences all took time off from their abuse-dances and spells to make that duty clear. Donald Dewar turned in a particularly notable performance last week. Yes, we can't let democracy down. The British Way demands we vote these wretches an assent at least sufficient to perpetuate their degrading quarrel for another five years.

Once the traveller is properly back Pa and Ma will both start in on him or her, of course. In an acrimony-drenched culture, neutrality stands condemned as cowardice (or worse still, as superiority). One is compelled to take sides. One may in fact take different sides every five minutes, but I have found that in practice this matters little. What really counts is the regular expression of a hatred-quota: the comforting certainty that this is political Hell, nor shall we ever be out of it.

But before being ground down there remains an interval of lucidity. The returnee cannot help briefly being aware that, after all, it is a unitary dramatic performance which is being enacted here: 'Scottish politics'. However hard Mr Punch and the Policeman beat one another up, they form in fact a single spectacle with an overall sense and effect. And before one· gets sucked back into the show, it is suddenly clearer what that sense is.

For a number of reasons the Scots still find it very difficult to unite against what has become their common enemy, the British State. Unable to vent justified anger and resentment outwards, in a rational fashion, they turn it inwards upon themselves. A history of will-lessness ('lack of self-confidence', etc.) predisposes them to this fate, as does the extraordinarily antique and British party system which they have inherited from a previous age.

The two main party-culprits are in this sense like pensioners in prams: unable to escape from formulae worked out (respectively) in the 1920s and the 1910s, the Scottish Nationalists and the Labour Party have become utterly locked into an incurably phoney war. Together they constitute what one might call the 'Snabs'.

The principle of Snabbery is that there must on no account be a compromise – or, a broad modernising alliance to replace the old structure in Scotland. No, having lived so long by the Old Constitution, these opponents would far rather die by it. As Britain declines they compensate with viler and more heedless abuse. Both long since came to identify the sectarian heat and fury of this shameful household quarrel with the reality of politics: the 'real fight', no quarter, victory next time (and so on).

The more such Hellish provincialism prevails, the worse becomes its basic cause: Scottish lack of self-confidence, that very apathy which the screaming and denunciation is (apparently) meant to counter. I say 'apparently' because, when perceived as a whole, the actual effect of Snab-politics is the opposite. Never mind what they say – what they *do* together is keep up a show guaranteeing the continued mediocrity and passivity of the Scots.

No conspiracy need be posited. The effects are unintended by either party, being simply inscribed in their respective natures. Like the scorpion in the fable who got a lift across the river on the frog's back and then stung it half way over, they just can't help being themselves. Stands Scotland where she did? Well yes – drowning, in the alien stream of Anglo-British politics.

CHAPTER EIGHTEEN

The Auld Enemy

Scotsman

9 MARCH 1992

'LEAVING THE ENGLISH to their fate': this was Brian Wilson's verdict on the new nationalism last week. In a *New Statesman* article he warned our southern neighbours that the SNP's main aim is 'the destruction of a unified labour movement and the permanent delivery of the rest of the UK into right-wing government'.

The 'ordinary people of Liverpool and London, Newcastle and Norwich' can only be saved from this fate by retaining the Union. Without us they would be doomed. Satanic Toryism will reign forever in a country deprived of its 40 or so Scottish Labour MPs. Then comes the guilt-pang, the awful accusation: how dare we do this to ordinary people, who suffer from 'problems and deprivations remarkable similar in cause and effect to those of their counterparts in Glasgow and Edinburgh'? How could we cheerfully go our own way and, simply because they're English, abandon fellow-creatures to Hell?

This argument has been repeatedly used over the past 20 years, and it's time it was taken seriously. Although its effects are less strong than in the 1970s, it's still capable of paralysing a vital nerve on the Left of Scottish politics. It imposes a kind of ethical *ne plus ultra* on thought about separatism. The mere contemplation of such a dastardly result comfortably rearranges the world into selfish nationalists and benign internationalists.

The most remarkable thing about the argument is its intense Scottishness. English Labourites have of course always accepted part of its content – the need to hang on to a Scottish power-base, and so on. But over the years I have often noticed how uneasy they are about its form and tone, as if some alien message were also being transmitted – something in between the lines which they don't like, yet can't quite understand.

The unease is justified. For only just beneath the veneer of an assertive internationalism there lies in fact an astounding moral nationalism. The underlying assumption is what might be called neo-Presbyterian primacy and rectitude. God's Labour Party among the Scots is seen as bearing a universal mission: the salvation of England, no less. This realm has since 1979 slid backwards into depraved materialist individualism. Its south-eastern heart is now so rotten that the sole hope is a kind of reverse colonisation – the redemptive message of a Scots-led Labourism.

The MP for Cunningham North now reluctantly accepts Home Rule as part of that mission. But only as 'a precedent for other parts of the UK'. Full accomplishment of the mission itself requires that the Union continue – 'as the necessary framework within which to deliver progressive change to all parts of the United Kingdom'. Thus there is a final temptation which those closest to God must refuse: to have Socialism for themselves and abandon the delivery of progressive change elsewhere, condemning London and Norwich to eternal perdition.

This arrogance has an ancient history. Usually nationalists are accused of raking up the past, but in Scotland the anti-nationalists seem to be much better at it. The instinctive attitudes of today's Labourite messianism echo those of the 17th century, when a Calvinist clergy sought to redeem the English with the Solemn League and Covenant. Then also London was held to have betrayed a cause – the great social change of the Reformation, sold out to the Devils of greed and Episcopacy. The answer was to be the 'strong and beautiful system of Presbyteries', the House of the Lord according to John Knox and Andrew Melville.

After their own revolution of the 1630s the Scots had that system. However, it was unthinkable to keep it to themselves and abandon fellow Protestants to the Antichrist.

Conscience cried out against such a course. Fortunately there was the Union of the Crowns, a necessary framework for its delivery to the English. After 1641, did the latter appear ever more reluctant to follow the corporate, disciplined model of the Kirk? Never mind – increased ideological activity in the South would soon put things right.

Move on three centuries. Following the 1987 general election – the first drumroll of another Doomsday – a similar set of delusions resurfaced among Scottish Labourites. Their lay version of the Kirk – Local Authority as Presbytery writ large – saw its power undermined by Southern deviance and the Thatcherite gospel. Again a Scottish (or Scottish-Welsh) missionary example was required, to root out weeds like Livingstonism and Trotskyism and restore faith in the greater Unified Movement.

The element of delusion here comes simply from identifying all possible Progress and democratic advance with Labourism. British Socialism is dying; so therefore is all hope for decency and compassion in Liverpool and Newcastle. The English, unassisted, cannot conceivably forge a new opposition or reform their own affairs. In the 17th century they were doomed without what Kirk leader Robert Baillie called 'the system of assemblies, higher and lower, in their strong and beautiful subordination'. So, in the 21st it seems they will be equally lost without Her Majesty's Labour Party, now speaking in the unmistakably Scots tongue of Claim, Convention and Community.

This is the tongue both Wilson and I were born into and (in different ways) accept: the national idiom. It shares grammar and syntax with Southern English, but not much else. We can't help speaking it, and (again in different ways) have to make the best of what we have been given by history. But – really – it is high time we assumed this historical burden (and opportunity) in our own right, and stopped imposing it on these long-suffering neighbours.

The fact is, of course, that they are perfectly capable of creating a new Left for themselves – even a new version of Socialism – with no 'help' whatever from us. Indeed (more uncomfortably still) they will almost certainly get on with it far better on their own. They did make a faltering start in the 1980s, with the Social-Democratic Alliance. But since then it seems to me they have impressively redeemed themselves with Charter 88, a reform movement parallel to our own. The movements are parallel, not unified, because in crisis two such profoundly different societies still have to seek strikingly different models of regeneration.

At present, the main obstacle in the way of both is an unreformed and (in Wilson's case) an unregenerate Labourism. He ends by quoting approvingly from Billy Connolly: 'I hate Nationalism. Anything that separates people, I have no time for'. This too is the old language of pulpit and excommunication. People (and peoples) are separated by ill will and devils, not by nature and history. Thank God (ours I mean, not theirs) British Socialism is now past saving by Scottish sermonisers.

CHAPTER NINETEEN

Second-Rate Unionism

Scotsman

23 MARCH 1992

'WHEN I WAS driving into Edinburgh last night I tried for the first time to think what it would be like driving into a foreign city, and that very idea filled me with sadness'. Thus spake Her Majesty's Foreign Secretary last week. He went on to explain why: 'It makes me sick at heart to see people so smugly preparing to demolish something much greater than themselves. The Union has achieved great things for all its people, to see it being chipped at and threatened in this second-rate way, it makes me feel sick…'.

Perhaps alone among his colleagues, Mr Hurd has enough imagination to see such things. Not enough, however, to grasp their meaning for others, or to perceive his own second-rate role in the whole drama.

The novelist in him senses that something big and irrevocable may be happening – that an epoch is ending. Yes: as they cease to be British, the very light will soon fall differently upon familiar scenes. We see what we imagine. Take the broad eastern vista from North Bridge, for example. George Steiner once remarked that the light round there always made him think of the Baltic and St. Petersburg. Wouldn't this effect be stronger if a working Scottish Parliament stood in the fore ground of the view?

But is there really no liberation, no awakening to new worlds in such thoughts? Hurd's perspective hides this behind the grandeur of what is forsaken – a tri-secular Union of States, greater together than either could have been on its own. He speaks of it as monumental, a fabric which bestrode the world and still towers over us. Something to be preserved (therefore) from the small-minded dwarves chipping away at it. Never mind that they represent 80 per cent of the Scottish electorate: midgets are midgets, sometimes to be protected from themselves.

By deploying this metaphor Mr Hurd merely sinks from the novel to the novelettish. Were the United Kingdom a monument his preservation order would in any case remove its meaning, as surely as demolition. But in fact it is a living state organism which happens to be ancient. In that sense one might compare it more aptly to a forest. It is the great wood left by the English and Scottish revolutions of the 17th century – the basic sheltering configuration of the Anglo-Scottish state. After the 20th century's wars and revolts, the oldest continuously living and breathing entity still standing on the political earth.

And what *is* happening to it now? All Englishmen are known to have at least one Scots grandmother, but Mr Hurd can claim two. As a veritable personification of Union, he is apparently entitled not only to judge but to wield a kind of spectral cane over post-independence behinds. Should there be midget trouble after 9 April, his prepared statement hinted at a tough anti-Scottish stance. A licking of dry Prefectorial lips preceded the ominous final warning: 'People in Europe regard this as so damaging to all concerned as to be inconceivable. I am not going to answer what the speculative attitude of a Conservative Government in the rest of the United Kingdom would be if Scotland seceded…'.

Such threats call for greater depth of field. Even forests have a history, and Hurd has overlooked vital parts of this one. He has forgotten just how British we were, politically speaking. Nowhere was Union more accepted than in Scotland. Until the 1970s, nationalism remained almost a crank belief-system, carrying the stigmata of long isolation and wilfulness. And indeed, it was just this fantasy side which he himself exploited in his sub-Buchanesque thriller, *Scotch on the Rocks*.

He has also forgotten how in the 1950s his party enjoyed a safe-looking majority among the Scots, not long before the Scottish Labour Party abandoned Home Rule. For decades the latter had clone nothing about the policy except mouth it; then it simply stopped, and formally abjured the old shibboleth for all time to come: A few veterans protested, but most thought it was just common sense – preparation for the left-wing modernisation of Britain, the mood which became Wilsonism.

Such were the assets of Union, a single generation ago. Today they have almost gone. The greater part of the forest crashed down in only 13 years after 1979, under the guidance of Mr Hurd's Conservatives and Unionists. In the name of radical renewal, most of the real constitution of Britain was over that period chainsawed away – the dense, ancient ecosystem of unwritten understanding and tolerant, tacit compromise. Denudation exposed it all to the raw atmosphere of the '80s, and it died. Nothing will bring it back.

Thus the Union destroyed the Union. But all Hurd can see is Nationalist midgets at work. Last week's feigned emotionalism at the dreadful sight is more than posturing, however. It helps conceal his own peculiarly repellent part in the business. For he, along with Whitelaw and Ridley, belonged to a select group of patricians who lent some traditional cover and style to the counter-revolution. They were the Von Papens of Thatcherism, as it were – the most corrupt of the demolition gang, those who should have known better and yet assiduously collaborated.

How dare he appear among us now to greet over our fate? Unfortunately this question isn't rhetorical. The totally bankrupt can fall back only on the totally shameless – in this case, on wooden histrionics straight out of *The Palace of Enchantments* (1988), a dire stab at political sexology set around the House of Commons. After failing to be Buchan, Hurd now failed to be Jeffrey Archer.

Christopher Harvie put it neatly in a review: 'extra-marital cuddling to compensate for the idiocies of Westminster'.

Of the forest grandeur, almost nothing is left. The plaintive rigidity of Hurd's 'emotional' 1992 Unionism speaks of defeat, no longer of the old wood's strength. While the last great trees groan in the new wind, Tory munchkins like Hurd and Major conduct a ritual dance around them, trying to persuade us by force of tears that all change is folly, and that the vandals are now conservationists.

What could more aptly persuade the Scots to leave than this disgraceful show? Out there, perfectly visible and more attractive every day, is that alternative landscape – a prospect which merges into the North Bridge view I mentioned earlier. It once evoked the Baltic, and now stretches eastwards through 14 new Republics to the Pacific, and southwards from what was once Leningrad to Skopje, the capital of an almost independent Macedonia. Soon this could be what driving into Edinburgh is like – an idea which fills me with anything but sadness.

CHAPTER TWENTY

Dark Forces

Scotsman

5 OCTOBER 1992

ABOUT TWO YEARS AGO, when Yugoslavia and the USSR still existed and people were wondering exactly where Slovenia and Slovakia were, I wrote an article suggesting that this world of the small battalions might be for the best. Troublesome maybe, even chaotic, occasionally evil. But still preferable to the big-battalion stability of times past, whose 'order' had reposed upon a joint threat to fry most of *homo sapiens* and freeze everyone left over in the nuclear winter.

'Hmm-m-m-m', said a metropolitan friend, 'good to see someone putting that argument in the *New Statesman...*'. Then came a pregnant pause, followed more menacingly by '...but you'd better be right'. At that time people could still recall the Cold War and what it was like to worry about being actually and hideously Dead rather than Red. Now they seem to have totally forgotten. Outrage over the sins of Nationalism has eclipsed those of the preceding era. Remember the time of Dr Strangelove? When the 'End of History' chilled our daily breath, before the phrase became trite speculation about a future we actually have?

What did he mean by 'being right'? Well, probably that these small-nation inheritors had better all be flower-people or there would be trouble. Trouble (notably) for opinionisers like yours truly, known already for his jaundiced view of Internationalism. The same friend has recently been in Sarajevo covering the war there for the *London Review,* and lamenting the end of Yugoslavia. He berates the Serbs for it; or the Serbs and the Croats; or nationalism, anyway – the fact that so many of these small battalions have come into the world with guns in their hands rather than flowers.

Even in a Scotland dispirited by setbacks to its national awakening, 'ethnic cleansing' is having its inevitable impact. A movement exaggeratedly constitutional and pacific in outlook is glibly aligned with genocidal murderers. In a recent attack on Scottish politics (also in *London Review,* 25 June 1992) the journalist John Lloyd admitted that during his travels here he had 'met or read no one who appealed to ethnicity'. A fact which did not prevent him concluding that he, as a Scot, 'does not now want to tempt up the forces which would warm me and 'my ain folk', and burn away or shrivel up those we define as outsiders'.

During the period when Lithuania was still under threat and the Yugoslav National Army was trying to browbeat the Slovenes, cosmopolitan distrust of nationalism did waver a little. The famous *Guardian* leader 'Don't Put Out More Flags' gave way to grudging admission that, well, all right, one or two more might be in order – but only if they behaved themselves. Reading Lloyd, one can see that this period actually endured for about five minutes. Overall, the movement of Responsible Opinion has been from convinced anti-nationalism to perfervid anti-nationalism.

Thus the dark forces of deranged metropolitanism are acquiring new life. All nationalism is again perceived as one: flower-people patriots are simply maniacs in waiting. If they got their way they would turn into Serbs. Do the Scots appear exceptionally meek and civil in outlook, with their claims about 'constitutional justice for Scotland challenging the rotten fabric of the UK state'? Don't be misled: such democracy is a disguise of the Dernon. Lloyd has a term for what lies behind it: 'repressive particularism'. The cure for this ailment is of course repressive generalism: bring back the big battalions, with the biggest stick they can find. Let Ukania lead the way: Yes – 'At a time of resurgence of the darkest nationalisms... we can appreciate what a triumph the Union is'.

Before he became Moscow correspondent of the *Financial Times*, Lloyd was Editor of Britain's venerable left-wing weekly, the *New Statesman*. I hope somebody is embarrassed by the fact today. For it has not prevented personal rebirth by total Tory-Unionist immersion. The born-again Lloyd is a break-dance Thatcherite, the sort of dervish which Conservatives have been trying to disown since 1990. 'Scots politicians, mostly of the Left, have not taken the point of Thatcherism', thunders the ex-Socialist, '... and in this respect I came to see them as not being in front of their English counterparts, but behind'. Surrender to nationalism, or even to Home Rule, would drag them still farther down. 'I fear a disturbance of the balance we Scots have reached', he concludes darkly. Any elements of continuity and corporate sentiment which sustain Scottish identity (as they do any form of nationalism) should be liquidated: harbingers of a possible Bosnia.

'Disturbing the balance': this is the point. Crass as he is, not even Lloyd has the nerve quite to say it: but I think what the *London Review* really pines for is that safe old world of empires paralysed on the edge of extinction – not just the Union but the entire old equilibrium of which it was a part. Émigré intellectuals like himself felt more at home there. Nowadays they feel uncomfortably pressured as individuals by any revival of collective feeling or aspiration on the home terrain. The article is eloquent on this theme, with its description of career and family supposedly at risk from SNP repressive particularism.

Given the volume of educated emigration from Scotland, Lloyd's posturing has far more weight than one might think. There are still plenty like him, and in positions of power. Anyone doubting this should reflect that he is, after all, merely up-dating the philosophy of that other intellectual emigre who some years back left a permanent and sinister impression upon the history of Scotland: George Cunningham MP.

'Internationalism' is a genuine morality, but it has always been separated by the most slender of membranes from righteous big-power chauvinism. In Lloyd's case – but not, I suspect, his alone – this membrane has been virtually torn away by the new stresses of post-'89. The émigré intellectuals have become open reactionaries. Probably what many of them would like to see is some English Metternich turning Europe into a second 'prison-house of nationalities', and re-imposing order on the Balkans (including Scotland). Fortunately, German democracy now looks strong enough to prevent it.

CHAPTER TWENTY-ONE

Demonising Nationalism

London Review of Books, vol. 15, no. 4

FEBRUARY 1993

TWO-AND-A-HALF years ago *Time* Magazine published a feature on the future of the world. Being on the cover of *Time* has always been an American honour: the cover of 6 August 1990 carried a portrait of Nationalism.

An elementary tombstone-shaped visage of plasticine, or possibly mud, glowers out from an equally rudimentary map of Central Europe. One primitive, soulless eye is located near Vilnius. Beneath the emergent snout a hideous, gash-like mouth splits the continent open from Munich to Kiev before dribbling its venom down across Yugoslavia and Romania. No semiotic subtlety is needed to decode the image, since a closer look shows the teeth inside the gash read simply 'Nationalism'. But in case anyone failed to register that, the whole image was crowned with a title in 72-point scarlet lettering: 'OLD DEMON'.

It wasn't an in-depth retrospect – it hardly could have been at that date – more an early, apprehensive glance during the first round of the ex-Soviet and post-Yugoslav tumult. In fact, it was what most Western or metropolitan opinion really expected, on the basis of these early stirrings. Sometime before the Baltic peoples, the Ukrainians or the Georgians had actually established their independence, when virtually all Western diplomacy was still devoted to shoring up Gorbachev and Yugoslavia, a pervasive sense of doom already lurked in the North Atlantic mind. It was summed up in a *Guardian* leader of the same vintage: 'Don't Put Out More Flags!' This editorial did become famous enough to endure mild mockery, but only because it was characteristically over the top, exaggerating what most readers instinctively felt: that if enough new national flags were put out the Old Demon would wreak havoc with the New World Order. The second springtime of nations was, in this glum perspective, already turning to winter, and a bad one at that.

Anyone could see from the outset that there were at least three principal strands in the gigantic upheaval against Communism. There was a popular, democratic rebellion against one-party autocracy and state terror. There was an economic revulsion against the anti-capitalist command economies which for 40 years had imposed forced-march development on the East. And thirdly there was the national mould into which these revolts were somehow inevitably flowing – the new salience, in post-Communist society, of the ethnic, or (as in Bosnia) of the ethnic-religious.

The *Time-Guardian* perspective on this triad is that the third element will most likely end by confining, endangering or even aborting the first two. And that perspective is what I am primarily objecting to – the instinctive notion that No 3 in the list is there by unfortunate accident, the bad news which has resurfaced alongside the good, an Old Adam who refuses to let the Angel of Progress get on with it. The conclusion to the *Time* article accompanying the front cover puts this point as well as anything else has, in terms which, since then, have been echoed thousands of times in tones of mounting hysteria: 'Not since Franz Ferdinand's assassination have conditions been so favourable for an enduring new order to replace the empires of the past. With a unified Germany locked in the embrace of democratic Europe, and the Soviet Union re-examining its fundamental values, the way is open for an era of peace and liberty – *but only so long as the old demons do not escape again.*'

But escape they did, notably in what used to be Yugoslavia and especially – as if some truly profound irony of history was working itself out – in and around the very town where Franz Ferdinand perished in 1914. The general view or new received wisdom soon became set in concrete: nationalism is upsetting everything. It has ruined the End of History which has come back like some evil shade, mainly in order to spoil the State Department's victory celebrations.

There were always serious difficulties in store in the East for both democracy and capitalism, of course, and no serious commentator has ignored them. But what has made these insoluble, according to the received wisdom, is the return and dominance of the third force – the atavistic, incalculable force of the ethnic revival, compelling peoples to place blood before reasonable progress and individual rights. Three years ago it already felt as if this might be the story: mysterious unfinished business of Eastern nationality wrecks any 'enduring new order'. And so it has proved. We (in the West) now face a prospect of interminable Balkan and post-Soviet disorder, where forms of demented chauvinism and intolerance risk arresting progress altogether. Putting out too many new flags leads only to *etnicko ciscenje*, 'ethnic cleansing'. Unless civilisation intervenes, the newly-liberated nations may end up by replacing nascent democracy with forms of nationalist dictatorship like those prefigured in Gamsakhurdia's Georgia or the Serbia of Slobodan Milosevic. As for economics, the consequences can hardly be anything but intensified backwardness.

This dreary tale is over-familiar: what 'civilised' coverage of Eastern folly perceives is primarily a re-emergence of archaism. It rarely occurs to the editorialists or reporters concerned that this enlightened, liberal perspective on the great change may itself be archaic. Yet I believe it is. Whether or not old demons are returning to haunt anyone in Bosnia and Nagorny-Karabakh, there can be no doubt that old theories – the conventional wisdom of the day before yesterday – have come back to haunt and distort Western interpretations of what is happening. This wisdom is easily dated. One need only head for the nearest available library shelf groaning beneath a set of *Encyclopaedia Britannica*. Turn to 'Socio-Economic Doctrines and Reform Movements'. The signature H.K. stands for Hans Kohn, a prominent writer in the Forties on the political history of nationalism.

The thesis which Kohn argued rested mainly on a distinction between Western and Eastern nationalism. The former was original, institutional, liberal and good. The latter was reactive, envious, ethnic, racist and generally bad. Western-model nation-states like Britain, France and America had invented political nationalism. But, Kohn argued, these societies had also limited and qualified it, linking it to certain broader, more universal ideals. Nationalism may have been a child of Western Enlightenment; but that very fact enabled the original enlightened countries to transcend it at least partially. As time passed, in spite of various imperialist adventures, a measure of tolerance and internationalism came to moderate any remaining crudities of Anglo-French nationalism.

Not so in the East. By the 'East' I think Kohn really meant the rest of the world, typified by Central and Eastern Europe. He was talking about all those other societies which from the 18th century onwards have suffered the impact of the West, and been compelled to react against it. That reaction bred a different kind of national spirit: resentful, backward-looking, detesting the Western bourgeoisie even while trying to imitate it – the sour and vengeful philosophy of the second or third-born. It was this situation (he claimed) which generated genuinely narrow nationalism.

Countries were hurled into the developmental race without time to mature the requisite institutions and cadres. Hence they were forced to mobilise in other ways. The intellectuals and soldiers who took charge there needed an adrenalin-rich ideology to realise their goals, and found it in a shorthand version of the Western national spirit. This was blood-based nationality, a heroic and exclusive cult of people and state founded upon custom, speech, faith, colour, cuisine and whatever else was found available for packaging.

Though originally drawn to the West, the Germans had ended by succumbing to an Eastern-style package. It was their blood-cult, developed into a form of eugenic insanity, which threatened to drown the Enlightenment inheritance altogether after 1933. Nazism was mercifully (though only just) defeated in 1945. Out of it, however, came the experience which stamped a lasting impression of nationalism's meaning on both the Western and the Communist mind. Nazism may in truth have been a form of genetic imperialism – in its bizarre, pseudo-scientific fashion universal (or at least would-be universal) in meaning – but its nationalist origins were undeniable, and keenly felt by all its victims. So its sins were inevitably visited upon nationality-politics as such. Since the largest, most important *ethnos* in Europe had gone mad in that particular way, the ethnic as such must remain forever suspect.

Such is the mentality which the post-'89 events have again brought to the surface. Instead of prompting a search for new theories to account for the extraordinary transformation of the world, these events have by and large resurrected the old ones. On the whole it seems to me that theory has contributed astonishingly little to an understanding of the New World Order, or Disorder, as Ken Jowitt, like nearly everyone else, calls it in the title of his interesting if eccentric 1991 study. The greatest revolution in global affairs since the epoch of world war is currently being explained almost wholly in terms of *Time* Magazine's Old Demons. Somehow a new age seems to have been born without any new ogres.

The creaky old ideological vehicles trundled out to cope with the post-Soviet and Balkan upheavals explain nothing whatever about their subjects. Gore-laden pictures of ethnic anarchy, of the Abyss and the Doom-to-come, start off by obscuring what is, so far, easily the most significant feature of the new world disorder. Since 1988 the post-Communist convulsions have drawn in about 40 different nationalities and a population of well over 300 million in an area comprising about one-fifth of the world. Thanks to the holding operation in Tiananmen Square they did not embrace an actual majority of the world's population, but it's surely reasonable to think that they will end by doing so.

When this scale and those numbers are kept in mind, the most impressive fact is surely not how much the transformation has cost in terms of either life or social and economic destruction. It is how astoundingly, how unbelievably little damage has been done. In one of the few efforts made at countering conventional hysteria the *Economist* did try last September to estimate loss of life in the ex-Soviet empire, and published a map showing that probably about three thousand-plus had perished, mostly in Georgia, Tajikistan and in the course of the war between Armenia and Azerbaijan. 'Fewer than most people think,' it concluded, and far less serious than what was happening in one small part of the Balkans. Social and economic disaster had been brought about by the collapse of the old Soviet-style economies, aggravated – rather than caused – by the political breakaways and national disputes.

This impression will be reinforced if any concrete time scale or historical memory is brought into the picture. The Old Demon mythology is essentially timeless – a dark or counter-millennium of re-emergent sin. In actual time the reflorescence of ethnic nationhood has followed a 40-year period during which humanity cowered in the shadow of imminent extinction. The demonologies of that epoch (anti-capitalism and anti-Communism) at least rested on something real, an array of missiles and other hardware which any serious clash between the empires – or even any sufficiently serious accident – could have activated, with the genuinely apocalyptic results everyone now seems (understandably enough) to have exiled from recollection.

But the old frozen *mentalité* did not vanish with the missiles. Instead it has found the temporary surrogate devil of nationalism. Another End of the World has been located: Armageddon has been replaced by the ethnic Abyss. It is a pretty feeble substitute, in the obvious sense that, even if some worst-possible-case scenario were to unfold – what Misha Glenny calls a 'Third Balkan War' or a Russo-Ukrainian war over the Crimea, or the break-up of the Indian state, or whatever – the consequences would not, by the standards of 1948 to 1988, be all that serious. Nobody would have to worry about taking refuge on another planet.

Almost by definition there is a great deal of anarchy in the new disorder, and no sign of its coming to an end. But there is (I would suggest) no abyss, save the ideological one in metropolitan craniums. As Benedict Anderson says in another of the more critical contributions to the debate (also entitled 'The New World Disorder'), the key misconception is that what's going on is essentially "frag-mentation' and 'disintegration' – with all the menacing, pathological connota-tions these words bring with them. This language makes us forget the decades or centuries of violence out of which Frankensteinian 'integrated states' such as the United Kingdom of 1900, which included all of Ireland, were constructed... Behind the language of 'fragmentation' lies always a Panglossian conservatism that likes to imagine that every status quo is nicely normal.' But as Anderson and anyone else making this kind of objection knows all too well, the immediate response to it is bitter recrimination. One is at once accused of apologising for savagery, or of indifference to the escalating Balkan wars. An appeal to Western Governments and the Secretary-General of the United Nations was published in the *New York Review of Books* last month demanding that the world take action to stop the Yugoslav wars: 'If democracies acquiesce in violations of human rights on such a massive scale they will undermine their ability to protect these rights anywhere in the post-Cold War world. And then, when, as has happened many times before, an armed hoodlum kicks our own doors ajar, there will be no one to lift a finger in our defence or to raise a voice.'

In this climate, to suggest that the nationalist course of history after 1989 may on the whole be preferable to what went before, and may not be treatable by any recourse to the old multinational or internationalist recipes, is to risk virtual excommunication. One must be lining up with the armed hoodlums. One is either a dupe of Demons like Tudjman and Karadzic or some sort of narrow nationalist oneself. (I'm not clear which of these is considered worse.)

The point at issue is really a methodological one which, though obvious, usually gets ignored in the new fury of the ideological times. Both anti-nation-alism and pro-nationalism are extremely broad attitudes or principles – the kind of important yet very general rules which are needed as signposts or reference-points. But signposts do not map out or explain the journey which they indicate. Attitudes on this plane of historical generality are bound to have – indeed, to demand – hosts of qualifications or exceptions. 'On the whole' inevitably leads to 'but ...'. What these broad attitudes 'mean' in any actual situation isn't, and cannot possibly be, just a deduction or a blanket endorsement or rejection. Exce-ptions don't exactly prove rules, but they are the lifeblood of useful principles.

This was blatantly true of anti-nationalism. Both in its standard liberal or Western form, and in the socialist or Leninist versions which used to hold court in the East, it was always acknowledged that occasionally, reluctantly, a few more flags had to be run up. This was permitted in cases of hallmarked national oppression. Colonial or imperialist dominance gave legitimacy to nationalism, at least for a time. The existence of 'great-power chauvinism' could morally under-write small-country national liberation – though only up to the point of inde-pendence, when universal values were supposed at once to reassert themselves.

The very least a pro-nationalist can say is that he or she is as entitled to exceptions. Conversely, to say that political and economic nationalism is, very generally, a good thing is not to say that there are no blots, excrescences or failures on the increasingly nationalised map of the world. To recognise that only broadly nationalist solutions will be found for what used to be the Soviet Union, Yugoslavia and Czechoslovakia is not to be an apologist for the bombardment of Dubrovnik or the rape of Bosnian Muslim women. To insist that the small battalions are likely to be 'on the whole' better than the large – particularly the multinational large – is not to imply there can be no pathology of the ethnic, or no cases where nationalists are wrong.

It seems to me that since 1989 the pro-nationalist is also justified in a measure of sarcasm. He or she can observe that, however many pustules and warts there turn out to be in the new world of nations, the small-battalion principle is unlikely to end up consisting of nothing but exceptions. Such has of course been internationalism's fate since 1989. The seamless garment always had to make room for tears and patches: but after 1989 it came to consist of almost nothing except holes, which no amount of lamentation or wish-fulfilment will repair.

For the first time in human history, the globe has been effectively unified into a single economic order under a common democratic-state model – surely the ideal, dreamt-of conditions for liberal or proletarian internationalism. Actually, these conditions have almost immediately caused the world to fold up into a previ-ously unimaginable and still escalating number of different ethno-political units.

Why has the one produced the other? Why has globalisation engendered nationalism, instead of transcending it? This is surely the fundamental problem of theory thrown up by the last three years. It goes far beyond what has become the obsessive question of Yugoslavia, and what should be done there to stop or lessen its crimes and cruelties.

To answer these questions may require some psychic effort of disengage-ment. I suspect that is necessary, above all, inside the countries of the European Community. Hans Kohn's theorisation of Western liberalism rested on a distinc-tion between West and East (or the West v. the Rest) – a distinction that was not simply resuscitated in 1989 but in a sense fortified.

The reason for that was what seemed to be taking place in the West End of the continent. Innumerable people couldn't help feeling, and repeating with varying degrees of self-satisfaction, 'just look at the difference!' *They* may be breaking up and disintegrating, but *we* appear to be doing the opposite – to be integrating, getting over at least some features of nationalism, pooling sover-eignty, looking rationally outwards, and so on. Extra complacency about the

North Atlantic dangerously fortified the old prejudices about the East, and made
the search for new explanations appear even less urgent. If Western advance and
superiority *was* the explanation, why waste time re-thinking history with elaborate theories about comparative conditions of development?

I suppose the worst single incident of that phase was the day Boris Yeltsin
turned up at the Strasbourg Parliament in 1991, and found himself (as he put it
at the time) being harangued like a backward school-kid by socialist MEPs. Why
couldn't he be more like Mikhail Gorbachev, they indignantly demanded, what
did he mean by being so nice to all those would-be separatists, could he not see
that breaking up the USSR would be a disaster? This outburst of daft parochialism
was a symptom of a phase destined rapidly to pass. Maastricht and the Danish
and French referenda were not far away, and were soon to produce an abrupt
change of climate. The sense of inevitable and uninterruptable progress towards
the post-nationalist light gave way to the doubt and uncertainty of the present.
It is (at least) not so clear now that never the twain shall meet, and that they
represent fundamentally diverging forms of development.

Other important blows to Western confidence have been dealt by events in
Canada and Czechoslovakia, especially the latter. This was the central, linking
country between East and West, which after its emancipation from Communist
rule was generally expected to follow a Western route and act as an example to
less fortunate neighbours. The fact that it has chosen the (supposedly) Eastern
route of division, civilly and without excessive commotion or animosity, is something whose significance has not been allowed to sink in. Eight weeks ago the
birth of two new democratic republics in the heart of Europe was greeted here
with a torrent of bile, commiseration and preventive accusations. Every single birth-
mark was seen as presaging doom. How dare they! Not only out of step but
going in the wrong direction! They'll learn, they'll soon be fighting like the rest
(and so on).

Liberal-capitalist complacency has been replaced by the mood, darker but
also more realistic, which Etienne Balibar conveyed in a 1991 talk about racism
and politics in Europe. *Es gibt keinen Staat in Europa* was his title, a remark
originally made by Hegel: there is no real state in Europe. 'Before there can be
any serious analysis of racism and its relationship to migrations,' Balibar wrote,
'we have to ask ourselves what this word 'Europe' means and what it will signify
tomorrow... In reality we are here discovering the *truth* of the earlier situation,
which explodes the representation that we used to have of it. Europe is not
something that is 'constructed' at a slower or faster pace, with greater or less
ease; it is a historical problem without any pre-established solution.' The evaporation of frontiers has not – or not yet – been replaced by the new definitions
and boundaries of a European state, one capable of establishing the social and
political citizenship so crucial to migrants. In a curious way, Euro-development
has led to under-development in this key area. 'All the conditions are present,'
Balibar continues, 'for a collective sense of identity *panic* to be produced and

maintained. For individuals – particularly the most deprived and the most remote from power – fear the state but they fear still more its disappearance or decomposition.'

I'm not sure about his description 'identity *panic*', but I agree the complacency of 1989 has been overtaken by identity concern, often coloured by anxiety and by a sharp disillusionment with the older European formulae. These features were certainly prominent in both the Danish and the French referenda over Maastricht, and they are also important in the much more smothered, inchoate argument now limping along in the United Kingdom.

Identity alarm can also be read positively, however. It is surely not wholly bad that it has replaced Western (and notably Britannic) identity somnolence. The new sense of dislocation and doubt, created by the new circumstances, may also prompt new initiatives and departures. Ethnic closure and brutal self-defence is one response to a loss of familiar horizons and signposts: but it is not the only one, and not one predestined either to return everywhere, or to triumph easily where it does.

To retain and cultivate a wider, more balanced perspective on the post-'89 transformation must be the task for serious theorists in this new world. Why has the End of History carried us forward into a more nationalist world? Why is a more united globe also (and almost immediately) far more ethnically aware, and more liable to political division?

In the years before 1989 significant advances were made in both the history and the sociology of nationalism. The central weakness of Kohn and liberal theory had been its neglect of economics, its failure to place the rise of ethnic politics within a more substantial framework of development. This failure was remedied by the important work of Ernest Gellner, Anthony Smith and others from the '60s to the '80s. They showed, to my mind conclusively, that nationalism was inseparable from the deeper processes of industrialisation and socioeconomic modernity. Far from being an irrational obstacle to development, it was for most societies the only feasible way into the developmental race – the only way in which they could compete without being either colonised or annihilated. If they turned to the past (figuratively to 'the blood') in these modernisation struggles, it was essentially in order to stay intact as they levered themselves into the future. Staying intact, or obtaining a new degree of social and cultural cohesion, was made necessary by industrialisation – even (as in so many cases) by the distant hope, the advancing shadow of industrialisation. And *ethnos* offered the only way of ensuring such cohesion and common purpose.

The strategy was high-risk, both because the blood might take over and drown these societies and because they might never really catch up. However, that risk was unavoidable. It arose from the conditions of generally and chronically uneven development – the only kind which capitalism allows, and the kind which has finally, definitively established itself since 1989 as the sole matrix of further evolution.

In this more rational but insufficiently appreciated perspective nationalism is therefore as much a native of modernity as are democracy and the capitalist motor of development. It is as inseparable from progress as they are. In his earlier work Gellner in particular stressed how vital the function of nationalism was in resisting over-centralised and monolithic development. Without 'fragmentation' and 'disintegration' some type of empire would long ago have appropriated industrialisation to its own political purpose.

I have already mentioned the standard triad of categories used to read the post-'89 changes: democracy, capitalism and nationalism – the third representing some kind of ghost or retreat from reason, an upsurge of atavism interfering with the other two. This view of nationalism is a piece of superstition; a superstition which has unfortunately grown so popular that it has come partly to define (or redefine) the task of nationalist theory. It seems to me that anti-Demonism is the pre-requisite of getting anywhere with the debate about ethnic issues and their future.

The fact is that, for all their weight and intellectual superiority to the old commonplaces, studies like Smith's *The Ethnic Origin of Nations* and Gellner's *Nations and Nationalism* have had very little influence on common perceptions of their subject. When the whole world was abruptly compelled to focus on it again, an older common sense took over and explained it all in terms of demons, resurgent fascism or the irrational side of human nature.

There is an interesting reversal at work here. Once upon a time (before 1989) the protagonists of internationalism tended to be over-rational creatures, professorial politicos who occasionally displayed nervous tics. Apologists for nationalism were supposed to be hirsute, romantic souls who took folk-dance too seriously and were liable to get carried away (especially by rogues). I can see little of this pattern in the arguments today. The shocked, semi-hysterical response of the West to the Eastern rebirth has plunged it into the style of unreason once supposed typical of rabid chauvinists and wild-eyed patriot-poets. By contrast, it's now up to the defenders of nationality-politics and *ethnos* to assume a cannier, more balanced point of view on the emergent world. It is they who should assume and develop a perspective based on the enduring theoretical and historical work I have cited. It's they who must look for the broader and more historically informed view, keeping their distance from the metropolitan virtual reality being pumped out in London, Paris and New York. This new perspective ought to find as natural a home in Glasgow as in (say) Kiev, or Ljubljana, or Riga – the newer centres of a more varied, more emphatically nationalist world which, in spite of all those pessimistic titles, and notwithstanding the abscess in Bosnia, will turn out to be more than just disorder and atavism.

Fifteen years ago I wrote something about 'The Modern Janus', likening nationalism to the two-headed Roman deity who couldn't help looking backwards as well as forwards. Since then the whole world has increasingly come to resemble him. But with an important difference. I believe that, on the whole, the forward-gazing side of the strange visage may be more prominent than it was in 1977. Perhaps because today the forward view is that much more open and encouraging than it was then.

CHAPTER TWENTY-TWO

Empire And Union

London Review of Books, vol. 17, no. 16

AUGUST 1995

Review of *A Union for Empire: Political Thought and the Union of 1707* edited by John Robertson (1995), and *The Autonomy of Modern Scotland* by Lindsay Paterson (1994)

Next time it will be different. Or so almost everyone in Scotland now believes, as they look forward to another election and back over the long trail of wreckage from 1979 to the present. The Conservative regime began by aborting Constitutional change and is ending in a state of Constitutional rigor mortis. John Major's Government contemplates no political evolution whatever on the mainland, as distinct from in Ireland, and advertises this rigidity as 'defence of the Union'. When it founders, however, such intransigence will be overtaken by long overdue movement, which can hardly fail to bring about parliaments in Wales and Scotland, as well as more European integration.

Just what is it that the Tories are defending? In Scotland they can be seen as trying to preserve what that sound Tory Sir Walter Scott called 'the silent way'. After the Union Scott thought that 'under the guardianship of her own institutions, Scotland was left to win her silent way to national wealth and consequence.' This is from his *Thoughts on the Proposed Change of Currency*, written in 1826 to defend the right of the Scottish banks to continue issuing their own banknotes and coins. But the context of the remark is more specific than is usually recognised. The Treaty of Union by itself had not brought wealth and consequence, Scott believed: it was only from 'the year 1750' that these changes had at last begun to emerge – that is, when Scotland was 'no longer the object of terror, or at least great uneasiness'. When, indeed, she had more or less sunk out of London's view altogether. Contempt had replaced fear, and Scott thought this was just as well. It was, he reckoned, 'because she was neglected... that her prosperity has increased in a ratio more than five times greater than that of her more fortunate and richer sister'.

Lack of a separate political voice was not necessarily an impediment to such distinctive prosperity. Certainly, the state is generally considered to be the key modern institution, but only under extreme totalitarianism is it all-important. Other, less important national institutions can, as in the Scottish case, furnish a separate national configuration of society and culture – an 'identity' in the contemporary jargon – quite capable of sustaining nationality, a degree of patriotism and even varieties of chauvinism.

So the way is 'silent' only in its wider international resonance. On the native terrain it has been associated with an uninterrupted cacophony of complaints, grudges and chip-on-the-shoulder moaning over non-recognition. In his *Thoughts on the Proposed Change of Currency* Sir Walter himself contributed powerfully to the latter: 'whingeing' would be the contemporary description. Alas, dignified mutism as a nation is compatible with and may even cause constant pandemonium at home. On that sounding-board of the national soul, the Edinburgh *Scotsman*'s letters page, I doubt if a week has passed since Scott's time without its quota of resentful jibes about non-equality and Southern arrogance. Back in 1925 we find MacDiarmid scorning them for it in *A Drunk Man Looks at the Thistle*:

And O! to think that there are members o'
St Andrew's Societies sleepin' soon,
Wha tae the papers wrote afore they bedded
On regimental buttons or buckled shoon,
Or use o' England where the UK's meant.

The Conservatives want to go on believing that political union is essential at once to the economy of the archipelago, to Britain's influence in Europe, and – in more mystical vein – to maintaining the civilised norms of British administration and culture. But what is the real historical nature of the Union thus defended? These two books represent very different new approaches to the question. They assume, surely correctly, that it is a genuine puzzle. There is nothing either self-explanatory or standard about the survival of a united kingdom based on England, from Early Modern times until practically the end of the second millennium.

John Robertson's collection of academic studies examines the origins of the Union's most important axis, the Parliamentary unification of Scotland and England in 1707. Lindsay Paterson's long polemical essay looks at the consequences of that for the Scots: a near unique form of 'autonomy' as unusual as the state of which it is a part. Scotland's silent way, he contends, allowed far more effective self-rule than most commentators have recognised. Nationalists have treated institutional autonomy as second-rate or instrumental. With their emphasis on all-British virtues, Unionists have also until very recently regarded it as relatively unimportant, or even as a mere relic. Paterson's view is that, though unusual, it was and remains a more respectable form of evolution than general theories of progress have allowed for. These have been based on the nation-state, and hence have overlooked the case of a stateless yet quite successful nation.

Both books bear on the current debates about devolution, Constitutional reform and Europe. Robertson's academic volume naturally disclaims partisanship, yet he cannot help hoping that better historical understanding may 'help to clear the way for the formation of a viable modern alternative to the Union'. For his part, Lindsay Paterson argues that a better grasp of the real story of autonomy may sanction moves to recover political authority in Edinburgh. But paradoxically, it may also render independence itself less significant. A new Scottish democracy demands more distinct political representation; but according to Paterson this need not lead to the restoration of statehood or a literal dissolution of the Union. Rather than being simply a forlorn pre-modern accident, the silent way may presage the post-modern development of other countries inside a European Union.

This places Paterson firmly among the nationalists rather than among the Nationalists. Politics in Scotland has turned into an orthographic battle between the upper and the lower cases. Almost everyone is some sort of nationalist, including even Michael Forsyth, the new Tory Secretary of State for Scotland. In retreat, the Conservatives have discovered that true Unionism awarded Scotland just as much nationalism as was good for it, via Scots Law, institutional autonomy and new devices like the National Health Trusts. Many of their speeches these days are devoted to extolling the modest merits of enough-as-is-good-for-you national self-reliance. One might almost think that the aim of Union and Empire had all along been to foster this better class of Scottish and Welsh nationalism. Some in their audience are of course bound to think, if it has been so marvellous then might not more be better still? Ah, it would bring disaster! is the official reply – the agonising abyss of separatism etc. But just why would healthy self-management lapse so swiftly into chaos?

Because the serpent will have bitten the apple, say Forsyth and his Scottish Office servants. They mean the serpent of politics. This is also the problem for a growing number of people occupying the intermediate stance in Scotland – those who find themselves somewhere in between the upper and lower cases (a position corresponding perhaps to 'small caps' in font design). These are people who, while not exactly yearning for a return to nationhood, perceive no likely stopping-place on the nationalist track short of whatever the European Union currently recognises as statehood or independence, and who have become increasingly matter of fact about the prospect. This is not surprising. It doesn't seem a great disaster in today's Europe to be a country similar to Denmark, or the Netherlands or Finland. Scots of this persuasion tend to be more definitely pro-European than similar strata in England, and for that reason also inclined to scepticism about the dread abyss of separate statehood.

And then there is full upper-case Nationalism, which does indeed yearn for the 1707 Parliament to be recalled, for the Scots to abandon their silent way and recover voice and presence as a nation-state. Many but not all Nationalists are in the Scottish National Party, or sometimes vote for it. However, there seem to be plenty of both upper-case and small-cap Nationalists in the Scottish Labour Party, and also among the Liberal Democrats, while an unknown number of small or tiny-n nationalists support the SNP less for its ideology than because it registers the most effective protest against Them. In existing circumstances They are of course bound to be mainly English, or at least perceived as held in Southern thrall.

Already confusing, the scene has become more so since the recent by-election at which Roseanna Cunningham won the rural and small-town constituency of Perth and Kinross for the SNP. Ethnicity-gaugers found the whole thing disorienting. Ms Cunningham is a vociferous Republican, Socialist and Feminist who refused to scale down any of her capital letters for electoral motives. This made no difference to the result. She thus succeeded one of Europe's outstanding politiclowns, the late Sir Nicholas Fairbairn. Normally garbed in tartanic garments designed by his own hand and inhabiting a nearby castle, Sir Nicholas had been famously critical of the SNP's open-door citizenship policy which would, for example, allow the illegitimate offspring of black American GIs stationed in Scotland to be as Scottish as... well, Sir Nicholas himself. Vote Tory to preserve the Scot-Brit race. This eccentric addendum to the Unionist creed was not openly endorsed by Fairbairn's successor as Tory candidate, a generally pitied young lad called John Godfrey. However, he did open up by routinely denouncing the Nationalists as Nazis, and the Tory campaign as a whole did little to redeem government fortunes. In fact all it did was mimic them, staggering from one gaffe to another like a Perthshire heifer struck down by mad cow disease.

The road from 1707 to this plight has been a long one. Neither union nor empire then meant what they came to signify for the 19th and 20th centuries. Robertson argues that the terms figured in a long and complex European debate within which the Edinburgh-London negotiations were only a minor episode. 'Empire' meant at that time not colonies and subject populations but something closer to today's notion of 'sovereignty'. 'Union' enjoyed a double-barrelled usage, as incorporation or confederation. The mounting absolutism of European monarchies encouraged the former, but at the same time 'there had also emerged a second, rival concept of union understood as a confederation of more or less equal states,' like the Dutch United Provinces. The rival sides in the 1706–7 argument looked back over these 17th-century disputes and struggled to adapt them to the new situation.

The 1707 deal was an 'Incorporating Union', but the main agency of incorporation, all-powerful monarchy, had been destroyed by the mid-century revolutions in both England and Scotland. A landowners' Parliament had risen to dominate one country and a militant Protestant church had become crucial in the other. Patriotic lairds like Andrew Fletcher opposed incorporation not with independence in today's meaning but with a version of equal-state confederation. Yet that position, too, was fatally weakened by memories of the revolutionary era. Everyone knew about, and a few individuals could actually recall, the dire events of the 1650s when, in Robertson's words: 'The armies of the Commonwealth succeeded where so many kings had failed, and summarily conquered both Ireland and Scotland. The experience of defeat, followed by enforced union, changed for ever the relationship of each country to England – never again could the Scots deceive themselves that the English lacked the will or the means to conquer them.' No really equal confederation of states was possible. Recent subjection had only emphasised a fundamental and inescapable imbalance. Today England represents about 85 per cent of the United Kingdom's population, Scotland about nine per cent. Scotland's population was relatively bigger before the great emigrations of the 19th century but its resources were relatively fewer. There never was a time when Scotland, or even when all the fringe nationalities combined, amounted to anything like the position of Hungary inside the Habsburg Empire, or even Slovakia within pre-1992 Czechoslovakia. Like German dominance in Central Europe, English domination of the British Isles came about because of a mixture of commanding geography, overwhelming demography and economic power. This did not mean that political mastery was equally preordained or natural; but English leaders could easily pretend or assume that it was.

The pretence was important above all for the English self-image. Most of the time, for most social purposes, nine-tenths of any group can ignore the remainder. They will do so all the more easily when their statistical superiority is amplified by advantage in other domains, such as ownership, social class, cultural or military achievement. The resultant hegemony appears more natural to those exerting it than to whoever is in its train, or under its wheels. 'Use o' England where the UK's meent' has always been an irritant to the fringe but inevitable for the majority. The latter rarely mean to rub in their authority. They just don't think about it nor, in most times and places, is there really much reason why they should. What *is* natural is that when they should be conscious of it, they usually have to be reminded.

This English absence of self-definition (or glib over-identification with Britain) flows from an ethnic dominance established well before ethnic traits assumed the central historical and political significance they came later to possess. The abolition of the Irish Parliament in 1801 was the final episode in England's ascendancy, but the 1707 Treaty of Union was arguably its most important moment. Through it the biggest rival *ethnos* of the archipelago was subordinated well before nationalism turned into a general motor of political discontent and mobilisation in Europe. The beginning of the 19th century – after the American Revolution, 1789 and the Irish risings of the 1790s – proved too late for another lasting incorporating union'. Instead, what became a quite standard form of European ethno-religious nationalism was pioneered there. Looked at in terms of the later mainstream of nationalist development, Ireland turned into a typical part of Eastern Europe, disconcertingly located on the Western seaboard.

At the beginning of the 18th century, however, neither democracy, nor Enlightenment, nor Romanticism had accomplished enough of their fertilising work. Since confederation was impracticable the Scottish governing classes fell for incorporation. Because absolute monarchy had been defeated, however, they were able to qualify and limit their subordination in remarkable ways, through what they (but not the English Government) regarded as in effect a written constitution: the Treaty of Union. Popular wishes had nothing to do with the 1707 deal. But that, too, was only part of the 17th-century or Early Modern package. Scott, firm Tory Unionist though he was, encouraged no illusions among his readers on this score. In *Tales of a Grandfather* he admitted that:

> the Union was regarded with an almost universal feeling of discontent and dishonour... The Scots felt generally the degradation, as they conceived it, of their country being rendered the subservient ally of the state, of which, though infinitely more powerful, they had resisted the efforts for the space of two thousand years. There was, therefore, nothing save discontent and lamentation to be heard throughout Scotland, and men of every class vented their complaints against the Union the more loudly, because their sense of personal grievance might be concealed and yet indulged under popular declamations concerning the dishonour done to the country.

He exaggerates the point revealingly. The two thousand years were fantasy, and it was not even true that the Scots and English had been mostly in conflict between the Wars of Independence of the 13th and 14th centuries and the time he was writing. Psychologically, however, he was right: that seems to have been the way most people felt. Dishonour was taken in a recklessly personal way which, under any form of democracy, would certainly have doomed the Treaty. He points out perceptively that the poor reacted more strongly than the wealthy, 'because they had no dignity or consideration due to them personally or individually, beyond that which belonged to them as natives of Scotland'.

A Union for Empire does not waste time going over the old story of sleaze. Scott's *Tales* covered that angle as well as anyone has ever done. Cash was sent up from London in waggons for the upper-class begging-bowl. When he has finished stressing how providential this whole event was, Scott concedes that 'the distribution of the money constituted the charm by which refractory Scottish members were reconciled to the Union' and 'it may be doubted whether the descendants of the noble lords and honourable gentlemen who accepted this gratification, would be more shocked at the general fact of their ancestors being corrupted, or scandalised at the paltry amount of the bribe.'

But still, these were the people who counted, not the mere dishonoured mob in the Edinburgh streets. What anyone today would recognise as a proto-nationalist fury might have inflamed the latter, but in Early Modern terms the former were the effective 'citizens'. The contemporary Scottish jurist Gersholm Carmichael pointed out how 'the composition of the citizens, properly so called, is to be gathered from the laws and customs of each state... When I use the word people I mean the citizens who are so called in a more eminent sense, 'those who by direct consent and agreement entered into with the sovereign himself originally instituted the state' and 'not all heads of households qualify.' That was the real point, of course, not the bribery. The eminent people had been rendered

structurally corrupt already by the previous century, during which royal authority had moved south to London and taken the great machinery of patronage
with it. They had got used to dependence, then had it confirmed by defeat – defeat
from below by religious enthusiasm, and afterwards from outside, by Cromwell's
army. As for the less than eminent, those who failed to qualify, their secular
national passion was as yet ineffectual. It still took the form of riot, not a
national movement.

John Robertson's collection contains essays devoted to Scotland's independent attempt at colonial empire, the Darien Scheme, and to religion, law and
theology. Two separate chapters are concerned with the operations of that wily
English rogue Daniel Defoe, and John Pocock delivers a thoughtful contribution
on the relationship of the Union to the American Revolution. But the book's
two key items are Robertson's own articles, particularly the second, 'An Elusive
Sovereignty', in which he traces the course of the arguments about Union from
1698 until 1707. In spite of the history of the two countries and the disaster of
the Darien Scheme, there were still many who sought to avoid incorporation.
Andrew Fletcher was not alone in his patriotic and idealist opposition. But such
opponents faced a fundamental intellectual problem. 'Radical and imaginative
as their thinking was,' observes Robertson, 'those who would uphold Scotland's
sovereignty, and preserve the kingdom from incorporating union, were faced
with the frustration of their efforts to identify an institutional framework equal
to the challenge.' The debate was in any case rigged by Queen Anne's ministers
and agents, determined to get their way this time. That they did so quite easily
merely underlined another weakness: the Scottish Parliament lacked the prestige
and wider popularity of its English counterpart. Hence there was no indisputable
focus of political mobilisation and resistance against London's manoeuvrings.
No single redoubt commanded either the traditional or the popular forms of
national feeling. Allegiances were profoundly fractured. The Glorious Revolution of 20 years before had united England, but divided Scotland and Ireland.

The exiled Stuart monarchy was still influential, and its supporters knew
very well that one essential purpose of Union was to keep it in exile. A non-state
institution, the Presbyterian Kirk, enjoyed something of the prestige normally
given to parliaments. But, although self-consciously national and hostile to
incorporation, it did not really think statehood was essential to its other-worldly
goals. The mental world of Scottish theocracy stopped well short of political
nationalism, and as later times would show, tended to be rather opposed to it.
The most democratic Scottish institution was therefore persuaded that, given
enough guarantees, it could cut its own deal with a unified British realm. The
Church of Scotland is unmentioned in the Treaty of Union itself, but this is only
because it was shrewdly promised its own separate legislation – a second treaty,
in effect, establishing its autonomous rights for 'all time coming'.

Nationalists have always denounced the Treaty as a sell-out for a mess of
pottage. What Robertson's book shows is the strength of the structural constraints

which forced decisions into this mould. The absence of a valid 'institutional framework' inevitably made short-term considerations predominate. Scotland's old institutions had partially collapsed, and yet it was too early historically for others to be improvised by nationalism. Thus an elusive sovereignty came fatally to be weighed against 'the prospect of material improvement... and the apparent benefits of participation in a British Empire', as well as against fears of Catholic re-expansion in Europe and the French 'universal monarchy'. The individuals who counted could all too easily perceive their own advantage as identified with the national interest. Saving one's estate from creditors coincided happily with the good of Scotland.

In Parliamentary circles, though not in the streets, this blessed coincidence had by 1707 already made the alternative – continuing the old unequal struggle for national honour – appear a dream. In the 1706 Parliament Lord Belhaven made his famous over-the-top lament for 'Mother Caledonia', piling one bit of myth-history upon another in a surfeit of sentimental metaphors. Englishmen present failed to understand what he was going on about, but he was trying to express a sense of incalculable loss, of a fate implicit in the Parliament's proceedings which lay far beyond short-range profit and party tactics. There was nothing absurd about that. It echoed the fury in the High Street and has been transmitted in one form or another, dimly yet hurtfully, as nostalgia or its opposite – hard-nosed realism – to each successive generation in Scotland. On the day, however, it provoked hilarity, and Patrick Hume of Marchmont's equally famous one-line put-down: 'Behold he dreamed, but lo! when he awoke, he found it was a dream.'

In truth the short-range advantages turned out to be themselves disconcertingly far off. As Scott put it sourly, after Union was obtained one delay and obstacle after another then 'interposed a longer interval of years betwixt the date of the Treaty and the national advantages arising out of it, than the term spent by the Jews in the wilderness where they attained the Promised Land'. Nearly 40 years later anti-Union resentment was strong enough to carry Charles Edward Stuart close to an overthrow not just of the Treaty but of the Hanoverian state. Only after the 1745 rebellion did conditions improve enough to resemble the changes promised an earlier generation.

This time-lapse is another feature which places the British Union in the Early Modern period. At no later era in history could any government have hoped to postpone benefits for so long and get away with it. With the revolutions of the later 18th century, in technology and agriculture as well as in America and France, time itself came to assume a different and more urgent meaning. The notion of measurable change entered more decidedly into mass awareness; expectations intensified and focused more clearly on futures realisable if and when social conditions were altered to allow them. The psychic world of nascent nationalism is one where all lands become promised, and not by divine intervention alone. An accelerated sense of the transitory and the possible makes any wilderness that much less tolerable; and hence mobilisation for exit that much more appealing and necessary. Such a consciousness would become general in the 19th century, then universal in the 20th. But in the 1707–45 era it remained embryonic, at least in Scotland. This is why the mechanics and arguments surrounding the Union Treaty appear so archaic. They did indeed occur 'in another time', or more precisely within another temporality where vital things were missing which we take for granted today.

A Union for Empire helps us understand more clearly what these things are, as does Paterson's *Autonomy of Modern Scotland*, from a strikingly different and contemporary viewpoint. His book follows two other recent general reassessments of Scottish post-Union society, Jacques Leruez's *L' Ecosse: une nation sans état* (1983) and David McCrone's *Understanding Scotland: The Sociology of a Stateless Nation* (1992). He gives a more political twist to these important analyses, attempting what amounts to a general ideological reassessment of post-1707 history: 'In effect, if not in constitutional theory or political rhetoric, Scotland had been autonomous for most of the three centuries since the Union – not a fully independent state, of course, but far more than a mere province. It has been at least as autonomous as other small European nations... closer to the partial independence of Norway, Finland or Hungary than to the dependent condition of the Czech lands or Poland.'

Most of the time, over most areas of social existence, a kind of self-management has prevailed. Until the 20th century London intervened very little. Rule was so indirect that the state seemed a remote entity impinging hardly at all on the native institutions left in place by the Treaty – the kirk, the law, the educational system and, later on a distinctive apparatus of local government. Scots liked to think of these bodies as 'civil society': it is no accident that this deeply mysterious term originated in Edinburgh. Originated, that is, in a lean-to social formation which, very unusually, had a powerful Treaty-guaranteed interest in the illusion of being self-supporting. Idealist philosophers like Hegel would later develop the idea further. It evolved into the general concept of a stateless or market-governed society, magically shorn of abstract or merely political authority.

Paterson reminds us that such generalisation had a concrete source, in the Scottish managerial belief that 'the whole point of the Union was to remove the oppressions of politics on the Scottish character. Government, it was felt, should have nothing to do with moulding the character of a people; on the contrary...the nature of a government should be derived from the pre-existing culture that it was supposed to serve.' Much of the author's effort goes into defending the resultant managerialism. He insists repeatedly that Adam Ferguson's conception of an oppression-free civil society was justified, and proven by the Scottish example. Caledonia's institutional bourgeoisie has often been scathingly denounced as servile, cringing, routine-minded and unadventurous. In Paterson's reverse image it shows up as rational, sensible, shrewd, 'showing a wise appreciation that there are multiple sources of social authority' and knowing where its true interests lay within the old British imperium. Thus 'canny' is transformed from accusation into general plaudit. Keeping one's head down was an inevitable part of the silent way; and rightly so, argues this book, since it preserved autonomy and the integrity of a system where 'the daily lives of people in Scotland remained thoroughly Scottish because emphatically local... By European standards Scottish autonomy was at worst normal, at best actually quite privileged.'

There is an interesting mechanism of psychic reversal at work in *The Autonomy of Modern Scotland*. In the course of only a few pages Paterson tells the reader that Scotland's élite is 'not abject', does not consist of 'dupes', does not deserve its 'reputation for cravenness', and is by no means always 'timid' and 'dependent'. He significantly labours the point. And the obverse of this is an over-emphasis on its supposed contrary, a near-infallible rationality. Our ancestors weren't just not abject, they were positively brilliant: they astutely converted weakness into strength and displayed 'sensible Realpolitik', a people that 'chose quietness, because it genuinely believed in the common destinies of all the British peoples', preserving the moderate demeanour of a 'dual identity' – 'British for formal and public matters, Scottish for the family and home and community'. Essentially, what today's all-or-nothing Nationalism denies is this complex if unromantic inheritance. It has 'forgotten about the partial, negotiated, but nevertheless real autonomy of domestic sovereignty'.

A series of comparisons with other 19th-century European countries is then used to underline the non-romantic virtues. Judged by progress towards independent statehood Scotland may have been backward: but in terms of broad liberal criteria it did rather well. Liberty, economic development and middle-class culture all flourished within the Union, encouraging Scottish intellectuals to go on cultivating their backyard autonomy rather than attempt organised political dissent. In Scotland civil society was after all a virtual *chasse gardée* of the intellectual trades: there were almost no English kirk ministers, lawyers or teachers in this job reservation, and hence no threat to Scotland's national integrity. Those who felt stifled by the backyard could emigrate. They did so in great numbers, bearing to London, Canada or Australasia what Paterson identifies as the virtues of apolitical Scotland – more or less the opposite of the Irish emigrant culture, with its inclination towards machine politics, conspiracy and grand rhetoric.

One result was the absence of a key social factor connected in most other countries with nationalism. A famously educated culture produced no intelligentsia. The circumstances of 'autonomy' bred intellectuals who were either over-employed managing 'domestic sovereignty' or in a curious sense lost to normal nationhood through outward osmosis. Paterson would probably not admit the dilemma implicit in his own analysis, but I think it can be seen in the social history of many Scots intellectuals. The choice inherent in the structure he describes can be expressed in the difference between John Buchan's father and Buchan himself: small-town stuffed-shirt or high-administrative panjandrum. Both very successful, of course, one cannily beneath nationality in the troublesome sense, and the other philosophically far above it, in the Tory club-land pantheon of those who have risen. The same point can be made in other terms, which the author also avoids. 'Nationality' in this sense came to mean politics. But politics is the one thing that modern Scots have been conspicuously bad at. Their best-known gift to 20th-century United Kingdom politics, Ramsay Macdonald, was also its worst calamity. Scotland had opted out of the 'oppressions of politics'; but out of its opportunities and collective rewards as well.

Now it is trying to opt back in. Autonomy has at last begun to yield to democracy, even in Scotland. Paterson describes how in the first half of this century 'the UK welfare state took a distinctive form in Scotland, to such an extent that Scotland can be described as having had a welfare state of its own.' Autonomy begat the Scottish Office – 'a uniquely bureaucratic form of national government' deploying vast powers of co-option and patronage, supervised only in dim and sporadic fashion by Westminster committees and late-night sittings. Though rooted in the older, simpler entities protected by the 1707 Treaty, such as Kirk Presbyteries, the Court of Session or the 18th-century sheriffdom, Scottish institutional identity attained its fullest flowering only in quite recent times.

What is institutional identity? What kind of National Character does it represent? Paterson wishes above all to dispel the familiar notion that Scotland is deformed or deeply defective in some way – a cripple or half-wit among nations, demeaningly glad to be allowed to run its own backyard without the usual accompaniment of a parliament, an army and so on. Speaking as one guilty of disseminating this libel in times past, I feel obliged to utter a few words in its defence. Institutional identity seems to me broadly the same as managerial identity or (less flatteringly but more familiar to theorists) 'bureaucratic identity'. The self-management of civil society historically found in Scotland implied a corresponding managerial or bureaucratic ethos, the customs of a stratum or class which administers and regulates rather than 'rules' in the more ordinary sense of political government or direction. Max Weber described its origins and character as one of the pivotal features of modernity. In *Economy and Society* he showed how superior such management is to all its predecessors, and how 'experience tends universally to show that this bureaucratic type of organisation... is from a purely technical point of view, capable of attaining the highest degree of efficiency and is in this sense formally the most rational known means of exercising authority over human beings.' No one would in this sense deny the rationality so strongly endorsed in *The Autonomy of Modern Scotland*. However, Weber also pointed out the drawbacks of instrumental or short-range reason. The very strength of such bodies and the kind of self-sustaining momentum they acquire poses a threat, the danger 'that the world might be filled with nothing but these little cogs, with nothing but men clinging to a little job and striving after a slightly bigger one... men who need 'order' and nothing but order, who become nervous and cowardly if this order wavers for a moment.'

Bureaucracy had an egalitarian side to it and within limits was a social leveller, especially in contrast to aristocracy or older, class-bound societies. But that should not be confused with democracy. It also lends itself rather to petty or low-level authoritarianism – sticking to the rules or, in the Scottish phrase I always thought of as timeless until I read Paterson's book, 'doing as one's telt'. Weber also remarked on how this sort of thing tended to 'parcel out the soul', before concluding that an over-dominance of the 'bureaucratic ideal of life' was something to be fought and averted at all costs. Simplifying for the sake of polemic, I would suggest that this dominance is indeed a fundamental trait of post-1707 Scotland. *The Autonomy of Modern Scotland* puts a spotlight on it much more effectively and passionately than any previous analysis, seeking to redeem and justify institutional identity as the bedrock of Scottishness – the explanation of Scotland's place within the British Union and of the relative satisfaction and quiescence which attended that position until quite recently.

But for many observers the spotlight will only deepen the surrounding darkness. After all, the most common identity stereotypes of Scottishness vary wildly. Nervousness and cowardliness are not ideas which suggest themselves to anyone who has witnessed the crowd at a Scotland-England international, nor do they feature in the Scottish Tourist Board's promotion of a castellated and kindly-peasant wilderness. Eagles, lairds, bagpipes and scones are the grist of Scotland's Heritage mills – not little cogs, canny cooncil-men or the quangocracy manipulated from St Andrew's House in such prodigious and democratically unaccountable numbers. At the literary level a similar puzzlement seems in order. What about the weird country depicted in James Kelman's stories, for example, where demotic-proletarian saints find themselves forever knackered by sadist-authoritarian bullies or preached at in Malcolm Rifkind English by *bien pensant* hypocrites and child molesters?

One easy answer now itself a form of cant might be the Post-Modern alibi: there are multiple or equivalently-valid identities co-existing in no special order of significance. Another, I believe more convincing, reply, is one from which Paterson also firmly averts his gaze. Since Walter Scott's time the Scots have indulged in chest-beating display-identities *because* the one Paterson singles out as 'real' has been in certain important respects both deeply unpalatable and functionally useless. In some ways institutional identity may indeed have been the blessing depicted in *The Autonomy of Modern Scotland*. In others it has been more like an unavowable curse.

In a large and growing number of characteristically modern situations, 'Who are you?' is inevitably a collective rather than an individual query. Its real sense is 'What do you *represent?*' as a sample of some broader entity. While one may of course be a Catholic, a stamp-collector or a Friend of the Earth, the most useful, all-purpose handle here remains one's nation. There is (literally) no getting away from it. Nationality is not in the genes, but it is in the structure of the modern world, much more prominently and inescapably than it was in ancient times, or than in the Early Modern world to which the Treaty of Union has for so long pinned down the Scots.

No one has ever responded to this interpellation with a short lecture on the beauties of the Sheriff system, the merits of Scottish generalist education or the advantages of not having one's own politics. Or if anybody ever did, it would only have been to see the interlocutor's eyes glaze over in bored disbelief. As Robert Louis Stevenson remarked in one of his letters home from Germany, in that situation you just find yourself gabbling on about clanship, tartans, Jacobites and whatever else will make the necessary effect.

Silence would imply oblivion – dismissal as an ignoble province, a mere part of England. Yet the long story is incomprehensible in normal conversation. It takes articulate theoretical animals like McCrone and Paterson around 250 pages to account for their oddity in the zoo. Shorthand is as inescapable as nationalism: the culture requires it. It must therefore be made up, with whatever materials come to hand. It is in this sense that the fakelore of Gaelicism and assumed Highland identity is by no means accidental, or simply the consequence of bad faith and culpable romantic escapism. Phoniness is the unavoidable accompaniment of this shorthand Highland identity, of course, as is the kind of uneasy half-belief which most Scottish Lowlanders have half-indulged in about it since Victorian times. However, all that really means is that since Paterson's 'real' identity cannot be deployed for certain important purposes, a display-identity is needed to fill the gap. Intellectuals are often terribly sanctimonious about the results, but should waste less breath on it. I speak as one who has in the past expended all too much of the precious stuff on the follies of tartanry. A cure will be found in politics, not in aesthetic disdain or standoffish intellectualism.

Paterson's analysis consistently counterposes these real interests and motives of domestic sovereignty to the external realm of Britishness. He argues that backyard autonomy is the main need of most people, most of the time, and so the Scots should congratulate themselves on preserving so much sage, short-range control over 'their own affairs'. Carried away by a commendable and intensely Scottish argumentative passion he ends by over-endorsing institutional identity and ignoring its awful shortcomings. It is quite possible – and in fact the common Scottish plight – to be attached to domestic sovereignty and yet unwilling to be bored to death by it. He fails to perceive how 'autonomy' itself has generated the more celebrated kitschland which now stands in for Scotland in the world's consciousness. *Rob Roy* is not all down to Hollywood, Michael Caton-Jones or Alan Sharp, nor even to Walter Scott's original tale of honour misplaced and traduced. Its nerve lies in a sense of intolerable loss which has always been as real as the short-term gains linked to silent-way managerialism. The same feeling animates Kelman's violent repudiation of a fallen middle-class universe whose increasingly nervous and cowardly cogs revenge themselves on underlings: the hell of a dead-end autonomy, as it were, from which an unseen God will permit neither advance nor exit.

A few years ago there was a Court of Session meeting concerned with the poll tax. The Edinburgh lawyer Randolph Murray had complained that it was illegal in Scotland since it contravened the Treaty of Union. As part of the proceedings photocopies of the original Treaty document were ordered up, and I recall vividly the eerie sensation of seeing the ushers solemnly bear in the large sheets and place them before Lord President Hope and his two colleagues. The judges then studied the relevant clauses for some minutes, only a few yards from the Parliament Hall where Belhaven and Patrick Hume had argued over them 284 years before. Unrequited ghosts hovered over the proceedings, their dispute still unresolved. Afterwards Lord Hope observed that this was a matter of such fundamental importance that the High Court would need a little time to reach its decision.

A fortnight later he published a verdict of exquisite moderation denying that the Treaty had been betrayed. Hume was still in charge (though other recent decisions suggest Fletcher and Belhaven may at last be staging a comeback). I think that few of those involved in the poll tax action ever paid the damned thing, but that was not because autonomy shielded us. We simply joined the mutiny against it, along with millions of others in both Scotland and England. Everyone there – small-p and large-P patriots alike – knew perfectly well that no Scottish legislature would ever conceivably have imposed such a tax to begin with, and that any Scottish representative body, were it no more than the equivalent of an old French *conseil régional*, would have denounced it. The only reason for our futile day in court was the complete absence of a political alternative.

One of Paterson's shrewdest points is his depiction of how often the Scots themselves have been responsible for Anglicisation. In true colonial situations the metropolis imposes its equalising will. But under self-colonisation it may very well be those indirectly ruled who seek assimilation as the way to equal treatment. Where the dependent or autonomous structure offers no alternative formula, then – paradoxically – a kind of self-preserving nationalism can move them towards integration. Nationalism's aim is equality with one's own first-class compartment. When the latter is ruled out, however, it may seem better to move into the majority's indisputably first-class accommodation than to lapse visibly into the second-rate. This is most likely to be true where assimilation in one particular sphere is not apprehended as too threatening. What does it matter being 'just like them' here or there, while, as Paterson shows, the main bulwarks of civil identity remain unassailable?

Recognition of this reveals another uncomfortable aspect of his position. If nationalism accounts even for assimilation, then it must really be endemic at some deeper level. *The Autonomy of Modern Scotland* counterposes a sage domestic-sovereignty outlook to romantic nationalism. But this is also a contrast between two sorts of nationalism: the canny calculations of self-colonisation versus the heedless and emotive assertion of equal status. Furthermore, the second must underlie the first. A sense of loss, limitation and separateness can help to explain the deviousness and main-chance opportunism of the Scots, but not vice versa. In any case, romantic is only a dismissive label in this context. The Patrick Humes have always employed it to keep politics out of court, as if it were an ailment or weakness to which the post-Enlightenment world had unfortunately succumbed. This is historical nonsense. Like nationalism, romanticism is more an integral element of modernity than a reaction against it.

Thus the road not taken haunts the one actually followed by a self-managing and self-limiting civil society. Nationalism is like a *deus* ex *machina* to Paterson's argument. It motivates the whole complex machinery he describes: institutional identity, self-preservation and (where needed) self-suppression. In that sense the Treaty of Union came just in time to bury a nascent Scottish nationalism, but could only put it into a shallow grave. Consent was the key to its remaining there. Yet to give such continuing consent it could never be really buried and forgotten. Robertson and Paterson show how the deal was meant to work out among the living, but neither accounts sufficiently for the illustrious cadaver of the seven-century-old Kingdom. In 1707 it was decreed undead, not dispatched to genuine oblivion. Embalmed by Union, it has not ceased to exert the most profound influence on each new generation. Has autonomy conserved it, as Paterson maintains? Or is it more accurate to say that that profound influence has kept autonomy working and in effective adaptation for so long? All recent experience suggests how persistent and apparently indelible nationhood can be. Once nationality reaches or crosses the threshold of modern development it is rare indeed for it not to attain political realisation, or at least go on struggling towards it. The autonomy of modern Scotland was intended to be a stable, self-reproducing system of dependency. But however artfully designed and maintained, dependency depends: it assumes the permanence of a wider system. If the latter collapses or shrinks, then it may only have been an odd way of cold-storing nationhood. The corpse may simply step out from temporary interment to resume his rights. He was never really sleeping anyway.

CHAPTER TWENTY-THREE

On Not Hating England

Independent on Sunday

SEPTEMBER 1998

Who would have thought it, and not me, not me…
It was a long road back to this undeclared Republic.
I came by the by-ways, empty of milestones,
On the roads of old drovers, by disused workings
… Allow me to pull up a brick, and to sit beside you
In this nocturne of modernity, to speak of the dead,
Of the creatures loping from their dens of extinction.

DOUGLAS DUNN, 'An Address on the Destitution of Scotland',
St Kilda's Parliament (1981)

At Dead of Night

JUST OVER A YEAR AGO, on 11 September, a referendum voted 75 per cent 'yes' for the Scottish Parliament to resume business (and also to pay for it, by 65 per cent). Knowing I would have to be up in the middle of that night, I had gone to sleep not long after the polls closed, and next morning wasn't awake enough to listen to the car radio until around 5am. And so the news reached me while driving along the High Street of Forth, South Lanarkshire (pop. 2523, alt. 286 mtrs).

A folk-tradition has grown up of recalling just where one was and what one was doing at historic moments. It's important to get the details right. On my way from Edinburgh to Ireland I pulled up for a minute or so to listen to the news, near Forth post office, between two dour-looking pubs, next to a family butcher's over the road from the '1st For Convenience' shop.

Then I got out of the car and walked a short way along the road, uncertain why, just turning over the details in my mind. A lot of Bannatyne Street – the High Street -seemed to be up for sale, right down to the long southward bend with its splendid prospect across Clydesdale and the Lanark Hills. The sale signs made it feel as if the whole place was becoming disposable. Not that Forth had ever been there for the views. The council houses on this wind-torn shoulder of bogland had been built only to serve a coal mine, until burrowing gave way to late 20th century open-cast.

What did I feel? 'Tradition' usually implies some qualified reconstruction of the past, which I'm trying to resist. Actually it was rather formless and confused – but at the same time, uneasy – along the lines of: 'No more damn-awful scenes like these, thank Christ'. Not one thing would ever be quite the same again, in Forth or any part of Scotland. The Proclaimers once had a hit single called 'Letter from America' which took off from the idea of 'Lochaber no more...' and then went into a litany of less familiar heritage-sites like Linwood, Renfrewshire and Methil, Fife. Just what was being thus wryly lamented, or exorcised? Old Jacobite Scotland, the rude shade of Scotch engineering, or both at once?

On the radio one could hear the excitement of hundreds of people in Edinburgh's new International Conference centre, where the final results had been counted and broadcast. And yet, I did not feel less in the middle of it that deserted morning, crossing Scotland's central morass in the hour before dawn. The road passed by so many fallen asteroids of the country's post-industrialism: Bell's Quarry, West Calder and Addiewell, then Breich, Wilsontown and Forth, places I know very few readers of these pages will have seen or heard of. I suspect they might be gratefully overlooked even by anti-guides to the solar system.

The cold, autumnal edge of the September wind was not lying. In the dead of that night a landslip had begun that would carry most of our previous habitations away. In a time far shorter than that of Empire and the boiler-plate engineers, their legacy in turn would vanish, or become a heritage-site like today's New Lanark, or the old Pictish stones. It had been a long, quiet process, and ended in a completely peaceful revolution. Many hearts had been worn down or broken by it, but no one had died. Scotland had upheld its modern civic tradition, and in the end had also managed to emancipate itself from the limits of that tradition. Thus far, an equivalently civic and decent nationalism had prevailed.

This was a low-profile success, in a world preoccupied by the military high drama of Kosovo, East Timor, Palestine and the former Belgian Congo. But the fact was, not such a small one either. An old nation – one of the original 'nation-states' of the early-modern world – had embarked upon the process of regaining its independence. Although located on the outer fringe of geographical Europe, it would do so within two very significant polities: the one-time industrial giant and former Empire-owner, Great Britain, and the emerging European Union. Like Slovenia, the Ukraine and the post-Czechoslovak nations, it had been able to seek emancipation through political agreement and negotiation, not via warlike exclusion or the forcible assimilation of someone else. The 'destitution' (in Douglas Dunn's phrase) to be remedied was internal, institutional and cultural in nature rather than a by-product of colonization or oppression. It looked forward to liberal confederation of some sort, and not backwards into the maw of vengeance and blood-sacrifice.

While many felt such a process starting up in the Autumn of 1997, nobody could have imagined the astonishing speed of the collapse. Within *six months* the Scottish National Party was revealed by surveys as likely to dominate, and quite possibly to control, the first Edinburgh Parliament. By 10 March the Glasgow *Herald's* System Three poll showed them overtaking Labour. 'Connery confident upward trend will continue' declared the front page ('speaking from his Los Angeles office', etc.) Far from home rule 'killing nationalism stone dead' (as Minister George Robertson put it), the very prospect appeared to be lending it new momentum.

Mr Connery's confidence has since then continued to be justified, right up to September of the following year, when the most surprising evidence yet appeared. An Edinburgh *Scotsman* poll (4 September) added a religious affiliation question to the usual ones about voting intentions, and discovered that a majority of Scottish *Catholics* would now vote for independence: 58 per cent as against only 51 per cent of non-Catholics (mainly Presbyterians). To grasp how surprising this is, it must be remembered that the popular Catholic vote was the traditional bedrock of the British Labour Party in Glasgow and right across the central industrial belt.[1]

This was an electorate that had seemed doubly imbued with underdog mentality: proletarian by fate and still half-foreign (Irish) by descent, always suspicious of nationalists as both 'tartan Tories' *and* somewhat Protestant (or even Orange) in demeanour. Although accounting for only a minority of the Scottish electorate, probably around 16 to 17 per cent, the Catholics occupied a peculiarly strategic position. Their much higher concentration in the old-industrial areas had made them crucial to Labourite hegemony there – that is, to the 'one-party state' set up in the 1930s, and which by 1997 had known a lifetime of unassailable (and unassailably corrupt) local power. It was this bastion which, in turn, had become so important to British Labour as a whole.[2]

If that has changed, then it is no longer an exaggeration to say that everything

---

1 A collective study, *The Scottish Electorate* (1999, Alice Brown, David McCrone, Lindsay Paterson and Paula Surridge) gives some idea of the previous situation, culminating in the 1997 general election. But it was in time to detect signs of the change in intentions for the referendum vote, when – 'Perhaps surprisingly there are few differences among the religious groups in their intended vote, with a majority of both Catholic and Protestant identifiers intending to vote Yes-Yes.' (p. 124) The figures were Catholic 60 per cent, Protestant 55 per cent. A year later the Primate of Scotland, Cardinal Winning, was actively defending the prospect of Scottish independence in Brussels!

2 Another paradoxical implication of this is that it was of course the very strength of 'Old Labour' in West-Central Scotland which had determined the Blair government's original move towards devolution. Since Scottish Labourism had during the '80s and '90s become converted under nationalist pressure to Home Rule, and it was necessary to 'do something for Scotland', a Scottish Parliament was the sole available answer in 1997. The prevalent belief was that Labour hegemony would continue unchallenged in the Glasgow area, and that a thoroughly grateful Party and electorate would afterwards dominate the new assembly and go on sustaining New Labour at Westminster. Such blind Britishness reposed in fact on a characteristic 'occlusion' of all that did not fit into its habitual world-view – an attitude with many different expressions, and discussed in other parts of this book.

will. A 'molecular change' was under way, rather than a passing shift in voting patterns. The underground workings must in fact have been far more decayed than anyone could have known only the year before. 'Class' was being transmuted into 'Nation' before our eyes. It seems to follow that the overall dynamic of the Parliament will be quite different from what was projected by the 1997 White Paper and the legislation which followed.

These had proposed a self-governing region in (as it were) harmlessly National uniform. By the following year, eight months before the first elections, what seemed to be arriving was a Nation already bursting out of the regional and devolutionary constraints. Most observers agreed verbally that the referendum was launching 'a process' rather than a fixed set of arrangements – that Devolution would require (in what was then a customary phrase) 'fine tuning' and a good deal of mutual adaptation in order to work properly. Indeed nobody could seriously think otherwise, given that the new authorities in Scotland and Wales were promulgated without any new all-British constitution to contain and circumscribe them.

However, it is one thing to calmly hold a door open to 'possible developments'; quite another when the first entrant proves unexpected, disreputable, and thoroughly ungrateful for being allowed into what he thinks is in any case his own house. And when he is, in addition, the very lout which the Open Door strategy was intended to keep out for good, or even kill stone dead, things begin to feel distinctly out of control.

Beyond Cosmopolis

Back in the '70s – when the Proclaimers would still have been at school – I remember someone who used to invoke Forth in arguments. Whenever this character saw pointy-heids like mine agitated by thoughts of rebirth he would lean stiffly forward from his well-worn perch at the end of a journalistic bar and object darkly: 'Aye... all very well that, but it's what the *man in Forth* thinks that really counts!' The point was difficult to deny: few could know where Forth was, let alone claim acquaintance with its manful sagacity. But of course his point was plain. Giddy dreamers should not delude themselves that the stalwartly canny Forthite would ever heed such nonsense: a Labour-voting Scot-Brit would he remain unto the end of time, or even afterwards, as Caledonian delegate to Nirvana (a spruced-up version of Glasgow Corporation). Man-of-Forth stood for the unalterable cosmos of grittiness in which Scotland's winning the World Cup (or even attaining the semi-final) would always mean more than fairy-tales about independence.

Parochialism is not just a state of mind, but a social structure. I had entertained theories like that before; but they became a real feeling only at that moment, in a 5am sensation of ground-shift too full of puzzlement, and too big for gladness or retrospective gloating. I don't know how many Forth electors voted for the change, probably nearly all of them. Not a shred of the old saloon-bar wisdom now remains. It is deader than the West Lothian shale-bings and a lot less decorative. Never was real defeat more utter, or reversal from a shaming like 1979 more complete.

Yet coming down from Forth to Lanark, then across the Border and then the Irish Sea, it was the sense of uneasy puzzlement which weighed most. In longer retrospect, I think that derived from something only half-formulated in my mind that morning. Time alone could bring it out. It was the sense of how, in fact, no side really wins or loses such big arguments -or at least, not in any sense subjectively imagined beforehand.

For 25 years in Scotland Unionism and Nationalism had contended amid notions of seeing the other side in flight, or with luck dropping stone dead on the spot: justified triumph with his foot upon the expiring, scaly monster. But history is not a courtroom or a newspaper Opinion Page. Things happen, and a die is cast – but always for partly accidental reasons, and never in a way or at a time corresponding to previous forecasts. Then the instant it occurs everything is too much altered, once and for all. Most of the old software of both sides is outdated on the spot. Although victorious, the dreamers then need upgrading almost as badly as would Scotland's nay-sayers and 'hairmless Harrys'.

Was this the cunning of history, in Hegel's sense, or just its daftly accidental nature? Whichever: in those small hours a country for too long too much outside itself would return into itself. Its former parochialism rested on a temporary equilibrium between places like Forth – John Gait's Parish, Dr Finlay's Tannochbrae/Auchtermuchty, Duncan McLean's *Blackden*, Andrew O'Hagan's Saltcoats – and a spuriously cosmopolitical realm, long deemed the equally natural habitat of Scottishness. On the one hand stood Blackden/Forth, 'the arse-end of the giant' as McLean describes it; on the other, a 'universalism' which was really the British Empire impersonating civilisation itself.

During that age a genuine Scotsperson was a sort of human shuttle, a back-and-forth composite of and between these things. Our *Heimat* had been both together, a package deal. The grimy, couthy old dump where nothing ever happened and no one bore a name like Jelly Roll Morton – not just a place, but a state of the soul. And then its busybody school leavers, out there in Hong Kong, Calgary or the Khyber Pass, explaining (or vending) Testaments and guns to other aspiring natives. These did not just gang thegither, they were an intimate condition of one another. Jointly they framed the special and awful style of parish-pumpery which was being condemned to oblivion last 11 September. James Buchan has called it the mental world of 'the Empire Scots', the imagined community of Scotland-at-large, a nation simultaneously far too wee and much too huge (or at least, over-extended) to require ordinary human statehood. It was the world of his grandfather John, and when that inheritance dies off (he concludes) '...with us will die a mental country that will astonish any future Scot who chances on this article' (Glasgow *Herald* E2 section, 7 February 1998).

Good riddance to it. Its cost was the blood of loss which I have tried to evoke elsewhere. It was that corrosive, underground stream which has seeped remorselessly down through the veins of one Scottish generation after another out of its source: 'the last day Scotland was Scotland'. The lands of George Lockhart of Carnwath were only a few miles south-east of Forth (in the area where Ian Hamilton Finlay's 'Little Sparta' temple and garden stand today). As we saw, those who accomplished the act could not have really known what they were doing either, in spite of the rhetorical warnings of Lockhart, Lord Belhaven, Andrew Fletcher and others in the last Parliament of 1706. Paid or not, for good and deplorable motives, they were opening a heart-wound that would run darkly underneath the whole span of the nationality-world lying ahead of them. However good it was to become British, this companion injury could only persist as well. As Lockhart felt, a nation could not cease being what it had become through such custom and the prolonged state-effort of centuries. It could only feign other and grander modes of existence, while simultaneously haunting all such departures with the question mark of its own origin.

Folklorists have thought of this souterrain nationality as the carrying stream. But this seems to me an over-romantic conception. Blessing and curse together, nationality is simply the fate of modernity. We know now how little genetics has to do with it, but the societal equivalent of DNA is another matter. There is a long-range transmission of community from one age into another, through a myriad of idioms and altering channels, which is too little understood. This can be seen as a cultural blood-stream too, sometimes blind or disguised in its impact, liable to assume unforeseeable shapes or even flow in reverse, and capable of rising to the surface when least expected.

I know that the literal blood of others counted too, alas, in the British-imperial existence which for so long ensued. Its charnel-house side probably had more impact on the Scots than anyone else.[3] But latterly more appears to have been pumped out of the national heart-stream itself. This has been symbolised through the beloved, itching, scabrous wound of so much 20th century Scottish literature. The latter's prolonged sojourn in Hell stands at bottom for the same loss, become reasonless: a national abnegation no longer explicable or sustainable by participation in a meaningful mission. I suppose British Socialism was

---

3   In 'Dressed to Kill' Douglas Dunn writes:
     For someone born in '42
     This subject sticks like rancid glue –
     All those wars, before and since...
     Rinse hands, and rinse, re-rinse, re-rinse,
     But still the blood just won't wash off
     As if the world can't get enough. No, by Jingo, no, I'm not
     A patriotic British Scot...
     Dante's Drum-kit (1993), pp. 143–4.

the missionary party's last throw. After such betrayal, remedy can be none. Well, none but (as Buchan ironically concludes) a common sort of Euro-prosperity via 'independence or provincial euro-autonomy' – that is, a normalization enviable by most populations on earth, yet somehow a bit ordinary to the Heaven-obsessed. To some of the latter, desertion by the imperium (God in disguise) leaves Scottish society beyond even the hope of redemption. It might as well blot itself out in drugs.

MacEverywhere, Farewell

In retrospect I can see that's what the prophecies of grittiness were (and still are) all about: explanations of how late it was, how late – vibrations from a parochial past rather than the future of Holyrood. This accounts for their extraordinary virulence, and their hatred of nationalism. They were extolling Forth less for what it was than for what it meant: a Scotland whose pawky misery was the reverse of Universality's coin, but also betokened a Glory to come. In his novel *Lanark* Alasdair Grey called Glasgow 'Unthank'. So, on the farther side of Unthank stood a heavenly city, a miles-better Jerusalem to which our nation should at all costs remain faithful. Nationalist chatterers were wilful – hence hateable – despoilers of this faith. They were a modern version of the Damned, protagonists of 'the world'. Especially after North Sea petroleum appeared, their selfish materialism enjoyed the kind of progress to be expected of Satan's seed, culminating in the decade of Thatcherite darkness.

To their credit, English observers never had much clue about the underground topography. Had Captain Kirk and Spock ever reached Scotland, their data-bank probes too might have been baffled. The expectation would have been to find nationalists frothing at the mouth and folk-dancing, pausing only to flout sober cosmopolitical reason and measured appraisals of the main chance. In this contraflow country it was in fact often anti-nationalists who fiddled and ennobled folklore, with steam jetting from their ears. The Labour Party's Norman and Janey Buchan presided over a prolonged anti-Nationalist *ceilidh* in the 1970s and '80s, and the former even composed and published a mock-epic poem about chauvinist folly, *The Dunciad*.[4]

Mild, secular, and almost entirely philistine, the SNP-style national credo exhibited by contrast a low-pressure if (in the long run) incontrovertible rationality. At bottom the fulminations against its fairly reasonable self-interest (or its thoroughly '*petit-bourgeois*' nature, as the Marxists said) were all because this wasn't good enough for Scots. It was as if the latter had been marked out for

---

4   *The Dunciad* (1976). Alongside many others, the writer was chided in it for his already misguided 'tendencies'. Owen Dudley Edwards replied at the time with a counter-mock epic on the theme of Labourite self-importance, which was broadcast on BBC Scotland, but (alas) remains unpublished.

some special extra- or supra-national role: an elect folk haunted by a God-given universality, for whom political independence would be but a selfish distraction. Since their true *ethnos* was the cosmos, it would be folly to settle for less. There was of course a bizarre kind of super-nationalism cached away somewhere in such numinous notions, like an unconfessable Zionism of almost Serb intensity. But by that time it had (fortunately) nowhere to go, and could only be defended in mounting fury and frustration.

Such was the Grail-quest of which Her Majesty's Labour Party (West of Scotland Branch) had been made the custodians. The denominational input to this mindset was variable. I think the principal impetus must have come from the old Reformed majority itself, diverted in its thrust yet still inclined to moral absolutism. But there was a prominent Catholic presence as well, stemming from 19th century immigrants wary of Protestant hegemony. Until very recently (as I suggested before) they couldn't help feeling that secular British Socialism might be safer than a possibly Orange-tinged domestic corporatism.

It was this kind of deep-structure inversion which conditioned surface political events until the 1980s, and the lessons of Thatcherism. Until then the most extreme version of nationalism around in Scotland was always anti-nationalism. Most of its disciples were on the Left, and habitually danced in rhetorical circles around British Socialism, their ineffably commanding consciences, leaky council-house roofs, the supposedly 'broader' (internationalist) view, and so on. But these were fig leaves. Underneath there lurked that simpler propulsive intuition of the Scot as chosen, and indeed superhuman: a nationality predestined to superb exemption from the vulgar nationalist path. Its visible justification on earth was still the Socialist Phase of the Great-British imperium; and its most important duty was to prepare for that coming by keeping the ever-falling English in line, and up to the mark.

There could be no mere parishes for such a race. Since its parochiality *was* the universal, the gritty judgement of Forth was indeed guaranteed to floor romantic haverings. The *Sunday Post* too was divinely ordained, mocked only to be ultimately exalted, the bleeding stigma of a Christ-ridden *Volk*.[5] No doubt that was why the present writer once felt it appropriate to rid Scotland of both that newspaper and its last Minister together, in a single liberationary outrage. They did belong together, and resumed the aberrant parochialism of an age. Not that I had worked it out at the time, 29 years before last year's referendum. In 1968

---

5 A Dundee newspaper more widely read than any other in the Scotland of the Imperial Captivity. Its populist parochialism and safe Britannic conservatism made it a byword for all that seemed inveterately and unalterably Scottish. It is still published by D.C. Thomson Ltd, who also brought out a range of comic and children's papers read all over the UK, like *Dandy, Beano, Hotspur* (and many others). Having been raised on Thomsonite hay, the present author was misguided enough to declare at one moment (1968) that liberating his homeland would depend, ultimately, upon 'strangling the last Minister (of the Presbyterian Kirk) with the last copy of the *Sunday Post*'.

it was more of a querulous desperado's hunch, which today I would defend only in much more qualified and second-thought terms.

With rueful introspection, moreover, I see that I'm actually doing so because the General Election result of 1 May 1997 so unmistakably cancelled the last custodial duty of the Northern warders. Middle England no longer needs us. In fact it has grown distinctly resistant to sermons about moral backsliding and Socialism. In fact it probably never really needed them (or us) at all. So isn't it time we left them alone? Shortly after the election the entire imperium-pretence was formally wound up in Hong Kong. It is long past time for the wandering preacher to return from his moorland hilltop, find an ordinary job and (as James Buchan implies) give his vocal cords a rest.

Labourism has remained the midwife of the delivery which followed. But (as I will argue below) we must hope that by delivering self-government it will also go on to deliver itself. Its unco' guid and well-meaning managed to retard development for nearly twenty years, before reluctantly giving way and persuading themselves they had always desired the outcome.[6] They too now deserve a break. On that level it's time we drew a line and forgave one another, for new-political rather than old-theological reasons.

On Failing to Hate the English

What has been happening in Scotland? For the metropolitan media, the simplest available answer was that the Scots are now possessed by a demon. It is the fashion to call the latter 'ethnicity' these days. Two months after the referendum a 19-year-old lad called Mark Ayton was beaten up and kicked to death in the posh Edinburgh suburb of Balerno. At that time I lived fairly near there, and can recall reading all the details in the local paper.

I did so with special and personal interest because I happened to know a bit about the area. Years before, a former partner had come from Juniper Green, another suburb-village adjoining Balerno, and she often used to talk of life there. There had long been an abrupt social contrast between the working-class communities at Juniper Green and Currie, and the older and more select Balerno. Juniper Green and Currie had been paper-mill villages, dependent on the Water of Leith factories in a nearby river-valley. Balerno was a traditional Pentland Hills small town, located up-river well before it got industrial. In the 20th century it had become a typical executive and retiral outer settlement at just the right distance from Edinburgh – a semi-rural *banlieue* of stone-built houses and large villas, set well apart from the industrial wastelands of West Lothian.

---

6   Some recent revelations in *The Herald* have shown this is almost literally true. Papers released under the 30-year rule show how Labour Secretary of State William Ross strove to keep Home Rule legislation at bay until the 1970s, when (following on the SNP's electoral successes of 1974) it could no longer be postponed.

One way of manifesting these contrasts was through traditional animosity between their respective schools, and tribal rules about who regularly drank in which pubs. Poor Ayton and his brother were caught up in a prolonged punch-up of that kind. Edinburgh as a whole remains, alas, chronically beset by such social chasms and resentments. Customary exclamations followed in the Edinburgh and local press about the surprisingly 'good background' of his assailants (i.e. upper-middle class, one of them actually *English*). They were given four years for 'culpable homicide', and Edinburgh's *Evening News* commented severely on the leniency of the sentences: 'Much was made of the accused men's claims that they didn't mean to kill Mark, and of their leafy, suburban background... The fact is that this incident and the ensuing court case would have been coloured considerably if it had taken place in Muirhouse or Pilton ...' (2 June 1998 – Muirhouse and Pilton are parts of the city now linked in the public mind to *Trainspotting* and *Filth*). The *News* ended with a ringing condemnation of Appeal Judge Hardie as 'Lord Advocate for the Upper Classes'. Neither ethnicity nor race-hate were mentioned in the *News* account.

It was therefore a good deal more than surprising to read in May 1998 that there had been *a race riot* in Balerno. The *Spectator* brought out a story entitled 'A Very Scottish Death' by Katie Grant, in which she claimed that Mark Ayton died 'for being thought English', and that what the whole incident laid bare was 'a rising tide of anti-English sentiment'. Why the tide? Because 'behind the mask of Scottish middle-class respectability there lurks a racist monster'. It is now loitering with more open intent, since the referendum 'Yes' campaign had been 'fought by New Labour and the SNP on an anti-English ticket'. Although invisible to most referendum voters on 11 September, and undetected at the time even by London media correspondents, this had none the less 'given anti-English feeling a degree of respectability in middle-class leftish circles'. Oh yes, with hindsight 'it is easy to see how death walked down the road to meet Mark Ayton'.

Even without hindsight, it remains a bit puzzling to see how the *Spectator* had given space to stuff like this, even when composed by Peregrine Worsthorne's niece. As Isabel Hilton commented acidly in the *Guardian,* if she was right 'it is only a matter of time before white-robed figures with burning torches are hunting out English settlers from their beds and hanging them from lamp-posts' ('The Ku Klux Klansmen', 10 June). Nor was Katie Grant alone in her demonology. In fact she seemed to have launched a mini-trend.

Monster-sightings were suddenly on the increase. The *Sunday Times* of 28 June last, for instance, led with the headline 'Anti-English Feeling Grows in Scotland'. The pretext for their front-page drama was another poll on the subject; but only a resolute minority of readers is likely to have followed through to the inside-page commentary on the findings. That was given by Professor David McCrone of Edinburgh University, and suggested that in fact anti-Englishness had 'grown' from the trivial to the insignificant:

The news for the pessimists is that there is not a lot of anti-Englishness about. Fully 83 per cent said they feel no dislike of the English, and this is true for all ages, social classes, and among men and women. There simply is not the animosity around, with only 17 per cent saying they disliked the English either a little or a lot...

But it takes more than this to divert a headline pessimist with the ethnic bit between his or her jaws. Andrew Neil returned to the assault in the *Spectator* the following month, with a piece talking of 'a pervasive and growing anti-Englishness... an outpouring of denigration and hatred'. He felt that this sort of thing was stealing his own country from him – the douce and decent British Scotland which he was reared in, and wants to keep going. Such a verdict is clearly of some importance, given that Neil is now Editor-in-Chief of *Scotsman* Publications (*The Scotsman*, plus what was then the country's only Sunday broadsheet, *Scotland on Sunday*). Not long before the incident Neil had also founded a 'Scottish Policy Unit' with money from his proprietors, the Barclay twins, in order to help stem the monstrous tide.[7]

At that time *The Scotsman*'s Westminster political correspondent was Iain Macwhirter, who was disturbed enough to reply to his own Editor-in-Chief with a testy 'Open Letter', in which he pointed out that there is so far no evidence whatever of increasing Anglophobia of the malignant or discriminatory kind which such tirades were signalling. Yet (he went on):

> *Spectator* columnists like yourself, Katie Grant and Bruce Anderson have been spreading fear and loathing in the Home Counties with tales of the tartan terror. You've become a kind of Scottish Tourist Board in reverse: 'Come to Scotland this Autumn, and be Beaten to Death for being English!'...

So (it seems right to ask) just what on earth *is* the panic about? Some people want there to be monsters. This must be because they explain, or seem to explain, something. The Scots appear to be going off the rails – that is, the rails of United Kingdom convention and expectation which all such critics (Scottish or English) took for granted, and to which they indeed owe their own formation and present status. A convenient way of accounting for the aberration is to imagine some kind of ethnic *Geist* or blood-instinct 'unleashed' by Labour foolishness. There may be little to support the idea in Scotland; but there is of course plenty elsewhere, not so much in the actual history of Eastern Europe as in mediocre journalistic musings upon its most violent incidents.

How inveterate such opinions are likely to be was shown later on, when an

---

7   The Barclay brothers are Scottish property millionaires living in the Channel Island of Brecqhou, off Sark, who have in recent years diversified as press barons, most famously with the *Scotsman* group (which they bought from its previous Canadian owners) and the now-defunct *European*. Their views are rigidly neo-liberal, anti-European and of course anti-nationalist.

article in *The Observer* repeated what was by now the script, verbatim. Their reporter Dean Nelson wrote on 8 November 1998:

> There is a good deal of complacency in Scotland on racism... there was reluctance to believe that the killing of English youth Mark Ayton in a middle-class Edinburgh suburb this year was racially motivated. The police have kept an open mind on the issue, while lenient sentences given to his killers were greeted with outrage.

The last sentence is true (as I indicated). As for the rest, Mr Nelson just hadn't done any homework, or read the cuttings. He didn't need to. Like other recent 'revelations' of this kind, his piece could hardly avoid ending somewhat differently – in this case by again citing David McCrone's evidence, and conceding that 'a sizeable number of English settlers in Scotland have joined the Scottish National Party'.

But that was the small print at the end. The big print over the top read: 'SOD OFF BACK TO ENGLAND: Scots no longer ashamed to be anti-English'. The crucial part of the message here is *'no longer'*. It means that things have changed because of current events, and will therefore get worse. The Union prevented (or at least restrained) such intolerance; hence its loss entails a fall into ethnic hatred and discrimination.

Northern Nihilism

There is plainly a pathology here that calls for more searching explanation. It seems to me there are two main causes for it, one among the Scots themselves, the other located much more profoundly, within the uncertainties of English identity. It is remarkable in retrospect how much of the most strenuous opposition to devolution has been the work of Scots, and particularly of Scottish intellectuals. Ever since the late 1960s, when Winifred Ewing unexpectedly won a by-election in Hamilton and showed that nationalism might become a serious political force, an influential minority of educated Scots has vehemently agitated *against* the very prospect of political rebirth. On occasion it succeeded in sabotaging the process, most strikingly at the time of the 1979 home rule referendum. The passage of MP George Cunningham's '40 per cent rule' at Westminster meant that the small majority won for devolution could then be disregarded by Mrs Thatcher's incoming government. Although Scotland had become a left-wing country since the 1950s, and resisted the tide of right-wing populism that had overtaken England, it was helpless against British government throughout the eighteen-year Conservative regime which followed.

In the end (we know now) this was to generate a stronger national reaction against Britain. But the point is, it was serious politics. This style of intellectual anti-nationalism had strong links with politicians, and it was noticeable in both dominant political parties. The question remains – what were such enduring and effective links founded upon?

One part of the answer lies, obviously, in the force of a fairly consistent 'rejectionism' in Scotland itself. The term 'national nihilism' may convey it best, by indicating what was being rejected. In occupied or colonised societies, intellectuals have most often been found on the side of the deprived population. There, nationalism has normally had the joint aim of political liberation and 'nation-building', a process requiring inclusion of whatever educated strata were available. The latter might be 'bought off ' or distracted by the imperial power with honours and trinkets, and seek to convince themselves (normally with metropolitan assistance) that all this was in the true 'best interest' of their people. However, it is simply a matter of record that such pretences were usually thin, and short-lived. They rarely resisted post-1945 decolonisation, and where they have survived beyond independence (as in French West Africa) it has been in a miserable *diminuendo* sustained at great expense by the former colonial power.

By contrast, Scottish national nihilism was founded upon being 'on the other side' in a far less usual sense. Although apparently marked out (like Wales and Ireland) for conquest and assimilation, the Scottish state sought to avoid that fate. It did so first by its own national effort at the end of the 17th century, culminating in the abortive project of colonising the Panama Isthmus in 1698–9: the Darien Scheme. When that was defeated, it agreed – albeit reluctantly – to a 'joint venture' with the vastly more powerful English state in 1707. And it was the success of this incorporating alliance which then provided a much stronger metropolitan platform for the intelligentsia of the lesser country to occupy and (before long) to exploit quite effectively.

This intelligentsia learned to reject its own country *in itself*, as a land bearable only when 'merged ' or extended by association with another – the England-Britain set up by the Treaty of Union. From this mentality came the fervent Universalism I mentioned above – that is, the identification of homeland and cosmos which suppressed mere local statehood as an unworthy side-issue. It then seemed to follow that the Scots could only 'be themselves' when thus broadened or leavened. Such postures have persisted strongly into our own time. Indeed there could be no more striking testimony to the durability of the pattern than the Blair government itself. Blair only became Leader of his party through the death of his formidable Scottish predecessor, John Smith, and in competition with the latter's equally impressive countryman Gordon Brown.[8] His subsequent government could not avoid remaining very Scottish, however. The Scots

---

8   At the time of writing there seems no way of estimating the significance of the deeply-rooted clash between Brown and Blair which resulted in the latter's victory in 1994. In spite of the great amount of speculation and argument over their rivalry, this may have to await farther disclosures or revelations, or even the memoirs and papers of the protagonists. However, there is one school of speculation which insists on the manifest weakness

may have attached themselves to the Anglo-British state as supplicants in 1707. By 1997 they were surprisingly close to being its masters. This was testimony to decline, admittedly – but also (obviously) to the vigour of such a transplanted or reverse-colonising elite.

Since the 1960s, however, taking 'the other side' in that sense has at least implied rejecting an alternative. Rejecting separatism just as a policy or strategy has never been enough. From the angle of the outward-bound elite, Nationalism was best presented as a vista of existential outrage. However quiet its language and aims, it was virtually a kind of damnation, propagated by fiends. Such has always been the sense (e.g.) of Labourite 'Nat-bashing', from William Ross down to the present regime's Helen Liddell. Whatever the pros and cons of a separate government it would inevitably threaten the life-support mechanisms of this quite substantial cultural and political stratum. It *is* a matter of life or death therefore – their own. Hence it is much more than a question of a few *vendus* or token metropolitan pets – the pretend-elites of most past nationalist dilemmas. A more extensive imbrication has taken place in this case, and one of its consequences has been this more visceral and impatient rejection, manifested in an emotive distrust or rage – itself so uncannily similar to nationalist passion.

Such anti-national 'nationalism' is certainly an unusual specimen in the ethnic gallery of modern times. But it may be more common than one would think. I think that varieties of its parodic humour are discernible in France and Italy, for example – other states of strictly forced centralism, where semi-alien elites have been co-opted into a majority hegemony. It was also found in the pre-1922 Irish-British rapport, much more strongly than is now easily recalled. But its most astonishing expression, surely, has been the UK one – above all on the British *Left*.

One should not forget that the Scottish branch of UK Labourism actually abandoned Home Rule *completely* in the early 1960s, in the period just before Scottish nationalism became politically important. Though a version of national autonomy had traditionally figured in Scottish-Labour manifestos from the 1890s onwards, it was formally renounced just as British decline grew unmistakable, and (simultaneously) campaigns of born-again *redressement* and greatness-support became more important in London. Scottish Labour's initial contribution to these was a renunciation of what it then dismissed as 'the Home Rule Shibboleth'. Thus it led the way to becoming more demonstratively British, as the trumpets of imperial distress sounded more loudly. Surviving elements of this same stratum are still pursuing the same campaign, under Blair. The 'shibboleth'

---

of the English component within the deteriorating British Socialism of the 1980s and '90s. After the electoral failures of Kinnock and Smith, it was urgently necessary to redress the weakness by (at least) not having another Scot. Blair, by contrast, was a practically identikit *British* individual in the sense most acceptable to English sensibility. Thus a subjacent national conflict may have been modulated (though not exactly resolved) by the residual rules of British identity. But is this ever likely to happen again?

has become reality (and they now claim to have always desired it); but it can still be prevented from 'going further' (and leaving England quite deprived of Northern moral guidance). Not long after the original save-Britain campaign got going, London was compelled to remonstrate gently but firmly over such excess of zeal – by pointing out how Britain's interests might be best served by *some* measure of local differentiation.

Southern Opportunism

Monster-viewing excursions are unlikely to tail off during the early years of the new Scottish Parliament. So it may be worth stocking up with some obvious facts. First of all, the Scots are *thinking about* England more, for obvious reasons. The subject occurs to them now, in a way which it previously did not, or not so often. How could this fail to be true? It is natural to wonder – not necessarily with antagonism – how Edinburgh-London relations will develop under the new circumstances. Problems *are* likely in what was, until 1997, an unnaturally changeless and stultified rapport. The Scots enjoy arguing, and ever since the referendum the Edinburgh and Glasgow media have indeed resounded with such speculative disputes. Some have interpreted this benevolently, as a sign of returning political life and intelligence. But with adequate ill-will it is also possible to see in such animation nothing but 'looking for trouble', or even looking for a fight of some – any – kind.

Secondly, there is *of course* antagonism towards 'England ' among Scots (though far less towards English individuals). It has been there since long before the Union, after which it settled down into a sort of steady-state grumbling and narkiness, a 'chip on the shoulder' due to the structural inequality which opposes 80+ per cent of 'Great Britain' to (now) less than ten per cent. As I pointed out before, Conrad Russell has shown how the Scots have largely supported the Union, more consciously and deliberately than the English – but have also read its meaning differently. What they wanted most was the one thing it could never supply – *collective* recognition and equality. They needed some kind of federalism, but found they had signed up to an intensifying unitarism – to an historical over-centralism, in fact, which would attain its unsurpassable climax only in the Thatcher years. Again, how could some ill-feeling fail to arise from that? But the 'England' being blamed here is in fact the British state, and the individuals who get its rough edge are *almost invariably* those easily identifiable with the ruling *moeurs* – i.e. the 'upper class', 'snooty', those automatically knowing best, and so on.

Undeniably, all this has fostered a rankling and cantankerous streak in modern Scottish identity. It is most liable to surface against what I suppose should really be called Home-County Englishness. But in my experience this is rarely understood by the English (of any class or region) who encounter it, and is then all too often aggravated by being ascribed to 'unreasonableness', or some kind of recalcitrant ethnicity. There are also liberal techniques of over-compensation –

striving to avoid the slightest suggestion of superiority. However well-meant, these can of course be in turn profoundly exasperating. Having little overtly English identity to call on, and unwilling to strike British attitudes, southern commentators of that kind sometimes resort to a facsimile of pure reasonableness -regrettably, the most superior of all postures. Thus instead of two ordinary national identities or points of view confronting one another, the result can sometimes be non-dialogue on an almost astral plane.

These are ugly dilemmas, and truly a part of 'the Destitution of Scotland' in Douglas Dunn's meaning. To my shame I can recall many incidents at University, or before that in school playgrounds, where such resentment would come helplessly to the surface and at least suggest the kind of violence which Iain Macwhirter's 'anti-Tourist Board ' is now scrounging around for with bell, book and candle. Yet the main point about all this is as blatant as its historical diagnosis: the incidents I can remember occurred (alas) 30 or even 50 years back. *They were part of 'the Union'.*

Far from being novel, or in any way linked to post-referendum consciousness, they were side effects of Britishness, and completely incurable within the latter's antiquated terms. By contrast, the current vogue of monster-hunting *is* linked to the notion of change: these intrepid scouts feel that the wish for 'devolution' or, still worse, independence *must* have provoked such reflexes – if indeed the whole business wasn't caused by them in the first place. Hence the Union must have been better because it restrained such barbarity. The uncomfortable truth is that the Union *caused* the 'barbarity' – that is, a petulant sense of frustration and incessant put-down which, under the old conditions, had no political mode of expression and sometimes assumed such irrational and personal forms.

Now, all these may indeed have been pretty small beer, compared to the kind of oppression suffered by most colonised countries; yet they were pretty disagreeable, and our own. Far from being a manifestation of 'nationalism' in the new, post-1960s sense, they provide a very powerful incentive to making nationalism more political – in order to at last escape from, or at least redefine such noxious dilemmas more tolerably. Scotland badly needs a cure for 'anti-Englishness'. But she can only find it civilly, by her own efforts. Here, what the ethnicscare scenario does is to confuse cure and cause. All efforts to achieve equality imply heightened consciousness of inequities and prejudice; but such awareness (including a greater awareness of things English) is then ascribed exclusively to prejudice itself – an unreasonable will to be different, as it were (or even better). I have mentioned some of the motives for the prominent Scottish collaboration in this new brand of witch-hunting – the fear of death, or at least of demotion and uncomfortable redefinition, among an émigré elite. However, the underlying sting in the process comes from a conjunction between such fears and the *emerging question of Englishness* itself. After all, a far deeper uncertainty attaches to post-British England than to any dilemmas currently experienced in Scotland, Wales or Ireland.

But one way of manifesting such anxiety is simply by displacing it, and projecting it upon others. The 'explanation' of troubling incidents and attacks then lies not in failures of state, or in the political system sustained by the UK majority, but in the ill-will or backwardness of minorities. The peripheral tribes are bringing trouble upon themselves, through unreasonable hatred of *us*; the childish dreads and charms of ethnicity lie within their nature, but never in *ours*. Such a form of self-exorcism requires the evidence of 'incidents' – or even their invention and (as in this case) heedless reinvention. The aim is reassurance: that is, peaceful certitude that the country of Stephen Lawrence and of so much malign Euro-scepticism is *not* succumbing to its own brutish prejudice or post-imperial exclusiveness. What Southern-liberal opportunism demands is above all to see ethnic cleansers tooling up for business... somewhere else.

The Lawrence case is especially relevant here. Alongside all the hand-wringing of summer 1998 in Scotland, the same readers and viewers were simultaneously being shown in dreadful detail just what 'racism' meant in practice, in a London suburb. Does anyone really think that people were less moved or enraged in Balerno or in Aberdeen, because Mr and Mrs Lawrence are *English*? On the contrary, I would like to think most of them knew the best of England when they saw it.[9] The English (like the Scots) have to get rid of their own venomous dregs – largely the deposit of a joint British imperialism which has been formally wound up yet still festers in the unconscious of both countries. However, the exposure and anger of the Lawrence affair have also been a way of combating that legacy. Would it not be *absurd* to see only ethnic monsters looming through it? Had Scottish pundits used such a diagnosis glibly to predict an advancing Bosnia in the streets of London and Birmingham, they would have been properly ridiculed. But that's the point: somewhat different standards were supposed to apply to 'ethnic threats' materialising in streets elsewhere – in non-heartland areas, even improbable sites like Balerno, where ethnicity is supposed to have a naturally higher profile.

A plausible overall depiction of what lies at the back of the different standards was given by columnist Magnus Linklater in *Scotland on Sunday* last November. Linklater is an informed witness of such matters. He lived in London for many years, where he edited English papers before returning to Edinburgh as Editor of *The Scotsman* in the 1980s. Looking back over this 'concerted and damaging campaign, conducted mainly by expatriate Scots' to convey the impression of a Scotland increasingly 'infected by anti-English racism', he pointed out that in the background had lain always 'the general idea of the Scots as a fairly muti-

---

9   This was recognised by Channel 4 Television at Christmas time, 1998, when a 'Christmas Message' from Mr and Mrs Lawrence was broadcast on 25 December to coincide with the usual Queenly message going out on other channels. It was a short and moving programme describing their son's murder and the police mishandling of it, and appealing for a different approach by both the law and the media.

nous lot – and growing more so'. Hence the profound constitutional argument being fought out around the Scottish Parliament, crucial to the future for England as well, gets by and large dismissed as peripheral bickering. Ethnic ill-will has become the standard way of accounting for it: 'they must hate us', rather than loving us for all we have given them:

> The prevailing English attitude remains, in short, a colonial one. It is conde-scending, biased and largely ignorant. Above all, it serves to fuel national prejudices north as well as south of the Border. It seems clear that much work will have to be done if Blair's vision of an inclusive Britain is to catch on. And at least as much of that will be needed in England as in Scotland.[10]

Region into Nation

It is now clearer in retrospect that the referendum vote of 1997 was for a direc-tion of affairs, rather than for any precise model of devolved government. The double 'Yes' was broad assent to a movement, and not (or not necessarily) to the delimited goals of the government's White Paper. And the movement in question was not that of a party, or even a coalition of parties. It included all the parties except the Conservatives, and reached far into the institutions of Scottish civil society. The latter have been the main support of national identity since 1707, so it is not excessive to claim that most of 'the nation' was involved. *The Claim of Right* (1988) and the Constitutional Convention were the obvious vehicles of that involvement – it was they who did most of the work on the self-rule scheme which finally turned into the Scotland Bill. But although the SNP had stood apart from that process, it was clearly that party whose influence (or 'threat', as both Labour and the Tories saw it) held such movements so firmly on course.

How conscious the electorate was of this became plain during the referendum campaign. A key episode of the latter was the agreement between Scottish Labour and the Nationalists on obtaining a 'Yes' vote, and the deep reverberations which that generated. I was not the only observer to be struck by the feeling – some-times almost the fervour – shown on the matter. It was like a kind of deep relief. A profound paralysis was being undone. After decades of snarling strife and denigration both movements had compromised on a platform enabling everything to move forward. But 'everything' meant the country, or the nation. It did not mean (or only mean) the autonomous region or the devolved local government foreseen by Westminster's final blueprint. Anyone who doubts the difference between region and nationality should study this alteration more carefully – and the history which has followed.

There was nothing dishonourable or wrong about Blair's plan (most of which had been thought up by Scots anyway). The only thing 'wrong' was that

---

10 'Anyone for an Inclusive Britain?', *Scotland on Sunday*, 8 November 1998.

it had finally been conceded to a people which, in the course of the prolonged struggle to obtain it, had recovered an identity and confidence going beyond what the plan finally allowed for. The final, vital touch was given to that confidence by the referendum campaign. It was as if a kind of subterranean fusion occurred, around a new-found sense of unity and legitimate common purpose. Once *that* had happened, however, farther progression was automatic – and passed, inevitably, a lot farther than what had previously been thought possible. All commentators have been struck, and rightly puzzled, by how rapid and near-unanimous this development has been. After all this was the nation which, in 1979, had suffered cold feet over dustmen's strikes and the antics of Alex Douglas-Home (he preached a 'No' vote at the last minute of the referendum that year). Yet only a few months after the 1997 vote, the route to independence was being taken almost for granted.

A lot happened in between to contribute to the eventual big shift. Before the 1997 election (for example) the Conservatives tried to make a mega-production out of taxation fears. They towed huge posters around showing Britain being torn into two parts by the imposition of a 'Tartan Tax': North Britons would lose their Union as well as their hard-earned cash, etc. When it came to the referendum, nearly two-thirds of them voted to pay the tax and were relatively unconcerned about the Union. What the Tories had suppressed from recollection was an earlier imposition which North Britain had mutinied against in significant numbers: Mrs Thatcher's Poll Tax.

The mutiny in England then became even bigger, and was responsible for its defeat (and Thatcher's fall from power). But the point is that both the way it was done and the resultant revolt had had a differential impact on Scotland. We see now that this impact must have sunk in, and left a living trace. There had also been a national element in the aversion to Thatcherism, strongly revivified by the anti-Tory campaigns of the 1980s, and still being borne forward in 1997.

When after the referendum vote Tony Blair came up to Edinburgh to thank the people for supporting him, he was still thinking in terms of gratitude. How could it fail to mean what he (and the Scots in his cabinet) wanted – reinforcement of Labour's ruling power in Scotland, and hence some strengthening of the UK? But on this point he was already being carried away by his own public relations and self-image. Many of those he glad-handed up and down Edinburgh High Street then turned to the SNP. But such 'ingratitude' arose from a different dynamic, quite unforeseen by his lawyers and constitutional experts. It derived from an abruptly repoliticised national identity – and not from 'democratic deficit' and regional economic needs alone. No one had known quite when or how this would take place in Scotland. But now it had, and irreversibly. The land of supposed '90-minute patriots' had carried the game outside the stadium, ignored the final whistle, and intended playing on to a real conclusion.[11]

---

11   Around 1992 the SNP fundamentalist leader Jim Sillars had castigated Scottish voters for

New Labour has also been consistently deluded on this score by mistaken analogies with national and regional movements elsewhere in Europe. What all such comparisons ignore is the crucial historical differences between Britain and most other states within today's European Union. With the exception of Sweden and Ireland, these are post-war regimes founded on elaborate written constitutions making provisions for devolved government.

On one hand the acceleration of a rediscovered national identity; and on the other an essentially unreformed framework making no real provision for containing or adjudicating clashes with the new centre of power – these are the divergent parameters at work. One need only set such internal and external conditions together to see how things are likely to go. But it is surely these structural factors which are also being registered by the electoral slide against Labour in Scotland, at least to some extent. An electorate long inured to British attitudes and political customs is perfectly capable of sensing its unease and decline over such a crucial issue.

And at the same time, one disintegration is also being spurred on by another – the local decline-and-fall which it was for so long intimately associated with. This is the fall of the old and corrupt 'one-party state' in Labour's Western-Scottish fiefdom. Scotland's first electoral campaign in 1999 has been preceded by the open rebellion of its most important city boss. Patrick Lally, Glasgow's Labour Lord Provost (Mayor), sued his own party for illegitimate removal from office, as part of the clean-up campaign. Spin-doctoring stands helpless before that scale of damage.

Scotland does have a great deal to be ashamed of. Douglas Dunn writes in 'The Apple Tree' of how 'Men' (including a lot of Scots) '... moaned of Scotland that its barren air and soil couldn't so much as ripen an apple':

> I can hear their croaked whispers reproach the stern and wild of Alba,
> Naming our Kirk, our character, our coarse consent
> To drunken decency and sober violence,
> Our paradox of ways...

But it's not so bad, he concludes. Apples could ripen there like anywhere else – if only it would regenerate itself, and do more to unravel such paradoxes by its own efforts. The trouble is that 'Devolution' has only limited value for this. It isn't up to deep-identity concerns like 'codes of courtesy' and ways of describing love, or constructing a better-natured land. For that it's independence or nothing.

In another poem, 'The Dark Crossroads' (*Northlight*, 1988), Dunn describes being cornered in an awful English pub by a gang of suede-shoed gin-swillers, delighted at finding an uppity Jock on their turf. He curls up in the corner, trying

---

their inconstancy and fearfulness, by calling them '90-minute patriots': fervent in momentary enthusiasm, they would go home and vote British the day after, still lacking in the confidence to run things for themselves.

to ignore the jibes with 'dreams of the moss-trooper, the righteous horseman', and feeling a bit ashamed of himself for it. 'Unwanted thoughts, but unaccountable', he concludes, a dark parting of the ways which nobody would ever want to cross again. 'Unwanted ' is right, but they were never unaccountable. However, they will be brought to proper and civil account only via independence. The alternative can now only be the rediscovery of a re-dimensioned civic nationalism *on both sides of the Border*. It can't remain the hopeless preservation of a Union which, in spite of the Blair rhetoric, is rapidly losing all purpose and direction.

CHAPTER TWENTY-FOUR

Hooligans of the Absolute: Black Pluto's Door after 11 September

Opendemocracy

OCTOBER 2001

Aeneas was praying and holding on the altar when the prophetess started to speak: 'Blood relations of Gods, bel Trojan, son of Anchises, the way down to Avernus is easy.

Day and night black Pluto's door stands open. But to retrace your steps and get back to upper air, this is the real task and the real undertaking.'

> The Golden Bough, Seamus Heaney, from Virgil's *Aenead*,
> in Opened Ground: Poems 1966–96

Demons of Yesteryear

AS BRENDAN O'LEARY has pointed out in a recent contribution to *openDemocracy*, one of the key things about 11 September is that no-one claimed responsibility for the atrocities. They were an ontological statement, rather than propaganda of the deed for a particular nation or oppressed class. The world was meant to stand revealed by them: 'reality' as God's ultimate struggle against Satan, exemplified by the martyr-hijackers. In such a cosmic phantasmagoria, a new world war is nothing. The bigger the Satan, the harder will he eventually fall. The perpetrators – attacking a society already so strongly inclined towards belief in UFOs, moral absolutes and the Christian version of 'fundamentalism' – must have calculated that they could hardly fail.

Yet fail they will, for perfectly mundane (and profane) reasons having little to do with the atavistic theology of either side. O'Leary is surely right to call for normality: '*Be normal*... think about being normal as a way of standing up for yourself and your values'. Keep the head, in other words. The object of the criminals was socio-cultural decapitation. They will not be allowed to get away with it.

But one might also observe how the silence O'Leary underlines is connected to another absentee from the excitable post-11 September cacophony: *nationalism*. In my view the two silences are intimately related. In fact, it is possible to argue that one explains the other. The atrocities can also be seen as standing for a new strain of nationalism – an 'ethno-cosmic' liberation movement, as it were, so grandiloquent in its goal as to require no apology or explanation. No 'responsibility' need be claimed for the Creator's will: it has simply to be made manifest. However, over-reach also implies futility: blood relations '*of Gods*' do not exist, and no actual nation is either divine or 'chosen'.

Less than a decade ago, most ills of humanity and of the coming century were being laid at the door of a more conventional 'nationalism'. Bosnias were seen coming everywhere, unless Reason (in the Atlantic-Trademark sense) prevailed. Rationality was then thought to be taking up a new logo: 'globalisation'. Selfish ethnicity was perceived as getting in its way. Throughout the benighted 1990s, no op-ed page was complete without this daily dose of spectral anarchy and pandemonium.

Now the tune has abruptly altered. I suspect most people would be quite happy to have the demons of yesteryear back, rather than these Horsemen of the Apocalypse. There was, of course, plenty of real anarchy and pandemonium in the '90s, as the post-Cold War thaw got under way. It would be shameful to excuse or exonerate any of the ensuing disasters. However, a decade later, it should be acknowledged that many of these disasters have either been resolved, or are on the way towards an answer.

The fact is that, to give just some examples, at the end of an awful ten years, Milosevic is in jail in The Hague, while Mladic and Karadzic are on the run; democratic peace of a sort is at least holding in Northern Ireland; East Timor is independent; democratic South Africa may be on the way to becoming the continent's first great success story; Iran is evolving steadily away from post-1980 theocracy – and so on.

Exit to the Underworld

Actual nationalism leads to actual solutions, in other words, even if these are clumsy, painful and approximate. 'Ethnic cleansing' was a particularly noxious side-effect of that kind. Terroristic actions were often involved, and the cumulative 'body-count' far exceeded that of 11 September. But none of it meant 'the end of the world'. An abyss separates it from 11 September, which was intended to signal just that. Humanity was being called through 'Black Pluto's door' into an antique Underworld of theocratic absolutes and paranoid finality. The saintly criminals were seeking to provoke a 'War against Terrorism', which would inevitably employ counter-terrorism as one of its tactics, thus setting up an indefinite spiral of outrages. God's will can then emerge from the ruins. It would be a pity to oblige them.

As Virgil's prophetess said, strip-cartoon apocalypse is the easy bit: for that, her dark door does indeed stand ever open. The information technology linked to globalisation makes it more visible, and even more 'inviting' (at least in the sense of imaginable). It encourages an inebriation of the collective soul, much in evidence right after the events. The harder part is finding one's way back into the 'upper air' of normality, where the majority can reassert their non-apocalyptic visions of the future.

Yet I doubt if this will prove so difficult. It is simply not the case that any mysterious 'Clash of Civilisations' is at work behind this crisis, rooted in immemorially divergent values or world-views. I suspect that something more like the exact opposite may be true. These hooligans of the Absolute were compelled to act because they (or those behind them) know that there is, in the 'globalising' world, a steadily advancing majority *against* fundamentalist or spirit-world politics. Unless they strike now, it will soon be too late. The genesis of 11 September lay in mounting despair, rather than conviction of real political or social victory.

The crux of their dilemma lies in the Middle East. This is the zone in which secular nationalism has worked least well, for a particular combination of social and longer-range historical reasons. The inverse of that failure has been the promotion of a pre-modern religious world-view into the breach: Islam, linked in collective recollection to a distant era of Arab conquest and supremacy, became the stand-in for both democracy and nationalism. The fall-back upon this ersatz concoction has been a misfortune for the Muslim faith as well as the rest of us, the infidels. It promised earthly Heaven to the former and humiliating defeat for the latter. Neither delusion has the slightest chance of realisation. But they have already generated vast mayhem on their way to failure.

A World of One's Own

In his moving account of *The Arab Predicament*, Fouad Ajami concludes bitterly that 'It is easy to judge but hard to understand the ghosts with which people and societies battle, the wounds and memories that drive them to do what they do... The renaissance of civilisations is used as a weapon because so many in the Muslim world and the Third World as a whole feel they live in a world constructed and maintained by others...'

Nation-states have been the main instrument of the real battle, and in the last quarter of the 20th century *democratic* nationalism has become its commanding credo. These are the effective means by which people and societies are coming to live in a world 'constructed and maintained' by themselves. Globalisation stands for the achievement and consolidation of that movement, not for its dissolution.

By far the best overview of its impact upon the Middle East is the one given by Roger Owen in *State, Power and Politics in the Making of the Middle East*. Owen's study originally came out in 1992, but his second edition, published in 2000, contains a new closing section on 'The Remaking of the Middle Eastern Environment after the Gulf War'. This makes it startlingly clear why the Wahhabites and *al-Qa'eda* had to undertake some highly visible counter-action: they are on the retreat everywhere – even in their Afghan redoubt and Saudi Arabian citadel.

Owen observes that, 'In a global economy with a well-educated middle class and virtually open access to information from abroad, it does not seem likely that (the region's) stick and carrot approach to political management can be maintained indefinitely. Sooner or later, issues which have always been implicit in both religious and secular discourse will be made increasingly explicit. These include notions of citizenship, the rule of law, religious toleration and a regime legitimacy that comes not from appeals to security, ideology or achievement but from popular representation and a consensus among the nation at large.'

All this is death and anathema to God-struck super-nationalists like Osama bin Laden. However, the influence of such ideas might be stayed, or even turned, if a suitably aggressive Western crusade could be provoked – a palpably Satanic onslaught which might drive the emergent middle class back into the fundamentalist fold.

I agree with Fred Halliday's account of US imperialism: compared to its European predecessors, muddled (and sometimes well-meaning) hesitancy has been its keynote, rather than the Captain America portrayed in so many left-wing diatribes (*Observer*, 16 September, 'No Man is an Island'). This must have worried the Islamicists too. Their foe was falling down on the job, and needed some stiffening. Would a few thousand deaths in the heartland do the trick?

In short, the murderous onslaught of 11 September was aimed most significantly *at the people of the Middle East themselves*. This is well described in Murat Belge's article in this issue of *openDemocracy*. The American and other victims in New York and Washington were made sacrificial lambs for a re-conquest of Muslim opinion. From Nigeria to Indonesia, the latter accounts for something like a third of the world.

Across the European Union, people are familiar with the concept of 'democratic deficit'. But there is also such a thing as 'nationalism deficit' – and the Islamic part of the world has suffered from a devastating combination of both. Mundane if mistaken calculation suggested to the perpetrators that big numbers could compensate for these structural failings. Properly led, might they not still 'bring down' Godless capitalism, via prolonged and brutal struggle? After all, Muslim insurgency had witnessed Godless communism collapsing in the 1980s (and played a minor part in its fall).

It beats me why anyone should expect anything better from a character like Osama bin Laden. He may look like old images of Jesus Christ, but is the seventeenth son of a crooked construction tycoon. No-one who has encountered him saw a hawk of the desert – rather, a soft-handed fixer and couch ideologist. His slaughter funds flowed from an odious version of Arabian state-fostered capitalism, not from Heaven's will.

Presumably the unfortunates who committed suicide on 11 September believed in the Heavenly vision; whether their backers and organisers did, only time will show – and this would be best shown in a court-room, before the steady gaze of humanity at large. Dubious acts of vengeance in remote corners of Asia will not achieve it. What we do know is that the 'counter-crusaders' want to restore or impose conservative theocracy, male-authoritarian hierarchy, the supposed warrior-virtues of antiquity, and *shari'a* law.

Retracing the Steps

The great, liberating thaw of modernity will never be turned back by such acts of despair. Another interesting contribution to *openDemocracy*'s debate described the affirmation of American nationalism which has followed 11 September. John Down drove from San Francisco to Los Angeles, reflecting as he travelled on the 'civic religion' of a stricken country, and its response to 'violation by an unseen evil'. I am ashamed to see how bargain-basement anti-Americanism has surfaced in some analyses; but what accounts like Down's reveal is surely a kind of grandeur – a solidity and humanity of outraged reaction, made up of new vulnerability, determination, and a sense of everyday sacredness. He does end up fearful of the immense power behind such displays, in case it 'leads the US further down the path of retribution that may well sow the seeds of a future terrorism'.

But since he wrote, these fears have not materialised. Of course vengeance was in order after 11 September. It is needed here as it was after the Srebrenica massacre in 1995, or after Pinochet's murderous coup in Chile in 1973. However, very many voices have insisted, in the USA itself as well as amongst its allies, that justice is the only true revenge. After all, it has come (or is coming) in these other two cases.

To strike back instantaneously is a natural impulse. But it is surely more important that justice should be inexorable, final, and public. No preposterous 'War against Terrorism' could achieve anything like this. It will do little but cast all the proverbial black cats into one indiscriminate bag in a darkened room, and (as Down dreads) provoke further atrocities.

What the extra-American world must fear is not US *nationalism* but the debility of the American *state*. The constitution linked to their 'civic religion' is a crumbling anachronism, as last year's Presidential election demonstrated. Some sense of proportion must be retained here, I agree: Old Glory is less of an archaism than the United Kingdom, for instance, or the nostalgic debris of Saudi fundamentalism. Still, both George W. Bush's position and his Texan machismo depend upon it, and might in the event of further disasters attempt to prop themselves up by mobilising appeals to the holy-smoke Christian conservatism which it also embodies.

This is another reason why defence of the positive side of 'globalisation' should not be an American prerogative. In an early contribution to the *openDemocracy* forum, David Held called for a new international body dealing with terrorist outrages, 'modelled on the Nuremberg and Tokyo tribunals' and under United Nations control. The idea has been amplified by his joint essay with Mary Kaldor, New War, New Justice. They argue that this new body should be 'an International Court (where) the terrorists must be treated as criminals and not military adversaries'.

In one sense, few would dissent while thinking of *this* example of 'terrorism'. But we already have international tribunals like The Hague, which could surely be adapted to the case at issue. The trouble is that any sweeping new formula takes us straight back to the black cats in the dark room. For instance, would the us Air Force's mistaken strike at a Sudanese medical laboratory have qualified for a Court appearance? Should the Real IRA bombers of Omagh go there, rather than to courts in Dublin or Belfast? What about the Palestinian human bombs who preceded the 11 September atrocities? And the Israeli counter-terror meted out in retaliation? Tempting as the concept of a single new institutional riposte undoubtedly is, it may be over-influenced by the climate of the moment – the feeling that '11 September is a defining moment for humankind', as Held originally wrote.

But it was not. A miserable old world near the end of its tether was hitting back, using new technology to amplify a brazenly antediluvian message. The new world – currently paraphrased as Held and Kaldor's 'globalisation' – should not think in terms of short-cuts and overpowering ripostes. Time is on its side, recession or not. The combined forces of development, democracy and secular nationhood are on its side – much more evidently than over the decades of Cold War concluded in the 1980s.

For example, as far as the mundane configuration behind these bombings are concerned, every news reader and TV viewer over the entire globe has known for decades what the 'real problem' is: Palestine. The general malaise of the Middle East, and by extension of other Muslim-majority polities, has been consistently focused on and envenomed by the incurable abscess of the Israeli-PLO conflict. The Arab failures Ajami mourns, and the 'general tone of bitterness and despair' described by Owen, have in practice constantly returned to and fed off this particularly disgraceful stalemate. There have been of course plenty of other big regional problems as well: the Iran-Iraq war, Kuwait, Kurdistan, the Sudanese civil war, and now the downfall of the Afghan state. But none has the staying power and sheer ideological resonance of the Palestinian war.

Back to the Upper Air

This war represents an *impasse* of nationalisms, to which the sole solution will be the formation of a viable, secular and democratic Palestinian state. American power has both imposed and fuelled the conflict, and yet has shrunk from imposing the solution (out of the motives Fred Halliday has described). Yet such an advance was *overwhelmingly* in its own long term interest, as well as that of Palestinian Arabs and everyone else – except the Holy Warriors. Had it been achieved sooner, it is doubtful whether the September assaults would ever have happened. Nobody wants a new world order regulated by a US gendarme; but what is at issue here is a poisonous remnant of the old world order, festering on into the more liberal age of globalisation. An acceptable nation-state remains the only way forward.

The current number of *New Left Review* (No.10, July–August) is devoted mainly to Palestine, and Perry Anderson's 'Scurrying Towards Bethlehem' is still another overview and set of proposals for Palestinian nationhood. Writing not long before the September attacks, Anderson concluded that 'The dismal political history of the Arab world over the last half century gives little reason for thinking (a solution) is likely in the short-run.' He saw small chance then of the Bush Presidency shifting its stance, or of 'the larger submission of the Middle East' ceasing to prolong the West Bank paralysis.

But since 11 September, something of a new start has been forced. Colin Powell's State Department has found it intolerable to preside over another round of the interminable feud, while simultaneously struggling to concert its new anti-terrorist strategy. Does the just-announced Bush policy in favour of a Palestinian state give us hope of a more permanent answer?

The general point here is that a meaningful response to Holy Terror lies upon this plane: real undertakings in the upper air of a nation-state world, which is still striving for traditional goals within the more fluid and liberating medium of the global market-place. As for the latter, the solid will go on melting into air, and bear the most heavenly ecstasies of religious fervour away with it. Its single unconscionable freedom – free trade, however naked and shameless – will continue to nestle, settle and establish connections everywhere, creating still more massive and colossal productive forces than have all preceding generations together, and enforcing the social and political constitutions required by the new empire of civil society. The true 'sorcerer of modernity,' it conjures up the power of future worlds, not the nether worlds of antique faith and superstition.

CHAPTER TWENTY-FIVE

Gordon Brown: Bard of Britishness

From the Book of the Same Name

2007

THE 1ST OF MAY 2007 will be a significant date. Modern Britain dates from 1 May 1707, when the Treaty of Union between the English and Scottish parliaments came into effect. This created both the United Kingdom state and much of the British Empire to be. Three centuries later the latter has disappeared and the former is in some trouble, in Northern Ireland, Wales and Scotland as well as Iraq. One would have thought the Tercentenary an appropriate moment for both thought and reconsideration, whether celebratory, critical, or both together.

But as historian Tom Devine has commented, practically nothing is being planned by either Westminster or the recently resurrected Scottish parliament at Holyrood. There will be some academic events and publications, but nothing *public,* as if despairing officialdom had decided that the indifference of general opinion were best left undisturbed. Since the Millennium commemoration farce, has the cadaver grown wary of farther disappointments?

But another historian, Kevin Sinclair, has pointed to political motives:

> ... the timing of the anniversary – which falls just two days before next year's Scottish parliamentary elections – may have rendered any public programme of commemoration a 'political no-no'.[1]

Deeply unpopular in 1707, the Union has come to be challenged again in recent times, and is currently sustained by the rule of a single political party, New Labour – the party whose hold over both Scotland and Wales is likely to be broken, or mortally threatened, by these elections. Hence, the prevalent apathy about even signalling a great historical moment. New Labour rule was only just kept going by the previous devolved elections in 2003, and it would be worse than embarrassing for defeated parties to face a possibly defeated (or reconstructed) Union state.

There has been one exception, however. Early in 2006 New Labour's Chancellor of the Exchequer, Gordon Brown, embarked upon a highly public and vocal campaign of Unionist rebirth and justification. The importance of this is of course amplified by Brown's position as heir-apparent to Leader Tony Blair, who has announced he will be standing down as Leader of the Labour Party and

---

1   Paul Dalgamo, 'No Plans to Mark Acts of Union, *Sunday Herald*, 23 April 2006, p.12

Prime Minister some time before the summer of 2007. Prediction becomes more hazardous than usual amid the crumbling structures of today's realm. It is possible (probable, some would argue) that the heir will never inherit, because over-attachment to vanishing imagined communities (like his own Party) caused him to wait too long.

On the other hand, whoever does succeed Blair will have to confront the issues raised in Brown's high-profile campaign: what he calls 'Britishness' is undoubtedly in trouble, and no Premier will be able to avoid rallying calls and identity antics of some sort. The London bombings in July 2005, the stalling of the Northern Ireland Peace Process, the aftermath of the Iraqi War, cynicism about the Special Relationship with America, dire uncertainties over the European Union, mounting restlessness over 1998s devolution of power to the Scots and the Welsh: all these will compel ideological, as well as economic, initiatives.

There's the rub: since the former Establishment failed for so long to reform the 1707 central state, no successor can avoid trying to half-reform *everything*. The UK's *ancien regime* prided itself on sensible, piecemeal evolution, to the point of disastrously over-playing this hand, in the circumstances that have followed the end of the Cold War. The new climatic environment of globalisation demanded something less piecemeal, a revolution, rather than ad hoc adjustments to such an archaic polity and foreign policy. Brown does understand the need, and has set out a ghost response – a fantasy nation suitable to the new age, which at the same time won't upset the ancient one too much. He proposes the selective resurrection of a Gladstonian-liberal England, without Disraeli's British-imperial bullying.

Unfortunately he has had to do so in the middle of a Disraelian war. Unable to denounce the latter (following the lead of his compatriot, the late Robin Cook), for reasons of Party and State, he has had to support it. Renovation of the out-of-date, collapsing state will have to wait. In the meantime, what else can be undertaken except renovation of the nation itself: *a new people* braced for the future?

Possessed of more imagination than most of his colleagues, Brown has been capable of at least rising to the level of Bertold Brecht's 1953 anti-hero, that Writers Union Secretary who urged redoubled efforts on the East Germans in the name of Party and Socialism. The poet commented:

Would it not be easier
In that case for the government To dissolve the people
And elect another?[2]

At the time of writing, nobody knows if Brown will be privileged to carry the election process forward from No. 10 Downing Street. However, no representative of ancient regime survival can now avoid something like it. Great Britain is conservable only through deeper cultural and ideological alteration, led from

---

2 'The Solution', in *Bertold Brecht: Poems 1913–1956*, 'Last Poems, 1953–56', Methuen, 2000, p. 440.

above by one or another Svengali. That is, some stage re-enchanter equipped with contemporary powers of suggestion and media influence.[3] Otherwise the centre is unlikely to hold. The key issue for the devolved elections and parliaments in 2007 lies here. Study of Brown's new crusade is a useful way of seeing what may be at stake.

From Keir Hardie to Svengali

Looking back over Gordon Brown's 30-year political trajectory, it may be useful to recall some features of his initiation into politics, with the publication of the *Red Paper on Scotland*. The book came out in 1975, after the period of nationalist break-through in Scotland, the same year as Harold Wilson's referendum on taking Britain into the European Economic Community, and following on some notable working-class agitation (displayed on the front cover the Upper Clyde shipyard occupation). Its editor was then the elected Student Rector of Edinburgh University; and both the man and his book seemed expressions of the restless, dissident spirit of the '60s, persisting into the '70s. It burst upon us after so many exciting indicators of change and new times.

So, naturally, its effect was great, and confirmatory: it seemed to unite the rediscovery of a long-interred nationalism with positive general ideas about the future, and suggested that the Scots might be a nation again, *and* equipped with a meaning capable of embracing the greater causes and visions of the times. That is, of a world still struggling out of the stale paralysis of the Cold War, and seeking new turnings. In 1975 it was naturally assumed that new kinds of Socialism were bound to find a voice there, as part of the rejuvenation. Such hopes informed the whole book, and notably Gordon Brown's 'Introduction'.

To this day, much of Brown's lingering Leftish aura rests upon a folk-memory of the *Red Paper*. This is why it may be important to recall that, whether behind the times or ahead of them, its left-wing and anti-nationalist assumptions were mistaken *at the time*. The entire *Red Paper* project was to be cruelly betrayed only four years later. In 1979, utterly different trends were to find a far louder voice, and a more decisive political will. With the Winter of Discontent, the failure of the first Home Rule referendum in 1979, and Mrs Thatcher's ascent to power, that will began to impose itself. It is ceasing to do so at present, but only after a 'generation' in the classical sense, an effective life-time of successful authority that has fostered assumptions and social instincts unimaginable to most in 1975. The prophetic fanfare turned almost at once into an elegy – indeed, almost an unintended funeral oration, the interment of impossible dreams.

---

3 A person who, with evil intent, tries to persuade another to do what is desired: 'a crafty Svengali who lures talented people with grand promises yet gives them little lasting operational authority' (Chris Welles). ETYMOLOGY: After Svengali, the hypnotist villain in the novel *Trilby* by George du Maurier, *American Heritage Dictionary*, 2000.

Many commentators have drawn an analogy between Brown's idea of his Party, and some inherited traditions of the Scottish Presbyterian Kirk. He does often speak of the former in terms reminiscent of the latter: indestructibility, bedrock, ineffaceable spiritual drive, a popular core 'returned to' in times of trial – and so on. This may sound vaguely reassuring to non-Scottish audiences, but is in truth somewhat alien to the instincts of a movement founded on the much looser, disparate inheritance of English Nonconformity and Methodism. The *Red Paper* was 'national' in a sense quite distinct from the SNP's ideology of political separation, as well as more recent notions of ethnicity. And the Presbytery based vision of 1975 was forced to confront an authentic time of trial – worse, a fundamental defeat of most of its assumptions and quasi-divine dreams. In that perspective, as 'Thatcherism' took charge of UK society and merged into the wider rising tide of US-led globalisation, little but ruins would soon be left. 'Success' lay elsewhere; on the other side of a Devil's terrain whose temptations would in any case alter its meaning.

Brown's own political success had been predicted from the days of his tenure as Student Rector in Edinburgh. But no-one then thought that such a career would be one of skilful ruin-management – that he would become the Jeeves of Great Britain's last days, a courtier of self-abasement, sleaze, insanely false pretences, failed reform and neo-imperial warfare. Unfortunately, this managerial fate couldn't help underwriting certain negative aspects of the Kirk inheritance. The latter combines both democratic and authoritarian elements. Individual souls had their say in the collective disposition, certainly; but the efficacy of such input lies in submission to the over-mastering will of God, and leadership's primary duty remains decipherment of His awesome power. He who reads the runes correctly takes on something of their authority – standing in for the Deity, an autocrat until some new prophet is elected.

Because *actual* election remains pretty difficult in the British system, Brown was effectively choosing to help that system down cemetery road. Because the runes of the '80s were so calamitous for the Old Left, the great abilities and personal charisma of the former Student Rector were to be deployed in a prolonged holding operation against what his Presbyterian ancestors would have diagnosed as the enemy forces of materialism: a 'way of the world' that had defeated not only Communism, but many of the assumptions of the Keynesian and social-democratic ideology so prevalent until the mid-'70s.

Such straitened survival was capable only of feigned rebirth. So the Socialism of the 'Introduction' was to re-emerge in a practical form worse than castrated. Losing the baby was bad enough; but behind the 'Third Way' curtains of the labour ward, something far worse was happening. A monster was smuggled in to take its place: 'New Labour' may have been shown proudly to the cheering crowds; but the creature was to burgeon into the prematurely aged infant of New *Britain*.

The Monster in the Manger

The *Red Paper* ideology had imagined a symbiosis of Socialism and Britishness. However, losing the former meant that the *British* ingredient was destined to grow ever more important.

In 1997 an effective over-arching belief system was urgently needed, above all by a movement by then unused to office, and with so much ground (and self-confidence) to recover. Party survival itself prompted this compensation, rather than popular belief. Over the same period most surveys have detected waning rather than reviving 'Britishness'. But still, a declining or contested *nationalism* offered (or seemed to offer) a far stronger chance of redemption than a socialism ailing unto death all-round the globe.

That's surely why Brown, the 'Party man' who took flight as a left-wing prophet, was to end up as today's strident UK nationalist. The Scottish Icarus felt his wings melting away even as he assumed office, and understood how the ungrateful way of *this* world might grant him almost no *terra firma* to return to. None (that is) without the restored or reconstructed 'greatness' of Britain. Hence service of the imperial state-inheritance, and improvement of its estate with minor changes, was the sole way forward. Or so dour realism seemed to indicate. A specific combination of Party vanity and self-confidence made him feel he could take the monster over. Unfortunately; it worked the other way round. The antique inheritance took possession of him. The result was a chain of compromises that have transformed him into the fulsome bard of a 'Britishness' none of his 1975 supporters dreamed of.

In mid-January 2006 Brown launched the latest round of the Save Britain campaign at a specially convened day conference in London.[4] His keynote address to this sold-out event was warmly acclaimed, and widely noticed by the media. The British nation would be safe in his hands, he reassured the (mainly) Southern intelligentsia. However, it would be safer still if a different, more patriotic spirit could only be infused into politics – a spirit of more self-conscious and positive patriotism, in which citizens flew the flag in their front gardens, and were given an annual British National Day to enjoy. It was no longer enough for Britain to just be there, like the old Crown and habitual Constitution that had prevailed back in 1975. Nowadays, a positive worship of these things is required, as in the USA, and we must learn to impart their values in school class-rooms and swearing-in ceremonies.

Another way of analysing the project is as a generalisation of Northern Ireland Protestant attitudes. Of course, among the latter there has long been an exag-

---

4   '*Who Do We Want To Be?*' *The Future of Britishness*, Imperial College, London, 14 January 2006. Accounts of the event can be found at: www.fabian-society.org.uk/, documents including Brown's speech www.fabian-society.org.uk/press_office. Also in the Fabian Review: the Britishness Issue, January 2006.

gerated emphasis on 'Britishness', as a form of communal self-defence against
the threat of Irish ethno religious domination. The 1916 blood-sacrifice for Irish
independence continues to be answered by a litany of Ulster Protestant war losses,
commemorations and ultra-loyalism. In the past, many main-island Brits were
suspicious of such extremism, seeing it is another oddly Irish phenomenon.

In Brown's new patriot-country, Britons had better forget all that. The tail
won't just occasionally wag the British dog, it's destined to *become* the dog itself.
Presbyterians, Catholics, Anglicans, Muslims, Buddhists and no-hope Atheists:
today all find themselves solemnly summoned to behave more like Paisleyites
– naturally without renouncing their previous *personae*. Many instinctively
rebel at the prospect. But they're behind the Brownite times. Have they not
understood that all such *personae* are tagged for rebirth within the New Patriotism, to be transported onwards by its multi-culturalist enthusiasm? ·

In this perspective, 'multi-culturalism' means something like: 'Be a whatev-
er-you-like and welcome here... as long as you pass Sir Bernard Crick's British
Citizenship test, fly the flag in the front garden, and go to war when requested'.[5]
A theatre of transacting minorities and nationalist contestations, played out
upon a contracting if not collapsing stage: such is the UK *société du spectacle* to
which the Queen's subjects were being formally invited in January.

Like the formal Empire and Commonwealth before it, Socialism has been
indecently given the last rites and had some concrete poured on top by Blair,
leaving 'Britain' even more naked than previously. Yet this nudity calls its meaning
into question more cruelly, if not terminally. Is that Little England knocking
timidly on the back door? Set the dogs on him at once. Yet a new call is required to
keep the wretch at bay: the glamour of backwardness must somehow be restored.
Enter the Magus from West Fife.

Nothing was more revealing on this front than the almost total absence of
monarchy from the Fabian January debates. Not so long ago, the Windsor Crown
was most people's idea of uniting Britain: the actual family that held the metaphorical one together. This was particularly important for the English, whose
narrower nationality had for so long been sublimated into a wider imperial view.
For them, the concreteness of Royalty voiced many of the emotive aspects of
nationalism, without posing awkward questions of identity and exclusion. Yet
now it had vanished from the scene of renewed Britishness, as somehow *passe* and
irrelevant – replaced by indifference, rather than an aggressive republicanism.[6]

---

5   Sir Bernard, an 'expert on British citizenship', was asked by Home Secretary David
    Blunkett (an earlier pupil) to think up a plausible 'compulsory test' for incomers seeking
    residence. It was at once labelled the 'Britishness test', and had the aim of making new
    Britons feel 'meaningful and celebratory' rather than just bureaucratically accepted.
    BBC World News, 10 September 2002.
6   Among the sessions I attended the subject only came up once, in a discussion of symbols
    and icons of the new-British identity, where a passing reference to 'getting rid of it'

Brown's ideological contraption is worse than no answer to the British dilemma: indeed it amounts to a cure via self-conscious exacerbation of the ailment itself. His weird mixture of sermon and us-style public relations hype may have been aimed initially at young British Muslims like the Leeds bombers of July 2005. But without reassuring the latter, it will end by annoying and disconcerting everybody else, including the vast English majority. The latter's acquiescent or puzzled silence remains vital to such an ideological venture. If they respond at all, it is likely to be with derision or hostility. The new Leader of the Conservative Party, David Cameron, put it rather well in the wake of Brown's recent outbursts of bad poetry: but, he objected...' we're not like that. *We don't do flags!'*

Pantomimes and Myths

Cameron was right, but irrelevant for the new show – other features of which he strongly backs, with his own rhetoric of novelty. Be a bit more *radical,* Cameron: enough of that dawdling in memory lane. Nothing the Conservative Party is currently advertising seems likely to save them from Neo-Patriotism.

The point here was in part occluded by the stage management of the January event; yet it must have struck some observers. There was something 'foreign' about it all, in an ancient but recognisable Anglo-British sense, something obsessive and strident about such a newly-discovered passion for things previously ignored, or taken for granted. Nor was this apprehension mistaken, however the effective content of 'foreign' here was actually *Scottish.* Brown's new fake Britishry is at bottom as Scottish as the old *Red Paper* had been. For, of course, the Scots and the Welsh *do* 'do flags', like the Republicans and the Protestant Irish. Their histories have configured them that way, a way closer to ordinary international practice than that of the Anglo-British majority.

The latter now finds itself chided and told what's good for it by a minority of know-it-all Scots, *and* cheered on by other vexed immigrant groups in the name of multi-culturalism. The latter would naturally like to remodel Britishness, in order to lessen discrimination,   and make principle replace racism. But as many know all too well, 'principle' is rather over-abstract for a *mentalite* so famously empirical and concrete. So can't it be clothed, and fortified, by new techniques of technicolour projection, by a British ideology made to healthier,

---

generated prolonged applause. The Queen's 80th birthday came along not long after, and Madeleine Bunting pointed out in *The Guardian* (21 April) that the low-key festivities were preludes to something else Elizabeth II's departure and: '... a constitutional crisis waiting to happen: the relationship between sovereign, church and state, which the Queen has managed to largely steer clear of public debate, would come under the bewildered glare of the global media, and who knows how it would fall apart under that kind of scrutiny?'

more enlightened orders? What would be wrong with such a reconstructed identity, fit for the multicultural times?

All that's wrong is that it rests upon a mistaken notion. Individuals and (with more difficulty) groups or parties may of course reconsider outworn ideas and argue over new ones. But *identities* cannot be confected in this way – and least of all by clever dodges and new-baked rituals or conventions. Only New Labour's odd fusion of narcissism and despair could have manufactured such a phony answer to a real need. What Frankenstein-Brown has done is to exploit the semi-conscious, taken-for-granted nationalism of the English with a specious formula, a made-to-order patriotic uniform stitched together from bits of the Anglo-British (imperial) past and misunderstood fragments of the United States.

But an identity is a cultural body, not simply clothing and spectacle. It has been made – or more accurately, has made itself – through societal struggles and experienced repetitions over quite long periods of time and via violent episodes like revolutions and warfare. It is the customs of living in common, dependent upon habits and 'unthinking' predispositions – the societal equivalent of 'instincts', built up over generations.

And of course such attitudes constitute every majority, even if the latter has emerged out of past or forgotten minorities and conflicts.[8] Within this contested sphere of discourse, 'minorities' has become a systematically misunderstood term. It tends to mean recent 'ethnic' or immigrant communities, groups in need of support or help, so they can 'fit in' better to the host culture, as well as succeed in their own terms.

Yet this myopic perspective does justice to neither the host nor the new additions. It disregards the majority story – as in the ceaseless platitudes about conflicts being the 'problem' of the host, rather than of immigrants. And it simultaneously neglects the creative force of the less-integrated cultures and (more important) their long-range persistence, and their organic effects upon both hosts

---

8   In this respect, much of Brown's mistake can be seen as derived from the popular misuse of Eric Hobsbawm and Terence Ranger's *Invented Traditions*, an attack on modern nationalism that systematically occluded all aspects not 'invented' by intellectuals and politicians. It ignored everything carried forward in other ways, and fostered a vogue for dismissal and self-conscious substitution. The issue has been recently examined by Eelco Runia in his essay 'Presence', in *History and Theory* No. 45 (February 2006), where he points out that *most* of the past is borne forward through 'metonymy' – the 'transfer of presence' that then makes invention or re-invention possible, and effective. The past is a 'stowaway' rather than a self-conscious, ticket-paying passenger who may be summoned to the intellectual bridge, reprimanded, and instructed to attire himself differently or (occasionally) jump overboard. Were this not so, humans would never be able to 'spring surprises on themselves', or suffer discontinuities, lapses and existential uncertainty. In this sense, rather than a renaissance, New Britishness may turn out to be the fag-end of a '90s ideological fashion, maggot-ridden mutton posturing as the spring lamb of globalisation.

and states. In such struggles, a new, changed or hybrid 'identity' is invariably making its way forward, entering the lists, as it were, for some future nationalism. But that only repeats the point, of course: neither side is likely to recompose itself according to Fabian Society or other blueprints.

It may be useful to remember some other examples: modern French identity is often regarded as an inherited majoritarian family of attitudes, combining the rigid universalism of some siblings with the racist comportment of others. Yet much of this contradictory identity itself has been the generational deposit of a Corsican family, who for two thirds of the 19th century imposed itself upon a highly variegated spectrum of ethnic and linguistic communities: the most, rather than the least, heterogeneous 'nation-state' in Europe. *Le chauvinisme* (1830s onwards) and then *le nationalisme* (from the 1870s) were progenies of Napoleonism, military conscription and incessant preparations for war, rather than simply of the Revolution itself. And in the course of this process, *La République* became fetishised into a secular (anti-clerical) nationalism, as part of such later struggles.

Something analogous took place in the post-Civil War USA. Both the sancti-fication of what was (even then) an archaic polity, the Union's takeover of Southern militarism, and the extension of reborn Christianity were all to become pillars of an emergent great power: untouchable blessings of the state that had found itself compelled to incorporate the Southern Confederacy.[9] And the active function of one minority or other in exaltation of these ideologies has been a constant aspect of the process – nowhere more clearly than under the rule of President George W. Bush.

None of Brown's New-British national identitarians show the slightest aware-ness of just how bizarrely parochial and inimitable is the 'patriotism' they have selected for imitation. They have taken Neo-Conservatism at its own valuation, in fact, seeing little since 2000 but the manifestation of the timeless constitu-tional values of 1776 and after – now imagined as not only universal, but virtu-ally one flesh with the Friedmanite capitalism of the '80s and '90s.

---

9   The results are described in Daniel Lazare's *The Frozen Republic: How the Constitution is Paralyzing Democracy* (1996). More recently, Bertram Wyatt-Brown has analysed other quaint aspects of American nationalism in 'The Ethic of Honor in National Crises: the Civil War, Vietnam, Iraq and the Southern Factor', *Journal of the Historical Society*, Vol v, No.4, 2005. None of these are ever referred to in Brown's pro-American sermons. He has either failed to read, or ignored, devastating accounts like Anatol Lieven's *America, Right or Wrong: the Anatomy of American Nationalism* (2005). What surfaces in such perorations is a kind of universal ghost, US Patriotism masquerading as universal model -on which of course an equally purged and New UK phantom must then dance attendance.

'Self-Colonisation'

The real point of the *Red Paper* was to choose the wrong nation. Its 'introduction' was a conjuring trick, reassuring both nationalists and anti-nationalists by claiming *both* peoples and countries were equally chosen. But in fact its Editor was going with the mainstream – or rather, with what *seemed to be the mainstream* from the 1980s up to the year 2000 (I will come back to this point later on). 1975's Editorial 'Introduction' strove to project a noble synthesis between Socialism and Nationalism. Brown figured there as a synthesiser of ideas, rather than an originator. But, it must be recognised, a synthesiser of a very imaginative and generous sort. There was a potential for leadership even then implicit in his willingness to seek and stress positive elements.

However, this was leadership of a special kind. Brown appears as an authoritarian 'moderator', in fact a strong-minded reconciler of ideas and initiatives in a sense more old-Presbyterian than New Left. Naturally the synthesis had a strong emphasis upon ideas about 'democratic-popular' transformation and socialism. I use Gramsci's famous phrase deliberately, for he was one of the dominating background influences in the performance. The transformation was envisaged as 'workers' control', and a Scottish Assembly was required (he wrote) partly 'to allow the framing of distinctly Scottish policies to meet social needs and requirements'. But then, and much more importantly, as well as 'reinvigorating the Labour Movement from the workplace and community outwards', it had to 'force the pace towards socialism in Britain as a whole' (p. 19). This would also 'give Scottish socialists a chance to lead and influence other regions and other countries', presumably by showing them how, in this way, nationalism could be subsumed or transformed into social or communitarian terms.

None the less, the collection was noticeably, if somewhat chaotically, open to Scottish nationalist and even 'fringe' opinion. It was in that positive sense eclectic, informed by a positive spirit of inquiry rather than just by hopes of compromise or deal-making among the different encampments of the Left. And, of course, this is what has kept it alive at some deeper level, however much the influence has now been betrayed by Brown's great-nation strobe lights and delusions about America.

In Eelco Runia's terms (mentioned above) there is still a 'stowaway' there, whom one would like one day to welcome back on deck. But he will have to find a different crew, sailing in another latitude, who have in turn forgotten all about the rejuvenated yet stable United Kingdom of Blair-Brown, homeland of the Welfare State, Liberty and Model-T parliamentarism.

By the time Brown reached office, Britain was already something different: an ageing Sorcerer's apprentice, pedalling harder to keep abreast of a cleansed and corrected age – indeed, claiming loudly to be its standard-bearer, rather than a mere camp-follower. Brown found leadership power at last, but in this crazily upside-down universe, as the champion of deregulation and privatisation, borne forward on a swelling tide of pro-American rhetoric. His first important step in 1997 was to abandon control of interest rates to the Bank of England – that is, to the City of London, formerly the deadly foe of all Labour governments.

The aim was of course, in the *argot* of that moment, to render London more fit and competitive, in the new world of 'globalised' capital and commerce. The corroded old iron of British Socialism emerged from Thor's new forge as alien steel – an unduly self-important side-kick of the Neo-conservatism reigning in Washington, DC.[10]

Such captaincy brought with it novel forms of allegiance and subjection. The Blair-Brown government was stepping into a train already formed in this sense, the willing 'subjects' of Clinton, then of George W. Bush. Earlier empires had rested on invasion, colonisation, and crude forms of punishment and coercion. By contrast, the US post-1989 imperium relies on self-colonisation. Typically, this rests upon some calculation of national interests normally aimed at 'fitting in', via the provision of credentials of commercial openness, entrepreneurial liberty and possible profitability. In the *huis clos* of American-led globalisation, such servitude was to be generalised.

But no servitude is likely to compare with that of former masters. After all the latter know servility from the inside, and are scheming not to set up a new country but to renovate an old one. In this way both shame and honour have been easily transcended, relegated by the imperative of survival. And this was, unfortunately, an existential enterprise in which the Scots were all too likely to distinguish themselves: who else had such a long history of self-colonisation, going back to the early 18th century, or even before?

It would be mistaken to single out Brown in this context, as if he had been particularly important or influential in the great climate change. His present-day eminence sometimes provokes this kind of accusation on the Left, voiced in sententious moral judgements about how he and Blair have 'betrayed' the principles of 1975, or even those of Keir Hardie and other founding fathers. Well perhaps they did. But then, so have most others, in most comparable countries, for good reasons as well as bad. Did he (and we) give up on Socialism; or was it not rather that Socialism betrayed us, because of certain inherent or incurable defects, or at least limitations?

Both versions have some plausibility, but neither (it seems to me) should be used to condemn Gordon Brown particularly.[11] No: another tragedy in the Greek

---

10 Just how really important can be gauged from the index of Francis Fukuyama's most recent recantation of earlier views, *After the Neocons: America al the Crossroads*, Profile Books 2006. There are precisely three mentions of Britain in its 226 pages, one in a footnote, the other two in a single paragraph on pages 96–7 (and one of these is only a list of side-kicks). Having paid so little attention to London so far, there will of course be even less need to heed such a camp-follower 'at the crossroads'.

11 I have tried to deal with the question in terms of the wider framework of Marxism's

sense was unfolding in this turn of events. And it still has some way to run. This seems to me both much deeper and more intimate than anything related to the vicissitudes of Socialism alone. It was *national* in essence.

In the most convincing general panorama of post-'89 so far produced, Yergin and Stanislaw's *Commanding Heights* (1998), it is shown how extensive and immediately irresistible were the general economic shifts that carried away the *Red Paper* world. But both in the *Red Paper* and in the mind-set of its presiding spirit a crucial weakness, or limitation, was revealed by their response to the earthquake. *Their* commanding heights were both inherently treacherous, and taken too much for granted. And this was much more serious than correct political attitudes towards Labour's old 'Clause 4', or the general retreat from Keynesianism. Neal Ascherson put his finger neatly on it in an *Observer* article. 'There were gaps in the Red Paper', he notes:

> There is almost nothing about Britain as such. This is striking, given the Labour Government's effort to package devolution as part of some wider programme to democratise British institutions (5 November 2000).

It certainly was. But I think the point can be taken even farther. What was being taken for granted was simply the British Constitution and State. It was assumed, notably by the Editor, that these *must* go on providing a perfectly reliable (and indeed the only possible) wider framework for any new Scottish democracy to function within. The passage of time has convinced Brown, belatedly, that the 'institutions' alone aren't sufficient. But instead of getting rid of them via reform, he thinks that the nation itself should be re-forged to fit.

In Brecht's famous sense, it's time to elect 'a new people': a more self-conscious nation worthy of the inherited robes. As Brown's current campaign for New Labour's leadership has illustrated, a reanimated British nationalism has become far more important than electoral reform. In fact, democratisation is becoming a threat to the American-style 'patriotism' now urgently needed to prevent farther decline and break-up.

Instead, an up-dated all-British nationalism is needed, to keep self-respecting self-colonisation going. The Sorcerer's Apprentice can't just tag along: he has some requirements of his own. And Scots like Brown know what they're talking about, in this sense. Looking back over the 30-year period in which Scottish and Welsh nationalism resurfaced politically, and the Ulster-Protestant equivalent acquired sufficient force to arrest the Peace Process, there is no doubt what the dominant strain of nationality-politics has been. The periphery may have got its assorted acts together enough to influence UK development. But incomparably the most determined, ruthless, militarised and life-or-death form of nationalism has throughout been the *British* one.

---

origins and development, in 'History's Postman', a review of Jacques Attali's *Karl Marx; au, l'esprit du monde, London Review of Books*, vol. 28, no. 2, 26 January 2006.

New-immigrant intellectuals have often argued that 'British values' (cleaned up a bit) have to be OK, and that British support for the Iraq War, ant-Terrorist hysteria and creeping authoritarianism are passing aberrations. Old-immigrant culture tells a different story, and not in Ireland alone: Iraq *is* the deeper current. And unfortunately; 'aberrations' can be detected more easily in the glib postures of a half-hearted multiculturalism, striving to measure and dole out just enough loyalty to keep Westminster in business. Which implies *not* reforming the foundations of the State, or UK *ancien regime*.

1975's mistaken assumptions had another in tow, which has proved deadly for the Left. A basic meme of modern Britishness is the idea that constitutional politics and ideas are essentially secondary, or 'superstructural', for socialists, or even for democrats. That is, they may be 'a good thing' (etc.), which wise reform will eventually find time to take care of (and so on). But they are never urgent enough to be tackled *now.* They are not necessary conditions of successful social, economic and cultural or other policies – those things deemed the 'real stuff' of politics.

In other words, there is no tradition of popular or radical *constitutional* agitation active here at all, no conception of the existing constitutional order as a standing offence or a humiliation, a form of repression or obfuscation intolerable in any new or improved social order. After the defeat of Chartism in the 1840s, a general acceptance of the endlessly liberal and adaptable nature of the United Kingdom state came to inform left-wing parties and most other movements, except in Ireland. The Women's Suffrage Movement was another important exception, but one which proved containable.

In 1975 there was in the *Red Paper* very little indication that the new Scottish restlessness was going to be different in this sense. The only real opposition on that score was coming from the Nationalists. But their claims were conventional in another way: a demand for national recognition *as such,* regardless of the nature of Anglo-British hegemony. The Scottish National Party was an elderly political movement, not much younger than the British Labour Party. It had inevitably been moulded by an older era, that of anti-colonial agitation and achievement, widely successful following World War II. But of course, the ideology of that period provided a very ill-fitting uniform for a non-colonised society seeking statehood, in very different historical circumstances.

As for the various Red contingents, these also clung to the conventional idea of socio-cultural change as not just coming first, but being a sufficient condition of all farther changes. The 1975 Editor's sole critical allusion to matters constitutional was the admission that British identity was a bit 'demoralised'. The implication was plainly that morale would be boosted by the book's various suggestions (once a properly revitalised, new Labour government got itself elected). So the fate of *Red Paper's* ideological venture was not determined solely by the misfortunes of Socialism after 1979, alarming as these were, but by what one can call the 'medium', or perhaps the vehicle, through which the Brownian synthesis was to come about. That is, the United Kingdom polity itself.

As a matter of fact, the United Kingdom state was at that time already launched upon an ever steeper downward slide into the present, where something far worse than 'demoralisation' is now disclosed to British subjects every day. Disclosed, and grotesquely parodied, as in the recent speeches and projects of today's Chancellor (and tomorrow's likely Premier). In this sense 1979 was to mark a decisive turn of the screw in that process. It was not just about defeating the Left, or the post-war welfarist consensus.

The world of the *Red Paper* on Scotland was indeed carried away by the rapids from that date onwards. But the mushroom-growth of Thatcherism was also to be the final confirmation of what I think one can call 'redemption politics' – that is, the rooted, unshakeable idea that the vital goal is to redeem or save the United Kingdom inheritance. 'Britain' must be kept going, *and* kept Great, or as Great as possible, as the prerequisite – and in a sense the meaning – of all other social, economic or cultural aspirations.

Regrettably, such redemptionism has become a common creed of all minorities trying to negotiate (or re-negotiate) their own rights or position within the foundering state. New immigrants perceive its supposed non-ethnicity as a bulwark of their own new roles; old minorities like the Welsh, the Scots and the Ulster Protestants see it as conservation of existing stakes and privileges, especially for the Left.

In the new globalising order, British nationalism was by now subordinate, trusting pathetically in a 'special relationship' with the new hegemons of world order. Since everyone else was becoming subordinate as well, did this really matter? The new network of *dependencia* at once evolved its own hierarchy: Capo, *sub-capi* and simple soldiers of the line. Ex-greatness entitled Britons to claim a priority of place among these sub-lieutenants: the land of unswerving entrepreneurialism and competitiveness, loudly (and where required, militarily) devoted to the new order. As the biggest traditional minority, it was quite natural for the Scots to take the front line – all the way from Niall Ferguson's vibrant eulogies of the New US Order, to Brown's aspirations for satrapy leadership.[12]

There still appeared no alternative. And if there was no escape route for British nationalism, there could be none for Scottish. The Scots were too profoundly inured to self-colonisation. How could they now question a British choice so similar to what their ancestors had opted for, in 1707? After three centuries of it, they understood the terrain better than the English majority. No nuance of creep, crawl and slither was unfamiliar to them: how to transform abasement into 'proud' assertion of National Identity devoted to the Greater Good of somebody else, in the imagined – if often postponable – long-term interests of all.

---

12 See Stephen Howe's incisive account of Ferguson's ravings in 'An Oxford Scot at King Dubya's Court', on www.opemocracy.net, 22 July 2004. I added some farther reflections on Ferguson's Scottishness in a review of Timothy Garton Ash on the same site: 'Free World's End', 1 December 2004.

Such, alas, was the real content of 'preserving the Union', by the time the *Red Paper's* Editor at length arrived in office. Then it became the real substance of 'Devolution', conceived as a risk-free endorsement of the same old subordinate identity and 'partnership'.[13]

In the past, an important delusion has obstructed our view of this process: the concept of 'decline', as the fate menacing what was left of the former British *imperium*. But 'decline' is rather like the 'demoralisation' referred to in Brown's 1975 'introduction' – a gloomy yet potentially comforting idea that leaves open the possibility of things being 'turned round', or rendered more tolerable by appropriate policies. Declining out of grandeur implies there must be some of the stuff left. Hence, suitable measures – meaning strong, colourful and, of course, centrally-managed, measures – may still reprieve and even rebuild.

When *The Break-up of Britain* appeared in 1977, it was not understood (least of all by the author) that 'decline' and disintegration – or the 'collapse' of an historic state form – *primarily* manifests itself as desperate, convulsive and in the end hysterical efforts to put things right. Blairism has exemplified this desperation, carrying Britain back to Mesopotamia to prove the point. And as that adventure concludes – most probably with the formation of three independent states, a century overdue – despair has turned into the cacophonous brass band of reanimated 'Britishness'. Undeterred by the accumulation of follies, Great British identity will still not go quietly into the good night. Its farewell is more likely to be a drunken drum-roll than T.S. Eliot's whimper.

Politically speaking, the main symptom of its terminal malaise is not falling graph-lines or questionable economic figures, mounting debility and melancholic withdrawal. All these may be present too. But the centre stage is occupied by bright-eyed relentlessness, an increasingly ruthless, loquacious and regimented determination to make things right, to resolve problems by ingenious new formulae or crafty devices, imposed by irresistible fiat (huge majority in Parliament, best Civil Service in the world). As for people, the subjects or citizens of a society in decline, they must never be allowed to slumber or feel wimpishly sorry for their fate. Rather they must 'soldier on'. No escape is allowed from the parade ground: *redressement* alone can keep spirits up, with help from tabloids and TV, but also by regular brow-beatings, colourful annual Government Reports, and interactive web-sites.

I mentioned recent precedents, like the social-sciences deconstruction and invention mania of the 1990s. But with longer hindsight, origins can of course be traced back to long before the *Red Paper*. Like so many other phenomena of the recent *fin-de siecle*, it returns us at least to the 1960s, and to what were in effect rehearsals of today's end-game.

---

13 Put in another way, Brownism can also be seen as the ultimate (hopefully terminal) chapter of what Graeme Morton has described as *Unionist Nationalism* (Tuckwell Press, 1999) – the reaffirmation of the devolved 'low politics' of Scottish civil society as support for the persisting (if troubled) high politics of a world power on the skids.

Here, the trajectory from Harold Wilson's redeeming 'white heat of new technology' in 1964 up to the disappearance of motor manufacturing and the collapse of British Railtrack, can easily be traced. But equally, on the Right, an analogous pattern was established from Edward Heath's 'Selsdon Man' in 1969 up to the excesses of Thatcherism, the wonders of deregulation and the Poll Tax.

Blairism and Brownism are merely later instalments, expressed in an ever more unhinged radical rhetoric. The new sermons are exercises in public-relations 'Sergeant-Majorism'. Their precursors stretch from the white-heat moment up to frankly mountebank spectacles like the Greenwich Dome, the farce of replacing the old House of Lords with a new one, or pitiable hopes that Prince Charles may yet modernise his Monarchy.

The political mechanisms of terminal Britishry demand *enhanced* reliance upon elective dictatorship, and hence on 'first-past-the post'. Round the world, all Neo-Liberal trusty regimes have indulged in increased centralisation of power, to hold democracy in check. I argued in *Pariah* (2001) that in the UK example this is especially acute: no redemption regime here can fail to be aware of the huge task confronting it. Changes are inconceivable without the vast power bestowed (or apparently bestowed) through the old, disproportional electoral system.

Only the latter can even seem to bestow the Sovereignty believed inseparable from historical greatness and world influence. By contrast, a proportional system might be fairer, but would certainly be 'weaker', in the sense of resting upon agreements and compromises, a potentially alterable 'consensus' of parties and leaders. More democratic, naturally: but that's exactly what makes democracy look intolerable, under the constraints of collapsing 'Britishness'. They might as well invite Little England into the drawing-room and give him sausage-rolls.

This is why constitutional reform has to be walled off by a Union Jack in every front garden, by citizenship ceremonies, and the pumped-up self-confidence that comes from sticking with the right body-building club, alongside the Americans. The next British election looks like being contested by two parties and leaders agreed on one all-important thing: refusal of farther reform for the *central* Westminster state.

Both Brown and David Cameron naturally have surrogates to hand, usually involving steroids for 'local government' and abundant provision of fertiliser for grass roots, that is, administration too feeble and distant to interfere with the higher authority of the elective dictatorship.[14]

---

14   David Miliband, Minister for Local Government and the most junior member of Blair's Cabinet, has been awarded the task of combating the mounting sense of 'powerlessness' among voters. This has of course nothing to do with being victims of Westminster archaism and unelected Lordship: it must be solved by regeneration of local, decentralised administration. As the *Guardian* wryly commented, junior recruits will soon out-do Cabinet veterans with this kind of nonsense, which amounts to little more than already existing local councils being exhorted to show more responsibility, mainly by privatising services (Leading Article, 22 February, 2006).

The real point of the 'revolutions' promised by the Blairites in 1998–99 (including devolution) was *to prevent* a political – that is, a constitutional – revolution on this deeper level. The fairly mild reforms suggested by Roy Jenkins's Commission on Electoral reform and long demanded by the Liberal-Democrats will not now be enacted, because these might threaten the very possibility of 'strong government' in Britain. They would obviously menace the saving of the British day, in the sense of 'clout', exceptionality, non-ordinariness among the nations. They would risk replacing dream-life with comparatively modest, realisable goals, and experiments with whatever forms of social engineering are appropriate in globalisation.

What Brownism calls for, by contrast, is Presbyterian 'realism': that is, teeth-gritted loyalty unto God's Will, as evidenced by Competitiveness, Market Forces, and Heaven's endorsement of an imaginary USA. What is the last ditch of this all-British nationalism? The alliance unto death of UK putrefaction and global Free Trade, represented by a government re-elected in 2005 by just over one fifth of the British electorate.

I mentioned earlier some features of the (stowaway) *Red Paper*, like its generosity and appetite for dialogue, its real openness to ideas, and the fertilising effect of Gramscian ideas upon the Editor, as well as so many of the contributors. In spite of the descending winter of the later '70s, it managed to convey an inchoate and yet unforgettable sense of a possible new Scotland. *That* is what really remains living about it: it was going in a different direction, unattainable in its time. And that direction was nothing like what's now happening. There was an abiding impulse and spirit about the enterprise, a stowaway not left behind by history, however grievous the disappointments in other directions.

The *Red Paper* staked out a claim, and somehow convinced many people that nationalism in Scotland could be more left-wing inclined, even if the Editorial blueprint for synthesis didn't work, and many of the particular formulae brought into play were mistaken. It sketched out the design of a Scotland (even an independent Scotland) that would be red, or reddish, in hue, and so quite distinct from older rural and conservative styles of nationalism.

Stowaways and Nationalists Beware

As for the coming period, no guesswork about the fate of stowaways is needed. The Chancellor himself has told us what's in store for them. In 1999 he published a brochure entitled *New Scotland, New Britain* with Douglas Alexander, another Presbyterian Minister's son, party member since the age of 14, and at the time of writing Minister of State for Europe. The argument was that devolved regional government had provided Scots with all they really needed or were entitled to; hence it was up to them to make the Scotland Act Parliament work, and, more important, to actively support the New Britain even then being commanded to arise from the ashes of Thatcherism.

The booklet consists largely of one morose cliché after another: 'better off together, weaker and worse off apart'; 'jobs at risk from separatism'; 'social justice versus separatism'... and so on, and on. It reads like a glossy election pamphlet, because that is what it was. The objective was the first parliamentary election in Scotland after the Devolution Act, where the Labour case was to be made primarily by daily TV and newspaper images of a homely-looking framed picture of Great Britain being smashed to pieces by a maniac with a sledge-hammer.

It was quite a step from Antonio Gramsci to this style of venomous alarm and brutal denigration. The combination of the Kosovo war and tabloid hysteria was credited with some effects upon the 2003 election results, no doubt correctly. But from our point of view today it's surely the sheer contrast between it and the world of the *Red Paper* which counts. *New Scotland, New Britain* did contain an obligatory summary of the history of Scottish Home Rule, from Keir Hardie up to Donald Dewar. But this version of the tale skips straight from 1929 on to the 1980s and Thatcherism.

It manages therefore to mention neither the ardent Home-Rule British Socialist Ramsay Macdonald nor – disappointingly – *The Red Paper on Scotland*. There is a hard-edged, heedless, brazenly party-centred tone to its narrative, an enclosure at the farthest possible remove from the creative inquiring spirit of 1975.

This drastic shift in tone and attitude arose basically from fear. That is, the fear (but now actually, the knowledge) that the existing framework of British authority, belief and prestige is falling apart so alarmingly that nothing whatever can be allowed to damage it farther. Hence, it seemed quite intolerable that Wales should elect a leader (Rhodri Morgan) who effectively voiced Welsh opinion; or that a popular rebel-figure like Ken Livingstone should become Mayor of London; or (of course) that the new Scottish Parliament should be allowed to chafe openly at the limitations of the Scotland Act 1998, and seek more power. The shakier Britishness becomes, the more fiercely it has to be defended, at least, by those who have in this way over-committed themselves to its management and survival.

The matter can be put in another way, still with reference to 1975. When the very elements of a grand, projected synthesis cease to be viable (in this case, both Socialism and the traditional form of State), synthesis can turn into mere compromise. But once compromise assumes charge, as strategy rather than tactic, no limit can be set to its operation. The imaginative fusion of ideas then turns into bottom-lining, or cutting a deal. If the State now depends utterly on a Party, then the Party can hardly help assuming the ruthless and commandist features of the State. Yet notoriously, the defence of a State sanctions saying and doing practically anything to attain its end, all the more so when the State in question has come to be perceived as (in Blair's terms) 'pivotal' to the entire world of marketolatry and (after 2001) the War Against Terrorism.

We saw all these things evolving within 'Thatcherism', and Blair and Brown have merely carried them farther. There can be, unfortunately, very little doubt that the Scottish electorate will face another assault-course of this kind in 2007, nor that the one-time student radical will be out there directing anti-nationalist operations. All will be in the name of the superior and more effective national-ism of 'Britishness', which his recent theatrical performances have at least had the merit of exposing to plain view.

For Britain's Sake

In practical politics, the conclusion that would seem to impose itself is paradox-ical, but I believe sustainable. The best, *and possibly the only*, way of saving many worthwhile features of the UK inheritance is for Scotland and Wales to become independent. One might, of course, say 'more independent', and deploy saving formulae like 'fiscal autonomy'.

Politics is about direction of march, as well as discreet policies. But whether its *de facto* or by-the-book independence, the main point is little changed. It is that whatever aspects of the UK past the electorates of its national components want to keep and continue *are no longer safe* in Westminster state hands. It has often been noticed how oddly 'British' and conservative peripheral nationalism has been in these islands (not excluding the Republic of Ireland). It has been (and still is) unlike the mainstream of 20th century anti-colonial liberation move-ments, for good reasons. 'Self-colonisation' then (like more recent specimens) had real advantages alongside its servility and shames. However, it has now run out of time.

Not having been colonised countries in the usual 18th–19th century sense, the Scots and Welsh do not enjoy – or suffer from – the usual compulsions to separate. 'Separatism' alarms them, quite reasonably in view of the widespread socio-cultural integration that has accompanied Anglo-British expansion. Nor is there any real incompatibility between such elements of assimilation and independent politics, except in the rhetoric of restricted elites over-committed to maintaining a unitary state (and their own authority) at all costs. Such sections of the Scoto- and Gallo-British communities would, of course, find themselves deprived: *they* would be shorn of their 'special relationship' to the overarching State. As independence, or separate membership of the European Union or the United Nations approached, they would inevitably find themselves displaced by normal representatives of the majority UK nationality, England.

Yet oddly enough, it looked for a year or so as if the Blair regime was at least half-thinking of such a direction, during the earlier reforming period, from 1997 to 2001, when it was partly carried away by devolutionary successes. After the legislation for Scotland and Wales, and the initial success of the Northern Irish Peace Process, a British Isles Council of elected governments was proposed. The idea was to co-ordinate policy formation and prevent clashes of interest arising from a more diverse United Kingdom.

The project was at once labelled 'the Council of the Isles', and it was claimed that the very different status of the participating units should make little difference. Two independent states, the UK and the Irish Republic, would be alongside a group of near-independent states, the Isle of Man, Jersey and Guernsey, as well as devolved parliaments with very different capacities, Wales and Scotland, and the new Northern Ireland assembly.

This Council marked the high point of New Labour's reformism and (almost at once) its fall into bathos and absurdity. Such a body was either signalling a profound redirection of political energies, leading on to some future confederation of Irish-British states; or else it was a *pretence* of liberal openness, to keep possible dissidence under control. New Labour's fog machines hinted at the former; but only to make sure the latter prevailed.

A confederation of Irishness and Britishness naturally entailed the equal self-government of all parties, or at least a process of movement in that direction: the possibility (at least) of devolution heading towards de facto independence – like, for example, the Isle of Man. Or (more to the point) like the status recently and quite successfully fought for by the Generalitat of Catalonia and (currently) by the Basque Parliament.

The Council of the Isles was an impasse. But that was because of its importance and its appeal, not its irrelevance. Irish President Mary McAleese liked the idea, and was naturally mocked for poetry and sentiment. But too many carapaced and vengeful identities were threatened by it, on the British side. In the longer run, 'Britain' will only survive as a confederation of independent states, probably seven or eight of them (including Man, Jersey and the other island dependencies); and that survival will indeed represent a 'new Britain', the things these governments and peoples have kept in common, and want to develop. However, this is wildly different from the Brown-Blair neo-American dreamland. And of course, it depends on actual self-governing progress around the periphery.

Things might be different if there were serious prospects of central reform, with a fairer PR system, outright replacement of the House of Lords, a written constitution, and so on. But since such prospects now appear non-existent in a Britain falling off its wall, the periphery has to come up with its own answers. *They* will never do it for us. Do it Yourself is the only way. And this is very far from a counsel of despair or utopia.

After all, *peoples have been doing it themselves*, since the '90s. The stalemate at the British-Westminster summit has been steadily undermined by electorates going their own ways, both negatively through mounting abstention, and (given the limited opportunities of devolution) positively, wherever fairer systems have allowed novel aims and ideas a way into government. It is absurd to think that the little-English electorate won't continue down roughly the same road, given its own devolutionary powers (which is of course why it has to be stopped in its tracks).

All that the Blair-Brown Isles pantomime was really concerned with was reassurance of the Northern Ireland Protestants, persuading them that devolution would never endanger that version of ultra-Britishness. A pompous Council might help to keep devolution toothless, and harmless to Dublin, Westminster and Protestant Belfast. Amidst much think-tank rhetoric, the avoiding-trouble principle thus set the constitutional tone for the remainder of New Labour's time in office.[15] Avoiding trouble has in turn led to the weird underworld of Brown's drag-queen 'Britain' – the country whose inverted commas signify pretentious self-parody, has-been grandeur, and international mockery.

For Democracy's Sake

This, which flickers at night

in the skullcap of my thought, mother of-pearl snail's trace or mica of crushed glass,

isn't light from church or factory to nourish

red cleric or black.

All I can leave you is this rainbow in evidence of a faith that was contested,

a faith that burned more slowly than hardwood on the hearth...

EUGENIO MONTALE. 'Piccolo testamento', from Collected Poems 1920–1954, translated by Jonathan Galassi (New York, 1998)

'Trouble' means England. All participants at January's Fabian Society event had to run a gauntlet, not of the British National Party, but of reasonable-sounding English protesters. They were complaining that the whole thing was an insult to Englishness, whether in the sense of all-English or of regional-English interests. The drag-queen was being artificially resurrected to prevent the majority national identity from winning any distinguishable or separate voice. The slogans suggested that a New Labour/Fabian conspiracy was under way to shut them up, and keep them out of any action. I was glad to see quite a number of them infiltrated the day's sessions, to make the same point over and over again.

---

15 It was the author's fate to sit across the table from Sir Robert Armstrong at one of this Council's preparatory meetings. He constantly muttered remarks like '... needs something to pull all this together', but wasn't on that occasion being economical with the truth. From an Establishment angle, the project would indeed be held together -by a resolute will that no real difference whatever should be made to 'real power'. Unable even to propose anything significant, the Council of the Isles stood for little more than Cheshire Cat grin goodwill, and almost at once vanished from history. Whatever reassurance it provided to Ulster Protestantism no doubt helped them later, as they moved to support Paisley's Democratic Unionist Party, preserving Britannitude by stalling the Peace Process.

The complaints were justified. In the latest Annual Report on *British Social Attitudes,* the question of self-consciously English identity is addressed, and their survey detects that, '… a still modest English backlash may be taking place. Though dual identities may still be common, more people express an adherence to Englishness now than two years ago.'

Peter Riddell commented on it in *The Times* of 28 November 2005 under the heading 'The Unanswered English Question cannot be ignored', and this is surely right. Whatever is causing the shift, Riddell points out, it isn't apprehension about Scotland becoming more independent, or even a separate state: 'More than half the English say they would be 'neither pleased nor sorry if Scotland were to become independent'.

They would accept it as a matter of fact, many probably puzzled by the screams of anguish emitted by Attorney General Lord Falconer, John Reid and other Scottish Westminster MPs.[16] Unionist fundamentalists claim that Welsh and Scottish independence would foist a polity upon the English 'rest of the UK', which they don't want. English *nationalist* movements have certainly been low key, as most voters there have understandably made little of the English-British distinction.

But it doesn't follow that the English electorate would not accomplish the matter-of-fact adjustment demanded of them perfectly well, probably without the histrionics predicted by minorities fearful of losing their own long-held niches, anchors, privileges and expectations. An English multi-cultural identity has in any case always represented around 85 per cent of what the unitary British one was, in reality as distinct from the new Brownite folklore.

Something of this has very recently been proposed in concrete institutional terms by the Liberal-Democrat Party, through their 'Steel Commission Report'.[17] This is a straightforward proposal for increased powers in Edinburgh, notably for tax-raising and the end of the 'Barnett Formula' that covers the costs of Scottish government out of UK Treasury revenues. Together with giving more normal legislative powers to the Welsh Assembly, as energetic ally advocated by the Richard Commission, a basis would then be laid for a Federal Britain.

This would be a great advance on the original devolution plans of 1998. And even before publication, the proposals won resounding endorsement from an important Westminster by-election in Scotland: On 9 February 2006, the formerly safe Labour seat of Dunfermline and West Fife was won by the Liberal

---

16 An admirable overview of the subject can be found in Robert Hazell's *The English Question,* January 2006, Constitution Unit. Hazell's University College Constitution Unit has consistently published the most accurate and thorough material on all UK constitutional matters, including the likely effects of Scottish independence on the 'RUK', or 'rest of the UK'.

17 *The Steel Commission: Moving to Federalism, a New Settlement for Scotland* (March 2006): Final Report to the Spring Conference of the Liberal Democrats, available from www.scotlibdems.org.uk

Democrats with a 1,800 majority – a swing of 16.24 per cent from Labour, and their first by-election loss in Scotland since 1988.

Cameron's New Conservatives did poorly, while the total vote for the purists of Britishness, the United Kingdom Independence Party, amounted to 0.6 per cent. It took little imagination to see the possibility of New Labour's grip on Scotland being broken at the coming round of Holyrood elections, on 3 May 2007. Over six months previously, George Kerevan of *The Scotsman* newspaper had envisaged the break-through as a 'Rainbow Coalition' founded on an alliance against Blair and Brown, and aiming at farther staged moves towards independence. The 'process' of devolution could then resume, linked to constitutional reform at the UK level.[18]

It's true that the new Lib-Dem recipe, which appears certain to do well in the 2007 elections, remains linked to their own fantasies of a reanimated Britain. Long in favour of reforming the over-centralised Westminster state and its preposterous election system, they continue to hope that light may dawn down there, as well as in Wales and Scotland. This is why quite substantial parts of the Steel *Report* give the impression of having been generated by a colony of voles, broadcasting out of some deep Thames-side sanctuary untouched by most recent events. There, they browse tranquilly upon the mouldering common-sense of past generations, and perceive independence as 'increasingly meaningless in the age of globalisation.'

This truth has yet to impress itself upon East Timor, West Papua, Tibet, Chechnya, Taiwan, Kurdistan and a growing list of other above-ground populations. In vole country, however, 'Britain' remains in a different league: inherently modernisable, since (alongside the USA) it *is* modernity, in a sense something like that of the Zionist factions who maintain that Israel and Jewishness simply *are* religion and universality combined. The next step is stern reminders of 'the significant benefits to Scotland of our ability to act on the international stage, as part of the United Kingdom'. Thirty years ago this was merely ambiguous; today it is ridiculous.[19]

---

18 See 'Somewhere Over the Rainbow Coalition', 3 May 2006. By odd yet telling coincidence, Gordon Brown's home is within the constituency where the upheaval took place, and he had taken a prominent part in the election campaign. The SNP, which has registered mediocrely in recent contests, including Dunfermline and West Fife, was imagined as part of Kerevan's 'Rainbow' and is actually a member of the more recent 'Independence Alliance' set up to contest next year's election, alongside the Greens and the Scottish Socialists.

19 As regards Brown's attitude to recent disgraces, he made it clear in an address to the Royal United Services Club on 14 February 2006 that he totally supports Blair's subservience to Bush, and the war in Iraq. As Channel 4's Jon Snow remarked on the same day: 'When it comes to the issue of terrorism and global security, you couldn't put a Semtex wrapper between them... Those who thought that Brown's firebrand university days might have left an overhang of concern for civil liberties were in a for a rude awakening...' snowmail_daily@channel4.com

Most Scots (and most other Crown subjects) have since 2003 wanted to *stop* acting on the international stage in this way. Yet such ghostly moans are now presented by Steel's Commission in support of policies that will – in spite of them – effectively modernise Scotland and Wales. Ideology and political reform have parted company; is there really any need to pay overmuch attention to the former?

The philosophy of 'Federalism' is an historical hangover, resting upon historical misunderstanding of what federal states have in the main been like, over the period between the American War of Secession and the end of the Cold War. They sometimes figured as 'liberal' (or at least as preferable) by comparison with older autocracies and military dictatorships, or with the communist parties of East Europe, China and elsewhere. But in the main, modern federalism has been a way of building or reinforcing the unitary command-states of the New-Imperialist era. Power devolved was always power retained, long before Great Britain belatedly caught up with this idea in 1997-98. Decentralisation and the encouragement of folk-dancing were techniques for the focusing and amplification of central authority, in the areas where power 'mattered' – and above all, for conducting warfare, the life-blood of modern international relations.[20]

Still hypnotised by the notion of federation as 'the normal constitutional set-up in advanced political societies', Lib-Dem ideology is quite happy to lump together Switzerland with the United States in its appeal for modernity confusing a *confederation* with the descendants of Lincoln's imposed post-1865 Union. It is conceded that England's problems are an obstacle to true Federalism, but this should not stop Scots from 'developing plans for their own role and status within a modernised UK ...', if necessary by some kind of 'asymmetric federalism' allowing the majority time to mature and catch up. The key thing is to avoid 'simplistic, separatist notions of independence' – presumably by non-simplistic, anti-separatist procedures that move voters towards *de facto* independent self-government, but with as little publicity as possible. Independence minus the billboards, as it were. Volespeak appeals to the 65 per cent or so of Scottish opinion that wants more powers for Holyrood... provided this doesn't mean being able to opt out of another UK war, for example over Iran.

However, it seems at the moment probable that voters will be supporting the independence-minded, rather than the voles. So will most Green and non-Labour socialists, and many ex-New Labourites reacting against the long agony of the Mesopotamian conflict. The ii way seems open for a watershed alliance or coalition, a 'rainbow' in Kerevan's sense devoted to movement in the

---

20 The only real exception is post-war Federal Germany -where the decentralised apparatus was not granted by a central state power, benevolent or otherwise. It was imposed by the Allied powers from outside, after a total defeat of the previous government and society. Such exceptional conditions mean that the German system is very difficult to appeal to as any kind of model -least of all, one would have thought, by a United Kingdom elite afflicted by success-complex rather than downfall.

direction of independence, even without definition of what exactly this will mean, or bring in some later wake.

'In a green constitution,' points out Robyn Eckersley, '...at the broad level of constitutional purpose, the green democratic state would be outward looking rather than parochial or nationalistic' – but it must of course be independent, in order to do so.[21] Her point is that globalisation has undermined Sovereignty, not sovereignties in the somewhat humbler but more durable meaning of diverse, recognised self-government and independent activity.

It is the capital 'S' that has been dissolved, not the real anthropological foundations of plurality or diversity. And the effacement of the former is in fact most likely to promote an enhancement of the latter. The morbid litanies of the 1990s about the vanishing nation-state were actually about the real or fancied humiliations of the Great, the once-Great and the would-be-Great once-more – conceived and relayed, naturally, by intellectuals of one metropolis or another.

In 2007 Scotland, more concerted rainbow politics will have another advantage: they are, after all, simply a continuation of what was promisingly launched – against the odds – at the last Holyrood election in 2003. In a paper delivered to the Humboldt University in Berlin just afterwards, Eberhard Bart and Christopher Harvie summed it up as 'A Small Earthquake in Scotland'. The result turned out disconcerting to both main parties', they pointed out, and the aftermath was to involve a constitutional aftershock w hose consequences were unfathomable then – and still continuing today.

'The People Bite Back' was how Iain Macwhirter, Scotland's premier political columnist, summed up the same result. 'Holyrood will soon swear in the most democratic legislature Britain has ever seen.' he continued,

> ... Scots had been offered more of the same brain-dead municipal mediocrity. They chose life instead. The Scottish people repossessed their parliament (and) a new democratic space has opened up in which the people can really begin to imagine a different future to the one presented by the monolithic party blocs

Sunday Herald, 4 May 2003.

Joyce Macmillan, the only rational voice at that time surviving on Andrew Neil's *Scotsman,* echoed the sentiment:

> I could almost sense, on the damp morning air, the feel of Scottish voters... beginning to experiment and play around with the new system of politics that has fallen into our hands.

By the time of the next election in 2007, the 300th anniversary of the old Scottish Parliament's decision to join the Union, she speculated on

---

21 See The Green State: Rethinking Democracy and Sovereignty (MIT Press, 2004) pp. 242–3.

... the likelihood of a harder-edged determination to vote tactically for the parties most likely to break Labour's long Scottish hegemony at last, and to usher in an era of major change

Scotsman, 3 May 2003

She was anticipating the watershed now clearly possible, and rendered that much more likely by the whole train of events following 2003, and culminating in Gordon Brown's campaign of salvation for the Union I have described. Labour's 'long Scottish hegemony' was also the hegemony of the Union, and of the ailing Great-Britishness that has been latterly propped up, by war and heedless rhetoric.

In 2003 the foundations of a broad alliance for moving towards independence were spontaneously laid by a deeply dissatisfied electorate, aware more clearly than party politicians that there could be no going back. Next time – surely – a more conscious, planned coalition of forces and opinion can surely build upon that, in both Scotland and Wales, and bring us into the era of major change so long needed?

New Britain or Easter Island?

But as for Britain, the prospect is more like a 21st century Easter Island. The inhabitants of that unfortunate place proved unable to change their ancestral customs, and continued the stone-quarrying, gross head-carving, log-rolling transportation and spirit-invocation that had held them back for centuries. The last trees were felled in the name of sacred tradition, because an inherited identity assured the people there was simply no other way. Divine intervention was the sole hope – hence as things got worse it was all the *more* important to remain themselves, and propitiate the far-off deities who had brought them over the Pacific in the first place.[22]

The British successor tale has recently been brought up to date by Ross McKibbin in some comments on the Blair regime's terminal decline. Some months after Gordon Brown's resurrectionist spasm, as things passed from bad to unspeakable in Iraq and the ground war escalated in Afghanistan, Blair's popularity fell badly enough to provoke revolt in New Labour's parliamentary ranks. He was forced to concede the approaching end of his 2005 government. 'Something has plainly gone badly wrong', notes McKibbin:

> The gap between what (the government) has not done and what it should have done is huge – in almost every sphere, but most conspicuously in reforming the country's decrepit constitutional structure... The present regime is slowly destroying the Labour Party, and it will not be rescued by a reasonable

---

22 Jared Diamond has recently recounted the story again in his comparative study *Collapse.*

competence at day-to-day management – any more than the Conservative
Party could be rescued by Major's government in its last couple of years.[23]

It will be remembered that Blair's predecessor, the once untouchable Mrs Thatcher,
was brought down by her own party in the wake of the Poll Tax disaster. It
dawned even on loyal supporters that they would never be re-elected as long as
she persisted in office with this deeply unpopular measure, and hence a more
moderate leadership was needed. The consequence was unforgiving feuds among
Conservatives, and the five years of decline up to the defeat of 1997. Even after
that, it would take the movement years to recover even partially. Nine years
later, most commentators have perceived David Cameron's leadership as not
only untried but in some respects equivocal (as well as quite ineffective in both
Wales and Scotland).

Once might have been an accident, twice in such a short time frame surely
suggests something else. For *both* ruling parties to succumb to Humpty-Dump-
tyism within a decade and a half surely points to system-failure, rather than
leadership idiosyncracy and policy errors. Breakage and wilful fragmentation
on such a large and persistent scale questions the United Kingdom's historical
identity – its in-dwelling self-image of exemplary stability and democracy. Here,
indeed, the New Labour collapse may be more significant than Thatcher's.

After all, it has come to rest much more completely upon the revival of British
nationalism. Early in her period, Thatcher won a minor war against the Galtieri
dictatorship in Argentina, a success that equipped her to win two further general
elections, in 1983 and 1987. Though that did depend on some American support,
few then saw such reliance as craven or unqualified. Many perceived the South
Atlantic War as, if anything, a recovery of initiative after the hidebound conformity following the humiliation of Suez back in 1956.

Blair was never capable of anything similar: his (and Brown's) conviction
was that their world role now depended on total support for us policies: a relationship 'special' only in fantasy terms, where influence might be obtainable as
a reward for courtier flattery and exaggeration.

As I indicated earlier, this was also a chosen American-ness based on delusions about the latter's universality, and hence its exportability. Brown has become
the fulsome Bard of this ideology. His passionate wish to serve the dregs of
Britishness has forced him to mistake everything about it: he occludes its imperial background, and its unavoidably English core, while clinging to the vulgar
self-importance of Scottishness as essential to civilisation. This latter trait naturally entails his own persona l suitability for Sovereign authority – indeed, the
conviction that both Party and People should bestow leadership upon him.
Inherent righteousness has blinded him, not only to the ridiculous archaism of

23 'Sleazy, Humiliated, Despised', in *The London Review of Books*, vol. 28, No. 17, 7
September, 2006

the UK polity, but to the curious parochialism and limitations of United States identity as well.

During the crazed disputes following Blair's concession of political mortality in September 2006, many of Brown's opponents were to reproach him with plotting, conspiring and back-stabbing from behind the arras. Of course these accusations are justified. But such 'loyalists' omitted to point out the obvious (and in this case the phrase deserves to be used) – *there was no alternative*.

A democratic constitution of both Party and State might have made a difference; but then, that's what both the Party and broader National procedures are all about – *avoiding open democracy,* by all means possible.

Why else is the UK electorate forced to contemplate another election in 2008 or 2009, with both great Parties of the realm in complete agreement on one thing: no serious reform of either constitution or the electoral system?

Both these Parties have become splintered ruins of their former selves, and the failure of the antique see-saw has been registered by mass withdrawal from the voting process itself. Yet this makes no difference to either Brown or Cameron. What they stand for is 'carrying on': the sacrosanct national vocations of huge-head quarrying, and terminal tree-felling to set up the effigies in proper positions – emblems visible from afar, and representing greatness, faith and (since 2001) War Against Terrorism.

It goes without saying that both have 'reasonably competent managerial proposals' for growing some more trees, slightly better imported tools, and the boosting of morale. But this isn't just managing capitalism. The point is to sustain traditional Greatness and status without risking overmuch change, or any return to political boat-building that might let people escape, or cease being 'British'.

It is sometimes thought that the British, American and other *anciens régimes* are embracing, or even guiding, 'globalisation' in such ways. Nothing could be farther from the truth. They are in fact ways of resisting, distorting and holding back a greater process which, *because* it is unifying so much, so quickly, will only be tolerable via an accelerated democratic reformation – 'democratic warming' (as it were) that in turn demands reconfigured civil societies, and new communities and nations.

Nor should it be thought that Anglo-American 'Neo-conservatism' is just a farther emanation of capitalism. Here, orthodox historical materialism is capable of mistakes as gross as those of its spiritualist and fundamentalist opponents. North-Atlantic Neo-imperialism is less a by-product of industry, trade and high finance than a desperate effort to keep (or revive) popular support for a decaying – indeed thoroughly anachronistic – ideal and political control of these economic forces.

What armies have been mobilised *for* is not (or not only) petroleum resources, or against fantasised Terrorism and ultra-Islamicism, but the preservation of the elite norms of the long counter-revolution that, in the 1960s and 1970s, had suppressed a previous revolt. That was the political reaction which was to benefit from the renewed and more transnational economic expansion leading to the end of the Cold War – quite naturally forming the quasi-religious orthodoxy of 'Neo-liberalism'. Its successor, Neo-conservatism, is merely the latter in arms – defending itself against failure, at first ideological but then, after 2001, directly military.

Gordon Brown is already a Centurion in this army, and now aspires to be a General. But he knows such a role demands above all maintaining the unity of his all-British basis. In the '90s he believed that Devolution was the way to accomplish this. Now (fortunately) he isn't so sure. In the end-phase of the Mesopotamian debacle, the task will become still harder. But it's important to note this won't be only due to more frightful events and losses, or (one must hope) to continuing anti-war protests and demonstrations. Something more fundamental has shifted, probably enough to disable British histrionics permanently.[24]

The *glamour* of Britishness has disappeared. I pointed out above how the monarchy has subsided from intellectual *view*, and was scarcely referred to in the Fabian Society's ideology exercise of January 2006. British Royalty once played a crucial role in Anglo Britain's curious surrogate for modern nationalism: secular yet manifestly 'worshipped', it stood in for the nation-state's mutation of transcendence – a personalised focus for many of the typical emotions of post-18th century nationality-politics. The Austro-Hungarian throne once had a similar function, and for analogous reasons. Such a focus reconciled both the dominant nationalities and the smaller or marginal *ethnies* of the imperium to a supposedly common ground. An actual family helped to control the more abstract and metaphorical 'imagined communities' of the romantic-nationalist era.

This 'symbolism' thrived by being the opposite of remote or emotively distant: a nationalism *not* concocted by intellectual malcontents in big cities. In the British case, 'the Crown' imparted a personal colouration and meaning – a 'glamour' of more than backwardness, which infused state authority and implied allegiance beyond the political and the narrowly personal or communitarian.

It was of course this mainstay that has made the great English majority 'silent'. Their over-identification with Britishness was not only imperial, in the overseas or colonial sense. It was also rooted in a popular royalism instinctively alien to 'all that' – to the kind of flag-waving David Cameron is worried about. The evaporation of such allegiance has become inescapable, and Brown's crazed

---

24 In an earlier essay (*Pariah*, Verso Books, 2001) this author argued that 1997 New Labour was at bottom not identifiable with Blair's strange mixture of Third Way policies: it was, rather, a 'second round' of Greatness-restoration (after Thatcher) designed to restore a supposed world-role. The motor was always British nationalism, not social democracy. Of course I didn't at that time imagine Blair (supported by Brown) would plunge the UK into a reoccupation of Iraq, and three years of futile warfare in Afghanistan, in order to fulfill this goal. The US special relationship was seen as a prop – not a way of making foreign policy all-important, and in the end fatal to British destiny itself.

pseudo-Britishness is an attempt to replace it. He wants to put a contrived civic virtue in its place – *without even reforming Westminster and the constitution of central power.*

The Devolution Brown supported so strongly from *Red Paper* times onwards was intended to give more latitude to folk-dancing in a discontented periphery. It 'worked' for a time in a country where there were already national institutions (Scotland); or where such institutions could quite rapidly built up around a common culture (Wales). It failed in the country where deeply discordant versions of folk-dancing prevailed (Northern Ireland). Now however, such times are past: the dancers must come round to Brownite sense and accept a suitably purged all-British identity.

The deepest impulse is at all costs *to avoid English Devolution.* Any serious tendency in that direction is likely to have an anti-Scottish and anti-Welsh side to it. Indeed, it already does. Writing in *Scotland on Sunday* on 10 September 2006, Political Editor Eddie Barnes observed:

'Across the shires …the anger is growing. In the blogosphere English voters rail against the coming man. 'He seems to be a dour Scots bully… OK as Chancellor, but may well be unacceptable, in England at least, as PM.' More acceptable English candidates will not be lacking, he concludes, and all Brown can do is 'thump the drum on his passion for the UK… There can be little doubt that his bid to emphasise his British credentials will gather pace over the coming months.'

'Passion' isn't too strong a word. It points straight at the most surprising recent mutation in UK attitudes. This has obviously crept up on British subjects themselves over quite a period of time, as a lack or blind spot. In truth, however, it is a novelty, instantly evident to anyone who has been long enough away from daily British culture. De-glamorisation has diminished a crucial 'passion' that used to be ever-present in all debates about devolution, particularly in Scotland – a high-tension charge that sparked whenever 'separation' was mentioned.

The theme represented something 'unthinkable' to a majority of partisans habituated to the Union: in effect, a desacralisation fraught with familial disasters as well as political and economic problems. That was the logic of making 'divorce' the key to the anti-nationalist assaults, notably during the 2003 Scottish and Welsh elections. The menace of a profane universe was conjured up, a crass and unreasoning hostility to 'being together', to marital stability and kinship. As I indicated earlier, this emotive pressure was essentially British: a majoritarian response to what has now been generalised as heedless and selfish 'terrorism'.

However, over 2005 and 2006, nobody revisiting these arguments (in my own case, from Australia) can fail to detect a certain lowering of tension. A tone of what one only call 'matter-of-factness' has somehow taken over: as if people were no longer so galvanised by existential threats. This effect is all the more striking because it departs from a general climate of aggravated fearfulness and alarm, the staples of post-2001 public opinion.

It is, of course, another reason why Brown now has to pedal even harder

than before with his ultra-British visions. Loss of glamour has had its consequences: the symbols counted because of their intimate, often semi-conscious
bond with mass feelings, and their loss of meaning has dulled (or even drained)
the latter. As Barnes points out, Brown 'called earlier this year for Remembrance
Sunday to be transformed into a national day of patriotism, the equivalent of
America's 4th of July.' What counted here was the sheer conceit of imagining
that nationalism can be 'invented' in this way, for the convenience of a government and state – invented *against* the tide of a population that, in all the British
nations, had demonstrated its opposition to the style of patriotism being propagated by New Labour.

By contrast, the political nationalisms at work in Scotland and Wales will
now surely benefit from 'matter-of-factness'. Where once the United Kingdom
monopolised common sense in contrast to the crazy sectarian passions of the
periphery, today something like the contrary prevails. The Centre has gone mad,
while 'out there' voters shrug their shoulders and rather calmly look for ways out.
The latter represent deeper processes of democratic warming that have withstood
and denounced the US and Blairite Great-Power hysteria of post-2001, and will
in turn defeat Gordon Brown's attempts to prolong and intensify the fever. Bush
and Blair have demonstrated just how different nationalisms can be: and the elections of May 2007 look likely to provide a useful way of choosing between them.

CHAPTER TWENTY-SIX

Union on the Rocks?

New Left Review, II/43

JANUARY–FEBRUARY 2007

Review of *The Union: England, Scotland and the Treaty of 1707* by Michael Fry

'THE NEXT NECESSARY THING', wrote Clifford Geertz in *The Anthropologist as Author*, 'is to enlarge the possibility of intelligible discourse between people quite different from one another in interest, outlook, wealth and power, and yet contained in a world where, tumbled as they are into endless connection, it is increasingly difficult to get out of each other's way.' New nationalisms are part of that connection, and part of the resultant structures of evasion, or 'identity'. Mongrels need new rules. And *all* nations are becoming mongrels, hybrids or foundlings, in the circumstances of globalisation.

This is the overall impression left by Michael Fry's definitive new book, *The Union: England, Scotland and the Treaty of 1707* – both a careful history of the Treaty of Union, detailing in particular the years from 1698, and a polemical argument for its repeal, and for the resumption of Scottish independence. Note, 'resumption' rather than 'claiming'. Its appearance could hardly be more timely. 1 May 2007 will mark the 300th anniversary of the 'United Kingdom of England, Wales, Scotland and Ireland'. This elderly piece of multiculturalism has endured alternative titles, 'Britain' and 'Great Britain' for example, all intended to make it sound more united than it ever was. People appear to be getting used to the idea of Iraq disappearing, divided between Kurdistan and one or more Muslim-Arab states. But an analogous fate may overtake Britain's faltering Union, if Scotland, Wales and Northern Ireland opt for new directions at the May 2007 elections to their 'devolved' assemblies. In that case a new acronym may soon come into play, the 'RUK' ('Rest of the UK'). This would be mainly England of course, though now with the curious sense of 'Little England' plus London – a cosmopolis with nothing little about it, outside of Westminster and Buckingham Palace.

About 20 years ago Eric Hobsbawm, annoyed by my own connections with what then seemed the hopeless cause of Scottish nationalism, reminded me sharply that it was the Scots who really made the British Union in the 18th and 19th centuries. He was implying that to withdraw from the UK would be a retrograde move, and that to try and reform it made more sense. Whatever is now thought of that political recipe, Hobsbawm's historical judgement was surely right. Though the British Kingdom unites a surprising number of countries and cultures, ranging from Wales to the micro-nations of the Isle of Man and the Channel Islands, its backbone remains the link with Scotland. That rapport, in turn, rests formally upon one thing. This is not an idea, or a sacred code or emblem, or even what sociologists call a 'habitus'. It is a sheaf of papers.

I recall vividly the first time I set eyes on the Treaty, at a court hearing in the 1980s on Scottish protests over Mrs Thatcher's Poll Tax. Some Scottish lawyers maintained that a head-count tax might be incompatible with the 1707 Treaty of Union, and hence illegal under Scots Law. The presiding judge testily decided that a copy of the Treaty was required, and dispatched a clerk to make a photo-copy from the Signet Library archives. Some hours passed before he returned with a handful of folded sheets – the nearest thing to a written constitution that British statehood has ever attained. A few days later the verdict came. There were no grounds for thinking the Poll Tax incompatible with any clauses of the Treaty, and Scots would have to put up with it. The Treaty hadn't saved them. The same miserable old sheets would be included, unchanged, in Blair's 1998 legislation on devolution. So the restored Scottish parliament was to go on being hamstrung by them, exactly like its ancestor of 292 years before.

This and many other absurdities can be made more sense of in the broader perspectives of *The Union*. Fry's close scrutiny of the motives for the 1707 Treaty underlines its unique character. It involved neither colonisation nor forced assimilation – of the sort displayed earlier in Wales and Ireland – but an inter-national agreement between two frequently battling kingdoms. They had been united under the same monarchy since 1603, but even this had grown precari-ous. Scottish in origin, the Stuart dynasty constantly threatened an armed come-back after twice being evicted, during the civil wars of mid-century and again in 1688. (The question would not be finally resolved until 40 years after the parlia-mentary Union, at the Battle of Culloden in 1746.) In 1707, Queen Anne's English parliament was demanding more serious political reform, a single assembly located (naturally) in London and supporting the new Protestant monarchy, fore-runner of today's Windsors. Their hope was for a more united Anglo-Scots ruling class, which would be easily dominated by the English aristocracy. At that time, poor and thinly-populated Scotland represented only a small part of the main island's population, and even less of its resources.

London's new urgency was fuelled by international problems. An expanding colonial empire could no longer tolerate home-island dissent, least of all from a regime that was showing alarming signs of wanting its own colonies and foreign policy. Scotland had often been allied with France, the dominant great power of the time and England's chief competitor. The Stuarts were in exile in France, and counting on diplomatic and military support from Louis XIV. At the same time, the condition of the Scottish economy had become pitiable. No-one will ever be sure what percentage of the population starved to death during the terrible 1690s, a period to which Fry pays great and deserved attention. In these circumstances, the Edinburgh political elite sought an over-ambitious remedy: launching a colonial enterprise of its own, by occupying the Isthmus of Darien (today's Panama).

A joint counter-attack by England and Spain defeated this venture in 1698–99 but, as Fry recounts, simultaneously emphasised the need for London to close the northern 'back door'. After the assimilation of Wales and Ireland, a different solution had to be found for the Scots. In contemporary terms, 'security' called for a political deal, rather than the dangers of occupation and repression. The English knew they could defeat Scotland's formidable clannic armies. They had done so already in Cromwell's time, but at huge cost; in today's world, comparable perhaps to recent assaults on Afghanistan. A much better solution was to buy off the northern aristocracy and warlords (including some compensation for their humiliation over Darien).

The Union is an updated retelling of the whole story, enlivened by the historian's own passionate and political involvement with the country that emerged. (Fry has described in a December 2006 *Prospect* essay his transition from prodevolution Conservative parliamentary candidate – he joined the Tory party in 1966 – to Scottish nationalist.) Such emotions aren't concealed by his conclusion, where the recent phase of devolution is dismissed as 'a flawed outcome' that has ignored 'deeper problems of the nation, of redefining its character and purpose'. He goes on to suggest that 'there may indeed be no satisfactory halfway house between the state of the nation as it was before 1603 and… as it was after 1707', so that today 'we are travelling back from the destination reached at the Union, if along a less bumpy route.' The question, then, is 'whether we should not make greater haste to the place where we started, as an independent nation'.

The Union deal was brokered before democracy and nationalism assumed anything like their modern forms. In the early-modern era, popular approval was not required – fortunately for the upper classes favouring the changes. Fry enjoys recounting the episodes of lower-class indignation and near-insurrection that accompanied the parliamentary debates of 1706–07, and makes extensive use of the reports compiled by an English journalist and spy, Daniel Defoe, better known today for later writings like *Robinson Crusoe*. Arriving in Edinburgh, Defoe was surprised

> to find a nation flying in the face of their masters, and upbraiding the gentlemen, who managed it, with selling and betraying their country, and surrendering their constitution, sovereignty and independency to the English.

Edinburgh was at that time poorly paved, with streets and alleyways that provided ample ammunition for the traditional form of protest: 'pebbling them wi' stanes'. Had the contents of the Treaty been better known, Defoe observed, few parliamentarians 'would have dared go home without a guard to protect them'.

Yet the pre-democratic, feudal-estates assembly of 1706–07 was by no means a contemptible body, as Fry several times underlines. Some did sell their votes, but many refused. Among the pro-Union ranks, some genuinely believed in their cause, and argued that short-term sacrifices would be justified by longer-term gains, more enduring peace and stability. In addition, he argues: 'The vigour of the Scots' existing traditions and institutions let them shape the Union too, for good or ill: it was a genuine choice in 1707, not just a factitious product of English expansionism.' All over Europe, small countries and city-states were coming under similar pressures to amalgamate and form larger units – a good example is Catalonia, whose assimilation to all-Spanish rule was in part forced (ironically) by a Scottish army under the Duke of Berwick. By contrast, the Scots were able to retain or even reinforce important native institutions, including the legal and educational systems. Surrender of the state did not entail that of their 'civil society' (to use a later term coined in Scotland). And it is of course the latter that has survived into the present, and reacted to Iraq and other failures of New Labour.

Survival of the nation was one thing; tolerable survival and popular accept-ance quite another. Fry also enjoys retelling the astonishing tales of bribery that punctuated the Scottish parliamentary debates and vote, finally made on 16 January 1707 (though not formally celebrated until 1 May). On that day the Duke of Hamilton, himself one of the most dubious figures in the aristocracy, comm-ented: 'And so the darkest day in Scotland's history has finally arrived. The point of no return has been reached, and nothing is left to us of Scotland's sovereignty, nor her honour or dignity or name'. Buying the elite was one thing, but convinc-ing the rising middle classes and stane-pebblers took far longer – well over half a century on most accounts, punctuated by both political and military revolts until 1746.

What made the real difference was not the Union Treaty, but the empire. Scots of all classes discovered that overseas expansion in the later part of the century, first to North America and then to many other countries, furnished oppor-tunities greater than their own abortive colonisation of 1698 could ever have done. To a great and sustained movement of population was added a striking cultural expansion, the Scottish Enlightenment. As Fry concedes, this first success-ful phase of Union (from David Hume's time up to 1832) 'saw glorious intellec-tual achievement, the one thing that gives Scottish history any universal signif-icance, and it ill behoves us now to complain about it.' The intelligentsia that had renounced its own statehood compensated by imagining a universal realm of progress, liberated from borders and inherited constraints. One of the most telling parts of Fry's Chapter 7, 'Fair Words – After the Union' is an account of Adam Smith's father, the 'Comptroller of Kirkcaldy', in Fife, for whom 'the Union proved a bit of a disaster'. But of course his son, Adam Smith Junior, would react to the miseries of the Customs Inspectorate with a theory about a tariff-free world: *The Wealth of Nations* (1776).

Contrary to some conventional views, it was almost certainly the Scots who headed the European emigration tables for the 19th and 20th centuries – a phenomenon Fry touches on, having produced a comprehensive account in his 2002 *The Scottish Empire*. Emigrants came from the rural lowlands and the towns and cities, not from the most traditional areas of clannic culture and less developed agriculture, as happened in Norway, and in Ireland after the 19th-century potato famine. The massive outflow came from all regions and classes, and continued for two centuries. The overall effect of such wide and enduring emigration was to constitute something like a 'haemorrhage society' at home – a nationality reconfigured by emigration, rather than just affected by it. The advantages for innumerable individuals had to be set against a mounting and decisive loss for the community, mourned by later writers like Edwin Muir, who complained in 1935 of seeing a country 'gradually being emptied of its population, its spirit, its wealth, industry, art, intellect and innate character'. The mythologies of nationalism are well known; but they should more often be set against those of migration and internationalism, still headier concoctions that rarely pause to measure this darker side of the process they extol.

It is, after all, that other side that partly explains the lateness of Scottish political nationalism, at which Fry's new history is directed. For all too long, the enterprising spirit of post-Union society was enthralled by the outward-bound impulse, which had plenty of time to itself become a tradition, and seem part of Scotland's 'innate character'. It was not just the absence of military occupation or police repression that distinguished post-1707 Scotland. Important as this was – when compared to Ireland, for example – there was also the positive sense of large-scale contribution and achievement made possible by imperialism. *The Union* describes the national shames accompanying the Treaty; but these were to be eclipsed by the greater, more structured opportunities that favoured one generation after another, until quite recently. The predominantly successful saga of emigration in turn encouraged a deeply conservative mind-set. Investment by all classes in the process made it practically 'unthinkable' to alter course against the 1707 Union bargain.

True, the empire finally shrank and converted itself into a relatively meaningless Commonwealth, nowadays a venue for sport rather than politics. However, the phasing out of imperial attitudes and 'Greatness' was a lengthy business which, after pulling out of India in 1948, took the form of many relatively minor disgraces and humiliations. These generated cumulative depression rather than wishes for a break – that English mixture of melancholia and ironic resignation, perhaps best conveyed in the post-war poetry of Philip Larkin. The defeats were not big or meaningful enough to force revolt: everyone put up with decline, Scots included. 'Decline' was nothing like the fate inflicted on France in 1940, or on the losers of World War II, or upon the Soviet domains of the 1980s. To an indurate general conservatism, such retreat could always be presented as something other than terminal. And it was compensated for by second-rung material prosperity, as well as by vaguer hopes of redemption. Union cohabitation obviously grew less appealing as a social option, and following World War I a growth of nationalism in Scotland and Wales reflected that. But surely nothing too disastrous or final could overtake it?

And indeed it did not – until now. For the order at which Fry's book is aimed is one currently undergoing collapse. Each day brings the crash of another wall or roof beam. On 12 January 2007, the *Daily Mail* (rumoured to be Prime Minister Blair's preferred breakfast reading) appeared with the banner headline: 'Union In Jeopardy: Majority of Scots See Independence as Inevitable'. More astonishing still was the second heading, pointing out that most English opinion apparently agrees with them: 'more than half', according to the opinion survey used. And the United Kingdom's life-expectancy? Five years or so, with luck and some prevarication. The doleful prognosis is if anything supported by the paper's editorial page, a compilation of half-dead clichés about 'losing clout', as well as the Security Council Seat, the throwing away of proud inheritances and 'constitutional vandalism'. One can almost hear them toiling away down in the Middle England boiler room, striving to raise some steam.

But there is no longer anything there. Defeat in the Middle East is the trigger, but it should be remembered that it is happening at a moment when all other recourses have proved disappointing, or failed. Thatcherism has been followed by Blairism; that is, over 25 years neither the Right nor the Left of Britain's political spectrum has managed to restore anything like the previous age of global distinction and domination, or redeem the old sense of meaning and self-confidence that 'Britishness' used to depend upon. Bizarrely, Gordon Brown – currently preparing for prime-ministerial takeover – launched an unprecedented campaign to boost not just New Labour but *British identity as such* at a Fabian conference in January 2006. Should he become Prime Minister, the 'Save Britain' movement threatens to raise US-style flagpoles in Ukanian front gardens for the restored Union flag; 'Britain Day' could soon succeed the former 'Empire Day'. But if Brown believes that old-style Britishness can be conjured up from the dead, he is mistaken.

From 1979 to the present, foreign policy has grown ever more crucial for London – the era of the South Atlantic War, a protracted (and unresolved) debate over European Union, and NATO's Balkans crisis, as well as of the advance of globalisation. Status and a global presence have shown themselves to be more important to the all-British identity than the post-war welfare state, or the conventions of liberal legalism. In the end, it is foreign-policy fixations and delusions that have dragged the state into the present abyss. A feared subordination to Europe has turned into actual subservience to George W. Bush's American neoconservatism, and condemned the UK army (with its large Scottish contingent) to the Iraqi charnel-house, and the hopelessness of Afghanistan.

But over exactly the same period, globalisation has been changing everything in quite different ways. A profound shift of outlook has encouraged aspirations for change and new starts – 'tumbled as they are into endless connection', in Geertz's phrase, great powers and poor devils alike. For all its pitfalls, the one world thrown up remains an authentically wider and expanding one; and bound, therefore, to resonate particularly strongly in a culture like Scotland's. In some ways Scottish society may have become over-committed to outflow and identity-switches – pathologically outward-looking, as it were. However, this same inclination may have attuned it to the new totalising perspective, and to both the secular and religious belief-systems that have accompanied it. Globality is a disconcerting successor to foundering imperialism. But however much the former must distance itself from the latter, the line of descent should not be occluded.

The UK posture under both Thatcher and Blair has been as a vocal leader of an unreformed global imperium, one that bases itself on the Cold War's conclusion. The descent upon Iraq should have been a victory for that would-be new, US-led world order. It has turned into an infamous and gory failure of the old, in which Great Britain's role has lapsed into a despicable mixture of bleating apologist and camp guard. Could any contrast be greater, or less controllable in its repercussions? In the old-Brit two-party system, both Tories and Labour supported the American neo-imperial adventure; but neither imagined that failure might impose intolerable strains, not simply on those in office, but on the grander system whose axis remains the 1707 Treaty of Union.

Fry's history crowns an ongoing debate about British identity and inheritance that includes Linda Colley's *Britons, Forging the Nation*, Thomas Smout's *History of the Scottish People*, Neal Ascherson's *Stone Voices* and Christopher Harvie's *Mending Scotland*. In Scotland at least, it looks as if popular instinct and response are now overtaking such 'history wars'. I cited above the question Fry concludes with, of 'making greater haste' to return to independence; and answers are already being given, by one opinion poll after another. In November 2006 the *Scotsman* published a survey,

> showing a clear majority of Scots favour independence, and illustrating a significant swing from Labour to the SNP. The *Scotsman* ICM poll found 51 per cent now favoured full independence with only 39 per cent against – the biggest level of support for separatism for eight years. The poll also forecasts major gains for the SNP at next year's Holyrood elections with the party on course to win enough seats to form Britain's first nationalist-led government.

In the run-up to the May 2007 elections for the devolved parliaments in Scotland and Wales – two days after the 300th commemoration of the Union, for the Scots – and with the worst of the Iraqi tail-end still to come, a majority is looking forward to independence. As in all similar surveys, only a section of the emergent majority can be regular voters for the Scottish National Party, though their support is now steadily rising from its normal 25 per cent. In other words, a broader movement including Liberal-Democrats, Greens, Socialists and many Labour rank-and-file supporters is already in existence, and likely to be allies of the Nationalists next year. Fry's book is in effect an argument for a reformed Scottish

Conservatism to join them, and secure an independent platform for separate democratic advance.

Stranger still, this Tercentenary election will itself be a by-product of New Labour's half-hearted constitutional reforms after its 1997 return to office. Then, the rising autonomist pressures within Labour's ranks in Scotland and Wales made it necessary to experiment cautiously with 'home rule'. It was taken for granted that a semi-proportional electoral system would be the best form for the devolved assemblies. Britannic mythology remained unshakably convinced that proportionality and fair shares are recipes for democratic anarchy and incompetence – the opposite of 'sovereignty', the stable and supposedly omnipotent authority cherished by the 1688 system. Thus a carefully delineated 'fair go' might help keep the discontented marginals harmlessly busy, and lessen the prospect of nationalism winning real power.

In fact what it provided was some breathing-space for new ideas to fight their way into Welsh and Scottish public opinion, and eventually into regional office. These powers are cramped, naturally, and counterbalanced by a gross reinforcement of central and increasingly authoritarian rule. But there's no mystery about this: such reinforcement had been one aim of the devolution strategy itself, from the start – 'a regime of provincial subordination', as Fry calls it. In that sense, 'devolution' can also be interpreted as another version of older historical models like the Soviet imperium of 1946–89: folk-dance as inoculation against serious political independence (and capacity for dissent).

On the constitutional reform front, the radical horizons of 1998 have taken on the dimensions of a disintegrating dog-kennel. In 2005, the ancient Westminster magic returned New Labour to office with a large majority based upon *less than 22 per cent* of the electoral vote. New Labour then returned the favour by making clear it had no serious plans whatever to farther alter the system that has 'served us so well'. In 1997 for instance, the preposterous House of Lords was to have been transformed into an at least semi-democratic, electable second chamber. But a decade on, this affront to democracy still awaits its nemesis – the only substantial difference being that by now nobody expects anything better, or indeed takes much interest in the farce. Blair's collapse has involved his interrogation by the police about an ongoing peerages-for-cash scandal. 'Modernisation' of this kind has generated a UK climate recognisable enough in many other parts of the neoliberal world: generalised scorn and despair of politics and politicians, and mounting anguish about what the country now *means*, in a shrinking world-web that somehow renders identity more, rather than less, important.

This is of course the background against which more and more Scots (of all shapes and grades) perceive 'no alternative' to resuming independence. Not 'claiming' it like an ex-colony, but (as Fry describes the situation) merely returning to a long-postponed normality, via renunciation of the Treaty of Union. At the opening session of the devolved Scottish Parliament in 1998, its first Chairperson, Winifred Ewing, simply declared that an assembly abrogated *sine die* in

1707 was back, and about to resume business. In spite of everything, against all the odds, the day had come. And found the nation still there. Her statement of presence was widely ridiculed at the time for its remote romanticism, and flight from practical reality. Nine years later, we can see that Ewing was merely slightly ahead of the times.

A bell was actually being rung, and not just for the media, or the attendant elite. Whatever the spores that coursed out from that day (other historians will trace them), they seem in the end to have reached and disturbed every obscure, puzzled, tongueless corner of this odd, relatively well-off *and* relatively deprived society: 'developed', and yet seriously lacking in communal will and self-confidence. That will-less void was of course the Union's achievement. And as Fry argues, the process of recovering and peopling it is now unlikely to cease. In other words, Scottish independence is about more than a 'democratic deficit' in general terms. A more specific history and discontent has brought acknowledgment that some democratic *nationalism* is the only way to carry it forward.

But *The Union* also omits, or skates over, several important themes. For all its merits, it remains the work of a thoroughly disgruntled conservative. More precisely, it expresses an unusual anarcho-conservatism: that is, a radicalism of the Right rather than the Left, but with quite similar shortcomings. Fry's forte is caustic impatience with compromises, half-measures, correctness and institutional stuffed shirts. Funny and liberating as this is, it leads him to underestimate the important part that equivocation and piecemeal changes have played in the formation of today's Scottish nationalism.

After the rise of the SNP in the 1970s, an initial referendum was staged on 'Home Rule' in 1979, under James Callaghan's Labour government. It failed, and was succeeded by 18 years of Thatcherite Conservatism. But throughout these years, movements quietly continued to keep the issue alive, and a left-of-centre Constitutional Convention was set up that planned a better kind of self-government, supposedly distinct from both the Unionist regime and straightforward separation. This won increasing support and respect, and naturally provided much of the content for Blair's Scotland Act in 1997–98. Scots themselves did most of the work for their devolution; and insufficient as it has proved to be, this process nonetheless created real foundations for today's parliament. It is not the case that it has *just* been a 'flawed outcome… all dressed up in tartan with nowhere to go', as Fry puts it, 'wasting its time and money on trivialities, on efforts at micro-management of personal lives'.

The author maintains that there can be 'no satisfactory halfway house' between region and true nationhood. Possibly; but an unsatisfactory halfway house may also have prepared the way for something better. Its emergent political class are no more all 'mediocrities' than were the parliamentarians of 1706–07 whom Fry describes. And its very existence has injected some confidence into a nation confined for three centuries to the most limited 'low politics' of town and county councils. Here, Fry's radicalism of the right seems almost as astigmatic as that

of the left-wing enthusiasts he has so often (and with reason) criticised. He has
confidence that a more distinctive Scottish conservatism will emerge, and be
another plus for independence. But its formation too is bound to depend on
gradual development, involving both alliances and contrasts with other movements of a new Scottish left and centre.

There is another absence from *The Union*'s police station line-up: 'ethnicity'.
The term has become inescapable, and at a time of recently revived nationalism
and conflict is especially important. In spite of its novelty (the 1960s), 'ethnic' is
today routinely applied to both separatist and minority situations: being 'ethnic
Albanian' or an 'ethnic Kurd' has become indispensable for deciphering respective problems, while multiculturalism has come to haunt every metropolitan
language. For Scots it is even more significant: as I said earlier, they have become
a nation of emigrants inhabiting a world configured by such stereotypes. And
one response has been the general adoption of what Tom Devine, author of *The
Scottish Nation* (1999), calls 'Highlandism': an exceptionally visible mixture of
tartan plaid, bagpipe music, folk-dance and the cult of Robert Burns. Like many
others, Fry may despise this ethnic mythomania, but in a work so focused on
the meaning of 1707 for the present (and immediate future), more should have
been said about it.

It is crucially important to stress the drastic variance of both history and
contemporary politics in Scotland from nearly all of what that mythology implies.
There is no single or even majority 'ethnos' among the Scots: the nation is irre-
trievably composite in origin, and to a striking extent unified more by institutions and past statehood than by either language, customs or culture. In the
conclusion to his *Scottish Nationality* (2001), Murray Pittock stresses that deciphering complexity is the difficult central task of anyone working in the field,
frequently against pressures from the London-based media. In November 2006,
the *Economist* carried a cartoon depicting Gordon Brown, of all people, dancing
about in a kilt with a discarded claymore at his feet. As Pittock observes,

> Cartoons in *The Times* and the *Guardian*... continue to show the exponents
> of Scottish nationality in the claymore-wielding, poverty-stricken garb of
> the Jacobites thus caricatured 250 years ago. Both elements feed each other:
> the self-congratulation of elements in a local elite are identified as provincial
> *bluster* by the metropolitan eye, which as a result sees no reason to alter its
> own perspective.

Everyone in Scotland knows in advance that each move towards a resumption
of independence will be treated to this kind of abuse: parochialism, call of the
blood, instinct taking over from reason, 'ethnicity' for its own sake – and so on,
and on. Only the previous week Lisa Vickers, the United States Consul in
Scotland, contributed to the knee-jerking when she announced that Americans
will always stick by England-Britain. The same hostility is quite normally voiced
as fear of a North Sea Bosnia, or as misguided opposition to the healthy style of

globalisation represented by President Bush and Blair's New Labour. That is what the 'Greatness' business is about – whether in Washington DC, or among its bed-raggled camp-followers in Whitehall and elsewhere. And 'ethnicity' is by contrast inherently narrow, a betrayal of greatness-defined progress: a mortal menace to the present, therefore, or a hopeless retreat into the past – or preferably both. Globalisation is meant for Greats, not tomfool left-overs and ethnic nostalgics. It's G8 stuff, nothing to do with West Papuans, Kurds, Chechens, Scots, Burmese Karens, Tibetans, Welsh, Québecois, left-out Muslims, Basques, Montenegrins, and all the rest.

It is quite true that a widespread and often unpleasant attitude surfaces among Scots: 'anti-Englishness'. This bears little relation to textbook ethnicity or blood-line inheritance. It is, in truth, anti-Britishness: something like latter-day anti-Americanism, a resentment of overweening state power and assumed superiority. Though Fry provides many examples of the mentality at work in 1706–07, and is good at situating the strange story of the Union in the broader framework of European history, he says little directly about England in this sense. The absence is all the more noticeable because of the book's urgently contemporary bearing. He reveals his own conversion to Scottish independence, but says next to nothing about the English nationalism this is bound to confront. However, The Union exposes how a placid assumption of England's ingrained universality ('ancient' even then) dominated the negotiations three centuries ago. Even before it assumed formal existence, 'Britain' was taken to mean Anglo-Britain, an imperially open society which all others should naturally accept, and indeed welcome. Such leadership was not to rest upon brute force, but 'hegemony'.

What harm can there be, after all, in a Great Power shepherding the way towards civilisation, along roads that all must, in the end, imitate and follow? The United Kingdom's hegemonic role (or 'burden') may have been merged into that of the United States, as Consul Vickers now reminds impatient Scots. But England's essence will remain true to the outgoing mission – as if the Protestant-ism of earlier Britons had now mutated into the neoliberalism of post-1989 victory. New times, however, call for a quite different style of outreach, beginning with emancipation from the paleo-imperialism of the Bush- Blair North Atlantic. Just as free trade was impossible without assorted forms of protection and barriers, so globalisation will only work via renewed forms of nationalism and identity conservation. I think the Scots know as much, if not more, about the outward-bound mentality. And they may be more aware of its pitfalls and temptations. Why else is the contemporary scene dominated by an ever-growing list of battling nationalist and irredentist claims, and 'rediscovered' identity concerns? Neoliberal correctness put these all down as fossils. But since consciousness-raising too is part of globalisation, the relics can't help growing more aware of their plight. And a self-conscious 'relic' is a nationalist dilemma. So far the burning-glass of Iraq has generated or concentrated three of them. Mobilised nationalities would not submit to high-command imperatives in the 20th century; they are surely even less likely to do so in the 21st. Seen in this way, Scotland's situation is typical rather than exceptional; and England's turn will surely come – 'turning inward' is only a part of doing this, necessary for any remedy.

Even so, outside observers are bound to ask: isn't *some* intermediate or compromise arrangement possible, among nationalities so long conjoined, and sharing so much – even with all the shortcomings of the Union? For example, a federal or confederal British polity where England, Scotland, Wales, one part of Ireland, and the micro-states, obtain equality of status and agree on common rules and norms, and shared representation where this is appropriate? As things stand right now, the answer has to be: 'no'. While such formulae are easy to imagine, they are difficult to sustain for long in practice because of one factor: 'England' – at once the largest component of any such state, yet without any separate political identity or institutions whatever and still so merged into a discredited Britain that few will even contemplate de-merger; or if they do, only via the shudder of a deprived, somehow shrunken 'little England'. New Labour's 'Council of the Isles' disappeared within months, when it became obvious that it could never function without more serious reform of the central power-apparatus, including its electoral system. In practice, therefore, the current turning away from Britishness has no alternative except straightforward independence, or separation – or (for the Scots) reversion to nation-state business as usual.

The move is depicted by Anglo-American leaders and Consuls as 'radical', extremist, and so on, but such phrases are self-serving rhetoric. To anyone like myself, following events from far away and returning only now and then for re-immersion, something else is far more noticeable. This is what I can only describe as mounting matter-of-factness. From the sixties through into the nineties of last century, most debate on nationalism was conducted in a furnace of mutual loathing and recrimination. Passions could hardly have been more intense – especially on the side of threatened Britishness. In Scotland, this led to institutional hatreds and vendetta-like feuds between SNP nationalists and British-Labour loyalists. Now, however, the returning native finds relative composure, and even a degree of resignation. 'Pros' and 'cons' are today – which now does mean almost every single day – listed and contrasted quite equably, in an atmosphere occasionally testy or bitter, but quite free from the explosive incriminations and lifetime sentences of a decade ago.

The passion of 'Britishness' has lost all weight and gravitas, except in Gordon Brown's sermons, or in strained liberal attempts to promote a civic patriotism supposedly inseparable from Britishness. As a consequence, a real openness has appeared, much more favourable to independence. This is why the Scottish Catholic electorate (about 17–18 per cent, Scotland's biggest cultural minority) has been drawn to vote for nationalism – and, of course, why Cardinal O'Brien appears so reconciled to independence 'before too long', as the *Scotsman* reported in October 2006. It is also why (as Fry's book and *Prospect* piece suggest) Conservatives are finding themselves in an analogous situation. Few now expect Great Britain to make a phoenix-like reappearance at the next UK general election; but nobody at all expects Cameron's neo-Toryism *not* to win in England.

Fry's book brings to mind a particularly revealing incident in recent Scottish history. In December 1992, when the European Council heads of government were meeting in Edinburgh, a big demonstration was organised in the heart of the city, the Meadows Park. Its aim was to remind delegates that a nation was missing from the assembly, one that wanted to be heard again. An open-top double-decker bus was used as a platform among the trees, and novelist William McIlvanney gave from there what became the most memorable address of the day. Neal Ascherson has provided an equally memorable account of it in *Stone Voices*:

> And then, in a tone of tremendous pride, he said this: 'We gather here like refugees in the capital of our own country. We are almost 700 years old, and we are still wondering what we want to be when we grow up. Scotland is in an intolerable position. We must never acclimatise to it, never! Scottish-ness is not some pedigree lineage. *This is a mongrel tradition!*' At those words, for reasons which perhaps neither he nor they ever quite understood, the crowd broke into cheers and applause which lasted on and on. What survives from those moments on the Meadows are his proclamation of Scotland the mongrel, and the joy these words released.

I was present at the event, and can recall the sensation vividly. It is true that nobody quite understood the thrill that made every nerve in the Meadows tingle. But that was because McIlvanney had touched something far deeper than the terms and conscious aspirations that had brought the crowd together, and still formed the official discourse of the day. He had broken through onto some unclaimed terrain, and given provisional voice to a pack of mongrels by rejecting the very idea of a pedigree 'lineage' (or ethnicity). He was speaking for people in a field or on a hillside, from nowhere or anywhere, with mud on their shoes and rain in their faces – yet some kind of different covenant in their hearts.

That was only three years after the fall of the Berlin Wall, and globalisation was still in its infancy. But in retrospect, wasn't it already fostering something different, far beneath the official chorus-lines of free trade and deregulation? Mongrelhood is also the asymmetric obverse of the older, uniformed identities of state and nationhood. In the Scottish context, it is also curiously like the positive assertion of what had been lacking since 1707: 'self-confidence', whose desolating absence was somehow converted into a virtue, even a sort of strength. The joy came from that acknowledgment of something real, the sudden awak-ening of a feeling that Scottish half-life was no longer fate – plus the obscure sense that altering circumstances might yet favour this change, rescuing it from the confines of pedigree and repetition. In Emma Rothschild's very apt phrase, a world of 'foundlings' was already on the rise, to which even a disabled country might hope to belong. Globalisation does not make all nations disappear, or become equally small. But it does make some permanently and irreversibly 'smaller', in the sense of rendering older styles of imperium and domination impossible. At bottom, the reason may be quite simple: in the new global dimension, not only are there vastly more mongrels than pedigree hounds – this was of course always the case – but the former cannot help acquiring voice and presence. Hence a process of democratic warming is going on, alongside global warming. And on that foundation, 'anti-global*ism*' is less an opposite than a modification of globality, and of the distinct yet open societies that will alone make the global tolerable. The '-ism' was the trouble, not the opening-up.

And new foundlings may be particularly useful in formulating these. In his account of the origins of modern Scotland, Fry several times makes the interesting point that Scottish anti-Union parliamentarians were not arguing for pedigree-preservation and protection, or the erection of new barriers, in 1706–07. On the contrary, some were demanding free trade, equal treatment and openness, and others a solution like the Netherlands United Provinces – with both perceiving the retention of national identity as necessary for such answers. The Union, on the other hand, stood for something simpler: 'incorporation' (the unvarying watchword of its devotees). That is, cementing troublesome diversity into one increasingly successful but quasi-mercantilist system: the armed imposition of laws convenient to *its* leadership, prosperity and empire.

The Union describes the process, and ends by arguing that it is time for our little country to de-incorporate itself. All genuine mongrels will agree with Fry on this. There is also a case for the more general and theoretical redefinition of what could be called the scale of nationhood. After a long period during which bigger was in some ways better, with the initial rise of industrialisation and the diffusion of global commerce, globalisation may have inaugurated another, in which smaller is, if not better, then at least just as good (and occasionally with the advantage over the erstwhile great, the muscle- and hidebound). The age of the body-builders has ended, as that of dinosaurs once did; that of smaller mammalian fitness is still being worked out. Is it really surprising that the United Kingdom should be one prime site for this to happen?

CHAPTER TWENTY-SEVEN

Globalisation and Nationalism: The New Deal

The 'Edinburgh Lectures', Edgelands Project

MARCH 2008

Life and culture continue to yield new emergent social entities, new adaptive forms brought into being in order to pursue survival and reproduction both through and in spite of the specific work of capitalism.

RICHARD N. ADAMS, 'The Dynamics of Societal Diversity: Notes from Nicaragua', *American Ethnologist*, 8/1, 1981

I KNOW, FAR TOO much has been said and written already about 'globalisation', *mondialisation, Globalisierung*, and also about their opposite numbers, anti-globalisation, 'glocalism' and so on. No one should propose adding to this untidy heap, without doubts and reservations (for a thoughtful mapping of the untidiness, see Perry Anderson, 'Jottings on the Conjuncture', *New Left Review* 48, November-December 2007).

Yet I would like to try my hand again. The only excuse possible is that of approaching the *Zeitgeist* from a different angle. Rather than adding one more interpretation, I will try to decipher something that is in course of being said, and said not (or not only) by intellectuals, academics and *intéllos*, the shamans of our age. The emerging message I'm after is the one that may be coming from below, from – to name one point on this compass – the electorate of Scotland.

Part of that message was delivered in May 2007, in the vote that returned a Holyrood parliament dominated by the Scottish National Party leading to the minority government that has followed. It was a message favourable to the independence cause, and seems certain to carry the Scots forward to one or more referenda on the matter fairly soon.

But I suspect that a great deal more than this was already being said, or half-said, or sought for, in this striking shift. At least part may have come from deeper sources, which surely relate to the current way of the world – 'globalisation' and all that – as well as to party struggles, the plight of the British and Scottish Labour Parties, and the weird dilemmas of Westminster's archaic constitution. Political leaders naturally hope people are voting for policies on this and that, after canny calculations of gains and losses; but of course voters are also concerned (often more concerned) with 'directions': general inclinations of society and soul, affected by passions or longings that may well be in the background of debate.

Scotland's People Flow

There is perhaps a feature of the Scottish electorate that may help us towards such a diagnosis. It's the one indicated by Tom Devine in his *The Scottish Nation 1700–2000* (1999), where he argues that the Scots have been the leaders in modern emigration. Comparatively viewed, they appear to have outdone the Greeks, the Irish, Jews, Italians and Norwegians from the 18th to the 20th centuries, and deposited a very extensive global diaspora whose size remains infuriatingly difficult to estimate. Most guesses put it at eight or nine times the size of our present-day population, and research continues today in north America, Australasia and southern Africa to establish both its numbers and its contemporary outlook.

But my point here is less the migrants than as what they left behind, a population unusually affected by so much departure, over such a prolonged period of time – around two and a half centuries. In Scotland, Romany or Gypsy nomads are usually called simply 'travelling people'; an appropriate label from residents who, if not travelling themselves, invariably have well-travelled relatives in Calgary, Cape Town, Nova Scotia, Auckland, Chicago or Perth (Western Australia) and who either go there, or receive fairly irregular visits from them and their descendants.

Michael Russell has some amusing phrases about this in his book *The Next Big Thing* (2007). Wherever you go, he points out, you find that 'Insecurity is part of the Scottish condition. We come from somewhere else, and settle where we feel least uncomfortable. We belong to places that we only visit, yet we are visitors in the place where we live…'

My recent travelling from Melbourne to Edinburgh gave me a personal stake in the long-distance-family culture. The dates of leaving my Scots-founded Australian city and university meant that I missed meeting up with a Queensland cousin; but on the other hand I was awarded the chance of catching up with another lot, who were just then visiting the homeland after prospering in the Republic of Ireland.

In his book *Devine* diagnoses what he calls 'Highlandism' as one by-product of this sustained communal haemorrhage: the projection of imagined origins, a famously synthetic folklore of 'Auld Lang Syne', an identity deploying the most colourful items from successive wardrobes and cabin-trunks, with appropriate music and displays. The least home-bound population on earth has generated the most home-bound and nostalgic ideology of *Heimat*.

But more than folklore is at stake here. This outstanding (and continuing) haemorrhage from such a small population may have fostered an unusually exposed and outward-looking mentality, a mind-set forcibly attuned to a wider view, and to contrasts of culture and custom.

More than most other nations, Scots have been so to speak 'pre-globalised' by such mundane circumstances. This matter-of-fact *Weltanschauung* has little to do with the new *intéllo* fad of 'cosmopolitanism' – the aloofness deemed ethically appropriate for the globalising times.

When Scots explorer John MacDouall Stuart reached the centre of the Australian continent in 1860, during his famed south-north expedition, the flag he proudly planted on a small hill there had to be the Union Jack, not the Saltire. Such was the old 1707 deal, the enchantment of that age. And what one might call the 'self-colonisation' implicit in such triumphs has proved much harder to recover from than other, cruder forms of imperial hegemony.

The Theory of Scale

At which point, let me return to the enchantment of today. In spite of the reservations about 'globaloney' I mentioned at the start, some theory of what global circumstances means is of course needed. And here, one way forward in the morass may be to look back more carefully at certain neglected views of nationhood. What I have in mind is the curious question of the scale of modern countries and states. This tends to be taken for granted in most commentary and policy-formation; but should not be. It relates quite directly to what the last century's main theorist of nationalism, Ernest Gellner, always posed as the crucial problem in his field.

The underlying puzzle has always been not why there are so many nation states and distinct ethnic cultures but why are there so few. In his classic *Nations and Nationalism* (1983) the social anthropologist Gellner observes that, although no one will ever know exactly, there can't be less than somewhere between 6,000 and 8,000 identifiable ethno-linguistic populations scattered round the globe.

Why, then, are there less than 200 or so national states? When he was writing in 1983 there were well under 200 United Nations representatives, and though this number has grown, forecasts for the later 21st century don't usually envisage more than something between 220–230 new (and naturally mostly smaller) independent states.

Gellner's characteristic explanation of this disparity was in terms of overall social and cultural development. The culprit, he argued, had been first-round industrialisation and urbanisation. These were not processes planned by some celestial council from a suitably all-powerful centre, such as Beijing, Delhi, Rome, Madrid (or wherever). No, industrialisation evolved chaotically, in fits and starts, out of the unlikely fringe location of the north Atlantic seaboard, and was marked throughout by chronic unevenness and widespread antagonism.

It was impossible for industries, larger-scale commerce, greater market-places and banks to develop at a small-town or region scale. Nor were they ever likely to be set up by the sprawling dynastic and military empires of antiquity, whose essential concern remained expansion, hierarchy and secure military dominance of an inherited rural world.

By contrast, capitalism (as it would later be called, notably by Scots) was able to evolve only at an intermediate level, within societies smaller than the antique dynasties but much bigger than most ethno-linguistic groups. It demanded the formation of relatively large socio-economic spaces, to be viable.

Viability in that sense may never have been a fixed or unalterable condition. However, in retrospect we perceive that for over two centuries it did come to mean (as it were) 'something like France' or like England (in the familiar 'Anglo-British' sense): not something like Brittany, Provence, Monaco, Wales or Ireland.

The Scots of course had already situated themselves within the bigger-is-better expansion, via the 1707 Treaty of Union. Their fate was to be the unusual one of successful 'self-colonisation' in that world. That is, they avoided conquest or assimilation, and conserved a distinct civil society – but only by accepting (and in fact eagerly embracing and preaching) the broader rules of the new age, as laid down by France, England and other more viable polities.

As Gellner points out, such rules required a sufficiently common culture and language, and the cultivation of popular assent. This should not (incidentally) be confused with present-day 'nationalism'. Nationhood and nationality culture and politics may have been primordial; but the '-ism' is a different and far more peculiar story. Nationalism didn't enter common parlance until the last third of the 19th century, after Abraham Lincoln's victory over the American secessionists, and the Franco-Prussian war.

Gellner always emphasised the general point, and newer historical analyses have strongly confirmed it. In all languages, nationalism became common sense in conjunction with 'imperialism', as part of the climate leading into the world wars, and finally the Cold War of 1947–1989.

'Nationalism is not the awakening and assertion of mythical, supposedly natural and given units...' is how he sums it up; 'It is, on the contrary, the crystallisation of new units, suitable for the conditions now prevailing', by which he means these emergent circumstances of primarily capitalist socio-economic development, at first in the north Atlantic area and then more globally. (3)

It was those conditions that favoured the norm, the typical scale and standards for the political entities of (approximately) 1789–1989. British nationalism was of course just one chapter in that story, a value-parade both enforced and widely exported – and defended down to the present with mounting desperation by New Labour governments.

From Fixed to Sliding Scale

But what I want to suggest is that it is precisely 'those conditions' that have changed, and are changing. Ernest Gellner was thinking in the 1980s, when the old identikit 'nation-state' rules remained in place, albeit shakily. But one aspect of globalisation has (notoriously) been the collapse of at least some of these rules. When commentators declare so confidently that it 'undermines' borders and flags, as well as customs-posts, they usually fail to make a vital distinction.

Yes, possibly blood is draining out of the '-ism'; but not out of nationalities, identities, cultural contrasts, and the wish (or the determination) to have, or to win, different forms of collective 'say' in the brave new globe. If we simply deconstruct his historic argument it follows, surely, that scale also must be changing its significance. However, speculation in this zone has been limited by a curious monotheism of outlook: the child, doubtless, of Christianity, Islam, and their kind, as well as of the odd theatre of the cold war's iron curtain.

Globality is decreed in advance to possess one overall or commanding meaning: either neo-liberal progress or some new universal oppression, choose your side. In fact, what globality may be ushering in is more like a range of conflicts, it may be too much to say 'battlefields' – but certainly terrains of decision, alternative directions and possibilities. Umberto Eco has identified one of these alternatives clearly, and amusingly, in his *Turning Back the Clock* (2007).

Look at the world since the first Gulf war of 1991, he asks: just who is so plainly clinging to past patterns and habits? We see the explosion and spread of what he labels 'neo-war', the curse of United States-led globalisation. That is, of threatened and actual incursions against largely phantasmagoric enemies like 'terrorism' and Islam or (on the other side) 'the west' and crusade-style Christianity or evangelism.

The aim of these is to maintain and mobilise the mass public opinion upon which great (or would-be great) power élites still depend, against the individualism, privatisation and indifference that accompany so many transnational blessings and successes. Societies have mutated far more than states. And this is why the latter find themselves tempted into another version of the 19th century restoration that tried to impose stability, values (etc.) between Napoleon the First and the 'springtime of nations' in 1848. Gordon Brown and George W. Bush can't literally put the clock back, any more than Prince Metternich could; but at least they can try to slow it down a bit, with plausible aggression (ideally involving mass-destruction threats), and of course the new forms of persuasion provided by the revolution in communications.

The guilty parties here are unmistakable: they are the old lags of Gellner's bigger-and-better epoch, plus new members and applicants to join the body-builders' club – countries endowed with that favourite attribute of British leaders, 'clout'. America First, naturally, but with Great Spain, Great Russia, Great Serbia alongside cheerleader Great Britain, plus rising muscle-flexers like India, Indonesia, Iran and China.

At the same time as it tries to take over globalisation, this great-at-all-costs club is busy acquiring its own academic credentials as well. That is, professors who seriously believe that the globe is safer – more secure – with well-padded, first-round veterans in control. An astonishing volume entitled *No More States? Globalisation, National Self-Determination and Terrorism* (Rowman and Little-field, 2006) appeared from the stables of University College, Los Angeles, arguing not only that there should be no more of these small nuisances, but that possibly a reversal of thrust may be possible, in the sense of 'agglomerationisand' – returns to one or other metropolitan fold by populations tempted astray by romantic delusion or bad verse. In case anyone fears I'm making this up, let me quote from co-editor Richard Rosecrance's summing up:

> Potentially dissident Scotland, the Basques, Quebec and other provincial populations have gradually come to see the federation-metropole as a less hostile environment, and their independence movements have declined in proportion... (hence) few new states are likely to be created... It is possible, even, that the number of fully independent states may decline as political units begin to merge with each other... .

This conclusion had the good luck to be published not long before the 2007 elections in the United Kingdom, and in that sense comment may be superfluous. But the general sense is unmistakable: global history must be frozen in its tracks, for the convenience of existing agglomerations, including the United States and loyal fan-club Great Britain.

Only thus will stability and reasonable global order prevail. 'Bigger is better' was therefore not just a phase social evolution had to go through, to improve the general lot. No, it has to be made permanent, virtually eternalised, in the imagined interest of the species, indistinguishable from the established interest of the body-builders' club.

The Stowaways Club

And on the other side, what about the no-hopers, nuisances and parasites? Here the list could hardly be more different, but in newly surprising ways. The best approach to it remains *Foreign Policy* magazine's 'Globalisation Index', a now long-running attempt to estimate and compare national successes and failures of the global times. The index takes a variety of social and cultural variables into account, not only 'GDP' and other strictly economic data. I only have the 2006 'top 20' list with me, and have only just received 2007.

But in fact its overall aspect has changed little from year to year: 'Singapore, Switzerland, Ireland, Denmark, Canada, Netherlands, Sweden, New Zealand, Finland, Norway, Israel, the Czech Republic' and so on and on, down to Slovenia, currently at number twenty (as well as providing us with the head of the European Union commission). I note that the new entrants for 2007 are Hong Kong, Jordan and Estonia.

True, there are also some exceptional entries. The United States appears in the top 20 because (as the editors apologetically explain), in spite of manufacturing decline and job exports, most of the new globe's spare cash has been washing irresistibly through it, at least until the regrettable 'sub-prime' property hitches of 2007. And the UK also figures, for related if more peculiar reasons: the inherited institutional role of City of London institutions in all such massive financial flows (at least, until the weird lapse of Northern Rock, now part of the state).

However, the broader picture remains unmistakable: a springtime of victorious dwarves, one might say. No more convincing illustration of globalisation's new 'sliding scale' can be imagined. And with equal ease, anyone can see Wales, Scotland and Northern Ireland queueing up to claim their places.

Sooner or later, one or more formal referenda will be of course be required for such entrants, but a kind of referendum movement, or direction, is already under way in Scotland, a gathering mixture of questioning and hardening conviction.

Among Scots this takes the form of a firming 'self-confidence', a kind of matter-of-factness I mentioned earlier. Again, Michael Russell puts it well in *The Next Big Thing*, where he points out the most significant trait of the post-May 2007 minority government may be its contribution to this cementing process:

> The real main purpose of our parliament may merely be to stop us moving back – to create the space in which we can get on and learn some other lessons. Lessons of confidence, and self-confidence. Lessons about who we really are, and what we really want...

Societal Diversity

As we have seen, the old question used to be: 'Are you big enough to survive and develop in an industrialising world?' The advent of globalisation is replacing this with another, something close to: 'Are you small and smart enough to survive, and claim a positive place in the common global culture?' Not too surprisingly, the most common answer coming up from the bowels and steerage accommodation of the common ship is: 'You bet we are... nor do we mean to be deprived of the chance.'

I think a sense of this may have been part of the election groundswell last May, in both Wales and Scotland – and maybe most notably in Scotland, for the historical reasons already noted. On the emerging global vessel, it's presence or nothing: speak up and act up, or the already existing officer and first-class passengers – the body-builders' club in charge of the bridge – will not only stay there, but reinforce their grip over the lower-deck rabble of dependents, servants and migrating stowaways. In a remarkable essay called simply 'Presence' (*History & Theory* 45, October 2006) the Dutch social historian Eelco Runia has made the point with a humorous metaphor.

Globalisation can't help meaning that we're all 'in the same boat'; but on this noble vessel, most of the occupants can't help being virtual 'stowaways', travelling either on fake documents and overdrawn credit cards, or just secretly, smuggled or bribed aboard at night or in disguise. Now however, as the global process continues its erratic and ambiguous course, the rabble has begun appearing on deck, in broad daylight. And not just for the fresh air, or to admire the views.

No, they want their tickets. It's time they were recognised, and released from the dank lower levels of ballast, coiled ropes and awful stairwells. 'Equality' is the standard demand, accompanied naturally by demands for use of the cafeteria and lounges, spare beds and some formal presence by representation on the bridge. There used to be bigger-is-best techniques for avoiding this nuisance: alibis like 'federalism', 'devolution' – home rule for the steerage classes, as it were. Allow them enough folk-dancing and local government, that'll keep them out of trouble.

But of course 'presence' in Eelco Runia's sense represents none of these palliatives. The spirit of Gertrude Stein is turning out to be quite strong up on deck, something to do with the democratic air. On this bigger, final boat everyone is now aboard, 'self-government' is self-government is self-government. What Charles Stewart Parnell meant in the famous remark about nobody having 'a right to fix the boundary of the march of a nation', in the sense of its will and sovereignty.

The motto prefixes the Scottish government's 'national conversation' on Scotland's future. In the new context this means not (or not necessarily) '6,000 or 8,000' states corresponding to Gellner's sources of human diversity. But it does imply that no court of fixers should decide who is in or out, or what their relationships with one another should be.

In practice, though, it probably signifies at least something like the foreseeable figures I mentioned before – around 220–230 sovereignties over this century and next. To an increasing degree these are likely to relate to one another via formulae of confederation, quite different from federalism, subsidiarity, devolved regionalism and other dodges of the bygone era. Scotland, Wales and Northern Ireland are, like many other smaller entities around the globe, simply joining the queue to be heard on that wavelength.

Across the Universals

And it's worth emphasising something else too, at this point – something fundamental that globalisation is bringing home, everywhere and to everybody. While the threats of globalising uniformity are often exaggerated, they do remain real enough to have brought something else, something really new, into recognisable perspective. One might call this 'the threat to Babel'. Globalisation can't help a degree of sameness; but, more strongly than empires of the past, the new mode may be forcing something more profound into existence.

The counter to 'all-the-same-ism' can only be cross-fertilisation, the societal equivalent of Charles Darwin's new species and forms. That's what 'the universal' has always been, the capacity to transcend, to fuse, to breed hybrid novelty rather than merely 'agglomerate' in Richard Rosecrance's sense.

However, the power to do this rests at bottom upon more than the maintenance of diversity – it demands that differentiation be favoured, be positively fostered, by globalisation. Globalisation will have to perpetuate Babel, as well as confronting all its difficulties and contradictions.

At bottom, the reason is that human universals arise only via contrasts, by the transcendence of borders, via cross-fertilisation, through hybrids and surprises, from the unheard-of, in communities not just 'imagined' in Benedict Anderson's celebrated phrase, but previously unimaginable, from presences whose spell makes the past into a bearable future.

And how on earth can anything like that be achieved without 'independence'? In this context independence surely isn't – or isn't only – backward-looking or inward-looking me-first, chip on the shoulder time, and so on. It's more like seizing the chance – and making sure it isn't the last chance – as the clock-hands move so decisively forward, the chance to contribute and to endure (or increase) with an emerging purpose not yet wholly known, because (as Eelco Runia puts it) societies must retain, or rediscover the power and confidence to surprise themselves. As (I would argue) both Scotland, Wales and Northern Ireland did in May 2007.

'Absolute Instinct?'

With all its daft twists and turns, and hopeless exaggerations, globalisation is providing new stimuli for nationality-politics. Not so much for 'nationalism' in the late 19th and 20th century sense, but definitely for the emergence of new, smaller communities of will and purpose – the nations of a new and deeply different age.

Mistaken theorists of an earlier time – myself among them – used to complain about Scotland missing or neglecting its national opportunities, or failing to participate in earlier waves of anti-colonial liberation.

But of course, the Scots were never colonised: as I pointed out earlier, they 'did it themselves' via 'self-colonisation', the subordinate affirmation of a kind of flightless or contained nationality, which implied exemption from many rules of the former imperial (and then anti-imperial) world.

But today that world, those rules, now are ended, and others are in formation. To resume the power of flight simply means participation in the new forms and rules, alongside many others.

It's a matter-of-fact need, neither too late nor too soon, and I suspect that something of this has already sunk into popular sensibility – the nascent 'common sense' of a different, dawning moment in history, the moment when Eelco Runia's 'presence' is possible for us, as well as for 'them' (up, out there).

There are endless problems and pitfalls as well, sure; but my task of summing up is also easy, since someone else has already said what I've been trying to put across this evening, only much more eloquently. So let the last word rest where it should, with our very own, dear Edwin Morgan. In 1991 he published a collection, *Hold Hands Among the Atoms* – gathered in 1994 in a larger volume, *Sweeping out the Dark* – that included the lines called simply: 'Difference':

The endless variousness is all for praises.
The faces, passing, never make an empire...
... You think not?
You'd rather have the second-best as long as
millions get it? – Mission, you cry, the mission!...
...
The endless variousness evolves, the empire
expires in frozen edicts, you can skate there,
but soon you're off the edge...
...
... The faces
pass, the individuals, how there can be such
difference we do not know but what we do know
is that an absolute instinct loves it different,
the world, the dialectic, the packed coaches
whistling at daybreak through the patched countries.

CHAPTER TWENTY-EIGHT

A Republican Monarchy?
England and Revolution

Foreword to the Enchanted Glass: Britain and its Monarchy

2011 EDITION

I'M WRITING THIS just after Her Majesty Queen Elizabeth II's visit to Dublin in May this year. And the Irish celebrations have come shortly after another British Royal Wedding Day, with schools on holiday, crowded streets in central London, and the media on full-alert for Kate Middleton and her husband-to-be, the Windsor Dynasty's future King William of the United Kingdom, Northern Ireland, Scotland, Wales and other remaining 'dependencies'.

The Enchanted Glass originally appeared in 1989, with the middle-aged Elizabeth II in a pink hat and white gloves waving from its cover; 23 years later she's still waving, and guaranteeing the British Crown for some years to come. Her son will then almost certainly succeed for a while as Charles IIIrd, with grandson William following on. So we find the principal Crown institution still hard at work re-establishing itself, and trying to look more plausible as a 21st century enterprise.

Nearly all commentators perceive Great Britain continuing to decline, as ex-imperial status turns into increasingly unavoidable marginality, screened by Special Relationships, the Commonwealth, and other old club subscriptions. This has so far striven to keep up appearances, via a kind of half-honourable decline: unwilling negotiations with retreat, rather than outright defeat, a piece-meal and staged withdrawal rather than mere eviction from the historical stage. However, the climate of accelerating decline brings other changes in its wake. I see now how at the end of the eighties I failed to focus sufficiently on one key motive for the successful working of 'enchantment': what one could call 'surro-gacy', in the sense of an English identity-diversion from standard-issue nationalism to the symbolic supra-nationality of a Royal Crown and Family. The unusual intensity and emotion of the latter has come from certain peculiarities of the former: as if a communal feeling unable to find appropriate modern expression has been compelled to find compensatory voice in another way, or upon a different (though related) level. Such deeper emotion contains a usually unacknowledged advantage. It absolves the majority English nationality from the customary '-ism' of recent history. No Anglo-national*ism* is felt necessary in the standard 19th-20th century form. Of course it manifests itself in sub-standard form, round the edges, as panic over immigration, and distrust of 'outsiders' and multi-culturalism. Yet its political expression has been very limited, in a 'British' National Party tied to extinct racism as well as to state decline.

Today's problems are the by-product of longer-range historical location. As Liah Greenfeld points out in her classic *Nationalism: Five Roads to Modernity*, England was 'God's First-born' in the formation of the Nation-state world: but this very priority meant that the English would not themselves become just another state, a national polity like all the rest. Naturally the English had to adapt themselves to the world they had set in motion and fostered, during the 18th and 19th centuries. But they did so in two main ways, both of which have now lost most of their sense. One was simply expansion: the 'greater England' represented by colonisation and the emigration of one generation after another over the era of empire. The other was a 'little England' of rurality and imagined roots, supposed to have both preceded imperialism and in some ways persisted through it – an enduring sub-stratum of earlier culture. During the later 19th and early 20th centuries the prime mover naturally sought to at least resemble the rest of the 'nation-state' normality it had fostered. Contrived timelessness was the answer. Thus the over-blown came to be counter-posed to an under-estimated essence, a fictive inheritance variously interpreted as genetic or socio-historical.

The point of monarchy was the way it suited this unique double life. Steve Pincus, in his major book, *1688 The First Modern Revolution* has shown how the improvisations of the 'Glorious and Bloodless Revolution' of 1688 led to a make-over: rather than Absolutism, an institution 'over and above' mere government was created. The resultant British 'Crown' then acquired quasi-global reach, to preside over a wide variety of countries and cultures. Such overplaying of 'nature' – as an actual family, a by-product of natural selection – then found new global amplification via Darwinism and related ideologies of 'blood' and lineage. The term remains mainly academic, but 'transcendence' is what this was about: a conduit from nature to the universal, from families to extended 'families', to nations and even to 'race' as an imagined future collectivity. In the 19th century the glass's enchantment thus seemed to reflect back a story that apparently reconciled the spiritual and the material – religion with economic progress. God's first-born now co-habited with Free Trade, industrial revolution and capitalism. All modern nations have done something like this, perhaps; but for God's first-born, monarchy offered the most convenient way of doing the trick – a trump card to be treasured across the age of nationalism and imperialism.

I'm glad to say that its workings are now better understood than in the 1980s. Following Pincus's 1688 a substantial re-analysis of the context within which both revival and transformation of the monarchy became central to Anglo-British statehood, Edwin Jones's *The English Nation: the Great Myth* has described how Protestantism was re-interpreted and mobilised for the task. As 'constitutional monarchy' the Crown mythology was an instrument for holding such a 'united kingdom' together. Three-quarters of the latter was of course England; but Scotland, Wales and Ireland remained too significant to be either absorbed or ignored. For a vigorously expanding North Atlantic polity, this 'periphery' had to be aboard, and actively participating. But earlier archipelago history – above all the recurrent wars with Scotland – had shown how difficult that could be, whether through force, dynastic alliance or both together. There was in fact no alternative to a symbolically 'reinforced' regal establishment. Republicanism had been attempted by Oliver Cromwell after the 17th-century Civil Wars, but abandoned: always unpopular with the aristocracy, it came also to be distrusted by the lower orders.

So crucial was this factor that the later ruling class *imported* foreign monarchies to make the grade and keep things going, not once but twice. After the 1688 upheaval, the Dutch William of Orange became king, and then (when that line ran out of heirs) Princes from the tiny German state of Hanover were invited to take over: the 'Hanoverians' of 1714 and later. Queen Victoria was one of them. Incomers can learn ways of making themselves more native than their hosts, and these Germans worked hard at it. They became the 'Windsors' during World War One, grafting themselves on to a still successful and expanding multinational enterprise. 20th century wars were very effective in consolidating the institution.

Warfare of course boosts nationalism, but this would never be straightforward for Englishness: neither the 'periphery' nor a dwindling Empire would easily accept 'little England' as a mere partner. The English represented three-quarters of the archipelago, and most of the colonial settlement. Again, the sole available solution was Royalty: an ever more pronounced and ceremonial 'enchantment' that at once allowed and qualified 19th and 20th century democratic advances. The Coronation of Queen Elizabeth IInd 58 years ago set new standards for the new age of TV and tabloid media, which we currently see the future King William learning to emulate.

But he and Queen-to-be Catherine do so in increasingly difficult circumstances. As ever the problem remains 'England'. The Crown is less popular in Scotland and Wales, and has a different sort of importance in Northern Ireland – for many in the latter, maintaining a United Kingdom appears vital, life-and-death as well as emotion and flag-waving. On 5 May 2011, local elections in England coincided with those for the Welsh Assembly, the Scottish Parliament and the devolved authority in Northern Ireland. Power had originally been given to these countries with the aim of strengthening 'Britishness', and carrying on Steve Pincus's 'First Modern Revolution'. But for the Scots matters can't help appearing quite differently. Their place in the early-modern 1688 upheaval was fixed by a Parliamentary Treaty in 1707: an international accord intended to underwrite the monarchical fusion of a previous century, and guarantee 1688 more thoroughly. Thus the new 2011 parliament in Edinburgh can't help seeing itself as more than an administrative convenience – the Scottish National Party did so well on 5 May that Alex Salmond's resultant government is bound to use its power to (at least) challenge and modify 1707. A referendum on independence has been proposed, possibly in 2013 or '14. This might be lost, of course, like the Quebec one of 1995; but the principle would nonetheless be established of the right to secede via popular vote, at some later time.

At such a juncture, some commentators have suggested another possible outcome: why not replace the 'Union ' with a federal or confederal structure, a 'looser' state form that might (so to speak) carry forward useful aspects of British multi-nationality? Though attractive to many, the notion simply cannot escape from the English ground: more than three-quarters of any such body don't care much one way or another. Not only is there no 'devolution' in prospect for England's majority, the latter is, not surprisingly, quite satisfied with the *de facto* authority Great Britain provides, and subscribes energetically to the colourful symbolism which monarchy bestows upon their preponderance. In Wendy James's terms, the English are specimens of *The Ceremonial Animal*, a nation for whom anthropological customs and observances have assumed the role that nationalism has provided for most modern-period states. By contrast, what Plaid Cymru and the SNP offer are aspirations towards this standard national identity – '-isms' akin to most other European and UN States.

It is also sometimes thought that Scandinavia offers a model. After all, the Baltic countries are also monarchies, where the 'nation' is symbolised as one with the shared but more abstract common ground of Social Democracy. Is there any reason why the British-Irish realm should not follow that example? What the position fails to acknowledge is of course inherent diversity of a different kind. I suppose Welsh or Scottish royal houses might evolve royalties of their own, like the Netherlands and Belgium. However, the English question remains – partly determined by a multi-national focus of allegiance much more like that of the 19th century Hapsburg domain in Central Europe.

Nor is this disparity likely to be resolved via any change of mind or movement, since it has longer-range or 'structural' elements which a whole population has inherited and used to define itself nationally. In other words, English majority identity *really is* 'different' for historical causes resistant to rhetoric and good-will ideology. No doubt English self-government would be desirable, and most conversations in the area disclose a touchiness, and a strong feeling of 'identity', if not of superiority. However, this isn't the same thing. England can't help clinging to priority, and invents new versions of it for each international epoch that has succeeded Pincus's *1688* modernity. London's last or latest thing is invariably other than the norm. It may appear old-fashioned and pseudo-feudal to outsiders, but justifies itself internally as renewal of an ageless, inherited secret. Thus a fossil remakes itself as ultra-modern thanks to Britishness, the original 'exception' to history's course. It stays just... well, different – 'above that sort of thing'. In recent times, both Tony Blair's New Labourism and David Cameron's New Conservatism have been redemptive convulsions of that sort:

new uniforms for the cadaver, as it were, preserving the tradition and spirit of congenital non-revolution. Pincus's book shows how there actually *was* an authentic revolution in 1688; but it was one that was then able – uniquely – to disown the rupture, partly via the adroit manipulation of a re-invented 'Crown', a monarchy salient enough to provide continuity without obstructing a new bourgeois régime.

And today, the same institution remains an important ingredient for continuing the performance, primarily among the English. *1688* points out how the monarchy was renewed, and quite effectively 'modernised', 19 years before the Treaty of Union. This made the resultant United Kingdom genuinely post-feudal – 'early modern', of course, yet reasonably adaptable to later episodes of evolution, as long as outright defeat and catastrophe could be avoided. These did threaten sometimes, but were kept at bay by significant *external* fortune, a combination of military success and one alliance after another with favourable foreign forces. From Empire/Commonwealth down to the Special Relationship and an obliging European Union, the English hegemony has been able to keep going, and even to maintain Great-Power pretensions notoriously far beyond its real capacity.

The sole important lapse was Ireland, under the combined shocks of World War One and the Dublin uprising in 1915. There, miscalculation was forced by the very factors underlined by both Jones and Pincus: the 'original sin' of a missionary Protestantism incapable of modest self-judgement and compromise. Religious absolutism resurrected ghosts that have now pursued the all-British identity to the very end of its days, in a Northern Ireland resistant to secularity as well as to Roman Catholicism. The forces that inspired Linda Colley's *Britons* (1992) outwards to global power have survived that power's shrinkage and general ridicule. But in this context of break-up, monarchy has become stressed to the limit: each new lapse or misfortune is accompanied by exaggerated flag-waving and over-rehearsed adulation. Prince William and Catherine Middleton can't help falling into the trap – the hysteria of counter-decline, and willful failure to quit a darkening stage.

Prince Charles has already prepared the way for this survival strategy, with his theatre of determined populism: too 'with it' by half, a modernising exhibitionism that deliberately underestimates the factors of tradition and retrospect that national identity also requires. His antics have marked a meaningful shift of emphasis – one that appears likely to prevail for some years, once Elizabeth IInd takes her leave. However exaggerated and ambiguous, it may be that the Prince of Wales's posture also echoes deeper shifts under way, to which I will return below. Decades of half-apologetic, 'ironical' Royalism are likely to leave their own diminished heritage, currently being handed down to the future King William. In *1688*, Pincus shows how 'like all modern revolutions… 1688–9 was a struggle ultimately waged between two competing groups of modernisers', which a traditionalist centre ground had to accept. But if the future brings a more self-conscious 'little England' with it – above all, with the departure of the Scots – then ongoing modernisation (or re-modernisation) could be quite different.

Most formulae for perpetuating the United Kingdom envisage some sort of 'federalism' or looser association of equal-status units, and are accompanied by redefinitions of 'independence' for Wales, Scotland, Northern Ireland *and England*. Occasionally this is hopefully modified by notions of regional autonomy, of the kind that John Prescott attempted without success to foster in the English North-East. However, the resounding defeat of that attempt by popular referendum makes the route seem most unlikely. Britannic 'confederation' (or whatever) cannot either avoid or minimise English nationalism. Four-fifths of the electorate would be invited to shift allegiance from 'Anglo-Britain' to a quite different model, one inevitably according much greater importance to 'the periphery' – and especially to Scotland.

The simply unlikelihood of this transfer puts Scottish separation and statehood in a different perspective – different and, it can be argued, simpler and more acceptable both in the archipelago and internationally, By comparison with reforming God's First-born it is, surely, a relatively minor change. Of course both the Scots and the Welsh need and wish to escape from 'the periphery'. And furthermore, one survey after another has shown English public relatively indifferent to the alteration. 'Westminsterism' attaches far more significance to Great-Power stature and the Security Council seat than do most English or British subjects. Also, the 'detachment' of the monarchy could prove useful, if the institution can distinguish itself more definitely from the disintegrating heritage of Union and Empire. It looks as if the true choice of Kings Charles and William will be between burial among the ruins of the *ancien régime* or some new, more modest function as symbol of 'federal' or other common clothes chosen to carry on some selected features of such lengthy coexistence and societal inter-penetration: the less-than-Great, less-united Kingdom of a European Union member, one that takes 'modernisation' and formal democracy more seriously.

'Republican Monarchy'? The term appears self-contradictory, and yet nothing else corresponds to what may be emerging right now, following the decisive SNP victory in the Scottish Parliamentary election of 5 May 2011. There will be a referendum on Scottish independence quite soon, and Premier Alex Salmond has repeatedly made it clear he does not want outright republicanism to be part of the bid. The future envisaged is therefore one of statehood equality over the former United Kingdom, in which a crowned head of state will remain, as the symbol of partnership and good will, established social and personal relations, and the historic closeness derived from 1688. It should also change – and probably moderate – the 'surrogacy' mentioned earlier, through which English national identity has been transmuted into Royalty-obsession, even adulation. One way the English have avoided 'little England' (the country on its own) has been the curiously amplified elevation of regal family dynasty described below, informally shared by the peripheral countries. A *formal* agreement between periphery and the core-majority, by contrast, could include acceptance of monarchy in a spirit different from what has so far prevailed. In effect, the replacement of 'enchantment' and emotionality by straightforward calculation of joint benefits and their costs. 'Constitutional' monarchy always contained that, of course – but transported by the singular fervour and (in the older sense) 'enthusiasm' for Royalty which 1688 and 1707 originally made part of the new corporate state-nation of Anglo-Britain.

As I argue below, this exceptional structure has then consistently sidelined all attempts at written constitution, helped by unceasing outward expansion and colonisation. No longer: Mrs Thatcher may have been concerned to restore 'Greatness' to things British, but the real question remains of removing it for good. What does 'resignation' from an older Great-Power club (Security Council position, et al.) truly mean? The Westminster-British political elite (including periphery members) will naturally cling on to it. Without an 'ethnically' English resignation from the outward-reaching model, therefore, the change has to come from the periphery, by a return to themselves of the archipelago's minority nationalities.

Fortunately, this seems to be under way, and has been given a great boost by the 2011 elections in Scotland. Different varieties of nationalism there, in Wales and Northern Ireland, are bound in turn to require a novel style of 'constitution' that could certainly include monarchy – but of a somewhat different style from the one imposed by what one might call the glamour of backwardness. A distinctly English input would be demanded from the four-fifths majority, as well as the assorted democratic minorities. There's nothing 'little' about this, in any demeaning or has-been sense: merely acceptance of reality in a rapidly globalising world. The latter's finality imparts a comparable importance to what 'we' all are, the distinctive deposit of past time or 'history'. First-round nationalism accompanied and voiced first-round industrialisation, and it can be argued that second rounds are now in formation, involving not the end but the renewal and advancement of 'who we are', of the collective identities derived from the 19th and 20th centuries.

CHAPTER TWENTY-NINE

A Nation's Blueprint

Foreword to the Case for Left-Wing Nationalism by Stephen Maxwell

OCTOBER 2013

NOTHING WILL MAKE up for Stephen Maxwell's disappearance. However, there remain some consolations, very important both to those who knew him and to those who will learn more about him from this book. He lived to perceive the political dawn coming, and in his final collection of texts this quiet man summed up much of what that should stand for. With good luck, his nation will come to embody it in due time, as a more distinct identity in the wider political world. I can't think of any other country – new or renewed – whose formation has benefited so much in this way, or in such a timely fashion.

I also have the strongest personal reasons for welcoming this posthumous contribution. For it was Stephen who put me right about both the cases and the likely character of Scottish nationalism, in a period when I remained over-attached to the fossilised remains of 'Internationalism'. Like many others I had imagined direct transitions from a personal level of faith on to the over-arching sky of totality, whether represented by capital-letter Socialism or Communism (philosophically hallowed by Marxism). And in this imagined passage, nationality was somehow by-passed, or treated as a hereditary accident – more likely to impede than assist individual progress towards humanity's capital-letter plane. In that sense, secular internationalists had simply taken over the deeper framework of so many religions: Hegel's 'Absolute' in 200 or so assorted tongues and disguises. Readers will find the episode referred to below, in typically forgiving style.

Nationality can't be glossed over or occluded, was the Maxwell message. It has to be incorporated into the contemporary, forward-looking mode of sociality. I think this is the sense of 'Left Wing' in his unceasing struggle to redefine Scotland's identity and its place in the post-Cold War world. He wasn't hoping to reanimate Soviet or other fantasies, or to re-invent Socialism. The struggle for Social Democracy in Scotland has been 'belated', inevitably. However, such a situation has advantages, too: the belated may be intertwined with the novel, the onset of a different age. The circumstances of 'globality' grow daily more distinct from those of 18th to 20th century industrialisation. The latter was a competitive and militarised transformation which had demanded everywhere what one might call 'high-pressure' identification. This demanded an over-intense devotion to the peculiar features and needs of each competitor: 'ethnicity', as it came to be labelled. Life-or-death turned into part of a deal from which escape was impossible, leading to incessant warfare – of which the 'Cold War' was the protracted but (one hopes) concluding episode.

Personally, Stephen would have laughed at the notion of being a 'prophet'. Nor was this just a matter of temperament. The prophetic period of Scottish nationalism came earlier, between the two World Wars, most famously in the work of C.M. Grieve ('Hugh MacDiarmid'), whose Drunk Man contemplated a Thistle persisting against all odds, and needing a violent revolution to evolve more freely. The Maxwell equivalent is non-violent, and democratic: a kind of 'Yes' to our collective being, and a restoration of the latter's self-confidence – what Carol Craig has called *The Scots' Crisis of Self-Confidence* (2003) in one notable survey of the terrain. However, there is surely something more deeply prophetic about the Maxwell oeuvre – expressed in works like *Arguing for Independence: Evidence, Risks and the Wicked Issues* (Luath Press 2012). The wicked issue is of course straightforward resumption of national statehood: a 'Union' originally opposed by so many, who are now given their chance to affirm a different course.

Such affirmation will be peaceful, and uncontaminated by inherited hatred or resentment. What was wrong wasn't 'the English', but the 'Great Britain' which an early 18th-century elite had signed up for, in pursuit of both industrial development and natural resources to be derived from more successful colonisation. The contrary of that union might of course be a differently articulated association, some kind of 'confederation' along Swiss lines. But any such reform would itself demand that 'sovereignty' be first re-located and diversified, among Scotland, Wales, Northern Ireland and a restored 'Little England'. This return of statehood would not be an impossible backward plunge into the epoch of extinct '-isms'. We can't help inheriting ideologies from the past; but 'nationalism' in that time-bound sense will itself alter and adapt, to confront the novel circumstances of 'globalisation'. Sovereignty means having the final word; but also, seeking more freely for the new words urgently needed, in such rapidly shifting times.

The prospective alteration has been under way for long enough. As well as Stephen's own *Arguing for Independence*, the academic W. Elliot Bulmer has produced *A Model Constitution for Scotland: Making Democracy Work* (2011). A little later, *Scotland's Choices: the Referendum and What Happens Afterwards*, by Iain McLean, Jim Gallagher and Guy Lodge (Edinburgh University Press) appeared, as did *A Nation Again: Why Independence will be good for Scotland (and England too)*, edited by Paul Henderson Scott (Luath Press 2008). There are already many forerunners of what will be a year's debate on the resumption of our country's up-dated statehood, considering the process in much detail. However, vision matters even more than the realism imposed by an oncoming age. And I doubt if anything more telling on the spirit of this coming moment will be published than the essays here, from the great thinker (and activist) who worked so long and determinedly towards his country's re-established independence.

The most recent addition to new nationalism's title-list has been Lesley Riddoch's *Blossom: What Scotland Needs to Flourish* (Luath Press, 2013). All classical theories of nationalism, like those of Ernest Gellner (Nations and Nationalism, Blackwell's second edition 2006) and Liah Greenfeld's *Nationalism: Five Roads to Modernity* (Harvard 1993), indicate nation-state formation as always arising from an alliance between popular restlessness and an evolving intelligentsia, inclining towards separate and independent development. 'Among ordinary Scots... the process has already begun', observes Riddoch, and 'the task is to let that flower blossom – to weed out the negativity and self-doubt' deposited by the half-history of an anachronistic Union. At the end of his *Scotland the Brief: Short History of a Nation* (2010) Christopher Harvie noted that 'a confederal covenant within the islands would be valuable', and the most obvious next step, if only the negativity could be got rid of. Stephen Maxwell's positivity is surely the answer, for dismissing 'the last enchantments of imperialism', and convincing the English majority of their own need to 'blossom' independently.

'Yes' is about the conditions required for such advance, which can't be 'cultural' or emerge from civil society alone. Scots invented 'civil society' in the 19th century as an alternative to the loss of statehood, but in the 21st century it's no longer sufficient. The prolonged recession between 2008 and the present has underlined the need for more political diversity, for new ways to tackle a 'cosmopolitan' capitalism no longer able to guarantee reasonable development and prosperity. Of course independence 'by itself' won't generate miracles; but the point is, surely, that no society is any longer 'on its own', and will only be able to contribute to a broader 'Common Weal' with the means to act, experiment, and be different. Independence was never a sufficient condition of societal success; but does it not remain a necessary condition of tolerable change and bearable identity?

CHAPTER THIRTY

Old Nation, New Age

Open Democracy

APRIL 2014

IT'S CALLED *Scotland's Future: Your Guide to an Independent Scotland*, and was published by the Scottish Government in November 2013. Shortly thereafter it arrived with a thud through our letter-box, all 649 pages of it, weighing in at 3 lbs 5oz (one-and-a-half kilogrammes). I can't add a price, since it's free (to all on the Scottish electoral roll): the 'White Paper' on our future – that is, if enough of us vote 'Yes' next September.

'A choice between two futures' claims the first paragraph... The door will open to a new era. Scotland's future will be in Scotland's hands' if enough of them tick the 'Yes' box on September 18 2014. Alex Salmond, the First Minister of the existing devolved government in Edinburgh, rubs in the main point again: 'Our generation has the opportunity to stop imagining and wondering and start building the better Scotland we all know is possible... It is time to seize that future with both hands.' Seven pages go on to list the advantages of independence, including removal of all nuclear weapons and bases, and 'a universal system of high quality early learning from the age of one to when they enter school' (p.09).

Who will be Scots following 18 September? British citizens 'habitually resident' in Scotland, naturally; but 'Scottish-born citizens currently living outside of Scotland will also automatically be considered... and others will be able to register or apply... based on clear criteria'. At the same time, 'the development of a Scottish overseas diplomatic and trade network will provide the opportunity to promote and share our culture and traditions with nations across the world' (p.19).

More important is the general wish for 'the process of becoming independent to stimulate new creativity and energy in Scotland'. The way forward is to be marked by 'negotiations with the rest of the UK and other international partners and organisations', in order to 'set out the timetable towards independence day in 2016' (p.20). The Windsor monarchy will be retained, and any new regime intends supporting 'amongst other Commonwealth States... rules to remove religious discrimination from the succession rules'. Initially the sterling currency will be retained, and Chapter 3, 'Finance and the Economy' provides an extensive justification for not following Ireland into the Euro system, as well as diagrammatic material on the existing economy –26 per cent 'Government and Services',

25 per cent 'Financial and Other Services' and 12 per cent 'Manufacturing' (from the Fiscal Commission Working Group Report: Macroeconomic Framework, February 2013).

At least that's the way it looked when Scotland's Future hit the door-mat a few weeks back. Since then, things have begun to shift. Keeping the UK's currency was interpreted as a gesture of reassurance and moderation. But of course that depended upon English acceptance of the deal. It's important to remember just what 'England' represents in the United Kingdom. The answer is: 80 per cent, approximately, of both land and population, a genuinely overwhelming majority. Nor should it be forgotten that this majority has inherited what could be called a psychology of primacy. All classical accounts (like Ernest Gellner's, and Liah Greenfeld's *Nationalism*) assume England to have been the original and model 'nation-state' of modern times; and of course it was this same state that adopted an equally overwhelming outward-directed path of development, leading it to rule so much of the globe in the 19th and earlier 20th century. Over that era, nation-states became the standard political form, leading to the present-day total of over 200 in the United Nations Organisation. In 1707 the Scots joined the transformation via a Treaty of Union that let them into the English-led 'Empire'.

But now many of them want out, somewhat belatedly. Or at least, that's one way of looking forward to the 18 September vote. However, there may be another. Could it not be the case that another 'age' altogether is dawning? And that the new times of 'globalisation' are already fostering different rules and possibilities, including those related to the problem of scale? Throughout the past era, the vital questions were posed by industrialisation: the emergence of manufacturing and commerce, on a scale which required dimensions larger than those of the city-states and regions within which capitalism first arose. Nation-states were the answer, and their spread fostered equivalent areas and (more important) cultures inside which sufficient homogeneity prevailed.

Such workable common ground implied a novel emphasis on scale. Not bigness as such (Antiquity was familiar with dynastic over-reach and land-grabbing) but societal cohesion into functioning 'identities' that could cope with rapidly altering circumstances: not 'bigger is better' but (in Benedict Anderson's phrase) 'imagined communities' able to conjoin inheritance with novelties previously unimaginable. 'Modernity' has become the normal label: the complex of such entities beset by an inescapable and competitive pressure of change, at the mercy of 'development' many of whose effects are only half-understood, if not quite misunderstood.

Yet in the evolution of a nation-state world, relatively big scale couldn't help counting. Capitalism may have started up in small city-states and marginal countries: but it was somewhat bigger entities that provided the combination of market-places and common cultures that favoured the rise of manufacturing, during the 18th and 19th centuries. Nor was there any pre-established scale for this process. The 'national' found itself propelled towards the 'imperial', and into take-overs and transoceanic expansion – which was of course a recipe for mounting conflict, and an increasingly war-like world. Was there any other way for the globe to develop? 'Industrialisation' may have been essentially peaceful in longer-term aims. But the route towards it could only lie amid the contrasts and diversities of homo sapiens, the house of many colours inherited from pre-history, a clash of tongues and customs only partly modified by religions and a speculative unity or one-ness.

Hence globalisation could only come 'before its time'. After the exhaustion of world wars there developed a 'Cold War' between differing modes of one-ness, or 'globality', which capitalism coldly won, and took over the last phase of Middle Earth's growth. China completed the process, and ushered in a 21st century where scale would count for less – and hence, become less significant for socie-ties seeking effective collective identity, or 'nationhood'. 'Bigger is better' lost whatever remaining sense it had.

Does this imply a reversal of the previously dominant scale-pressures? Not necessarily – it doesn't follow that smaller is becoming automatically preferable. However, it is most likely true that globality has (so to speak) left a new door ajar, or openable: societies once held to be 'unviable' may become imaginable, and capable of formation, or reformation. As I write, it can be argued that events at both ends of Europe, West and East, are indicating at least the possibility of such new developments: one is of course the British-Irish archipelago under discus-sion here, and the other is in Ukraine and the Black Sea peninsula of Crimea.

There, Russian-speakers are demanding either reforms or alterations of statehood more favourable to their collective interests. Is an independent Crimea any more or less likely, or possible, than an independent Scotland and Wales? Russia's President Putin seems inclined to military intervention, to invasion and the risk of war with the government of Ukraine: '19th century' formulae that almost no-one would have dreamt possible very recently.

At the same time, a new government in the cross-Pyrenean country of Cata-lonia appears to demand recognition and independence: as do the people of the Basque Country farther West, 'Euzkadi'.They want 'Independence in Europe', to cite the familiar slogan of the Scottish National Party now dominant in the Edinburgh Parliament. Isn't a recognisable trend emerging in several otherwise quite different countries, and acquiring a common voice? And isn't there also some common ground among their opponents? That is, the former or would-be great powers of Spain, France, Russia and Great Britain? The latter all built up historical 'nationalism', culminating in the world-scale warfare of 1914 to 1946, as well as its 'cold' successor conflict down to the end of the last millennium. Madrilenos, Parisians, Londoners and Muscovites are naturally hostile to the novelty, and anxious to preserve the nationality-politics of previous times: the 'realism' of viable scale and standing, hard-won institutions that confer both visibility and rights.

However, it may none the less be time to argue that 'internationalism' now manifests itself in new entities and demands: a globe of even greater diversity and variety, a house of many more colours, shades and possibilities than the ones historically registered and 'approved' by the existing United Nations. Are not 'Great Powers' history, as much as the old colonies, dependencies and hangers-on? As Tariq Ali has recently written, urging the Scots to 'undo this Union of rogues' and realise their own, distinct potential in the name of 'sovereignty, honour and dignity': 'The notion that an independent Scotland will be parochial is risible...' It 'could be far more internationalist and would benefit a great deal from links to both Scandinavia and states in other continents'.

The implication seems to be: '*reculer pour mieux sauter*' – the Scots should take a step back into statehood, in order to leap forward and embrace the new age, a globality where there are certain to be many more self-governing units rather than fewer and bigger. The 'Yes' won't be to some out-dated or renovated self-government, but to a necessarily new form of self-rule, a polity framed partly by the new circumstances themselves. Of course we can't know just what the new 'potential' will be – or at least, all we can be reasonably sure of is that it will be different, more democratic, and will require a correspondingly reformed Kingdom (or even a Republic?). 'Yes' means: 'Let's get on with it', whatever follows the never-ending decline, the 'Special Relationship' to Washington that was in truth a way of avoiding changes, and of clinging to the shade of by-gone times. Little England, let's hear from you, and not via fossils like the British National Party and the United Kingdom Independence movement. It's not chance that such outfits over-play Britannitude in their titles: this is, rather, a way of evading a long-overdue re-framing of Englishness. Boris Johnson appears to think London should turn into the Capital of Europe, if not the World: any absurdity to avoid a modest return to itself, and a real exit from the over-growth of a long-defunct imperium.

At least the Scots will have some chance of getting through (or at least moving towards) the Exit later this year. Let's do it, rather than hang around for more decades of brooding about it, and trying to sum up enough self-confidence to take on the new age. The confidence will come from doing it, and helping to foster the incoming tide of real inter-nationalism in our own way: new colours in the rising house, new tunes that Robert Burns might recognise as he sees the parcel o' rogues in the removal van at last. The end of 'Internationalism' is within sight: that '-ism' has already sunk half out of sight, and been replaced by the internationality visible in (for example) the *openDemocracy* web-site, where inter-nation discourse is taken for granted, and no longer a disguise for one or other great-power ambition or nostalgia – the sour half-world of Great-British 'special relationships' refusing to go quietly, and forever half-commemorating an irredeemable past. That's part of what the Scots will have the chance to vote for on 18 September, by saying 'Yes' to a world of many more open nations arriving to govern themselves, not just Catalonia, Wales, the Basques, the Crimeans and the other familiar cases.

Luath Press Limited

committed to publishing well written books worth reading

LUATH PRESS takes its name from Robert Burns, whose little collie Luath (*Gael.,* swift or nimble) tripped up Jean Armour at a wedding and gave him the chance to speak to the woman who was to be his wife and the abiding love of his life. Burns called one of 'The Twa Dogs' Luath after Cuchullin's hunting dog in Ossian's *Fingal*. Luath Press was established in 1981 in the heart of Burns country, and now resides a few steps up the road from Burns' first lodgings on Edinburgh's Royal Mile. Luath offers you distinctive writing with a hint of unexpected pleasures.

Most bookshops in the UK, the US, Canada, Australia, New Zealand and parts of Europe either carry our books in stock or can order them for you. To order direct from us, please send a £sterling cheque, postal order, international money order or your credit card details (number, address of cardholder and expiry date) to us at the address below. Please add post and packing as follows: UK – £1.00 per delivery address; overseas surface mail – £2.50 per delivery address; overseas airmail – £3.50 for the first book to each delivery address, plus £1.00 for each additional book by airmail to the same address. If your order is a gift, we will happily enclose your card or message at no extra charge.

Luath Press Limited
543/2 Castlehill
The Royal Mile
Edinburgh EH1 2ND
Scotland

Telephone: 0131 225 4326 (24 hours)
email: sales@luath.co.uk
Website: www.luath.co.uk